THE ETHICS OF BEAUTY

TIMOTHY G. PATITSAS

THE ETHICS OF BEAUTY

ST. NICHOLAS PRESS

Copyright © 2019 by Timothy G. Patitsas
All Rights Reserved.
First Edition. 2020.

This book may not be reproduced in whole or in part (except copying permitted by the U.S. Copyright law, and quotes by reviewers for the public press), without written permission from the publisher.

St. Nicholas Press is an imprint of the Road to Emmaus Foundation. Road to Emmaus Foundation/St. Nicholas Press publications may be purchased in quantity for educational, business, or promotional use. For information on ordering, write or call: Road to Emmaus Foundation/St. Nicholas Press.

Mailing address: St. Nicholas Press, PO Box 198, Maysville, MO 64469
Phone and Fax: (+1) 816-449-5231
Email: stnicholaspress@gmail.com
Web: www.stnicholaspress.net
                   www.roadtoemmaus.net

ISBN: 978-1-63551-100-0
Library of Congress Control Number: 2019943423

The first three chapters of this book were published and copyrighted in earlier forms in *Road to Emmaus: A Journal of Orthodox Faith and Culture* between 2013 and 2015. "The Opposite of War is Not Peace: Healing Trauma in The Iliad and in Orthodox Tradition," Winter 2013, #52; "A Feeling for Beauty: The Aesthetic Ground of Orthodox Ethics," Spring 2014, #57; and "Chastity and Empathy: Eros, Agape, and the Mystery of the Twofold Anointing," Winter 2015, #60. Although significant content has been added to each of these chapters, their most important arguments and discoveries were already present in these earlier versions.

Selection from Colm Liubheid, translator, *Pseudo-Dionysius: The Complete Works* on page xvi is reprinted with oral permission from Paulist Press. All rights reserved.
Selection from Jane Jacobs, *Systems of Survival* on page 561 is reprinted with permission from Random House. All rights reserved.
Selection from Roy Rappaport, *Ritual and Religion in the Making of Humanity*, on pages 715-17 is reprinted with permission from The Cambridge University Press. All rights reserved.

First printing: December, 2019
Second printing: January, 2021
Third printing: August, 2021
Fourth printing: October, 2021
Fifth printing: July, 2022

Printed in Thailand.

Front Cover: Christ healing the woman with the issue of blood. Catacomb of Marcellinus and Peter, Rome. Photo courtesy Wikimedia Commons.

Layout and Cover: Bruce Petersen Art Direction & Design

For my mother and father

Contents

Preface — i

How to Read This Book — ix

Acknowledgments — xii

Chapter One: The Opposite of War Is Not Peace — 1
Healing Trauma in the Iliad and in Orthodox Tradition
    I. The Cost of War
    II. After Combat
    III. Afterword: Responding to Reader Comments

Chapter Two: A Feeling for Beauty — 45
The Aesthetic Ground of Orthodox Ethics
    I. Attaining Freedom through Love for Beauty
    II. Creation's Origin in Eros for the Beautiful

Chapter Three: Chastity and Empathy — 101
Eros, Agape, and the Mystery of the Twofold Anointing
    I. Chastity
    II. Empathy
    III. The Twofold Anointing

Chapter Four: Shame and Sacrifice — 183
Rescuing the Soul from the Empire of Therapy
    I. Ethics as Therapy
    II. The Triumph of the Therapeutic
    III. Shame
    IV. The Soul in Orthodox Christianity

Chapter Five: Only Priests Can Marry 297
The Reconciliation of Men and Women in Christ
    I.   The Shape of Gender Reconciliation
    II. Love for the Sexual Enemy
    III. Personhood

Chapter Six: The Mystical Architect 405
The Conception of the Crucified Logos in Art, Science, and Nature
    I.   Motherhood
    II. Logoi, Forms, and Patterns
    III. Hospitality

Chapter Seven: Beauty Will Save the World 517
Social Justice, Judgment Day, and the Human Need to Forgive God
    I.   Symphonia: Fidelity to the Prophet-King
    II. The Ancient View: Guardians and Traders in War and Peace
    III. The Wedding of Christ and Jerusalem

Chapter Eight: The City as Liturgy 623
How Jane Jacobs Used the Beautiful Science of Complexity to Explain Cities, and Unknowingly Reconciled Science and Religion
    I.   Jane Jacobs, City Theorist
    II. The Beautiful Science of Complexity
    III. The City is a Liturgy
    IV. The Gentle Reconciliation of Science and Religion

Epilogue: The Joy of All Who Sorrow 725

Bibliography by Chapter 731

Preface

This book attempts to recover a lost way of doing Ethics, one in which love for Beauty played the central and the leading role.

What is attempted here is not only a description of this forgotten way but also a demonstration of what an aesthetic approach to ethics might mean for everything from war, to psychotherapy, to our identity as men and women, to the biology of conception, to art, to social justice, and even for the reception within the academy of the science of organic complexity.

But is there really a need for such an Ethics of Beauty?

Contemporary Ethics is defined as "the rational investigation of morality," a description which is so spare and exact that surely there could be no hidden bias lurking within it. It is only when this definition is cast in terms of Socrates' three transcendentals that its ominous character becomes visible: at once we find Ethics identifying itself as the investigation of "the Good" by "the True" … and we realize that an entire Socratic transcendental, "the Beautiful," has been invisibly barred from our consideration of what constitutes the best life.

Much of modern Ethics, following Spinoza and even Kant, claims or at least implies that the investigation of the Good by the True is the whole of ethics. Even seemingly "goodness-first" ethicists like utilitarians conform to this "truth-first" rule of doing Ethics as if it were at bottom a problem in logic.

When Beauty, or feeling, does dare enter into ethical deliberation nowadays, "she" is regarded as a temptress, a siren distracting the rational mind. Reliance upon Beauty is taken as *ipso facto* proof of bias, cultural prejudice, or superficial romanticism.

But in discarding Beauty, Ethics itself risks becoming not only unlovely but also an affront to loveliness, and it loses its power to motivate the human soul except through the force of argument, backed perhaps by the armed force of civil legal power.

I was never explicitly taught the Beautiful Way described and employed in the present volume. It was in a process of fits and starts, accidents and coincidences, and in the chance happening to read books from unrelated disciplines which somehow illumined each other in unexpected ways, that a dim vision of what Ethics once was – and again could be – gradually gathered itself before me, one element at a time.

Only now that I have unexpectedly assembled some of the pieces of it for myself have I become aware that an Ethics of Beauty has been present with me all along, often even within formal academic Ethics itself. I never noticed it, though, because its essence had been only partly transposed into the truth-first language of academic ethics and philosophy. Indeed, Beauty's presence in Ethics is often deliberately hidden "for fear of the Greeks" – that is, out of conformity to the prejudice against Beauty that eventually followed the later Enlightenment's use of a reductive and mechanistic version of Hellenism.

To be sure, there are limits and patterns governing the transposition of Beauty into Truth, such that it can never be mapped fully in the reductive way some would insist. It was never my desire to write a truth-first book about the Beauty-first approach to ethics. Beauty creates its own structure, a form that may not be perfectly linear and symmetrical, but which is still harmonious and beneficial and, in its odd way, perfectly accurate. Through the surprising order of the Beautiful, reason participates in and discloses living mystery *as* mystery; that is, when it starts with an eros for the Beautiful, reason is able to announce to the world what mystery is: that which interprets and changes us, just when we manage to engage with and interpret it.

To the extent that this book has entered into this lost way of doing Ethics, I hope that the reader will find himself not only convinced by what is presented here, but actually renewed, released from certain false constraints, and more fully alive.

The above is a brief defense before my fellow ethicists of a Beauty-first approach to moral life; let me now address another cohort, Christian theologians.

Preface

The written tradition of Christian dogma began, even in the letters and books that would become the New Testament, as a response to theophany. The resurrection and the crucifixion of Christ the incarnate Son of God shone out to the world and all but compelled a response in action as well as in thought.

Since those first witnesses to God's appearing were found to be faithful and true by still other faithful and true witnesses, in a succession lasting from apostolic times until today, the theology of the Christian community has ever remained a reflection upon Beauty. It matters not whether we experience this revelation directly or if it is conveyed to us by earlier or later witnesses. Either way, without its first appearing, there is no basis for Christian theological reflection.

For example, it is sometimes stated that in the patristic period, Western Latin theology worked from the concept of the essence of God before deriving the three Persons of the Trinity, whereas the theology of the Greek Fathers began with the three Persons and thereafter derived the intellectual concept of the common divine essence.

But it is not at first a question of what object or concept or even Person we contemplate but of whether we allow Christian theology to be rooted in the gift of revelation rather than in speculation. Christian theology can only begin with God's self-offering in the Divine Economy. On this point, Protestants, as well as Roman Catholics and Greek Orthodox, would broadly agree.

The theology of the Church did not begin with considerations of intellectual method nor with concerns about the wider relevance or usefulness of the Gospel message; Christian theology began with Beauty rather than with Truth or Goodness. Similarly, Christian Ethics must begin with what is Beautiful – namely, Christ's self-revelation in his resurrection, crucifixion, and incarnation, whether this appearing comes within history, creation, Scripture, or in the Church, which is his body.

To be sure, theology also does not *end* at Beauty, for a faith that refuses to unfold into the Goodness of a purified self-offering for others will not save – and will be in no position to move yet further, to become itself True and in consequence a further revelation of the Beautiful to the world.

Besides ethicists and theologians, I have had two other audiences in mind while writing this book.

One is the reader looking for a comprehensive summation of the Orthodox Christian ethos. Growing up as a Greek Orthodox Christian in the United States, I had always wondered about the distinct "feel" of life in the Orthodox Church, quite unlike anything else in my childhood experience. The intangible quality of spirit which makes Orthodoxy distinct from her many companion Christianities is fascinating because this feeling of difference persists even when the doctrines of other churches seem all but identical to Orthodoxy, or when the outward forms of worship are in fact identical. Even in these cases, there exists some unmistakable "taste" of Orthodox life, a fact which to me has always been a source of puzzlement and wonder. The attempt to acquire an epistemology that could describe and account for this intangible alterity has been the pursuit of my life, in many ways.

The answer I was looking for is in large part to be found in the preeminence of the Beautiful within the Orthodox ethos. The central text about Orthodox Christian prayer life, *The Philokalia*, itself means "the love of the beautiful." *The Ethics of Beauty* is best conceived as a prose companion to that spiritual collection – certainly not on the same level as that classic text, but hopefully recognizably in the same family. Where *The Philokalia* is an aid to the pursuit of the Beautiful Way in prayer, *The Ethics of Beauty* is a discussion of why the Beauty-first Way is preferable, and an examination of that Way within as many areas of life as possible.

There is yet one more audience for this book about Beauty which commands my attention. I was originally moved to write this book out of empathy for the community of people who either are trauma sufferers or who are their allies in recovery. Ultimately, it is those who have encountered the very antithesis of Beauty, who have endured the type of shocking and horrible experiences that threaten to degrade and disintegrate our human identity, who must be the judges of whether an "Ethics of Beauty" can be more than a sly mockery of actual human life.

I would never have set out upon the journey that led me to the *The Ethics of Beauty* had I not read Jonathan Shay's observation in his *Achilles in Vietnam* that contemporary analytical psychotherapy has been largely unable to heal the suffering of the soldiers afflicted most severely with post-traumatic stress disorder. I have slowly come to see that another way to read Shay would be to say that the initial focus of soul-healing must be on Beauty rather than on truth, on a living vision of a loving and crucified God, rather than on an autopsy of the broken self.

This is not to say that I have written a book about trauma or that every chapter in this rather long work has something to say about trauma. In order to answer the questions I had about trauma's healing, I was forced also to answer questions that I had had all my life about what exactly is the Orthodox ethos. These answers might be of interest to any reader, and especially to those looking for a renewed understanding of Christian spirituality.

Still, it would be wrong to describe my concern for trauma victims as something other than the very center and heart of this book. Imitating St. Paul before the people of Corinth, I have aspired in this book to "know nothing among you, but Christ – and him, crucified." That is, I believe that Ethics must address plausibly the experience of the "least of these" if it is to be valid for any of us. And I have tried to show that it is Christ, and indeed the Christ of Orthodox Christianity, who is our best hope in the healing of any human soul but most especially the souls of the victims of trauma.

It seems to me that the Christian Church has always understood that both the personal spiritual path and the path to social justice are meant largely to trace this ancient Beauty to Goodness to Truth trajectory, if they are to be truly life-giving. The fatal flaw of soul-therapy since Freud, by contrast, has been its insistence that truth and not beauty be our first concern; the repellant aspect of today's political ideologies is rooted in a similar insistence.

Contemporary American psychotherapy largely relies on what I would call a truth-first method, but in fact no such method could ever truly liberate man. To partly paraphrase and partly quote Lev Shestov's evaluation of the entirety of the Western philosophic project (excepting, in his view, Plotinus and, in part, Plato), rationalist methods can only claim intellectual validity if they first posit a predictable, miracle-free, and self-contained universe. Only upon such a fixed and settled basis can the philosopher (or in today's case the therapist, the most ubiquitous and successful type of philosopher in our culture today) reliably exercise human reason to chart out a predictable and stable ethic of human life. The original move of philosophy, said Shestov, had therefore been the brutal subjugation of the world and of the human being to blind, unfeeling Necessity.

Referring to the temptation and fall of Adam and Eve in the Garden of Eden, Shestov went on to say that philosophy since Socrates had in effect chosen to cast its lot with the serpent rather than with a personal God, by accepting that "the knowledge of Good and Evil" is man's best destiny and would make us the equivalent of gods.

To make Shestov's assessment of philosophy sting still more, one now unavoidably hears within this cause of the fall of man in Genesis – the desire to eat of the Tree of the Knowledge of Good and Evil – our current definition of Ethics: "the rational investigation (the knowledge) of morality (of good and evil)." Far from being a guiding light, such a truth-first Ethics can easily increase our blindness and our estrangement from God; it can easily become a way towards death.

The knowledge of Good and Evil, no matter how systematically or thoroughly consumed, will by no means make us gods. Rather, modern ethics, modern psychotherapy, and modern political ideologies all tend to produce not superhumans but pitiable slaves to the rationalizations generated by our distorted human desires. In order to gain control over the world, we have been too willing to renounce essential aspects of our own freedom.

The inability of truth-first methods to liberate the human person is apparent above all in contemporary therapy's failure to heal trauma, which is one reason why trauma therapy is the starting point and the ending point of this book. Traumatic experiences are themselves *already* a terrible force-feeding from the Tree of the Knowledge of Good and Evil – no other *ethical* definition of such horrible phenomena is more accurate – and are among the most bitter and oppressive experiences of the human soul. Therapy as we now generally conceive it seems to attempt a gentler repetition of the same transgression, and to the extent that it does so, cannot be trauma's cure.

Christians should be extremely cautious about truth-first methods whenever approaching issues of social justice or Ethics, as well as when attempting to heal the broken-hearted. When we do not begin with Beauty, it is all too easy to miss the full complexity of human personhood and thus to diminish and dissect men and women made in the image of God.

Truth-first methods can take the soul apart; they cannot put it back together. But the trauma victim is that person *par excellence* who does not require any further dismantling. He or she frequently already subsists at an almost atomic level of disintegration, division, and excommunication. What can further dissection offer such a person?

Rationalist approaches to the soul tempt us because they promise easy understanding (truth) and effective action (utility, or goodness). In practice, however, they so often lead to tragic confusion and wasted effort. Indeed, reductionist methods applied to any living system may be examples of man's perennial attempt to live away from God, for they are often the attempt to substitute sure though partial knowledge for a living relationship. Such an attempt is the repetition of the primordial error of Adam and Eve.

Christians know all too well from dealing with our own temptations to replace the living God with either the idol of religion or with our perfect ideas about God, that truth-first approaches quickly lead towards eternal death.

Therefore, in the healing of trauma, as in Christian dogma, as in the ethical consideration of the best life, Beauty will be our first concern.

"For I resolved to *know nothing* among you, except Christ [that is, the one whom we know to be the Anointed because He rose from the dead, ascended, and is seated at the Father's right hand] – and him, *crucified*" (I Cor 2:2).

And if the ultimate trauma victim, Christ himself, cannot heal this persistent pattern of separation which the trauma sufferer endures – if the Beauty of his resurrection cannot unfold into the Goodness of a soul therapy that makes the person again whole, or "true," – then the Gospel would be "of no account" (Mk 7:13).

But Christ *can* heal trauma, and the radiant beauty of his resurrection *does indeed* unfold into the Goodness of a perfect soul therapy, as has been shown in the lives of countless people from all ages.

And so:

One Lord, one faith, one baptism in Christ Jesus, to the glory of God the Father, by the grace of the All-Holy Spirit, both now and ever and to the ages of ages. Amen.

How to Read this Book

Behind the writing of this book lie hundreds of conversations conducted over more than five years between myself (the author) and the editor. Many of these discussions took place in person, others by phone, and still others in writing. Although all of the material in this collection began as interview-formatted essays which I wrote while alone, even these earliest drafts were composed in the light of these dialogues with my editor, Mother Nectaria McLees. Mother Nectaria is also the editor of *Road to Emmaus: A Journal of Orthodox Faith and Culture*, which is why the interviews are presented as a conversation between "RTE" (Road to Emmaus) and Dr. Patitsas.

The editor responded to my original drafts with comments, objections, requests for clarification, and follow-up questions. Almost always this meant that I returned to my writing desk to add still more points of my own, which elicited further rounds of discussion and revision. The interview format was chosen precisely to give room for and evidence of this unfolding process.

As a result of this dialogue form, however, the precise thesis of a chapter will not always be clear at the outset of a topic. In these conversations, meaning emerges through the natural give and take of the discussion. This is not a mere artifice; for the most part, it was only in the writing of the original interview-essays that I figured out exactly what I thought, what I wanted to say, and what I believed was being overlooked by other commentators about the important matters discussed in these pages.

Although I am a professional academic, this is not an academic book. It casts its net too widely and its form is too nonlinear for the narrowly-focused, richly-footnoted style which is the hallmark and strength of research work. My conclusions are not so much presented as they are discovered and developed within the full view of the reader, who can trace the process by which I followed hunches to the conclusions that I reached.

At times, the deviation from academic structure may frustrate. For example, although Beauty is the heart and soul of the entire book, it is not until Chapter Three that I managed to delineate for myself what I think Beauty is. Similarly, I was not quite certain until the very end whether brief discussions of complexity and information theories belonged here, but finally I concluded that they did. This, in turn, required me to say something about the late urbanist and economist, Jane Jacobs, whom I see as the most important proponent of a Beauty-first approach to science itself.

Mostly, however, I think that the natural way in which the discussions unfold here makes them easier to follow and more inviting. *The Ethics of Beauty* presents a seamless worldview, one in which love for what is beautiful guides human life, and the dialogue format allows these insights and intuitions to come forth in a humble, unassuming sort of way. Also, interviews are ideal for presenting difficult ideas and thorny topics without overwhelming the reader, since they provide many natural breaks for the reader to sit back and reflect before moving on.

Thus, the many little temporary confusions the reader may experience along the way, as important names and ideas are dropped in profusion, are an intentional part of the book. The jokes, the exclamations, the expressions of frustration, the musings, and the author's heartfelt cries – all of these were deliberately kept in the final version so that the text would remain alive. The discussions presented here meander, flow, and reverse course at times, just as real conversations do. Probably the best way to read this book is in measured doses (although some readers have kindly reported being unable to put even the longer chapters down).

The eight interviews here cascade one upon another with a gathering momentum. Themes just hinted at in earlier interviews are expanded and clarified as the book unfolds. Some ideas that are mentioned in passing in earlier chapters will later turn out to be decisive keys to the book as a whole. Nevertheless, an attempt was also made to keep each interview somewhat independent, understandable on its own. Thus, when key concepts from earlier chapters are re-introduced, they typically receive some kind of brief summary.

As a contribution to serious thought, *The Ethics of Beauty* doesn't claim to be the last word on any of the many themes it touches. It is designed instead to be a "first word" or a "further word" for the person in search of an alternative way of thinking about the world. Even certain places where for the sake of brevity I don't develop my ideas to their final conclusion have been deliberately allowed to remain. The hope is that the reader will use whatever seems unclear as a catalyst for his or her own further thought about what has been presented.

In short, although these interviews never "took place" in the final form gathered here, they are nevertheless very much the record of a lively, dialogical, and interrogatory process that has lasted over years.

Acknowledgments

This book was born out of the experience of teaching Ethics to our seminarians at Holy Cross Greek Orthodox School of Theology in Brookline, Massachusetts, and in the light of three ongoing encounters with the broader life of the Christian Orthodox Church beyond the campus of Holy Cross: twelve years of leading the school's annual St. Helen's Pilgrimage to Greece, Mount Athos, and the Ecumenical Patriarchate; my own many pilgrimages to Orthodox monasteries in the United States and around the world; and time spent with my spiritual father, a married parish priest in Moscow, Russia. The indispensable background for all of this was the normal course of family, friendship, and Sunday parish involvement.

Organizing our school's annual embassy of graduating students to the Ecumenical Patriarchate, coupled as it has often been with the reunions of the alumni of Halki Theological School, has had a lasting impact on my development as a theologian. I am very grateful to have had this opportunity, and for the witness offered to me by the Orthodox Christians of Turkey, in particular by His All Holiness Ecumenical Patriarch Bartholomew I.

I could not have completed this book except for my father's hospitality during periods of summer writing in Greece. My dear mother energetically encouraged and supported my education from my earliest years until her passing in 2011. The members of my extended family, from Samoa and Fiji, throughout the United States, and in France, Germany, Russia, and Greece, also have given me their love and encouragement. As this is my first published book, I want to mention that major funding for my doctoral education came from the late Aspasia Lemos, and from her daughter (my aunt) Marigo Patitsas-Lemos.

The following friends read earlier drafts of this work and contributed feedback: Elyse Buffenbarger, Lukas Bühler, Alexandra Drechsler, Jonathan Gardner, Andrew Gould, Theodore Nottingham, Thekla Raney-Kagaris, Rebecca Safley Clark, Maria Sanderson, Georgia Williams, and Steve Zabak. Two colleagues, Dr. Joel

Kalvesmaki of Dumbarton Oaks Research Library and Dr. Robin Darling Young of The Catholic University of America, also commented on the book as it neared its completion. Needless to say, none of these readers is responsible for the final contents.

Dean James Skedros of Holy Cross granted me the sabbatical semester in which the principal work for this book was undertaken. I also thank our school's president at that time, Fr. Nicholas Triantafilou, as well as His Eminence Archbishop Demetrios of America for blessing this leave.

The prompting to write this book came from my editor, Mother Nectaria McLees, who during her student years at Holy Cross became a close friend. The staff and many of the readers of her magazine, *Road to Emmaus: A Journal of Orthodox Faith and Culture*, encouraged me to publish with their responses to the earlier chapters.

Since I first discovered *The Death and Life of Great American Cities* in 1996, Jane Jacobs has been perhaps the single most important thinker for my intellectual development. Our correspondence and acquaintance from late 1999 until her passing in April of 2006 was one of the treasures of my life. As I say in the text of these interviews, she was not a religious person, nor do I try to make of her an "anonymous Christian." Nevertheless, I am grateful for the example of profound wonder and moral purity which guided her own attempts to make sense of the world.

Rev. Dr. Stanley Harakas, the professor who established the study of Ethics at Holy Cross, at the end of his career remarked that he had reached a point in his academic work where he increasingly felt compelled to rely on a trans-rational category, "fittingness," to demonstrate the validity of Orthodox ethical positions. "Fittingness" is an aesthetic quality, I have since realized, and so I hope that by beginning with Beauty, I am continuing precisely where Fr. Harakas left off.

THE ETHICS OF BEAUTY

From this Beauty comes the existence of everything,
  each being exhibiting its own way of beauty.
For Beauty is the cause of harmony, of sympathy,
  and of community.
Beauty unites all things and is the source of all things.
Beauty is the great creating cause which bestirs the world
  and holds all things in existence by the longing inside
  them to have Beauty.

And there it is ahead of all as Goal, as the Beloved,
  as the Cause toward which all things move,
  since it is the longing for Beauty which actually
  brings them into being.
Beauty is a model to which they conform…

From the One, the Good, the Beautiful –
  the interrelationship of all things in accordance
  with capacity.
From the One, the Good, the Beautiful –
  the harmony and the love which are formed
  between them but which do not obliterate identity.
From the One, the Good, the Beautiful –
  the innate togetherness of everything.

From the One, the Good, the Beautiful, also –
  the intermingling of everything, the persistence of
  things, the unceasing emergence of things…

– St. Dionysios the Areopagite
Divine Names, 4.7

CHAPTER ONE

THE OPPOSITE OF WAR IS NOT PEACE

Healing Trauma in the *Iliad* and in Orthodox Tradition

It may seem odd that an Ethics of Beauty should begin with the discussion of beauty's antithesis in war and in trauma, or with critiques of just war theory and of our current approach to healing psychologically afflicted veterans.

However, when I was first interviewed by Road to Emmaus Journal *on the subject of Orthodox Christian views of war, my intention was not at all to write an "Ethics of Beauty." Rather, my main concern was for the victims of war trauma. Troubled by reports that our conventional approaches to the healing of their souls were failing, I offered educated guesses as to why this might be so, and suggested an alternative path towards spiritual wholeness.*

In this chapter I begin to discuss this other approach to healing the psychic wounds of combat, at the same time laying out the very ancient Christian view on war to which it corresponded. This spiritual method I term the Beauty-first way, and it is relevant not only for those suffering from trauma, but for anyone concerned with human soul development.

I. THE COST OF WAR

ROAD TO EMMAUS: It's not surprising that as a seminary ethics professor you have a theoretical interest in the Christian ethics of war, but do you also find this topic compelling as an *Orthodox* Christian?

DR. PATITSAS: As both an Orthodox Christian and as an American, yes. I was born and raised in the United States, with its huge military – now slightly larger in terms of expenditure than that of the next thirteen countries combined. I was raised to respect this might, to be grateful for it, and to honor our soldiers. This may sound strange, but the Fall of Saigon in 1975 made a huge impact on me, even though I was not yet nine years old! I really felt that a terrible tragedy had befallen not just the South Vietnamese, but the world. By the age of 13 or 14, I understood with pain something of the unique situation of Vietnam veterans upon their return to society. This gives you some sense of how long I've been thinking and even worrying about these types of issues.

And of course as Americans we are not only experiencing the aftereffects of wars fought in the twentieth century, but already in this new century we've been fighting in Somalia, Iraq, Afghanistan, the Philippines, Pakistan, Yemen, and other places – sometimes mainly with our drone strikes.

We may not think about it, but for centuries the Byzantines waged similarly amorphous struggles against similar opponents, and if this were widely known, many more people would wonder what that civilization might have to teach us. The one book to draw this comparison explicitly is Edward Luttwak's *The Grand Strategy of the Byzantine Empire*.[1] Byzantinists have qualified portions of Luttwak's work, but, in the main, his arguments seem plausible to anyone who knows Orthodox Christian theology and Byzantine history.[2]

In reading Luttwak, I was most impressed by two things about the Byzantines. First, the great lengths they went to in order to avoid actual combat engagement with their enemies. What we call the Byzantine army was really the Christianized Roman army, the most experienced army in history to that time, and yet their attitude was, "Even if you are really powerful, in battle things can still go terribly wrong." They also knew that war is a morally questionable

---

[1] Edward Luttwak, *The Grand Strategy of the Byzantine Empire* (Cambridge, MA: Belknap Press of Harvard University Press, 2009).

[2] For a highly regarded Byzantinist who largely supports Luttwak's work, but with many corrections and qualifications, see Anthony Kaldellis, "Edward N. Luttwak, *The Grand Strategy of the Byzantine Empire*" in the *Bryn Mawr Classical Review* 2010.01.49.

enterprise, and although they certainly fought wars, they also used all sorts of negotiations and devices to avoid them.

War Is a Great Evil

RTE: What else impressed you about Luttwak?

DR. PATITSAS: How eastern and western Christians each thought about the ethics of war. For the West by the time of the Crusades, war might in certain cases not be morally ambiguous. A blessed cause for war makes the war an unqualified good, and therefore participating in it is not a sin. Even killing in war is not a sin but can in fact be part of a holy service that absolves you of your sins.

What the Orthodox Byzantines retained was an older notion that war inevitably damages the soul. Even in a just cause, in self-defense or to protect innocents, participation in war still harms the soul in some measure; in Old Testament terms, "blood guilt" is incurred in battle.

And so I came to the realization that the Byzantine employment of religious rituals around war – inviting priests to bless troops and weapons, to pray before battles – was not a blessing of warfare as such (although they certainly prayed for victories, partly because they saw them as the quickest route to peace). Rather the reverse: the primary purpose of such prayers was to inoculate the soldier against a particular kind of damage that could occur to his soul during war – what we would refer to as traumatic stress.[3] These acts of blessing, still retained in Orthodox countries, are not to be understood as the Church pronouncing war good, but exist precisely because she knows that war is always evil.

---

3 Or "moral injury," or again, "blood guilt." Alice Linsley, author of the "Just Genesis" blog in which she applies anthropological research to the first book of the Bible, in a phone call in May of 2015 pointed out that even most of the heroes in Genesis had direct experience of killing, or at least of war. They expressed their subsequent spiritual state in terms of "blood guilt." The leaders of Genesis knew from experience that a warrior, in order to serve and save his people, would incur a spiritual cost. Even if "trauma" and PTSD are somewhat culture-specific descriptions of part of the soldier's burden, the difficulty of living with having killed is universal. See my afterword to this chapter for a discussion of "moral injury" as an alternative term for the spiritual impact of war.

Let's put this more intimately: these soldiers aren't strangers to us. They are our sons and daughters, our relatives. And, moreover, they are not disposable – we want them back when this evil has passed. So of course we don't just send them into battle spiritually defenseless. We give them every armor, so that when they experience the horror of war, it won't destroy them spiritually, psychologically, or emotionally.

Again, the Byzantines were not saying that war could be made holy, but that its innate destructiveness would overwhelm us unless we bind ourselves tightly to our ultimate holy values. For the Byzantines, that meant the cross of Christ, the Church. American soldiers also defend their psychic integrity by binding themselves to their most sacred values when they face combat. Since we Americans are influenced by Calvinism, that means above all that we interpret battle in terms of "work": it's not "killing"; it's "completing the mission." Cartoonist Gary Trudeau quipped in the first Gulf War that so many soldiers were describing their own involvement with the words, "I've got a job to do," that the NBC News "theme" for its television coverage of the war should be amended from "America at War" to "America at Work."

Other supreme American values are also called upon to make the chaos meaningful and save the soldier's soul: cleanliness – and we say of the enemy, "Waste him"; discipline of the weak as an unavoidable duty, and we call upon our soldiers to "hurt those little people"; self-reliance, and of his own fallen comrade a soldier in Vietnam might say, "He screwed up"; and of course sex, as in, "We ****** them up."

Clearly work, cleanliness, discipline of the errant, self-reliance, and sex can be positive values, but they won't safeguard your soul in a time of trouble the way the cross of Christ will.

Today in the secular West, we are recovering some of the ancient understanding. For every war America has fought for which we have data, we have sustained far more psychological casualties than physical casualties. In his book, *On Killing: The Psychological Cost of Learning to Kill in War and Society*, David Grossman – a lieutenant colonel in the U.S. Army and a practicing psychologist – talks about periods in World War II where the Army was discharging the psychologically wounded as fast as it could bring new soldiers in.[4] Gone now is the old notion that because a war is "just" it is somehow not going to hurt you. No serious person in the psychotherapeutic or American military community accepts that at this point.

Maybe we will also persuade other Christians of the Orthodox Christian view and maybe we won't, but for now a major component of this Orthodox position has become both accepted psychological science and official U.S. policy. Although they don't yet know how to inoculate people psychologically against war or to treat them once they have returned, everyone accepts that war always causes some setback, or at least imposes some cost, spiritually and psychologically.

Just War and Bad Moral Luck

RTE: How much of our Orthodox view is from the New Testament and how much goes back to the classical Greek philosophy that also fed into Byzantium?

DR. PATITSAS: In his Epistle to the Romans, St. Paul commands Orthodox Christians to respect soldiers and the government, and to cooperate with their divinely appointed mission to keep the peace. In the narrative of Christ's crucifixion and in the martyrdom of St. Ignatius of Antioch, there is respect for the office of a soldier. "This is what you have been appointed to do" – and even Pilate is reduced to that necessity. A soldier is in a position where he may be ordered to use violence, and there's not much he can do about it.

More positively, in Church hymnography we understand that the timing of Christ's incarnation was related to the fact that most of the known world was then gathered into one polity by Caesar Augustus. The Christian empire came to be seen as an image of

---

4 David Grossman, *On Killing: The Psychological Cost of Learning to Kill in War and in Society* (Boston: Little, Brown, 1995).

God's oneness – there is one God, and with a Christian emperor, there is one earthly ruler.

And yet, the Church still maintained that killing is always wrong and that Christians should not, if possible, get involved in these things. We have many examples of those who practiced the absolute refusal to kill, including the Russian passion-bearers Boris and Gleb. As the sons of Prince Vladimir the Great (958-1015), they were raised and trained to battle, but as Christians, they wouldn't fight to save themselves or their birthright. They knew that to do so would simply unleash a wider circle of vengeance and hurt many more people.

RTE: Do you have any thoughts as to why the East and West diverged in their ideas of warfare? Even before the schism, the West constructed their just war theory and then went on to develop the idea of a Christian holy war with the Crusades.

DR. PATITSAS: Just war theory provides a necessary checklist so that our fighting will rise above the level of pure brigandage and murder. For example, there must be a legitimate authority involved, and the cause must be defensive or at least have a moral validity to it.[5]

But where does this go wrong? You know, once while I was picking up my godson from elementary school, I overheard two fathers speaking. Both were apparently well-educated professional men. The first dad was very earnestly making the point that, if something couldn't be avoided, if acting in some way was a part of nature, then clearly that act could not be immoral. The other father wholeheartedly agreed. As men of the world, this made perfect sense to them.

But of course as Christians the argument from nature is insufficient, because nature itself is now subject to fallen influences. There is a tragic dimension inherent in our existence, such that we are often forced to do wrong things in order to survive or to protect our children. Rationalism, however, lacks this appreciation for trag-

---

5 For a full list of just war criteria, see footnote 23 below.

edy, tries to talk itself out of what poetry, religion, and music know so well: the world is not what it should be, and life is not reducible to linear syllogisms.

Ethicists have a concept known as "moral luck" – that sometimes we are held blamable for our action or character, even though we were powerless to act or be otherwise due to bad circumstance. Rationalism hates luck, and ethical rationalism hates moral luck; luck, if it exists, would frustrate logical reflection.

Well, war involves whole skeins of bad moral luck, and so any attempt to create a perfect intellectual ethical system about it is going to drive you very quickly away from the tragic (and let's face it, sometimes tragi-comic) reality of actual war. It is going to lead you, albeit in rational, logical steps, to completely absurd conclusions.

Jews, Greeks, and Romans: Balancing Three Cultural Styles

RTE: If the West is more rational, more linear, how then would you describe the East? Irrational? Ortherworldly?

DR. PATITSAS: Orthodox Christian Rome – Byzantium – aimed for (and frequently achieved) a mature blend and balance of three modes of being in this world. They had the mind of the Classical and Hellenistic Greeks; they had the heart and personalism of the Semitic world, of the Jews in particular; and they had the practical rationality and organization of the Romans. And while the Greek mind and the Jewish heart might both seem to us more important, in fact it was the Roman body, the Roman system, that lent them their primary cultural identity in Christ.

Some have argued that further West, Christians gradually lost one aspect of this triad, the Semitic personalism, even while retaining the Greek respect for intellect and the Roman reverence for law and power. What Western Europe either lost or minimized with time was one dimension of the way of the heart. The intellect became primary.

RTE: Yet the West has had mystical saints down to the present day.

DR. PATITSAS: Yes, of course. Ultimately, it is difficult to get the balance of mind, heart, and body just right. Whenever the balance of an idea falls away from the heart and toward the mind, we have taken to referring to it as "Western," no matter where it transpires geographically. Western Europe was once Orthodox; among Orthodox theologians today, the question of whether a new idea is consistent with the tradition, or has become "Western" because it is somehow no longer mystical in the right way, is always an open one. These terms are not nationalist or tribalist.

At some point, though, there did occur a slight separation between the mystics and the theologians of medieval Roman Catholic Europe, a gap between the cloistered prayer of the heart and the theology of the university scholars. The slightest such gap would be fatal for truly Orthodox life. When the mind is no longer submitted to the heart, it becomes irrational through an excess of rationalism, while at the same time the heart becomes dull through an excess of passion and imagination.

The unity of mind and heart, of a mind stationed in the heart and focused on the Name of Christ, is far more than a matter of having the right attitude. Rather, it is a hard-fought, spiritual force-against-spiritual force, bodily achievement. For this reason the true Orthodox Christian must always be a Roman first, at least in his *élan*.

Without experience or victory in this struggle, a university scholar like myself will arrive at the false conclusion that the intellectual sins (pride in particular) are the primary sins, since the intellectual power of the soul is itself higher than either the appetitive or the incensive powers. But in the East the memory endured because the practice was preserved – it is in the lowest part of the soul, in the appetitive powers, where the battle will be won or lost. Sensuality – which in the context of the Jesus Prayer means chasing after images, sensations (even holy ones), failing to keep the basic fasts of the Church – is the gateway to all sin. Such self-love is the mother of the passions; pride, merely her most developed and insidious child.

RTE: But how does knowing this affect ethical deliberation about war?

DR. PATITSAS: You can't do the ethics of war with your mind in the first place, nor even with your heart, if by heart we mean something like the emotions.

Rather, starting with your body, in the light of your duty to protect your loved ones who are forced by circumstance into combat, you must not deny your bodily instinct that they return from war *wounded* and yet *through no fault of their own*. They have changed in some way, and many of them will struggle terribly in trying to re-enter society. Everything begins with accepting these facts about people whom we love.

Putting the intellectual sins first misses the point of everything, because if on paper you can justify that a war is necessary, then supposedly these intellectual sins aren't involved and participation in a war won't hurt you. From our eastern, Orthodox perspective, just to witness combat is already a terrible burden on the soul. Whereas the mere fact that a particular war can be proved intellectually to be the lesser of two evils – and therefore unavoidable, or perhaps even preferable to not fighting – doesn't in itself resolve the spiritual or emotional wounds suffered in combat.

It is still individuals who kill or at least experience those images and passionate feelings, and it is individuals who have to be cleansed, as St. Basil the Great says when he has soldiers who kill in battle refrain from receiving Holy Communion for three years.

RTE: So you are saying that war remains evil, even when justified. Is killing in war then murder?

DR. PATITSAS: Some early Christians called it that, but St. Basil the Great did not agree, and his penance for a soldier is not the same as the penance for a murderer. So, the motives outlined in the West's just war theory certainly do apply in the East as well, when you are distinguishing types of killing according to logical criteria. Killing in war is ethically distinct from murder. However, the fulfillment of the just war criteria is not sufficient to inoculate us absolutely and completely from war's evil; war still hurts us.

Achilles in Vietnam

RTE: Then what do you think is the spiritual reason behind St. Basil's penance? Many people see it as a sort of punishment, but perhaps it has more to do with healing.

DR. PATITSAS: Yes, St. Basil was concerned with healing. Today, our best thinker about war and the healing of the soul after war is Jonathan Shay, an M.D., Ph.D. in clinical psychiatry, who wrote *Achilles in Vietnam: Combat Trauma and the Undoing of Character*.[6] Shay says that the *Iliad*, our oldest western epic, was designed as therapy for post-traumatic stress.[7] It was written and recited to fulfill this role, and it did so successfully. Simone Weil said that the *Iliad* is also the only epic in western history that doesn't take sides between the two warring parties.[8] It mourns the death of the Trojans as much as it does of the Achaeans, the Greeks. Shay thinks that this may have been because it was performed for and in order to heal descendants of both sides.

Shay's point is that a culture that recited the *Iliad*, that had its combat veterans listening to the *Iliad*, was a culture that still thought that war is, as Simone Weil says, something that hurts not only the losers but also the winners. The Orthodox Christian position naturally complements this older Greek view. In a sense, this view is older than the Church. Cultures that have taken the view, "This is for the

---

6 Jonathan Shay serves as Visiting Scholar-at-Large at the U.S. Naval War College and holds the Chair of Ethics, Leadership, and Personnel Policy in the Office of the U.S. Army, Deputy Chief of Staff for Personnel. In 2008-09 he was appointed to the Omar Bradley Chair of Strategic Leadership at the U.S. Army War College and Dickinson College. In 2007 he received the MacArthur "Genius Grant" Fellowship to further support his work with trauma victims. Shay is the author of *Achilles in Vietnam: Combat Trauma and the Undoing of Character* (NY: Maxwell MacMillan International, 1994) and *Odysseus in America: Combat Trauma and the Trials of Homecoming* (NY: Scribner, 2002).

7 Alexander Pope, trans., *The Iliad of Homer* (New York: Macmillan, 1965).

8 See Simone Weil, *Intimations of Christianity Among the Ancient Greeks* (Boston: Beacon Press, 1958) for her essay, "The Iliad, Poem of Might."

glory of Rome, the other guys deserve it, and let's get on with it," tend to be cultures where off-duty soldiers spend a lot of time getting drunk. They are self-medicating in some other, less effective way.[9]

RTE: Is the *Iliad*, then, an expression of remorse for the destruction of war?

DR. PATITSAS: Yes, the Trojan War was a total disaster. The *Iliad* is a celebration of the bravery of both sides – the youth, the strength, the beauty – but the epic also tells us that these heroic men in fact are all too weak to escape being trapped in this conflict. It is a profound text that already has (that, in a way, originates) this Orthodox Christian view of war – that no one wins completely.

RTE: Would you call it a religious text?

DR. PATITSAS: Fascinatingly, the entirety of the *Iliad* occurs within a space marked by two profound desecrations of the classical liturgical program, of the religious belief and observance of the Trojan and Achaean peoples. As it opens, Agamemnon, one of the Greek commanders, has offended Apollo's priests by taking a priest's daughter as his concubine. As a result, plague has struck his army. When the seers divine that Agamemnon must give the woman back, he grudgingly does so – but instead takes Achilles' war-prize, a maiden named Briseus whom Achilles loves.

Achilles then withdraws from battle in bitter protest and, without him, the Greeks begin to lose until his friend Patroclus puts on Achilles' armor and goes into battle pretending to be Achilles. When Patroclus is killed, however, Achilles begins to suffer a complete breakdown, spiritually and mentally. He becomes a monster. Where before he had always shown compassion to enemy prisoners, now there is no stopping him; he's just a murderer. His murderous thirst for revenge is not slaked until he kills the Trojan hero Hector, desecrates his corpse, and then himself is killed.

---

[9] For a very brief look at this issue, see Matthew Gault, "The Problem of Drug-addicted Soldiers is as Old as War," on the respected *War is Boring* website, May 8, 2015; accessed on August 8, 2017.

While Agamemnon's sacrilege opens the *Iliad*, the hero Odysseus' sacrilege ends the Trojan War itself. In fact, Odysseus ends not only the war, but the entire Heroic Age because he is so very human and because he intentionally subverts the ancient liturgy. In his case, he does so not out of passion, but almost as an act of moral superiority over the capriciousness of the gods, who have caused the war to drag on for a decade. So, he devises the Trojan Horse, which in fact is not only a ruse aimed at his human opponents, but a deceptive liturgical offering. But because the sacral order is thus violated and Troy destroyed, Odysseus will be punished for ten long years.

Nevertheless, this also says something good about Odysseus, because although that old heroic world was somehow superhuman, it was also therefore subhuman. The heroes were demi-gods, comic book characters of superhuman strength and virtue and manliness, but they lacked some humanizing element. Odysseus doesn't. He's just a man who wants to get back to his wife, and by his action he brings the ancient world to its end. He is really our first modern, the first European. His only "super-powers" are devotion to home and his amazing cleverness.

Odysseus is a precursor of Christ, Who also subverted the liturgy of His people.[10] When Christ was mistaken for a mere man and crucified, He is hidden in plain view on the wood of the cross, just as Odysseus is hidden within the wood of the Trojan Horse. They are both subverting liturgy (indeed, the Chief Priest who sentenced Christ was entirely unaware that this was the liturgical act for which he had been appointed) with the aim of making peace. If you take the Greek gods as demons, or as simpler, more childlike versions of the demons, then both heroes have tricked the demons.[11]

---

10 Steve Zabak, who read this text in advance, pointed out that St. Paul seems to be making some sort of connection between Odysseus and Christ, through his choice of words in the opening lines of his Epistle to the Hebrews. For a meditation on what exactly that connection might be, and how strong the literary echoes are, see Jared Calaway, "Polutropos: Much-Turned Speech in the Odyssey and Hebrews," on his *Antiquitopia* blog, March 18, 2009. Accessed August 8, 2017.

11 This idea of Christ's being hidden upon the cross in order to trick the demons is from Nicholas Constas, "The Last Temptation of Satan: Divine Deception in Greek Patristic Interpretations of the Passion Narrative," in *The Harvard Theological Review*, vol. 97, no. 2 (April 2004), 139-163.

There was something doubly brave in what Odysseus did. He and his men could have been discovered inside the Trojan Horse and wiped out, so in a sense they *are* dying; they are a part of the sacrificial object which they offer. It's a liturgical death that they simulate.

Of course, we don't depict the story like this. We depict them as "clever guys," but theirs was a culture saturated in ritual. They knew what they were doing. They were both desperate and willing to be damned, not just physically, but also spiritually, because they had to end the damned horrible thing that is war.

The Widespread Reluctance to Kill

RTE: How does Jonathan Shay take all this? Does he also admire Odysseus?

DR. PATITSAS: Yes. Shay's first book is *Achilles in Vietnam*. His second book is *Odysseus in America: Combat Trauma and the Trials of Homecoming*. In his first book, Shay's empathy and focus are with Achilles himself, and in the process Shay gives us this amazing corroboration of the Orthodox Christian view that war may sometimes be the lesser of two evils, but it still remains evil, and it is harmful to our souls.

A strain of research decades before Shay pointed in this direction. After World War II, S.L.A. Marshall, a U.S. army historian,[12] organized interviews with thousands of American soldiers who had been on the front lines, actual infantry who were doing much of the ground fighting in Europe and the Pacific. I can hardly believe that this is true, but he and his team of combat historians found that about 85% of trained soldiers would either not fire their weapons in combat or, if they did fire, would aim high or wide so as to avoid directly harming the enemy. Other historians subsequently found this to be true not only for World War II for the Americans, but for the other side, and in fact for any other war for which we have firm casualty statistics. When ancient battles are reenacted, historians find that the number of deaths that were actually generated would

---

12 S.L.A. Marshall: A commissioned officer and U.S. Army World War II and Korean War historian who authored some thirty books about warfare.

have been many times higher, had all soldiers really sought to harm their enemies. It also seems that soldiers' nearly universal reluctance to kill was well-known to non-commissioned officers from the time of the Roman legions until now. Historically, officers have had to force their enlisted men to actually kill, or very little killing would be happening in combat.

RTE: This is so unexpected. Can you tell us more of the soldiers' perspective?

DR. PATITSAS: Many soldiers feel that they are killing a part of their own soul if they do kill, and when it comes right down to it, most people would rather die physically than spiritually. There are a tiny minority of people who are psychopathic or sociopathic, and there are also a minority of sane people who can kill in war or in self-defense without much apparent damage to themselves, but that is a very small percentage. David Grossman's estimate of psychologically healthy soldiers who can kill without suffering spiritually is very low – far less than the 15% who will fire at all.

Grossman said that in studying Marshall's numbers, he was ashamed of American soldiers who didn't take the chance to help their cause, their nation, and their friends, but he was also proud of them for this human response. As he points out, these non-firing World War II soldiers were not cowards. In fact, they were exposing themselves to great danger, treating their fellow wounded, and bringing in more ammunition under intense fire. They were doing all these brave things – but they weren't killing.

Grossman's book is now required reading for new DEA and FBI Agents, and, I think, non-commissioned officers in the U.S. Army, because one of his findings is that many men won't fire unless their commanding officer is right there forcing them to fire. Meanwhile, Shay's book has become very influential for classicists, who now almost all agree with his premise about the *Iliad's* therapeutic purpose. No scholar now feels that they can understand the *Iliad* without Shay, but *Achilles in Vietnam* also changed the way in which the U.S. Army is organized and deployed.

RTE: Because the army wants to find a way around this human reluctance to kill?

DR. PATITSAS: Yes and no. After Marshall's WWII-era findings, Grossman tells us that the U.S. Army went to a new method of training, which was really as much psychological conditioning as training, by having soldiers shoot at human-like shapes that pop up at you, and so forth. Subsequent to this, the incidence of post-traumatic stress in Vietnam skyrocketed and hasn't stopped yet. But many of the changes in Army practice adopted from Shay are done in order to lessen the psychological burden of war. It has this positive, prophylactic side as well.

The danger would be that we moderns would understand this ancient and Orthodox view but then become worse than we were before, by using it only – as you say – to kill more effectively and to involve still more of our young people in killing.

RTE: Have the firing percentages changed with the new conditioning?

DR. PATITSAS: They claim it has, but I see anecdotal evidence that in a war like Vietnam, firing percentages rose when you couldn't see the enemy in jungle combat anyway. Snipers and infantry with confirmed kills were still a small minority of even front-line troops. If the percentages have risen, it might be because today's soldiers are farther from traditional Christianity or because they are all volunteers.

Grossman also thinks that videos and computer games work exactly the way army conditioning now does. He says that through these games, we are conditioning our young to kill but without any of the social controls the army has in place. Conditioning that makes people more apt to kill will only deepen the psychological trauma and impact society as a whole, as we are seeing ever more clearly.

RTE: If Grossman is saying that our innate respect for life is being conditioned out of soldiers, how does this affect them as individuals?

DR. PATITSAS: Grossman focuses on the moral cost of learning to kill and of killing. Shay is looking at a related experience: When in combat you have seen the violation of the moral order sanctioned by your own chain of command, what does that do to your character?

In reading Shay, you tend to focus on moral violations that are egregious – such as being ordered to endanger civilians – whereas in reading Grossman you are reminded that sanctioned killing in a justified war is itself a violation of human morality. Killing in war, even in a situation where the enemy soldier is about to kill you, will strike Marshall's non-firing 85% as a violation of social morality. The army perhaps didn't do anything *per se* that was a betrayal of its own code, as was the case when Agamemnon wronged Achilles. However, when a young pure-hearted person who perhaps grew up as a Roman Catholic altar boy or as a devout Protestant sees the reality of killing, he feels that the moral compact with which he has been raised is broken. He has been betrayed by the society that raised him, because it made him a soldier and told him to kill.

The Berserk State

Let me stress this point: Post-combat spiritual wounds are by no means sufficient proof that someone has committed a violation of the laws of war. All war is a violation of human morality, on a very deep level. As the ancient Church taught, even when war is the lesser of two evils, still it remains evil. A returning soldier will have to do penance not because he is deserving of punishment, but because he is deserving of forgiveness and cleansing from the realm of sin into which his society sent him. He has faced a moral dilemma – either to kill his enemy or allow his society to be ruined – and he has made the wiser choice, perhaps. But he has entered a zone of blood and impurity and will need God's grace through the cleansing of confession.

Shay's brilliance lies in describing what can happen when you experience the violation of the social moral order. A chain of events can be unleashed in your soul that culminates in "post-traumatic stress." What happens, says Shay, is that you may undergo a progressive shrinking of the sphere of your concern for others, until the circle includes no one – not even yourself.

RTE: What would that look like?

DR. PATITSAS: Shay describes a phenomenon in war known as "berserking," in which a soldier undertakes desperately fearless actions but without regard really for his cause or even for the safety of his brother soldiers. At that point, the trauma victim has moved outside of human social relating; he is part animal, part god, and feels himself to be such, as he exposes himself to danger even if it compromises the mission – for example, by triggering an ambush so as to maximize his own heroics before his unit is ready to defend itself. This is the state to which Achilles fell when his moral order began to unravel through his commander's betrayal of what was right.

Shay says that trauma *always* starts with the feeling that the moral order has been betrayed. It's not merely the carnage or the killing that harms us.

To begin with, the soldier will experience the shrinking of his moral horizon in positive terms – he would do anything for his brothers, those in his own unit. He is fighting for his buddy. He does not recognize that his deepening attachment to them may be a sign that his attachment to the rest of humanity – including his enemy – has weakened. But when this inner circle is violated – that is, when the hell of war results in one of them, particularly a best friend, dying – then the sphere of moral concern can become quite narrow indeed. The person may eventually lose all interpersonal connection, which culminates in the berserk state during which a traumatized person attempts to destroy everything around him in a god-like rage.

In Achilles' case, he first withdraws from the army of the Greeks, but he remains attached to his company and to his friend Patroclus. When Patroclus is killed in the mix-up that follows, then Achilles' field of concern shrinks even more. Prior to these events, Achilles would defend or at least show compassion to the enemy prisoners he took, but he now just slays them, ten or twelve at a time, overcome with lust for blood in this berserk state.

This berserking is a kind of ecstasy – or rather, its parodic reversal. It is not communion with all men and with all things, but is rather the final death of communion. Berserking is, we Orthodox would recognize at once, the very opposite of that which saves us – communion with God and others in liturgy. Shay doesn't use the word liturgy, of course, but he does show how this totalizing experience leads to a cutting of communion and the unraveling of character.

War, for the berserker, has become an anti-liturgy, and of course, many soldiers experience this in some lesser degree. As in liturgy, all five senses are fully employed; a kind of divinization is experienced; a letting go of earthly attachments occurs; there is a ritual of bloodletting. But the berserker, unlike other soldiers, undergoes all of it in the service of annihilation of the self and the other.

Shielding the Soul from Trauma

RTE: How has the U.S. Army used these insights in a good way, to inoculate soldiers from this ex-communication?

DR. PATITSAS: I'm glad you called it that. Now you know why the Church "excommunicates" the soldier who has killed in combat or has even experienced close combat. She is not "punishing" the soldier but rather "staunching" the spiritual wound he has received. She is *not only* imposing a limit on Communion until his soul can be purified for re-entry to society, but, by saying that the ban from the Eucharist will last no more than three years, she is *also limiting the extent* of the excommunication. The Church bans the soldier from the chalice – particularly in these kinds of extreme cases – temporarily, because the traumatized soldier himself will be tempted to make the ban permanent. I was so relieved when I understood this.[13]

[13] One of my students, Bryce Buffenbarger, reacted to the matter in this way: We are meant to think of St. Basil's three-year penance not as the minimum but as the maximum length of excommunication. That is exactly my point: we are dealing here with a limit. Confession is required, but the actual period of time without Holy Communion comes down to the question of how best to heal the soul of the particular combat veteran before you.

But back to the United States Army. Post-Shay, soldiers are rotated into and out of combat as part of the same unit with which they train and will be debriefed afterwards. Unbelievably, in the Vietnam War years, we had actually been rotating soldiers individually! The cutting of communion and of combat brotherhood was built-in. It was a system custom-made to produce deep combat trauma.

More could be done. For Shay our major remaining mistake is the speed with which the bodies of dead soldiers are vanished out of the combat theater. Grieving for brother soldiers must be more prolonged, and more physical, if we are to heal properly.

By the way, Shay isn't saying that every soldier or every soldier in direct combat experiences trauma. It depends on factors that can't be predicted. But he is saying that when trauma occurs, it occurs in these specific stages: almost always, the person first feels that something immoral is going on, and then comes this progressive shrinking of the social horizon. But we also have to remember that no matter what a person did in war or in any situation, it's not the end.

RTE: What about other forms of traumatic stress – say after childhood abuse or a plane crash?

DR. PATITSAS: Although Shay is very respectful of the uniqueness of the combat experience, he believes that when trauma victims insist that their own brand of trauma was uniquely horrible, that this itself is a result of the trauma. One way of excommunicating ourselves is to show that we have suffered as no other person ever has; if no one can understand or share my suffering, then my godlike aloneness is total. There is a danger, in trauma, of being seduced by this forbidden fruit, this access to ultimate isolation, that promises me an almost godlike knowledge of good and evil. We could even become proud of having suffered some evil in complete and divine aloneness.

In fact, though, studies of the brain demonstrate that chronic neglect of an infant or child can be as traumatizing as more explicit kinds of child abuse or adult trauma. Trauma actually rewires certain aspects of the internal connections within the brain. Certain brain scans that map the trauma wound cannot really distinguish people who have been attacked, assaulted, or just plain neglected. In every case, communion has been profoundly broken, and the brain and soul are deeply wounded. Shay believes there is also a commonality in successful therapy, in that it relies not on the intellect but is based in new patterns of relating to the self and others.

RTE: This is all so heart-wrenching. How do your students react to it?

DR. PATITSAS: We now have students who are combat veterans. And their major reminder to me is that war can destroy character, but it can also refine it. The soldier is by definition a victim of what Simone Weil called "The Empire of Might." But in the right circumstances this will make him stronger and wiser than the man or woman who stayed at home. Many soldiers feel that they have risked their sanity and salvation for the sake of society, that there was a real sacrifice of self in that intent. As a society, we do respect that. We think, "That guy has been in combat." We look up to him because he has been tested in a way we haven't. One of my friends confessed that he was ashamed to still be suffering traumatic outbursts since the war. But I told him that some of the men who did not face the dangers involved in protecting their country also feel ashamed.

An attack by armed injustice presents us with a moral dilemma: If we do not fight, the injustice and evil may increase; if we do fight, we will cross a line by shedding human blood. Moral dilemmas are like that: most of us will not come out of them without something to repent of.

And we should see other victims of trauma with respect, as well. At some point, we have to look up to the person who was abandoned to an underfunded orphanage and rarely held for the first three years of their life. Their whole life may now be nothing but suffering, and they can't get well, but that person is more than us in a way. Their identity with that ultimate trauma victim – Christ, and him crucified – is different and perhaps greater than ours. Nevertheless, what Shay is after is not just the proud display of trauma scars but genuine healing. The Church would agree. After these disasters, the resurrection must be permitted to come.

II. AFTER COMBAT

The Opposite of War Is not Peace

RTE: Taking all this together – Shay's work, Grossman's meditations, your students' responses, and your wider awareness that many more people than just soldiers suffer the psychological wounds of trauma, what have you come to?

DR. PATITSAS: Above all, this: that the opposite of war, or of any kind of trauma, is not peace, and that it is bootless to try to find peace after these events. Our psychology, with its excessive faith in the therapeutic power of "getting it out," has reduced the human soul to a steam engine and emotional healing to an elaborate system of hydraulic adjustments – "venting" about sums it up. This approach is reductive; there is something deeply wrong in it. Modern psychology has nearly destroyed friendship in this country – we say too much, we analyze too much, and, worst of all, we do all this "in cold blood."

After trauma there can be no return to a category as neutral as "peace." The opposite of war is not peace, but liturgy – the cognitive, bodily, totalizing act that steadily increases communion, instead of cutting it. Liturgy is an act that purifies and knits the character together, whereas trauma unravels our character. In liturgy, I give my life for my brother and sister, I renounce retaliation, and I give my very body and blood for the life of the entire world.

It's like that wonderful saying that you must "either get busy living or get busy dying." Well, sin and trauma keep us enormously busy but slowly kill us, while liturgy keeps us busy *and* makes us live again. Trauma is more than busyness – it can have a kind of infinite effectiveness in excommunicating us, splitting us even from our own selves. Liturgy, especially the Divine Liturgy of St. John

Chrysostom, is the precise opposite; there, your communion and integration just increase and overflow, and all is taken in and reconciled. For the trauma victim, there isn't some third choice beyond these two poles; you have to, best as you can, try to choose liturgy. Moreover, Orthodox Christian liturgy enacts and teaches you actual doxological truth, whereas trauma teaches you a heretical truth. War, then – like every form of trauma experience – has always been an anti-liturgy.

RTE: Then war is not just the opposite of liturgy, but it actually enacts a false liturgy?

DR. PATITSAS: In any all-engulfing experience, you obtain a knowledge that totally overtakes you, but when such an experience includes trauma, other effects are added, including the *cutting* of communion, the unraveling of character, and the learning of heretical truths. The heresy taught by war is that a) my brother is not my life, but rather the opposite of my life, and b) that God is not all-powerful, or at least will not exercise that power in a loving way in my case.

Now, does my awareness that this is a lie mean that I myself wouldn't fight to protect my own? I would, but I also must know that ultimately it is not my enemy alone, but other dark powers who lie behind his actions. I must therefore recognize this fighting as, in part, misdirected. And moreover, even in a fallen world, the enactment of these partial truths is a deep tragedy.

As something of an aside, let me just mention how in the arena of sexual temptation we also see false truths being disclosed by very intense experiences of seeming communion. Sexual activity outside of marriage is still cognition ("knowing" the person, as Scripture says), it's still totalizing, but even at the moment that it's supposed to be the most intimate and ultimate experience, sexually immoral acts can "flip" and become the cutting of communion. This is why sexual addictions and promiscuity unravel our character, whereas sex within marriage helps us to knit it together. Sex outside of marriage teaches us a kind of heretical truth, even about – especially about – the goodness of sex itself, because people are left with these awful aftershocks of shame about their bodies and their desires; everything is inverted.[14]

Healing of Trauma

The point is that what we've "learned" as trauma victims in any of these traumatic experiences isn't completely true, despite how real it feels, because there is a partial, distorted truth transmitted to us in the moment of trauma. Trauma is practically the ultimate teacher; few other experiences so powerfully form our view of the world. And yet what it teaches us is mostly lies. To be sure, it has a part of the truth, though, so the issue isn't to erase it, because that would be going too far in the other direction.

But the trauma victim is driven towards a point where their only communion, in a way, is with that false knowledge, that lie, that says God is unloving and my fellow man is my enemy. Trauma therefore imparts a kind of reverse gnosis. And this applies not only to traumatized victims of war, but to any trauma sufferers, or to all of the trauma that you or I may have experienced in our lives.

We can't expect the world to equal the Church in its understanding of trauma. But now there is an awful lot of fresh understanding of trauma for the Church to work with, a whole improved array of evidence around which to reflect theologically. We say often among ourselves that to have Orthodox Christian theology is to have a "cheat sheet," to have all of the answers already, because everything in life can be explained so much better.

When we experience trauma, our very being is thrust away from coherence and solidity and towards non-being – and this is hell. But Christ's liturgy can absorb any amount of chaos and bring it back towards being.

---

[14] Certain of our sexual desires are God-given, while others are a fallen form of these God-given desires. In those cases where we become tired of resisting such fallen desires or intellectually convinced that they are not wrong, the "heresy" or wrong belief about our healthy sexual desires might then go in the other direction; no longer plagued by shame over our sin, we become impudent, declare our sin to be righteousness, and rebel against God or morality more openly.

Freud's Ambivalent Impact

RTE: Do Shay's observations on healing trauma apply to psychotherapy more generally?

DR. PATITSAS: To be frank, I think that we don't have much of a psychotherapy in the modern West and that we will never get one unless we are able to "master" trauma. The principles of healing taught us in the cases of trauma victims will then have to be used in every psychotherapeutic situation, although of course in appropriate ways.

Let me take a little detour, here: My mentor, the city-planner Jane Jacobs (1916-2006), said that the clues to what problems are piling up unsolved and will destroy a society are always to be found in the sufferings of a society's poor. Mother Theresa thought caring for the "poorest of the poor," including especially the unborn, was the gateway to social peace. Muhammad Yunus thought that lending to the very poorest was the only hope for real economic development.[15] Paul Farmer based his approach to universal social justice on serving the remotest and most medically deprived populations; among these, he identified women in childbirth as the most vulnerable and set their welfare as the lynchpin of social progress.[16] And our own St. Silouan summed it all up when he understood that he must simply pray, "All these will be saved; only I shall be lost."[17] To me, the witness of the twentieth century is unanimous: We will find our answers in solidarity with those who are at the negative apex of suffering and excommunication.

Well, among the poorest, the weakest, the most vulnerable person psychologically is the sufferer with PTSD. Not only are they ut-

---

15 See Muhammad Yunus, *Banker to the Poor: Micro-lending in the Battle Against World Poverty*, 1st ed. (NY: Public Affairs, 1999).

16 For the story of Dr. Paul Farmer, see Tracy Kidder, *Mountains Beyond Mountains*, 1st ed. (NY: Random House, 2003). Dr. Farmer specializes in establishing hospitals offering a First World standard of care in areas of the globe where there are almost no medical services of any kind.

17 Saint Silouan the Athonite (1866-1938) was a hesychast and ascetic of the Orthodox Christian tradition.

terly excommunicated, but all of their human energies are recruited to the fundamental task of deepening and preserving that excommunication. You can't threaten this person with hell; they already live there, and they will fight with their last breath to remain there.

Shay is finding ways to re-commune these ultimately vulnerable people. I am arguing that Shay stands with this list of twentieth-century thinkers who discovered that the essential key to their disciplines was to be found in what was thought to be the least likely place. Shay discovered that for trauma victims, the older psychotherapeutic techniques of exposure, self-revelation, and self-analysis only dug them further in. That is why I say that we don't yet have a psychotherapy in the contemporary West: if our most common approach, which is talk therapy, can't heal trauma, it's a sign that it probably isn't doing very much else correctly.

RTE: Then, out with Freud?

DR. PATITSAS: Freud's contribution to a genuine healing of the soul is extremely ambivalent. He can be taken as the first step toward the recovery of the way of the heart in the West. But he can just as accurately be interpreted as the final step of a rationalism that wanted to kill the power of the mystical heart.

So on the one hand, Freud is the death of the West. At least, what he helps to kill – as do Darwin, Marx, Nietzsche and others – is the Greek-Roman West of the Enlightenment. That movement intended to rely upon reason to the exclusion of the aesthetic sense and the moral sense for its understanding of the world. Like these other revolutionaries, however, Freud deploys rationalist scientism to deconstruct rationalism itself. Freud and these others demonstrate that reason is always grounded in modes of relating that are themselves not strictly reasonable – in Freud's case, what he termed the "unconscious." In this sense, we can say that Freud is the pivotal figure in the Western recovery of the way of the heart.

Now, why was such a recovery even necessary? From the standpoint of Orthodox Christianity, we might say that the West had became too Greek and insufficiently Jewish, the moment it lost the science of the human heart represented by the Jesus Prayer. When Western monasticism began to focus on the intellectual sins over the sensual sins, it in effect privileged the mind over the heart. Later, it would favor intellectually interesting categories like divine or human nature over the mystery of the actual divine or human person. You can see that this last statement is a fair description of why American psychotherapy feels somehow "off" to Orthodox Christian eyes. In therapy, the intellect barges too boldly and shamelessly into the inner hearts of people.

Nevertheless, Freud identified the core vulnerability of the Enlightenment: the fact that reason itself turns out to be reliant on non-rational forces. In Christian terms, we would say that without the heart and personal communion, the mind cannot even preserve the basic presuppositions of its own rationality. Freud, in his way, proved the same. Darwin and Marx, too, showed how all sorts of non-rational factors had to be in place before the human mind could come into being or start thinking.

In general, the discovery of the reliance of reason upon non-rational factors has not been taken well by the West. Without prayer of the heart – without an alternative account of reason's origin and role – you are really in trouble. The discovery that the "truth-first" way isn't working is driving the post-modernist West in a number of contradictory directions – religious fundamentalism, nihilism, hedonistic materialism, three-blind-mice scientism, gender dysmorphia, and, most especially, political messianism.

But, again, Freud and the others could also be taken in a very positive way, as signposts that without the way of the heart, the other ways of science and of engineering – the Greek and the Roman – are adrift, rudderless. Through his idea of the unconscious, Freud gives you back something like the Jewish heart – the non-rational motivation for human action.

And yet, Freud doesn't place the mind *in* the heart as does Orthodoxy. Rather, he just tries to drag the heart into the mind, which is what much of modern therapy does. And in this sense, he only takes you halfway home. In fact, one could even say that Freud makes matters worse by rationally dissecting what is most sacred, the inner chambers of our hearts. Shay found that for trauma victims, this approach was especially destructive, but the basic idea applies to all of us.

A Much Deeper Integration of Mind and Heart Is Necessary

And this is what Shay found: The merely intellectual retelling of traumatic experiences by his veterans led to an epidemic of suicides among his patients. That mentalist approach is always bad, but the trauma sufferers are your poor, your canaries in the coal mine. They are our best and first clue as to why modern psychotherapy is so flawed.

The trauma sufferer himself or herself seems at first to agree with the conventional psychotherapeutic approach. They imagine that through something like analytical talk therapy they will be able to weep, cry, get it out, purge it all away. But Shay found that for trauma it doesn't work this way. Although the therapist might think, "Wow, he really opened up to me today…", the problem seems to be that this talk therapy is only cognitive in a weak sense. It's just brain; it isn't yet a restoration of communion.

As I said, initially, Shay and his predecessors tried the reflective listening approach with their veteran patients, but they found it went horribly wrong. For severe victims of trauma, it led to a rash of suicides among the people who had been encouraged to talk about what they had seen and experienced. Mere talking was not yet a restoration of liturgical communion. Instead, it left them in total, killing isolation. As I said before, trauma is a deep excommunication, but this also makes it the unraveling of your very being, which is constituted only through interpersonal communion. The worst thing that can possibly happen to a person who has been excommunicated in this ultimate way by trauma is to be treated in this cold intellectual manner by their therapist.

Only one kind of listening helps – listening in which the hearer is deeply empathic. The trauma sufferer is isolated even from himself; the therapist must actually feel *for* him, until he can feel for himself.

RTE: But we've all listened with our whole hearts to friends who tell us the painful scenes over and over, but it doesn't seem to help. What is lacking in our empathy?

DR. PATITSAS: I'll tell you how it's done by the people who still know how to do it. But they are a small vanishing breed these days.

What they seem to somehow do, and really it turns out to be Christ acting in them, is that they take *all* of your pain, *all* of your isolation and trauma. They may do this through weeping where you can't, being outraged where you can't. Or, they may do it through a depth of inner life that I can scarcely imagine. What is crucial, though, at this phase, is that their intention is not to change you, to heal you, or even to help you, in a sense. Their only aim is to suffer for you. Only then – and this may take years of close spiritual friendship – does it begin to dawn on you that they are suffering in your place, that they are taking on your burden. And then you yourself will demand to take some of this burden back. But now you will be ready.

But this process is, as I say, a vanishing art.

RTE: This reminds me of Greek and Russian village life, where people really stop and listen to you.

DR. PATITSAS: Yes, they don't listen "efficiently" like we do, getting so quickly to the main points and the actual root issue and the "real heart" of the matter. Friendship cannot be done efficiently. So when in the Greek village you try to go too fast and say your story too completely and too all at once, they just won't let you. They'll stop you, and they'll try to make up what is lacking because of what you've suffered. Because you're in a state of excommunication, they will also try to re-commune you in any other way – through food or touch. The talking is limited, placed in proper proportion to the other paths to re-communion. You are not *allowed* to tell your story just yet. You are not silenced, but neither are you permitted to detach from yourself by treating your life like a story.

Shay points in the same direction. He says that what is needed is not cognitive processing – a listener in a hurry to download all your personal data, find a solution, and move on – but a listener who weeps where you can't, a listener who feels your hurt in ways that you can't yet. And even before you get to this, Shay says we need to establish good patterns of self-care for the person: a daily routine, decent food, a job to go to, friendships.

Once the good patterns are in place, then comes the empathic listening – which should be reflective not in the sense of providing a more organized or intellectual retelling of your story, but reflective in that the listener is touched without being overwhelmed, and then enfolds you into his own life, which is a life rooted completely in Christ. And this is not about our "story" but about an unfolding adventure which renders large parts of our pasts opaque: We can't yet predict what Christ is going to do with all that has gone before in our lives.

You don't want to be cold while the other person reveals himself to us. You want to be touched, and this guy, who maybe even isn't saying too much, sees that you are touched. He may not acknowledge what he's seeing in you, but he's secretly touched that you are mourning with him. That is the aim of this therapeutic relationship: to feel the emotions that he can't feel – to recommune the person whose trauma has placed him outside of human communion.

Of course, if an expression of empathy is overdone, then the sufferer resolves, again, not to share. A look of "patient concern" can be enough to let the sufferer know that our helper has cut themselves off from him or her, for such an expression of empathy could only come from a person who feels themselves "well," and the other person, "sick." Our empathy for others should be an icon of Christ's empathy for us. It is not about the healer, in the end, but about the mystery of Christ's own crucifixion and resurrection.[18]

---

18 In July of 2017 at a health clinic on the Greek island of Paros, I asked a physiotherapist in her early twenties if my joint pain and general exhaustion were related to the fiery car

RTE: You started our discussion by saying that the *Iliad* actually healed combat trauma. Is this how?

DR. PATITSAS: The *Iliad* did this, according to Shay. It brought large numbers of veterans together, who would have had varying degrees of emotional wounds from war. The people hosting the recitation created a safe space, with regular breaks for meals, rest, and so on. And within this space, war's survivors were taught by the poem to love beauty again and to awaken within themselves their empathy for all soldiers. The result, Shay postulates, was that the veterans thus learned to practice a more complete empathy for themselves.

Think of how many of our own war movies today tell the story of war in terms of heroics and blood lust. But though the *Iliad* contains such elements, its larger message is a noble sorrow for the soldiers whose lives are cut short, who experience bad leadership, privation, homesickness, confusion, fear, and pain. The poem was recited to a group of veterans who felt all these emotions again, but on behalf of Achilles, Ajax, Hector, Odysseus, and all the other warriors who in the story go through just what these later soldiers had gone through. The listeners are healed because in grieving for other, heroic and ideal combat veterans, they learn to grieve for themselves.

The first step in healing, of course, is to remove the person from further encounters with trauma-inducing events, but then we engage this social aspect. If there are very good relationships in your life, then the bad relationships can be assimilated. In the Church,

---

crash I had been in six months before. I told her that I had not been the same emotionally or physically since the accident (which, though frightening, was not extremely injurious; the burns I suffered were mostly first degree).

Although I did want her perspective on the effects of the accident (and I do think that some of its effects lingered on), in fact one of the reasons I mentioned it was that I wanted to see how a person from an Orthodox culture (indeed, from a Greek island which until recently was quite isolated) would react.

Her reaction was textbook Beauty-first. She instantly, gently, and yet very firmly deflected my attention from the past event, and at the same time somehow conveyed in her manner and tone, deep love. Then, she quietly commanded that I not give any attention to such memories, but instead focus on the positive beauty of my life since the accident. Once further positive experiences had multiplied, she said, this past event would become simply that – a single negative day in the sea of a generally very good life.

if the person has a closeness to Christ, to Panaghia,[19] to the saints, as well as to other people, then little by little, other things can be digested and find their place, because the person is not done. No one is done, especially at age twenty-two or twenty-five. But there have to be enough good patterns and relationships in place to help these other negative things fit in. The forces re-communicating you have to outweigh the forces ex-communicating you. Also, for those who are helping, God's grace has to be a living experience that is transmitted, not just talked about.

The *Iliad* has no "truth" in it, no facts not clothed in a mystical and sacramental glory. Rather, it is theophany in dark relief. The hearer of the *Iliad* becomes Panaghia at the foot of the cross, gazing upon Christ's unjust crucifixion. For the fact is that all the men in the *Iliad* die unjustly, Simone Weil tells us, in the sense that they are all trapped within the same world of blind might where they must kill or be killed. And the poetry, the language, and the spirituality of the *Iliad* are all superb.

This *beautiful* story arouses our *empathy* for its warriors, for all warriors, and for ourselves if we are warriors. And thus we *become true* – we return to sanity. This is our program: Beauty, Goodness, and finally Truth.

A society that has such a means of therapy for traumatic stress is going to recruit into its functioning self-awareness many restored victims of such experiences. But these people are not like us, these people are better than us because they've been through hells that, God-willing we haven't experienced. So now, when they receive this healing and are transfigured, what they offer to the Church and society is really great. Now you have these people at your councils of war, and this is what Shay says that the healing offered by the *Iliad* leads to. You've got people who are healed from traumatic stress in the council deciding, "Is this next war we are considering worth it?" That's not where we're at now. How many of those in command have faced what these people have faced?

---

19 In the Greek Orthodox tradition, Panaghia is a title ascribed to Mary, the mother of Jesus Christ.

From the *Iliad* to Christ

What Shay is arguing is that the performance of the text was itself the therapeutic act for Ionian society,[20] 700 years before Christ. That act of listening to the recitation of the *Iliad* from someone who knew it by heart over days or weeks worked because it took place in a communal setting among other veterans and it showed a kind of universal compassion to all of the soldiers equally. Since in the *Iliad* there are no good guys or bad guys, its performance helps you to renounce resentment and villainization. It is the beginning of reversing this excommunication of resentment – "the wind of hate" that Grossman talks about. In the *Iliad*, the wind of hate (the spiritual shock of realizing that another human being hates you enough to want to kill you) is itself the villain. It is a force and everyone is the victim of the empire of naked force.

RTE: So, to bring this amazing conversation to a close, can you pull together Shay's principles of healing trauma in the context of Christ and the Church?

DR. PATITSAS: The first level of those who truly help is not only listening but mourning with you. If the healer is able, he can go further and take your traumatized life on his shoulders and carry it, but this is much harder because you are often going to lash out at the person who tries to bring you back into communion. You may hate them before they are done loving you.

Thus, with healers in the Church you will notice that there is no visible "trying" to help you. The right hand does not know, as Scripture says, what the left hand is doing. Everything is handled with great subtlety.

In a sense the Christian priest or therapist or friend doesn't have to take on the burden of the person they are helping, because Christ does it. And in fact, if they do it in a wrong way, it could

---

20 Seven hundred years before Christ, "Ionia" referred to a network of Greek-speaking city-states located on the shores of the eastern central Aegean, both in the areas of Asia Minor between and beyond Smyrna and Ephesus, and on what are today such islands as Chios, Samos, Ikaria, and Naxos.

harm them both. They have to let Christ do it, and that is exactly what Christ did on the cross. It's not only his trauma Christ is experiencing there – his torture and crucifixion – but all of our trauma from all of human history past and still to come.

This is real divine justice: you've been traumatized and you have, in a way, the right not only to *not* forgive, but to strike back somehow. The striking back doesn't accomplish anything, but that impulse for self-defense is God-given, and Christ lets you do it to him, if you must. This is also the mission of the priest. He goes into a parish, he receives the chaos into himself and converts it into life. If he is able to do this, it is because liturgy has become innate for him. He is not just the priest, but he is also the victim because he is going to take it from everyone.

The Anointing Stone

When you go to the Holy Sepulchre in Jerusalem, it's an all-encompassing experience because Golgotha, the tomb of the Lord, and the place where St. Helen found the cross are all under the same roof at varying levels. But one thing you may not have heard about is a stone slab near the entrance. This is the anointing stone. The present one is from the fourteenth century, but it is located at the traditional site where they anointed the Lord's body after taking him down from the cross.

All kinds of people have experienced trauma or read about trauma and they think, "Where was God when those people were suffering?" Our intellectual, rationalist conception of God is that He is up in his remote perfection and we're down here taking it on the chin. But when you see that anointing stone, it is a visceral experience. If you are a trauma sufferer yourself, you may feel, as Shay says, "the overwhelming urge to weep, cry, vomit." You feel very much that Christ was the ultimate trauma victim, in particular because He was so innocent and took on his torture so willingly.

(But notice that the Orthodox Church does not replay these events in a dramatic way; Holy Week is not a hyper-realistic passion play. For those who get it, the restrained way in which things are said is enough; and for those who don't get it – well, I hope they never do. In film today, if they are going to show you some traumatic event, it's a writing in flesh, almost a kind of pornography. They so spell out the traumatic event with music and camera angles that they try to put you through it yourself. The only way they know to tell you the story is to make you also suffer. That is not what Homer or Holy Week is doing, but that's what a passion play, or a certain type of retelling of Christ's life, can become.)

But when you see the anointing stone, it all suddenly hits you and you wonder, "How can one person take that much?" There's even a message here for those wounded by rape, because on Holy Thursday when we process with the cross we sing the antinomies, such as, "The One who hung the clouds... is wrapped in a shroud...." But another one is, "The Son of a Virgin... is pierced by a spear." His body is violated and abused, but we don't stop there. The point of Christ's suffering, of his liturgy, is that He can take all of the chaos of the world – not just the chaos of non-being, but the chaos of fully-formed being acting evilly. He can take all of that, everything, and convert it into life. Now *that* is liturgy, and *that* is the opposite of the hell of war. I suppose that it is peace, also – but a dynamic peace that is both hard won, and a free gift of grace.

III. AFTERWORD: RESPONDING TO READER COMMENTS

Since the first version of this interview was published in *Road to Emmaus Journal* in the Winter of 2013, three main themes have emerged within the reactions of readers. These have shaped this book as it unfolded after Chapter Three.

Say More About Healing

The first response was more like a demand, or even an accusation, and it came from combat veterans: "No other words about our experience have touched us as these have; not even in reading Shay or Grossman directly did we see the import of their insights so compellingly. You therefore have a responsibility to say more about how we can be healed. You cannot go as far as you have, without trying to take this all the way."

In ways either small or large throughout this book, I have tried to respond to this challenge. However, in the end I could come up with no particular recipes or techniques. Instead, all I could do was to write the book that was given to me to write, with the hope that, like the *Iliad* itself, encountering *The Ethics of Beauty* as a whole will be a therapeutic act for those suffering from trauma. I do not offer concrete advice, but, perhaps for some, a living encounter.

Moral Injury vs. PTSD

The second response came not from veterans but from practitioners of trauma healing among veterans. It happens that therapists have arrived empirically at an important distinction between trauma disorders, on the one hand, and the existence of a spiritual wound that can be termed "moral injury," on the other.[21] Specifically, they note

---

21 Chaplain (Maj.) Sean Levine, an Orthodox priest and U.S. Army chaplain, brought the "moral injury" concept to my attention, spelling out its usefulness for the Orthodox Christian conception of war's harm.

that many soldiers do not have the persistent mobilization for danger associated with PTSD but still report the feeling that their souls had been wounded by what they did, witnessed, or contributed to in war. Unable to resolve this spiritual feeling, the soldiers were left, in ways either small or large, incapacitated by their experience.

In other words, the treatment community has discovered that a soldier needn't be visibly, intrusively, "traumatized" in order to feel a deep wound in his soul from what he has seen, experienced, or done. Therapists themselves are noting that if every time a soldier confesses his soul wound from combat we then label him with PTSD, that we will find ourselves recommending psychological therapies and prescribing psychiatric medications when what is needed is something like a religious ritual of purification and forgiveness. Somewhat at a loss as to how to respond, secular healers are looking both to ancient cultures and to contemporary religion for guidance about healing moral injury.

My approach, even in the revised interview above, however, is to continue to include the soul harm, as well as the physical and psychological harm, within war's impact on the soldier, and to label it "PTSD." Some of my reasons for this decision are described in the next few pages.

Moral Injury and Sin

Clearly, "moral injury" is close to the Orthodox Christian concept of "sin," because moral injury includes more than just what you did wrong. It also involves the wrongs that you may have witnessed, tacitly consented to, or even tried to stop others from doing but couldn't. Just as an Orthodox Christian who accidentally killed a pedestrian while driving would seek the sacrament of confession, even if the pedestrian had been suicidal and purposely threw himself in front of his car, so too "moral injury" includes any participation in moral wrong, however innocent. The wound is real, and it must be addressed.

It is especially relevant for this interview, in other words, that therapists have found that even lawful killing in war can inflict deep soul harm, a sense that one's own heart has been wounded. And so the discovery and classification of "moral injury" confirms the Orthodox Christian view that war – even when the lesser of two evils, even if it does not involve the commission of war crimes, even though it may include many acts of valor and virtue – is still evil and still affects the soul.

Caution About Sharp Distinctions

However, while the distinction between PTSD and moral injury is helpful and important, it should not be pressed into an outright division; trauma and moral injury are distinct but are probably not completely separable. For example, in my understanding of therapists' use of the moral injury concept, it almost seems that some feel that "trauma" should be viewed as a physical phenomenon, localizable to the brain or body, while "moral injury" describes a wound to the soul that is more religious.

Therefore, a sharply divided formulation of the problem would leave therapists out of a job: the doctors would be tasked to heal the brain, and the priests or shamans would be brought in to cure the soul, with the therapists having nothing to do. The job of the therapist, in my estimation, is to be a bridge between medicine, religion, and philosophy/ethics, with sufficient competency in each area to recognize when to offer treatment himself, when to refer to specialists in those disciplines, and when to effect a working alliance with others. No formulation of the soldier's situation that does not respect the integrity of this three-fold task of the therapist, will allow therapy its potential due in healing.

As an Orthodox Christian theologian, meanwhile, I have always been taught that the wound of war affects both the body and the soul. Having distinct names for the two aspects can be useful only provided the point is not pushed too far. Too sharp a division between the brain and the soul is not supported by actual human experience. In general, we must not separate the traumatic ugliness of war from its spiritual badness. War's violation of Beauty and its violation of Goodness are of a piece. Moral injury cannot be completely separated from trauma, nor vice versa.

This is because the cosmos, while beautiful, is also good. Therefore a traumatic event — a shocking event — is not only a marring of that beauty, but also an affront to the moral order. In a car crash, not only might your body and your vehicle be mutilated, but your stable sense of the social and physical order around you — in other words, your trust in the inherent goodness and "friendliness" of that structure to you, in particular — is at least temporarily shaken. This, too, constitutes a *moral* injury, whose severity or superficiality depends on many factors, but which is nevertheless real.

Again, the cosmos is not only beautiful, it is also good. Therefore, its violation or destruction — even by natural forces — not only says something about our bodily survival, but also impacts our soul's deep sense of justice. This is why even after a "non-moral" event like the Christmas Day Tsunami of 2004, some people questioned the goodness — the morality — of God.

Too sharp a separation of trauma from moral injury would not, therefore, correspond to the way we as human beings actually experience the world. To be human means to see almost everything through the lens of both body and soul, both beauty and goodness, both brain and heart. Plenty of trauma sufferers already experience a false division between body and mind, and adding a further false division of brain from soul into the mix will not help.

The Implications for Recovery

Trauma reactions involve our ongoing participation — mentally, physically, and spiritually. They are not merely "brain disorders," with the brain now reduced to a biological organ within the human body.

Those of us afflicted with trauma may not be able to stop our reactions — I mean, we are not reacting to triggers or even spiraling out of control "on purpose" – but we do find these reactions corresponding with our inner soul states, with at least part of what we sense to be the real moral order of the world. In fact, without even realizing it, we actually feed these reactions, protect and intensify them, precisely because they correspond to our deepest beliefs – learned in the traumatic event itself – about the fundamental character of reality.

We should therefore expect patients to resist the "healing" of their trauma so long as their souls remain morally injured. The persistence of trauma reactions makes the sufferer a prophet regarding the moral outrage of what he or she has experienced. The trauma sufferer is a warning sign to the rest of us and may even feel himself a protector of others from the sort of events that traumatized him or her. Their sensitivity to triggers means that trauma sufferers are literally our first responders to certain kinds of physical or moral mortal danger. Of course, their help may be at times irrational and, in fact, unhelpful, and their first response unwarranted since the danger they perceive has long since passed. Yet and still, they stand as watchdogs, in a way that is nevertheless not *completely* distorted, and their reactions are not to be disrespected.

Again, in the absence of a realistic avenue for the healing of the moral injury aspect of post-war psychic wounds, the accompanying biological-brain trauma reactions can be a certain kind of safeguard, both for the person and for those around them.

Besides all of this, in the real world one can guess the painful paradox that will unfold if we assign the bodies exclusively to the doctors and the souls exclusively to the priests: The priests, frustrated and confused by the fact that your trauma/moral injury is not responding to their ministrations, will conclude that your problem is medical. Meanwhile, the doctors, frustrated and confused by the fact that your trauma/moral injury is not responding to their medications, will conclude that your problem is spiritual. The trauma sufferer will fall through the cracks.

Instead, both the doctor and the clergy will have to look at you and say, "Your condition is both. And I am both. And by modeling for you how to be both, I will help you to remember that you are both. And this is close to the essence of your healing." Of course, the doctor and the clergy will differ in emphasis, but woe to us and to them if they adopt a sharp dualism.

In general, professional healers, whether doctors, nurses, or clergy, should beware of anthropological divisions that lead in directions a theologian would call Nestorian (or which a philosopher might term Cartesian). We should not separate the soul from the body in a dualistic fashion.

I would guess that what therapists will eventually find as they remain dedicated to an empirical resolution of this problem, is that almost no one with a "moral injury" has avoided certain brain impacts as well, usually including something that looks at least faintly like "trauma." And medical researchers will also find, if they look a little more closely, that those who have been traumatized almost always understand profound issues of morality to be at stake in what they have suffered. The distinction between PTSD and moral injury should take us to the point where we see the necessity of both the moral and the physical elements of healing, but with primary emphasis almost always on a third term, the "spiritual" – a term that for Orthodox Christians should signify the union of body and soul.

The union of soul and body is experienced in many places – religion, of course – but also through music and through our most ancient sense, our sense of smell.[22] One reason why healing in the Orthodox Christian Church has been effective for two thousand years is that it employs both music and the sense of smell within a sophisticated program addressing body and soul. A spiritual ther-

---

22 I refer to smell as "our most ancient sense" for three reasons. First, biologists believe that the sense of smell evolved before the sense of sight or sound. Second, the sense of smell is also deeply connected to pre-rational parts of our brain, as well as to memory. Smell can bring us back to a long-ago experience with intense vividness. Thirdly, because smell is the first sense which enables us to recognize our mothers, and therefore is connected with our earliest ability to recognize where our true help and salvation lies.

apy that does not access these two primary avenues of soul-body integration will struggle to equal what goes on in the Church – even before we mention the divine and uncreated grace of a loving God in the mystery of the holy sacraments.

Therefore, while the distinction between moral injury and trauma is for therapists a major step towards the Orthodox Christian understanding of the human impact of war, I would invite them to come still farther. The idea that trauma is essentially a brain disorder, while moral injury is exclusively an injury to the soul, does not conform to the ancient Church's understanding of the unity of body and soul and, if pressed, would lead to bad results in therapy.

Contemporary Rejection of the Just War Tradition

The third response among my readers was to make me aware of recent Western commentators who have also grown suspicious of the just war tradition, arguing that all wars are evil, and therefore that there is no justification for war. Some are speaking out against this tradition, and against war and militaries, much more strongly than I have. They are neglecting the fact that the attempt by wartime leaders to adhere to just war standards is a necessary, even if not sufficient, element of preventing the violations of themis which can trigger spiritual harm in soldiers.[23]

---

[23] As we have said earlier in the chapter, just war theory elucidates principles according to which a country may legitimately go to war without egregiously violating *themis*. Abiding by these principles can lessen (but never completely eliminate) the spiritual harm of war fighting. The final criterion, "The Duty of Military Competence," is my own.

Jus ad bellum (The law for going to war)
1) Just Cause: To protect the weak, innocent, and in self-defense when the offense is grave, certain, and lasting. 2) Last resort: Only if all non-violent remedies, diplomacy, and negotiation fail to stop the injustice. 3) Right Intention: To stop injustice, not to realize other goals of national interest. 4) Legitimate Authority: Only an established and recognized government can declare war. 5) Proportionality: Cannot perpetrate more harm than the evil being stopped. 6) Prudence: Reasonable hope of success. 7) Duty of Beneficence: To end extreme injustice towards other peoples (i.e. genocide). 8) Deterrence: To show perpetrators that they will be thwarted, thus preventing further fighting.

Jus in bello (The law for fighting justly)
1) Discrimination: Non-combatants, wounded soldiers, and prisoners must be neither harmed nor mistreated. 2) Proportionality: No force disproportional to attaining goal. 3) Duty of Military Competence: Officers must master diplomacy, negotiation, strategy,

As anti-war writers rejecting the just war tradition, we should not go too far. Yes, pacifism and the total rejection of war are the first possibility for the Church. But defensive war, understood as the lesser of two evils — understood as "laying down one's life for one's friends" — is still a path that is also allowed to us in our human weakness. Not everyone has the strength to walk the way of martyrdom, and Christian Scripture itself allows for police and soldiers to "restrain the evildoer" (Rom 13:4). A rejection of the just war tradition should not lead to extremes that condemn all soldiers as murderers and all statesmen as monsters. The original, if implicit, tradition of the Church on this difficult issue was a balanced one.

Guilt-stricken soldiers often come to clergy or to healing professionals more than ready to execute themselves for the crime of having killed in a lawful war.[24] The Church must be prepared not only to offer forgiveness but to insist that the soldier may have simply chosen the lesser of two evils, was too young and inexperienced to know better, or was following lawful orders. Besides, the Church can, through her prayers for the dead, even offer the possibility of reconciliation between a living soldier and his fallen enemy.

The soldier has risked his very soul to save the lives of other people; now, let him seek forgiveness from the Only One who can forgive, and let the soldier renounce his right to serve as his own judge and executioner. His sin was a result of being caught up in a fallen world and may well have been done out of love. Although this wound may have left scars upon him, these can be healed, in this life or in the next.

I hope that for some, this book will be a small part of such healing.

---

tactics, and use of offensive and defensive weaponry including non-violent alternatives, in order to end conflict quickly, and with minimal damage.

Nevertheless, even killing in war that meets these criteria is morally momentous. It involves great evil and impacts our souls in a way that requires repentance and divine forgiveness.

24 A student, Elyse Buffenbarger, pointed out that such an impulse may stem from the desire to return the moral order to balance: my own eye, for the eye that I have taken. But for Christians, such blood sacrifices would be ineffectual; it is Christ's blood alone that can pay such a terrible price.

CHAPTER TWO

A FEELING FOR BEAUTY

The Aesthetic Ground of Orthodox Christian Ethics

Following "The Opposite of War Is Not Peace: Healing Trauma in the Iliad and in Orthodox Tradition," we trace the contemporary difficulty in healing trauma to an early difference between East and West regarding how the human soul is meant to be purified and saved. Orthodox Christian spirituality has always followed a Beauty-first path uniting the mind with the heart, rather than taking an approach focusing on the intellectual powers of the soul.

The consistent failure of analytical, or "truth-first," methods to resolve severe trauma makes the trauma victim a kind of canary in the coal mine: What we see sharply in such cases about the ineffectiveness of a certain approach to soul healing is a warning to our entire culture that we must find an alternate path for the development of our souls.

This other way is a retracing of the sequence by which the world was originally created, according to St. Dionysios the Areopagite and the Fathers who followed him: the beautiful appearing of God over the face of the deep kindled a fiery eros in non-being that inflamed it with the longing to transcend its formless state. Overcome with love for God's beautiful theophany, non-being willingly left its nothingness behind and rushed towards the Creator. In this ecstatic rush towards the divine, all created things became differentiated, specific, concrete, real — and gloriously alive.

Rather than attempting an intellectual dissection of the heart, the Orthodox Christian path of soul development trains the penitent to fall in love with the same divine appearing that once drew the world into existence, until a similar experience of fresh life, clarity, and individuation is experienced and the person is born again.

Intellectual examination of our hearts, by contrast, can thwart the erotic drive towards Beauty and leave us imprisoned in the self. Too often, self-analysis leaves us further mired in the chaos out of which the world was made, rather than catching us up in an eros for the Super-Divine God.

Orthodox Christian Ethics, a close sibling of Orthodox soul healing, also begins with Beauty. In this chapter, I try to show how through this focus on Beauty, Orthodox Ethics resolves a thorny challenge in secular ethics, the opposition between "moral agency" and "moral luck." Academic ethicists ask whether "morality" itself would still have any ultimate meaning if our moral lives were in large part determined by events beyond our control. This dilemma is resolved in a surprising way within the words of the Jesus Prayer, which is so central for Orthodox Christian spirituality.

Trauma victims, wounded by events that were entirely or at least partly outside their control, find afterwards that their moral agency has been lastingly diminished, as certain reactions and responses toward the world elude their conscious control. Thus, they are the double victims of bad moral luck, and their struggle for healing is bound up with their struggle to regain their moral agency.

Finally, it is appropriate to start a book on Orthodox Christian Ethics with the subject of trauma because the Orthodox way is Beauty-first, while the traumatic event in contrast is an experience of anti-Beauty, of ugliness-first. To live governed by trauma is to live governed by an experience of ugliness, which unless we can incorporate the Resurrection into this gruesome crucifixion, cannot lead to health. Trauma is the exact opposite of Beauty-first: it is ugliness, first, middle, and last.

I. ATTAINING FREEDOM THROUGH LOVE FOR BEAUTY

Ethics and Aesthetics

RTE: We return today to follow up on our previous discussion, "The Opposite of War Is Not Peace: Healing Trauma in the *Iliad* and in Orthodox Tradition," so that we can hear more of your insights into recovery after trauma. Your desire to add aesthetics and beauty to the discussion is even more intriguing, because it brings us to the question of spiritual as well as of psychological and emotional health. Exactly how do Ethics and aesthetics relate?

DR. PATITSAS: Ethics, put very generally, is the contemplation of what would be good to do in a particular situation – and of goodness itself, if possible. Aesthetics, by contrast, is the examination of why certain things are considered beautiful or of the rules and principles that underlie Beauty's creation and appreciation.

In Orthodoxy, Ethics and aesthetics are closely related. Personally, I find Ethics much more exciting when it is also resolving questions I've had all my life about the healing of the soul – and for this we need to begin with Beauty (aesthetics) and only then follow up with Goodness (ethics and morality). When I first began reading Jonathan Shay's description of the failure of a certain kind of widely used approach to healing trauma victims, I could see at once that what was going wrong there wouldn't just apply to combat veterans. Even if we are not trauma victims, we still shouldn't rely on a fundamentally flawed approach to soul development.

Whereas Orthodox Christian theology and soul healing call us and encourage us to begin with Beauty, it is obvious, once we think about it, that trauma has just the opposite effect: Trauma results from a very powerful encounter with ugliness, especially if that ugliness strikes us as a kind of revelation, disclosing to us the *real* truth about the world. Consequently, the Church will have much to say about trauma and about why certain approaches to soul healing will or won't work.

So, I hope that these interviews will be life-saving not only for trauma victims but for many people. The Beauty-first way represents an alternative and deeply sophisticated worldview that almost all of us can relate to in part, once we've heard it, but which we rarely find expressed coherently in one place.

Whatever we've been through, whoever we are, the broad contours of the way forward are to be found in the way of Beauty that I am trying to describe here. The practice of love for Beauty can become our response despite the circumstances that have oppressed us – the events that seem in many cases to have taken away our very free will, our "agency."

Moral Luck and Divine Providence

RTE: Can we begin then with an idea from the previous interview: the ethical concept of "moral luck"? How can Christians believe that luck could ever be central to moral life? Don't we instead trust in a divine providence that never permits us to be tempted beyond our strength?

DR. PATITSAS: Now, regarding moral luck: this is a technical term, used in Ethics since about 1976 to describe what the ancient Greeks called "tragedy."[1] It is the idea that our character sometimes can be determined by what happens to us; i.e., by circumstance. Our human moral agency is not so strong that it can overcome every conceivable shock and influence thrown at us. Sometimes, human character turns bad owing to things beyond our control. "Moral luck" is thus a way to raise the question of whether we truly possess a meaningful freedom and true moral self-determination. If the right temptation could bring any of us down, in what sense is one person truly "good" and another "bad"?

We all can relate to the idea that circumstances sometimes overwhelm our integrity. "Do not be deceived," St. Paul says, "bad company corrupts good morals" (I Cor 15:33). Two such examples of bad company could be being sent to the front lines of a shooting war, and growing up as the victim of neglect or abuse. Your moral life may suffer in such circumstances, and if that has been the case for you, the Orthodox Church is able to help. In fact, its whole life is geared to just this, to helping and healing and saving.

RTE: How then do we relate these circumstances to divine providence, which Christians understand as innate to our tradition – unlike "luck," which seems purely pagan?

---

1 Thomas Nagel, "Moral Luck," in, *Proceedings of the Aristotelian Society Supplementary*, vol. 50, 137-155, 1976 (Reprinted in Mortal Questions, Cambridge Univ. Press, 1991).

DR. PATITSAS: Divine providence has operated most beautifully for me in two relationships that are conveying to me a new way of thinking about the healing of the soul and about my own moral responsibility in the face of circumstance.

These two spiritual fathers have been a profound gift of God in my life, but precisely because their help is so beyond what I could have done for myself, I struggle very hard to cooperate with it, to apply it, and not dishonor it. It isn't anything I could have imagined or come up with on my own. To me it's "out of left field," so to speak – completely unanticipated. It is God's grace, but to me it feels like pure luck: I'm quite sure I did nothing to deserve it.

RTE: So is moral luck just another way of saying divine providence?

DR. PATITSAS: Moral luck is divine providence, viewed through the eyes and experience of someone who, like me, is spiritually undeveloped. It is divine providence in hazy outline, before it has come into clear focus. But the idea of moral luck also includes the things that God does not will for our life, but that He somehow permits in a fallen world – tragedies and disasters of various kinds. And it includes things that we may understand as part of God's providence only once we have become sanctified – or even only once we have received the heavenly reward for whatever crosses we have been forced to carry in this life.

In a sense, through our spiritual work, we ourselves help convert such disasters from bad luck or tragedy into providence. Even the act of forgiving changes the moral status of what has happened: Christ said to the sinful woman, "Is there no one left to accuse you? Then neither do I accuse you" (Jn 8:10-11). In other words, how badly another person hurt me in my past is in part only discoverable in seeing whether or not I am able to recover spiritually from that injury later on.

Boys on the playground know this – it's one reason you shake off the injury you receive in play, because to collapse from it is to accuse the one who hurt you of something more serious than they perhaps intended. And even so, my spiritual recovery is an element easing my tormentor's condemnation. By the same token, our refusal to recover may sometimes seem like our only recourse to justice, or this refusal is our revenge, or it is even our way of staying in solidarity with others who have suffered like us – including our "earlier selves," which we may imagine ourselves to be protecting by not growing forward.

These are complex webs, and as we prepare for the Judgment we must beg one another for forgiveness. God forbid that any of us face the Judgment while still owing such unpayable debts on what we have done to others. But might it be the case that many of us are not only trauma sufferers, but also trauma perpetrators, through our participation in the passions leading up to wars of every kind? Much prayer is needed.

For all of these reasons, I prefer to use the technical ethical term "moral luck" rather than "divine providence" when discussing trauma. I don't want to give the impression that God is to blame for the evil in the world, nor accuse him of being capricious.

Synergy with God

RTE: And how would you differentiate between bad moral luck that results from the chaos, ignorance, and folly that we find in the fallen world and bad moral luck that comes from the action of the evil one?

DR. PATITSAS: You can look at moral luck from another perspective, seeing it not as a thing in itself, but as a simple description of the fact that we are weak, that we need the support of others, that human personhood does not flourish in isolation. Certain invisible powers are indeed relating to us with wholly malicious intent, and they even use accidents and the weakness of those around us to further their aim of destroying us both physically and spiritually. We call out to our guardian angels, the saints, and the Mother of God to frustrate these attacks – to grant us good moral luck, so to speak.

More prosaically, we can all relate to the idea that two persons in life might take utterly divergent paths, seemingly with no otherworldly interference, merely because different things happened to them which were outside their control. And yet we can all also accept that an utterly passive dependency on circumstance is something *that needs to be overcome*. As Orthodox Christians, we acknowledge something like "luck" in a fallen, chaotic world, so that we can assimilate that chance into liturgy and thus render it meaningful, providential, and in some cases, ultimately life-giving. We recover our human agency not through greater exertions of willpower but through participation in Christ's liturgy; although willpower does figure as one element within liturgy, it alone is not sufficient.

"Luck," in the sense of brute randomness, is just a sign that the world is still being created out of the watery deep of non-being and chaos – and bad moral luck reminds us viscerally that we are necessarily co-agents with God in that ongoing creation. That is, we've got to do something about it, or bad moral luck *will* drown us.

Ultimately, any kind of luck just says to us: pray without ceasing, for chaos and malice are still around us, and only the liturgy of our Lord and Savior Jesus Christ on the cross can master them and turn them into life. Liturgy is stronger than luck; it is stronger than trauma. Christ's voluntary passion (his liturgy) was the stake in the heart of our subjection to bad moral circumstance.

The question that remains, though, is how to assimilate Christ's liturgy within the conditions you face, to overcome your own challenges. Those challenges will include, as you say, outright evil; "Deliver us from evil," the Church prays many times every day in the Lord's Prayer.

RTE: Wouldn't believing in luck, like believing in fate, lead us to inaction and passivity?

DR. PATITSAS: I hope that knowing how "lucky" we are – how blessed in positive ways (if we do see it as "luck," as unmerited) – will make us tremendously vigilant, resilient, and decisive. We won't let those good moments slip by, but rather will pounce on them like mountain lions. The best advice I've ever received was from His Eminence Metropolitan Sotirios (Trambas) of Korea: "If you have a good thought, you must do it at once!" Because, ultimately, that good thought didn't come from us – it was a theophany. Moral luck is another way to describe the centrality of synergy for our spiritual lives.

That's why I thought to mention two of my spiritual teachers when you asked about divine providence. I don't want even to sleep – I just want to run after the grace they share out so abundantly, because I remember what things were like before they came along!

In the case of bad moral luck, thinking of it as "luck" just says, "Well, these things happen. I'm not to blame for that. It doesn't define the whole of me, to the very last farthing of my soul. It is what happened *to* me. Now let me run to Christ, and see what He has to say about it." A child reacts this way to harm, running straight into the arms of his mother.

But trauma is a bigger harm, sometimes even designed with ultimately evil intent to collapse any distance between you and what happened to you. We so belittle people for being "victims," but hold on. What they suffered may have been very cunningly designed to render them utterly passive, an object. Obviously, it will take some art to heal from this, and our piling on with rejection makes us an accomplice to the evil inflicted upon them. Not to say that when we are victimized we should give up. Rather, from the other side, in trying to help the suffering, it takes rare spiritual skill not to blame the victim while simultaneously holding out the hope that they can overcome.

RTE: When (infrequently) someone refers to me as a "victim," I have a perverse sense of being robbed, as if a door had been shut on my moving forward. Since calling someone a victim is an attempt to be empathetic, why would it ever feel wrong?

DR. PATITSAS: I suppose there are good and bad ways to be empathetic. A bad empathy skips a prior stage – the presentation of beauty, which would arouse hope and movement. Bad empathy goes straight to a moral consideration of what happened and pronounces the victim blameless, perhaps even justified in not getting up. It is like what we said in our last interview, that an intellectual investigation of the morality of a particular war leaves untouched the actual effect of being involved in that war. The problem with bad empathy is that it doesn't begin with beauty and respect for the image of God in each person.

Personal Background

RTE: Can you tell us why you are personally concerned with this issue of moral luck and trauma in general?

DR. PATITSAS: Well, because I'm an *American* Orthodox Christian, and thus I want to see more souls healed, more quickly *(laughs)*. No, this actually is the case, which is obviously not totally positive. It's great that we Americans are so Roman – we are determined to find a way, to solve the problem. But the wise and healthy soul is not a hamburger to be mass-produced by the billions through the application of some efficient technique! Such an attitude is part of my dissatisfaction with our current American psychology.

Also, when I was in sixth grade in Kent, Ohio, and I first heard that there was a secular, socially-revered organization that centralized God and catalyzed profound human transformation – Alcoholics Anonymous – I was fascinated. I wanted to be an alcoholic, so that my spiritual life could also be real, deep, and socially admired – in a way I thought was not always true for ordinary religious people. I even felt that traumatic experience was the key to authenticity. Fortunately, God did not grant my wish! Traumatic experience can be a key to authenticity when it is assimilated through Christ; outside of him, it can be just the opposite.

Christ is my focus now, anyway – not authenticity, nor even spirituality, per se. But my focus on Christ also makes me troubled about the lack of spiritual doctors in today's world.

RTE: So you are an American, but also Greek...

DR. PATITSAS: ...and German, and very, very faintly Italian, and I would like to learn to be deeply at home in many other cultures, too, but simply don't have the time or strength – we all must live where God has placed us.

Also when I was in high school, I didn't have the language of moral luck but certainly felt my bad moral luck was not to have been born an African-American. That seemed to me like the one American culture that had a cohesive identity, a proud experience of noble suffering, a music, and a way of life that were coherent and compelling. I was too young yet to see that America itself is such a culture, such a way of life.

Eros: The Love that Makes Us Renounce Ourselves

But I tell my undergraduates that you can't consider yourself educated unless you at least once have longed to have been born wholly other culturally – to have been born in another time, language, country, whatever. In fact, for many people, it's reading the Tolkien trilogy that first gives them that deep, erotic longing for a transcendent cultural otherness. His significance for education, for modern Western civilization, is therefore deep.

Eros is the beginning of human moral life, and Beauty in art and literature are oftentimes more effective than religion in awakening eros within us. Religion can just seem like God coming down at us, scolding us, telling us to stay where we are, but just do better. But real religion must awaken the movement in the other direction, must make us come out of ourselves and move towards him, fall in love with him. It's about beginning an adventure, becoming a pilgrim, an exile, a lover.

RTE: Why is eros the beginning of moral life? The ancient Greeks used the term philosophically, but for westerners the term "erotic" usually signifies unrestrained sensuality and a consuming selfishness.

DR. PATITSAS: By eros we mean the love that makes us forget ourselves entirely and run towards the other without any regard for ourselves. Allan Bloom described eros as "love's mad self-forgetting." Eros is the beginning for us, because in fact religion doesn't begin with us; it begins with God. God's initiative is primary. The Gospel begins with his call, not our search, and what He calls us to do is to fall in love with him first of all. Once we do, then the rest begins to fall into place. All that I have to say today is contained in this sequence, this "typicon."

Hubris and Human Agency

But let's go back to Greek tragedy, and to *Oedipus Rex*, the one play in particular that helps us best understand the centrality of eros for moral life. In the process, we may be able to say something more about the healing of trauma.

Oedipus was the victim of bad moral luck. Events beyond his control – his fate – meant that his very attempt to be moral and to act morally went awry. Alcoholics can relate to this when they discover that the more they exercise willpower against the desire to drink, the deeper their addiction becomes. Many times, starting with goodness – with the attempt to be good and to stop sinning – is a recipe for moral disaster, as we shall see.

At Oedipus' birth, a prophecy foretold that he would kill his father; a later prophecy added that he would also marry his mother. Despite the effort of others to avoid all this by leaving him to die as an infant, and later, when he is a man, despite his own decision to avoid this fate by fleeing the couple he thinks are his parents, the unfolding of his life meant that the prophecy would be fulfilled.

At the root of bad moral luck, for the Greeks, was *hubris*, a kind of pride by which we forget our place in the world. The tragedians warned that we might imagine that we can overcome our dependency on the gods and master our fate, but we cannot. Our human agency is limited, circumscribed within the bounds set for it. To attempt to rise above this is to provoke the gods, and we then receive a just punishment. For Greek civilization, bad moral luck *always* implies that a person had somehow, through *hubris*, provoked the gods.²

While the *Iliad* was lumped in dismissively with the other tragedies by Plato, in fact, on one point the *Iliad* and the philosophers are in alliance against the tragedians. For both, man must be liberated from the passions of the gods. Plato attempted this liberation through reason and recourse to a more rational God; Odysseus attempted it more wisely, subverting pagan liturgy itself with the offering of the Trojan Horse.

Homer *achieves* this liberation from fate, or "the gods," (he has to do more than attempt if he is to heal actual combat trauma, since trauma represents the loss of our freedom and our imprisonment

---

2 In fact, though, thinking of "hubris" as "pride" may result from a bias within the truth-first approach (the approach that begins with analytical reason rather than with eros) itself. In reading a recent encyclical on the environment from His All Holiness Ecumenical Patriarch Bartholomew I of Constantinople, I noticed that in the living tradition of the Greek language, *hubris* seems to signify not pride but rather a failure of the aesthetic sense; the hubristic man is the man who cannot see that his life, his talents, and his virtue are *mostly gifts*. *He cannot see* that these goods *are a kind of theophany*, evidence of divine good favor. Rather, the hubristic man takes his life and virtue *as a given* upon which his mind and efforts then go to work, charting out a "secular" and self-reliant path. According to this reading, Oedipus' primary sin is more like ingratitude than pride; he lacks an erotic connection to the world, and thus returns to the chaos out of which he was born, even re-entering his mother's womb! His eros reaches no true "other"!

If *hubris* in fact had this aesthetic meaning in their plays, then the tragedians would be doubly opposed to the Greek philosophers. On the one hand, the playwrights begin with the aesthetic sense rather than with intellect and truth. And, on the other hand, they despair of the human capacity ever to see with a completely whole and chaste eye exactly what is required of man before the gods. The poets think that vision is primary, but that perfect vision often seems impossible.

Christians would express the danger of a vice like *hubris* by saying that our human condition without Christ is that we can neither discern nor do what we must do if we would have life; this is exactly why we need a Savior. Without Christ's Light, we would never see the world as it really is, and without his Blood and Body inside of us, we could not act according to pure vision, anyway.

The philosophers, in contrast to the playwrights (and the Christians), thought that: a) such a correct discernment was possible through unaided Reason; b) once known, this better path could be followed; and c) man's happiness did not include the possibility of real freedom, anyway; intellect only promises the possibility of conformity to "Truth" – in reality, to blind Necessity. There is nothing tragic for the philosopher about the loss of a freedom that was always an illusion. Thus, the philosophers lost their tragic consciousness in three ways.

Authentic art therefore will seem ridiculous to the philosopher, for art's power lies in its trans-rational or pre-rational reference to Beauty. Today, the truth-first view has advanced to the point that there is no one left to make art; "graphic philosophy," much of it of the cynical school, predominates.

by "fate") by capturing the human condition more clearly than the philosophers: Homer saw that we are trapped in a Necessity that mars human dignity. He saw that "the gods" are part of the Necessity that enslaves us and makes us less than fully human.

Simone Weil wrote that the *Iliad* was itself, however, the theophany in dark relief of the real God, Who is dispassionate, empathetic, and true.[3] Only such a God could heal trauma because only a God who neither compelled nor could be compelled could offer us an escape from the "empire of might," as she called it. Jesus Christ, alone in all of human history, was a being truly free of compulsion and thus of trauma.

The tragic plays, on the other hand, seem to say the opposite of the *Iliad*. They seem to say that we had best not transgress the limits set by these capricious gods, that we cannot fight our luck. Only the proud man challenges his fate. But Odysseus challenged it and eventually *did* arrive home – he was freed from the trauma of the war, in other words.

Martha Nussbaum's *The Fragility of Goodness: Luck and Ethics in Greek Tragedy and Philosophy*[4] was the book that alerted ethicists to this opposition between the playwrights and Plato and the philosophers who followed him. In fact, Nussbaum locates the most important fault-line within Greek civilization here, regarding the reality of human moral freedom. Could our moral status be determined by things that happen to us outside of our control, as the tragedians believed? Or, would sufficient information and moral willpower in every case be sufficient to help us choose the good, as Socrates and later philosophers insisted? And, if we aren't completely capable of determining our own choices, do we really have "moral agency"; that is, are we free, are we ultimately responsible and accountable? Does it even make sense to praise good character, if it is always partly accidental?

---

3 An excellent collection of her essays is *Intimations of Christianity Among the Ancient Greeks* (Boston: Beacon Press, 1958), which includes her famous essay, "The Iliad, Poem of Might."

4 Martha C. Nussbaum, *The Fragility of Goodness: Luck and Ethics in Greek Tragedy and Philosophy* (New York: Cambridge University Press, 2001).

Although living more than 2600 years ago, Homer gives the best argument that, in practice, we are heavily dependent on others and on circumstance for our moral state. The tragedians expand on this point, which is why, according to Nussbaum, Plato calls Homer, "the first of the tragedians." But the philosophers push back and argue that the intellectual life can save us from the gods in a different way than just by avoiding the mistake of *hubris*. The intellect can be rightly trained and ordered through philosophy to master the passions and achieve a liberated life wholly independent of these absurd "gods" and wholly independent of the need to see all our virtues and our very reason as themselves gifts.

Moral Agency and the Cross

RTE: Then what do Orthodox Christians believe? That our moral status is dependent on such outside forces? And if so, how are we responsible for our actions?

DR. PATITSAS: According to our tradition, moral agency is quite dynamic. We begin by acknowledging severe limitations on our freedom, and then implore the exercise of God's *ultimate* freedom – his ability to work miracles – to augment and purify our own free will. And rather than using our current lack of freedom as a way to justify our sinful actions, we take on the responsibility of even other people's sins, in order to see our own agency strengthened.

At the beginning, of course we want to throw off "the weight of sin that clings so closely" (Heb 12:1); tragically, we can't. It turns out that we aren't fully responsible, even for our most free-willed choices and actions; our passions run so very deep. And yet we wish we could be more responsible because we wish we could embrace Christ more consistently, overcome circumstance, and help others. We want to overcome temptation and circumstance so that we would no longer deny Christ, not even a little bit. Thus, for us the problem is how to become *more* responsible, even if that means taking on a more developed sense of our own sin, not how to *deny* responsibility when our agency has been compromised.

Our Savior shows us a miraculous way forward. He alone shows us the path to become "free indeed" (Jn 8:36). That path is the Cross, which is the real conquest of tragedy; philosophy cannot equal the power of the Cross to restore human agency, although it has its role in response to the Cross.

RTE: So, rather than trying to avoid responsibility – "It was my bad childhood that made me do it" – we want to become more responsible? But wouldn't that make us more guilty as well?

DR. PATITSAS: A rock is passive. A plant has some power to react but within careful limits. An animal reacts but largely according to instinct. We want to be human, and that means overcoming the causes of our passivity. We want to acquire the agency which "the gods," "the fates," the human passions, and other spiritual opponents all wish to deny us.

Better to be free and guilty – and thus weep – than innocent and sub-human. Besides, it is our "fate" to be free. This may be a paradox, but it is still reality: our destiny is that we will be judged for how we have lived our lives.

Christ shows us how to use the freedom we have (or, after a lifetime of sin, still have left) in order to become freer still – and more innocent, too. But this becomes harder especially when, on the way to adulthood or within young adulthood, trauma intervenes.

So, the simple Orthodox answer to moral luck is that, a) we are subject to moral circumstance, in particular through the sinful influences of those around us. We do lack perfect and complete self-determination. But, b) if we are determined by others' actions, then so must they be determined in part by ours. In fact, others may be sinning against us because of mistakes that we have made towards them.

Therefore, c) *could it even follow that sometimes those causing us to sin are doing so because of the impact on them of our own prior sins, whether of commission or omission?* In that case, even what looks like our dependence on others still contains an element of our own freedom.

There are so many possible angles of interdependence and mutual influence at work in human action that we could never hope to untangle them all. So, finally, d) Orthodoxy counsels us to repent not only of our own sins but of the sins of the entire world. That way, we address our responsibility more accurately, account for the influence of anything that might weaken our moral agency, and become free.

Again, only if we are willing to repent of the sins committed *by others* – since they also possess a limited moral freedom and we *are* in part (perhaps in many cases the decisive part?) responsible for their sins – can we ourselves become more fully free.

Moral Luck Is Completed at the Last Judgment

To be clearer about this: although I may not have contributed directly to the sin of the person hurting me, I probably *have* contributed to the general world atmosphere of sin, which in turn affected this person. Of course, they are still free in some ultimate sense, but we can only really see the full extent of their moral status when we take out all the negative influences upon them put there by us and by other outsiders.

Thus, it may be only at the Last Judgment that we see our freedom clearly and find out what exactly we have made with it. This is because only there will we each receive that ultimate *good* moral luck of seeing Christ face to face, the One crucified and resurrected for our salvation. Only there can we see completely whether we have cooperated with this grace or not because only there will we enjoy a perfectly positive "moral luck."

Do others cause us to sin? Yes, but let us repent of the sin in us, that caused them to cause us to sin. That way, we become free of both our own sin and of the sin caused in us by others.

The path to our freedom is the taking of responsibility for the sins of others; there is no other path that actually works. In taking the sins of the entire world upon ourselves, we are freed from all circumstance.

And this is precisely what the saints do. They have repented so completely of all the lovelessness and harm committed by anyone, anywhere in the world, that they not only overcome moral luck, but they attain a deified agency; they can calm storms, heal the sick, stop wars, freeze criminals in their tracks. A passionless saint is a saint who is no longer *determined* by passionate states in himself or in others – nor by natural chaos nor by "luck." And such a person is not determined precisely because he is actively taking full responsibility for himself and for others.

"Have Mercy on Me, the Sinner"

This is why in the Jesus Prayer – "Lord Jesus Christ, Son of God, have mercy on me, the sinner," we pronounce ourselves "the sinner."

RTE: Some variations of the Jesus Prayer don't include "the sinner," or "a sinner" and, in fact, adding that can seem like a return to focusing on oneself after reaching up to Christ in the first part of the prayer. Wouldn't pure prayer mean forgetting ourselves?

DR. PATITSAS: I would say that there are three levels, all important, of what we might mean when we call ourselves "the sinner" in the Jesus Prayer. The third of these levels will be especially significant in helping us master the challenge of moral luck.

First, by calling ourselves "sinners," we are simply confessing our creatureliness, our total dependence on God. We were created out of nothing, and our very existence is a result of God's mercy and love. Second, we are, indeed, sinners; we do bad things. No man lives without sinning. Saint Paul, in fact, called himself "the chief of sinners." Of course, he meant in particular that he had earlier persecuted the Church of Christ. But we all must admit that the limitation of our sinfulness has more to do with God's mercy than with our own good character. Thus, identifying ourselves as "the sinner" is not unrealistic.

But most importantly of all, by calling ourselves "the sinner," we willingly identify ourselves with Christ who "became sin" for the life of the world (II Cor 5:21). Christ's expiation of our sin consisted in his willingness to take all human sin upon himself. The result was that He conquered death, and was seated in glory at the right hand of the Father. He was willing to die as if our sin were his fault. It is this that makes him our Savior.[5]

Heaven is the place where everyone has become willing to be lost for the salvation of the other. Hell is the place where no one is so willing. Pronouncing ourselves "the sinner" is what we do when we share in Christ's readiness to give his life for the life of the world. In fact, calling ourselves the sinner may not have much to do with how many sins we've actually committed.

When we don't make ourselves lower than the worst by seeing ourselves as *the* sinner, then we are denying Christ – and denying him at the precise moment, his crucifixion, when such a denial would be most hurtful to him. On the cross He "became sin" so that there his anointing as *the Christ* was the most costly and the most perfectly revealed, though in a hidden fashion. If we would be saved by his Cross, we must try to unite ourselves to him when He is on the cross.

---

5 These three meanings of "the sinner" in the Jesus Prayer correspond to the three stages of the spiritual life, which we shall see later in this chapter and in Chapter Three. The sense of "sinner" as being made *ex nihilo* is the Beauty stage, at which we acknowledge our nothingness and run to Christ. Because this involves the renunciation of *hubris* and the clear discernment of who we are and who God is, this is the aesthetic phase. "The sinner" as a moral failure, of course, corresponds to the stage of Goodness, or morality as it is usually understood. Finally, confessing ourselves as "*the* sinner" completes our journey through discipleship to friendship with Christ; we are now willing to die for the world, to take on its sin, just as He did. As we shall stress throughout this book, this sequence is not successive; we don't leave the earlier steps behind as we ascend. Rather, the sequence is an unfolding because the later levels include and amplify the earlier ones. To be joined to Christ is not to lose one's independent, created identity.

"Becoming Sin" as Christ Did

This is why our religious lives are so weak. We proclaim Christ as King and Savior, but we aren't willing to join him as the very thing He became for us: the Person who, though sinless, bore the burden of sin for the sake of man's salvation.

In our American mentality which is influenced by a kind of Calvinism, I suppose that terming oneself "the sinner" could imply "total depravity," guilt, perhaps worthlessness. That would be spiritually destructive. No, instead, we are "the sinner" not because we are worthless but because "my brother is my life." I want to take the fall for him because I love him. That's all; calling ourselves "the sinner" has very little to do with how sinful we've actually been. After all, Christ did it best!

Notice that on the cross Christ didn't call us sinners, but instead He claimed that we were innocent, even as we crucified him. "Forgive them, Father, for they know not what they do" (Lk 23:24). There is only one "Sinner" in his universe at that point. I think this will help us see in what way "the sinner" of the Jesus Prayer is Christ himself; it isn't referring only to you because you have done wrong. It is also referring to Christ who, though blameless, was willing to let sinful human beings condemn and punish him as a sinner, for the life of the world. You call yourself "the sinner" because He is your Bridegroom and you want to be one with him, especially there on the cross where He poured out his life for all mankind.

When you recite the Jesus Prayer, you unite yourself to him who became sin for the life of the world. You join yourself to his person by entering into his act of self-emptying love for the entire world. This journey to perfect oneness with Christ is fulfilled when you call yourself by his "assumed name" – the sinner. Don't shy away from this part of the prayer – it's the answer to the first part, the calling upon Christ for mercy.

Paradoxically, the mercy that we are asking for is exactly this: the strength and the clean joy to do as He did, to empty ourselves to the farthest extreme out of love for others. The mercy we ask for, you see, is nothing less than a share in Christ's own anointing by his Father – the descent of the Holy Spirit upon him. When that hits us, we find ourselves overwhelmed by the sweet longing to do what Christ also did in that anointing, which was to suffer for the life of the world.

We receive that mercy as we join with him who received it on the cross as well as in the Resurrection. The Cross and the Resurrection are inseparable; this is St. Paul's whole message.

Elder Sophrony said that the Jesus Prayer fulfills *both* of the two greatest commandments. In this prayer, we love the Lord our God with all our soul, our mind, and our strength, *and* we love our neighbor as our self. The Jesus Prayer fulfills the second of the two greatest commandments when we pronounce ourselves "the chief of sinners," because in so doing we pronounce ourselves "lost" and everyone else "saved."

We think it's called the "Jesus Prayer" because it has the name of Jesus in it. But the real reason is that it is a fractal of the Son's own primordial prayer to the Father – the "moment" when the Son received the Holy Spirit, proceeding from the Father in order to rest upon Him as Son, and when in that receiving of the Spirit the Son poured himself out for the creation of the cosmos – as He would later for its salvation.[6] For St. Maximos the Confessor, this describes the way the world was created.

Yes, Christ alone is *the* "sinner," so that He could make us "the saved" in an exchange. But we see already in St. Paul the ardor among Christians not to accept this gift passively. No, like St. Paul we long to use our being saved in order to "become lost" for still others, in imitation of Christ. Our being saved is our being anointed, and like the Anointed One himself, we desire to offer ourselves on behalf of the world from within that anointing, by seeing others as innocent and ourselves as responsible. In the Holy Spirit, that is

---

6 Fractals are irregular, self-similar shapes which appear at many different scales within the same phenomenon; for example, the branches of a tree, or your body's system of arteries and blood vessels, at each scale within them, have the same rough pattern. Coastlines also have a fractal shape, such that without some outside frame of reference it is impossible to know whether a photograph from above is showing miles, or hundreds of miles, of the coast. Clouds are fractally shaped, too, and thus pilots are taught not to estimate their distance from clouds visually, but instead to use man-made landmarks or their instruments.

to say, we thirst for moral agency. And this thirst is granted, miraculously. We become more than free. We become sons and daughters of the Creator himself.

In the Orthodox Church we live so completely the Resurrection that each time we are "lost" for another person, we feel a total fullness and an abundance of life in the Holy Spirit. It is not something self-destructive to sacrifice for others but our joy and our resurrection. Even when he "keeps his mind in hell," accepting himself as "the one man lost" (to use the words of St. Silouan the Athonite), the Orthodox Christian does not feel despair nor that he is earning his own salvation. Rather, he knows that to be *saved by Christ is to be joined to Christ* in the Holy Spirit – and *to Christ's own self-offering for the salvation of the world*. We have a pentecostal certainty of grace and salvation in these moments of self-emptying for the salvation of others.

Thus, the Jesus Prayer reverses the whole problematic of moral luck. We embrace our dependence upon others and upon circumstance because, guess what, *we also contribute to the circumstances affecting everyone else and the entire cosmos*. Seeing our total dependence does not make us slaves, paradoxically. Rather, it gives us the dignity of sons and daughters of God who help determine the fate of the cosmos.

So moral luck for an Orthodox Christian simply means that we live and are meant to live *perichoretically*[7] just as the Father, Son, and Holy Spirit do – to see that our life rests in others and their life rests in us. And, like Christ, we are called to repent on behalf of all for the sins they have committed.

Christ's Reversal of Oedipus Rex

RTE: Can we catch another thread? How would the path traced by Christ in his own life compare to the one recommended by classical antiquity?

---

[7] The Greek word *perichoresis* – co-inherence – is used in Orthodox Christian Trinitarian theology to describe the shared life and substance of the three Persons of the Holy Trinity. When we apply this term to human life, we are attempting to describe the life of communion, the fact that we find our lives in and through one another.

DR. PATITSAS: Whereas Oedipus killed his father and married his mother, Christ reverses this exactly by preserving his Mother's virginity and accepting his own death as the will of his heavenly Father. Oedipus blinded himself at the conclusion of his terrible path; Christ is revealed to be the Way, the Truth, and the Life.

This reverse parallel is so exact that you can see *Oedipus Rex* as a prophecy of the kind of Savior the world needed: the Son of a virgin, the obedient-unto-death regent of his Father, a perfect Teacher. Indeed, the Christian Gospel did liberate the classical world from the gods worshipped by the priests, from the tragic human condition depicted by the playwrights, and from the realm of Necessity posited by the philosophers.[8]

Again, Christ kept his mother ever in virginity, and even in childbirth preserved her wholeness. Then, He accepted death when

---

8 As I was completing the final draft of this book, a copy of Lev Shestov's *Athens and Jerusalem* (New York: Simon and Schuster, 1968) was placed in my hands by a monk at I.M. Xenofontos on the Holy Mountain. Shestov (1866-1938) was one of the four main founders of existentialism, along with Kierkegaard, Heidegger, and Sartre. Although Shestov remains well known on the continent, in England and America he barely receives mention. This is unfortunate, because for Christian existentialists Shestov should be more important even than Kierkegaard.

As Shestov saw it, the aim of philosophy from Socrates onward (although Shestov excuses Plotinus fully and Plato in part from these charges) had been to conceive of the universe completely in terms of Necessity so that human reason could analyze the world without impediment. By taking the world as a given, reason could guide us to a conformity to the world's structure – to an ethics – that would bring our highest possible happiness. But in order to arrive at a nature so completely settled, the philosophers had to be willing to renounce both man's freedom and the possibility of miracle – i.e., God's freedom. Shestov finds this a terrible price to pay for rational ethics.

We can thus see that Christ liberates the philosophers by smashing the terrible realm of absolute Necessity, putting us instead on the road of Abrahamic faith in the reality of God's ongoing intervention in the world. But the price of freedom in Christ is the renunciation of an air-tight rationalism, or of the truth-first way; i.e., freedom requires that we embrace faith. What my writing is trying to show is how faith unfolds into both ethics and the use of a purified, transfigured, reason.

To Shestov's damning critique of philosophy could be added the observation that, just as a truth-first philosophy enslaves man to the necessity of the world as a "given," so a truth-first psychotherapy will tend to enslave the soul to the "given" of its innumerable complexes, which are discovered, enumerated, and carefully nurtured in therapy. Moreover, because a person with a traumatized condition already lives as a "slave" – in the sense that when the traumatic flashback comes upon us it is seemingly inescapable and it masters our best attempts to respond differently – a truth-first psychotherapy (the talk therapy analysis that predominates in our contemporary American practice) will naturally only worsen the trauma victim's feeling of hopeless unfreedom. This must be why Jonathan

it was the will of his Father. He did not jealously react to his Father's preeminence as Oedipus did to that of his own father; rather, Christ was the Father's obedient regent. Christ did not fight the prophecies made about his life. Rather, He was careful to fulfill each and every one of them.

Oedipus's name even means "swollen foot," for his father had maimed his legs at birth as a preparatory step before killing him, in order to protect his own kingship. But Scripture stresses that Christ's legs were untouched at his death (Jn 19:36),[9] and that his death was as the beloved Son of his Father, not as a victim of his Father's jealousy.

Father Michael Meerson,[10] who emigrated to the United States after some daring exploits as a layman in the freedom underground in the U.S.S.R. during the 1970s, once told me that when Christ quotes the opening of Psalm 22, "My God, My God, why hast Thou forsaken Me?," He is expressing the theological meaning of the entire psalm: even though I suffer unjustly, nevertheless, God is justified. So at the moment of his deepest darkness, Christ isn't blaming the Father, but rather exonerating him. He is acting in the exact opposite way that Oedipus did.

Shay had observed that the talk-therapy approach so often provoked despair among his most traumatized veterans. In the name of "healing," they had been boxed in on every side by terrible, cold Necessity.

For Shestov, meanwhile, man's choice remains the one given in the Garden of Eden: whether to live by faith and relationship with the God of the Old and New Testaments, or whether instead to "eat of the Tree of the Knowledge of Good and Evil" by trusting that rationalist analysis will give us the status of gods.

But anyone can see that "trauma" consists precisely in a person's already having been force-fed the bitter fruit of the Knowledge of Good and Evil. It defies all humanity to offer the trauma sufferer a cold plate of more of the same, by insisting on a primarily analytical approach to their experience.

Now that the Western psychotherapeutic truth-first approach to the soul and to theology has come to control the pastoral formation of clergy across all American religions, and from there invades the confessional and the pulpit, religious encounters, too, will cease to liberate and will become deadening. The serpent offering the Knowledge of Good and Evil has slipped in to the consciousness of the American Christian through this cold approach to the soul.

9 I thank Prof. Olga Meerson for noting this contrast between Oedipus and Christ.

10 Michael Aksionov Meerson, author of *The Trinity of Love in Modern Russian Theology* (Quincy, Illinois: Franciscan Press, 1998).

RTE: Would a Greek have seen Christ in this way, as a clear reversal of Oedipus?

DR. PATITSAS: Not quite, because Christ reverses Oedipus in a second way also. And this is where things get really interesting, as we begin to see the deeper pattern in the Orthodox way. Here is where we will see why a primarily cognitive approach to healing trauma not only doesn't work but can't work. In fact, it can't work as the primary tool for *any* meaningful soul-transformation, which is even more of a bomb to drop in our culture – a culture which is so classically Greek, in the sense of being overly dependent on intellect, that we Greek Orthodox can barely comprehend it.

To the Greek tragedians, Oedipus's mistake – the human person's mistake – begins in the mind, in the intellect; his *hubris* undid him. Next, Oedipus encountered his father along the road, of course not knowing him; the two argued, and he slew his father. Finally, he journeys to his real home and unwittingly marries his mother.

Thus, all of his mistakes seem traceable to two intellectual primary mistakes, pride and ignorance. Since pride is a form of ignorance, the Greek tragedians aren't so different than the philosophers in this respect; both could be interpreted to mean that the intellectual virtues of awareness and intelligence will be sufficient to safeguard your soul. After pride, for Oedipus, came sins in the realm of anger and, finally, in the realm of desire.

About Face: Reversing the Order of Battle

RTE: Don't we agree? Surely the Orthodox Church gives first place to the humility of her saints?

DR. PATITSAS: Lars Thunberg writes in *Microcosm and Mediator*, his book about St. Maximos the Confessor's theology and anthropology, that we Orthodox don't agree. In fact, he says that very early on, by the fourth or fifth century, monasticism East and West differed exactly on this point. In the West, the intellectual sins like pride were taken as primary and as the first line of spiritual defense. In the East, the sensual sins were taken as primary; the battle should be fought and won there.[11]

The tradition of the Church often makes use of the idea that the soul is tripartite – has three distinct sets of powers: the rational or intellectual, by which we apprehend truth; the spirited or incensive powers, with which we hate evil and fight for the good; and the desiring or appetitive powers, with which we desire what is good for us because it is beautiful.

These powers can go wrong, can become fixated on the world as an end in itself, and then we term them passions. Incensive, fighting powers gone wrong are then known as irascible passions; appetitive powers gone wrong are known as concupiscent passions.

Well, the idea in the West became that Oedipus fell into intellectual passions, then irascible ones, and finally concupiscent ones. And this is held by many to show us the order of battle today.

RTE: It seems pretty logical. We all struggle with pride, and "pride goeth before a fall."

DR. PATITSAS: I thought it logical, too, but once a student pointed out to me Thunberg's remark about this essential difference between Orthodoxy and the West, I started asking around and looking around.

Our Savior followed the path that we follow in the Orthodox Church. First, He was born in virginity, preserved his mother from the moment of his conception ever in virginity, and himself lived a virginal life. Thus, He defeated the concupiscent passions, the temptation to sensuality. Next, He faced the temptation to kingship, the wrath of kings, and the sentencing to death. By bearing his death without wrath, He conquers the irascible passions completely and utterly.

---

11 Lars Thunberg, *Microcosm and Mediator: The Theological Anthropology of Maximos the Confessor*, 2nd ed. (Chicago: Open Court, 1995), 246.

It is only at the very end, in the grave, that we depict Christ when we describe his "extreme humility." Victory over the passion of pride comes last.

Similarly, in our own life: First we fast; then we give alms or are otherwise reconciled with our enemies; and finally we are prepared to pray in all perfection, to humble our minds in receiving the perfect vision of God's glory.

RTE: And when you looked around, did you find that Orthodox Christians knew about this "order of battle"?

DR. PATITSAS: I discovered that in general we don't seem to know what Thunberg is talking about, when he says that in the Eastern Christian tradition you fight the sensual sins first. To very much oversimplify, we might react, "Wait, isn't it the Roman Catholics who think sex is sinful, while we Orthodox are all about humility?" We either think Thunberg has it exactly backwards or that he simply doesn't make sense. I *should have* understood, based on everything I'd been taught in seminary, but I certainly didn't.

So I went to a monastery and asked the abbot. Not only did he know what Thunberg meant, he said that Thunberg's point is a life or death distinction for Orthodox. In fact, he started by saying that the entire purpose of a monk's life rests upon this precise distinction! I felt an immediate rush of gratitude, knowing that we live in a Church where the inside knowledge of the fourth century is still the most important knowledge of the twenty-first.

What the abbot said is that the purpose of a monk is to keep the mind in the heart, focused on the name of Jesus. When he attempts to do so, the great temptation will be from images and sensations. Any of us, when we try to pray, find that pictures come into our minds, even holy ones, to distract us from prayer. Feelings arise and take hold of us. Or, we are too hungry or tired or cold to pray. In one way or another our first battle is with sensations and images.

But the Christian who stands fast in devotion to the name of Christ will find that he has conquered self-love, which itself is known as the "mother of the passions." "As for pride," the abbot said, "it is a passion like the other passions. You can't give it any particular significance."

Well, I know now that you can't fight any of the passions head on but must rather cut off their source, self-love, by falling in love with Christ. You begin with chaste devotion to him. The Old Testament prophets had a lot to say about our eros for God being disrupted by adulterous attachments to many other things.

Unfortunately for puritan misinterpreters of this tradition, who think you can cure bad eros through a kind of anorexia, the only real cure for bad eros is good eros, and plenty of it.

And incidentally, this is why you can't be the only referent of "the sinner" in the Jesus Prayer; in that case, the prayer would leave you enclosed within yourself, rather than promoting your ecstatic union with Christ.

From Adam and Eve to the Good Thief

RTE: So the abbot's short answer sufficed to open the door?

DR. PATITSAS: Yes, because I saw at once, even before the abbot had finished speaking, that his answer puts the story of Adam and Eve in a universal light. Eve represents the concupiscent passions which desired the attractiveness of the fruit more than company with Christ.[12] Don't I do the same thing, many times a day? Next, Adam represents the irascible passions, seeking to cut himself off from Eve and God to save his own life after the bitter taste of sensuality. This is what happens when he says, "The woman whom you gave me, caused me to eat" (Gen 3:12). He sacrifices God and Eve to save himself, says St. Silouan, by accusing them of a sin that was known to be punishable by death! And isn't this what I do when I am filled with hatred for myself and for my own body, and even blame God, after I have fallen into concupiscent sins?

12 The Orthodox Christian tradition holds that Adam and Eve's company with God in the Garden was, in fact, company with the pre-Incarnate Christ, in a mystery that we cannot explain.

Finally, to prevent Adam and Eve from living forever in their passionate state and growing irredeemably proud, God expels them into the world outside paradise. Outside of his easy company, the difficulties of life in a fallen world will prevent them from attaining to a demonic level of pride and being lost forever.

If the abbot was right, then this is a drama that we each repeat many times a day. We are all taken away from focus on Christ by sensuality, come to war with ourselves and others as a result, and then are only spared from a demonic pride and total spiritual destruction when God allows us to suffer – and accepts our repentance. Knowing that we do the same thing continually, we should feel a lot more compassion for Adam and Eve!

Or look at the Epistle of James. "Why is there war among you? Because of the passions of the flesh" (Jas 4:1). Concupiscence leads on to irascibility, and then our deception grows.

Saint Silouan even says that if Adam had not tried to sacrifice Eve and God to save himself, then the Fall and expulsion from Paradise would have been averted! So, if we fall into the concupiscent passions, our next backstop is the irascible ones – at least don't blame God and others, don't lash out and grow resentful, nurse rage, reject your very self, lose all peace. Saint Seraphim of Sarov says that when we fall, "we are not to be our own executioners" through indulging in self-hatred over our weakness.

But if you do even this, then allow the intellectual powers to be the backstop of that. At once humiliate yourself and run to your confessor, and say openly what you have done and thought.

This is our Orthodox way, and however often we fall, we cannot attack pride directly as our first priority. Rather, we return to the front lines: our simple devotion to Christ, our fasting, our chastity, and the sacred beauty of the icons. This is always the first order of business, once the dust settles on the last spiritual battle. Your spiritual father, the saints, Christ himself and his All-holy Mother will move mountains for you – only don't neglect your daily struggle with images in prayer, your fasts, nor the many simple adventures in chastity. We think those are the least of our obligations, but they are where the battle will be won or lost.[13]

RTE: I like this very much because this calmness in the midst of spiritual storms is what I see among the pious in Orthodox countries. But what if we don't have the time or energy left to fight our passions – like the thief on the cross? How was he the first to enter Paradise?

DR. PATITSAS: First, he was somehow able to fall in love with Christ, renouncing the vain outer appearance or image of things, rejecting all the sensual evidence that obscured Christ's glory. Instead, he glimpsed Christ's perfection and fell in love with him. This was the Beauty stage.

He was thus prepared to take the next step, of Goodness. He became able to defend Christ from the unjust judgment of the bad thief, to stand up for Christ, to "fight" or contest for him. The thief is so firmly anchored in Goodness at this moment that he speaks with the perfect authority of a lawgiver about his own state, that of his brother thief, that of Christ, and about the fittingness of the punishment he endures. In fact, the thief speaks for all of sinful humanity in pronouncing himself worthy of punishment. He was able to recognize goodness in the world and he enacted this goodness by confessing Christ openly.

---

13 I have heard it remarked that vanity, rather than pride, was held by some Fathers to be the primary sin, the cause of all falls. I would guess that the Fathers who say this are not conceiving of vanity as an intellectual passion, as we do, but as a concupiscent one. "Vanity" as the primary sin would, for these Fathers, mean the obsession with both inner and outer appearances; that is, a falling into sensuality. We now tend to conceive of a vain person as being obsessed with his own appearance in the eyes of others and "vanity" as a complement to "pride," but these particular Fathers must have seen vanity as describing a running after sensuality and appearances in general. Vanity would have been the polar opposite of "unknowing," in other words; or, it would have been another word for "self-love."

Another common scriptural meaning of "vanity" – the fruitlessness of running after fleeting this-worldly goods and pleasures – is similar to what I am surmising was the patristic meaning. Moreover, this carefulness around vanity should remind us of Plato's analogy of the cave, where *all* appearance was in fact *deceptive shadow*. Thus, Plato is allied with the general mind of the Fathers on this point, when read in a certain light, and is less a rationalist than an ascetic. Shestov himself went so far as to defend Plato from the charge of dualism, interpreting him to mean that it was a non-iconic interpretation of the world (here, I am paraphrasing Shestov quite liberally), not the world itself, from which Plato wants us to flee.

And finally, he was willing to humble himself utterly, asking a dying "criminal" for mercy. This confession of Truth guaranteed his entrance into Paradise.

Worldly "Virtue"

In the Orthodox Christian approach to salvation, the sequence is chastity (Beauty), empathy (Goodness), and humility (Truth). It is important, whenever possible, to pursue these three virtues in this order.

The world today is going with a version of the classical approach of the Greek philosophers, which cannot work for the spiritual life. Society tells you to *start* by attacking your pride. Humble yourself by renouncing your claim to an intellectual hold on absolute truth. In other words, embrace relativism. Second, work for world peace – which should be easy once no one any longer holds passionately to their own ideas about truth, the logic goes. Or at least *imagine* you are working for world peace, perhaps by hating those who seem not to be. As for the pleasures, the world says you can have as many as you like, so long as you continue the prior renunciations of truth/exclusivity and of self-defense/jealousy.

In other words, be a relativist; have a vague commitment to passivity and peace; but above all don't get involved in a long-term Christian marriage in which things like chastity and exclusivity are worth fighting for; do all this, and the world will be happy with you.

Our young people feel the pressure of this inversion very strongly when they attempt to be chaste and virginal. Their friends will respond, "Why? Do you think you are better than us?" That is, the young person is accused of pride, an intellectual passion. "Are you rejecting us by not joining in our hopeless fun? Are you separating yourself from us?" In other words, the young Christian is next accused of enmity, an irascible passion. "Besides," they say, "concupiscent passions are the least important of the three, and in fact are a good thing." If we fall for these lies, the result is predictable.

Such an approach is poison. We must spit it out at once.

II. CREATION'S ORIGIN IN EROS FOR THE BEAUTIFUL

St. Maximos and Christ's Beauty in Creation

RTE: How does this approach to spiritual warfare reflect the cosmology you spoke of earlier?

DR. PATITSAS: We have already hinted at the answer. It started with the original "Jesus Prayer." "When" (we cannot use words for time in these mysteries, except allegorically) the Father caused his Spirit to proceed and rest upon his only begotten Son, the Son "at once" became willing to share out his Life with the world – a world which was then roused into existence through this very shining out, this self-emptying of Christ in the Holy Spirit in obedience to the Father.

To put it another way, St. Maximos says that God was so good that his goodness could not be contained within himself. It poured forth "outside" himself in a cosmic Theophany over against the face of darkness. The appearing of this ultimate Beauty caused non-being to forget itself, to renounce itself, to leave behind its own "self" (non-being), and come to be.[14] All of creation is thus marked by this eros, by this movement of doxology, liturgy, and love. Creation is a movement of repentance out of chaos and into the light of existence.

Creation is repenting from its first moment, *for repentance does not require the prerequisite of sin*. It simply means that we put our attention still more deeply upon Christ, to love him much more than we have before.[15] Of course, compared to that "more deeply," the prior state looks like sin, but this is partly relative.

---

14 This idea was brought into the theology of the Church by St. Dionysios the Areopagite; See *Divine Names*, 4.7.

15 That repentance does not depend on prior sin is obvious to the noble soul, Christian and non-Christian alike. I had a Tae Kwon Do instructor who, each time before we sparred, would make us bow and apologize to our opponent. "Sorry," he would say, "is too late. You must say sorry *before* your mistake." Analogously, repenting prior to sin or *independently* of sin in everyday life partly just means asking, "How can I improve the situation in which I find myself? How can I rouse myself from sloth and become a force for creativity and love where I am?" This question does not imply the presence of existing sin, per se; or

Thus, first comes the battle with concupiscent passions, which we win by fasting – in other words, by falling in love with Beauty itself and not with false beauty or with the chaos around us. But what is real Beauty except Christ himself in his self-emptying love? And so through Beauty we learn the Goodness of the Cross (that is to say, Ethics), and we ourselves long to pour out our life for our brothers, sisters, enemies, and all of creation. In order to contemplate this goodness, to be illumined, we must give alms. We are then illumined in both senses: we contemplate correctly, and our light "shines before men" (Mt 5:16).

Thus, we arrive at the knowledge of Truth and at a union with the Truth, Who is the Logos of the Father. Here, we become our true self. We participate in Truth by our very being, each according to his own unique calling. We are genuine. There is no longer any "falseness" in us. This is what it means to arrive at Truth, although various insights will surely follow as well.

Only in this three-fold movement do we come to be, for St. Maximos says that every existing thing is created according to its own particular logos, its own unique sharing in the ultimate Logos, the Truth who is the Son.

RTE: And this movement toward Christ is why you said that eros is the beginning of moral life?

DR. PATITSAS: Yes, and that was actually my point in bringing up how Tolkien helps us to experience the eros involved in falling in love with other cultures and civilizations, or with something beautiful that can make us forget ourselves. Our lives only begin, our moral struggle only commences, once we've loved something enough to want to leave ourselves behind. That can be painful – but ideally it's never worse than bittersweet.

---

rather, the prior state will only come to seem sinful in comparison with what we were able to accomplish once we were ready to repent in the absence of sin. *In fact, one reason we resist improvement in our current weak states is that we don't want to make our "prior" self look bad.* The cultivation of repentance in the absence of sin is characterized by the Greek term *philotimo*, a term that we shall return to in Chapter Four. It describes the noble, or royal, soul.

Adam and Eve, by contrast, failed in their pursuit of Beauty, fell into a war with each other, and then were expelled from the Garden because their pride threatened to become absolute and permanent.

Incidentally, a wise educator always trades in Beauty and Goodness before Truth.

The Gates of Truth – The Tomb of Christ

RTE: How does this all relate to trauma? It seems that everything you've mentioned could be a help.

DR. PATITSAS: All I can really tell you about trauma is how I as an Orthodox ethicist read Jonathan Shay, perhaps our culture's best expert on trauma.[16] I am an ethicist, not a psychiatrist with daily experience interacting with trauma victims. It may turn out that I don't know anything about how to heal trauma, and on that point I'll let you and the reader judge for yourselves.

In fact, if the reports coming back from the field of mental health were positive; if a MacArthur Genius Award-recipient like Shay were not reporting that, in fact, we don't know how to heal trauma; if a recent issue of *The New Yorker* magazine hadn't spelled out what an utter chaos of treatment approaches – many of them already debunked in their approach by Shay, few of them empirically verified – are being currently employed across the Veterans Administration to heal PTSD[17]; if I couldn't see with my own eyes how wrong we as a culture can go when it comes to comforting the broken-hearted victims of bad circumstance – if all this were not the case, then I would leave this to the experts.

But since it is, I will share what Orthodox Christianity, in my limited understanding, might have to say about trauma. What is crucial according to Orthodoxy is the "order of battle" in the spiritual life, the way that we conduct ourselves in the spiritual struggle.

---

16 See Footnote 5, Chapter 1.

17 David Finkel, "The Return: The Traumatized Veterans of Iran and Afghanistan," *The New Yorker*, September 9, 2013.

This is an order that flows from the unique and almost unknown (even among Orthodox) account of how the world was created that we just now mentioned. Our anthropology of soul-healing is inseparable from our account of creation. Since so few know the second, the first can easily go astray without our noticing.

Creation results from God's self-emptying over the face of non-being. God appears, He shines out, as Beauty. This Beauty is so compelling that not even non-being can resist falling in love with it. Overcome with eros, non-being renounces itself, repents of its chaos and self-absorption, and arises into being. As it does so, it "learns" to behave as the One it loves behaves – full of self-emptying Goodness for everything around it. Thus, everything that exists is marked by a cruciform love – for God, as eros, and for all creation, as agape. In these two movements, rocks, stones, stars, plants, animals, electrons – all of it – becomes what it is, becomes true.

That is how the world was, and still is being, created. And that is the path that anyone who wishes to be born again (Jn 3:3) will also have to follow.

RTE: People found the first interview not only helpful, but providential. So we accept your disclaimer about not being a healing professional, and promise to judge for ourselves.

DR. PATITSAS: Thank you. Elder Porphyrios, who as of this very day has been canonized and acclaimed a saint by the Holy Synod of Constantinople, said it best. "No one ever became holy by fighting evil. We only become holy by falling in love with Christ."[18]

We said so much in our last interview about trauma, but let's focus on what we said near the end. We talked about war in general, and trauma specifically, as an anti-liturgy. Whereas liturgy knits our individual character together and integrates us; whereas liturgy promotes communion and deepens our connection to others and

---

[18] Saint Porphyrios (Bairaktaris) of Kapsokalyvia and Athens (1906–1991), canonized on November 27, 2013. The greatest contemporary example of "Beauty-first," St. Porphyrios' discerning spiritual counsel can be read in *Wounded by Love: The Life and Wisdom of Elder Porphyrios* (Evia Greece: Denise Harvey, 2005), 156.

God and the whole of nature; and whereas liturgy teaches us the profound truth of who God really is, and thus who we are and who the world is – well, war and trauma reverse all this. They unravel our character by breaking our connection to beauty, drive us from close communion with others so that we don't have the opportunity to be good, and teach us lies about God, the world, and ourselves.

The healing of the soul begins with noticing God's many theophanies and with falling in love with them. In other words, it begins with eros for Beauty. In renewing our love for authentic Beauty, we are slowly cleansed of the ugly images of trauma and the false images of worldly pleasures. Our character, unraveled by what we have experienced, begins to be knit together and becomes whole again. We begin to be "created" again.

After this we can discuss Goodness. By embracing what we find within authentic Beauty – the crucified Savior and the Cross – we attain Goodness and become good, and find our communion to others restored. We do this through almsgiving, or empathy. We contemplate Goodness through action as well as thought, and are able to see any and all culpability we have for the state of the world – but now in a spirit ready to embrace that culpability through repentance. With time we come to wish that we could be still more culpable so that we could do something about it all. In other words, the empathy that Shay so emphasized comes more and more into play in this second stage.

Finally, through these two steps we are brought to the gates of Truth, which is to say, to the tomb of Christ. And here we bow down and accept our own humiliation in a spirit of surrender, finding ourselves resurrected and renewed. We begin to receive our crown for what we have suffered, already in this life. We are, that is, engraced.

Why We Don't Start with Truth

RTE: How then will this "order of battle" help the trauma victim?

DR. PATITSAS: I think it shows why the classical Greek approaches contained in tragedy, philosophy, and our contemporary analytical psychotherapy will not be sufficient; truth is not the first order of business for the soul. Especially when it is not the truth of the self, but simply the truth about certain events or impressions. Nor should we try to begin with goodness; that attempt to do the right thing is also doomed, as we see most clearly in the case of the addict. This is what makes their disease so distinctive.

Trauma represents a kind of paralysis within the irascible passions; addiction, a paralysis within the concupiscent passions, usually with a corresponding trauma wound, perhaps self-inflicted as in the case of resentment.

But trauma signifies being trapped in this defensive crouch. It is important to remember that this defensive posture of the traumatized person is not by any means the ultimate step of pride and spiritual death. From that, it is light years away in fact.

Rather, for the trauma sufferer, a concupiscent attachment to something perceived as irrevocably lost has resulted in the irascible event of a narrowing of all attachment, a war against all, including finally one's own self. Even the berserk state, which we mentioned in the first chapter, is not yet the prideful state, although it mimics it. But I assure you it is not. There is still so much hope there – the berserker is still so very far from damnation.

So this freezing within the irascible passions must be addressed.

Addressing the Irascible Passions

First, the Beautiful: Shay says we begin when we take the trauma victim out of the ugly circumstances inflicting the trauma. We bring them to good patterns of life, to friendships, to self-care. All of this represents the return of Beauty to the life. Good Patterns –

in the Christopher Alexander[19] sense of Patterns in architecture, but applicable to Patterns of action and self-care and relating – are really nothing less than the Platonic Forms, the direct visitation of Divine Beauty in our lives.[20] These Patterns must be cultivated first.

Can we then see the Goodness within this Beauty? Do we see the care being shown us by others as pure Goodness in our life, as good moral luck, as a precious empathy coming at our benefactor's expense? This is what I emphasized in the last interview. Some people know how to heal trauma, and if we meet them we will see that they are the very opposite of a person inflicting trauma. In fact, what they do is accept our abuse out of love for us. But they are only able to mimic Christ so completely because they are well-practiced at giving everything to Christ. It is He who is carrying you through them. Such living saints are simultaneously afflicted yet free.

Shay knew that the *Iliad* was the crucial text; so did Simone Weil. I love the way that this text combines beauty and goodness, art with empathy. In it, in its profound hearing, brother soldiers came together for a week or so, to listen to a beauty that made them forget themselves, in a safe context of hospitality and unity. Within that Beauty was Goodness, empathic love. As we said last time, there are no enemies in the *Iliad*, only noble soldiers, trapped in war on both sides. Before such a monument of Beauty and Empathy, we can safely weep, practicing empathy for others – and by extension for ourselves.

You know, Truth isn't really a "third moment." If you have Beauty and Goodness, Truth is right there, inside them both. That noble weeping in the hearing of the *Iliad* is one of the moments that you are most alive – most true.

---

19 Christopher Alexander is Professor Emeritus of the University of California at Berkeley. An architect noted for his remarkable theories of design, Alexander is the author of *The Timeless Way of Building* (Oxford Univ. Press, 1979) and *A Pattern Language* (Oxford Univ. Press, 1977). *The Timeless Way* has this mystical quality: it is a book about good design that nevertheless frees the reader from vanity, in the sense that we defined vanity in Footnote 6, above, as an obsession with the superficial look of things.

20 We will return to the subject of the Forms at length in Chapter Six. For now, let us just note that the Forms are the "typical" ways that things have of being beautiful, or good, or merely existing. In this present context, what I am calling for is the cultivation of such order, when possible, to calm the chaos that we feel inside.

The hell of the Trojan War, we must remember, was put down by Odysseus's willingness to die upon the wood – the wood of the Trojan Horse, I mean – for had he been discovered inside, he would have been killed. This sounds so much like Christ, who stretched out his body upon the wood of the cross. The Hellenes were very close to Christ. That was their suffering – to have been so close and yet still so far away. Thank God for St. Paul!

RTE: And it seems that you are using "truth" in the sense of "genuineness," rather than knowing the facts about things.

DR. PATITSAS: Yes! That genuineness is the real meat of truth. Truths "about" things, and about people and ourselves, can foster that killing isolation we spoke of last time.

But as we heal, we do arrive at certain truths about ourselves, our enemies, our torturers, about God and life. These are manifold and not to be treated lightly; let me just mention one. We come to find that when we replay trauma tapes in our heads, we are actually inflicting damage upon ourselves. We are getting ourselves stuck more deeply in the mud. We are hurting ourselves. This cannot be known at first; we initially experience the flashback as a continuation of the attack, as something external, and in many senses it is. But with time we learn to master this response, to develop some space between the impulse and our cooperation with it. With time, a person can even stop playing the tapes.

But that doesn't mean you can intellectually talk someone out of this replaying before having done the work of Beauty and Empathy and Genuineness; heavens, no. In some cases, such a rushed, cold, forced approach to "healing" is the approach of a sociopath; it can be a soul crime.

Anyway, a person who has advanced so far is still not "cured" of trauma. So then why does it matter? Because he or she can then return to square one – focusing on more beauty, more empathy, more truth, without the distraction of these ugly tapes running on the mind's view screen. At that point, time begins to flow again;

time is on your side, and you see more vividly what was hidden though present before – hope.

At times, we will not be able to follow this order of battle. A person may have an attack of pride, for example, or seek moral guidance about a pressing question. We respond where we have to, where the crisis hits us. But we always re-start with Beauty, with the spiritual senses, with chastity and eros, because that is where it all began when the world was first created, when we were first created.

What the Body Knows

RTE: Shay says that the truth-first approach could work with patients who have conditions less severe than trauma. Why is trauma so much different a challenge to healing, other than the very shocking or overwhelming source event that produces it?

DR. PATITSAS: Because, as Bessel van der Kolk says in *The Body Keeps the Score: Brain, Mind, and Body in the Healing of Trauma*, trauma is not just a mental or emotional fact.[21] Rather, it actually induces a rewiring of our brains. Moreover, it also recruits other systems in our body into its preservation. Biologically, various bodily systems and the brain are themselves the places where trauma is being "remembered" or stored. This makes healing more complex. The intellectual part of the brain is almost beside the point in attacking trauma.

Let me tell you a story that illustrates the mysterious ways in which we know things. Back in 2003, I was asked to be the tenth man in a pick-up basketball game. I had never seen any of the other players play basketball before. I just happened to enter the gym when another player was needed; the game was about to begin in a few seconds. Therefore, no more warming up was happening, and I had no knowledge of these men as athletes. I took my place on the court, the ball was thrown in, and everyone started to move at once.

---

21 Bessel van der Kolk, *The Body Keeps the Score: Brain, Mind, and Body in the Healing of Trauma* (NY: Viking Press, 2014).

Hoping to get acclimated quickly to what I was dealing with, I had positioned myself to observe the entire court. Well, within the first five steps taken by each player, I saw in an overwhelming flash that I was in serious trouble. Of the ten players, at least two were professional-level players, and two more were at a semi-pro level. Within their first steps, I could see that the court sense and body control of these four players were quantumly different than that of anyone else on the court. In fact, these were the kind of guys I almost never see on the basketball court unless I have paid to get in. Afterwards I found out that one of them had played professionally overseas, another had played on the national team of his communist country in the Olympics, and so on. But going into the game I had no idea; these expert men were of all ages, so their conditioning was no tip off to what I was about to see.

Of course, there on the court, I was trying to react and adjust and keep up with the game itself, but at the same time, my mind was churning. What is the knowledge of how to play the game of basketball that some people possess, such that this expertise is evident within even a fraction of the game? Where exactly in the body or the brain of an expert athlete is that kind of information and insight stored so that it shapes their every movement?

Last winter I was invited to a college hockey game at Boston University, and the same thing happened. One player, known to be destined for the NHL, was acting and reacting in some completely different way from every other player on the ice, even when he wasn't near the puck, even when he was just standing there. He just looked different, in some way you could hardly describe, at every moment he was on the ice, no matter what he was doing. What is that knowledge of the game that he possessed? Where in his mind or body was it stored? What was he actually doing differently than the others?

Moreover, do you think that a player like that could *ever* unlearn such knowledge, could ever be made to forget it? In forty years when he skates with his grandkids, won't it still be obvious who he is?

But in fact, all of us are like this in many ways. It is hard for a young woman to fake being a mother if she has never had or adopted a child of her own. She often lacks a subtle knowing, and when you see her with a child, she allows some psychic distance between her and the child that mothers never do. And in many other areas of life, there are levels of knowing, acting, training, habits, and dispositions that are far below the cognitive brain – the simple brain of rational analysis. The first month I came back from teaching in South Korea, it was disorienting when I would see an American-born Korean woman standing on a street corner begin to walk. Because nothing about her walking is like the way a woman raised in Korea walks. All cultures are like this – they change us on levels below even the so-called subconscious.

Well, *what if what the trauma sufferer knows, he or she knows better than almost anything that you know with your conscious mind?* Van der Kolk says that cognitive neuroscience – the neuroscience looking at the brain as it undergoes various psychological states – tells us that when a trauma flashback occurs, the person's brain can actually change into a different chemical and hormonal profile, almost as if the trauma sufferer were then a different person. So the trauma sufferer knows in their endocrine and adrenal systems and in various parts of the brain that most of us have never accessed with our weak religious practice, far more about their trauma than I might know about the love of God. Of course, I would in that case struggle to heal them or to advise them!

Now, trauma is also stored in the parts of the brain that are accessible to rational analysis, says van der Kolk, but we must stress that *it is not only stored* there, *nor mainly* stored there. Rationally, you may be able to observe your trauma, realize what caused it, understand how much its continuation is harming you, and even recognize when you are replaying it and how unsuitable this is. But because you cannot change hardly any of this from the rational vantage point, the growing awareness of all this tragedy – of course! – will then coincide with growing despair. You both see the dark situation more clearly and become at the same time more convinced that change is hopeless since rational awareness has no impact on fixing it. Van der Kolk is quite insistent on these points.

The understanding of truth (of Necessity, if you are a secularist) does not produce a goodness, an ethics, that is of any use. Quite the reverse; it makes all ethics seem impossible.

RTE: This does not sound encouraging because if the expert athlete can never erase that extra something they know about their sport, how can a trauma victim erase this bodily memory?

DR. PATITSAS: The stupendously intuitive athlete can't ever forget his hockey or his basketball, true enough. But perhaps because he is so "natural" at one sport already, he might then be taught to fence? Or to box?

That is why I said in our first talk that "the opposite of war is not peace"; physical knowledge like this cannot be erased, but it can often be assimilated into some even more sophisticated practice. It may be that some trauma sufferers may never get anywhere trying to process complex trauma (i.e. developmental trauma[22]) unless they are also learning some new and more challenging skill, some even deeper set of reactions. Only through grace can an even deeper level be accessed. And noetic prayer, the prayer of the heart, is that ultimately sophisticated skill.

Meanwhile, the very primitive approach we often use now, of talking and talking about traumatic experiences, actually involves a reliving of the trauma in the synapses and chemicals of your brain – which the talk therapist encourages, thinking that otherwise you are detaching from your experience and "not dealing with it." This re-living then further intensifies the hold of these events over you as you re-fire the neurons and chemical reactions that made them so powerfully present in you to begin with. At least, this is what van der Kolk reports.

---

[22] Van der Kolk distinguishes between "simple trauma" induced by a single event, or by a series of discrete events, from "complex trauma" generated by more sustained patterns of traumatic experience, especially if it occurs in childhood or young adulthood. For example, a pattern of sexual abuse over the course of childhood generates a traumatic profile in the brain and body that is different from a single act in adulthood of sexual assault.

Thus, talk therapy moves the trauma patient toward despair and hell on three fronts: by a) increasing your rational awareness of b) an increasingly bad configuration of your total brain and body (the re-living through discussion is actually strengthening the physical presence of the trauma in your brain) that c) cannot be amended through the reasoning process you are being powerfully conditioned to rely upon. For van der Kolk, the brain is actually getting more and more steeped in the chaotic mess as you relive it.

Nevertheless, what the trauma sufferer knows so well, what he knows perhaps best of all, is a lie. Well, not a lie exactly, but rather, the "absolutization of a partial truth," as I was taught to define "heresy" by Fr. Emmanuel Clapsis, my dogmatics professor at Holy Cross seminary. The thing the trauma sufferer knows most deeply is actually a kernel of truth wrapped in an accretion of lies or some subtle blend of truth and falsehood.

In general, American psychotherapy wants us to start by trusting our feelings, by analyzing our feelings intellectually, and, through the expression of our feelings in the light of reason, to commence the route to health. *None of this* applies to the trauma sufferer when his brain begins to enter its flashback profile. Instead, he has to avoid the triggers that unlock these deceptive feelings and take active steps to counter-feel when they do arise. Expressing the feelings generated by the flashback profile, especially with the wrong people, is a route to all sorts of problems. And the last thing you can do is to trust such feelings indiscriminately.

No, the heart is deeper than our feelings, and within our deep heart we will find our conscience itself telling us to exercise very great care with the acceptance and expression of trauma-style feelings, even in therapy.[23] We are not meant to relive these events, nor to induce others to do so. Our heart and

---

[23] Steve Zabak, one of our proofreaders, called my attention to the Church's version of the Old Testament, the Septuagint, which makes this point beautifully in Jeremiah 17:9. It reads, "A human heart is deeper than anything, and this heart is the essential core of a human being; and so, who shall really know a man?" (Author's translation.)

The later Masoretic version of the same verse is far less inspiring: "The heart is deceitful above all things, and desperately wicked, and who shall know it?"

The next verse, Jeremiah 17:10, makes a further point, that the Lord alone knows men's

our feelings are in open warfare against each other when we do – a sign that we have entered the realm of the passions.

All of this, by the way, rules out some huge percentage of "serious films" these days, which so often revel in their capacity to mimic trauma-inducing experience and to evoke the feeling of being traumatized within the viewer. The pornography of trauma has come to dominate the film-making art.

Well, it's not just Hollywood. So many people these days seems to be trying to score points in an argument by inducing trauma in their audience or referencing the absolute vantage point of their own trauma experience. And the f-word is the most laconic way of doing that, which is why it is gaining wider usage. But that tendency didn't start with our degraded political and ethical debates; it was inculcated in us by film after film glorifying the berserk state, from "Deer Hunter" to "Rambo" to "Good Will Hunting" to "The Horse Whisperer."[24] And at the back of that is the berserk sins we've committed against foreign civilians and the souls of our own soldiers in our wars of the last century.

In many places within art and in education, you run into this notion that beauty is a lie, and this belief that trauma and traumatic experience alone vouchsafe authentic truth. I felt this, too, growing up – that somehow only the person who had been a dramatic sinner had anything to teach me about spiritual life.

One other thing: have you noticed, really consciously thought about, the fact that our American flag has been "footnoted"? In so many official places, the flag can't be flown unless the mournful black flag commemorating POW's and MIA's is flown underneath

---

hearts and "tries their reins," and thus is able to do what we cannot: accurately judge our true state.

"The reins" is a biblical term which we might smirk at; really, it signifies what Bessel van der Kolk also thinks is decisive for our understanding of the human person. "The reins" signifies the inner biology of feelings and attitudes which we identify with the adrenal and endocrine systems or with the autonomic nervous system. In other words, the biblical conception of the human person, untouched by the Enlightenment's biases, is more scientifically accurate than that used by much of contemporary psychology.

24 See the classic study by Kirby Ferrell, *Berserk Style in American Culture* (NY: Palgrave Macmillan, 2011). In 2015, an updated edition of this work became available: *The Psychology of Abandon: Berserk Style in American Culture* (Amherst, Massachusetts: Levellers Press, 2015).

it. This footnote to our American flag was added by federal statute in 1990, but the movement to adopt it grew out of our post-Vietnam feeling that the American nation had not been able, had not even tried, to "bring home" the very soldiers who actually live amongst us. The "prisoners" aren't in some jungle encampment in Southeast Asia – they're right here, trapped in post-traumatic stress reactions that our psychological science struggles to heal. Have I gone too far by saying that we can't heal war trauma? For heaven's sake, we've agreed as a nation to add a shadow to the American flag to express that very belief!

Trauma Is an Anti-Theophany

RTE: How can we think of this theologically? What is going on in these cases?

DR. PATITSAS: According to the Beauty-first doctrine, both our original creation and our salvation from death and sin begin with theophany. To live and to be healed both mean that we have been drawn away from self-love and toward some positive vision of Beauty. Theophany sparks within us a dynamic motion towards God, and this motion structures the very content of both being and salvation. Faith – chaste and ardent eros – really is sufficient for our salvation, containing within itself already the seeds of perfect works/agape and true love for God and others!

Well, a traumatic experience exactly reverses the process by which we were created and saved. The cause of our being traumatized is that we have beheld, whether briefly or for a prolonged period, some overwhelming vision of anti-Beauty, some naked ugliness. This ugliness then becomes our guiding black hole – if we experience this hell more powerfully than the real Beauty and theophany present in our lives. It is not just ugliness, death, or shock that causes trauma but the sense that these experiences are actual anti-theophanies, that they actually reveal to us in an overpowering and ultimate sense the real shape of both God and being. Traumatic experience may seem more real than our saccharine religious experience, for example.

When we see a real theophany, we naturally liturgize and experience both increasing inner coherence and social communion; eros for the Beautiful arises in our heart, and we find our empathy for others increasing almost immediately.

But when we behold traumatic events, we are frozen out of liturgy (we usually curse, in fact, so we see how literal this excommunication from liturgy is), and we experience both inner dissolution and the loss of empathy that will result in social isolation. We lose faith (eros) and find empathy (agape) difficult even years later when we fall into those moments when the trauma reaction has been triggered. All of this together makes me believe that, theologically, traumatizing events are akin to an anti-theophany.

If we have encountered such an anti-theophany in that full sense, then anti-Beauty may begin to draw us backward and down towards the non-being from which we were created. The traumatizing event or events form a new, negative attractor that pulls us toward nihilism. In other words, in trauma we behave as if we have beheld an anti-theophany and we go in the opposite direction that creation does. We fall away from integrity, wholeness, peace, and healing. This is the opposite of being created and being saved; we are progressively dismantled.

So there are really two reasons why we've begun this book on Orthodox Christian Ethics with the subject of trauma. First, in trauma we find our lives organized around an experience of ugliness, the polar opposite of the Beauty given to us in our relationship with God.

Second, the failure of analytical modes of therapy to cure trauma shows us that a truth-first way of soul healing or soul development is not going to be sufficient for anyone. The excessive rationalism about the soul, the naive Enlightenment faith in truth-first approaches to the heart, are simply counter-indicated. Yes, analytical modes can help in cases of milder shock, of milder trauma, because they can be sufficient to help us incorporate the ugliness into some larger hope and structure so that we still keep moving forward. But this requires that the person have some other, certainly-not-acquired-in-therapy, Beauty-first discipline within their lives. And now that Enlightenment-style therapy has conquered the American soul and even American religion so completely, where is this trust in eros and respect for Beauty to come from?

Analytical modes of relating, meanwhile, are unlikely ever to be the main answer in cases of severe trauma since they increase focus on ugliness and neglect Beauty. Soul health for all of us requires a program of *actively* taking steps not to focus on ugliness, and this is doubly so for the trauma victim. We all need training to increase our commitment to the Beauty-first way, a training which in the Church we call "asceticism."

Three Crucifixions

Recently I read something which may apply here. In his theological essay *Ambiguum 53,* St. Maximos the Confessor writes about the three crucifixions on Golgotha: that of Christ, that of the unrepentant thief, and that of the good thief.[25] Since, as we said, the trauma victim has been and is being crucified by his experience, the saint's explanations may show a way out.

Of the three crucifixions on Golgotha, says St. Maximos, that of Christ was undeserved, yet received willingly. That of the bad thief was the opposite; deserved, yet received with curses. The third crucifixion, however, that of the good thief, begins as unwilling and deserved, but then changes. The good thief comes to see that, despite his sin, it is Christ who is being crucified with him. And he accepts his own crucifixion as deserved.

Now, this is not at all to say that we deserve to be traumatized in the way the thief deserved his punishment! *My point is not that traumatic things happen because of our sin but that we must be careful not to*

---

25 The "Ambigua" of St. Maximos the Confessor (580-662) are his treatments of ambiguous passages in the writings of St. Gregory the Theologian. See Saint Maximos Confessor, *On Difficulties in the Church Fathers: The Ambigua, vol. II,* in *Dumbarton Oaks Medieval Library*. Nicholas Constas, editor and translator. (Cambridge: Harvard University Press, 2014).

add our own sin to them later. We must strive to take the crucifixions we involuntarily endure as weak creatures and assimilate those crucifixions to the voluntary and blameless crucifixion of Christ. *We must strive to suffer so blamelessly and innocently that we come to see not only that we are suffering with Christ but that He is suffering with us, in us, and for us.*

And through all of this comes peace. First, because should there be any trace of sin in our response to the traumatic experience or experiences, our clinging to that sinful reaction will keep us imprisoned in the trauma. Second, because in beholding Christ's suffering with us in such innocence, we may even forgive our tormentors as He did.

And third, because the tragedy of our own crucifixions is assimilated to the non-tragic crucifixion of Christ. A tragic figure is a moral failure – that is the whole point of the "moral luck" concept, that for reasons beyond our control we fail morally and come to ruin. This does *not* describe the Crucified and Resurrected Lord of Hosts. His traumatic death does not traumatize him. Seeing him crucified alongside us, our own trauma is still real, it is still hell, but since Christ bears it with us, it now becomes a hell in which the light of the Resurrection shines and consoles.

In the midst of his own crucifixion, the good thief sees that the Savior of the world is dying with him, and for this reason, he allows his own crucifixion to be transformed into something else. *The good thief is even still being traumatized at that very moment, but he catches sight of Beauty and so is able to assimilate the ugliness afflicting him into his own salvation and recovery. He sees Theophany in the midst of anti-theophany.*

RTE: What do you think became of the bad thief?

DR. PATITSAS: It's a good question and one which seems to have concerned St. Maximos himself. Although at the beginning of *Ambiguum 53* the saint seems to accept that the bad thief was lost, by the end of the discussion he proposes, rather, that the bad thief's not having responded after the good thief's rebuke is proof that he has humbly accepted the rebuke. His final silence is not defiance, but rather represents peaceful submission. He, too, is saved by the Theophany of Christ amidst trauma.

But St. Maximos also says that we could be condemned as the bad thief is usually thought to be, if in our suffering we cannot allow ourselves to see that the Word of righteousness is suffering, blamelessly, with us. This is a hard teaching, and for some of us it may not be resolved before the Last Judgment.

Saint Maximos, at any rate, is speaking somewhat metaphorically here. He is telling us that this third type of crucifixion is the one that we hope our own crucifixions will come to resemble; we will never equal Christ's absolutely blameless suffering. But this is the question of healing for most of us who suffer trauma: how do we move from the isolating and killing crucifixion of trauma to a new possibility, which is the bearing of the aftereffects of trauma as a life-giving co-crucifixion with Christ? The good thief somehow beholds a theophany amidst his pain.

Might it not help us if we believed that the hell we are experiencing involuntarily, Christ himself took on voluntarily? He did it out of love, to save us from the hell we all have created for ourselves and for each other. We do believe that God is suffering with us in our trauma.

Shay found that the truth-first approach to trauma was not helping. Talk therapy easily increases our sense that the self is split, thus intensifying our sense of lost agency. Analysis reminds us that we are unable to control our own persons and our own identity. We start to feel as if we were brain-damaged – which as trauma sufferers we sort of are. We begin to think that if we could just go berserk then at least we would feel some temporary wholeness and integration.[26] But we also know from past experience that the price to be paid for such public nakedness is high, that in fact the price increases with time, and that any relief is only temporary. There has to be another way out.

---

26 As K. Farrell says in his notes to *Berserk Style*, "Berserk abandon is terrifying yet also alluring. It promises access to extraordinary resources by overthrowing inhibitions." Exactly. Farrell goes on to say, "Berserk style has shaped many areas of contemporary American culture, from warfare to politics and intimate life." If true, this would be a bad sign, a sign of barbarism.

Seeing ourselves as suffering with Christ, seeing that He suffers with us, reverses all of this. It stops the panic and reintegrates the soul. In consenting to suffer with Christ as He consents to suffer with us, we overcome all possible attacks and find our integrity being restored.

Faith, the Determined Memory of Theophany

RTE: In your last interview you emphasized the helpful role of relatives, friends, and spiritual fathers.

DR. PATITSAS: What the existence of moral luck shows, in the end, is that we don't make sense morally until we receive a kind of *ultimate* anointing by God's grace. We need mercy, we need perfect mercy in every possible dimension of our life, before it will become clear who we really are. Before that point, it is possible that our sin is not really our own doing.

On our own, before we've been "chosen," it's all a bit chaotic, isn't it? In a perfect world, we would all have that perfect anointing, feel ourselves at every moment to be the apple of God's eye. But then, there would be less wiggle room when we fell; there would be no excuse.

And in fact, at the Last Judgment *we all will have* that much love from God; we will be anointed fully as little "christs." Which is why only then can we be really and accurately judged. There alone is God's share of the synergy totally revealed to you in all its splendor – and you find out whether or not you have cooperated, even a little. It's the Last Judgment because it's the ultimate good moral luck, and thus only there can we see what we have made of our freedom.

When you encounter something beautiful, even if it's in a third-hand re-telling of the cosmology and battle plan of the Fathers of the Church, it means your luck has changed, ever so slightly, for the better. If this account strikes you as beautiful, it's a re-starting.

The ideal situation for a trauma sufferer would be to confess, to be baptized, chrismated, to commune the Body and Blood of

Christ, and to have a spiritual father who is a saint – as well as to have whatever help medicine and doctors can provide. The saint can give you back a space between you and the trauma which you are suffering. They do this by invisibly absorbing your trauma and showing you Beauty, by showing you God. This "arouses" you, gets you moving forward and thus away from the frozen state, and is the beginning of hope. It redeems you.

RTE: What if a trauma sufferer can't find the dreamed-for spiritual father? Is there no hope?

DR. PATITSAS: Anything that tells you that there is no hope is the returning presence of the evil force that initially traumatized you. Like wolves, they are returning to hunt the wounded while they are weak, to finish them off; the other side wants you to renounce hope and die. Don't give them the pleasure.

I am asking you personally: don't dishonor the nobility of your own suffering – even if it looks like your life is a disaster, a hell, a void of meaninglessness, a failure to achieve anything. Forget it. Believe me, that is all to your glory, and in time this will be revealed. The only ones who should be ashamed of the wreckage that your post-trauma life has become, are the ones who inflicted the trauma upon you in the first place – or perhaps the forces behind them. You just run to Christ. He will get you in order. The disorder is probably not as bad as you think.

Anything that says that a long delay in healing, the absence of the longed-for saintly spiritual guide, is unbearable and a reason for the madness of despair – well, this panic on top of panic is flowing from your passions. Don't listen to it.

All kinds of things are going on invisibly within us when we pray, though outwardly nothing has changed and we feel only the same. Although you mean everything to God, and He welcomes your urgent cries, sometimes He may be arranging things with your long-term interest in mind. And in the meantime, when you are being crucified by the trauma flashbacks, know that you are with

God; you are his icon.[27] But your strength is also limited, and He will descend.

RTE: This is comforting. Further observations?

DR. PATITSAS: You know, I used to accept the whole faith vs. reason conflict, the idea that some things you can figure out and others you just accept. What I see now is so much different; not necessarily completely opposed, but completely different.

Beginning with Beauty means beginning with feeling – not with passionate emotions or opinions, but with purified feeling. I mean a theological sensing, the innate ability we have to recognize theophany even in its hidden manifestations. In relying on that intuition, or in recognizing that within the Beautiful story of Christ is goodness, and therefore almost certainly truth, we fall in love with beauty and step out in faith toward it.[28]

Is faith any different than eros? Abraham stepped out of his land and onto a journey of exile not because he worked it out intellectually but because he had received a theophany! Perhaps faith is just the memory of theophany, the continuing to launch out towards that divine supernova when it seems to have gone dark?

And when we find within Beauty the miracle of empathy, and contemplate this Goodness by imitating it, we see that the first feeling is not left behind. Rather, it is amplified and becomes contemplation, a feeling that includes discursive thought, or a faith that is expressed as reason. And finally our sense of truth is but an amplification of our sense of Beauty and our sense of Goodness or morality. The three are just one clear channel, one pure stream, flowing from feeling to contemplation to knowing Truth directly. This is why

---

27 One of my readers, Elyse Buffenbarger, took this phrase to mean that the trauma sufferer is an image that God himself would venerate, an icon that God would tenderly caress and kiss and honor.

28 In Greek, what we are talking about here is the distinction between πάθος and αἴσθησις, both of which are legitimately translated by the word "feeling." The first term, however, connotes something more emotional, while the second in Greek usage describes the kind of feeling that is already insight, something rational. Cf. Marcus Plested, *The Macarian Legacy* (Oxford: Oxford University Press, 2004), 134-40.

Orthodox theology looks the way it does, so pure and free, so elegant and aesthetically satisfying, rather than cold, logical, and hard.

My first teacher in the doctoral program at Catholic University, Prof. Eric Perl, was, I think, trying to teach me all this twenty years ago, but only recently have I understood him a bit better.[29] In his book *Theophany*, he says that our aesthetic sense, our contemplative sense or reason, and finally our mystical insight are the same power in us, but along a "continuum of cognition." Your sense of the beautiful is already an intellectual power, and your final knowing of truth will still be a falling in love with the beautiful through feeling.

This is why Orthodox ascetic struggle, and Orthodox theology and ethics, do not begin with intellect and truth, nor with the intellect investigating goodness. Or, they may temporarily begin there if challenged to do so, but they will always return to their real beginning, which is Beauty, followed by Goodness, then the appropriation of the self-revelation of God (his Truth). We begin with theophany, then add correct praxis, and finally we investigate dogma.

Imagine an ethics that was nothing more than Truth investigating Goodness, with no thought for Beauty? Who would even care about what it discovered? But isn't this exactly how we define Ethics today?

Or, imagine a psychotherapy in which Truth investigates Truth, asking only whether what we feel is true, always seeming to denigrate concern for Beauty and Empathy in the form of its very practice? Can there even be a Truth without Goodness and Beauty? Well, this is just what we call "objectivity," and it is just a kind of hell.

---

[29] Dr. Eric Perl, Professor of Philosophy at Loyola/Marymount University in Los Angeles, is the author of several works on classical and Christian philosophy and metaphysics, including *Theophany: The Neoplatonic Philosophy of Dionysius the Areopagite* (State Univ. of New York Press, 2008).

Purification, Illumination, Deification

RTE: This sounds like the "purification, illumination, deification" sequence of the Church Fathers. How does that relate?

DR. PATITSAS: Yes, that is an ancient name for the Beauty-Goodness-Truth progression, although we must always beware of sequences if they are too discrete, with each stage too separate from the others. And moreover, purification comes not from moral struggle, but from ascetic struggle, which is the attempt to fall in love with Christ and him alone, to be chaste, to energize our eros. And illumination is a contemplation not yet of theological truths, but of goodness, of the empathy and compassion at the heart of beauty. Thus to purify our reasoning, we emphasize not logic, but the giving of alms; only this will clarify our judgment about goodness and render us illumined.

Deification is not separate from the others. To attain Eros (for Beauty; the first commandment of Christ's two greatest commandments; cf. Mt 22:36-40) and Agape (in practicing Goodness; the second of these two commandments) is *already* to be deified. Or, we must see that even the first rays of Beauty in our lives represent the onset, incipient but real, of our deification.

We know the theologian to be deified because when he speaks, it is God speaking with him, with one voice human and divine. He is *theologos* because he has found his own logos in the Logos who is *Theos*. This could be anyone.

Conclusion

RTE: A final word to bring it all home?

DR. PATITSAS: We must not discount the role of doctors and medicine in healing trauma. But even they cannot succeed in defiance of the ancient order: Beauty, including a life suffused with excellent patterns of self-care; Goodness, and the steady practice of empathy; Truth, but truth primarily in the sense of being just who we were made to be. Retelling of the traumatic events should be done very gingerly, and never out of proportion to our progress in the other two realms.

We all go wrong from this progression in different ways, and a self-defeating response to trauma is one example of that.

But we all can go right, too. We might fall in love with someone; see in that person their powerful compassion for us, and begin to imitate that compassion toward them and towards all; and finally, become willing to accept the truths necessary – and just those truths, not rushing too fast in a cognitive way – that we need in order to *be* true, to be our *true selves*. We will then look back upon that first vision of that person's beauty as the moment when our lives started, when we "came to be" out of a kind of nothing. We will know for ourselves what it means to be created *ex nihilo*, and we will weep.

It doesn't have to be marriage we are describing here. And it doesn't have to be a spiritual friend or a spiritual director. But it will be someone in whom, for us, Christ becomes the Great Physician.

I asked a spiritual healer once, an Orthodox priest with the gift of confessing thousands, "How do you do it? How do you take on so many burdens and not become crushed?" And in fact, he is the freest person I know. He answered very simply, "Everything is to be given to God." Have I seemed in our interview strident, rather than ardent? But to fall in love with Beauty is really just the opposite of a straining for health, for clarity, for truth. It is rather an intoxication, a liberation. I wish that genuine Orthodox Christian spirit to all of you – and to me, too, some day!

CHAPTER THREE

CHASTITY AND EMPATHY

Eros, Agape, and the Mystery of the Twofold Anointing

Until God reveals himself, be it ever so slightly, man can find no stable ground upon which to stand nor solid reason for which to commence any action. The Beauty-first approach to Ethics and to life naturally follows from the unavoidable reliance of all creation upon God's free-willed self-disclosure.

But amidst the many claims upon our attention and affection, how are we to develop the discernment to know whether what draws us is genuine Beauty and the action of God or if something else is at work? And what happens when, after a theophanic vision has ended, either the memory of theophany starts to fade or negative outside influences begin to compete for our loyalty?

These three earliest challenges of spiritual life – discernment, constancy to our calling, and faithfulness amidst temptation – all concern our response to theophany. In the light of theophany, the first human task is to refine our eros, to strengthen it, and to stabilize its orientation toward Christ.

The Church calls this first stage of spiritual life "purification," and it has this paradoxical requirement: on the one hand, we have to rouse ourselves and cultivate our desire for Christ. We can't remain lukewarm but must instead become genuinely hot. On the other hand, we must become "cold" to all worldliness as we cleanse our eros of anything self-interested or false. Our eros must be wholly for Christ.

In simpler terms, we need to develop an eros that is simultaneously both ardent and pure in its pursuit of the Beautiful. We must learn both to feast and to fast – and to understand that these two moments are inseparable; they *condition each other. A pure and ardent eros will then become for us both a clear sense of sight and an unwavering focus on Christ. Such an eros is the heart of spiritual discernment.*

Chastity is a good general name for the quality that eros attains in its entirety, when it overflows before the self-offering and self-emptying of the Beautiful God in the midst of his creation. Chastity as a spiritual virtue should always have this paradoxical character of being both pure and ardent.

The stage of spiritual life which follows purification is termed by the Church, "illumination." Here, Chastity naturally unfolds into empathy, or almsgiving. The refined sight granted to us by Chastity glimpses the deep content within Beautiful Theophany: the ultimate Goodness exercised by the Son of God in his voluntary crucifixion.

Seeing Him as He is on the cross – extended in the ultimate Goodness of self-offering love for the world – we are caught up in the very same orientation toward all of creation. We "contemplate" Goodness not through theoretical reflection but by imitating it in our practice. In other words, inspired by the life of crucifixion found within Beauty, we learn to offer our own lives for the life of the world – and, like Christ, we take that life up again, now renewed and transfigured.

All of this is not our own achievement but rather results from the two-fold anointing which is always granted to those who will know Christ. This unique anointing makes us not only powerful "kings" but also sacrificial "lambs." The characteristic action of the Holy Spirit, proceeding from the Father in order to rest upon the Son, is to bestow just such a paradoxical and trans-rational experience of crucified-yet-resurrected love for God and for the world. This twofold anointing is our destiny, both now and in the endless age to come.

It is the Holy Spirit who guides us along the Beauty-Goodness-Truth continuum with and towards Christ, so that, having loved both beauty and goodness, we might become true. As we do, we shine out unto the world as beautiful. We ourselves then become "theophany" for those around us, drawing them toward eros for God, in a process that never ends.

I. CHASTITY

RTE: One of the most confusing questions that we face today is about chastity. For many, chastity seems naive or even disingenuous, and is too often dismissed as false piety, a denial of the body, or even as a judgment against those who are not chaste. What is the virtue of chastity once we remove it from the wrappings of moralism?

DR. PATITSAS: Chastity *is* a tough issue. I struggle both to understand it and to live up to it. And failure in this realm can lead to a general loss of self-confidence, especially for young people. I have a lot of empathy for people struggling to be chaste, for people who suffer when they fail, and even for people who don't appear to be struggling at all. Although these latter seem to be "getting away" with a sinful life completely untroubled in their conscience, they, too, are created in God's image, and are worthy of something better.

I'd like to start by just saying a number of things, and then we can discuss how they relate.

Christ Came to Conquer Death

Many theologians, especially the late Fr. John Romanides (1927-2001), have pointed out a difference in orientation between Orthodoxy and other Christian doctrines on the matter of what exactly Christ came on earth to accomplish. Orthodoxy gives so much emphasis to the Resurrection and the conquest of death, and in fact to the Paschal service itself. In comparison, Western Christianity seems to focus more on the cross and the expiation of sins, while the celebration of the actual Resurrection has until recently been more subdued.

And why is this? The Orthodox Church hews closer to the ancient Church's sense that the first problem in human life since the fall of Adam and Eve is death, even more than sin. Moreover, we hold that it is Christ's death and resurrection *together* that conquer death. I think that in our time many Christians are starting to move back to the Orthodox understanding of the Resurrection's evangelical and catholic significance.

Still, though, in the West the theology about Christ's salvific work focuses mostly on the problem of how God in Christ managed simultaneously to punish us for and forgive us of our sin. The entire atonement is reduced to how Christ cancels our sin through his death on the cross, with the Resurrection almost as an afterthought.

But, as we have said in our previous two interviews, Beauty *first*: first we experience Christ as the Resurrected One so that through his beautiful theophany over against the face of the deep He can draw us out of the death of non-being and chaos. In the holiness of baptism, we dare to "put on Christ's death" (cf. Rom 6:4) and "take up his cross" (Lk 9:23) *because* we know him as the One who conquered death.

Clothed with the crucified and resurrected Christ, we thus possess his power within us. Only after that, after receiving this gift of his resurrection in baptism, will we have the grace to begin to grapple with sin.

I think that this is why the icon of the Resurrection shows Christ hovering above Hades – for his conquest of death shines out like the original Theophany over the abyss that created the world. We first repent of death, as it were, and then we repent of sin.

Repent of Death

RTE: How do we repent of death, for which we are not necessarily responsible?

DR. PATITSAS: Sin is the sting of death, St. Paul tells us (I Cor 15:56). So much of our sin and our temptation to sin comes from the fact that we are terrified of death. And not just the death of losing our biological life, but the fact that it feels like death when our wills are frustrated, or each time that choosing one thing inevitably means foregoing another, or when we are rejected, poor, or sick. We come to these moments of "death," and we look for an escape – even if it means defying God and hurting others.

Fear of death, or fear of the fact that our life is so dependent on God's sovereign will, is the main driver of human sin. This is how the serpent tricked Adam and Eve – he promised a way for them to end their dependence on God.

But Christ came to conquer the death we so fear. He granted us a share in his resurrection and gave his own divine-human Body and Blood as our food. Now we can look differently at all of these moments where we seem to be "dying," with eyes not clouded by fear and the egotistical grasping at our survival. The Resurrection begins to impart to us a chaste vision of the world because we no longer see this world as the final word. Instead, we begin to understand that the world is an icon of a heavenly world that has been prepared for us and freely given to us.

In a sense, the Resurrection comes before the Crucifixion. That is, there would be no Church and no gospel, no apostles or heralds of the gospel, had Christ not resurrected from the dead. Therefore, we today actually "see" the Resurrection first. If Christ had not risen, no one would be preaching his cross.

Once we have accepted the fact that Christ has risen from the dead, only then are we ready to see the Cross and to understand that the Cross is *our* destiny as well. Because only in the light of the Resurrection can we see the Cross as life-giving, as a dimension of our future resurrection in transfigured form.

To give a mundane example: if my friend pays me a surprise visit, the first thing I will see is his arrival at my door. Only then do I know that he has left his home. Even though his arrival came second in time to his departure, in my experience it actually comes first.

Even so, the Resurrection is "the Beautiful," while the Cross is "the Good" that we should only try to discover in the light of the Resurrection, lest the Cross overwhelm us. Without the Resurrection, the Cross would be invisible, unable to be interpreted properly.

It should tell us something very important that when St. Paul first preached Christ in Athens, the Athenians thought he might be preaching a new god named "Anastasis" (Acts 17:16-21). It was really Christ's resurrection that astounded everyone, whether Greek or Jew, and it really was the Resurrection that St. Paul emphasized first of all in his preaching. Many of the prophets before Christ had been martyred. But Christ alone rose from the dead and conquered death; on the basis of his resurrection alone can we begin to both master our temptations and not overreact in those moments when our temptations master us.

Find the Orthodox Church

If sin – if morality – were the first order of business in our spiritual lives, then the Cross alone would be sufficient for our salvation. But if the conquest of death received in baptism comes first, then you need, as we just said, the Cross *and* the Resurrection, and you need them inseparably; their unity is what we receive in Holy Baptism. What Orthodox Christian has ever celebrated the night of the Resurrection and not understood that the power of death is no more? Christ has vanquished death; we know this empirically.

Anyway, this is part of what St. Elder Porphyrios meant when he said that we "will never become holy by fighting evil," and that, rather, "we must first fall in love with Christ."[1] "Beauty first" is another way of saying that first we receive Christ's resurrection, his victory over death, and only then do we begin our struggle to be good, by standing firm against sin's now undermined (although still terrible) presence in the world. After embracing the Resurrection, we struggle against sin on new terms, on terms advantageous for our salvation. We have put on Christ in baptism, we are armed with his sacramental grace, and our eyes are illumined by an uncreated Light. Something deep has been renewed within our natures by the baptismal washing, the chrismation by the Holy Spirit, and by the partaking of Christ's Body and Blood. We are a new creation.

---

1 Saint Porphyrios, *Wounded by Love: The Life and Wisdom of Elder Porphyrios* (Limni, Evia, Greece: Denise Harvey, 2005), 156.

In the sin-first description of what Christ has done to save us, Christianity may collapse into a moral system. We act as if being good were our first order of business. The struggle with Chastity then becomes destructive, precisely because it is so hard to win it head-on and it can be so debilitating when we fail. I mean, people are bruised not only in the normal way that corresponds to active spiritual warfare with physical passions but from having picked up the spiritual struggle by the wrong handle.

So although we think that Chastity is equivalent to sexual morality, in life we come to find that sexual immorality is really the consequence of a failure to be chaste, rather than simply another word for the loss of Chastity. If the eye is sound, then the whole body will be full of light (Matt. 6:22); Chastity comes before sexual purity. Fighting sin is not our first order of business, but rather receiving Christ's victory over death by entering the Orthodox Church through her mysteries (the sacraments), because with that victory comes a new power and fresh eyes.

Chastity includes a life lived, body *and* soul, in devoted eros[2] to the Ultimate Lover, the Incarnate Christ. While Chastity includes the need to live that life with a view to concrete, practical, and timely decisions about the disposition of our God-given and blessed

---

[2] In our first two interviews, we defined "eros" as the kind of love that responds to divine Beauty by making a complete gift to the Beautiful of all that we have and are. Eros is not a sexual love *per se*, even though it is a gift of the *whole* self, soul and body alike. Allan Bloom's phrasing (see Footnote 7, below) is very good; he described "eros" as "love's mad self-forgetting." "Agape," meanwhile, we characterized as the love whose concern is the brother or sister, or the creation.

It should be noted that there is an influential strain of thought that accuses eros of being a selfish love, in contrast with agape, a supposedly more Christian form of love that thinks only of the other. This is not at all the Orthodox Christian experience, for we understand eros as the complete *renunciation* of self-love and thus a prerequisite of healthy agape. Nevertheless, agape can be considered as "higher," not because it renounces eros, but because it is the natural unfolding of eros.

Moreover, if eros for God includes a certain spiritual "pleasure" or blessing, this is not a sign that we are being selfish. God's blessing may be a sign that He is "well-pleased" in us (Mt. 3:17). Should we refuse to be "well-pleased" in him? And thus while a wrong kind of self-love is something negative, in Christ we do learn to honor and love ourselves in a non-selfish way. I mean, a fallen self-love will drive me to overeat, but a *proper love for myself* will help me to resist this temptation. Eros for Christ, meanwhile, may so fill me that I forget to eat at all; here, too, we must be careful and show balance.

sexual powers, Chastity is first of all a dedication of our eros, our power and attention, to Christ.

Chastity includes the proper use of our sexual powers, but it is not *limited* to this; in fact, if we do limit Chastity to sexual purity, we shall fail at both Chastity and at sexual purity.

If this is still not fully clear, please stick with me: this will be the focus of our discussion.

Chastity Is a Special Kind of Eros: The Sort of Eros That Is Also the Seed of Agape

RTE: So then, how does chastity work with eros?

DR. PATITSAS: Chastity is a special quality of eros. If we perfect the energy of eros wisely, it will be available to empower our union with a monastic brotherhood or sisterhood, or with a husband or wife – but first of all with God. And through these choices, we will begin to find our total place in society and in the world. Let me also just add that even for monastics Chastity is inseparable from the mystery of gender – the other great terror of our contemporary culture.

The problem that the Church sees today is not firstly the prevalence of extramarital relations but the death of genuine eros. Without an eros that has matured through the struggle for Chastity and that has grappled wisely with the challenge of gender, no true agape, no empathy, can arise. Sexual sin, which is exploitation of our neighbor and of the bodies and minds God gave us, besets and troubles us until we have acquired Chastity.

This is why Chastity is of life and death significance, not only personally, but for our Church and for our civilization. Without people whose sexuality is chaste, social justice in the home and in society will be not only unattainable but unthinkable. For example, what kind of world can we provide our children when we cannot master our idolatries of sex, money, food, pleasure, luxury, and ten thousand other things which occupy our eros, set us at war with each other, and weaken our families?

Of course, some people live a life of sin when young and then discover this Chastity after they marry and feel that they have found a better way. But the better way is shown by what they matured into, not the childish habits they grew out of.

We can see clearly this link between chaste eros and selfless agape in our poverty statistics. The greatest cause of poverty in our nation is divorce and illegitimacy. Most American poverty occurs in families of single mothers, and in the case of sons, the lack of a father in the home will account for the lion's share of why a young man ends up in jail or as a high school dropout. Next to this, the gamut of other very real influences – racism, exploitation, bad governance, faulty welfare policy – play only a contributing role to poverty.[3] When the blessing of eros unfolds into marriage or monasticism, we can take care of each other. True eros, by which I mean chaste eros, leads to agape.

For those of us who live lives of wealth and comfort, the importance of Chastity for social justice may seem like an abstraction. But just read Theodore Dalrymple's *Life at the Bottom* to see the sexual predation that has befallen women and children in the British underclass ever since sexual morality was jettisoned.[4]

Eros itself, of course, begins with God and at his initiative. It is a response within us that is provoked by his appearing. We do not search for God, but rather, "the people who sat in darkness have seen a great light, and for those who sat in the region and shadow of death, light has dawned" (Mt 4:16). That is, we mustn't take *our* existence as a given, while imagining that God's existence or love might or might not be real; over time, all the evidence is the other way round.[5]

---

3 In a typical year, the poverty rate among American families where both parents are working full-time and both have at least a high school diploma, is marginal. See Myron Magnet, *The Dream and the Nightmare, the Sixties' Legacy to the Underclass* (NY: W. Morrow, 1993).

4 Theodore Dalrymple, *Life at the Bottom* (Lanham, MD: Ivan R. Dee, 2003).

5 Well, I realize that in fact this can seem like a terribly idealistic statement. It can take years of searching for God before we come to a point where God's presence is direct, even

Chastity is eros in its holy form. And Beauty is the light of Chastity, the radiance enabling this holy form of eros, because Beauty is the only thing that can make the eye chaste. Many people experience this in a literal way: when they look upon an icon of the Mother of God they at once become chaste, if only temporarily. The pure eros, the divine eros for God and his life, is aroused within them and they are whole.

The Completeness of the Virginal State

RTE: How do you begin if someone says, "I have no idea of what Chastity is, and I'm not sure I've even seen it?"

DR. PATITSAS: We begin with positive appreciation, by seeing riches where others see only poverty. As one of our theological students, Andonis Prayannis, so insightfully remarked, to see abundance where others see only lack is a practical apophaticism. I thought that was brilliant, since we normally use the term "apophatic" for the theology that describes what God is *not*, and Andonis was describing a particular Christian who was able to see what "lack" is not – not proof of God's absence, nor even of real poverty![6] Rather, poverty is often the prerequisite for the riches of God's kind presence.

A similar apophaticism is needed here. For the secular world, sexual virginity is an empty state; a virgin is someone who isn't

---

insistent. Only then will we remember (and perhaps even miss) the way God was present in our earlier years through this salvific pain of his seeming absence.

But this doesn't mean you could realize that fact cognitively at the time of your earlier existential struggle, like reading an entry in the encyclopedia: "This utter misery you are now feeling is in fact the surest sign that God is very close to you – so cheer up!" A normal person would either respond, "Well, if that's how it feels to be close to God, then perhaps I'll look for fulfillment elsewhere," or, "You make no sense. If right now misery is the sign of God's presence, why would I cheer up, if it's really him I want?"

6 The particular Christian whom Andonis was praising was Dr. Paul Farmer, who establishes his medical systems in precisely those places which are the most poor. In the process, he unlocks resources hidden within both his contributors and in the poor people of these places. See Tracy Kidder's *Mountains Beyond Mountains: The Quest of Dr. Paul Farmer, a Man Who Would Heal the World* (NY: Random House, 2003).

experiencing some fullness, some pleasure, something wonderful. Chastity is a zero, a nothing. But you can't build on nothing.

My mentor Jane Jacobs said of city design, "The hardest place to start is where there's nothing" – or, where people dismiss a troubled neighborhood as merely a slum, a ghetto.[7] And of course, to the city planners, bankers, and philanthropists who wrecked our cities in the decades following World War II, the city indeed was a nothing. They saw only ghettos, pollution, traffic, poverty, and a jumbled mass of chaos. They did not start with love for cities, neither with care for the fine social order existing also in the poorest neighborhoods, nor for the commerce and culture that already existed there; look at the harm such planners then caused.

In the same way, people who mock sexual purity, or who just see the innocence of childhood and early adolescence as a blank neutral state, have no foundation upon which to build their mature attitude toward sexuality, have only shifting ground upon which to construct the "city" of an adult life, a stable family, and a just society.

In life we must always look into the poverty or the difficulty confronting us and give thanks for the life that *is* present there, if hidden; the rest will then have the chance to unfold in an organic way, like a flower growing from a seed. Similarly, we must learn to see within virginity a fullness that is destined to flower, perhaps into marriage or monasticism or into a celibate life in the world; at any rate, into a life of loving relationship with others.

Chaste eros is the seed of pure agape. This is so clear to anyone who has experienced it in themselves or in another. It is the indispensable beginning! It is a holy joy and a divine potentiality. If we manage to be chaste in our younger years, our agape for our spouse might unfold more naturally.

The transition is difficult, however, from eros to agape, and we all need social support and divine help to take that step. Nor should

---

7 I communicated regularly with Jane Jacobs, author of *The Death and Life of Great American Cities* (NY: Random House, 1961) and six other books about cities and their economies, from 2000 until her passing in 2006.

we lose hope if we have fallen or even fall many times but rather be always ready to start anew in trusting God. As our suffering increases, so does God's grace, to paraphrase St. Paul (Rom 5:20).

Thankfully, we in the Church begin with our vision of the virginity of Christ and of his all-holy Mother. And so we can easily understand that even a Chastity that does not include blessed sexual relations can be the greatest fullness, the greatest joy. We love the Chastity of our saints, whether they are married or monastic; and, if we are raised in the faith, we also have this positive experience that purity and pure thoughts are not a burden, but a freedom. They are not a "missing out" but a "partaking in" something divine and awesome.

Selfish Eros Is Not Eros

RTE: Now, can we retrace this wonderful view of Chastity from the opposite direction? Eros has such a bad name in our culture, and is synonymous with a lack of Chastity, whereas you are saying that chaste eros is the strongest and holiest eros. Why this disagreement, and what practical steps can we take to be chaste?

DR. PATITSAS: Christian eros for Christ is both a self-forgetting and it is the ultimate fulfillment and contentment. Analogously, this is true of romantic eros as well. But we may be tempted to seek eros only for its one side, for the way it fulfills us. This is why eros has gotten a bad name.

In chaste eros, because our focus is so tenderly and purely on Christ, it becomes natural to unfold this love and imitate Christ's self-offering for the world through agape. An unchaste eros, on the other hand, will not lead to pure empathy, because it is an incomplete eros. Although outwardly resembling "love's mad self-forgetting,"[8] its concern remains the self. It is a weak eros or even a fake eros –

---

[8] Allan Bloom's description of eros in his book, *The Closing of the American Mind* (NY: Simon and Schuster, 1987), 122.

and if it is fake, then it is a form of theft since we pretend to be in love but do not leave our selfishness behind. Rather, we try to take the beautiful and run off with it or consume it. A false eros is discerned by the fact that it does not lead into this willingness to care for the other.

Theft is the primordial sin: it is one description of what Adam and Eve did at the Fall in taking the forbidden fruit. Rather than continue the movement of eros out of non-being into the arms of God, we try to pluck some blessing and return to the formless abyss with it. In fact, the first parents in the Garden of Eden are symbolized by the two thieves between whom Christ was crucified. Theft is the opposite of thanksgiving, of the Eucharistic liturgy that gives us life. Moreover, thanksgiving is so much the opposite of stealing that even ingratitude is a kind of theft. But to really be grateful for the person with whom we are in love is to be willing to let go of everyone else and to love only him or her.

Many times bad eros starts with forgetting one's self, which is good, but it never matures into agape. That is, it never comes to include the genuine regard for the other because it is not willing to pay the full cost of loving. We may fall in love, but then we stop ourselves for selfish reasons and so refuse to follow through. At a certain point we simply discard the victim of our self-love. Without agape, eros remains stunted, partial – finally it collapses and isn't even eros; the fire goes out and all that remains is the original concern with the self. Such eros has never completely risen above self-love.

Right now I am reading Sarah Ruden's *Paul Among the People*,[9] a tough look at the depravity of classical culture and at St. Paul's message to that culture. The apostle's concern was that sexual relations be mild, mutual, just, other-regarding, chaste, an act of agape and not just of self-pleasing. This is what we are saying.

---

9 Sarah Ruden, *Paul Among the People: The Apostle Reinterpreted and Reimagined in His Own Time* (NY: Pantheon, 2010). This book contains some hard-to-read descriptions of ancient cruelty.

For those who will marry, we may feel eros for ten thousand others, but only for this one can we translate this eros into the full and permanent care for the entire soul and body of another person and be physically yoked with them unto death. Ideally, this happens only once, but we could say, "up to three times, though of course not at the same time," since the Orthodox Church allows a person to remarry twice out of awareness of the need that arises from the death of a spouse or from divorce. Of course, monasticism is another means (I Cor 7:7-8).

The Ideal as a Theophany

RTE: There seem to be two kinds of "moral ideals" in life. In one, the ideal is somehow oppressive; it leaves no room for the average person and is somehow untrue or only partially true. In the other, the ideal is unfolded in the presence of Christ with such a brotherly "we're-all-in-this-together" compassion that it seems natural and attainable. Although it is high, its very idealism consoles.

Since we are all imperfect, how can we see this chastity as a liberation, rather than being weighed down with impossible moral imperatives?

DR. PATITSAS: When we are younger and we face these things, our shame over our falls is often mixed-up with anger at ourselves. We think if we had tried harder we could have avoided the fall. But these temptations turn out to be so intractable, that we eventually come to accept our complete dependence on Christ. The passion of vanity gives way to a calm acceptance of our creatureliness. In this way we experience the beginning of peace, even before God grants us victory over the temptation. Our struggle with temptation can then unfold with more success.

But whenever we are called to teach, our proclamation of goodness should be so wrapped in beauty as to console. This should apply to our daily actions as well, and it is an art. A sermon or an ethical text should not leave us feeling, "Why bother? It's too late."

I have found for myself that it is not virtue but rather sin that really is the heavy thing. Especially over time it is sin that leads me to despair; not the reminder that, yes, there is another way that I can follow, if only I can access the miracle. Virtue carries with it a lightness, even when the struggle to attain it is hard. Our virtues are a sharing in Christ's own life, and "his yoke is easy and his burden is light" (Mt 11:30). Though we struggle to attain virtue, we must always see that success here remains largely a gift.

Sometimes people have a little motto which is meant to be consoling and liberating: "Orthodoxy is not about ethics; it's about ontology." I am not fond of this saying. In fact, we need three things: faithful eros, hopeful works of empathy (ethics), and true love. Meanwhile, God's uncreated grace, his own life, permeates us "ontologically" at every one of these three steps.

But what the people who say this mean is that salvation in the Church comes not from moral perfection but rather from union with Christ. If they also mean that we start with the gift of Theophany and Beauty and God's Uncreated Energies conveyed to us in baptism and in the mysteries (St. Paul's term for the "sacraments"), rather than with Goodness and moral effort, then they are right: Beauty first.

And what does this ontological union with Christ look and feel like? The simplest way to put it would be to recite the Beatitudes (Mt 5:3-12), *because when Christ pronounces them these sayings are autobiographical.* "Blessed are you," He says again and again in these verses, but, in fact, He is the "Blessed One," the "Anointed One," the Christ. When the Beatitudes describe the "blessed" person, they are describing *Christ*, and therefore they also describe what, as we share in his life, we too will experience.

For when we are united with Christ through our chaste eros for him, we begin to more than resemble him. We have "put on Christ," because He has given us a share in his very life and being. Our lives thus begin to resemble his in their perfection, purity, and Chastity. The general character of our lives becomes like his – priestly, liturgical, an offering of ourselves to God for the life of the world. We then see how the commandments can be the lightest burden and how freedom from sin is the ultimate freedom: "For freedom Christ has set us free," St. Paul writes (Gal 5:1). We see truly that, "It is more blessed to give than to receive" (Acts 20:35). We walk as Christ walked, we die as He died, we live as He lived – in grace and truth and in "the peace that passeth understanding" (Phil 4:7).

What I am trying to say is that *this* is why we discuss Chastity in such high terms: we are describing not ourselves when we describe the virtues, but Christ. "Virtue ethics" should be mostly Christology, if we are doing it correctly. Extolling the virtues should drive us into the arms of Christ for consolation and for liberation from the crushing weight of sin and of continual regret and sadness. In the embrace, we will find that Christ grants us his own virtue.

Nevertheless, sometimes when I look upon this vision I am consoled and uplifted, even if also a little ashamed. But other times, I am so ashamed that I won't receive the consolation, and I don't want to try any more. At still other times, the vision is beyond words.

I remember once arriving at a convent in the Dodecanese Islands in Greece with a priest-monk. I was there less than five minutes when I saw the faces of three nuns entering the divine services. How can I describe what happened next? From their faces I understood at once that I had *no* spiritual life, that I had not even *begun* to live a spiritual or Christian life. Not because they looked down at me – they hadn't even seen me. But *their faces were on fire* with a purity, a sobriety, a maturity, a love, a strong joy – it was a theophany worth more than all the words that I might ever say to our seminarians. And the whole experience was not only a judgment, but a consolation, a revelation of hope.

What can I say? Should I pretend that such people don't exist? Should I pretend that my way is good enough? Should I pretend that the most difficult gospel teachings are a kind of nice picture, but not really a criterion for our judgment? Should I refuse to admit that although I do not wish to become a monastic, still I do wish to imitate the innocent freedom and purity of those nuns? The answer is not to roll over and go back to sleep. Whatever the answer is, it's not that.

Mildness in Confession

RTE: What did you do? What should someone do who has already fallen?

DR. PATITSAS: I texted my spiritual father another time, after some kind of fall into sin – I can't remember what, but it was something that was the struggle of that moment. I just typed, "I fell."

And he texted back, instantly, "Get up."

Yes, we can't present the gospel in a way that seems like it's only for the perfect. But people aren't made of sugar, either; they won't melt in the rain. If the confessor has mildness, the soul is saved. There were years prior to that text saying, "Get up," when my confessor offered *only* consolation to my sins. But if a spiritual guide lacks mildness, the soul of even the person with only very small sins to confess will become more self-reliant and harder. The shame that we experience in confession must be directed toward eros for Christ, not toward increased self-reliance and self-obsessed moral effort. It should be a shame that leads gently upward and outward to worship, and not inward and downward to despair.

When the struggle besets us, we are to run to confession. In the Orthodox tradition confession is not firstly a focus on sins and morality, but a letting go of sin, the refusal to remain fixated upon ourselves, and an embrace of Christ. It is not only a confession of sin but is even more a *confession of faith* in Christ's humanity and divinity and of our total dependence upon him. Thus confession naturally leads us to commune the Body and Blood of Christ, to take the divine strength to keep going, to know that all is forgiven and that we are saved and loved. This is our medicine, and in this way, Christ acts in us. Confession and Communion are a unity because together they offer such perfect recommunion with Christ.

And guess what else besides Chastity isn't a zero? Your fall. In that fall you did gain some insight about how sin operates, how much it hurts, and how to avoid it the next time. Through experience, infused with divine grace and power, in a synergy of effort and grace, we arrive.

What does arriving look like or begin to look like? It looks like a miraculous coincidence of effort and grace – being brought to a point where our hardest trying is *inseparable from, though unconfused with,* God acting in us. Amazingly, our own trying harder now becomes one crucial part of the answer to our prayers for help, whereas before our moral efforts often seemed to somehow make us more obsessed with self, more self-reliant, and more prone to fall. Now, your self-discipline becomes the Crucified One acting within you; such a divine-human union of wills comes only through Holy Communion, and with time. We *do* arrive at that point; there is no more distance, we are saved. Of course, there will then be a longer period, after we have been given to taste such a state, before it is more stably "ours."

Let me say something else about those Dodecanese nuns. There was one nun at that monastery – this was years ago – who was the most gifted Byzantine chanter on earth! Her voice was from the next world. And yet in the many times that I prayed there, I could never once discern *which* of the several nuns at the chant stand was the one with such a miraculous ability. Her execution of the hymns was so mild that only its fruit was discernible and no attention was drawn to her own self.

These kinds of stories are theophanies. They both chasten us and lift us up; they accuse us of our sin so mildly and with so much hope that for a while we seem almost to float in our journey toward the New Jerusalem. This is the way to console ourselves if we have fallen.

Christ Invents Chastity in Both its Marital and Virginal Forms

RTE: Are chastity and virginity the same thing?

DR. PATITSAS: No. However, we also shouldn't make the simplistic distinction of saying that virginity is of the body while Chastity means that the soul is full of light. When we discuss virginity in the Church, we mean both a bodily state and a spiritual one. And when we discuss Chastity, we apply the essence of virginity – purity of intention, the refusal to be an idolater or an abuser of creation, the proper use of all our powers – in describing the bodies and souls of both virgins and of those who are married. In the Church, this purity is firstly a gift and only then a matter for struggle.

Our Lord and Savior Jesus Christ invents Chastity in both its marital form and in its virginal form. Before him marriage was, and still today without him marriage often is, difficult or even impossible. (Incidentally, the divorce rate of those who worship every week together in the Divine Liturgy is very low, so let us take courage.[10]) At the same time, before Christ adult virginity was an option for almost no one. Chastity in these two realms is among the first signs of Christ's in-breaking Kingdom, of the next world breaking through here, for "in heaven they neither marry nor are given in marriage" (Mk 12:25), while already in Christ, "the Kingdom of Heaven is *at hand*" (Mt 3:2). Paradoxically, the purity of heaven is needed for marital relations to become life-giving and sustainable here on earth.

Christ invents Chastity by preserving the wholeness of his mother physically during childbirth, spiritually during all that she suffers for him, and also by blessing the wedding in Cana. He invents Chastity, in fact, by being the revelation of that Beauty in whom and through whom *all* our powers and desires find their fulfillment; He himself is that Beauty, and especially He himself as crucified, resurrected, ascended, and come again.

---

10 For divorce among Christians in general see: S. Feldhahn, *Good News About Marriage: Debunking Discouraging Myths about Marriage and Divorce* (Colorado Springs, CO: Multnomah Books, 2014).

Interestingly, when Christ establishes Christian marriage at the wedding in Cana, in the very same moment He gives his Mother the blessing to overcome the last attack on her Chastity, on her monastic purity; I am speaking about the attack on her heart and mind presented by the sight of his crucifixion. It is not only marriage but also monasticism that Christ blesses at Cana.

RTE: Why would seeing his crucifixion be an attack on her chastity?

DR. PATITSAS: We often fear the cross hidden within Beauty. When that cross begins to become visible, this fear may cause us to betray the Beautiful and act unchastely.

In Chapter Two, "A Feeling for Beauty," we discussed how God created the world in this mystical manner: a Theophany appeared over the face of chaos and the watery deep, and this Theophany was so beautiful that non-being itself fell in love with it. Eros for this divine appearing moved so strongly within unformed matter that it repented of its prior state of being neither well-formed nor beautiful, dropped its "nets" (its pointless "concern" with itself), and moved towards the Light, taking on being and thus beautiful form in the process.

In other words, when our Savior says in first-century Palestine, "The Kingdom of God is at hand" (Mk 1:15), and "Follow me" (Mt 4:19), He is repeating the moment when He created the world, when He summoned non-being to repent in the face of his appearing. And just as "Let there be Light," in Genesis 1:3-4 leads to a separation of darkness from light, so his gospel leads to a choice of whether to stay in darkness or to walk in the light.

I suspect that the Theophany that originally called the world into being out of chaos was already the appearing of Christ and of him "crucified" – that is, it was the Son of God himself in an attitude of victorious self-emptying love for the world Who appeared before the face of unformed matter.[11] "Let there be Light," and, "his light was the light of men" – and of every created thing. We don't know how or in what manner, but the Son of God really is "the Lamb slain from *before* the foundation of the world" (Rev 13:8), and his victorious self-offering was the Beauty that drew us into being.

I am not sure if I am alone in believing that the initial Theophany was a revelation of Christ crucified, or if this is established patristic doctrine, or if this message lies hidden within the Fathers.

Of course, this vision of Christ crucified did not reveal a dead God, but a death-conquering God. And so we must indeed think of this primordial Theophany as a vision of the Resurrection! The Resurrection is the radiance of the Cross; it is implied in every vision of the Cross.

But only the perfectly chaste can see this radiance always and in every case, and even then, this deeper seeing does not annihilate the tragic aspect of the crosses borne so painfully by mere human beings in a fallen world. Jesus wept for Lazarus, the gospel tells us (Jn 11:35).

The Garden of Eden

There is something else, though, that I believe. In the Garden of Eden, Adam and Eve also saw Christ in his self-emptying love. There was a section of the Garden that was forbidden to them – they were told that it contained a forbidden fruit. And there, when they transgressed its boundaries, they beheld Christ hanging upon the cross. They were accustomed to conversing with Christ daily,

---

11 Saint Paul famously reminded the Corinthians that he had preached nothing but "Jesus Christ, and him crucified" (I Cor 2:2). We must remember that Christians only knew Jesus to be the Christ, the Chosen One, the Anointed One, for several concrete, specific reasons: He had resurrected from the dead, had ascended into heaven, was seated at the right hand of the Father, had sent the Comforter, had performed miracles, had fulfilled the prophecies, and had been accompanied throughout his life by various signs. The cross itself was not initially the proof to them of his being the Messiah, except as they came to see that a) this death fulfilled the Scriptures, b) the Messiah was the perfect blood offering for our sins, and c) the cross was the instrument of the conquest of death. Therefore, when St. Paul states this formula for his preaching, "Jesus Christ, and him crucified," he is telling us that he preached first of all the Resurrection and power of the Messiah, while never leaving out the Crucifixion and the humiliations endured on our behalf.

but in that forbidden place they saw Christ in a different state. This shock was what broke their faith and confidence and made them lose grace – the grace that had clothed them with Uncreated Light. And that is how they discovered themselves to be naked, because they were no longer dressed in this Light.

Before they entered the secret realm of the Garden, they knew Christ; I mean, they conversed directly with their Creator and the Master of creation. But they did not know Christ *crucified*. They were not yet meant to take that step from the "Resurrection" (the understanding of the Son as all-victorious and divine) to the Cross (his self-emptying love, his vulnerability, his granting to them of their own freedom vis a vis his sovereignty).

They lost their Chastity – by being scandalized by Christ's vulnerability, by turning their focus away from the crucified Christ and looking instead to this world and to pleasure, to wisdom, to power, to themselves, and even to dark powers, for the source of their existence. Adam and Eve turned, that is, to anything which seemed in their limited understanding to possess an unbroken strength, unlike their Creator whom they now saw crucified. After all, how could they accept that the source of their life was a Creator who himself hung dead upon a tree? They were not yet ready for this vision because they were still like children. In fact, after they were exiled from the Garden they themselves probably forgot what they had seen or could talk about it only in metaphors.

The serpent deceived them with a partial truth. He told them that in trespassing the forbidden section of the Garden they would become like God. *However, he did not tell them that to become like God they would have to die with God*. Such a total self-sacrifice would have been too much for them in their childlike state, so we can see how mocking and cruel his words were. The enemy was jealous and insanely malicious, knowing that the dying Son was more lofty than his own angelic resplendence and power.

Saint Symeon the New Theologian tells us that Adam and Eve were like children, that their friendship with Christ in the Garden lasted just forty days from the moment they had been created until they fell, and that when they fell they lost the Uncreated Light that had been their original clothing. But it is just my own opinion that what they had seen was Christ crucified, that the forbidden fruit was a section of the Garden they were not permitted to enter – and I could of course be wrong.

Mysterious Words at the Wedding in Cana

RTE: How do these events in the Garden relate to the purity of the Virgin Mary? And how is monasticism blessed at the wedding of Cana?

DR. PATITSAS: At Cana Christ not only blesses human marriage, He also blesses monasticism by preparing his Mother for her own encounter with the "Tree of the Knowledge of Good and Evil." He readies her for the instant on Golgotha when, as the New Eve, she will behold him crucified, just as Eve did in Eden. He does this in a subtle way, a way hidden to us.

When she asks him to perform a miracle to bless the wedding, He references a short verse from the Old Testament, changing it slightly. Christ does this in order to alert her, to reassure her, and, perhaps, also to purify her understanding. He says, "Τί ἐμοὶ καὶ σοί, γύναι; οὔπω ἥκει ἡ ὥρα μου" (Jn 2:4) – in English, something like, "What (is it) to me and to you, Lady? My hour has not yet come." However, it is actually impossible to translate the first five words of Christ to his mother; or at least, we can see that translators do not know what to do with these words.[12] But what if Christ is actually quoting an Old Testament verse in answer to his mother's question? In that case, we could see what He was really saying.

---

12 Four English translations cover the possible variations in meaning of Christ's words and show the translator's difficulty. KJV: Woman, what have I to do with *thee*? RSV: Woman, what have you to do with *me*? NASB: Woman, what does that have to do with *us*? NLT: Dear Woman, that's not our problem (i.e., what do we have to do with *it*?) All four possibilities miss the fact that the five words are a paraphrase of the Septuagint Greek of I Kings 17:18, a passage read as one of the fifteen prophecies on Holy Saturday just after Christ's "hour" has indeed come, *and has come without harm to his Mother's faith, since from the moment of Cana, at least, He has been preparing her for this challenge.*

I think that here in Cana, Christ is making a reference to a story from I Kings 17. In that story, the only son of a pious widow at Zarephath had died, even though she had taken a great risk in offering hospitality to Elijah the prophet. She apparently held the prophet responsible for not preventing this sad loss.

This widow blamed the death of her son on the prophet himself – or at least implied that for the good she was doing in hosting Elijah, she deserved better treatment from him! "Τί ἐμοὶ καὶ σοί, ἄνθρωπε τοῦ Θεοῦ;" are her words to him (I Kings 17:18). In the NIV, the widow's plea is translated, "What do you have against me, man of God?" In other words, she was asking him, "What have I done to offend you? Is there some strife between us that I am not aware of that would cause you to allow this to happen to me?"

Elijah humbly accepted the widow's "judgment" and stretched himself three times upon the boy, and by God's power raised him from the dead and restored him to his loving mother. This three-fold prostration was an image of Christ's three-day burial and resurrection from the dead.

So now here in Cana the real "ἄνθρωπος τοῦ Θεοῦ," turns this saying of the pious widow back to another perfect "person of God." The Virgin Mary's guardian Joseph is now deceased, making her in the world's eyes a widow, as was the woman in I Kings 17. Of course, the Virgin Mary was not technically a widow, since we Orthodox do not believe that Panaghia ever married Joseph. However, we do recognize that in Joseph's death she had lost a guardian and had become more vulnerable.

By paraphrasing this Old Testament passage when speaking to his mother at Cana, Christ is thus hinting that if He performs the "small" miracle she is requesting, it will commence a series of events that will end in the death of his "widowed" mother's only son! In other words, I think that Christ is saying, "My Lady, do you wish that I reveal my divinity to the world in this miracle, even though once I do so, a sequence will unfold that will be difficult for us to bear?"

It seems wise to assume that both Christ and his Mother knew the Holy Scriptures inside and out, and even that they may have spoken to each other through scriptural quotations at times.[13]

But as we said, Christ is not accusing his mother with these words but rather preparing her to withstand her most painful moment, his future death. That is why He at once changes his emphasis and reassures her, "My hour is not yet come." In the Gospel of John the "my hour" of Christ always means the moment of his glorification upon the cross. So Christ is reassuring her that He can perform this miracle, and that she shouldn't worry because the hour of his full enthronement as king, his death upon the cross, is not imminent; it is only eventual. Most of all, by quoting the passage from I Kings, Christ was telling her that she shouldn't worry in another sense – that when "his hour" does come, it will be followed by his three-day resurrection!

And so, both warned and comforted, the Theotokos turns to the servants and directs them to do whatever her son says. In a few words Christ has conveyed so much meaning and love and nobility and mildness, so much of his divinity and his humanity, He has so thoroughly both reminded his mother of his vulnerability and simultaneously acted strongly to protect her, that she stands there like Job after Job's deeper vision of Christ; no further speech is possible. In Christ's few words, she has seen both his crucifixion and his resurrection, and his entire identity as the Messiah, the Son of God.

In other words, Christ's words to his mother in John 2:3-5 are pastoral, and their purpose is to prepare her for her own moment of supreme temptation, which she will face when she sees her only

---

[13] Perhaps Christ even said this one phrase in Greek, as Palestine had been a Greek possession for much of the three centuries from Alexander the Great until Pompey. Intelligent and literate people in other eras and places have often known certain foreign languages, as people outside English-speaking countries in our time know and occasionally drop words or expressions in English. In many cultural contexts throughout history, limited recourse to a particular foreign language has been a part of high-class speech. For a synopsis of the use of the Greek Septuagint in first-century Palestine, see http://www.gotquestions.org/septuagint.html

I always admired the kids in my high school in Kent, Ohio, who would communicate entire paragraphs of shared meaning amongst themselves through a short quote from some book they all knew and loved. This is what I think is happening between Christ and his mother in John 2:3-5.

child hanging from the cross. By referencing this verse from Scripture, Christ is not accusing her, but reassuring her of the certainty of his own resurrection. After all, the widow's son was in fact raised by Elijah from the dead. Christ is giving his mother courage for what will follow in the chain of events starting with this first miracle.

Thus, when the New Eve later sees what the Old Eve saw – Christ hanging upon the cross, upon the ultimate Tree of the Knowledge of Good and Evil before which we are all tempted and shall all be judged – she manages to bear this temptation, this attack upon her Chastity – that is, upon her perfect devotion to Beauty, even in his most difficult guise. I recently read somewhere that an early oral tradition first put in writing by St. Maximos the Confessor held that the Virgin Mary waited two nights at Christ's tomb, that she never left the tomb, and that she was the first to witness his resurrection.

Even though the water of our earthly love be changed to wine by Christ's grace, our wedding is not complete without Christ's wedding: "My hour has not yet come" – the hour in which He would be glorified, by receiving the twofold anointing of the Cross and Resurrection in all its strength. When it comes, his death and resurrection make Christian marriage possible. And because He quoted Scripture in order to teach his mother there in Cana, she endured with hope and she saw the Resurrection first. At Cana, alongside marriage, the special Chastity of the hesychast, the monastic, is made possible too.

Eros Becomes Difficult When We See that We are Meant to Carry the Cross Hidden Within the Beautiful; this Co-Crucifixion Is the Essence of Agape

I realize that it appears that I've changed the topic here, because we think of Chastity as exclusively applying to the realm of sexuality. And here I go saying that the Crucifixion was an attack on the Mother of God's Chastity – an attack she negotiated successfully in part because of her son's words at a wedding in Cana.

Again, Chastity is the purified form of eros. But eros is not only the first love, but also the first cognitive power, and therefore Chastity is a special quality of sight that is necessary if we would fix our eyes upon theophany. Chastity is the unswerving love-filled gazing upon Christ without any trace of selfishness.

But this devotion becomes difficult the moment "our eyes adjust" to the vision of Beauty, and we glimpse the Cross within the picture of the Beautiful. It is as if we are in love with Beauty, but once the Goodness within it – the Holy Cross – comes clearly into focus as well, we falter in that vision; we avert our faces and head in other directions. For the Mother of God, this vision of Christ's self-emptying love was experienced in the most direct way possible, at Golgotha. To the sexually tempted person, on the other hand, it is the crosses within the beauty of the other person which trip us up; these crosses are manifold, but if we fail to carry them, we fall!

For example, we see someone who is so very beautiful to us, only to realize that they are not for us. Perhaps it is not for us to look at them at all. But how can we embrace the cross of not looking, of not possessing, when confronted with such Beauty? We falter, and so we try to grasp greedily in lust and fantasy and sentimental hopes that can waste years of our lives.

Faced with a temptation, we must look instead to Christ. However, can we imagine what it meant to face temptation in the age before Pentecost, before the outpouring of the Great Comforter into the world? In Panaghia's case, the Beauty of her Divine Son led her to a horrible scene, a scene that seemed to prove to random onlookers that her son was not the Son of God, that his beauty was not divine. She faced the temptation to despair, to look away, to run away, to question even the circumstance of his miraculous birth! But she did none of these things. Her eye remained chaste, and though the outward Beauty of her son was fading in the Crucifixion, with her noetic eye she never wavered, she never failed to see him as her beautiful son.

"If the eye is sound, the whole body is full of light" (Mt 6:22). When we first speak of Chastity, we aren't yet speaking of sexual morality; rather, we are speaking of the wholeness of all our powers, including our gendered sexual ones, in an undiminished vision of the Son of God. The Chastity of Panaghia at the cross is that she does not waver from this difficult vision of Christ, she does not flee physically or in her heart. Before we can be faithful to each other, we first of all have to be faithful to Christ.

The Role of the Body in Salvation

RTE: Once our powers are whole and the body is full of light, does purity automatically follow?

DR. PATITSAS: This becomes a big question in our context, where in the attempt to live by faith alone, some Christians have unwittingly tried to live by their minds and spirits alone. If your body suddenly starts to express faith through the prompting of God himself, they will accuse you of trying to save yourself through good works! The result is that we become like gnostics, acting as if our spirits are the real us and our bodies are an accidental shell. Of course, lately our brother Christians have learned with dismay the very long-term consequences of their theology – people don't even anymore understand the proper connection between bodily gender and marital love. Many live by a disembodied, genderless, faith.

The Church Fathers were wise. They said that the spiritual struggle is with the body and for the body. And in fact, the Resurrection is precisely a sign that the body and the soul belong together. Now, I know that, insulated by technology and comfort, I sometimes become a functional gnostic, thinking of myself as a mind, and not as a mind, heart, soul, *and* body. Let me give some examples.

It's not always easy to live ascetically. I don't like fasting – it is inconvenient and uncomfortable, and because I have no culinary skill it is hard for me to fast and still work. I don't like making prostrations, because they are difficult and I don't have the time. I would rather sleep early than attend an all-night vigil. To preserve our bodily wholeness is also difficult and, in today's world, confusing, since sleeping together seems to have become almost an expected part of the worldly version of courtship. When it is time to pray the Jesus Prayer, I would rather wait until my commute to work and listen to a spiritual audiobook, than stand in front of my icon at home in the darkness of early morning.

But then I ask myself: If I don't want to fast, nor make prostrations, nor stand in front of my icon corner nor attend vigils, nor even light the charcoal and cense my house, and if the struggle for Chastity seems to me like something wholly negative and not a positive achievement, if pilgrimage to holy places near and far is too inconvenient and expensive, then what role exactly will my body play in my spiritual life? Do I want a spiritual path and a salvation that does not involve my body? Because if so, then my spirituality may be gnostic or classically Greek, but it is no longer Christian.

If I allow my body no role whatsoever in my service to God, let alone the central role it deserves and demands, then what is the point in confessing faith in God Incarnate, of celebrating Christmas, of professing that Christ is risen bodily from the dead, of hoping for my own bodily resurrection, of receiving the Body and Blood of Christ, or even of being baptized? What would be the point of reverencing our martyrs, the point of the bodily sufferings of our Savior upon the cross, and of the millions upon millions of Christian acts undertaken throughout history to heal and feed the bodies of the poor, the sick, and the elderly? Despite all my own personal emphasis on fitness and health care, apparently to me my body matters only when it gets in the way of my real center – my vanity, my ego, and my intellect.

If, like me, you don't fast much, nor make prostrations, nor pray in such a way that brings bodily fatigue, nor receive sufferings due to illness or old age as a spiritual "medicine" from God, then let us together ask ourselves what still remains of the apostolic faith that is so centered on the incarnate body of the Word – and try to do better. And if Chastity, too, is no longer meaningful to us, then let us with piety and mildness reverence the God who became man through a virgin birth, and who himself remained a virgin, so that He could restore us.

With the spiritual use of the body, with our willingness to be in some small way co-crucified in our bodies for Christ, our Christian belief can become more practical. For if we exclude the body from any real role in our spiritual practice, we may sadly lose even our hope for the body's resurrection. So often, people who don't fast or struggle for sexual purity do lose respect for the bodies of their beloved dead, a sign that they have lost any interest in their own future bodily resurrection. We then have a disembodied faith for a disembodied people.

Allow me, if I could, to make one final comment. Why is the Church's most precious collection of texts about prayer called *The Philokalia*, which means, "love for the Beautiful"? It is because the Jesus Prayer is focused first on loving Christ who is the Beautiful. And the careful focus on his name in the prayer is our chaste and ardent eros for Christ. In cultivating the prayer, we cultivate Chastity before the Beautiful, and this is the first step in Orthodox Christian life, always and forever.

II. EMPATHY

RTE: Your title today is "Chastity and Empathy." How does empathy fit into our discussion?

DR. PATITSAS: We should not think of eros and agape, or love for God and love for our neighbor, as two separate things. Instead, we should see that eros for Christ is the seed of agape for our fellow man and for all creation. Chastity is the quality of eros that we are striving for, while empathy is a nice term to help us see agape with fresh eyes. Since our eros is for the Crucified One, it will lead us naturally to a co-suffering love – an empathy – for all those around us.

Christ's primordial self-revelation, the one that drew the world into being, is already his "taking on flesh." He appears to the world and also in the world; i.e., He lends his being to creation, in a way. And therefore our eros towards him will lead us into very concrete decisions and actions about our bodies, about the bodies of the people we love, and about creation. Chastity, if it is pure, will always lead us to empathy for the physical, concrete world around us, including the bodies and souls of the people in it.

The Discarded Image[14]

These days, however, we are trending in a different direction, inspired perhaps by the technology of virtual reality. We want to be free of our bodies, to no longer be determined by them. We don't express Chastity with our bodies, because we so often behave as if our bodies were the "vehicles" of our real selves, rather than inseparable from our core identity. Down this path lies certain danger.

This tendency to disembody the human person has even hijacked the women's movement, leaving it seemingly unable to agree that there is such a thing as "woman." I mean, the movement has become terrified of saying what is unique about women or of defining a woman as anything more than "a human being oppressed by men," for fear that any concrete discussion of the differences between men and women will lead to the stereotyping and thus the oppression of women. But then we are back at square zero: a woman is defined wholly in terms of what men do to her! This larger cultural drive toward the disembodiment of human identity now tries to remove even marriage from a firm connection to gender.

Many theologians have traced this decoupling of the person from the body to the Reformation, Descartes, and the Enlightenment. Since about that time, the thrust has been to strip the human person of his or her basic nature, leaving only the intellect and the will as the "real" human being. This of course is gnosticism, and it is destructive of both men and women.

---

14 C.S. Lewis, in his *The Discarded Image: An Introduction to Medieval and Renaissance Literature* (Cambridge: Cambridge University Press, 1964), discusses the older Western vision of the world as an icon and laments its loss.

In fact, however, the denial of basic human nature, the distancing of our "real self" from our bodies, has roots hundreds of years before the Reformation. It is traceable to new emphases in sacramental theology in the West that began centuries before Martin Luther was born.

The disconnection of human personhood from physical human nature actually began the moment we forgot that the reality of our world depends on its being a sacrament, a symbol, of heavenly realities. Because if the world is not an icon, then neither marriage, nor gender, nor anything else about us is an icon. In that case, our human form would be as arbitrary as the form of the world itself, and chastity would no longer make sense.

Reality vs. Symbol

RTE: How have we arrived at such a discordant view?

DR. PATITSAS: What would seem to be the first moment of this blindness about the world, and our human bodies, is connected to a confusion about the body of Christ himself. It was when theologians began debating whether the Eucharist was *really* Christ's Body and Blood or *only symbolically so* that a fatal disconnect between our bodies and our identities began to appear.

In the West, the manner of the sacramental change in the Eucharist was discussed periodically from the ninth to the sixteenth centuries at various doctrinal councils. The many smaller resolutions dealing with this issue culminated for the Roman Catholic Church at the Council of Trent, where transubstantiation was officially defined in 1551.

What you can see from almost the first moment of these discussions, however, is the question of whether the change of the bread and wine into the Body and Blood of Christ was to be considered as real or only as symbolic. Reading these disputes now, one senses the outline of the much-later split between Roman Catholics and Protestants on the Eucharist. More importantly, one discerns something similar to the philosophical opposition between nominalists and realists that began to take on its full force in Western European philosophy with William of Ockham in the 1300s – and which plagues us still today. One feels already very early on, in other words, that the West will have some trouble in holding on to the idea that our world is real because it is a symbol, an icon, of heaven.

This requires a bit of explanation, and first of all let me say that there seem to be very few voices at the outset in the ninth century who would balk at saying that the Eucharist is Christ's Body and Blood. A theologian like Paschasius Radbertus (786-860), who wrote the first major Western treatise on the Eucharist and who is a saint canonized by the Western Church, wanted to emphasize the reality of the change effected in the prayers of consecration. Somehow, his explanations of how this transformation happened provoked other clerics to insist that the change had a spiritual, or symbolic, dimension as well. Both Radbertus and his respondents (and the Western Church more generally) were seeking an orthodox formulation that could convey why the real Body and Blood of Christ still looks like bread and wine after the consecration – that is, why it appears to us symbolically.

The issue for me – and the reason I bring it up in our discussion of the importance and goodness of the human body – is that in these early theological discussions we see a struggle to capture both the symbolic and the real aspects of the Body of Christ in the Eucharistic mystery. Eventually, the larger problem of such a coincidence of opposites (that a sacrament is at once both real and symbolic) cannot be handled, and we have the emergence of full-blown nominalism in William of Ockham. At that point, we begin to lose both the world and the body as icons of eternal significance.

Now, what do we mean by nominalism, and why is it important? There are many aspects of the nominalist position, but the main one is just the denial that this created world is an icon of a heavenly reality. Instead, nominalists hold this world's form to be arbitrary, a product of sheer divine will. As Orthodox, we still comfortably assert that the world is an icon of heaven, or is meant to be. But in the

West this union of the symbolic and the real became rather vexed. Now, we have even developed this destructive iconoclasm around gender, the human body, human sexuality, and so forth. Outside the Church, we have come to think that we can simply posit whatever reality we wish about these things.

The nominalist and the realist positions must be reconciled. We must see that the reality of the world depends upon its being a symbol of heavenly realities. If creation is not a symbol of heaven, then its essence, its substance, would be of little importance. For example, if the world is just the arbitrary product of God's will, then God could have made some other world, or not have given us gender, and so forth. And if the world's form is arbitrary, then it is no longer "good," no longer beautiful and holy.

RTE: So what is the significance of these Eucharistic controversies in the West, since they did try to express both the real and the symbolic nature of the change occurring in the consecration?

DR. PATITSAS: The miracle of the Eucharist is resistant to analytical dissection. The more one tries to analyze it, the more that one-sided (and therefore dogmatically incorrect) explanations loom on every side. We know that there is a change of the bread and wine; we know that this is a mystical change. We also know that after the consecration, the bread and wine have become Christ, who alone is the real Bread of Life, despite perhaps not looking any different to our eyes.

But the Eucharist is the mystery of mysteries. It is the mystical center of the Church, and as such it cannot be defined. Here, more than anywhere else, the symbol conveys the highest reality – the reality of a change into the life-giving Body and Blood of Christ. We cannot say much more than this. The actual shape or the precise structure of this transformation remains veiled to us.

Our larger intellectual issue, of whether the world is really an icon of divine realities, or is instead arbitrarily designed, is simply surpassed in our experience of the Eucharist. Here at the Mystical Supper, we know that when the bread and wine become the Body and Blood of Christ, we are seeing far more than an icon; we are partaking of the cup of immortality. As Palamas would later say, even in heaven we cannot go past, or further than, the chalice.

And this means that the mystical "symbolism" in the Eucharist – the fact that even after the change our eyes see bread and wine rather than Christ's mystical Body and Blood – does not negate at all the reality of the change. Above all, we must stress that "symbolic" should not mean "fake," but, rather, "the highest level of reality."[15]

---

15 Should we, then, adopt Fr. Alexander Schmemann's language that the Eucharist is both really bread and wine and really the Body and Blood of Christ? And indeed, that the bread and wine only become fully bread and wine after the consecration? [As he implies in his "Appendix Two" in *For the Life of the World: Sacraments and Orthodoxy* (Crestwood: SVS Press, 1970) and again in his *The Eucharist: Sacrament of the Kingdom* (Crestwood: SVS Press, 1987), 226.] I think that we cannot. Here, in the central Mystery of the Church, we must say simply that after the change what we have is the true Body and Blood of Christ.

For this, we have precedent in Church history. When Pope St. Gregory VII of Rome asked an esteemed monk for guidance on this issue just before the Roman council of 1078, the elder prayed and was visited by the Theotokos. He "received as an answer that nothing more should be held or required on the real presence than what was found in the Holy Scriptures, namely that the bread after consecration was the true body of Christ." This holy vision took place in the context of the Berengarian Controversy about the Eucharistic transformation, which for Fr. Schmemann is a, if not the, central event in the decline of Western sacramental theology.

Cf. https://www.ccel.org/ccel/schaff/hcc4.i.xi.xxiii.html; namely, the Christian Classics Ethereal Library, "128. The Berengar Controversy." Accessed October 20, 2017.

Schmemann's position, by contrast, seems to be rather close to the Lutheran doctrine of consubstantiation, according to which after the consecration the gifts are both still bread and wine and yet now also the Body and Blood of Christ. By comparison, Trent's phrasing of the doctrine of transubstantiation is merely, from the Orthodox perspective, unfortunate, because it could be interpreted to mean that the gifts are only partly changed – that the accidents are not changed while the substance is changed, and that therefore a split has occurred between the inner and the outer reality of the elements of the offering. And that is why, in the Orthodox Church generally, the teaching of Fr. Schmemann on this point is received somewhat gingerly, while the Church has historically been willing to adopt the Latin term "transubstantiation," so long as we drop the substance/accident explanation of it.

If the Roman Catholic Church had a doctrine of the uncreated light, and of the possibility of theosis (rather than of the beatific vision), then even this substance/accident phrasing of the meaning of transubstantiation would be of small consequence. In the end, it is its potential inference that the divine and created realms are not fully unified that makes us reject the substance/accident distinction in the description of the Eucharistic miracle. Father Georges Florovsky thought that *the* theological problem of the West was Nestorianism – that somehow Western Christian theology could not quite express the reality of the full unity of God and man achieved in and by Christ. We wonder about this point in general regarding the West, and so we are sensitive to it, here, in the substance/accident distinction.

To make this point just a little clearer, consider a contemporary Roman Catholic explanation of transubstantiation: "What appears to be bread and wine in every way (at the level of "accidents" or physical attributes – that is, what can be seen, touched, tasted, or measured) in fact is now the Body and Blood of Christ (at the level of "substance" or

We know empirically that the change is "real" because in receiving it we experience a new life. We know empirically that sacraments are "symbols," in the sense that they employ material realities. And, we know that symbols are not empty shells, but realities which participate in their archetypes. But we do not know the precise mystery of how this change takes place in the Eucharist itself, the mystery of mysteries.

The Western Church correctly discerned that to say the Eucharist is only a symbol and not really the Body and Blood of Christ, is clearly heresy. But to phrase the question in this particular way is a trap and has no good answer. Once you pit the symbolic *against* the real, once you forget that this world is real only because it is the symbol of the heavenly realm, then everything about the created order becomes by definition arbitrary. If creation is not a symbol of heaven, then its beauty and its goodness are no longer anchored in an underlying and eternal truth. In fact, an arbitrary world is somehow not only "false," but also neither beautiful nor good.

Instead, the physical form of the world would just be the imposition of a capricious divine will. The world would be nothing more than a power play, in other words, a dead object of God's creative whim. And once we have the power (through technology), we can change the world to whatever suits us. The world is then no longer a "second book of revelation," no longer an icon. This view of creation will underlie the philosophy of the Enlightenment, but its source was centuries before, in an accidental turn within sacramental theology at these councils held at Lateran in the 1070s.[16]

---

deepest reality)." I think that an Orthodox theologian might agree with this statement, while amending its conclusion to read, "in fact is now the Body and Blood of Christ at *every* level of reality; and that is what makes the Eucharist the mystery of mysteries..."

[16] The biggest sign, for me, that the Great Schism of 1054 was indeed part of a deep spiritual wound to the West is the fact that just twenty-five years after this particular break with the Orthodox, the Latin Church in this council at the Lateran can no longer sustain certain crucial theological paradoxes. Moving forward, the entire next millennium for the West will be marred by an irresolvable dispute between the Nominalists (for whom the sacrament is merely symbolic) and the Realists (for whom the very reality of the sacrament means that it is not a symbol at all). Today, the Nominalists are the deconstructionists, those who think gender a mere social construct, etc., while the Realists are their conservative opponents.

Now, the Enlightenment was based on a major inconsistency, as C.S. Lewis argued again and again in his Christian apologetics. The secular philosophers of the seventeenth century still thought rather naïvely that the human mind was, unlike the wider world, somehow exempt from being a mere product of power. I mean, the Enlightenment came to see creation as a mere artifact of the power wielded by natural processes, and yet still believed that the mind had access to godlike reason in an absolute sense and was therefore capable of seeing truth in an ultimate sense.

As we said in Chapter One, Darwin, Marx, and Freud expose the materialist position as nonsense. Either the *whole* world, including our minds, has some ultimate significance, or our minds are also a product of the natural forces of biological and social evolution, and are therefore not capable of more than an instrumental, accidental grasp of ultimate truth. Thinkers like these who reveled in this discovery may seem sinister to us (and they are, in part), but they were right to show that the Enlightenment was based upon the self-contradictory idea that we, alone of nature, were somehow not part of nature.

RTE: Then, in what sense is the world itself a living symbol of the heavenly realm rather than a dead object? For instance, is there an "England in heaven," of which the earthly England is an icon, as C.S. Lewis once wrote?

Politically, the Nominalists are the progressives, who intend to remake human nature itself, and the Realists are the conservatives, who insist that this is impossible.

Faith vs. Works is a closely allied false division; Luther argued that we are not "really" saved in the sense of having our natures transformed but that the Christian is simply "declared" by God to be saved. The Roman Catholic argument for "works" responds that the grace of God in salvation must have some actual effect on human nature or it isn't real.

Orthodox Christian theology and philosophy are not trapped in this war between Necessity (Realism) and Freedom (Nominalism). As we shall see in a later interview, in Orthodoxy freedom and necessity coincide, and go under the name of something higher: "Life." When Necessity and Freedom aren't made by grace to coincide, Freedom comes to be defined as the exercise of an arbitrary and capricious will, while Necessity is held to govern, in the end, even God – who must conform to the logic of the theologians and the philosophers.

The architect Christopher Alexander can help lead us out of this thorny thicket of Nominalists versus Realists. He is a practical Neoplatonist, in whose work Freedom and Necessity coincide within a true twofold anointing. We will come to him in Chapter Six.

DR. PATITSAS: It is interesting that in trying to address this flaw in Enlightenment thought (I mean, the idea that the human mind, unlike the rest of the natural world, is godlike and not determined by accidental and self-interested processes), C.S. Lewis went so strongly in the Neoplatonist direction. Lewis was very much a person who thought that the world exists through its participation in the divine life, and who also believed that the world is an image of heavenly realities. Lewis's whole literary and theological project was to argue that if the world is not an icon, if our minds are not made by God in the image of God's own mind, then an ultimate understanding of truth would be impossible, our minds themselves would be nothing more than survival mechanisms. If our minds are solely the products of blind evolution, then they would be able to reason only by accident.

To use your example, there are at least two ways to think about the basic fact that the world exists by participation in God. One is to say that the earthly England is an icon of the heavenly England. The other way is to say that the England below (or anything else in this world) exists because God has imparted being to it, has given as a gift certain heavenly attributes which, when mixed with creation, look like England.

Either way of expressing it is fine, but consider the matter instead from the divine perspective: the world and all of creation are, through Christ, a window, a potential window, into heaven. And thus the world's order is not arbitrary, for God made the world, and He made it good (Gen 1:31). But as we know, God alone is good (Lk 18:19). If we meditate on these two verses, we will see that the world is an icon.

This vision of creation as heaven's icon begins to be lost, albeit with a glacial slowness, from the moment when, already in the eleventh century, a Western council pitted the real *against* the symbolic. The opposite is the truth: the more symbolic we become – the more we can say, "It is no longer I who live, but Christ who lives in me" (Gal 2:20) – the more real we become, the more ourselves we become. This is Christian faith: that the world becomes real through an ever-deepening infusion of God's uncreated grace. We must therefore reject this awful vision of the world as something dead, as something stripped of divinity and separated from God, whether such a misinterpretation of the world is perpetrated by the Enlightenment or, almost six hundred years before, inadvertently by sacramental theologians. As C.S. Lewis insisted, that way lies the abyss.

The Natural Law as Icon of the Logos

RTE: But by emphasizing the Natural Law, which holds that the truth about God and morality is partly knowable through creation, doesn't the West retain an understanding that the world is an icon?

DR. PATITSAS: Saint Paul himself tells us in Romans 1 that we can learn about God and our human condition through nature, and so for us Orthodox, the Natural Law is an icon of Christ the Logos. It is an icon both in the sense of being a means of participating in Christ and in the sense of being a foreshadowing, an image of the real, divine law which will absorb and transfigure the Natural Law itself.

But as the West very slowly, over those eight hundred years or more, loses its sense of nature's iconicity, the Natural Law itself comes to seem a dead thing. It may still be true, it may still have powerful repercussions, but how many are arguing that the Natural Law is beautiful? If nature is dead, if it is not a sacrament or an icon, then therefore neither is its inner principle, the Natural Law, any more alive. We now study the Natural Law not in order to commune with God (who, by the way, remains free to transcend this Law when He so chooses), but in order to put our human intellect in the driver's seat and in fact to dispense with God entirely. We come to prefer a fixed Law over a free God, and the Law becomes a truth which can liberate us from God, or make us gods, rather than leading us to God. Studying the Natural Law becomes the equivalent of eating of the tree of the knowledge of good and evil.

For example, the greatest strength of a Natural Law argument against artificial birth control is to be found in the refined Beauty of the sort of spiritually mature marital relationship that could forego its use, that could even accept to fast from sexual relations at certain seasons. But the argument against contraception instead came to seem merely an arbitrary statement flowing from the power of the Latin Church, derived from its mastery of Truth. We have come to read the Natural Law as Truth and Goodness – i.e., as "Teaching Authority" – with Beauty in an ancillary position. Beauty has become like the oppressed wife who is forced to walk ten steps behind her husband, Truth, and his favorite son, Goodness.

This is partly a stereotype and, in fact, a stereotype that many Roman Catholic theologians are working against. But this caricature had enough grounding in reality that few modern people could realize how much was at stake in the Latin Church's recent stances against birth control. And only now that the utility (i.e., the goodness) of the position that is skeptical of contraception is made evident in the collapse of populations throughout the developed world, and even now in the developing world, are we taking the teaching seriously again.

A teaching, by the way, which was held universally (although with a Beauty-first emphasis) in Orthodoxy also, until there was wavering by a minority starting in the 1970s. Since the earliest decades, the Orthodox Church has been wary of birth control that did not rely upon abstinence and the natural rhythm of fertility.[17]

But when Beauty-first is lost in the West, the Natural Law flips and becomes something onerous. When you are forced to defend the Natural Law from a Truth-first or a Goodness-first perspective, it is all but impossible to both maintain the validity of a moral teaching and yet still allow for the necessary pastoral exemptions that a wise confessor would discern. If you put Truth or Goodness ahead of Beauty, then to allow an exemption to the Natural Law is to commit an act of logical inconsistency which places you upon a slippery slope to its total unravelling. When the Natural Law is

---

17 Cf. Tikhon Pino, "Contraception and the Orthodox Church: Contemporary Theology and the Sources of Tradition" (paper presented to the Orthodox Ethics course at the Holy Cross Greek Orthodox School of Theology, Brookline, MA, December, 2010).

approached in the wrong way, to permit an exception is to lose the entire teaching. Whereas if you put Beauty first in teaching the Natural Law, then the teaching remains as a shining theophany, an inspiration and living guide, a Guardian Angel almost, *even for those too weak to follow it.* Loving and respecting the unattainable Natural Law transforms us from the inside out, even while we are as yet unable to live up to it. Eventually, either we or our descendants *will* have the strength and opportunity to follow the Church's teaching on contraception, is my belief.[18]

Right? The Orthodox Church does not condone artificial contraception; her father confessors know empirically that its use usually *does* impact the spiritual state of a couple. But no one is rushing to condemn those who use it, nor seeking to press a point that is beyond the spiritual strength of the average person at this present difficult moment. In that sense, the Church really does allow that the use of contraception is "between the couple and their confessor." And yet the standard remains unchanged and, in fact, beckons enticingly to those who have ears to hear it.

Forgive me, but I could almost laugh just now, thinking of the ways that my own confessor, trained through immersion in the Beauty-first approach to the Natural Law by the old masters of the Pskov Caves Monastery, has "overlooked" certain sins I could not part from, until all at once they no longer held such an absolute power over me. I laugh because there is such a tremendous release of false tension when you "enforce" the Natural Law in a Beauty-first way.

---

18 Why isn't the Natural Law approach the perfect example of Beauty-first ethics? After all, this approach takes God's creation as a kind of theophany, and then discovers its principles of Ethics within that, right? I think it is because Natural Law may start with a certain kind of Beauty, but it is so anxious to strip that Beauty away and just get to the core principles of Truth; from that Truth, it will then derive its "Goodness," its law, never again returning to Beauty. Remember: Beauty-first means that you unfold Beauty into Goodness, *without at all leaving Beauty behind.* And then, the Beauty and Goodness together make you True. Natural Law as practiced in Roman Catholic moral theology seems to be more of what Shestov most decried in secular philosophy: the taking of the world as Necessity rather than as Gift, and then the derivation of ethical laws from that Necessity through unaided human reason. Stripped of its primal Beauty, such a process then misunderstands what it might possibly accomplish – the elucidation of a moral icon that can catalyze our participation in God's uncreated life in potentially unpredictable ways. Natural Law theology, in contrast, seems to imagine that it has unlocked the engineering code to the machine of the world, which must henceforth control our every action.

In fact, you find that the cross imparted by the Natural Law literally is "natural" – the easiest thing you could do, in the end!

Rebellion: What Happens When the Natural Law Becomes a "Necessity" Governing Even God

It will help us to see that the Natural Law is living, is an icon, if we call it by another name which C.S. Lewis uses for it in another of his books, *The Abolition of Man*.[19] There he calls the Natural Law the "Dao" (or "Tao"). That sounds more accurate to our deadened ears than the term "Natural Law," which we nowadays hear as an arbitrary imposition handed down from a scholastic, logic-chopping elite. No, the real Natural Law is what we understand the Dao to be: a mysterious principle within created order, a principle that is beautiful and good and true, and that imparts life. Our highest joy is to live according to it. It is an icon of the Logos, of the Divine Law, and of the Way.

However, if the Natural Law is this Dao, this beautiful Logos, then why do the Protestant Reformers tell us that they felt like wild animals with their legs caught in the trap of the Natural Law Empire? Precisely because the West had lost a full and proper sense of the world as an icon, as a second revelation of God granting us the opportunity for communion with him. Natural Law had become a power, an intellectual force to be obeyed, a weapon wielded by a Church which no longer saw even itself precisely as icon.

I mean, in the West you can hear people still today speaking of the Church as if it were the "means" of salvation, rather than as the very event of salvation itself. All real contact with the Uncreated has been pushed out of the frame. From such a system, humankind had to escape. Such a false distance between man and God represents the defeat of the gospel.

RTE: How did the Reformers make their escape, as you put it?

---

19 C.S. Lewis, *The Abolition of Man* (London: Oxford University Press, 1943).

DR. PATITSAS: If nature is dead, if nature is not an icon, if it is just the imposition of a tyrannical will, then let's try to cut around it and go straight to God – who will save us not through any transformation of our natures, but merely by *his* will to declare us arbitrarily saved. We'll get rid of the sacraments, we'll jettison tradition, and we'll even begin to cut ourselves free of human nature. That way a person could be free of arbitrary church authority, and even free from a world that itself seemed arbitrary. All this was the route to free man and God from the iron grip of abstract intellectual systems which were held to govern even divinity itself!

It is the ultimate irony that the Reformers were all such terrible iconoclasts, that the Reformation leads to the greatest destruction of art in European history, and that the Reformation has now morphed into this destruction of the body, of gender, and of marriage – when all along it was the very lack of a Beauty-first approach, of the remembrance that the world and the Church were icons, that had caused their crisis to begin with!

It didn't happen all at once, but the trend in Protestant thought, all the momentum, was to deny human nature entirely, and to place the center of a person in his will – the same sort of will that in God's case could supposedly make any world He liked, or call any sinner a saint if He wished, without bothering to actually transform him.[20] The entirety of the spiritual life was reduced to the cultivation of a finely honed and tough willpower for God, which then became misidentified with the "faith" of St. Paul.

But what is a human will without any defined human nature as its source? In effect, the Reformers were willing to chew their legs off (our fixed human nature) to get free of that trap of a non-iconic

---

20 This is, or appears to be, the position of Martin Luther: The sinner is not so much changed, as he is simply declared saved by God's omnipotent will. Calvin seems to reach a similar conclusion from the other direction: you were already made by God either to be condemned or to be saved, before you'd even heard the gospel. Again, in neither Protestant father's view is the real transformation thought to be effected by the sacraments of the Church. Rather, God's arbitrary will simply pronounces or creates the person to be saved or damned. This whimsical God is the only God, in the Protestant view, who retains his freedom from Greek philosophical systems and is thus a worthy object of Hebraic biblical faith. But St. Dionysios offers a better balance of nature and will, necessity and freedom, which we are discussing throughout this book.

Natural Law. But this turned out to be a path with no logical end, as today people even surgically alter their gender, or try to, and claim a right to disturb the natural order of marriage. They have tried to free the human person completely from nature.

But there is a better way, a balanced Christian anthropology that takes both human nature and human will into the realm of the human *hypostasis*, or person.

Well, this is a big topic, and I promise to come back to it later. But the point for now is this: Christ came to save us as *persons*, which means not just our wills or our intellects, but also our bodies and our entire natures as well. Our bodies, and purity, and gender – all of this functions as an icon with eternal significance. And they are all beautiful, deeply and permanently beautiful, as well, since their very reality is inseparable from their being symbols and disclosures of heavenly life.

Reasons Why Chastity Has Become More Difficult

RTE: In our war and trauma interviews you said that we theologize firstly not with our minds nor even with our hearts, but with our bodies. Is that what you mean here?

DR. PATITSAS: I think so. Our bodies are part of this wonderful gift of creation that God has given us. If the world were not an icon, then where would we find beauty? And why would beauty matter even when we did find it?

But what is more beautiful than the face of a truly chaste person? So we can see right away that the spiritual life for Orthodox Christians is unthinkable without the radiant beauty of the sexually pure. I mean, before we make any intellectual investigations about it, we can see that the luminous virginity of the Mother of God is the *sine qua non* for Orthodox life. We can't imagine a way of life that was not consonant with her chaste, majestic beauty, as being at all ethically or theologically sound.

You and I have discussed many times the absolute purity that we have seen on the faces of chaste people. This Chastity will be present even in a child who is pre-sexual, but only if that child is spiritually pure; therefore, Chastity is not mainly about sex. And, of course, we also know with sadness how the face of the person who loses their purity often changes so completely. Before, they were naïve, but happy; now they are wise, in the sense that Adam and Eve became wise, but they feel themselves naked of grace; they hide from God in the cool of the evening night club. They may even stop coming to church until they begin to recover their Chastity in marriage and wish to raise pure children.

We wouldn't need elaborate moral theologies if we could just stop insisting on being so blind! The person who falls for the first time enters a new realm of worry, anxiety, sorrow, sometimes bitterness. Their very appearance often changes. Anyone can see this – anyone who is not blinded by twisted moral reasoning, that is. And anyone can recover their hope by seeing the extent to which repentance can utterly renew the face, the countenance that is the window of our personhood.

Empathy: Engaging the Body in an Agape Based in Eros

However, the important transition from chaste eros to agape and empathy takes art. Because it could be exactly out of empathy for their beloved, and in attempting to celebrate the goodness of bodily nature, that the young person might rebel against a gnostic anti-body culture and consent to lose their virginity – not realizing, meanwhile, the holiness of marriage. But eros and agape are not different things. *Agape is the amplification of eros*, and so love for our spouse must include Chastity, not leave it behind, nor discard it as a naïve stepping stone to wisdom.

Sex outside of marriage may seem to be celebrating the body, but so often it ends by destroying it, and always it mars it. It may be undertaken as an attempt to show empathy for the beloved, but it may not end that way, and always it implicates our beloved in mortal sin. As another one of my students once told me, Orthodoxy is about balance; in this case, the attempt to balance agape with eros, romance with chastity.[21]

Our young people are not meant to face the transition from eros to agape entirely alone, but today to face it alone would often be an improvement. In fact, they may now face the transition in the teeth of opposition to Chastity from the culture and deceived by the abandonment of a living belief in Chastity by those around them.

What if it turns out that young people today start out just as interested in Chastity as their more religious forebears were but that we adults have designed an economic, educational, moral, and even urban system that makes young marriage all but impossible, officially "irresponsible," a kind of crime against society? Well, I think this is exactly what we have done. The collapse of sexual purity among young people is but the punishment for the idolatry of the older generations. It is bootless to moralize at the children without also repenting ourselves.

So who has the greater blame? We who have renounced idealism can scarcely parent a pure child into adulthood. And even if we have regained that idealism, we may have not yet completely recovered the thread of an Orthodox worldview.

RTE: Then are you suggesting that an entire social change is necessary before a person can be chaste?

DR. PATITSAS: "Marriage is a social institution, and it works best in the context of broad social support." That is something my dissertation director, Robin Darling Young, once told me, and she was right. Social organisms like nations and families and communities live and die according to complex webs and pathways of interaction.

One feedback loop is that sexual immorality weakens marriage, while in turn the weakening of marriage makes sexual morality

---

21 Actually, Orthodoxy is not really about "balance," but about the grace-filled coinciding of what to the world seem like irreconcilable opposites. This may look like balance, but it also may look like the wild abandon of the artist.

harder to attain.²² And when either is weakened, religious faith suffers, which then makes both morality and marriage even harder to understand. Also, when there are few jobs, or when education is organized as endless progress into impractical generalism, or when welfare payments include cruel incentives not to marry and not to work, we can then see what happens to the family – because since 1965 it *has* happened: 40% of American children are now born to single mothers. Many times the parents of the child marry soon after, which is very good. But for many marriage has become an unaffordable "luxury good," in the words of a recent book.²³

Fighting Smart

RTE: Then what encouragement do you offer to the young person who sees all this and says, "I want to follow the Christian path, but everything is arrayed against me?"

DR. PATITSAS: We must not emphasize the obstacles we face, although they do exist, but rather the power of the Cross to conquer all. I would say, "If you see that the course is hard and full of obstacles but still wish to succeed, then I have a counter-intuitive suggestion: run to your Heavenly Father, and accuse yourself for the ways in which you have consciously or unconsciously participated in sins against chastity. Of course you are not to blame for what went before, but by going against the grain of self-justification, by taking the responsibility even for sins that did not originate with you, you will become stronger. This is the shortcut to adulthood and you will amaze the world by what you will accomplish." The fact is that many of us among the older generation are praying exactly for this, that you will do better than we did. In this, we too would be saved.

---

22 Mary Eberstadt's *How the West Really Lost God* (Philadelphia: Templeton Press, 2013) lays out a web of feedback loops through which moral practice and belief influence each other and is worth reading.

23 June Carbone & Naomi Cahn, *Marriage Markets: How Inequality is Remaking the American Family* (New York: Oxford University Press, 2014).

The world is only messed up because there's something wrong with us, with each of us. Since those who love us and those who live alongside us put up with us and help carry the burden of our mistakes, let us do the same for them. When we are willing to repent – cheerfully – for other people's mistakes, we find ourselves liberated from many of our own temptations. So, no, I don't think that we have lost agency, or the ability to do the right thing, in the area of Chastity. We just have gained the possibility of even more heavenly crowns from actually doing it!

RTE: You mentioned that it is an art to move into relationship while preserving our chastity. Can you say more about this?

DR. PATITSAS: The world doesn't understand and has lost hope in the possibility of Chastity, partly because it seems impractical, even unrealistic. How can someone expect to remain pure for the many years until they are economically and educationally ready for marriage? It seems impossible, and is it even important? You and I have both heard young people say that they just wanted to "get it over with" and lose their virginity. This doesn't seem very erotic or wonderful. It is as if we face an awesome and holy challenge, and our only response, before we have even tried, is to ask where we can turn in our weapons and surrender.

Moreover, people just don't remember how to win the battle with sexual temptation, and this we see acutely in the most destructive forms of sexual sin. These temptations are like uninvited guests that, if we let them in much at all, may soon claim our very identity for themselves. Since we've forgotten how to keep them at bay, we've bitterly concluded that these temptations must be natural. That is to say, we blame our Creator for their victory over us, and after that we may even become full-blown blasphemers. Look, even when we surrender to these alien forces, we aren't happy to function as the "hosts" of such parasitical powers; a bitter estrangement from God might arise in our breast, because we secretly blame him for not delivering us from these sins.

In the case of same-sex attraction, in particular, the rules for resisting the temptation are almost entirely different than those for resisting temptation in general. To fight it in the way you fight many other temptations will guarantee that its force only becomes stronger in you over time. But who is left to know these things, to show these ways? And thus many have fallen and will continue to fall. The tradition of successful spiritual combat still exists, though, and is even being strengthened among some spiritual fathers.[24]

Well, we weren't meant to live in sin, and there is a royal part of us that will always resent this slavery, however much we call it freedom. And that resentment can spur us to a more concerted search for a genuine spiritual doctor – but it may instead result in an ever-growing desire to re-crucify Christ by opposing and destroying his Body, the Church. I wonder if this is why Elder Aimilianos of Simonopetra Monastery said, "Wherever you see schism in the Church, know that there is scandal (meaning, usually, sexual scandal) behind it."[25]

Some people who have lost their Chastity have wound up on anti-depressants, or soon thereafter mutilate themselves with absurd tattoos and inappropriate piercings, or in some way act out their sorrow by damaging their bodies further through promiscuity and drug use or just smoking. And this sorrow is no small thing, for although we were meant to be royal sons and daughters of God, through our passions we have instead become enslaved to hostile powers. This sorrow and these acts of self-mutilation and self-medication are in fact part of "the whole creation groaning for deliverance" in the Holy Spirit (cf. Rom 8:19-22). They may be a kind of proto-repentance, a cry going up that is honest and direct and can be answered if we will let it.

---

24 Some people who are facing same-sex attraction recommend the "Redeemed Lives" program. They say that this kind approach comes close to the heart of how traditional Christian morality liberates rather than suppresses our deepest identity.

25 Elder (Abbot) Aimilianos (b. 1934) is the re-founder of Simonopetra Monastery, of Ormylia women's monastery in Chalkidiki, and of monasticism in Meteora.

Gnosticism and Economic Fears

Another reason we have lost respect for bodily purity is that we moderns have a tendency towards gnosticism, the belief system which in the early years of the Church was the greatest competitor with Christianity. Gnosticism privileges the mind and denigrates the body; its first practitioners were intellectuals, false mystics, pagan Greeks – and not Jews.[26] And the gnostics often descended into either licentiousness or self-mutilation when it came to sex. In either case, they could not accept the significance of the body for eternal salvation. The Jewish Christians knew that the teaching on sexual purity would be almost too much for "the nations," which is why they insisted upon it up front, in the very first Apostolic Council (Acts 15:1-30).

But while we moderns are gnostics in our spiritual lives, our economic science is comically materialistic. Despite every evidence that economic development is mostly about innovation – that it is centered in the "artist's moment" wherein we discern the "logos" in some thing or material or problem, and embody that insight or principle so that it may be shared with others[27] – we remain terrified that the finitude of today's resources must inevitably lead to the lack of tomorrow's bread. People are so terrified of overpopulation that they try to break the link between sex and children by promoting only those uses of sex that will not lead to children. For these sophisticates, lust is our only defense against starvation.

But I think another reason why people are not choosing Chastity is that we in the Church have not always based our instruction

---

26 When the *Da Vinci Code* films and books came out, based loosely on the Gnostic gospels, I asked myself the question: Isn't it true that the actual Gospels were written by Jews, from Palestine, who knew Christ personally – or, if written by a Greek (St. Luke), by one who knew the earliest Church and its Jewish leaders? And isn't it also true that the later Gnostic accounts of Christ's life were almost all written by Greeks who'd never set foot in Palestine, who lived a century or more after the actual events? For salvation "is from the Jews," not from Gnostic philosophers who have no idea what to do with either the body or with sexuality. Greek Orthodoxy is distinctive among Christian faiths for its mature embrace of Hellenism – that is, for an embrace of Hellenism through the filter of a strong *Semitic* emphasis on the unity of soul and body and on the way of the heart.

27 Cf. Jane Jacobs, *The Economy of Cities* (New York: Random House, 1969), 59-63.

about Chastity on Beauty, but instead may base it on a goodness divorced from Beauty; and goodness understood solely in bourgeois worldly terms. "Sex outside of marriage is bad because you will get a disease, drop out of school, and go on welfare. When what you should do is not burden the healthcare system, become economically productive, and pay lots of taxes so the State can buy a shiny new coat of armor." Is this an ecclesial message or a public service announcement?

Well, I shouldn't overdo it here, because the concern with disease and poverty is an expression of the fact that fornication so often leads to dissolution. And in the old days, before abortion and birth control were so freely available, the Beauty of the Church's teaching lined up perfectly with the practical Goodness of making it in the world; you couldn't take sex outside of marriage and expect anything but poverty and humiliation.[28] Now that link between practical life and morality seems to have been broken.

But some in the Church do really seem to be motivated by a moralistic impulse that reduces Orthodoxy to concern with individual piety. In particular, I find it disturbing that some spiritual fathers can be so bold in their direct contradiction of St. Paul's command that abstinence within marriage be only by mutual consent and for a short period. For example, some even bless the husband or wife to impose abstinence upon their unwilling spouse during Lent. This is wrong not because "the church does not belong in the bedroom" (for the marital union is an icon of Christ and the Church, and so of course the Church blesses some things and not others), but because neither is the confessor to make alliances with the wife against the husband, nor with the husband against the wife.

Instead let us try to inspire: marriage that unfolds from a pure life is a tremendous adventure and an enormously counter-cultural act. Few things will throw you more directly into maturity than a Christian marriage when the entire world is screaming at you, not to wait, *but simply not to believe in love*. Few adventures are more dan-

---

[28] So argues Ross Douthat in his *Bad Religion: How We Became a Nation of Heretics* (New York: Free Press, 2012).

gerous, more rewarding, or more of an inspiration to the Church than a young marriage that follows on the successful fight for Chastity. And in contemplating entering into marriage, just as when you are thinking of buying stock in a company, or in any of a thousand other cases in life, once all the danger is gone, also gone is much of the reward. If you have your parents' blessing, then just jump and start reaping those rewards and facing those dangers together.

Also, we adults might try taking the main responsibility for the loss of Chastity today, since we have designed our society so that people sometimes reach adulthood with no real economic abilities, shielded from reality, immature, and with no attention having been given to the formation of their eternal souls. They may not even know what the teachings of the Christian faith are in these matters, or why they matter, or how to win the fight.

To sum up, we Christians are not meant to oppose sex but to promote eros.

III. THE TWOFOLD ANOINTING

The Fractal of the Twofold Anointing

RTE: Let's go back to your idea earlier in the chapter that to love Beauty in the right way means that we consent to the cross that we find within it. You implied, for example, that Adam and Eve were able to love Christ as they walked with him day by day in the Garden, but that they were overwhelmed when they saw him, in some mysterious way, already crucified there within a forbidden section of Eden.

Meanwhile, in your lectures you've emphasized that "Anointing is always dual," or that within any genuine anointing from God there is both the Cross and the Resurrection. Are these ideas connected?

DR. PATITSAS: Yes, and in two ways. First, within the Beauty of God's appearing, which can lift us up and exalt us, we will find a call to Goodness, or a cross. Therefore, divine visions are not all sweetness and light; they carry difficulty and responsibility with them. Often, the visionary receives a sacred wound along with their theophany, as did St. Paul himself.

But earlier, also within eros itself, we can see that the visitation of God has this twofold character. Eros is sweet, but it is so sweet that it makes us deny ourselves, leave our "old selves" behind. It, too, has a cross hidden within it.

However, when eros leads on to the cross of agape, the unity of the Cross with the Resurrection unfolds from the other angle. In empathy, in co-suffering love (even should it be to the point of martyrdom), there is always eventually a fullness, a completeness. In loving another person self-sacrificially, we do feel some reassurance and joy.

Because this unity of Resurrection and Cross is found within both eros and agape and also between them (seeing eros, for the moment, as the Resurrection and agape as the Cross), we must admit that we are dealing here with a fractal. Indeed, I argued in my dissertation that the entire universe is structured according to the same fractal, the particular quality of unity between death and life in Christ's cross and resurrection.

In other words, the unity of Chastity and Empathy is intrinsic to the structure of the universe. We cannot live except according to this principle.

What Is the Twofold Anointing?

RTE: What does it mean to say that anointing is "dual"?

DR. PATITSAS: For Christians, it means that when a person is genuinely anointed by God's Holy Spirit, he or she becomes both a king *and* a sacrificial offering: the two states are inseparable. To be called out of non-being into being, for example, is for human beings a great gift, and yet we must admit that it is an adventure with many struggles also. To be elected president grants one many privileges, but these are inseparable from the burdens of serving others self-sacrificially. To be married is a joy, but it also carries with it sorrows and restrictions.

In fact I've been told that such a duality within anointing was understood throughout all ancient Indo-European, Near Eastern, and other sacrificial religions. It is a human truth present in the Natural Law as seen in many places, which finds its final expression in Christ and his cross and resurrection. As the title of one novel about Ancient Greece put it so powerfully, *The King Must Die*.[29]

But the example I received from the person who first taught me about the twofold anointing was the anointing of animals before ancient sacrifice. The anointing by the priests would seal the perfection, the unblemished state, of the bird or beast being offered. This "christening" was given only after the priests had inspected the animal for flaws and found it to be a perfect offering. But the very moment that the priest anoints the offering as perfect, as "the best," he is in this same gesture also marking the animal for death.

We personally may want to be "the best," but, in fact, in true religion we only sacrifice "the king" of what exists; we give our very best to God. The thing which is the best is also destined to die, to give its life for the renewal of the cosmic order. To be chosen, anointed in Christ, is exactly like this, and thus to follow Christ is both to be counted worthy of eternal life *and* to be called to give our lives here and now for those around us. We receive a cross to carry at the same time that we receive the foretaste of our resurrection!

This is why in icons, Christ's halo is unique. It includes the circle of perfection as do the halos of the saints, but it also includes the cross. While a saint-martyr may be depicted with the cross in his or her hand, there is only one with a cross inside the halo: Christ, the only perfectly anointed one! Incidentally, *every* icon of Christ is an icon of the entire Holy Trinity, for Christ is the express image of the Father (Col 1:15) and his halo is the symbol of the Holy Spirit, proceeding from the Father in order to rest upon the Son (Jn 1:33).[30]

---

[29] Mary Renault, *The King Must Die* (New York: Pantheon Books, 1958).

[30] Every Orthodox Christian icon of Christ is thus a presentation of the Orthodox doctrine that the Holy Spirit proceeds from the Father in order to rest upon the Son. According to

Joining the Resurrection and the Cross in Our Lives

This idea that anointing is always dual applies to our eros as well. If we have seen what is Beautiful, if we have sensed it and have fallen in love with it, this means that we have been anointed as "little christs" – that we have been chosen by God precisely both to die and to be reborn through our love for that Beauty. And so we know a thing to be truly Beautiful because in the ecstasy of loving and desiring it some self-denial arises. We forget ourselves, at least for some moment. The depth of its beauty corresponds to the depth of that self-denial.

The concern that the object of our eros should include the Cross means that for Christians desire and Chastity are inseparable. They are one thing, a single movement. Eros in Christ implies Chastity. Fasting and feasting seem separate to us in our fallen state, but they form a single twofold response to the Beautiful.

Living in Christ as we do, our cross and resurrection are not always sequential. Rather, we may experience them simultaneously, in the ecstasy of at once living for our beloved and dying to ourselves. This coincidence of the Cross and the Resurrection is what is so uniquely characteristic of Orthodox art and Orthodox spirituality.

To fast is to feast chastely; it is to so feast on Christ and on what Christ brings you, that nothing else can tempt you. To feast is to fast chastely; it is to leave behind every false beauty and partake of only what is given to us in Christ. Cross and Resurrection coincide.

Or in terms of eros, to fast is to be so overcome by eros that we forget to eat. It is to be so intoxicated by the divine wine that you cannot drink wine here. Thus, St. Paul cautions St. Timothy to be careful how he fasts, lest he damage his body (I Tim 5:23) – the body which your Bridegroom desires!

Aristeides Papadakis, this formulation was the Trinitarian teaching developed by the Orthodox Fathers in response to the *filioque*. See his *Crisis in Byzantium: The Filioque Controversy in the Patriarchate of Gregory II of Cyprus (1283-1289)* (Crestwood: SVS Press, 1997). I believe this is the best expression of what will ultimately become the universal Christian belief in the Holy Trinity: the Spirit proceeds from the Father in order to rest upon the Son. This, for example, is the picture of Trinitarian life that we see at Christ's baptism in the Jordan.

In terms of beauty, to fast is to leave behind every partial beauty and all partial estimations of what is beautiful, and to love the ultimate beauty. What first drives us to fast is a vision of Christ's Beauty.

Yes, many times this vision of his perfection will remind us of our present, and we hope temporary, ugliness. And thus out of mercy Christ proclaims, "Repent, for the kingdom of heaven is at hand." That is, He does not just show us the Kingdom, leaving us with despair at our own unworthiness, but He also promises us that repentance is possible and that He will help us to repent, since in Christ repentance is not a "self-improvement program" but *an act of obedience for which He himself provides the main energy*.

Twofold Anointing in the Holy Trinity

RTE: Earlier you have emphasized this twofold character as a way to know whether an anointing is genuine, and you've used the well-known terms "joyful sorrow" or "bright sadness" – χαρμολύπη in Greek – as that special quality which marks the Orthodox Christian aesthetic.

DR. PATITSAS: In my Ethics course lectures, I try to connect these terms to the duality of any genuine anointing, and I argue that we can tell whether an action is truly ethical by the degree to which it embraces both the Cross and the Resurrection.

The person who taught me that "anointing is always dual" – an idea I'd never before heard, although it felt exactly right – was my dissertation director and mentor, Robin Darling Young. She was advising me at a crucial moment in my research about Orthodox Holy Week. I was connecting what I was reading in Holy Week to St. Gregory Palamas' teaching about the Holy Trinity. He emphasized that the Holy Spirit proceeds from the Father in order to rest upon the Son; earlier Orthodox Fathers had begun to speak the same way, using the *filioque* as a positive opportunity to clarify a position that both Orthodox and Roman Catholics would hopefully recognize as correct. But St. Gregory Palamas also pointed specifically to the Gospel of John for a scriptural proof of this teaching. St John the Baptist had been told that only him upon whom the Spirit descended *and remained* should be recognized as the Christ, as the truly anointed one (Jn 1:33).

I believe that at Christ's baptism in the River Jordan we see the view of the Holy Trinity that all Christians will someday agree upon: the Holy Spirit proceeds from the Father in order to rest upon His Only Begotten Son. Well, when I said this, Robin responded rather cryptically, "But you must first of all remember that anointing is always dual." And then she went on to give those examples of ancient cultic sacrifice.

It's a wonderful idea, because a twofold anointing – an anointing that confers both a cross and a resurrection – explains so much about the gospel, about iconography, about the way Orthodox Christians conceive of faith and piety. The twofold anointing is the joyful sorrow, the bright sadness, the sober ecstasy of our faith that we just mentioned. It is the clear measure of the Orthodox sense of aesthetics; neither too light, nor too dark, nor a dull middle. Rather, our sense of beauty bears a fullness and a clarity and a coinciding of being both king and sacrificial lamb – a balance and coincidence of opposites that is synonymous with Life itself, for only Christ the Life-Giver achieves it fully.

By the way, in Greece the term I hear used more recently for "bright sadness" is the *Stavroanastasimo Ethos* – the Cross-Resurrection Ethos. This is a beautiful way of expressing this coincidence of the opposing aspects of the twofold anointing. For those of us who know this coincidence from our experience of the Church's life, it is our most precious possession – which it should be, for it is the very life of the Holy Spirit, bringing Christ to us.

From Beauty to Goodness

RTE: Is a vision of Beauty always an anointing?

DR. PATITSAS: Yes, very much so! And it is also true that in some cases the cross within this vision is easily carried, while in others we find Beauty's cross all but impossible to carry. Some beauty is so intense that it can wound, for it startles us too greatly with its reminder of how unworthy we are of it. Saint Silouan said of an ecstasy granted to him that, if it had lasted even a second longer, he would not have survived!

And some beauty that we see is not meant for us in particular, or for us in the first place, so the cross of glorifying God, of giving everything back to God, can be overwhelming in that case. We would so love to be the owners and occupants of that perfect house we just visited! But instead, the blessing granted through this particular unpossessable home is not for us to live in it, but just the assurance that, "In My Father's house are many mansions; if it were not so, I would have told you. I go to prepare a place for you" (Jn 14:2). So, it can take some really hard work to get there in our response to Beauty, to see everything beautiful truly as an icon and not as an idol, as something leading upwards and not downwards.

If our first criterion of real Beauty is that we always find the cross of Christ within it, then our second and twin criterion is that it is at least within the realm of possibility that this beauty will inspire within us an eros that is in fact chaste. Such a response is possible when we see our own spouse in privacy, but not when we invade other couples' privacy; I think you can see what I mean here. In a healthy response to real Beauty, we experience a coincidence of the two opposites of feasting and fasting.

These are then two simple rules for evaluating what appears to be beautiful: Is the cross of Christ within it? And, is it possible to love it chastely?

When we urge each other to "begin with beauty," we are of course talking about cultivating a pure eros for Christ. And this eros – "love's mad self-forgetting" – makes us wild and free at the exact same moment that it brings a deep and unbreakable order to our lives. On the one hand, in the presence of Beauty we become exactly who we are and are thus free of everything false; but on the other hand, we find that we "could not be otherwise" than what we thus become. Although eros releases us from every false rule and false imprisonment, it also makes us more specific, more concrete, in a way. This is another example, and a lovely example, of the twofold anointing, when in Christ we experience a wild abandon that is also infinitely precise and ordered.

Pastors, parents, teachers – they may all be afraid of urging us in the direction of cultivating eros. Part of the fear is wise and justified, for to give oneself wholly to this total love is to risk so much. But if we do it right, if our eros is pure and for Christ, then it always includes this cross, and it is chaste. And that is what keeps us stable, what grounds us and prevents us from "going off the deep end." Coldness is not the answer to temptation, but the fire of Chastity.

Saint Paul said as much in II Cor 12: "Because of the abundance of revelations – because the ardor of my eros for Christ was so all-encompassing and total, I was given a thorn in the flesh, to remind me that I was still human! That I was still a mortal man with a body and limitations! – And to show me, too, that even the greatest saint will often need to rely on 'non-saints' when he is sick." Well, I may be implying some of that quote, but I think St. Paul wouldn't mind.

In other words, the twofold character of anointing is what pushes us into the second step after Beauty, which is Goodness. For in the cross that comes within eros, we see our dependence not only upon God, but upon others and upon the whole of nature.[31] Eros for Beauty makes us see that we are radically implicated in the great cosmic liturgy of self-offering and poverty, of need and desire, of life and death. We see that Beauty is the radiance of the Good, just as the Beautiful Resurrection is the radiance of Christ crucified. We know for sure that if we are to gain this beauty it will be only because we have consented to become beautiful in the same way that it is – by living out the Cross!

---

[31] This, too, is an approximation of the quote about eros in Allan Bloom's *The Closing of the American Mind*, cited above. In editing this interview, it occurs to me that Bloom's argument must also be broadly allied to the Beauty-first approach, or he would not have defended eros so strenuously.

The Beautiful Art of Asceticism vs. the Good Fight for Morality

Besides, individual moral effort doesn't take us very far. We need ascetic effort as the bigger share of things. Ascetic effort is not exactly the same as moral effort.

RTE: What is the difference?

DR. PATITSAS: Look, for example, at the issue of sexual morality. Giving the moral advice, "Don't do it," no matter how many scare tactics we put behind it, has no effect if we haven't shown a young person a real experience of Beauty and Chastity. Even the person giving the advice has to possess Beauty and Chastity, or the moral advice will be a dead letter. There is nothing in empty words to draw them upwards towards Christ.

Jane Jacobs, the city-planner, said that you can't directly fight emptiness or poverty or blight in a city neighborhood. When you try to, for example by knocking down bad buildings, the area often just becomes more empty and the blight gets worse. You have to encourage, instead, the good things that are happening commercially or culturally within a so-called slum. You have to find the life and feed it.

In spiritual terms, feed the good eros by pursuing beauty and don't fight the morality battle as your first priority. Or, as Christ said, "The devil driven out finds his old house empty, so he comes back with seven of his friends" (cf. Mt 12:45). This is the message for our time, for our struggle, and it is as true in spiritual life as it is in urban planning. You almost never win by fighting many kinds of temptation head on. As we said when we opened this interview, death must be conquered and hope reawakened before sin can be defeated. Let Christ come and drive the demons away for you – that way no dangerous vacuum will follow, as it may in any of our self-help efforts.[32]

---

[32] And, of course, this again points to the strong connection between the sacraments of Holy Communion and Confession; both are a turning to Christ and a touching of the hem of his garment. Confession should be followed quickly by Communion, as a unity. In this way, He will allow the power to go out of him, staunch our wounds, and fill us with himself.

Understood accurately, asceticism is about Beauty; it's about attempting to be the sort of artists who won't betray what they have seen of the beautiful. For example, we don't fast in order to be good, but rather so that our devotion, our eros for Christ's Beauty, will be absolute. Moral effort only matters when it expands that ascetic effort into the arena of Goodness. Moral struggle has to be an amplification of asceticism, never a substitute. It has to be the working out of all that Beauty entails. In fasting, you love the Lord your God with all your heart, soul, mind, and strength, and then this unfolds into your ability to, like Christ, die for your brother as if he were yourself, by "giving alms" in many senses of the term. Fasting prepares you to serve others both because it leaves you with more resources to give away and because it is an early training in enduring hardship.

What if We Can't Fast?

RTE: What if we can't fast due to medical or other physical reasons?

DR. PATITSAS: Yes, and how did I even get onto the topic of fasting, you might ask. Fasting is how we purify eros, while feasting is how we intensify it. The two only make sense together. And fasting and feasting both involve the body, showing that the spiritual life involves the total human person. Finally, fasting and feasting, although they are the heart of this first stage of spiritual life because they help us to develop Chastity, are also this good preparation to serve our sister or brother. These practices also grant insight into your neighbor's situation; as an ascetic yourself, you won't sentimentalize or ignore their challenges.

But back to your question about whether to suspend the fasts if you are sick. Spiritual fathers generally will say that you have not done something bad in weakening your fasts in those cases – it may often be even necessary and good. They also warn us to be careful of a danger from the other direction, that when you do fast you aren't looking to Christ, but are only shoring up your own self-control, self-regard, and general sense of moral superiority.

Fasting may strengthen your willpower, but it also may exhaust it. Therefore, what is important is that it gives you something deeper than willpower: the firm habit of self-denial. I'm told that in the army there is a saying that you don't "rise to the occasion" in combat through a burst of willpower but that you "sink to the level of your training." Fasting is training for spiritual warfare and it prepares a part of our minds and souls that is more basic than willpower.

Now, sometimes people react to the possibility of self-righteousness by stopping the fast completely. But the answer is to see that if fasting and asceticism are about the Beautiful, then you must use them to fall more deeply in love with Christ and not to fall more deeply in love with your own moral excellence. Self-love is the defeat of eros, the mother of the passions, and fasting is meant to cure us of the bad forms of self-love.

But if your moral struggle should ever betray the good eros which is the foundation of morality, then you will have sawn off the branch you are sitting on. This is what happens when we focus on the evils of sexual immorality instead of first supporting the movement towards Christian marriage and family, or towards monasticism; really, towards Christ. Our message becomes nihilistic. "Don't" is all we have to offer.

Sexual Sin Is Often a Result of the Wrong Response to Theophany

Saint Paul looks at sexual purity in both of these ways, as both the right response to Beauty and as a struggle to preserve our moral Goodness. But we only seem to remember the second and overall much harder way. Yes, sexual sin is something that can keep us from God, which can lock us out of the heavenly kingdom: "[Although they know] the righteous judgment of God ... [they] not only do the same but also approve of those who practice them," he says, referring to homosexual acts in particular (Rom 1:32). And, "Neither fornicators, nor idolaters, nor adulterers, nor homosexuals, nor sodomites, nor thieves, nor covetous, nor drunkards, nor revilers, nor extortioners will inherit the kingdom of God" (I Cor 6:9). This is the ethical side: temptation comes to every single one of us, and we must fight against it.

But for St. Paul the other direction was more important, and to me far more surprising. In the first chapter of Romans, St. Paul says that sexual immorality isn't so much a sin, as it is the *punishment* for sin! It is the *consequence* of a prior sin: sexual falls are the handing over of our lives and bodies to humiliation because we have already sinned in another way. If we are having trouble in our own battle with temptation, it may be because, although we struggle and struggle to be good, we have skipped a prior step. This is such a wild perspective on things!

Saint Paul describes the typical four-part sequence through which we descend into sexual immorality. First, there is the revelation of Beauty – God's Theophany. Second, is how we respond. What if we fail to respond to Beauty in an orthodox liturgical way? What if when we see the Beauty and self-revelation of God in nature or in the Church, we don't give praise or repent? We may fail to leave ourselves behind and entrust ourselves to this vision, this Good News of Christ. We might not respond in faith and eros, in other words.

Third, if we have failed to acknowledge Christ's Beautiful Theophany and have not fallen in love with him with all that we are, so that our very lives become a liturgy, we instead become idolatrous, says St. Paul. We worship created things, whether in the form of idols or by becoming materialists. But another form of idolatry could be obsession with our own moral perfection, when we regard our virtue as our own achievement rather than as a gift and a fruit of synergy with God!

Following idolatry, as the fourth step in the sequence, St. Paul describes a kind of mystery. In a sense, it is God himself who allows us to be turned over to sexual uncleanness, allowing this out of love, so that in our humiliation we might return to him.

"You Don't Become Holy by Fighting Evil"

So if we are going to defeat sexual sin, and while we are at it clear up our confusion about what Chastity is, then we have to return to Theophany, to Beauty. We have to fall in love with Christ more deeply. This is what the Greek elder St. Porphyrios meant when he said that "you don't become holy by fighting evil" – he was reminding us of the first step of Christian life in St. Paul: doxology, which Paul usually called "faith." In other words, what St. Paul calls faith, we are calling "chaste eros."[33]

This is what St. Porphyrios called the "easy way": struggle ascetically first, and then struggle ethically. Struggle easily to be faithful in your devotion to the One God – Father, Son and Holy Spirit – by falling in love with God's amazing beauty. Then, virtue will be given to you, in large part.

So now we can see that asceticism comes before moral struggle, and that asceticism is the struggle of the artist to create honestly and within the bounds set for his art. Asceticism is Chastity in our devotion to God. It is rejection of self-love and every other form of

---

[33] Since "faith" and "chaste-yet-ardent eros" are the same thing, we can see that St. Paul's "we are saved by faith," and St. Porphyrios' "No one ever became holy by fighting evil; instead, fall in love with Christ," have the same meaning. And we can also see why "faith without works is dead," for our chaste eros/faith is for the Crucified One, and therefore loving him always results in our having the living desire to be crucified with and for him. Thus, true eros always unfolds into agape/works. We then become true – that is, are saved, and become the full human person we were called to be.

Taken together, this sequence shows us that the state of salvation is to liturgize; i.e., to practice an eros of self-offering to God that alone has the potential to unfold into the right agape/service to our fellow man and the creation. As we are saved, our lives become liturgy.

Still, "faith alone" is sufficient, for within true faith is already found the full kernel of both agape/works and philia/friendship with Christ. "Chastity and Empathy," the title of this chapter, could therefore also be written, "Faith and Works" – but with the understanding that works are an *amplification or flowering of* faith, not a substitute *nor even exactly a counterpart* to faith, just as agape is an amplification of and a more developed form of eros.

But all of this can be taken another way. The Protestant rebellion against the Truth-First Empire of Moral Duty was, in its way, a return to eros – faith – and thus to Beauty. Although not a Beauty-*first* way (for it sometimes aims if possible to stop right at Beauty, hiding there beyond the reach of the stormtroopers inhabiting the realms of moral goodness and dogmatic truth), it is recognizable to Orthodox Christians as far as it goes.

Our question to Evangelicals, though, is a difficult one: Do you resolve to know only Christ? Or do you resolve to know only Christ, *and him crucified*? Because in the second case – the path that St. Paul commands – faith must unfold into the desire to be co-crucified with Christ (Mt 16:24).

idolatry. In other words, we should struggle to keep our eye sound, rather than focus on resisting the negative.

It is easy to conflate ascetic struggle with moral struggle because we naturally feel guilty when we eat meat on a Friday, for example, and so our lack of asceticism seems like merely a moral failure. But we must preserve some distinction in our understanding: we fast because we choose not to idolize food and instead to feast on our vision of God, and to feast, in fact, on God's very Body and Blood. Asceticism is first of all for Beauty, and only then is amplified into a struggle for Goodness.

If we take Scripture's warning against sexual sin seriously, then we have to accept the whole sequence that St. Paul describes in the first chapter of Romans. We have to see that sexual immorality, serious as it is, is usually a punishment for sin, even more than a sin itself. And that our primary and initial battleground against such sin is in the focus on theophany – Beauty First. This is what I meant when I said earlier in our discussion that sexual immorality is not equivalent to the loss of Chastity but is rather the consequence of losing Chastity – of losing our focus on theophany.

Saint Paul also shows us how to combine his two understandings of sexual purity, as being both a gift and an arena of struggle. If the primary sin is the failure to respond to God's self-revelation with faith (that is, it is our failure to liturgize in an orthodox manner and thus we instead become idolatrous), then St. Paul shows that the unethical use of our bodies is also a sin against liturgy, for "your bodies are the temples of the Holy Spirit" (I Cor 6:19). Sexual sin is the failure to use our bodies liturgically; it is a kind of idolatry of the flesh, a usurping of our own or another person's flesh. It is a kind of anti-Eucharist, a theft and an unlawful appropriation of something not made by us, an underestimation of a gift belonging also to God.

If our lives really begin with God's self-offering, and if it is his will that we leave ourselves behind and run to him chastely in response, then the opposite of Chastity is not a rich erotic life; far from it. The opposite of chaste and ardent eros for God is always some version of the bad kind of *self*-love, or the total defeat of eros.

Eros requires Chastity or else it pours itself out in dissipation and leaves us trapped within ourselves. Chastity always means the forgetting of self and the discovery of the other.

At that point we can discuss agape, empathy, and being crucified together with Christ for the life of the world.

Imitate Creation's Eros for Christ

By taking the universe as a given, or as the "last word" on what is out there, science inadvertently commits a kind of idolatry. They have made a material thing (the material universe) the final reference point of human existence. But St. Paul tells us that idolatry, or not seeing in God the real meaning of the world, leads to bad problems in our sexual practice. We can see that this is happening today.

The Enlightenment project did not intend to idolize the world. Rather, it hoped to desacralize the world in order to liberate man from the power of religion. As we said, the first scientists attempted to complete that western journey which so alarmed C.S. Lewis, away from seeing the world as an icon. In a non-sacred world, reason was supposed to reign supreme and men would no longer serve mythic powers or church officials, the philosophers of the Enlightenment promised.

But if there is no divinity beyond this world, then creation becomes the ultimate frame of reality. At that point, we are more idolatrous than the pagans and the primitives ever were.

But this means that the Enlightenment, despite the fact that it partly raises up nature and its wonder, was launched upon a negation of eros and beauty, of icon and theophany, and thus of freedom itself. It freed us from God and left us slaves to the world. Freedom from religion was purchased by making the world – and thus eventually man as well, who is, after all, also a part of the world – a fixed, predictable, un-free thing.

That is why we moderns only talk about two of the three Socratic transcendentals, truth and goodness. Truth, we call science, and Goodness, we call technology or public policy. But there is no room for aesthetics, for letting Beauty spark our souls into life. To moderns, aesthetics is just opinion, prejudice, oppression. Beauty tempts us, we moderns think, to do bad things.

And so Beauty is the only thing we moderns agree is ugly, because disagreement about it will divide us – especially Beauty that rises to the level of theophany; vision is the only thing we moderns agree cannot be seen, because it would undermine our rationalism; eros is the only love we are denied, for it dislodges the self from its position at the center of the world; and Chastity, by demonstrating the iconicity of the cosmos, is seen as our greatest enemy, the thing which must be minimized, ridiculed, and vilified.

RTE: Is the distrust of eros also based in the fear that love for the beautiful, or theophany, will cripple our exercise of reason? Or, do we fear beauty because it will make us look ugly in comparison?

DR. PATITSAS: Well, we do have to be careful. In earthly beauty there may well be elements of human sin. Some of these can lead a person to reject the beauty itself. For example, the city of St. Petersburg is a jewel of Russia, but so many tens of thousands of indentured workers died in its construction in the early 1700s. Knowing this, how do you not feel something tragic there? And when the communists took power in Russia, of course they used tragedies such as these as a reason to reject the beauty that the old Empire had achieved. It is often the case that the beauty we have managed to achieve in a culture is bound up with our sin.

But yes, we might hate pure spiritual beauty and even try to wreck it in others, simply because it does rebuke us for our falls.

Our culture, though, is not so troubled by its sin; it is so madly pursuing power, that it can't be so easily shamed. Chaste eros promises freedom, but if it is truth a culture desires (and only such truth that will enable us to exercise power in predictable ways), then eros will only frighten us. And if we are willing to sacrifice even our freedom and humanity in order to acquire a different kind of power, then we will pretend to find chastity ridiculous, since it implies that the path to freedom is vulnerability.

I think that in the Epistle to the Ephesians St. Paul makes it very clear that Chastity is a necessary preparation for marriage (Eph 5:1-33). In that epistle, he argues that in pursuing Chastity we are training ourselves to see the world as icon, as gift. After that, we can see our husband or wife as an icon, of either Christ or of the Church. Our stage-one total eros for Christ, "Love the Lord your God…," is proper preparation for stage-two agape, "Love your neighbor as yourself," because loving that neighbor is inseparable from understanding him or her to be an icon of Christ. Beauty first, then Goodness.

And then we can see the real challenge that Chastity brings: you love Christ so completely, only then to discover that since He is the Crucified One you must now fulfill this love by consenting to be co-crucified with him. In that next step of co-crucifixion you have Goodness as well as Beauty, which is what makes you True. But we might be too scared to proceed.

Our main problem with the spiritual life these days is that "we just don't feel like it" – we lack eros. A world without true holiness is good enough for us, so long as we have an abundance of the technological fruits of the Enlightenment.

RTE: How do we overcome our complacency?

DR. PATITSAS: Saint Seraphim of Sarov was asked what differentiates our age from the age of the apostles. He answered, "Only one thing is missing: a firm resolve." And this resolve comes from gazing again and again at ultimate Beauty, especially in the lives of the saints. This resolve is not "willpower" as we use that term today, but a fiery love; it is, in fact, the bright fire of chaste eros, or faith. Such a faith is sufficient to save us because it is the living seed of true Christian liturgy.

RTE: We are often urged to use willpower to attain both spiritual and material goals, but it can be very isolating. How does willpower differ from a Beauty-driven resolve?

DR. PATITSAS: "Willpower" in the sense that it is used outside the Church is aimed at goodness or truth. We know an effective way to lose weight would be to eat differently, and so we struggle to be good by dieting. We know that pornography is bad, so we disconnect the internet. This is fine as far as it goes, but our main focus ought to be outside ourselves, on Christ, or on the joy of healthy foods and exercise, or on the chaste beauty of the Church services.

By making our bodies instruments of liturgy – in other words, by loving the Lord your God with all your heart, all your soul, all your mind, and all your strength – we arrive at total eros for God. This all-consuming eros for Christ and the Holy Trinity is, as we have said, Chastity. When this is realized, unclean desires will find no place in us, will be pushed aside. Chastity only has meaning for us Orthodox when we "begin with Beauty." We are not to make a display of our virtue for its own sake or to subsume it into some worldly social purpose like "lowering the rate of teen pregnancy."

Moreover, out of the first of the two greatest commandments flows the second, "to love your neighbor as yourself." Agape should always be anchored in Chastity. This is why, while we welcome good done from anyone, we in the Church are cautious about love shown in some name other than that of Christ. Out of eros for Christ flows agape for our neighbor; out of Chastity, genuine empathy can arise, be sustained, and be without blemish.

Otherwise, the same voices who speak for women's rights will denigrate men; or the same voices who will speak up for the child in the womb will bless wars and invasions that result in the deaths of other people's children. Of course, people can love Christ – Perfect Beauty and Goodness and Truth – in ways we don't understand. And we are ready to make common cause with anyone who does, or even tries to, join agape to eros.

But let us be wary of do-gooders who lack the erotic dimension, who lack the consequent wildness of real persons.

We must learn, rather, from the creation. The famous Elder Aimilianos experienced a vision in which he saw that all created things – rocks and trees and animals – are in fact continually reciting the Jesus Prayer, by virtue of their very existence. They, too, exist erotically when they cry, "Lord Jesus Christ, Son of God, have mercy on me!" for in praying this, they leave themselves behind and run to him. And for them, also, this eros is amplified in agape, when they conclude the prayer by identifying themselves as "the sinner!" – in other words, as a creature made out of utter nothingness, yet also wishing to join in the overflow of Christ's self-emptying love for the world! They, too, trace the path through Beauty to Goodness, and in so doing arrive at their logos – that is, they exist, or become True.

If the elder's vision was genuine, and I certainly believe that it was, then all of creation prays this way except for us! We alone are the missing link.

Distinguishing Real from Apparent Beauty: The Presence of the Holy Cross

RTE: Until now we've spoken about our response to Beauty as being a chaste yet ardent eros, which is what you believe St. Paul meant by "faith." If from the beginning you had directly called Beauty "the Gospel," or "Theophany," or "Our Lord and Savior Jesus Christ," I don't think we would have been as challenged by the idea of "Beauty first." Having taken it from this slightly different angle, the whole picture is new. And it reminds me of what the gospel is supposed to evoke in us: delight, joy, and a desire to turn towards Christ.

DR. PATITSAS: I really wanted to emphasize Beauty, to cast the gospel in this light because I feel that in denigrating Beauty, as we do when we reduce all of life to science and technology – our culture's names for what are in fact only very limited pictures of Truth and

Goodness – we in the West are suffering. We are losing our respect for the feminine. We are losing our sense of being at home in and belonging to the world. We are making family life impossible, and because we can't worship properly or celebrate deeply, we are making Church membership as the Bride of Christ impossible. Millions of people are lost in either legal or illegal drug use precisely because we have lost our joy through these self-inflicted cultural wounds. We often resemble robots, as we attempt to conform ourselves to this picture of the world as a machine.

And I wanted to emphasize Beauty-first in solidarity with C.S. Lewis, who devoted all of his novels and his theological writing to this one point: that the world is beautiful because it *really is* an icon of heavenly life. Lewis did not follow the decline of our Western vision all the way back to its origins in the eleventh-century Lateran councils that first separated the symbolic from the real.[34] However, he did insist that we should try to trace the failure in Western Christian theology back to its origins, or we would never really overcome it.

RTE: For those who feel that they have never deeply experienced the Beauty you speak of, or seen real Chastity, or encountered Christ, how does one start to take this first step? God can seem very far away.

DR. PATITSAS: He can, and then in his seeming absence we may panic and make things worse. But, in fact, Christ is closer to us than we are to our own selves.

Beginning with Beauty can be done very practically, in a simple moment-to-moment application. Although eros is actually a cognitive act and the first stage of reason, it operates in us like feeling – but in the sense of intuition. Or, it operates like that certain knowing that we all possess, which goes beyond all opinions and emotions.[35] So often Christ stands at the door and knocks (Rev 3:20) – I mean, He imparts to us some spiritual prompting – but because we don't yet see a moral or logical dimension to this prompting (neither

---

34 See Fr. A. Schmemann, "Appendix Two," *op. cit.*

35 I learned this from Eric Perl in his *Theophany: The Neoplatonic Philosophy of Dionysius the Areopagite* (Albany, NY: State Univ. of New York Press, 2008).

Goodness nor Truth are as yet clearly in play), we don't respond, we don't react. We are tragically cold to Beauty – we have not cultivated our intuition and our theological senses. And in the case of these intuitions, by the time we find out *why* we should have prayed or helped or changed our course, it is often too late.

I think this is the meaning of the Parable of the Sower and the seed that falls on different types of soil (Mt 13:1-23). This parable isn't only about whether or not we accept Jesus Christ as Our Lord and Savior on the first hearing of the Good News. In reality, the Sower continues to sow beautiful seeds of theophany within our hearts on an hourly basis, such that even those outside the Church have the divine law almost continually written on their hearts (Rom 2:13-15). But do we listen? Are our hearts ready to receive and bear fruit in the most practical sense, by welcoming these promptings and joining our own efforts to them?

God's initiative in our spiritual life is always primary, and his prompting in our hearts is a kind of theophany. This inner prompting is in fact the *usual* way that He speaks to us. And it is precisely through our aesthetic sense that we can most immediately recognize these seeds as his action, and not as something else at work. We learn what his prompting "feels like," "tastes like" – as opposed to when it is our own passions, dark forces, or just our emotions or bodily feelings operating.

This is why "discernment" as a category of insight in Orthodoxy is not about reading a crystal ball that shows the hidden states of others, the world, or ourselves. It's not magic. Discernment just means that our aesthetic sense is so refined by grace and asceticism, that we know at once *which* promptings are from the Holy Spirit and which ones aren't. Discernment, even for elders, is not about reading other people so much as it is about reading the movements of the Spirit.

But for someone like me, while I am ignoring these small promptings that are the actual encounter with Beauty in my life, I am giving in to all kinds of "pleasures" and opinions and emotional highs and lows that really aren't Beauty at all. Isn't it amazing how just a glance at an icon can often wake us up from such temptations!

"Beauty First," we have been saying, implies developing a healthy Chastity. If we're going to hear the "still, small voice of God," we'll have to give no mind to (i.e., not direct our *nous* toward) the clamor of our own passions, opinions, and prejudices. One problem I have with contemporary psychology is that it encourages us to devote so much attention and significance to that clamor.

Beginning with Beauty means that you start by cultivating and not suppressing the divine eros at work within you. But eros toward what? And so fasting is immediately part of eros – we've gotten so attached to so many false beauties, or to true beauty but in false – selfish – ways. The Church talks about fasting, almsgiving, and prayer: This is our three-part psychotherapeutic program, and although to our dull ears it sounds pietistic and weak, in the interviews on trauma, and then on Beauty, we could begin to see the awesome power of this sequence: cleanse your ability to appreciate Beauty through fasting; contemplate Goodness by actually practicing empathy/almsgiving; and in noetic prayer steadily become one with Christ, who is Truth.

Yes, our culture is wary of beauty. It is afraid of being seduced. But is it afraid of being seduced because it wants to be faithful to God, as Eve failed to be in the Garden? Or is it afraid of being seduced because it is afraid of that conversation with *actual* Beauty that will follow our fall into socially-accepted but false beauties: "Who told you that you were naked?" (Gen 3:11). I think our culture is afraid of Beauty because, while it can learn Truth and it can master Goodness, genuine Beauty will always render it vulnerable and interdependent with others and dependent on God.

So, yes, we have scriptural warnings that false beauty can pull us away from God. But falling in love with real Beauty is the sign that we are on the way to ultimate truth or that we are ready to put away our selfish desires and pursue something outside of ourselves. Falling in love with Beauty is sometimes even the proof that we are leaving "the world" behind entirely and are becoming ready to dedicate ourselves to God without counting the cost.

An Eye for Beauty

RTE: Can you repeat which guidelines we can use to distinguish the Beauty that saves from the merely pleasurable sensation that seduces?

DR. PATITSAS: At the heart of genuine Beauty we always find the same Principle, the same Logos, the identical Someone: Christ; and in fact, Christ crucified for the life of the world. I mean, within true Beauty we always find the ultimate Goodness who is Christ in his dying for us on the cross. So Christ crucified is our measure, our criterion, of whether or not what we see is truly Beautiful.

The ancient Greeks called the Beautiful "the radiance of the Good." Just so, all beauty is the radiance of Christ's cross. Just read some of the hymns for the feast of the Exaltation of the Holy Cross on September 14th; I think, in fact, we do sing exactly this.[36]

Let's say that you tell me that this building, or this painting, or this musical composition is beautiful. Then show me now Christ, and him crucified, within it. I once thought this standard was too high, too literal, to cover every form of beauty in music and painting and building, but the Austrian-English architect Christopher Alexander, in *The Timeless Way of Building*, convinced me otherwise – although he does not speak of Christ in literal terms, and may not even be thinking of the historical Christ in what he says.[37]

RTE: In *The Timeless Way of Building* and in his other writings, so many people have found a reconnection to their innate ability to recognize and create beauty. But before we speak about Alexander and his ideas, can you say more about how Christ's cross is present in what we find truly Beautiful?

---

[36] Exaposteilarion at Matins for the Feast of the Exaltation of the Holy Cross: "The Cross is the guardian of the whole world; the Cross is the beauty of the Church. The Cross is the might of kings; the Cross, angels' glory; and wound to demons."

[37] Christopher Alexander, *The Timeless Way of Building* (New York: Oxford University Press, 1979).

DR. PATITSAS: This presence of the Cross can be relational – not relative, but relational. I mean, my wife will remain beautiful to me precisely because I am crowned to her. Through the sacrament of marriage, my desire for her beauty includes Christ and his cross of self-sacrificial love for her. It is possible, within limits, to find someone else's wife beautiful also, so long as an appreciation of her beauty includes the cross of not desiring her in an improper way, the cross of resisting sexual expressions of love for any beautiful person who is not my wife, the cross of not acting in ways that might make her husband jealous.[38] This is how we are to understand the beauty of someone who is not available to us through marriage.

If, however, we pass into sin, then we ourselves will have converted God-created Beauty into the wrong kind of beauty, into something that negates the Cross. Stolen beauty turns bitter in our mouths; it becomes ugly because we ourselves have attempted to remove the Cross from within it.

The existence of the Holy Cross within Beauty is relational in other senses. For example, the ascetic calling that we respect the seasons of life – when it is and isn't proper to eat, marry, and so forth – shows us that the beauty of a thing exists to the degree and in the way that the thing relates to Christ and to his will for us to become "priests," his desire that we join ourselves with him as concelebrants of his eternal liturgy for the life of the world.

Therefore, the same object (food, for example) may be truly beautiful if we eat it in a spiritual way, or at one season, and a mere appearance of Beauty if we eat in a worldly way, or at the wrong season. Moreover, how we relate to what we encounter also partly *determines* whether it is truly Beautiful. We are called to be co-creators with God of the world, and thus we ourselves will help to determine whether a thing is formed – that is, whether it is truly part of the "cosmos," the Greek word that means both "created order" and "beautiful thing."

---

[38] I don't mean primarily physical beauty. Infidelity can also begin with admiration for the beauty of the spirit or of the mind of someone beside our spouse. Locate the cross within that beauty, and find a mature balance.

How often do we see a holy person showing appreciation for some overlooked person or place or even object, such that suddenly its inner radiance is almost blindingly bright! This is the meaning of proper "nationalism" in the Church, by the way, just that we should love all nations equally – and yet also have some of the fervor of a partisan for each!

RTE: I've seen this with experienced spiritual fathers in Greece and Russia who are able to to bring out the beauty of something that before seemed rather ordinary.

DR. PATITSAS: Related to this shifting presence of beauty in a person or place is the fact that if the cross is at the center of the thing for which we feel eros, it will be because either we or God have put it there. And if it is placed there by God, the presence of a cross is meant to be confirmed by our assent to it; this happens when we are willing to embrace the part of loving something beautiful that involves the Cross, and not just the part that makes us feel like "kings" and "lords" in a worldly sense. Our calling as Christians may be to rule, to lead, but then it is also always the calling to rule and lead at our own expense, as a friend at Georgetown once put it.

So, yes, "Beauty First" means that we've got to distinguish between Real Beauty and merely apparent beauty. We need a threefold spiritual development: of our discernment, of our artistic skill at ignoring false beauty, and of our passion (in the wonderful American sense of passion, meaning "sustained and committed longing") for the really beautiful.

"Beauty" includes all that God has done throughout salvation history, throughout the life of the Church, and in our own lives up to now. "Beauty First" is another way of saying, "Pay attention to theophany." And where do you most readily find theophany? The list is not brief, especially when you multiply the particular instances of nature and good art, as well as liturgy, Holy Scripture, pilgrimage, saints' lives, hymnography, Church art and architecture (indeed, all the ecclesiastical arts, including incense and vestment making), family, friendships, romantic love, and so on. But do we approach these sources as if they were beautiful and fall in love with them? Or have we lost that wonder from our lives?

RTE: How do we cultivate this?

DR. PATITSAS: This takes experience and training. And one form of training comes from just being immersed in the Tradition. Tradition is a record of prior theophany, of Beauty, and a living Tradition is able to re-present that Beauty to us. As we enter that current and learn to swim in it, we learn what is real Beauty and what is false.

When a child is raised in the Church in a healthy way, what he has above all is an unshakable sense of how Orthodoxy "tastes." He grows up knowing the theological aesthetic of the Church, and this will carry a person most of the way home if he is faithful to it. This is part of what Dostoevsky meant when he said that "Beauty will save the world." He was talking about the saving power to an adult of the memory of attending Presanctified Liturgy as a child.

We start with eros and the willingness to fall in love but also with the readiness to have our eros purified through fasting. When we begin with Beauty, we make Chastity and Unknowing our first allies and friends.

RTE: Is this "unknowing" the same as the willingness to be surprised? C.S. Lewis seemed to be renouncing Enlightenment rationalism when he called the account of his conversion, *Surprised by Joy*.[39]

DR. PATITSAS: "Unknowing" is another term for chaste yet ardent eros or for the fasting that is also feasting – for faith. Therefore it is very much an openness to surprise, the act of real listening – but a listening balanced by an ability to ignore the clamor of the world. Saint Mary of Egypt also "unknew" herself and turned to the beauty of Christ.

---

39 C.S. Lewis, *Surprised by Joy: The Shape of My Early Life* (London: G. Bless, 1955).

Afterword: The Practical Path to Agency through Eros

RTE: In our first two discussions you spoke about the concept of "moral luck," the idea that our character, for which we will be praised or blamed, depends at least in part on factors outside our control. Then you showed how Orthodoxy resolves the challenge of true moral responsibility, of how we can be free and responsible even though our lives are also a product of our times and environments. How does moral luck relate to Beauty, Chastity, and marriage?

DR. PATITSAS: The term "moral luck" may be unfamiliar, but marriage is the perfect example of the practicality of the idea. People fear the loss of control that will come with marriage, and some marriages do end disastrously. But we all also know couples who have more freedom, more financial success, and even more fun than we do as single people precisely because they *are* married. In a happy marriage people take the Orthodox path: rather than trying to be free by escaping responsibility, they become freer still by accepting responsibility for the care and even the mistakes of others.

In the Orthodox way, you overcome moral luck – you attain your full human agency, your capacity to act freely in the world – by forgetting yourself, by taking on more responsibility than you have to, by taking on the weaknesses of another, by seeing that the whole world is a vibrant offering from God meant to be joined by us to the body of Christ. In the secular world, you attain moral agency by going in the opposite direction – by focusing more and more narrowly on yourself, by cutting off the weak and troubled around you, by seeing the world as something dead that can be manipulated.

In short, in the Enlightenment you deny both eros and agape and move straight to the truths of science, the usefulness of technology and of an ever increasing willpower, while all along denying that Beauty even exists, so that you can be "free." You may end up helping many people along the way, and for this the rest of us should be grateful, but this approach also always threatens to descend into inhuman permutations that cancel out all the good that science and technology offer. Of this we have had too much proof.

And such a world will tend to see marriage and eros as the loss of agency, whereas the Church says, "No. Move into the choice of your particular cross, and you will attain real agency." Besides, to deny both eros and agape is like imprisoning yourself in the berserk state, in a cold fury of isolation.

RTE: Could such an emphasis on eros make us impractical, or incapable of coping with the ordinary aspects of daily life?

DR. PATITSAS: Well, we are starting with love, the eros love, but then we move on to expressing the agape by thinking how to make this pursuit something sustainable in and for society. That is, having seen our vision of the Beautiful, we then have sufficient motivation to ask what sort of cross will be hidden within that. No good path is broad; no Orthodox path is without crucifixion. If we can just commit to carrying that particular cross, we will become Good and at the same time the Beauty will be ours.

In a consumerist culture that is really hand-in-glove with this Cartesian view – which believes that the world is not an icon, that the world is not a gift, that it's not bound up with a self-offering of God to us – the erotic dimension is cut right out of creation. Creation is seen as just a dead object, a fixed thing. People are taught to look at the world that way, at themselves that way, at their lovers that way (by pornography, for example). Now people begin to feel that eros itself is a sin, rather than the one thing that could deliver them from our contemporary secular idolatry!

Now, of course, in an Orthodox Christian culture, parents are also trying to be careful of whom their child will marry, to help them make a practical decision, but that's in a Christian culture where there is a widespread rejection of materialism and reductionism. So, no, eros does not make us impractical.

We said before that, "The only cure for bad eros is good eros, and plenty of it." Well, this works in reverse, too. If you condemn the healthy erotic impulse in your children, then what follows is that people fall into sexual sin. If when your son or daughter falls in love and wants to get married, if you don't bless them or haven't at all prepared them for that moment, if you manage even somehow to prevent them by appealing for them to be reasonable and cold, then they are less likely to remain on the Christian path.

Well, the young people sort of draw their own conclusions in that case, and those are: "What the Church is asking me to do isn't blessed by my parents or really possible within my society anyway, so we have to have sex when we can and get through college. Doing that, of course, probably means it won't work out permanently, so later we'll have sex with someone else." Then that becomes the new way.

What the parents don't see is the way many preceding generations of idolatry (to go back to our reference to Romans 1) have led to the punishment of sexual sin being committed by their children. We have idolized money or career or our particular educational system or whatever created thing, and God says, "Fine. You want to live in those places, go ahead." These things are all necessary, but how much thought have we given to more creative ways that would allow our young people to have both Chastity and these other necessary things?

Although there are many factors to it, I think that one reason behind the growth of homosexuality in America is that traditional marriage seems impossible, so people prefer to pursue something that seems safer because it does not promise children and it does not involve the dreaded mysterious challenge of gender. Well, traditional marriage seems impossible because we have neglected Beauty and criminalized eros.

RTE: In Greece there is a saying, "Either marry young, or get tonsured young," with the implication that this will lead to a good life. But there are some Christians who do neither. What can you say about this?

DR. PATITSAS: A single person in the world can be that good son or daughter who provides solace to his or her parents in their old age. In that way they resemble a married person, present for nieces and nephews and providing invaluable help in their communities. A single person in the world can also often give more attention to the Church, and in that way they resemble a monastic. It is often a middle state.

When St. Anthony the Great became the "first monastic" (as he is often called) in Egypt in the early third century, his first act was to get the advice of... more experienced monastics. Now, these holy people were not technically monks or nuns, but they were people who lived unmarried in the world and yet also were dedicated to God in prayer, almsgiving, fasting, and vigil. From the example of St. Anthony's life, therefore, we see that this third way of life is highly blessed. It is the very wellspring of monastic life, in a way, since celibates in the world were the earliest teachers of a saint who is sometimes called the founder of monasticism.

RTE: So we have that freedom, too?

DR. PATITSAS: Well, it's not clear how much freedom we have in any given situation. I mean, God's providence circumscribes our choices so that our life in him is truly synergistic. I spent my late teens and early twenties trying to join the military but each time developed problems with my health so that my entry was proscribed for a limited time. I finally understood that God had other plans – although when I got my Greek citizenship, I tried one last time to enlist somewhere and was again denied, this time on account of my age!

Also, those who had the freedom to marry or become monastics while they were still young, but did neither, may regret to find their choices narrowing later on. Finally, a person may wish to do one or the other but simply must acknowledge that they can find neither an appropriate spouse nor an appropriate monastery. Single life in the world is the hardest calling in a way because of its uncertainty and ambiguity, but it can be so fruitful for society and for the Church.

Salvation is interpersonal; it comes in community. But it is true that some just know, from the beginning, that for them this communion will be best realized by a single life in the world. There are people with special callings.

CHAPTER FOUR

SHAME AND SACRIFICE

Rescuing the Soul from the Empire of Therapy

The oldest psychotherapy of the West, the psychotherapy that in its inventing by Socrates founded the West, is the discipline of Ethics. When Socrates applied a relatively strict rationalism in order to analyze everything about the worldview of his contemporaries, he did so with the aim of establishing what it is that makes the human soul truly healthy and alive. For the next two millennia, ethical behavior and soul health were considered to be of a piece.

Ethicists today, therefore, must not evade their responsibility to evaluate the mode of psychotherapy that has displaced their discipline as Western civilization's guide to the health of the soul – the professional therapeutic approach which descended from Freud.

The power of Freudian influence is partly due to another trend in Western thought. From at least the time of the Great Schism of 1054, the Western European worldview steadily became more based in an appreciation of science first learned from the ancient Greeks, combined with a thirst for effective technique inherited especially from the classical Romans. Ethics itself, though more than a millennium older than the split between the Orthodox East and Roman Catholic West, originally developed through a similar combination of emphases, promising that the rational investigation of the world and of the soul would deliver a system infallibly promoting human happiness. The influence of Christianity provided a powerful corrective to these emphases. After the Great Schism in the eleventh century, however, one component of Jewish influence, the so-called way of the heart, was somewhat eclipsed in the West.

To some, the arrival of Freudian psychotherapy in the early twentieth century seemed to reintroduce the way of the heart to a Western European civilization that, despite its devotion to Semitic Christianity, was increasingly tempted to cover over the trans-rational dimensions of human life with a reductive rationalism.

However, Freud managed to achieve this return to the heart only in a rough, distorted form. The therapy that descended from him and which rules us today in fact wavers between a Semitic side and a Classical Greek-Roman side. On the one hand, it somehow promises to touch the deep heart, but on the other hand, it cuts a truth-first path into the most mysterious inner chambers of this heart in the search for an effective fix to emotional suffering.

Moreover, contemporary therapy's attempt to be scientific about the heart is flawed even in scientific terms. Secular psychotherapy was born in the late nineteenth century, at a time when only one of the three essential types of scientific problem-solving had been discovered. It will therefore be necessary for us to say a little about what the three kinds of science are and about the tragedies that inevitably follow when we apply earlier, simpler methods of science to complex entities like the human soul.

An Ethics of Beauty offers a third way to the healing of the soul, beyond both the reductive approach of philosophical Ethics and our current misreading of the heart as little more than the "unconscious." The Orthodox Christian approach to soul healing and soul development strikes a balance between Greek rationalism, Roman method, and the Jewish heart. According to the principles of this approach, the spiritual father is hesitant both to analyze the heart of the spiritual child and to make prescriptions based upon any kind of abstract system.

Instead, he is called to shield the penitent's heart from a wide array of assaults. These attacks come from invisible powers and from human passions, to be sure, but they also include the judgments launched by the spiritual child's own self-criticism and self-analysis. The spiritual guide teaches us to deflect such destructive barrages and to be cautious about placing too much hope in self-knowledge, while gently bringing the soul's focus back to Beauty – to Christ.

The ultimate goal of the Church's soul healing is that the soul should become "orthodox," and on this decisive point the Beauty-first way diverges irreconcilably from both the secular truth-first mode of psychoanalysis, and the rationalism of philosophical Ethics. For the Church, the healthy human soul is characterized by three concentric states of healthy shame, which we can term shyness, boldness, and glory. The soul possessing such healthy shames will naturally and joyfully express eros for God and agape towards God's icon, the human being. Fulfilling these two loves, the soul becomes true and is saved.

The soul is never to be sacrificed, which has been the inevitable outcome of its cold analysis using the rules of the reductive kind of science. Instead, the healthy soul gives sacrifice, caught up ecstatically in the liturgy that constitutes all created being in its emergence from nothingness in the pursuit of Christ.

The healthy soul, in other words, again and again traces that moment when the world came to be ex nihilo through falling in love with the primordial Theophany of the victorious self-emptying of the Son of God. The healthy soul is, in this process of returning to Theophany, continually born again (Jn 3:3), becoming ever and again as pure as a child – "for to such as these belong the Kingdom of Heaven" (Lk 18:16).

I. ETHICS AS THERAPY

RTE: Dr. Patitsas, in our previous discussions you've sketched out several crucial and underemphasized aspects of the Orthodox soul-healing tradition. But you've also made some pointed comments about contemporary American psychotherapy, including the statement that therapy has "all but destroyed friendship in this country." Because these remarks were made in passing during our discussions of the ethics of war, trauma, or chastity, can you explain them in more detail?

Would you now move across disciplinary boundaries and describe what psychotherapy within an Orthodox ethos would look like and how this would differ from secular psychotherapy? You obviously have strong feelings about this.

Ethics: The Psychotherapy that Founded the West

DR. PATITSAS: I'm not crossing any boundaries when I critique the methods therapists or other moderns use to heal the soul. Ethics is not only the oldest psychotherapy of the West, it is the psychotherapy that *founded* the West!

When Socrates used reason to analyze morality, religion, and politics, he had one ultimate question: What makes the human soul truly healthy, truly alive, truly blessed, and truly happy?[1] For most of the 2,500 years since, the question of the soul and of its development and health was thought to be first of all the province of philosophical or theological ethicists.

In other words, Socrates not only invented the West by giving reason the pride of place in our approach to the world, but his first example of how to use rational analysis in this way was in his philosophical investigation of moral feelings and beliefs. That is why *Ethics* was felt to be the indispensable *soul-guide* for members of European civilization.

In the Christian Church these ethicists, although certainly with a different emphasis and approach than that of Socrates, were the bishops, the spiritual mothers and fathers in the monasteries, the holy lay men and women, the priests, and sometimes their wives. Although these men and women in Orthodoxy kept a Beauty-first way quite different from that of Socrates, still they shared his assumption that an unethical life brought unhappiness. They also believed that a life of holy communion with God and man, together with a virtuous spiritual path, would calm and heal and develop the soul. Further West these counselors may have at times counseled moral effort, while in the East they would have begun with Beauty, but both agreed that ethics was an important part of soul-healing.

So we ethicists (I mean, people like me who make our livings as professional academics specializing in Ethics) should consider ourselves in something of a competition with therapists. We should feel a responsibility to challenge therapists' complete domination of Americans' inner life. Ethicists should not cower behind academic borders or give up their responsibility for the soul without a fight. This is not to say that we don't have something to learn from therapists as well, but certainly we also have something to teach.

[1] Peter Kreeft, *The Modern Scholar: Ethics: A History of Moral Thought* (Recorded Books: 2003).

Orthodox Christian ethicists, in particular, should know that the old map of the soul – the one which described the three main types of soul powers as being those of desire, of defense, and of intellect – was formulated for therapeutic purposes. You can't understand human motivations or heal them properly without this knowledge of the soul's three-part structure.

As proof of this tripartite structure, I offer the fact that Freud himself ran aground on his inability to employ this old map of the soul. He saw the reliance of conscious thought on the unconscious, but when he went to map the unconscious, he couldn't decide where to locate its bottom, its final ground. He vacillated as to whether what he called the soul's "death instinct" or instead its deep sexual desires were the final ground of the soul. But Orthodoxy remembers that there are *three* "final grounds" within the human soul: the desiring (including the sexual) powers, the fighting powers (including the willingness to risk death), and the rational powers. So, at the very beginning of modern therapy, we see that Freud was bumping up against a science that was far older and much more sophisticated than he knew.

Anyway, even if some of my comments against therapy become hyperbolic, that is only because the other side is crowding the plate. I'm just brushing them back a little.

American Therapy Avoids Mentioning Man's End – The Judgment

RTE: Is the domination of inner life by secular psychology specifically an American problem? Freud, Adler, Jung, Piaget, Levin, and Pavlov were all Europeans.

DR. PATITSAS: I spend about two months a year in Europe teaching and writing. But that is not my home culture and I don't know it well. My impression, however, is that the old Christian liturgical consciousness is more alive there, even in Protestant countries. Europeans express this as, "Americans don't know how to enjoy life like we do. They are in a rush." But what Europeans mean is that the liturgical way of life is more innate there.

Now, it is true that people are taken with therapy in Europe, too, and with the therapeutic culture, but whether there are larger pockets of resistance within the culture there, I'm not sure. It is still the case in most Orthodox cultures, at least, that no sane person would consent to be the object of a "reflective listening" session. They would not allow themselves to be objectified like that.

So my impression is that the therapeutic culture has gone farther in America. They liked it in Europe, but here we just show no mercy with it.

In general, because we Americans are more of a blank slate in terms of our connection to history, and because we are more welcoming to new ideas and are always ready to solve big problems, we are in a somewhat perilous state. On the one hand, when some good idea comes along, our entire country might become an "early adopter" relative to the rest of the world. But we also sometimes lack a filter; the membrane of the national body is porous. Read Allan Bloom's 1987 *The Closing of the American Mind*, for example, for his analogy between America and Germany, on the one hand, and Sparta and Athens, on the other.[2] Like Sparta, America won the war, but German philosophical nihilism conquered the American university, in the same way that Athenian culture conquered Greece despite the Athenian military defeat. Through therapy, Bloom tells us, German nihilism then invaded the American soul.

RTE: Can we go back to your earlier point for a moment? It is certainly true that today we don't think of Ethics as a soul therapy.

DR. PATITSAS: Nor do we think of even religion as soul-therapy! It so frequently happens that faith is quickly reduced to correct dogma or to outward moral perfection without our understanding how right belief and right praxis affect the inner life. Meanwhile, what has replaced both religion and ethics as the ultimate healing for the soul?

---

2 Allan Bloom, *The Closing of the American Mind* (New York: Simon and Schuster, 1987).

The culture of therapy is now the main guidance for the soul formation and self-reflection of almost all Americans – even those who don't see a therapist. We think in its terms, we speak to our friends about their most intimate problems through its assumptions, and we even judge our religious life according to whether it leaves us fulfilled and balanced in psychotherapeutic terms. The total dominance of this new mode is shocking.

Therapy as a cultural force teaches that our primary concern should be neither sin nor death, neither the Last Judgment nor the promise of life eternal, but rather the maintenance of an inner equilibrium while we live the life that pleases us. Am I saying that we Americans should abandon therapy wholesale, when so many people have genuine issues that need expert semi-medical care? Well, the vast majority of people are not in dire states of mental illness but nevertheless look to therapy rather than to religious tradition for their soul development.

The mere fact of therapy's total, unchallenged, and unexamined victory over American inner life should give us pause.

Think about this: No matter what type of mainline Christian or Jewish faith you practice in America, at seminary your pastor, priest, or rabbi was probably taught the practice of pastoral care along lines that were broadly Freudian. That alone has to tell you that our theologians and ethicists have been asleep at the wheel: Did their prior traditions all have *nothing* unique to say about soul healing? Or, was everything that those unique traditions had to say really so effortlessly compatible with reflective listening and the paid intellectual analysis of subconscious motivations? And, do the professionally religious actually imagine that their doctrinal differences over Scripture, revelation, mysteries, and tradition really matter to anyone, when at the end of the day all 300 million of us are turning to Oprah and other talk show hosts for actual soul guidance?

One of my older brothers, an Orthodox priest, was taking a Clinical Pastoral Education course at a major city hospital, alongside experienced ministers from twenty different religions and denominations. A facilitator had them going around the circle, with each minister relating how they would typically approach a parishioner facing a terminal illness. The circle comes around to my brother, who says, "In situations where the parishioner's end is so close, I always begin by talking about the death and resurrection of Christ." Whereupon all the nineteen other ministers respond, "What? You talk about theology with your people in pastoral situations?" As we said, today American pastors from all traditions are tempted to follow the same vacuous and a-theological approach to the care of the soul.

Some people are worried that ecumenism will lead to one syncretistic and humanistic religion, but, in terms of the pastoral care offered by America's mainline religions, such an outcome is already in place, and this development had nothing to do with ecumenism.

The disruption in a genuine Christian ethos is evident from the other direction, too. Almost all of the Church Fathers were pastors. Once upon a time theology was being done mainly with a view to spiritual guidance and soul formation. Now that we theologians are being held prisoner in the universities, to what extent is that true? And if it isn't being done with the healing of the soul in mind, why would theology even matter?

Freud never really wavered between whether he believed there was a trans-rational ground to human life, or whether he would instead continue to promote the basic secular program of the Enlightenment: to reduce every human being to a utility-maximizing rational actor in a desacralized world.[3] Freud's basic ethos was individualistic, reductively analytical, and irreligious. How could any Orthodox Christian, therapist or not, adopt the methods that have descended from him without asking some rather pointed questions about a soul therapy based on such a desacralized view of the world and of the human being?

---

3 The term "utility-maximizing rational actor" is used by economists and philosophers to describe the person who seeks his own rational self-interest in order to lessen his sadness and heighten his happiness (his "utility"). The effect of the term is a view of the individual stripped of moral depth; such a person has not transcended self-love. Of course, if we were to see that our real happiness is found in the twofold anointing by the Holy Spirit discussed in our last interview, then the "maximization of utility" would require that we seek a fuller mystical life in the Church, that we seek to suffer for those whom we love. Then we would desire to be persons, not mere individuals.

And, yes, I am aware that many therapists are trying hard to leave behind ploddingly analytical models and reach the real heart of a person – although I am just as aware that many therapists *think* that is what they are doing, when they certainly aren't. They are just floating in outer space.

RTE: What about someone like Jonathan Shay, a therapist you've spoken about in such positive terms?

DR. PATITSAS: Shay proves the point: The kind of therapy that I would term "Freudian-Socratic" – because it is a primarily analytical and mind-centered approach to the heart – could not heal trauma. This is what drove Shay to remark that other cultures knew better than ours how to heal the soul. Thank God, concern for the trauma victim may someday provoke a transformation in the entire field of psychotherapy, led by certain trauma specialists themselves. These practitioners are far more frustrated than I am with the state of American therapy and for the same exact and really vexing reasons. Their assessments are far more blunt than mine.

Western psychotherapy is approaching a watershed moment wherein it will be able to choose very explicitly those rare times when it will use a truth-first, Cartesian approach, and the more frequent need to rely upon a Beauty-first, way of the heart approach. Yes, I do think that there is a limited scope for the more analytical method – provided you don't confuse it with the heart-centered way, and provided that you know which of the two is more important.

Some Orthodox Christians think that American therapy is already following the way of the heart just because it pays attention to some of our deeper, hidden motivations – but it's really not. If anything, it is having the opposite effect – tending to produce, as C.S. Lewis once said, "men without chests." It is making us less erotic, and that is a tragedy for the human person and for our civilization.

Greek vs. Semitic Soul Therapy

As I have said in our other discussions, "Ethics" is defined by ethicists themselves as "the rational investigation of moral belief or of moral feeling"; no one disputes this definition. And yet, at some point in teaching Ethics, it occurred to me that this definition is potentially disastrous, for it means that Ethics amounts to little more than "the True" investigating "the Good." But of course anyone who remembers that in Socrates there were *three* Transcendentals – the True, the Good, and the Beautiful – will demand to know what has become of the third one.

The way of Orthodoxy, the way of "right glory," is to begin by giving glory to God's Theophany (the Beautiful) and then to practice the Good glimpsed within that Theophany. Through this eros which unfolds into agape, we participate in the True, and thus we become true. Even the Ten Commandments were received within a glorious theophany, a mountaintop vision and loving encounter between God and Moses.

Outside the Orthodox Church, Ethics is done backwards, moving from the True to the Good, and it is often done only part-way, never managing or bothering to reach the Beautiful. This is all right for certain purposes, especially in a secular society where reason is the only thing we all recognize in common. But when this truth-first approach occupies all of Ethics, it renders Ethics largely powerless to move and thus heal the soul. That which does not stir the soul in dynamic movement toward its *telos* cannot heal the soul.[4]

In other words, we can see clearly the problem with Ethics today – it runs backwards, and it leaves out the Beautiful.

Well, isn't it clear that the problem with American psychotherapy is that it makes exactly the same mistake? Therapy is so completely stuck in a mind-centered approach to the human person that it, too, amounts to the True investigating the Good. Therapy heavily emphasizes the aspect of the Good that includes utility, or the usefulness to the person's emotional equilibrium of a particular set of

---

4 *Telos:* The purpose for which something is created.

beliefs about the world, but the same broad pattern applies. Therapists are analyzing your moods and dispositions for their accuracy (their truth) so that you can live life in a more satisfying (better) way.

The American therapist is trying to be Socrates, in other words: asking questions that gently lead us along to insight; acting as though all learning is actually remembering, a journey into the past or the previous self; trusting that the soul will be healed once it can process cognitively all that is really going on.[5] Socrates thought it was impossible to knowingly do wrong – whereas St. Paul saw that, "the very good that I would do, that I do not do"; in this alone you can see why therapy today cannot be the main answer for a Christian person.[6] Therapy is broken, and, I will argue, it is harming the human soul. It has not placed the Beautiful in the driver's seat but instead over-relies on Truth.[7]

---

[5] For Socrates, even geometry was to be "remembered," because he thought that the human soul prior to its bodily birth had already beheld the Forms. Just so, today some therapists even claim to bring us all the way back to the womb in the search for the causes of our problems. But remembering a prior vision of perfection *a la* Socrates is not at all like trying to remember the chaos of your deepest childhood. So, on this point Socrates actually resembles a Beauty-first practitioner, or at least allows for the potential priority of this approach.

[6] Why have we come to believe that the source of our problems – of our passions, in actuality – lies in our pasts or in our deep childhoods? Well, because our passions *are* partly rooted in the passion in which our parents conceived us. But our passions cannot be healed through *returning* and analyzing the primordial chaos *out of which* we were formed; rather, renewed vision of our *telos* (in other words, of Christ himself) will turn these pasts into the elements of a new creation.

Incidentally, Orthodox Christian legends recount that some holy saints were conceived dispassionately by their loving parents; that is, the sexual union in which the saint was conceived was entirely free of selfishness. This is not the case with the origin of every saint by any means, but this does indicate a) the importance of this marital act for our children's souls, and, b) how our fallen passions *can come* from our childhoods, all the way back to the moment of conception. So therapy is partly right in this instinct, but it applies the insight in a counterproductive way, leading us to the contemplation of chaos and not out of it towards contemplation of the Beautiful.

[7] For Plato, most of what you learn in American therapy would just be the shadows on the wall of the cave; it isn't the Forms you behold in analysis but the fallen world. A proper reading of Plato would warn us that the more accurate and true the self-knowledge that you gain in therapy, the more securely you would be trapped in the cave. A completely different kind of vision, a different set of eyes, is needed in order to bring us out of the cave. We should be cautious not to let our eyes "adjust" to the current state of soul – lest we find ourselves blinded forever....

The therapist is so smugly confident that if he can expose your lie, then you will be free. But this is naive. In actual fact, you *need* your lies until you know Christ. Stripping yourself from the entirety of your misconceptions about the world is not really possible all at once; we see how wrong it is, for example, when people try to make children grow up too fast. The answer to partial truth isn't a violent exposure to full truth; that would just spell the complete crippling of our ability to believe in any truth whatsoever. When therapy strips away your false constructs, it threatens to leave you naked – and, much worse – shameless. Therapy can't heal trauma because so often therapy itself is traumatizing.

A therapist lightly connected to Christianity might push back at my critique by quoting Scripture, "Know the truth, and the truth will make you free" (Jn 8:32). But truth is a person, not a collection of facts; in fact, truth is a person who cannot be known fully and meaningfully all in one moment of intellectual analysis. No real person can be known like that. The truth which makes us free in Scripture is a Person who appears to us first through theophany, as Beauty.

Of course, secular therapy today *does look* at non-rational factors in the human soul, and so it has certain apparent commonalities with the Beauty-first way. The matter is complex, but the essential principle is simple: To the extent that therapy returns us to the way of the heart, it is much needed. To the extent that it centralizes the way of the mind even within the realm of the heart, or to the degree that it silences healthy movements of the heart in favor of a desiccated rationalism, its impact is more than a little negative.

Yes, in some cases all the soul seems to need is clear intellectual explanations of what is happening or happened to it; to say otherwise would be to damn all of human reason – even this discussion would be pointless. But "of many books there is no end," and if there is not some door for the soul *beyond* the way of the mind, if there is not contact with the Logos who lives through crucifixion and a song that is sung in the silencing of the mind, then our soul healers are leading us to a sterile dead end. We need a true way of the heart. A book like the one you are reading at this moment is fine if it offers a glimpse of the divine life and emboldens you to pursue that life; otherwise, it is worse than useless and should be tossed aside.

Orthodox Christian soul healing, while allowing for the possible though certainly partial usefulness of this Socratic approach, concentrates its energies on a more Semitic path – a more "way of the heart" path. Our approach is Beauty-first rather than Truth-first. A wise confessor guides the mind not to analyze the heart but to a profound stillness and silence of the mind *within* the heart. In this way, the mind is humbled, and the mind and heart together behold an even deeper vision of the free, personal, and loving Triune God.

Although the vision of this Beauty will certainly lead to greater intellectual understanding of the self, it is sure also to render the vast majority of a person's possible current self-understanding obsolete, as the self is first forgotten in, and then miraculously transfigured by, the fire of divine love.

In this process, what the soul acquires above all is a love manifested in three successive, concentric waves of healthy shame, which we can call shyness, boldness, and glory. The soul ceases to resemble a mechanism that can be analyzed or coldly dissected and instead becomes a living, surprising, and free organism engaged in the worship of God, empathy for others, and ceaseless doxology. The more lively the soul, the more impotent will reductive analysis be to explain its movements.

For trauma sufferers on the way to recovery, it will be the displacement of diseased shame by the strengthening of healthy shame that will indicate the end of their sensation of excommunication and their re-entry into life-giving relationship with God and other people. Just as the only cure for bad eros is good eros, so the only lasting cure for unhealthy shame will be healthy shame.

Analysis, in contrast, threatens to rob you of your healthy, humanizing, shame. Because American therapy is an Enlightenment science, its first task will always be to desacralize the world, your soul included. It is sacredness that inspires shame, so the denizens of a non-sacred world are, of course, shameless. The idea that the world and your soul are not sacred is a lie, which if we accept will prove fatal for our salvation. Even when contemporary therapy becomes aware of this danger and explicitly tries not to do this, its very use of a truth-first method almost guarantees that this will be a part of its effect.

The Threefold Way of the Heart

Orthodox Christian soul development and healing have always been structured in a particular way: the task of the soul is to retrace consciously the steps by which creation itself first arose from non-being into existence, took on form, and became beautiful.

When we begin Christian life in baptism, we are plunged into water, returning to the watery chaos that symbolizes non-being. This indicates that the way the cosmos itself was first created out of nothing is exactly what is about to happen to us, now. Of course, there is a major difference between our baptism and the creation of the world, for in the meantime Christ has become incarnate in history. Therefore, the transformation of a Christian from "non-being" into being will be even more radical.

In this Orthodox Christian way of the heart, God acts first – I mean, his theophany does not depend on us but is his pure gift to us. As the Bible says, "This is love: not that we loved God, but that He loved us and sent his Son as a fragrant offering for our sins" (I Jn 4:10). Theophany, including the Resurrection and the Crucifixion, is the starting point.

RTE: How does this work in us?

DR. PATITSAS: Starting with theophany means falling in love with what is beautiful. Saint Porphyrios, the contemporary Greek spiritual father, expressed this by saying that we must cultivate our eros for Christ, first of all. Or, as St. Paul said, "Whatsoever things are true, whatsoever things are honest, whatsoever things are just, whatsoever things are pure, whatsoever things are lovely, whatsoever things are of good report; if there be any virtue, and if there be any praise, think on these things" (Phil 4:8). Or, showing the unavoidable necessity of the Beauty-first way more directly, "Whatever does not proceed from faith [that is, from eros] is sin" (Rom 14:23).

A simple way to begin with theophany and beauty is to read more saints lives. If the average person were looking for a way to improve the health of his soul, it would be far more valuable to devote fifteen minutes a day to a really good collection of the lives of the saints, for example, than consuming almost any amount of contemporary psychological literature. Lives of saints are theophanies; in fact, that's why we consider some people to be saints in the narrow sense of being uniquely holy – because they have followed the threefold path of eros-agape-philia, have become beautiful, and so reveal God to us clearly.

Practically speaking, theophany can mean many things, slightly different for each of us. It could mean, for example, that we don't wait until we are "ready" to go to church but trust that just by showing up, the Beauty there will begin to change our minds, enlighten our souls. Another example I always try to give is the wise saying that I once received, "If you have a good thought, you must do it at once." Inspiration is also theophany. Paying attention to God's promptings in our heart is a good way of beginning with Beauty, with theophany.

If a person still protests, "But what about me? I have no such inspirations and have seen no special visions." Well, what is this desire that you have for inspiration? That did not come from you, but rather is a gift from God! Even if you are just sad that you don't have a spiritual father, this is already evidence of a theophany! It is the beginning of God calling you forward. Now, by joining that longing, that eros, to a concrete action of any positive kind, you will be well on your way. You may feel like nothing has changed, but your journey has begun, and in fact you will be travelling forward at the speed of light!

After theophany must come the human response, which is chaste eros, which we can also call, "love's mad self-forgetting," or repentance, or asceticism, or faith, or our total self-offering to God.

These are all different words for the same thing, which is our response to God's beautiful appearing, whether we discern that appearing in the world, in the gospel, in people around us, in our lives, or in our hearts.

As eros prompts us to leave behind all that we have – including an obsessive concern with our own failings, or even with self-knowledge and self-awareness, or even with truth when its role is wrongly perceived – we learn to imitate Christ's self-emptying love for the world. That is, we amplify eros by embracing agape. We practice self-sacrificial love for others and for the whole creation. The ardent chastity of eros becomes the courageous and longsuffering almsgiving of agape.

Finally, through the consistent cultivation of eros and the steady practice of agape, we become true, we become our true selves. This is the third step of the path, which can also be stated in this way: the person who, based in a powerful eros for Christ, consistently practices *agape*, also learns *philia*; that is, they become friends with Christ. Such a person may sometimes feel God's absence, but often when they do, it is because they are so close to him that He is no longer "there" – no longer "over there," because their union with him is so total. At such moments, Christ is not absent, but rather has taken us to him on his own cross. Such an identification is part of our goal in Orthodox Christian soul healing.

An equivalent term for *philia* is "theosis," or deification. It means to become like God. However, in our contemporary gnostic culture we might mistakenly hear the term "theosis" as being the individualistic experience of spiritual perfection. True theosis means to become friends with Christ, because you have walked and are committed to walking, whatever the cost, the way which He walked, which for us means ardent eros for the Triune God and the joyful way of the Cross on behalf of all those around you. One of the most common uses of the term "theosis" among the earliest Church Fathers, for example, was to describe someone who was helping the poor, someone who was *philanthropos* like God was. Such a person was described as having achieved theosis.

This is the threefold path of Orthodox soul development, or of Orthodox soul maturity, by which the soul becomes healthy, vibrant, and comely. The path is, Beauty; then, Beauty plus Goodness; then, Beauty plus Goodness plus Truth. Or, eros; then, eros plus agape; then, eros plus agape plus philia. Or, faith; then, faith plus empathic works of hope; then, faith plus hope plus love perfected. The earlier stages are not left behind but rather are unfolded, intensified.

There is no other path, although other paths might well serve as ancillary aids, as helps, to this fundamental trajectory. A person who follows this path again and again *becomes true* more than they *"know the truth about"* themselves and their inner life. The intellectual analysis of subconscious motivations is *not yet and not precisely* the way of the heart; beyond a certain point it rapidly becomes a sterile substitute for the holy way. The way of the heart is far more self-forgetting; it is a total focus on Christ within which we discover both ourselves and the people around us.

The way of the heart means that again and again we are not knocked off course by our sins or failings, nor by the temptations that arise around us. It means that when we fall we do *not* panic and shift our primary focus to worldly pleasures, nor to moral effort, nor to self-knowledge.

No, for no matter how dark the night of our own failure becomes, no matter how flattering our own virtue seems, no matter how brightly the promise of apparent self-knowledge seems to shine, we *always* turn our focus to our first love – Christ, and him crucified – and practice small gestures of asceticism and even agape.

In American Christianity, however, the danger is that the person who is trying to be born again spiritually either will be beguiled by the truth-first way of analytical therapy *or* will interpret religion as being a goodness-first path of moral rather than ascetic effort. Even asceticism becomes grim and joyless, a moral duty, rather than the joyful joy of eros. So in critiquing what I see as therapy's truth-first emphasis, I am certainly not advising a shift to moralism. American Orthodox Christians can spend their whole lives bouncing fruitlessly between a truth-first and a goodness-first approach, finally becoming exhausted and concluding that the spiritual life is hopeless. Approached by the wrong handle, it certainly is much harder, but the Beauty-first way awaits!

A Preliminary Word on the Value of Healthy Shame

Besides all this, we must add a further twist. Because the actual way of the heart is based in our response to theophany, the feature that we in the secular world will find most odd is its insistence that soul health is inseparable from healthy shame.

Proper shame is not easily defined, but we can begin by saying that it is the glow of a worshipping and healthy human soul. Secularism, on the other hand, is the attempt to strip the world of all religious meaning and to put man in God's central place. Secularism tries to stop us from worshipping, and in order to do that it has to stop us from feeling healthy shame. Shame and secularism are mortal enemies.

When we see theophany, and especially as we develop and are able to see it more clearly, we want to praise, to worship, to be pious, to have a holy and healthy respect for God and the Church. All these responses grow out of a healthy shame. Healthy shame is quite complex. Many of us get it wrong at first, but it is our most personal energy, in a way, and therefore its development and cultivation are synonymous with our becoming our unique and true selves. Healthy shame is the *sine qua non* of a spiritually developed person! And this reverent shame is what inevitably grows through the Beauty-first approach of focusing on Theophany rather than on self-analysis or on our moral failings.

By way of contrast, the Truth-first approach to the heart tends in practice to kill healthy shame; can anyone deny that our therapized culture is also a more shameless culture? In fact, the pride of therapy seems to be its ability to erase all shame from the human heart; this is supposed to mean that you are free and that you love yourself properly and can deal with your issues without becoming overly emotional. But the effect of losing our shame is dehumanizing. Truth-first approaches have the effect of making us irreverent because they take for granted what they analyze. The secular knower is more than a god, because God at least loves and cares for what He "analyzes."

Beauty-first approaches always strengthen healthy shame. Truth-first approaches always seem to blunt healthy shame. And therefore the real goal of Orthodox Christian soul development is that the soul become... orthodox. The soul only develops through a correct and healthy response to God's pure Theophany – that is, by feeling the right kind of shame in the face of God's glory. The soul only lives and becomes pure by learning to give "right glory." When it does so, it itself becomes glorious in the right way. None of this is possible unless the soul is brought face to face with the Beautiful, with God's self-revelation – and even then the soul may need very much guidance and prayer in order to leave behind unhealthy shame and cultivate healthy shame.

The great hospital for the soul is liturgy because in liturgy we are invited to fall in love with what is most Beautiful. Meanwhile, through the mysteries of Church life, we are being strengthened to experience the proper sort of shame, which is not a burden, but the greatest freedom. "Save us, O Son of God, who did arise from the dead, *in that we sing to Thee, 'Alleluia!'*" This hymn that we sing at every Divine Liturgy is telling us that only those who doxologize, only those who react in healthy shame to God and to others and the world, will be saved. This is the way of the heart, this is Beauty-first, this is how we are saved, we remind ourselves at every Divine Liturgy. This is the "liturgical soteriology" of the Church; we are saved by God as we glorify him in faith. "Faith" is eros, and eros is most naturally expressed in *the* work of faith, the Liturgy for the life of the world.

One final general comment. As a product of the Enlightenment, American therapy often seems to take the world as a "given," and of course it also takes soul health as a "given." It therefore continuously asks after the causes of bad mental health – whether these causes be physical, or someone else's mistakes, or our misinterpretation of events. But for Orthodoxy, following the core notions of the best of biology and organic order, *health is not a given*; no, not at all. Rather, *health is a gift* which, when it comes, invites and demands our cooperation. We have to train our souls and minds to receive health and to practice it, to cultivate it. Having "issues," or being confused in your youth, is to be expected.

For Orthodoxy, the health of the soul is a challenging and complex task, a sacred mission, an adventure for the intrepid. It requires a willing spirit, perhaps a trained guide, and that we follow an effective program. Soul health is not a given whose absence proves that someone else has failed or betrayed us.

We can't really have mental rest without the eros of faith and without developing the virtues of agape. It is in using *all* our powers properly, it is in loving God and man in the right way, that we develop healthy shame and go forward.

RTE: Then to what extent is the Orthodox way an ethical way, a Semitic way, a Greek way, and so forth? What is the blend or the balance there?

DR. PATITSAS: Orthodox Christians must fight for their salvation, by gathering their concentration into an imageless prayer, that represents the mind's sabbath rest with the Savior in his life-giving tomb. They must engage the Greek mind, Roman spirit, and the Jewish heart. This total path we would call our ethic, our ethos.

II. THE TRIUMPH OF THE THERAPEUTIC

Having said, although very briefly, some of what Orthodox Christian soul development looks like, let me turn now to this imperious culture of psychotherapy which has so beguiled us here in America. If we have an insufficient idea of our own Christian tradition of soul-healing, then when we try to help our friends, we easily turn to a style of thinking adopted from therapy. Even Christian ministers are tempted to see the people in their congregations as "objects" of their pastoral care rather than as disciples of Christ.

First of all, let me state that it isn't just what goes on in a counselor's office that I have in mind when I push back against therapy but rather "therapy" as the cultural force that has largely replaced religion and ethics in guiding the inner lives of Americans. Christian scholars are still reacting to the seminal work on this tectonic shift in American spiritual consciousness, Philip Rieff's 1966 *The Triumph of the Therapeutic*.[8]

If every single therapist in America were to find Orthodox Christian Jesus tomorrow, it would scarcely make a dent in the cultural mores spawned by therapy in the past. These cultural attitudes reverberate in everything from dating practices to corporate ethics codes to the script writing of children's cartoons. So, it is mainly this therapeutic culture I am talking about, although of course I also have quite specific concerns about the actual "truth-first" approach within the therapeutic session.

A most helpful book on these points is Ross Douthat's *Bad Religion*;[9] many of us probably have the broad impression about our culture that he describes, but he states things very well. He shows that in the 1960s many intellectuals believed that "religious man" would soon give way to "political man/ideological man." Even though the 1950s, Douthat tells us, were the zenith of organized Christianity's appeal and influence in the United States, many observers came to

---

8 Philip Rieff, *The Triumph of the Therapeutic: Uses of Faith After Freud* (London: Chatto & Windus, 1966).

9 Ross Douthat, *Bad Religion: How We Became a Nation of Heretics* (New York: Free Press & Simon and Schuster, 2012).

the conclusion that people would soon wake up to the fact that religion was really about social justice and that social justice could be better handled through activism than religion. Thus, they predicted that this heyday of church involvement would give way to increased political action.

But Rieff went hard against the grain and predicted that "therapeutic man" would replace both the strong religious emphasis of the 50s and the emerging social consciousness of the 60s. Rieff was prescient, says Douthat: as traditional religious faith began to wane in America in the early 1970s, people did not then become even more politically active than they had been in the 1960s. Instead, they turned inward and looked for mechanisms (including practices and beliefs offered by Eastern religions) to adjust their souls to the new worlds of sexual and financial freedom that were developing.[10] A new "me" generation was spawned, the birth of which was midwifed by the self-regard training conducted in the therapist's office.

What Rieff meant by the "triumph of the therapeutic" was not that we would all go to therapy but that as a people we Americans would abandon categories like sin and repentance and the Last Judgment. Instead, we reinterpret our inner worlds and moral obligations such that the problems of sin and guilt are explained away without any real cost to our self-fulfillment and pleasure. Was Rieff not correct? No serious theologian can ignore this shift in the souls of contemporary people.

---

10 Some churches followed the trajectory of what seemed by the late 1950s to be the future of American faith, adjusting their preaching and practice away from judgment and dogma and toward political progressivism. Although the basements of such churches may be occupied night after night by Twelve-Step meetings, this is not, in a surprising twist, evidence of the rise of "therapeutic man." There are sharp distinctions between therapy and work in a "program" which make these two movements, in some ways, rivals or even adversaries. The "anonymous" programs (AA, CA, DA, SA, etc.) are closer to the Beauty-first way than to therapy, even though therapists are anxious to claim such programs' success as vindication of their own ethos.

Accepting Medical Help

Let me stress that in attacking therapy, I am not talking about the treatment of the mentally ill. Unless, that is, you accept Thomas Merton's prediction in the 1970s that our country "would soon become one vast lunatic asylum."

Medicine certainly is needed in its place. We are not to reject medical science but to challenge the replacement of Orthodox Christian soul healing by a quasi-science, therapy, which in controlled studies is shown to be not much more effective than friendship at alleviating emotional suffering.

Both in the Orthodox world and in the Evangelical Protestant world, the false notion that, "Christ can heal your soul and emotions; you will never need medicines or therapists," has captured a small subset of believers. In some cases, this has even led to tragic suicides and deaths when a person has a bona fide chemical or biological imbalance.

It's crazy to deny a person medicines in favor of exorcisms or home-grown or herbal remedies when a medical issue is indicated. No; we must let mental health professionals handle these cases. We must never be interpreted as denying people who need emergency hospitalization or medicine their reliance on these helps.[11]

---

[11] Incidentally, in a Hollywood culture we have no clear idea as to how to do exorcisms with a sober spirit. I offer the example of what I have learned of wise practice on this matter in Russia and Greece today.

First, most priests won't themselves make the extremely rare determination that someone is possessed; these judgments are left to those very few priest-monks who have been found to have a special charism in this area.

Second, priests rarely do exorcisms alone; rather, they do them in groups of two priests or more, or the possessed person is taken to particular monasteries where such exorcisms are done.

Third, the exorcism is not even necessarily done in the presence of the person who is sick. In this way the matter does not become an occasion for histrionics, restraints, and other problems we see in movies. In fact, in many cases, when a person is facing something insidious, it is thought better not to inform them at all that an exorcism is being said. Taken together, exorcism in a mature spiritual culture is not a dramatic matter, normally speaking.

Of course, far more common is the simple reading of prayers by a priest over a person who is not possessed but who is being harassed by some sort of darkness. This latter is a practice that could be used in many situations.

A Lengthy Aside on the Three Kinds of Science

But for most of us who aren't mentally ill, American psychotherapy feels reductive; i.e., it feels as if the therapist were reducing the vast complexity of our inner life to some simplistic explanation. It feels like an attack on our soul. Even when the therapist tries to avoid this, something of this reductionism comes through and we recoil. It isn't just that their explanation of our behavior is reductive (for it may not be), but something within the encounter can make me feel that my soul is the cadaver and the therapist is the forensic pathologist.

RTE: Is reductionism in science always bad? Can't it just be a simpler approach that allows you to deal with one topic at a time?

DR. PATITSAS: Reductionism has its place; but in dealing with living systems, it is not usually the primary place.

Reductionism is just one of the three main ways of doing science. In fact, I would like to make some very general remarks about the way reductionism can either harm or help our understanding of the world, depending on the situation.

The reason I would like to go off on this tangent is simple: people today often find therapy helpful but only to a certain point. The answer is simple to explain, and I don't want to linger on it for long. It is that there are three kinds of science, reductionism being one of them, and they all have their place. Reductive methods can be useful when they are enfolded into a larger program.

RTE: Then why critique therapy as energetically as you have?

DR. PATITSAS: Because when reductive methods run amok and become the main approach to a living system, they might easily kill what they analyze. This is what happened to our cities, it has happened to our farming communities in America, and it often seems to be happening to our souls. I am not trying to eliminate a formal approach to healing the soul but to retool it along the lines of a more sophisticated, non-reductive kind of science: organic complexity.

It will be better if I simply go on and explain what the three kinds of science are.[12] Then it will make sense that I can be both alarmed at what therapy is doing to us and yet still look upon it with appreciation, and even fondness, in certain cases. But in brief, it has a limited place, and it needs to be very firmly put back in that place or it becomes destructive.

I promise that we will come back to the Orthodox Christian approach to healing the soul and that I will say more about why I distrust therapy. But we need to press the pause button and look at the history of science itself, for just a moment.

A Bit of Science History

Freud himself was trained as a neurologist in the nineteenth century. Thus, he was schooled principally in what we would now call "problems in simplicity," the reductive two-variable approach to science. You are looking in this kind of science for a single cause of a specific effect, in other words. For example, when you change the weight of an object, does that or does that not impact the speed at which this object falls from a given height?

In Freud's day, reductionism was equivalent to science itself because the other two kinds of science hadn't been discovered yet. If you couldn't show the one final ground to which something was reducible, then you hadn't really explained anything about the subject you were studying, went the logic.

Once again, during Freud's formative intellectual years reductionism – the explanation of one factor solely through the behavior of another factor – *was* science, since neither complex statistical

---

12 Jane Jacobs presents the three main classes of scientific order in "The Kind of Problem a City Is," in *The Death and Life of Great American Cities* (New York: Random House, 1961), 428-48. She, in turn, borrows her account from Warren Weaver, "A Quarter Century in the Natural Sciences," in *The President's Review, including A Quarter Century in the Natural Sciences by Warren Weaver, from the Rockefeller Foundation Annual Report, 1958* (New York: The Rockefeller Foundation, 1958), 7-15. Although to me it seems that Weaver's schema is *the* indispensable touchstone for understanding the after-history of the Enlightenment, I am aware of only one other writer who seems to see its pivotal significance – Steven Johnson, author of *Emergence: The Connected Lives of Ants, Brains, Cities, and Software* (New York: Scribner, 2001).

analysis nor a developed biology had as yet been discovered. Science was just "increase the mass, and the speed at which the object falls does or does not increase" – two variables were in play; that was all science could handle.

Science has moved well beyond this simplicity in the last 115 years. Although, in fact, it turns out to be *incredibly* difficult to go beyond two variables using rational analysis. And so from the years 1600 to 1900 science couldn't do much more than that, despite laying the groundwork for more complexity through the development of calculus, for example.[13]

Every child from elementary school will someday learn about the main three different *kinds* of scientific problem that modern science is capable of handling. Nowadays, they aren't clearly distinguished even in most universities. But knowing what all three kinds of science are is one of the most important aids to understanding the clash between the old Beauty-first liturgical way and the new truth-first modern way.

To put it simply: science first learned to handle two-variable problems. Then, starting in the twentieth century, science discovered how to handle billions of variables using statistical analysis. Finally, about ninety years ago science finally began to see how to look at organic problems, where there are a middle range of variables, and where, far more importantly, the "whole is greater than the sum of its parts," as in a living system.[14]

---

13 There is something called the "three-body problem" which arises when you try to use classical Newtonian physics to predict the precise orbits of three celestial bodies. With just one planet and one sun, you can do it with full precision. But it turns out that the moment you add even one extra object, the orbits become "non-repeating" – which is a calm way of saying that the orbits are literally *impossible* to predict. Imagine that! Reductive science and mathematics can't predict with absolute precision the motion of the moon around the earth under the influence of the sun, but this same science aspires to explain individual human behavior in exhaustive detail.

14 With "problems in simplicity" style science, we invented the telephone, the radio, the automobile, the airplane, and the diesel engine, for example. With "problems in disorganized complexity" style science, we can plan a telephone exchange or stabilize a life insurance company. With "organized complexity" science, real advances in medicine become possible because an organic system is determined by metabolic processes that unfold in time; such systems exhibit feedback in a way that non-living systems do not. Cf. Jacobs, *Death and Life, op. cit.*, 428-32.

For each of these kinds of problems, science has to rely on different tactics of analysis. All three types of science have their place, but if you choose the wrong kind of science for the problem you are studying, then the smarter you sound, the more wrong you will be.

But again, we do need all three kinds of science. And once we see that we do, then even reductionism is rescued from its bad reputation, since there are uses for which it is clearly the best approach. And with that, let me get back to Freud, for whom only reductionist methods were available and who lived at a time when such methods were thought to be most or even all of science itself.

Freud kept vacillating as to whether it was the drive for sex or the drive for conflict and death that was the single and ultimate ground of the soul's motivation. In other words, he waffled between the desiring powers and the fighting powers as being the final ground to which all else in the soul should be reduced. But the soul doesn't have *one* final ground, unless that be its archetype, Christ. Within itself the soul has three poles, three starting points – the desiring powers, the fighting powers, and the intellectual powers. We call this the tripartite soul. Every Orthodox Christian knows that, or used to.

Reductive Explanations for Living Organisms

RTE: What good, then, did Freud accomplish?

DR. PATITSAS: On the good side, he was one of a constellation of nineteenth-century thinkers who upset the applecart of the primary Latin mistake, the privileging of the intellect – a mistake that the Enlightenment was designed to expand and make permanent *until* it ran into people like Freud, Marx, Darwin, etc.

We mentioned in our earlier interviews how the emphasis in the West on intellectual rather than sensual sins had led already by the fifth century to confusion about what a monk was supposed to be doing at prayer, for example.[15] The theologian could easily become detached from the ascetic life and the way of the heart, or the spiritual life itself could be seen as primarily an intellectual task.

In Freud's case, he helped upend the hyper-rationalist order that had produced him, by insisting that non-rational motivations outside the conscious mind heavily determine human thinking. As I emphasized in our first interview, he represents the return of something like the Semitic heart to a too-Greek and too-Roman Western Europe.[16] So far, so good, an Orthodox Christian might react; this is why so many Orthodox are drawn to the therapeutic mindset that derives from Freud.[17]

But then Freud undoes his own insight by imagining that the subconscious can be rationalized through intellectual analysis and a kind of Cartesian mapping. Well, it can't be; the soul is too intractable for that. And, moreover, it isn't just any kind of rational analysis of the soul that he conducts but this very primitive two-variable analysis that we mentioned above.

---

15 See the first two chapters for the early disagreement as to whether sensual sins or intellectual sins were the first line of defense for the soul. If the sensual sins are the origins of spiritual danger, then the use of the imagination in prayer must be extremely restricted, for the nous (the mind in the heart) should focus entirely on God in imageless prayer. If, on the other hand, the intellectual sins are the primary danger, as the West believed, then such mental pictures might be encouraged as long as they are done for religious or humble reasons, and monasticism steadily becomes more akin to the philosophical and intellectual life than to the ascetic life. Religious life is then centered in the mind outside of the heart, and even when exceptionally pious sentiments and ideas follow, they will strike an Orthodox Christian as somehow dangerously off-track – although he or she may not be able to say why.

16 In Chapters One and Two we argued that the Latin West lost one leg of the Orthodox Christian triad of the classical Greek mind, the Semitic heart, and the classical Roman body; specifically, it steadily lost a feel for the way of the heart from the very moment it concluded that the intellectual sins were the primary line of defense for the soul. Therefore, Freud is both good, because in him the heart returns under the guise of the "unconscious," and bad, because this heart is then invaded, colonized, and denuded of life through Greek analytical therapy and Roman social conformity. We need all three cultural styles, but we need them in the right sequence and balance.

17 Orthodoxy is the most Semitic of the major Christian faiths, so the affinities between Orthodox Christianity and Judaism are strong and sometimes surprising. For example, a believing Jew will often know two essential elements of Christian dogma that some Western Christians seem not to: that God's glory (the shekinah) is uncreated; and that God's Spirit has at least a quasi-personal status.

Freud's explanations are reductive, that is to say, and this is why therapy seems at once so powerfully persuasive and so shockingly wrong; it's quite confusing. But in fact *any* time a reductive science tries to explain living order you get that combination of powerful persuasiveness and shocking wrongness. Reductive analysis can only capture all of a living system if it first succeeds in killing the organism it seeks to explain, thus rendering it inert, inorganic, dead – but, hey, at least now it can be mapped!

To see a larger-scale example of how two-variable reductive analysis tends to mangle living organisms, consider that this is exactly how we almost killed our cities in America between 1949 and 1974. We applied a reductive style of urban planning in massive acts of city demolition and rebuilding, even though a city is a living organism. The result was vast suffering and bitter sorrow. And that is the danger of therapy: In applying cognitive analysis to the soul, it risks turning your living, breathing, complex heart into "the projects": dysfunctional, surly, and hopeless – but simple and linear, too (perhaps with a small patch of green grass for show), and in theory fully understood and clear.

American therapy always wavers between these two emphases – its Semitic side, whereby it represents the liberating return of the way of the heart to our modern world, a huge breath of fresh air and sanity, on the one hand; and its anti-Semitic Enlightenment Greek and Roman side, on the other, in which our therapists are essentially the Roman army occupying and oppressing first-century Palestine, while maybe constructing a few Greek amphitheatres and passing some good laws along the way. American therapy is trapped in this ambivalence between its Semitic and anti-Semitic tendencies.

RTE: So, how would an "organic" psychotherapy differ from the one we use?

DR. PATITSAS: Oh, that's simple. Now, we have a therapy that is asking what the soul is made of; in other words, it is trying to discover the causes of why you think and feel the way you do. Therapists conceive of the soul as a mechanism, a machine, that can be taken apart, checked out, corrected, and re-assembled.

That won't work for the soul because the soul is alive. Instead, you've got to ask, "What does a soul do? What inner processes are intrinsic to a soul fulfilling its natural function? If the soul seems not to be doing those things, how can we jump-start it, or re-catalyze it, so that it does?"

What a soul does, of course, is get caught up in eros for God and agape for our fellow man. And it is usually bootless to look for the reasons why it isn't caught up in eros and agape because to actually do those things takes a saint. They are really hard to do consistently. It's not someone's fault, per se, when they don't happen. It's just par for the course in a fallen world, and we have to find the motivation and the techniques that will get us back on track.

Poverty Has No Causes

We see a similar absurdity in our Cartesian and thus reductive economic science, by the way. It is always looking for "causes of poverty" (the "bad childhood" of an economy, to create an analogy relevant to this chapter!), instead of realizing that an organic system like an economy can neither be taken apart like a machine, nor planned, controlled, commanded, and finely mapped. A living system must rather be pruned and cultivated to grow in new and better directions. It's the processes which generate wealth, whether in a nation or in a soul, that should be scientists' first concern, not the "causes" of poverty.

It was my mentor Jane Jacobs who wrote, "Poverty has no causes; wealth has causes. Poverty is just evidence of the lack of the causes of wealth."[18] She was an economist, but this principle is true spiritually as well.

---

18 Jane Jacobs, *The Economy of Cities* (New York: Vintage Books Edition, 1970), 120-21.

In fact, Jane Jacobs' insight about material poverty is a modern rediscovery of the Orthodox Christian (and Neoplatonic) idea that evil is *meontic* (from the Greek words for "non-being"). Evil is lack, it is just the failure to love, since loving was, as the Beauty-first way teaches, what made us consent to God's creating us. It is being loved and loving that made us come to be. Poverty and evil, by contrast, are the failure to exist fully and properly; they are parasitical. They have no causes, per se.

The situation that describes material poverty, or that describes evil in the world, also should govern our thinking about lacks in our emotional equilibrium. In my own soul it is obvious that, yes, negative elements in my past did influence my character. The other cause is that I have never bothered to cultivate enough eros towards God the Father to become a full adult – something Jesus managed to do by the age of twelve, by the way, despite growing up in a destabilizing environment of foreign occupation and terrorism.

Speaking for myself, I can say that the processes and patterns and routines that I have cultivated most in my own life are not religious ones but inner habits of self-pity and self-justification regarding challenges left by my past. And my time in therapy was not even designed to train me in the good patterns, which are Beauty's presence in our lives, but to help me understand the bad patterns and the sources of poverty in my past. Therapy often strengthened the hold of those forces over me by turning my attention in the wrong direction.

Let us jump back to another pole of our analogy, material poverty. Although we've said that poverty has no causes, to be completely fair, there are three ways in which we can think about the sources of economic poverty. I'd like to say that poverty has three "causes" *which, though contradicting each other, are nevertheless all true*: 1) injustice, such as when members of a religious, ethnic, or racial group are denied basic economic or legal rights and thus cannot get ahead financially; 2) "acts of God," such as hurricanes or epidemics or wars; and, 3) . . . no cause whatsoever – poverty is just the absence of wealth-generating processes. This final "cause" was Jane

Jacobs' main emphasis, although she took seriously the influence of the other two, as well. This third point is the most crucial one, and the starting point of the Beauty-first way.

Almost always, elements of all three causes of material poverty are present; almost always, we focus on only one or at most two of these causes when we confront material poverty (or sin), and this imbalance partly negates the efforts that we do make to heal poverty. It is hard to balance all three ideas in our heads at once, since their being, a) contradictory, yet b) all true, requires a transrational grasp of life (i.e., wisdom), not the reductively analytical narrow-mindedness which decades of sitting in regimented classrooms – and, sorry to say, church pews – tends to inculcate. A liturgical worship can help to break us out of some of that reductive absurdity (despite the fact that today, some liturgical scholars are offended by this very character of Orthodox liturgy, which to their linear analysis seems merely messy or chaotic).

And, again, almost always, it is the third thing, the fact that poverty has no causes, to which we must give the first and greatest attention.

Let us jump back to the subject of our emotional poverties. Those who are most wounded psychologically must be especially protected and have it made safe for them to again pursue Beauty-first. They especially must be permitted to ignore certain causes, instead revitalizing the processes that will generate spiritual and emotional wealth and dynamic equilibrium in their souls. The other two causes of emotional poverty, injustice and bad luck, must take a second place in our consideration if we are ever to become well.

Did our families hurt us? Perhaps. But the other contradictory and yet still true take on our childhood may be this: even while all that was going on, or at least when we got a bit older, God was very near to us, but perhaps we did not know how to approach him. This is the other side of our spiritual poverty. I can say for myself, at least, that in the crises of childhood, I did not have the capacity or usually even the thought to turn to God.[19]

Of course you could ask, "Are you even blaming the victim of childhood sexual abuse?" But Christ himself answers this question. He says that the angel of this little one who is being abused is always before the face of His Heavenly Father, pleading for them, and that it would be better if their abuser had had a millstone tied around their neck and been thrown in the sea than do what they did. But for the rest of us, and even for those of us who did suffer such things but have begun to regain our health, we will want to look to what generates spiritual health, not at these incidents and their effects, most of the time.

Sometimes reductive approaches can be ok, but only when they are incorporated into the erotic drive for God. That must remain primary. By way of analogy, we can see that when reductive and statistical approaches became primary in the war against material poverty, this resulted in hurting the poor, in the "sack" and destruction of our cities (as Jacobs said), in greater racial tension, and in the destruction of poor families. Let us not rely on statistical and reductive approaches to the poverty of the soul if we do not wish to foster spiritual disaster.

Good Secrets

RTE: How should a spiritual father use this understanding?

DR. PATITSAS: The soul healer (perhaps a "spiritual father") is to be a safe harbor for the wounded soul, not a cold forensic pathologist

---

[19] The sting of death is sin, and even before we are adults, we might almost kill to avoid death. Saint George Karslidis of Drama, Greece (reposed 1959) was nearly starved to death by his caretakers in childhood. Soon after the moment that his little sister did indeed die, at the age of three, from this same episode of maltreatment, her grave was bathed in uncreated light. Having in some hidden way conquered the fear of death and forgiven her tormentors, this little girl apparently became very close to God. Moreover, her relics when later exhumed showed additional signs that she had been spiritually perfected. See Herman Middleton, *Precious Vessels of the Holy Spirit: The Lives and Counsels of Contemporary Elders of Greece* (Thessalonica, Greece: Protecting Veil Press, 2003), 177-87.

dissecting every single one of our motivations and past experiences. Confident through experience in the healing power of the sacraments, he takes an attitude of "unknowing" towards our pasts, and he invisibly imparts to us the ability to adopt a similar attitude. With time, the very brain chemistry of the victim is calmed. The past is not erased, but it does become *the past*, something that is neither happening now nor controlling us now. We become, eventually, regular old sinners like everyone else, more or less, and can repent of those things for which we are responsible.

RTE: And what is your own relationship to therapy?

DR PATITSAS: As for my own relationship to therapy, I can say that when I was younger I thrilled to it. After all, it is someone talking about the person in a deeper way than just ordinary conversation. Later on, I realized that there was something missing in it and that many of its hidden assumptions (hidden even to therapists) are quite damaging.

Today, however, some of my trusted friends are therapists – but they are also intense Orthodox Christians, so that their blend of Freud and the ancient Church carries them past the faults that I am describing here. But I am much more careful now. I know now that even in its innocent uses, the secular therapeutic approach can make the soul more dull, less alive.

But in fact I go to such friends precisely because, as therapists, they are interested in the soul, in the deeper motivations that are at work in my students and myself and in themselves. Many times they are the ones who are looking out for the way in which some problem we face externally is almost entirely caused by our own internal disposition towards it. Thus, they remind me of the centrality of Beauty-first, that I must empty my mind and heart of false motivations by first falling in love more thoroughly with Christ.

Until we become full-on Orthodox Christian Romans (I am referring here to the Byzantines, who saw themselves as Romans, and who combined the three cultures of their world), we will often be forced to rely on our current weak and ambiguous American therapy, in order to correct our natural Enlightenment tendency to be so mind-centered. But this in many cases is a devil's bargain, and we should instead make more progress in our understanding of the Orthodox way to heal the soul.

Anyway, two things I don't do: I don't go to confession with anyone who *really wants* to hear my confession, especially if they are a monk at a monastery to which I am making pilgrimage. Bad problems will result. And I don't share my very deepest motivations with therapists; there has to be something hidden between me and God that only one other person – my confessor, if I actually happen to have a good one, a non-analytical one – will know. But in that case, this old-school confessor will himself be the one insisting that my secrets not be discussed or mentioned unduly, nor before their time.

Our inner worlds – we must exercise caution about how and with whom we share them. Some secrets hurt us, but other secrets make us stronger. Good secrets are, in fact, an indispensable marker of our human dignity and even of our basic identity as humans. The Book of Revelation says that in Heaven each of us will be given such an essential secret – a new name that for all eternity will be known only to us and to God (Rev 2:17).

Oprah and our modern therapists will just *die* in heaven, wanting to know what everyone else's secret name is!

Ultimately, American psychotherapy is a product of the Enlightenment and thus is bound up with so many false presuppositions about the world – that the world and the soul can be explained through a strictly materialistic account; that rational self-interest should be the guiding principle of human behavior; that the center of the person is the intellect; that shame is almost always unhealthy; and so on.

The reality is quite different: the world is sacred; the center of a man is his heart and not his mind; the heart is far deeper than our feelings and emotions; in a real sense emotional and spiritual poverty have *no* causes; and, in a way, the *only* purpose of soul guidance is to arouse eros and teach us a cult, i.e., a program of self-offering.

The fact is, one individual person is not a person. Therefore, *only* a rich relational life – not an obsessively self-analytical one – will make us fully human. Furthermore, self-sacrifice is so important for our soul's well-being that we can even say that we are meant to be priests, nothing more and nothing less. And finally, as persons and as a society we are meant to glorify God and to become beautiful.

III. SHAME

RTE: What does this mean practically for the trauma sufferer? What role does the healthy shame you mention above have in the healing of a combat veteran?

DR. PATITSAS: If we can understand how shame goes awry during a traumatic experience – and, man, does it ever – and if we can also see what the Church does to help us recover healthy shame, then we are at the beginning of our answer.

The Church is a hospital that will provide you with uncreated grace. By ushering in the mild advent of a consoling and healthy shame, this grace will slowly displace the unhealthy shame that is the brutal echo of your trauma. And the Church won't re-traumatize you in the process, imagining that it would be wonderful and more efficient to get in there and rip out all your unhealthy shame in one go. We simply need to cooperate as gently as possible with the advent of this healthy shame. If healing starts to come too quickly, we may need to slow things down. We want an organic and lasting transformation, not a fix.

But all of this takes a miracle – it may even take the miracle of finding a true soul healer in the Beauty-first way. The Church is a place of miracles, not systems.

But let us begin with the work of Jonathan Shay, whom we discussed in our first two interviews for his work with traumatized veterans of war. By beginning with him, we can put the Orthodox mystical approach into language appropriate to our culture.

Achilles and Priesthood

Shay asks a question: when Achilles "lost it" and went berserk, what precisely did he lose?[20] His humanity, his character, yes. But what does that mean? What is lost when a person loses his humanity?

I don't think that Shay can answer this question as well as the Church can. In our earlier interviews we saw that war is a kind of anti-liturgy because of the way it employs all five human senses in the cutting of life-giving communion with God and with our fellow man. We also heard Shay say that it is specifically as a berserker that Achilles stands at war's bottom point.

Combine the insight that war is a kind of anti-liturgy and that the berserker is its negative apex, and it becomes clear what Achilles has lost: he has lost his priesthood – he has in fact become an anti-priest at the center of an anti-liturgy. What Achilles could no longer do was to make a sacrifice of himself to God for the life of his fellow man and for the world.

Before the chain of events that destroyed his character occurred, Shay says, Achilles was exactly capable of making such godly sacrifices of himself for others, even in the midst of war. In fact, Homer tells us that Achilles excelled all other soldiers in this regard.

Priesthood is the core quality that we lose when we lose our humanity. The reality that war is not *entirely* evil (or is not perfectly impervious to the exercise of virtue within its evil), we can see from the fact that when we honor soldiers, we do so because of their priesthood. No one in Arlington National Cemetery ever killed for their country; no, they all "gave their lives for their country."

And not only for our country but to liberate the captive oppressed in Europe, Asia, or the Middle East. We think our soldiers more noble than those of other nations because we believe that our warriors exercise this double priesthood on behalf of both their own and foreign peoples. Don't think I'm being ironic or cynical;

---

20 Jonathan Shay, *Achilles in Vietnam: Combat Trauma and the Undoing of Character* (New York: Atheneum, 1994), 77-90.

I think that this is the motivation which usually drives Americans to enlist in the military, especially in its more dangerous specialties.[21]

What if, however, once in combat the soldier concludes that this priestly drive is not motivating those who have sent him to war? Things can become quite confused in his soul; Shay calls unjust actions by wartime leaders, at any level in the chain of command, a violation of *themis*, of "what's right."[22] Shay says this violation of *themis* is the first step toward serious combat trauma among the soldiers under their command. Of course, as we said in Chapter One, for many soldiers, the reality of killing will be enough to convince them that they are caught up in the violation of *themis*.

Risking Spiritual Injury for Our Sakes

Something else is coming to be understood in the treatment of war trauma, although it isn't expressed in the terms I will use here. And I think it is a great insight and really something crucial. We are remembering now that one element of a soldier's priesthood is a paradox – the wound of post-traumatic stress disorder comes through a wounding of his priesthood, yes, but because of the way this wound was received, it's also the *proof* of priesthood. It's one more way that you've accepted to suffer on my behalf, American Soldier, and I thank you and promise to stop wasting so much of

---

[21] I was visiting my Dutch cousins in Holland in 2012, exercising the typical "non-ugly American" apology for our interventionist foreign policy, but they stopped me right away. "Wait a second," they said, "If you weren't the sort of people who enjoyed sacrificing for others' liberty, we in Holland wouldn't be free right now. You are the only ones who are willing to protect the little countries, and we are extremely grateful for that. We really admire you." So we are seen differently, in different parts of the world. Right now, in parts of the former Yugoslavia, in parts of Ukraine, and in much of the Middle East, we are seen in quite a different light, as troublemakers fomenting conflicts that kill thousands and drive millions of people into exile, in order to keep our enemies off balance. But even if this is partly the case (and I would guess that it is the case, but only partly), it's certainly not our soldiers who would be to blame but our statesmen. And in other places or at other times, our statesmen, too, have operated with more clearly altruistic motives. Enough of politics, though, for the moment.

[22] In a democracy, all citizens fall somewhere within this chain of command. Our seeming obliviousness to our soldiers' sacrifice is a violation of *themis* by us in our role as "wartime leaders," a violation which American soldiers have reported to be one element in their feeling of betrayal and subsequent trauma.

the life that you won for me. At any rate, PTSD is not a shameful condition but an honorable one, in this paradoxical way.[23]

I don't remember whether Shay says this, but soldiers who call the berserker "the best," as he tells us, are probably in part saying this very thing: some soldiers will sense that the berserker is "fighting hurt," and fighting very hard while (psychologically) *very very* hurt. And, guess what, this does indeed make him "the best," even if it also means that the berserker will need to be removed from battle before he harms himself or his own comrades.

And this paradox is true of every trauma sufferer, that their humanity was wounded precisely through that part of them that was most humane. We are a noble race, we humans, and we can find the meaning and purification of that nobility in Christ.

Humanity Is Made in the Image of the High Priest

Anyway, despite the paradox of how trauma both demonstrates and denies the priestly identity of a trauma sufferer, it turns out that the losing of one's priesthood is equivalent to the loss of one's humanity; priesthood is an essential element of humanity. We aren't just created "in the image of God," no; we are created in the image of Him who is the express image of the Father – I mean, in the image of Christ. Moreover, we are made in the image of Christ resurrected, but also crucified. Christ is a priest, He is *the* priest, He is the one whose whole mode of being in the world is to offer himself and the world to God the Father in the Holy Spirit upon the cross, for the life of that very world.

Do that too, however partially or humbly, and you have regained your humanity, also. You are a priest, and therefore have come more closely to the likeness of Christ.

---

23 In June 2015 I had the honor of speaking on Shay's and Grossman's views on war at the Aristotle University of Thessaloniki, Greece. This was an unforgettable experience because the *Iliad* is taken very personally in Greece. For many people there, the interpretation of that text is crucial for their own personal identity. There was a strong and articulate minority of perhaps five percent of the hearers for whom Achilles' berserking actions were seen as being deliberate. For them, the rage of a berserker is directed so squarely against war itself in the service of his comrades that it remains a noble and heroic act.

Any of us, if we have a poor character or are stuck in some emotional *cul de sac*, are limited in the exact same way, i.e., in our ability to make a pure and non-destructive offering of ourselves to God on behalf of others. Are we limited to the extreme extent that Achilles was? Probably not. But to *some* extent we are so limited – and this is why we must overcome. Your childhood issues and all that do matter, especially to the extent that either you can or can't fulfill your priestly identity to love God and others self-sacrificially.

Healthy Shame vs. the Passion of Shame

Or, we could put the matter in terms that are even more jarring to our contemporary desacralized ethos: the reason Achilles lost his humanity was that he lost his shame. At his worst, he became utterly bold and shameless towards his enemy, before his own comrades in arms, and before the gods. It is shamelessness that describes the berserk state, and this shows us three things.[24]

First, it tells us that close to the essence of our humanity is our sense of shame. We have to be careful how we define shame, but the point remains that to lose all healthy shame, is to risk losing one's soul. Second, it reminds us that man's destiny is a liturgical one, for liturgy is the proper expression of healthy shame. And third, the identity between berserk and shameless shows us that to be healed in our soul (especially of trauma, but also more generally) is to recover the proper kind and expression of shame. It is to become "orthodox," in other words – to give glory and see glory and feel glory in the right way. You can't be a priest if you have no shame.

Why is shame so necessary for a specifically human identity? Well, we can see that a person with no shame has no antennae by which they can relate to other human beings or to God. They are just a wrecking ball. They have no receptors by which they can receive the relating being conveyed by God and by their fellow man. They are blind and deaf. Thus, they are utterly excommunicated

---

[24] In *Achilles in Vietnam*, Shay tells us that in the berserk state what is lost is "all restraint"; see page 86. The berserker loses his mercy and his regard for all others.

even when surrounded by those who love them; they have "left the city." They become, as Aristotle said of those who live outside the city, either beasts or gods. They are not acting from their identity as humans.

RTE: Then, what would shame look like in the life of a holy person, since we think of saints as being more fully human than non-saints?

DR. PATITSAS: What distinguishes a holy person is the precise quality of their shame. They are dignified where they should be, humble where they should be, and reverent in just the right ways and at the right times, to put it in terms that Socrates or Aristotle might recognize. Or, we could say that their shame is much stronger than ours, and utterly transfigured, since its source is in the direct vision of Christ in his self-emptying love.

Healthy shame limits but does not oppress. Indeed, it liberates you by freeing you of neurotic or psychotic extremes, and it liberates your neighbor because they are no longer under attack by the passivity or aggression emanating from your unhealthy shame.

American therapy, of course, sees itself in similar terms, as a way to free us from unhealthy shame. But what is therapy replacing unhealthy shame with? How does it define healthy shame? This is the core question for the health of the soul.

Is American therapy really in possession of an Orthodox understanding of healthy shame? "Right shame" in Orthodoxy is so complex, so deep, and such a rich phenomenon that it is hardly likely that therapy has captured its insights. Only the uncreated grace in the sacraments of the Church can create such a beautiful state.

RTE: Doesn't therapy try to replace unhealthy shame with self-esteem?

DR. PATITSAS: Right, it may not even think there is such a thing as healthy shame. At any rate, it is so busy promoting self-regard and, ultimately, self-love, that it can't possibly also teach us to look to the source of healthy shame outside ourselves.

To replace the wrong kind of shame in us with the pure quality of shame, soul therapy must bring us face to face both with God *and* with other human beings who've seen what we've seen and yet have done better than us – that would be, in one person, Jesus Christ. Or, if you like, God and the saints.

Such healthy shame cannot be ideologically or analytically constructed any more than you could build a real city out of static parts, while denying the underlying organic processes that generate actual city order. Healthy shame is a fruit of deep organic processes; it is the glory upon the face of Moses when he descends from Mt. Sinai. And we must also see Christ crucified, or else we will never overcome our false ideas about what is and isn't shameful. Without seeing "the King of Glory" hanging from the cross, a person will never be able to understand those times when accepting to be shamed by others is a necessary part of receiving God's glory.

Healthy shame is the power within awe, reverence, and wonder. It is the engine that drives both worship and repentance, and it is the power that makes us philanthropic, human, sane. It drives us to love what is better than us, to hate what is unworthy of us, and to care for all human beings irrespective of class, gender, race, religion, nation, or the level of their sexual sin, since shame reminds us we are in no position to look down upon anyone. Healthy shame is encapsulated in the beautifully untranslatable Greek word *philotimo*, which describes a disposition that, a) could not bear the shame of doing even the tiniest thing wrong towards God or others, and b) would be ashamed to count the cost of doing good.

Shame, I think, is the broader name for the energy of the soul that senses our proper limits in our relationships with God and man in order to connect us with our neighbor; "proper," meaning neither overdone nor underdone.[24] Shame is an energy at once of connection and of privacy, of openness and concealedness, of closeness and of distance. Healthy shame combines the freedom of the child before an understanding and loving parent, with a virtual

---

[24] I have been asked how shame is related to the conscience. Healthy shame characterizes the healthy conscience; i.e., shame is an attribute of the conscience.

unthinkability in regards to committing sin. Shame is to our human nature what the divine energies are to the divine essence. Or, rather, healthy shame gives a grace-filled character, even an uncreated quality, to all of our human energies. With it, a person can be "naked and yet not ashamed," as we were in the garden – but let me return to this paradox later.

RTE: Then, does the experience of healthy shame also play out in communities and nations?

DR. PATITSAS: Think how much the struggle for international human rights rests on the humanizing power of shame. All we have to do is point out to the world that such and such country jails its poets and writers or permits human trafficking or practices female feticide, and the shame is often enough to provoke repentance – or at least more caution in their future evil acts. And it's also why attempting to shame Russia for jailing the women who desecrated a church got nowhere: the shamefulness of the women's act was too obvious to Russians for it to be possible to make the average Russian feel ashamed to punish it. But when President Reagan termed the U.S.S.R. an "evil empire," that bold pronouncement stung the Soviet leadership deeply, we are told, and provoked a degree of moral crisis that helped lead to the end of that empire.

To repeat, the identity between berserk and shameless shows us how close shame is to being the essence of our humanity. Sensing an identity between berserk and shameless tells us a second thing: It reminds us that man's destiny is a liturgical one, for liturgy is the proper expression of healthy shame. Heaven itself is a city, the New Jerusalem, where nothing but liturgy goes on, night and day, forever. And people are happy there. In contrast, the berserker is an anti-priest conducting an anti-liturgy.

And, the identity between berserk and shameless shows us, thirdly, that to be healed in our soul is to recover the proper kind and expression of shame. It is to become "orthodox," in other words; not as a confessional label, but as the best description of the healthy soul. Such a soul is what we want to have.

RTE: How then does unhealthy shame impact liturgy?

DR. PATITSAS: Look at how terrible shame's complete absence became in the case of Achilles. The loss of all shame makes our priesthood, our humanity, impossible. This shows us that shame itself is not the problem but *distortions* of shame. The issue is not to eliminate shame but to drive out false shame through the growing power of healthy shame.

During his berserk state, Achilles insults the gods while also making blasphemous sacrificial offerings. Achilles is then literally acting as a priest because he kills dozens of his captives as a terrible human sacrifice to honor the dead Patroclus. However, this liturgy is an offense to gods and men; i.e., it is not "orthodox," not an example of "right worship." Rather, standing at the negative apogee of the anti-liturgy of war, Achilles comes near to the negation of human priesthood.

Orthodox Christian psychotherapy, both for the average person and for the saint, must be built (has of course always been built) around this particular human energy: shame. This shame is expressed and cultivated through an ever-deepening and ever more natural expression of reverence. And that is why it is centered in the divine services and not in a doctor's office.

We all have healthy shame and unhealthy shame; unhealthy shame we Orthodox could term the "passion" of shame, if we wish. The goal of therapy should be to cure this power in the soul – to make us ashamed where we ought to be but aren't; to make us free of shame where we are ashamed but shouldn't be; to make us exactly as ashamed as we ought to be, no more and no less, in all areas.

Shame, priesthood, our humanity – they are inextricably bound together. Our shame will have to be purified, cured, and healed if our humanity is to be healed.

Three Phases of the Shame that Saves

RTE: That is beautifully clear, yet shame does sometimes play a negative role, such as keeping us from going to confession or turning for help. What then?

DR. PATITSAS: Well, this could even be partly the fault of the confessor. These days, a healthy shame may itself restrain us from confessing since the confessor may treat us in this truth-first, cold Socratic way. When, in contrast, a confessor develops the reputation for really knowing the way of the heart, there are no shortage of people willing to confess.

Of course, even when offered the opportunity to confess to a saint, a person could still be shy; this modesty is an example of healthy shame, and a wise confessor will find ways to help the person through this.

But other times, when we say we are ashamed to tell the priest, this is just a polite way of indicating that we are not yet ready to let go of a particular sin. In that case, it is not healthy shame that is to blame but its lack.

But if we can find a good confessor, and if shame still blocks our path to the healing power of the sacrament, then we can pray about this, and surely God will hear our prayers.

It is best to think about shame in traditional Orthodox Christian terms. Any feeling we have can either be healthy or can be distorted; distorted versions of feelings we call "the passion" of that particular emotion, especially when they become habits. "Be angry, and sin not," says St. Paul (Eph 4:26). When anger becomes sinful, then it is the passion of anger at work. The answer is not to destroy healthy anger, but to heal the passion of anger so that healthy anger can work a holy purpose.

Ever since about 1989 when I first read Gershen Kaufmann's classic work *Shame*,[26] and then with this feeling reinforced through

---

[26] Gershen Kaufman, *Shame: The Power of Caring* (Cambridge, MA: Schenkman Publishing Company, 1980). Also important for my thinking in the late 1980s was John Bradshaw, *Healing the Shame that Binds You* (Deerfield Beach, Fla.: Health Communications, 1988).

twelve-step work, which itself is so obviously about restoring a person to proper shame, I have believed that the drama of Orthodox Christian therapy is to heal the "passion of shame." The goal should not be for shame to disappear but rather that it be converted from negative shame into healthy shame. The healed person is then "orthodox," or possessed of a healthy and right shame. Only the advent of healthy shame can displace the unhealthy shame.

Recently, though, I have been challenging myself to be more precise. After all, was Christ ashamed to be hung from the cross for our salvation? Was Joseph in Egypt ashamed to leave behind even his clothes and run from the temptation of Potiphar's wife? And what about the designation "King of Glory" for the icon of Christ hanging from the cross? What does it tell us that in Christ the very thing that was most shameful has now become glorious?

I now believe that healthy shame has three concentric phases, or types, and that these phases trace the Beauty, Goodness, Truth continuum. Therefore, when Achilles lost all three aspects of shame, his very existence, physically and spiritually, was endangered.[27] Remember, the three-fold path of eros-agape-philia is the path by which we were created, so to fall off this path is to begin to fade into non-being.

The first phase of healthy shame is chaste yet ardent eros; this is the shame that prevents us from doing something ugly in the eyes of God. It is shame at loving anything that is unworthy of God, shame that we are directing our eros toward something that is *not beautiful* in the real sense of beauty because we love real Beauty so much. This is the beginning of true reverence.

Then there comes the second type of shame, which in some ways reinforces the first shame, but in other ways seems to contradict it. This is the shame at not doing good, and it is a shame so intense that we are even willing to be embarrassed in the eyes of the world so long as we do not betray *goodness*. This makes us bold, forbearing

---

[27] We have been saying all along that both being created and continuing to exist are synonymous with following the path of these three loves, of these three healthy shames. To violate them intentionally is to risk one's very existence.

– and, in a sense, "shameless" because we are willing to be rejected by society as the cost of doing what is right. If the first shame is chaste yet ardent eros, then the second is courageous yet longsuffering agape. This level of shame includes the first kind of shame, but now it also adds doing good. Here, we are not afraid to appear shameful in the eyes of the world in the course of working justice.

And finally comes the third healthy shame, the shame of the fully-formed person. Here the other two kinds of shame coincide completely and permanently, so that we experience the twofold anointing at a higher fractal level and in a permanent way; permanent because such a paradoxical union of opposite types of shame is finalized only at our death.

Awesomely, the name of this third kind of shame is ... glory.

A Death Without Shame

Part of what we are asking when we pray for "a death without shame," as we do in every Divine Liturgy, is for the grace to heed the warnings given us by the first two kinds of *good shame*, even under extreme duress. In this way, we will die *in glory* or at least die destined for glory. We pray not to be deprived of glory eternally.

Well, what is truly shameful? To transgress the limits imposed for us by the first two healthy shames. But if we *do* cultivate and honor those first two kinds of shame all the way through our death, then we shall also receive the third healthy shame, which is called "glory." We could then be said to have attained a death "without shame."

The English here is confusing, so let's try to clear up what is going on. If we lose either kind of healthy shame or transgress it (for example, by eating of the forbidden fruit because we want to dare to be like gods), then naturally we feel ashamed. This ashamedness is something healthy; it is a sign that our healthy shame is still functioning. God designed us to feel this way so that after sin we would repent. We feel ashamed when we have transgressed against chaste, ardent eros (for example, by being drawn to impure things or by being cold to pure things) and also when we have transgressed against courageous, long-suffering agape (for example, by not sticking up for our friends when they are unpopular).

But if we transgress either type of healthy shame at the moment of our death (for example, by cursing God in our pain or by denying Christ), then the danger is that we might have no time left to repent. Of course, we can't say for certain, as some say that time slows down as we approach death and that even the person committing suicide may repent utterly of his mistake before their soul leaves their body. We must never lose hope for those who have gone before. But if we die doing something shameful and don't repent, then our being "ashamed" might even last for all eternity, to no good effect.

So, in this prayer for "a death unashamed," what we are mainly asking is for the strength not to transgress the healthy shames at the hour of our end. This does not mean that our manner of death won't necessarily look shameful to others, however. If we have offended the first two kinds of healthy shame in the course of our earlier life or have not really cultivated them, then God may permit this to be corrected through a difficult or even shocking manner of death. Thus, the arch-heretic Arius, presumed by many of his heretical followers to be holy, died in a way that indicated to Christians that his course of life had not been a blessed one. However, in this way God may have also given Arius a last moment to repent before he died, as well. Thus, an outwardly shameful death may be part of the way God heals my soul so that I am not ashamed at the Last Judgment.

Yet, we mustn't be simplistic in these matters. Even people who are saints or who have lived pure lives may die in great pain or suffering. In that case, the final cross is simply an additional crown sealing their perfection.

The Glory of Healthy Shame

Another name for the first kind of shame, the shame that is expressed as eros toward God, is "unknowing," and it makes us shy; it looks like the blush. It means to "know *nothing* except Christ…"

It makes us ascetics and chaste visionaries. This first kind of shame also makes us overlook the sins of those around us because we are so focused on the person, who is made in the image of Christ. Unknowing means to leave behind love for objects and for our passions, and instead to love persons, and especially to love Christ. This is the first phase in healthy shame: an eros that is simultaneously *ardent* yet *chaste*. This, I submit, is what St. Paul meant by "faith."

Another name for the second kind of shame, the shame that is willing to be humiliated rather than fail to serve others, is "one man lost." This shame makes us simultaneously *courageous* yet also *long-suffering*. Here we amplify the first shame, so that we "know nothing except Christ, *and him crucified*"! Here we are "shameless" in doing good because all our life is hid with Christ in God (Col 3:3), and we are willing to be humiliated with him. We don't care if the world derides us or if we seem in their eyes to be lost, so long as we do good. Hope is stronger.

At its extreme, this hope is so strong that even when we see *no* hope, we are not tempted to despair. "Keep thy mind in hell, and despair not," was the divine command given to St. Silouan.[28] He had already seen an ultimate theophany, the vision of the living Christ, and in response the saint's stage-one shame, his eros, was as full as it could be. But it took many more years until that eros could unfold fully into agape. And this happened only when his hope was so perfected that his willingness to be "lost" for the salvation of others was tested and found complete.

This is why I say that the first two types of shame seem to be opposed. One makes us shy, while the other makes us bold. One is clear ecstatic vision of heaven; another is sober-eyed and wary calmness in the midst of hell. And yet somehow we are meant to cultivate both types of shame, and even to take the matter further.

The name for the third and most complete form of shame is the most surprising: We can just call it, as we said above, "Glory"; it makes us complete. In the coinciding of shyness and boldness, of

---

28 St. Silouan the Athonite (1866-1938).

the desire for heaven with the readiness to risk even hell for the sake of love, we know more deeply now what it means to love.

That is why we depict this third kind of healthy shame only on icons; I mean, the halo around the saints. The halo is a way of saying that this person has fulfilled irreversibly the goal of the Christian life, which is to acquire the Spirit of Peace, the Holy Spirit. In other words, saints are those who have perfected holy shame at all three fractal scales. Shame is conveyed to us, in all three forms, through the descent of the Spirit who bears uncreated grace.

Or, we can say that the person possessed of healthy shame is extremely careful not to offend the Holy Spirit, neither to do, nor to omit, the slightest detail that would result in the loss of grace.

Examples of the Three Shames in the Holy Bible

The Gadarene Demoniac

In Holy Scripture we can see these three phases drawn out in crucial encounters. The Gadarene demoniac is the closest thing in the gospels to a berserker (Lk 8:26-39). He dwells far from the city, possessed by spirits and therefore godlike, in a sense, but also living like an animal, without clothes, barely subsisting. His humanity is being lost in this division between demonic and beast-like existence. The demoniac is also like Job, in terms of being permitted by God an ultimate testing at the hands of the adversary. Like Job, he cannot be healed until he sees Christ face to face – until he sees Beauty.[29]

And this encounter rekindles the Gadarene demoniac's chastity, his devotion to the *one* God and not to *a legion's worth* of demonic "gods." Even the demons within him see past all appearances to Beauty and Theophany and confess Christ's true identity! Thus, when Christ casts out the many spirits which are ruling the man,

---

[29] Job is a better example of the trauma sufferer than the demoniac, while the demoniac is more like the berserker. The heart of Job's story is that he refuses to "berserk" – i.e., to "curse God and die." But he does experience the sudden, complete, and unjust loss of all that he loves.

this man is now found to be "clothed, and in his right mind." In other words, he has recovered his primary shame and thus his human identity.

To be found "clothed and in his right mind" is also an accurate description of someone who has recovered from a terrible shamelessness and from a destructive posture towards others and himself. Such a person in recovery has found his limits, and has also rediscovered his limitedness: we are naked; as human beings we need clothing for protection. Or, for those of us who are addicts, we see that we are powerless over our addictions, that we are naked before their force and therefore need to be clothed in a program and in the support of others working a program in order to survive.

In the case of the Gadarene demoniac, we see the coincidence of the first kind of shame, when it is healthy, with spiritual recovery. In recovering his first shame, the demoniac has recovered his human dignity and become *single* again; he is no longer half-animal, half-god – a fair description of any of us when we are possessed by our passions or when we suffer trauma flashbacks. We see here that healthy shame, by delivering us from a false glory, begins to raise us towards true glory.

Notice the reaction of the friends and family when a berserker like the demoniac is healed: they ask his healer to depart at once. This tells us a lot, you know, about why it is not so easy to overcome PTSD, nor a correspondingly difficult challenge in the realm of concupiscent passions, such as same-sex attraction. The holy person who is able to heal same-sex attraction will in fact be driven away, perhaps from our country itself.

To see the second kind of shame, the holy boldness, we might notice that the healed demoniac now wants to leave his town and become "stateless" a second time – in order that he might follow Christ! Recovering chaste eros gave him the strength to live again "outside the city," but now in a holy way. Fools for Christ also have this second kind of shame, the holy "shamelessness," because down deep they are so perfectly chaste.

Joseph in Egypt

Or look at the story of Joseph's encounter with Potiphar's wife. Joseph in Egypt was a slave and a victim of sexual advances, but when the fallen lady grabs his cloak, he simply leaves it behind in order to avoid sin. He was not ashamed to be naked, rather than sin against chastity. In his case also, one shame – Joseph's sexual purity, his chaste and ardent eros, his faith – already held within it the seed of the next shame – courageous and longsuffering agape, his dedication to justice, his hope. His nakedness here is not shameful but rather counts to his glory. If the choice is between sin and shame in the eyes of the world, then we must choose shame.

The Samaritan Woman at the Well

The woman at the well also traced the three phases of good shame through her encounter with Christ (Jn 4:6-42). Apparently not chaste, she was not ashamed to do evil. But Christ cut off the unnatural boldness of her personal life and appeared as divine to her, enkindling once again her chaste eros. In other words, she was granted a theophany, and this helped her recover her first shame.

Immediately, the Samaritan Woman follows up this recovery of chastity with a courageous agape and asks the God-man about the deepest mysteries of worship, since these had pitted the Samaritans against the Jews. She is becoming a bold peacemaker, in other words.

Finally, she combines both shames, makes them coincide perfectly before her fellow villagers, when she repents of her sin before them while also boldly proclaiming that Jesus is the Christ. She later dies a martyr, a saint of the Church, thus sealing her in this third kind of shame, which we called "glory." In the Orthodox Church she is known as St. Photini, and her memory is commemorated every year on February 26th and again on the fifth Sunday following the Resurrection.

The Practical Importance of Teaching Both Kinds of Healthy Shame

RTE: What about children who are shamed by their classmates for healthy or innocent instincts, such as compassion for the weak, sexual innocence, or their faith in Christ? We usually try to tell them not be ashamed of what is good. But should we instead show them how this shame is to their glory?

DR. PATITSAS: I think that American cinema often does a good job on one point. In a movie, the final glory of a visionary is shown to be all the greater because of the rejection and humiliation that they have undergone along the way. In some cases no one in particular is ridiculing the striver, but the sacrifices they are making for their principles or their art still lead them to places that are not as glorious in the short term as what they would have had had they compromised themselves. For example, they may give up a coveted position, or wealth, or prestige.

The problem is this: if we don't teach our children the necessity of enduring the second kind of shame with dignity, then sooner or later they will have to give up on the first kind of shame as well, and betray their own virtue or what they believe. The first shame has to unfold into the second, or it will not mature and become truly virtuous. But "the nations" of eighth-graders can be quite cruel when they rage (Ps 2:1) and can really gnash their teeth at us quite convincingly.

We can show our children how, in Joseph's case, his purity and then nakedness led all the way to the third kind of shame, his glorious enthronement. He became a type of both Christ crucified (once by his brothers and a second time by Potiphar and his wife), and of Christ resurrected and sitting at God's right hand (although for Joseph it is the right hand of Pharaoh).

Again, easy to say and hard to do. I recently heard the true story of a woman who was deceived by distant relatives into sexual slavery in a foreign country. When on her first day with her new "employer" it dawned on her that no real job awaited her but that the cousins whom she trusted had all along only intended to sell her into this slavery, she immediately flung herself from an open third story window onto the streets of the foreign city below. She spent six months in the hospital and struggled to get the government of her native country to replace her passport, stolen by the satanic slavers, and bring her home. They say that her body will never heal completely.

But we might pray for women like this when Holy Week opens each year with the remembrance of Joseph, as we remember his nakedness and death sentence, which were a necessary part of his avoiding being ashamed in the eyes of God. Such people are very close to Christ; they are his living icons. I sometimes even ask in my heart for saints like this woman who have not yet passed from this life to somehow hear my silent request that they pray for me.

Shame and Philotimo

RTE: Do you have another example of the third shame?

DR. PATITSAS: Our Lord and Savior Jesus Christ, dead upon the cross – but still King, still God, still the One to be Resurrected.

This third and ultimate shame includes the two lower levels of shame – of reverent chastity before holiness, and of intrepid defense of the good – but takes them all the way to the point of death, and beyond. As I said, we call it "Glory," and it is the halo on the saint. It is the Holy Spirit. We call Christ, in the icon of his being dead on the cross, the King of Glory. The Holy Spirit proceeds from the Father *in order to rest upon the Son, in time anointing him as the Christ.* This resting of the Holy Spirit is the Sabbath rest of the Father, and of the Son, and of the Holy Spirit.

To remain perfectly chaste, while being wrongly accused of and willingly suffering for the sin of someone who is not chaste: this is the perfect coinciding of the two shames, and of course this is just what Christ came to achieve and did achieve. And every Orthodox Christian ascetic longs for the same fate as Christ: *to suffer for the sins of the world yet without adding anything to the sum of that sin.* Moreover, this coinciding of the first two kinds of shame is so difficult and so rare that it actually is something more. In fact, it is a third kind of healthy shame that we can only call "glory."

Saint Seraphim of Sarov said, "The goal of the Christian life is the acquisition of the Holy Spirit" – in other words, a full two-fold anointing by the Holy Spirit, received through both kinds of healthy shame. This acquisition would be our glory. This is why I think that the central concern of Orthodox soul therapy is the cultivation of all three phases of healthy shame. These phases are the sign of the Holy Spirit moving within us, carrying us from naturally possessing the divine image to supernaturally attaining the divine likeness of Christ. In the Holy Spirit, we long to be at once all-pure *and* to take on the sin of others and die for the world. That is just what holiness often feels like.

You can see, by the way, why the Greek word *philotimo* is so important to a saint like Paisios of Mount Athos. *Philotimo* is St. Seraphim's "acquisition of the Holy Spirit." You can also see why this word is so impossible to define exhaustively. Within it are contained a shy reverence, a fearless boldness, and a glorious fullness of human identity, all at once. A person with *philotimo* is truly a force to be reckoned with. If you want social justice, fill your society with people who cultivate this quality.

Achilles' Lost Priesthood

RTE: Earlier, you spoke of Achilles' lost priesthood. How does his path relate to the loss of healthy shame?

DR. PATITSAS: It took a while to figure that one out, even though Shay is pretty direct on this precise point, because I was just too readily condemning Achilles as having "lost all shame." (How unjust of me; Achilles seems to have actually existed, and he was a noble warrior.) I had to understand shame better before I could understand such a rare person. He didn't just "lose his shame." Healthy shame is complex, and losing it means directly opposite things in each of the three phases we just mentioned. I now see that it would be more accurate to say that Achilles' shame was inverted rather than lost.

To Agamemnon, Achilles himself had counseled healthy shame of the first type when he told the king to respect the gods, the priests, and the holy things.[30] In fact, this fidelity to healthy shame was what so angered the foolish Agamemnon that he took revenge upon Achilles. But when Achilles goes astray, he is no longer shy before the gods and religion but instead is shameless. He makes blasphemous offerings of cruel human sacrifice and will not heed the gods' commands to stop his destructive acts. He is no longer shy before divinity in the healthy human sense.

And, where Achilles should have *not* been ashamed – in doing the good, in having done so much good for the Greeks *and* for his enemies (he had always allowed his prisoners to be ransomed and had respected the noble families of Troy) – he now "repents" of this brave nobility. Instead, he is ashamed of the mercy he showed to his enemies in the past. Again, his healthy shame has been inverted.

Finally, whereas until the point of his berserking Achilles had been an anointed hero and champion, he instead became despised even by his own allies. Achilles mars his kinship with the Crucified One and becomes instead a crucifier of the innocent. He loses his glory and becomes, instead, infamous.

Meeting Christ Crucified – in Us…

Achilles' berserking is to the classical world what Adam and Eve's eating of the forbidden fruit was to the biblical world.[31] After Achilles, the age of the hero ends. Innocence was lost in the Garden

---

30 The *Iliad* opens with a plague in the Greek camp, which has occurred because Agamemnon has violated the sanctity of a temple and its priest. Achilles rightly rebukes him and, though Agamemnon repents and the plague ceases, he then takes revenge by seizing Achilles' honestly won prize and love, Briseis.

31 In Chapter Three, "Eros and Agape: Chastity, Empathy, and the Twofold Anointing," I related my pious belief that Adam and Eve's "eating of the forbidden fruit" was a metaphor for their having entered a forbidden section of the Garden of Eden. There, they

and it is lost here for the same reason: the untimely encounter with Christ crucified has overwhelmed our hearts. We need preparation and maturity for this meeting, we need an apostle who can present it to us in love and in the light of the Resurrection.

A berserker loses his innocence, he unravels, when the crucifixion that he is forced to witness – in fact, to carry – overwhelms his still-forming character. The PTSD sufferer's vision of Christ crucified is especially tough because it is not at all external, but rather it is within himself, through and in his own body, mind, and soul, that he finds Christ being crucified. This is a profound and sacred truth, I believe.

I do admire Odysseus, who in the end finds his own way to defy the demonic "gods" and end the war. He was human and the first European, and it just so happens that as I add these notes to our interview here in Greece on my family's balcony, I can look south across the Ionian Sea both to the island of Ithaca and almost to the northwestern Cephalonian peninsula that others believe was the actual ancient Ithaca. And, yes, I admit that the other heroes in the *Iliad* are comic book characters compared to Odysseus' sophistication. Still, I like them more, and something is lost for Western civilization in the very real fall from Achilles's innocence to Odysseus's cleverness. Having defied the gods, Classical man goes on to live by his wits.

Shame and Democracy

Shame is a royal emotion, in the Christian sense of royalty, because in feeling it we find a coincidence of two opposites – equality and natural hierarchy. For example, when overcome with grace during a vigil in church, we are both more aware of our sinfulness and

---

beheld Christ crucified since He is "the Lamb slain from before the foundation of the world." This vision was more than they could bear. Seeing it before they were ready, they lost faith and thus grace. And this is why in the daily prayer of the Hours we return now to this same vision of Christ crucified and then take rest "in the cool of the evening" at Vespers, but now *with* Christ and *without* distorted forms of shame. In fact, we ourselves are at Vespers clothed anew in the Uncreated Light, the "Gladsome Light."

createdness and yet closer to God than at other times. Analogously, at such times we both feel our oneness with all men and see ourselves as lower than all.

But because healthy shame makes us comfortable with natural hierarchy, it logically follows that in democratic America shame is a disposition with which we would like to dispense. If no one is ever ashamed, then no one ever needs to feel less or more than anyone else. To put it more gently, in America the kind of unhealthy shame that we most fear is the kind that puts one person too much lower or above another. In fact, we may tend to mistake *all* shame for unhealthy shame, just to be on the safe side and "not judge" anyone else, not even ourselves.

American therapy serves the American project of complete democracy just the way Transcendental Philosophy did in the context of post-Revolutionary War New England, or Baptist Soul Conversion did on the early American frontier.[32] These earlier movements, like the Empire of Therapy, in effect promoted the absolute identity of the human soul with God. Therapy adds to this the idea that if we are each loved by God just as we are, or if we even are gods just as much as Christ was (as is held also by American religions like Mormonism), why would we then ever feel ashamed, or shame?

RTE: Then how do you see the conventional and more analytical "truth-first" therapy handling shame?

DR. PATITSAS: When we meet a therapeutically reengineered person, our first reaction is often exactly right – we sense in some cases that, like the berserker, they stand outside of the community by being either too detached or too in our face. Either they are remote observers of the situation or they become instantly too familiar and invasive about our personal business, perhaps with a look of patient concern as well.

---

[32] According to Harold Bloom, in his *The American Religion: The Emergence of the Post-Christian Nation* (New York: Simon and Schuster, 1992).

Their shame is off, somehow, yet they insist that we should abandon our normal shame reaction of wanting to flee them and instead submit to their brand of plastic shame. They both stride like gods among us and at the same time they devour our souls through their brazenness; they cannot find their bearings as normal human beings. In this sense, though intending to serve the American democratic project of a shame-free non-hierarchical world, the therapy process tends to create a self-anointed aristocracy who are unsuited to the honest give and take of civil society.

To be charitable, psychotherapy here, as an Enlightenment science, tries to take out your organic, unhealthy shame and replace it with something better. But the replacement it offers may not be the shame flowing naturally from encounter with God, but a synthetic, mentally-manufactured shame that is promoted as being less painful and intrusive on your freedom of movement. It's hip replacement for the soul, and in ten years it will have to be redone, as our society expands its definition of the things we should no longer feel shame about.

To get real shame, you need a real encounter with the real God; then, healthy, liberating shame just flows naturally. It can't be "assembled" by anyone, not even by a clergyman.

RTE: But we also can't manufacture an encounter with God. Nor is it a commodity that we can order online.

DR. PATITSAS: Well, that is why we try to get our liturgies right. If we do, they are the most natural schools of healthy shame. That, and the long versions of lives of saints. Together, they go a long way toward restoring our natural humanity.

Therapy Beyond the Therapist's Office

To be more confrontational about the loss of shame in American society today, American therapy has morphed into a larger cultural force, the one demonstrated in Philip Rieff's *The Triumph of the Therapeutic*, that kills all healthy shame, leaving us in a state at once superhuman and subhuman. It so often tells you that your sin is not the problem but rather that the shame that you feel about your sin is what is diseased. If you can just get over that, this attitude says, then you will be healthy. This is madness, spiritual lobotomy. We see it in the realm of sex and promiscuity and greed, of murder in the form of euthanasia and abortion and torture and endless war, and in the realm of the intellect. The things that should make us ashamed no longer do. Therapy as a cultural force is the enemy of Christian shame.

Since the purpose of the Enlightenment was to desacralize the world, to render the world flat and scientific, then it should not surprise us that the purpose of this broader therapeutic cultural force is of course to root out the sacred from the soul, leaving it similarly empty. If the world is not the icon of something holy, why should we ever be ashamed? Why would we ever feel reverence or repentance? Therapy is the Enlightenment applied to our inner life.

Two hundred years ago, the former President George Washington had his death hastened in part by the then-craze in American medicine – bloodletting. The idea was that bodily illness could be cured by releasing blood from different parts of the body, in different amounts, depending on your condition. What is in fact almost always the vitality of the person (our blood), America's best doctors somehow mistook for a harmful substance.

Today, the leeches bleeding us are the vast army of "truth-first" therapists and the ministers they've trained; the blood they take is our sense of healthy shame, which is the main vitality of the soul, precisely because it is the worshipping and philanthropic energy of the soul; and the bloodletting happens in ten million talk shows, entertainment commentaries, therapist's sessions, "Christian" sermons, and in the private conversations of therapy-drunk Americans. Collectively, we are committing a slow-motion spiritual suicide on account of our pseudo-scientific therapy's poor ability to distinguish good shame from bad.

The privacy of the confessional is only partly aimed at the priest, who can scarcely remember from one penitent to the next the precise details of identical passions, failures, sins, and scandals he hears confessed – identical not only among penitents, but with his own sins. Instead, the privacy of confession is aimed at the person repenting, who tells these things privately precisely so that he may learn that sin is shameful, not to be repeated, and not to be discussed too boldly or glibly or openly.

RTE: Yet, the secular attempt to rid us of shame hasn't worked either. People are constantly ashamed and, as you say, are even ashamed to be themselves. Think about teenagers who commit suicide because they have lost all sense of their infinite value. This is even more apparent when you contrast this with cultures where people are not self-conscious – non-therapy cultures where people somehow stand more deeply and solidly inside themselves, without the self-dissecting introspection.

DR. PATITSAS: Yes, there are cultures and subcultures like that all over the world. Shame is a social emotion, after all, and so to get it right takes cultural support. Right now the support we are getting here is all mixed up, a blend of good and bad.

At times it would even seem that we have taken out the healthy shame, the real blood of the soul, and replaced it with a synthetic solution of paralyzing shame about nonsense. Some therapists are embalming your soul while you still live, and charging you $150 an hour to do it. And, by denying the power of even our eventual death to make us repent and feel shame, they promise us that we will live in this deadened state forever. No wonder our films and television these days are obsessed with zombies and the walking dead.

Many therapists seem, in effect, to teach us to live from our head and not from our heart. When they do so, they are killing the voice of our conscience. Does therapy so desacralize the world and the soul that the human vocation to priesthood has become impossible?

RTE: But what if someone who reads this is benefitting from his therapist's guidance? Or has been fortunate enough to have a Christian therapist who has a healthy sense of shame himself? I have friends who believe that their sanity was saved by someone who was willing to listen and give advice.

DR. PATITSAS: That's called "a friend" or "a mentor." And yes, analysis is sometimes helpful, no matter who it's done with. We do have a cognitive side, and we do need to think about things.

But you just can't let what you do in therapy spoil your fundamental orientation of reverence and unknowing, of justice and boldness. Fundamentally, what healed you was the face of Christ in that therapist. Another person was loving you in the best way they knew how, given the blindness of the culture in which they were raised.

For God's sake, be careful! This is your one and only life, and we will be judged. The Orthodox Christian in therapy might consider adding regular pilgrimage as a complementary way to become whole, through the recovery of their deepest identity as children of their loving Heavenly Father. They had better give some thought to the cultivation of eros and of shame before God.

Therapy has claimed preeminent sacredness in our society. Like its close cousin, consumer capitalism, it tends to dissolve every other attachment in its path. However, that is no reason for the rest of us to bow down uncritically before the supposed inevitability of its triumph, even if it sometimes does do some good. And for some, the endless visits are just a trap.

IV. THE SOUL IN ORTHODOX CHRISTIANITY

Some Alternatives to Failure

RTE: Previously you've said that Shay found that conventional cognitive therapy – talk, processing of memories, reflective listening – was extremely destructive for his PTSD veterans.

DR. PATITSAS: Yes, on top of everything we've said so far, comes Shay's experience that a naively analytical therapy which encouraged combat veterans to "get it all out there" led to the suicide of his most vulnerable veterans. The vaunted "scientific neutrality" of the truth-first method turned out to be a further infliction of the very thing the soldiers were already dying from: isolation, excommunication, dehumanization, and objectification.

In war, our enemies are trying to objectify and dehumanize our soldiers, to turn them into corpses or at least to destroy their subjectivity, their morale. There is no need for us to finish the job for them upon our soldiers' safe return by imposing upon them this horribly objectifying analysis, just because they are having trouble adjusting to life at home.

Using a reductive or statistical approach to the human person is so risky. It is taking apart your soul as if it were a toaster, when in fact it is not a toaster but a living thing.[33] The patient has to be pretty strong for such "surgery" to not be very harmful, and even then, I think we shouldn't usually do it.

But in trauma cases, especially: for God's sake, why should a therapist re-emphasize a cognition divorced from empathy and beauty, when the one thing a trauma sufferer has in superabundance is an awareness of things other than goodness and beauty?! As for reflective listening – it feels so awful to be on the receiving end of it, even though it's a perfectly Socratic practice and shows American Therapy's roots in an Enlightenment West that was creatively re-

---

33 Cf. Douglas A. Hall, *The Cat and the Toaster: Living System Ministry in a Technological Age* (Eugene, OR: Wipf and Stock, 2010). This book applies complexity science to pastoral ministry.

newing its appropriation of the classical Greek tradition. But I don't want to cross mental swords with my confessor (I mean, to the extent that my therapist is in a sense my confessor) when I am at my most vulnerable. And isn't the ability to understand someone else's pain without feeling it the very definition of a psychopath? Why in the hell am I confessing to someone impersonating a psychopath, or to someone who even might thrill in their ability to overlook my suffering and press on with their deconstruction of my soul?

Many people turn to the priest because they sense that something is wrong in the ethos of therapy; especially when a person is young and more vulnerable, they realize that to submit to this ethos completely would be to risk their soul. They sense that the process is both shameless and likely to make them lose some aspect of their healthy shame.

And yet the therapist alone claims to really know them and to have an answer to their crisis. So, they come to the priest not just for listening and prayer but because they genuinely want to know if there is an alternative approach to soul healing consistent with the ethos of the Church. They want, in other words, an elder who can "bring forth a word" that will actually save them – from their own sin, their own complexes – *but also from the therapist*, whom they often see as the purveyor of an alien ethos which, although it may have much to recommend it, seems not quite right and even potentially harmful. They want their unhealthy shame to be replaced by a stronger, bracing, healthy shame – not to lose shame entirely.

Bessel van der Kolk

I have been criticized for expressing my suspicion that analytical therapy is not appropriate for many trauma sufferers; the fear is that my words will keep vulnerable people from getting the help that they need. But Bessel van der Kolk, author of *The Body Keeps the Score: Brain, Mind, and Body in the Healing of Trauma* and one of the preeminent experts on trauma recovery, is far more critical of his field of psychotherapy than I am.[34]

Van der Kolk says that therapy in general objectifies the patient; that the therapeutic community refuses to define trauma holistically and therefore misreads it; that pharmaceutical-based approaches have taken over the field of psychotherapy; and, that therapists are short-circuiting the emotional recovery of large numbers of patients by so readily prescribing drugs. He has been working for more than twenty years to get the classification of "complex trauma" added to the DSM (the Diagnostic and Statistical Manual of Mental Disorders, which guides psychiatric diagnosis), and the reasons why his proposal was not accepted in DSM-5 (made public in 2013) had nothing to do with real patient well-being, in his opinion.[35] All the evidence for this new diagnosis is on his side, and still no success.

As for a technique like EMDR (Eye Movement Desensitization and Reprocessing Therapy), van der Kolk says it often works well for simple trauma (trauma that comes from one awful incident) but not so well for complex trauma (trauma that is more all-encompassing or that occurs while we are still developing emotionally in childhood or adolescence). The overall feeling in van der Kolk's book is that therapy as a science would rather be Cartesian, precise, and wrong than switch to something organic, complex, and helpful to patients.

Van der Kolk's book is not encouraging for defenders of therapy from my, admittedly amateur, critique.

Orthodox Christianity does have another way: the unconditional free love of a guide-confessor who is rooted in an *unknowing* of himself or herself that is perfected in noetic prayer. This unknowing is the precise opposite of what is offered by a therapist or

---

[34] Bessel van der Kolk, *The Body Keeps the Score: Brain, Mind, and Body in the Healing of Trauma* (New York: Viking/Penguin, 2014).

[35] "DSM-5 has hinted at symptoms of complex PTSD, but in the end has left them out of the manual. DSM-5 continues to opt for a universal reaction to stress, as presented in the diagnostic criteria." Cf. James Phillips, in "PTSD in DSM-5: Understanding the Changes," September 25, 2015. Available online at psychiatrictimes.com, accessed on June 15, 2017.

spiritual father who is not only a big-time knower of himself but who is anxious to analyze and know you, as well. An encounter with a master of unknowing is the best way to inculcate proper shame within someone, without making them feel ashamed in the bad sense. We want to avoid further unhealthy shame, which would only be a furtherance of the excommunication that trauma already implies. There is a kind of infinite *mildness* to a true elder that slowly lets the air out of every false shame afflicting us, while steadily strengthening every holy shame within us.

Here I diverge from my main guide, Jonathan Shay. Shay is careful to say that cognitive approaches don't work with trauma victims in particular, while I fear that these victims are really the canaries in the coal mine: *none* of us are meant to share our deepest selves with people who respond with emotionless analysis.

"Well," you could say, "we aren't meant to be anesthetized and have our bodies cut open, either, but if that's what it takes to remove a tumor, it saves our life and we are grateful." But I can't imagine how we could apply such an approach to our soul without harming it. In general, self-examination has its utility in the context of theophany and eros. On its own, we must be careful with it.

From the beginning of their helping us, an Orthodox soul healer is giving everything to God, and God is healing silently and painlessly, through the presence of this saint.

A better medical analogy is this: before a surgeon cuts you open, he first sterilizes everything that will come near you so that he doesn't accidentally wind up killing you through an infection. Now, show me the therapist who is giving equal thought to cleansing his own soul through eros and agape, and I will give you my endorsement of your going to him. Otherwise, you may pick up his "germs" at your most vulnerable place and wind up worse. If he isn't cleansing his soul, even though he is acting calmly and analytically, the therapist can't help but be advising you out of his own passions.

How Orthodoxy Does Influence Some Contemporary Thinking about the Soul

RTE: Can you say something more about Orthodoxy having had a psychotherapy of sorts long before Freud? We see it in places like *The Philokalia*.

DR. PATITSAS: Yes, the Church has a psychotherapy dating to Christ and to St. Paul, a tradition continued by the mystics and the Fathers. This approach is focused not so much on our subconscious or on our family-of-origin issues but instead notes the mixed motivations that we all possess, our tangled web of positive and negative devotions to God, to those we love, to our own passions, to the things of this world, and so forth.

This realism about the lies we tell ourselves regarding our motivations (see, for example, the Samaritan woman, Christ's rebuke of the Pharisees, and numerous other examples from the gospels) is continued within the Orthodox system of soul care in the desert fathers and the elders.

In the sixth century, that approach was condensed in writings like *The Ladder of Divine Ascent* by St. John Climacus, but in fact it is older and is found throughout desert and patristic literature.

This long Orthodox Christian tradition eventually does show up in Western Europe and America through the vehicle of the great Russian novelists of the nineteenth century. We can see the spiritual relevance of this Russian literary tradition in the more recent writings of Metropolitan Anthony Bloom (1914-2003), for example, whose spiritual books are loaded with dissections of the various stories we tell ourselves, the hidden motivations that are really driving us. Each lie is exposed gently, often humorously, so that healthy shame can be re-kindled and drive us toward God and each other.

The effect of this kind of analysis is not to increase focus on the self, but to lessen obsession with the self, and in time weakens even the focus on our endless rationalizations. "Go, and sell *all that you have*," Christ tells the rich young man; here this means that the whole of our self-knowledge is stripped to three facts: I was created *ex nihilo*; I am a sinner; and, my destiny is union with the Resurrected Lord who gave his life for the life of the world.

Although this Orthodox Christian approach to psychology does expose the half-truths we trust in, it is not a truth-first approach because the exposure of the false reasoning is simply an invitation to renew our attention to theophany. Of these sorts of self-deception there is no end – and no beginning, either. These false motivations are just the fading echo of weakening eros and agape, and had our mothers and fathers all been saints, we still would have generated these insidious rationalizations for sin on our own. So the point of this ancient Orthodox Christian therapy was never a more accurate map of the self (although some improvement in our self-conception will certainly be a byproduct) but rather a more chaste and ardent eros for Christ.

This ancient tradition differs decisively from the tradition of Freud because it never tries to reduce the human being to his or her mind, as though *any* irrational motivation were false. No: love and pure love are still the best motivations of all. And this ancient tradition, growing as it does from Christ and from the Hebrew Scripture's emphasis on the heart, is expert at promoting a clean heart and at strengthening the *right* irrational attachments (really, transrational, not irrational). So, rather than de-mythologize our motivations, Orthodox psychotherapy seeks to re-mythologize them, but with a "myth" that is in fact an icon of eternal realities.

As I said, the patristic psychotherapeutic tradition shows up in the Russian novelists in the form of a brilliant frankness about people's motivations and self-deceptions. In both the desert and in the monasteries of Holy Russia, this mindfulness teaches us the self-deceptions of the mind; it teaches us our dependence on grace, on the mysteries of the Church, and on forgiveness; our need for checks and balances; the depths of the heart; the importance of ignoring *logismoi* and of devoting ourselves to noetic prayer.[36] It does

---

36 *Logismoi:* A technical term in Byzantine spirituality that can mean fruitless, even though apparently rational, thoughts either self-generated or suggested by others.

not trace most of our identity to our childhoods, perhaps because people had different childhoods in those days. Saint John Climacus himself was a monk by the age of fifteen.

C.S. Lewis follows this Russian-novelist/Orthodox Church approach to the soul in *The Screwtape Letters* and elsewhere.[37] And although this approach looks pretty starkly at our false motivations (and is backed up by the daily prayers of the Church, which also prompt us to confess our confused motivations and hidden agendas every morning and evening), it doesn't lead to depression, because the idea is never that you could be completely free of this mess by trying harder.

Or rather, you try harder by warming your heart more and more with eros for Christ. So, if you want, you can just laugh at your crazy thoughts. This tradition shows us how ridiculous we all can be. We are meant to find our true self in Christ, not in a better map of our personal falls and passions.

RTE: It's a temptation for new converts, especially those from strict or punishing Christian traditions, to try to emotionally feel what they are reading in such penitential prayers and then to be depressed and morose about the sins enumerated there, or rather, what they bleakly think of as their real spiritual condition.

DR. PATITSAS: Yes, we even think that we are supposed to feel bad, maybe make a long face, as we pray such prayers. We are so convinced that guilt is the way to go, not shame. Oh, if only I had tried harder, we say! Go ahead and try as hard as you want, you still won't get anywhere!

Shame – healthy shame, not diseased or toxic shame – is the way to go. Rather, let us acknowledge that we are created, we are dependent, we are weak. We cannot live except through an endless outpouring of divine mercy upon our troubled selves. Accept your

---

37 C.S. Lewis, *The Screwtape Letters* (New York: Macmillan, 1943).

creatureliness, and then you can read these prayers of confession with some sighing, but not with dark despair.[38]

In this Orthodox Christian approach, seeing our false motivations exposed with loving mildness is supposed to inculcate a healthy shame. We see how false we are, and we begin to pray noetically in another sense. In fact, we can see what "noetic" prayer means in this case: not the forced accession to a supreme mystical state but a prayer said in complete dependence on God and in independence from all false, created, helps and hopes. No images are allowed, because "naked from the womb we came" (Job 1:21), and so must our minds dare to flee worldly attachments, the Potiphar's wife of the passions, and run naked towards God.

Noetic prayer need not yet imply the perfection of the Jesus Prayer *but is simply prayer that in some small way is set against conscious thought:* "Lord, I know that even my asking for spiritual enlightenment is mostly a lie, as my motivations are so mixed. And I know that even in this moment of repentance and during this precise prayer, part of me is secretly thinking only of how wonderful I am for being 'so spiritual.' Nevertheless, hear my words O Lord, di-

---

[38] The same caution applies when we say that we overcome our own dependence on moral luck by accepting responsibility for the sin of the entire human race. We mustn't take on the guilt of others, per se, but rather the proper shame. After all, I cannot exactly feel guilty for most of what other people do; I didn't do it, they did.

But I can feel sad when I see them fall, and in the spiritual mourning of my soul for them, willingly repent on their behalf. This is not a false guilt, which would make me neurotic and destroy me, but a healthy shame: "Lord, your creature is sinning, and I too am a creature. Help us!"

This response is not based on actual guilt; in fact, it is usually only the relatively innocent person who will take on this expression of healthy shame! To claim that all shame is toxic is just a trope of the desacralizing Enlightenment-style thinking about the soul.

The secular approach also tells us that "guilt" is a better way than shame to think about the soul because within guilt is the idea of something I can fix, something I can change. This is such a dead-end street! Both shame and guilt have their place, but our moral agency is both limited and limiting: I both cannot fix much of what I know I am guilty about, and I am not guilty about most of what I can fix. I mean, I am not guilty of your sin, but it is so often the case that by loving you, I can make a decisive contribution to your being freed from that sin, whereas my own bad habits simply ruin me despite my perfect awareness of how they operate. Therefore, we can see that guilt is over-rated in our thinking today, while shame is underrated. So many people seem to think that the antidote to toxic shame will be guilt because then they can focus on what they can control; no, the antidote to toxic shame is healthy shame, full stop. And to those who live the way of the Cross, the promise of control solely through individual effort is revealed for what it is: an illusion.

vorced from all the falseness with which I say them, and help me to love you more and never to count the cost of loving you more – whatever that might mean! And Lord, I am not closing my eyes as I pray this, nor scrunching up my face and emotions with spirituality, as if on my own I could change myself, or as if, having made this awesome scrunchy-faced effort, *it won't be my fault* when *you* don't answer this prayer for my renewal. Rather, I am genuinely accepting that I don't know what precisely would have to change in me for me to love you more. This unknown change, which you do know, is what I pray for. I pray against myself. Amen."

I have been in twelve-step meetings where everyone has years of sobriety in multiple programs, and you can hardly imagine more joyful, peaceful, sane, and humorous gatherings. One after the other, each person confesses their own absurdities, makes a fool of themselves in front of the others, and without any trace of false shame or guilt. "That's just my disease talking, telling me these crazy thoughts," each one notes. Contrast this with the somber atmosphere of the therapist's office, where the disease is mistaken for the self, where the client's attempts to distance himself from his disease are patiently and universally defeated by the "caring" therapist who labels this desire to peel off sin a form of "denial," or what have you!

The older system of Christian psychotherapy is inseparable from shame and from worship and from God. You just will get nowhere until you pull God into the picture – and push yourself right out of it! Self-knowledge attained through relationship with God enervates your self-love; therapeutic self-knowledge often strengthens your self-love, your self-obsession, your isolation. It can make you more mechanical, not less.

Orthodox Christianity and American Therapy – Friends or Enemies?

So our two main choices today are Orthodox Christian psychology and Austrian psychology: in the first, the failings of the mind are self-evident proof of our need for a Higher Power, for something outside ourselves. In the second, the failings of the mind are self-evident proof of our need to think harder, more clearly, and to analyze the source of these deceptive thoughts. American psychotherapy trends much more towards the analytic style. The Twelve Steps are more Orthodox, although today, due to the rise of therapy, even people working a program sometimes become paranoid about codependence. They may lose entirely the original Alcoholics Anonymous vision that they can only become well by helping another addict. I mean, AA was born through embracing a fully Orthodox approach to bad moral luck; an alcoholic could only become well by attempting to help another alcoholic.

I think that "codependence," this great terror for us, is just our modern term for "friendship," but now turned into something pernicious and negative. Codependency is supposed to mean that we have become addicted to the feelings or opinions of another person or are enabling their destructive habits. But to a large extent, similar actions are a natural part of love.

"Loving your neighbor as yourself," if it does have risks (and it certainly does), cannot be corrected by "not loving your neighbor as yourself." And it cannot even be fixed by loving the friend more accurately. It can only be corrected by going in another direction entirely, by "loving the Lord your God with all your heart, soul, mind and strength." Chaste eros alone can form the impetus for the right kind of agape towards those around us. Then, an unhealthy love of neighbor will be replaced by a healthy one; and, incidentally, one much warmer than we display nowadays, when our friends have become disposable and interchangeable aids to our individualistic self-actualization.

You can't cure codependency by "maintaining healthy boundaries," unless these boundaries are naturally flowing from a positive internal eros for Christ.

Earlier in this interview we reported Douthat's saying that at the heyday of organized Christianity in America in the early 1960s, some thought that Religious Man would give way to Ideological Man, in the form of a more politically active Christianity. That happened for mainline Protestants, but with the result that the numbers of their adherents crashed. Instead, says Douthat, Therapeutic Man arose to fill the void left by Religious Man's demise.

To Orthodox Christian eyes, it was hard to know whom to root for. Since Orthodox Christianity was not about moralism or individualism to begin with, it couldn't relate to Religious Man, an Enlightenment artifact of individualist salvation. Orthodoxy's social and ecclesial concern had always been central, so it cheered for Ideological Man, even as it regretted the loss of potential transcendence signified by Religious Man's demise. And, since Orthodoxy had also always been about healing and therapy, the turn toward Therapeutic Man would, a) not have enticed it to leave transcendence behind; and yet, b) would have seemed a welcome relief from the pietistic side of Religious Man.

I mean, you can understand how an Orthodox Christian would see the shift to Therapeutic Man as, "Hey, this is something we can work with, a less moralistic and more healing-centered way." In fact, the rise of Therapeutic Man is a relief from this tremendous Western rationalism around dogmatic differences which, when not arrived at through a vision of uncreated light and theophany anyway, and thus having only a limited basis in empirical mystical experience, can be exhausting and demoralizing. Also, therapy appears to offer a relief from the wearying moralism and pietism of Religious Man. And you can see how Orthodox Christians would say, "Yes, our faith never functioned as a penal system of rewards and punishments around morality the way 'religion' does, but as healing for the soul."

For these exact reasons, many Orthodox Christians welcomed the rise of therapy in America over against "religion" but without really seeing the Enlightenment roots of American Therapy and thus its ultimate incompatibility with a Beauty-first approach to the soul. The question should have been: to what extent is the new soul-healing allied to or opposed to the soul-healing of our own Tradition? What elements within it can and can't be used? Can a truth-first approach to the soul be reconciled with a Beauty-first one? If so, how, and in what way?

Those questions were rarely asked, and when asked, they were asked by people who really didn't know the old way.

To be sure, there is a sense in which American therapy seems not to be truth-first. Its emphasis on feelings and on our irrational motivations seems to take us past an intellectual approach to the soul. Or, as we put it earlier, it wavers between a Semitic side and a Greek-Roman side.

But even here there are problems. An emphasis on our feelings is nice if it means following our pure hearts, not so nice if it means giving attention to misleading feelings or to our hearts in those moments when they are darkened by passions. They say in Alcoholics Anonymous that "feelings are not facts." Well, Orthodoxy has a lot to say about the ways such a statement is and isn't true. And, in fact, recently psychological research itself has begun to move away from the analysis of feelings and towards the importance of cultivating such emotional habits as love, gratitude, and compassion.

But if therapy traces every feeling back to some "truth" about ourselves or our past, then the whole process devolves into just another truth-first, reductive Enlightenment science – which is just the very science that even well-educated people today are so tired of. They are sick of this approach in other areas of life because it is not organic, not complex, and therefore does not tell the full truth about life. Therapy is overdue for its own back-to-nature movement, and Orthodox Christians should not wait around for this to happen but simply get on with it! We don't need to ask permission from the wider culture in order to follow the brilliant aspects of the gospel, for heaven's sake.

As for the humanistic emphasis of therapy, we can simply ask if removing God from the conversation ever would have worked in therapy? Not completely, that's for sure. You can't know yourself until you see what you were supposed to have been. We are icons of a divine being, and we can't close our eyes about what we are really meant to be and still hope to know ourselves.

Would an individualistic approach ever have worked? It will never work: you aren't going to feel more human until you're in more perfect communion with God and others. I don't even like the way the therapist sits across from me, pays attention to me, and encourages me to pay attention to myself – I don't really need that, I do that well enough. I really need training in paying attention to Christ and to others. And as for a truth-first approach? We are rational beings; it has a role – but not usually the primary role.

So, what is left that is good in therapy? The return of something, in the form of the unconscious, that at least suggests the existence of the heart. The compassion therapy shows in trying to understand even the greatest sinner with respect and without judgment. Even its emphasis on our pasts, if we see in this emphasis an affirmation of the fact that we hardly exist except as we are and have been in relation with others.

But my response to anyone who might protest my criticism of the Therapy Empire would be, "Why should I sit around and defend therapy from its own painfully obvious flaws and pernicious effects, when secular psychological research itself is moving in directions that will completely undermine the current practice of American psychotherapy?" Researchers are seeing that executive function and willpower are *extremely* limited in what they can do for us. A truth-first analytical approach is often relatively ineffective at helping us live better lives, they are finding, when compared to inculcating the right "master emotions" and feelings – of love, gratitude, wonder, and compassion.[39]

---

[39] For example, David Desteno, "A Feeling of Control: How America Can Finally Learn to Deal With Its Impulses," in the online magazine *Pacific Standard*, Sep 15, 2014. Desteno argues for the cultivation of a range of what I would call "liturgical emotional habits," in the sense that these feelings are involved in praise and worship, a fact not noted by him.

The science of psychology itself is now poised to arrive at a Beauty-first approach. Everyone is fed up with this outdated nonsense describing the soul as a machine or a hydraulic system venting this and that. For God's sake, the Age of Steam ended long ago, and we need better metaphors. No one has time for that absurdity, and we need to call people to something divinizing, not something steam-engine-ifying.

RTE: What then about Orthodox therapists who believe they are practicing Christian psychotherapy?

DR. PATITSAS: I am sure that they *are* helping people, just the way a loving friend would help. So, of course, are many non-Orthodox Christian therapists. It is even possible that at times what they do is equal to what elders do because the attentive love of one person for another can often overcome egregious faults in method. Parenting itself shows us that!

But why should people who claim to be scientists cower and tremble behind the justification of the partial good they do, rather than boldly experimenting with newer and more ancient and more accurate paradigms? At the least, I think, American therapists have to consider fresh approaches that are based on helping their patients cultivate emotions of gratitude, wonder, healthy shame, and worship. These are the best route for soul healing. Therapy is a science, or claims to be, so let it develop and incorporate new discoveries.

Among experienced spiritual fathers in Russia today, for example, it is widely accepted that the practice of soul healing is almost always acquired from within the millennia-long stream of earlier generations of soul healers. If a therapist were to meet one of these people and see no difference between their ethos and that of the elder, then they should keep doing what they are doing.

I am not condemning, but I am predicting that a new way is coming within therapy itself. This new way will be more Orthodox in the sense of trying to achieve a more helpful balance between the Socratic truth-first method and a Beauty-first sensibility.

Beauty-First and Talking Backwards

RTE: Can you give us an example of how the ethos of the Orthodox soul-healer is different from that of an American therapist?

DR. PATITSAS: The ancient-way therapist is fully and properly clothed, for one thing. I mean, they aren't so shamelessly in your face, so naked of shame and proper limits within themselves, that they feel free to transgress the patient's boundaries with a million investigative questions. Even when elders are blunt (which they may well be), they aren't forgetting their own limitedness. There is very little of that bluff and bluster by which the American therapist affects this great confidence about what he knows of your inner life. Does he or she do this because they are conducting reconnaissance by fire, trying to provoke us through their boldness, or do they actually imagine that they know me within three sessions? When I have been in therapy myself, I can never tell which it is. Elders, meanwhile, are less like hot-shot surgeons or fighter pilots and more like super-wise and patient older brothers.

Or, if elders *are* like surgeons, their main job is to transplant into you some of their eros for Christ, while drawing off some of the passions that are keeping you self-obsessed.

The subtle presuppositions within the Orthodox approach are not trivial to discern. It took me years of monastic pilgrimage, for example, before I realized that in Orthodox monasteries they tend to "talk backwards" and "think backwards," too. What I mean is that in the world we use conversation to establish communion and come closer to each other, to convey information. But when you start every day in the Divine Liturgy, and not just in the Liturgy but in profound noetic prayer within a Liturgy celebrated for the life of the world, you already start out with the experience of intense communion and friendship. You are nourished on the Body and Blood of the Logos, and therefore information, too, will acquire a different significance after that.

At that point, your main use for language is not to "connect" or share with others. In fact, among your first priorities is that your words should not disturb the already existing communion amongst us and within our hearts. You just try not to say anything that would be unworthy of that communion because then you might see it slip away.

In my brief monastic stint in Greece, I never could quite get that right – I was too precious about it, for one thing. Noetic prayer and communion are primarily gifts, and we cannot become paranoid that every chatterer coming to the monastery is going to knock us off course. Many times the visitor feels free to chatter because their link to the noetic way is stronger than ours, not weaker.

RTE: So, is this backwards way of talking in a monastery another example of Beauty-first? I mean, the monks or nuns start with this free gift of communion, not with a rational pursuit of it. In other words, they go to church.

DR. PATITSAS: Yes, it is one of the best empirical proofs of the Beauty-first approach: start with the gift of theophany, not with mental or ethical or scriptural gymnastics designed to earn the gift. This is what St. Paul meant when he said that we are saved by the gift of grace, through faith, for a life of good works (Eph 2:8-10): First, theophany (the gift of grace); then, chaste eros (faith); then, carrying the cross through empathy (for a life of good works). That is, you move through Beauty into Goodness *without* leaving Beauty behind. At that point, you are "saved"; that is, you join the Logos according to your own particular logos, are true, and permanently exist. The Fathers termed this same continuum being, well-being, and ever-being.

The same principle applies to our thinking when we enter the realm of noetic prayer. We aren't then speculative in our thoughts, but rather intuitive, direct. We just know the few simple things that God has given us to know, and the rest we leave to God. Most of us couldn't do an hour of therapy twice a week with an Orthodox elder for very long. What would he let us talk about? And most of us, probably, do not have that much to say about ourselves when language is used in this "backwards," Beauty-first, way.

Truth-first therapy (I mean, our contemporary rational approach to mapping each individual heart) will eventually flesh out a super-vivid picture of the patient's soul. But at that point the very accuracy of this account is what will end up hindering us. The more truth it contains, the more we forget that it's not actually the real us. To develop an accurate picture of a person, you need to paint an icon; i.e., you need to leave gaps, fractures, wounds, and spaces in your depiction and in your rational account that allow for continual surprise, mystery, freedom, theophany – and, for forgiveness. Therapy's account of you becomes a super-accurate lie when it's too convincing, because each person *is* an icon – of the Son of God, a mysterious figure that no amount of analysis can ever capture.

If you want to depict accurately someone who is an icon of Christ, you are going to have to paint an icon. If you want to depict a dead, unsacred object, a truth-first approach will do.

And anyway, the desire to build "the final and complete map of you" is also based on a mistake within rationalism that postmodernism exposed already ten million times: the therapist isn't just studying us, but he is already changing and forming us by everything he does and says. He attempts to be detached in the interest of objectivity, but in therapy he is remaking you in his own image nonetheless. The more he examines you, the more he ought to see his own influence in your identity because this is exactly what is happening.

In therapy, my therapist is constantly bringing me back to what he and I earlier discovered about me. He is forcing me, he thinks, to deal with the truth about myself and confront it. In Orthodox confession, the opposite applies: the Beauty-first confessor is continually insisting that I desist from making or referring to such mental maps of myself, and instead is asking me to return to the moment of my original birth in Christ, my original creation, which occurred in response to the vision of Christ, and of him crucified. The Orthodox soul healer is asking me to be born again, and again, and again, and again – from within whatever I am experiencing. "Unless you become as children, you will not enter the kingdom of Heaven" (Mt 18:3). Thus does the soul retrace the original path of creation.

Sex and Revenge: There Is More to You Than That

RTE: Isn't there some benefit to self-knowledge about our weaknesses, their causes, or our habitual failures?

DR. PATITSAS: Saint Porphyrios said, "The soul is so deep only God can know it." Of course it is good to have some awareness of the traps that often tempt us. But if our relationship to Christ is actually vibrant, many times the picture of our self will be changing so quickly that no map can keep up. That is why in Orthodox therapy they don't form the map of *you* but the map of the rationalizations and falls that just absolutely *everybody* tends to fall into. This is why Alcoholics Anonymous isn't therapy, either. It's more general in its description of the soul's weaknesses because by staying general we can avoid the self-obsession (really, the self-love) that is the mother of *all* the passions. The map of typical mistakes that apply to everyone is sufficient; you can afford to leave your soul undisturbed in its inner mystery.

Saint John the Theologian reminds us that "God is greater than our hearts," so that at times even our conscience will not tell us the full truth of our inner state (I Jn 3:20). And an awareness of our faults is helpful mostly because it helps us *to ignore*, with a subtle art, both the faults and the enemy's attempts to exploit them, so that instead we turn to Christ. At least, this is my own experience. We must remember St. Paul's warning that the very good he knew, that he could not do. The saints show the way around this, which is eros for Christ.

The Enlightenment comes directly out of Scholastic theology and the medieval notion that there is a nature that is all right on its own, to which grace is then added. That is totally heretical, just nuts. In Orthodoxy we think that no existing thing would exist for even the tiniest moment were it not sustained by uncreated grace.

The Enlightenment sciences (of which American psychology is one) take the medieval notion of nature a step farther and say, "Ok, let's look only at the nature and leave grace to the clergy."

Well, in Orthodox cosmology this wouldn't make sense. We won't completely understand *anything* in nature unless we also see it as an icon and as existing because God's grace sustains and permeates it. So, to think that you can know your true self through objective analysis and only afterwards turn to God is a category mistake: *there is no such self to be known.* Absent your purified communion with Christ, there are just the fading echoes of a self, clouded and degraded by passions and demonic influences and complexes. The only version of yourself that is actually knowable, because it possesses a really stable essence, is the self that is firmly anchored in Christ! And talking about that self usually seems to chase the grace away.

Look, who do you imagine that you are? What is this "real self" that you would know? You are an icon of Christ, and your identity is only knowable in knowing him. And moreover, your identity is in its deepest well *inexhaustible* since you are an icon of the God-man himself. Such a self cannot be "known" in the way that the secular world imagines knowing.

Self-knowledge about our weaknesses may be necessary so that we can make amends to others, so that we can realize whom we've hurt, so that we can stop hurting the people around us. Such knowledge is also helpful if we would have a good and honest confession. But self-awareness alone won't lead to transformation. To have that, you have to *unknow* yourself by forgetting yourself and falling in love with Christ. This art of becoming a child again, of having the self-forgetfulness of an innocent child, is the art of spiritual life in the Church, when that childlike innocence is then focused not on toys or games but on the loving face of Christ.

Religious people, because they are putting morality first (goodness first), and therapeutic people, because they are putting truth and analysis first, are both trying so hard to be adults, so hard to be grown up and grim and take responsibility for things which are in fact none of their business. They are inventing causes and moralisms and concerns, fleshing out elaborate self-depictions, forming committees and establishing non-profits, but forgetting the one thing needful – their right to be children of their Heavenly Father.

RTE: How does attaining a more childlike stance to God affect the way we know other people, then? That is, when we stop forming mental maps or constructs of others – the super-accurate lie, as you called it – but still want to know them better, how do we go about it?

DR. PATITSAS: There is a rhythm within Orthodoxy of knowing and unknowing. This rhythm is mirrored in the bodily life by feasting and fasting, or by seasons when sexual relations among married couples are either celebrated or not promoted. You aren't meant to know people through an all-at-once intellectual account of their origins and motivations; or, you must balance such awarenesses by periodically forgetting these insights, allowing room for mystery and movement, for breath.

You know, during the six months I spent in a remote monastery on a Greek island, every day in church all I thought about was sex and revenge (the concupiscent and irascible passions, of course). For the first few weeks I could pray, but eventually the long hours of boredom were just too much, and I was off in a million directions, thinking about world military history or whatever for the whole time I was in there. I absolutely could not shake the grip of those fantastic thoughts from my head for the four hours a day I stood in church. It was so bad, that leaving the services was actually a relief many times. At the end of the six months, I came out of the monastery and a very close friend commented, "You've changed completely." "How?" I asked – because I wanted to know what she was seeing. "You are free of rancor." And yet I would not have described myself chiefly as a person of anger before, because I was hiding that even from myself.

So, as we deepen our relationship to Christ we become better known to others and to ourselves, precisely because now there is movement, there is change, there is the possibility of *comparison*.

Under normal circumstances, one reason that you can't "know" yourself is the simple fact that there is only one of you, and so there is nothing relevant to compare you with. Only as you mature and grow can you or others come to see who you are. Without movement, without difference, there is no information. Meaningful, real movement comes only with eros; nothing else makes it happen. So, a static analysis is pointless.

The Free Gifts of God

RTE: Do you credit that freedom from anger to your practice of noetic prayer during your time in the monastery?

DR. PATITSAS: You must be joking. If I could practice noetic prayer, I'd still be there.

However, when we are in church services for long vigils, the background noise that normally masks our inner state is switched off, and at first just the static of our passions comes through. Our inner channel out here in the world may not be clear, but normally we don't notice because of the external noise in our life. And then, there in church, we turn off that noise and find that we feel worse than ever – but at least now the game is on!

Well, for an entire year (I spent the other six months in a different monastery), I lost that game every day, every time, and still the grace and beauty in liturgy was enough to overcome all lack of cognitive success or my failure at "noetic prayer," if even that is understood in a mechanistic way. I mean, noetic prayer is not a technique, even if technique can accompany or aid its arrival, but a falling in love with Christ. It's the mind of Christ, and why any of us is *ever* given that is the greatest mystery of all.

And other people also said that I had changed completely, despite my total failure at anything that could be considered my own contribution to the path of spiritual development. You don't have to do anything, you can fail completely, and still be given some of these gifts. It is arriving at a point of utter defeat, but a defeat reached at the feet of Christ, that helps you to live by faith. And at that point, spiritual vanity and charismatic talents will be the last thing on your mind.

If You Aren't the Whole Problem... Then You're Just Part of the Problem

I tell you one thing that happened during those six months, though. I had been reflecting for years on a particular injustice that I was suffering, really turning it around in my mind from every angle. Not only out of resentment, but really asking God why He was allowing this, had allowed me to suffer in that precise manner. And suddenly, almost at the end of my monastic retreat, I saw the time when I was in grade school, a particular incident, where I had allowed someone else to suffer in precisely the same way for five minutes.

I felt God telling me that this years-long sorrow I was experiencing was in fact no different than my not having intervened for five long minutes to help another child when I was less than twelve. An incident "from my childhood" that I believed had "happened to me" – because the event was in fact overwhelming and there were teachers present, too, who might have helped – had actually been a scene of moral responsibility on my part. I could have helped but didn't, and now was experiencing slowly what that other child's pain had been briefly. I am not saying that God had been punishing me, but that He showed me that my former stance about my own cross – that I was the aggrieved innocent – was a dangerous fiction, since at other times I had hurt people in the exact same way. Once I saw that, a way out opened.

You know, before that revelation in the monastery, I guess what I really thought was that God loved me and that that meant that the entire story of my life was about me. Other people's minor mistakes towards me loomed large, while I acted as though even my most morally criminal acts hardly mattered, to me or to the people I'd betrayed, since I had acted under difficult circumstances. It was sobering and shattering of a false kind of childhood to realize that

God loved me and that He had been expecting me all along to do everything within my power to overcome from within whatever chaos and lovelessness I faced.

As I tell my students, transposing a great 60s saying into Orthodox terms, "If you are not the whole problem, then you're just part of the problem."[40] Eventually we do have to become adults, in other words. We must see not only what happened to us, but whom we happened to. And it is important to see that *this kind* of adulthood is inseparable from a recovery of our childlike status before God, because genuine innocence should help us see more clearly that sin is childish.

In Orthodox Christian therapy, we reactivate the priesthood within a man or within a woman or within a child through the sequence of Beauty, Goodness, and Truth. In Orthodox therapy three to five hours per day of beauty are prescribed whenever possible (I mean, our physical presence in the divine services), and we learn a mildness that is the opposite of our berserk culture of shock. Protopriest Artemy Vladimirov, a confessor in Moscow, says that mildness is the single biggest missing piece in both our monasteries and in our parishes, for we have knowledge, patience, and zeal – but we fail to express all of this with a mild heart. "Mildness" captures the combination of boldness and shyness – healthy shame – if we do it right. *Philotimo*, too, includes a kind of infinite mildness amidst bright strength and joy.

In Orthodox therapy, we are taught to minimize the emphasis given to the causes of spiritual and emotional poverty, in ourselves and in others, and to instead refer everything to God. We promote a rich relational life with God and man in Christ by seeing the best, or at least hoping for the best, in everyone. We don't analyze the self to exhaustion but balance self-awareness with unknowing. I

---

40 Of course, the original saying was, "If you're not part of the solution, you're part of the problem." But I think that the original saying's heavy emphasis on busy activism is not always helpful. People have a right to live their lives in peace.

Also, if we were to follow the rule, "First, do no harm," then we would have to admit that much activism is worse than doing nothing. There are many poor people who would rather be left alone than be "helped" by arrogant outsiders.

mean, even if I understood myself and knew what was right to do, I still wouldn't do it!

Noetic prayer is the hardest work, the saints say. But they also say that it is the sabbath rest of a mind grown weary with the world, and that it is often received in repose from the attempt to "pray" with one's mind. So, let us rest, knowing that we are icons, and lean more on Christ, our archetype. Only as we grow closer to him, will we find out who we are.

The Church's two millennia-long experience is that the mind becomes much healthier when it can take periodic rests from all analysis, from discursive reason, and especially from rationalizations. These vacations of the mind can be achieved through noetic prayer, and when the mind descends from such noetic prayer, we find that it has been "re-booted," has received new default settings, has become more an icon of Christ's mind and less a dangerous weapon firing powerfully yet wildly.

When To Force and When Not To

RTE: So what does it mean when the Fathers (both patristic and contemporary) say you must "force yourself" to pray? In the framework you are talking about, what kind of effort needs to be made, and how does one rest in Christ while at the same time exerting such effort?

DR. PATITSAS: To everything there is a season, says Holy Scripture (Eccl 3:1). Although the Church Fathers who teach on prayer of the heart often invoke the verse that says, "... the kingdom of heaven suffereth violence, and the violent take it by force" (Mt 11:12), they also often warn that forcing the spiritual life or prayer in the wrong way or at the wrong time can lead to problems. The bad kind of force can bring on spiritual delusion, madness, or just a cold and judgmental heart.

Saint Porphyrios employed "violence" in his spiritual life in the following sense: he did not coddle himself, he was not lazy, he did not indulge himself, and of course he took the monastic habit. But he also taught that it was wrong to force prayer when it was not coming. He counseled that it would be better to stop for a minute, collect oneself, and warm up one's heart by meditating on love for God. Then, one could pray without injuring one's soul or damaging one's heart. He seems to have thought that we never outgrow the need for a Beauty-first approach of beginning our session of prayer with eros for theophany.

I would guess that in our own climate, where in general we don't have spiritual experts of the caliber of St. Porphyrios, that the best "violence" is to insist madly on the Beauty-first approach. Even when you are so angry and tired with your own sins or with the state of the world that you want to descend into intellectual analysis and moralistic striving, "Be still, and know that [God is] God" (Ps 46:10). Avoid berserk gestures, however pious or rational they look, for they invariably generate no end of trouble. Use the gentle violence of insisting on the way of eros instead.

For example, when we find ourselves in church (perhaps after having negotiated traffic and whatever obstacles at work or at home which nearly caused us to conclude that it would be a mistake to come to church at all), sometimes our main psychic energy then becomes immediately focused on our sins or on the reactions of other people in the congregation. If instead we can collect ourselves for a moment and see how beautiful everything is, then our time in church will be both more restful and more dynamic, more productive. If the service is short, there may not even be much of a need to "pray"; we have already prayed with our bodies by showing up. Now we just need to settle in. We must try to balance our examination of conscience with our awareness of God. We don't want to make even the divine services the scene of an individualistic moralistic striving that cuts us off from others. It can be instead both a sabbath rest and a more mystical encounter that will truly leave us transformed, if we are a little more clever about it.

Also, I have heard it said that sometimes we have what we think are dry periods of prayer but which are really God's giving us some other task to accomplish. Here again we must not worry but rather understand that lack of inspiration in one area of spiritual endeavor may be God pulling us toward some other aspect of spiritual life.

A simple story from the life of Elder Amphilochios of Patmos (1889-1970) gives us a memorable example, but I am sure that we can all relate in our own way. He was trying to pray, and was in fact in intense prayer, when an intrusive image of a young widow in distress kept entering his mind. At first he tried to regain his concentration, but suddenly he realized that God was leading him. He ran from his cell and down to the harbor of Patmos island, where a boat was leaving at that precise moment for the island where the woman in his vision resided. He jumped aboard, and upon arriving at the island (Ikaria), he hastened up from the harbor, asking if anyone had seen her. He located her at the edge of a cliff, about to throw herself to her death. Her husband had died some time before, and she was so distraught at the burdens she faced, that she could not go on. The saint was able to save her because he had given up his "prayer life" and followed the life God was showing him.

This is a dramatic example, but as we grow in prayer we come to see which of our failures in prayer are opening us for some other work in Christ, which need to simply be ignored as we rest, and which failures have to be overcome through "force." There isn't one answer.

Noetic prayer is a gift, ultimately, and is best approached through pilgrimage to places where the atmosphere of this prayer is present. In such places we might catch its spirit, and we might also learn how to continue it elsewhere in unobtrusive ways. Even if we are in one place, in our homes or in our monastic cells, we might think of the times set aside for noetic prayer as pilgrimages where we shall wait until, if God wills, we receive the gift. Confessors, therapists, or others to whom we turn for spiritual guidance, especially, should have this gift.

At any rate, they should at least not be training their spiritual offspring to investigate every rationalization that pops into their heads, granting such temptations significance, existence, and the central role in their spiritual lives. Other terms for the empty ideas and feelings that plague our minds are "thoughts" and "*logismoi*."

Logismoi

RTE: *Logismoi* is a very common term in Greek Orthodox writings, but it is less frequent in English translations. Can you give us an example?

DR. PATITSAS: A simple one, but at my own expense. Once I was standing in a bookstore in Seoul, Korea, and some salacious books caught the corner of my eye. Here was the *logismos* that followed: "Those are the sorts of books I shouldn't be looking at; let me just go closer to make sure I shouldn't be looking at them." Then, I laughed at how "rational" a total lie could appear to my fallen mind.

By the end of most days, many such thoughtless thoughts have passed through our minds and wounded, even if slightly, our hearts. That is why we end the day with Compline, to unknow all such rationalizations and know again our Savior "Jesus Christ, and him crucified." The prayers of the Church are designed to help us pass beyond the exhaustion and futility of mere thought, to the oasis of noetic knowledge.

People who do not have the opportunity or cultural awareness for Compline often watch the late night comedians' monologues instead. Comedy can have the same effect of robbing "thoughts" of their power, showing that these impressive idols have feet of clay. Late-night comedy, at least in some forms, functions as a kind of weak substitute for Compline.

The goal of Christian therapy is recommunion with the Church, not the cure of the individual, it has been said. It is an open question to what extent only re-entering communion can cure the individual or, on the other hand, the extent to which some cure of the individual is necessary before they can more fully re-enter communion. But our focus is always on Christ and his Body, the Church. We will find ourselves as we leave ourselves behind, and as we also leave our psychotherapeutic self-obsession behind.

In Orthodoxy, it is expected that no one can fill, by themselves and solely through mental work, gaps which were meant to be filled in the unspoken loving embrace of others, such as our early families. That would be just impossible by definition.

Consider two ways that in Orthodoxy we deal with the problems we might have had with our families of origin. First, we address our fellows in the Church by family names such as "father," "sister," "brother," or "gherondissa."[41] In other words, we allow new relationships to heal the hurt of old ones, without necessarily emphasizing analysis of what went wrong before.

And second, in many Orthodox Christian cultures we are encouraged to honor our parents by naming our children after them. Some people find this oppressive because they want to be creative with their children's names. However, the custom seems designed not only to honor the parents, but to liberate us from them, because it makes the young married couple right away into "the parents of their own parents." It is aimed at the transfiguration of a relationship that is so powerful that it can easily become idolatrous. The young parents can visualize every day that their own parents were children once, too, in need of guidance and of help in growing up. This naming practice both honors the parents and lessens any negative hold that they had on us.

Salvation by Faith Alone:
From Martin Luther to the Power of Positive Thinking

RTE: Something like the idea of *logismoi* was addressed by American self-help groups of the late twentieth century. These groups claimed to be scientific about dealing with negative thoughts, insisting that a person could employ rational tools outside of a religious frame-

---

[41] "Gherondissa" is Greek for "female elder," and it typically describes either an abbess or a simple nun of great wisdom.

work to clear the mind and transform one's "inner being." These approaches are still immensely popular, and range from secular self-improvement literature to older, more complex religious-based practices like Christian Science, and even include the exotic system of Scientology.

DR. PATITSAS: These movements which focus on our inner disposition are interesting to an Orthodox Christian. They have hit upon the vital relationship between the overcoming of "thoughts" and the cultivation of a more potent moral agency. Americans have made this connection especially since William James (1842-1910) and his interpretation of religious experience as a special moment of insight that could unlock new power and health in an individual. But even earlier, in Benjamin Franklin, we saw a non-religious version of the idea that controlling one's thoughts could lead to a fuller life.

In William James's account, it is sometimes unclear if the empowering "religious insight" is triggered by a genuine theophany, or whether it is merely the individual's own self-realization. The movements that you referred to above, however, almost certainly don't employ a true Beauty-first approach. That is, they reinforce our attention upon ourselves rather than on theophany and so, by definition, they lack eros.

Nevertheless, there is something positive in this concern for "thoughts." We are called by God to master inner temptations and to actualize our human agency. The many volumes in the self-help section of a bookstore are really aimed at helping us attain a more complete self-determination, usually under the name of "effectiveness" or "success." They represent, as does much of psychology, the effort to overcome the slings and arrows flung at us by bad moral luck.

The self-help impulse itself, which is what motivates this secular concern with the *logismoi*, begins when we say to ourselves, "Technically speaking, I am free; I can determine my own fate. But why don't I, then? Why am I so often the victim of bad circumstance?

Why are my bad habits so impervious to my efforts to overcome them?" So, this popular culture advice on cultivating better habits, better thoughts, or even on acquiring virtue is, at bottom, advice about liberty. We want to amplify our agency, to gain more power over circumstance, and to become truly free.

Whereas, for the ancients, good habits mattered as a path to liberty and virtue, or better still as a path toward liberty, virtue, and finally God, for us the matter of habits and thoughts is usually focused more squarely on agency, or freedom, for its own sake. Saint Paul does say, "For freedom Christ has set us free; stand firm therefore and do not submit again to a yoke of slavery" (Gal 5:1). But the freedom the apostle is preaching always has its aim in Christ-likeness.

But to get back to the matter of *logismoi*, specifically: Prayer and faith have always been central ways that Christians dealt with "thoughts." And we Orthodox, of course, know about this broader issue of thoughts through the monastic tradition and teachings on combating thoughts contained in works like *The Philokalia*.

As Americans, however, we might also trace our concern with "thoughts" to the life of Martin Luther. At the beginning of the modern period, Martin Luther broke with the Roman Catholic Church precisely because he was having so much difficulty in resolving his own "thoughts." While still a Roman Catholic priest, he felt a growing anxiety around the idea that he might not be saved. Any theological system or ethical practice of which he knew seemed to leave a debilitating doubt on this point. Finally, he resolved to vanquish all such "thoughts" through reliance on "faith." In other words, Martin Luther built his theology and later his church around his personal necessity to conquer a particular *logismos* about his own salvation. And this is why mission work in the churches Luther fathered often begins by trying to inculcate a similar *logismos* in the would-be convert – a similar anxiety about one's eternal salvation. The American Evangelical solution to the spiritual life presupposes a particular Lutheran problem – the problem of deep emotional agitation about one's eternal fate.

Luther was right to take the battle with *logismoi* away from philosophy and argument and toward faith because no truth-first system can ever completely defeat "thoughts"; *logismoi* find so much fertile ground in any intellectual construct that we need the aid of a meditation that silences the mind in order to find solid spiritual ground. Indeed, the inadequacy of a "Socratic" approach to salvation is why I remain cautious about American psychotherapy; I wonder if it doesn't often entangle us still more deeply in various *logismoi* by encouraging us to enter into conversation with them.

Martin Luther set out to reject both the truth-first emphasis of the late medieval theologian and the goodness-first emphasis of the late medieval preacher. Reliance on faith, he realized, would put both dogma and morals into a lesser place. The interesting question is whether we can therefore describe Luther's system as being Beauty-first. After all, living faith among evangelical Protestants is expressed through a focus on Scripture (in other words, on theophany) employed to combat "thoughts." This resembles what we observe in Christ's own temptations by Satan, just after his baptism in the Jordan. Clearly, something very good is involved in this Evangelical approach to the spiritual life.

Is Reliance on Faith the Beauty-First Way?

The matter is tricky, however, and although I am sympathetic to the Evangelical witness, I think that on three points it differs from the Beauty-first way as understood by the early Church. These three points are all facets, in turn, of the idea that our faith ought to be not only in Christ, but in Christ crucified.

First, there is the question of whether the approaches that have followed Martin Luther are Beauty-first or merely "Beauty-*only*." There seems to be no way within the American Evangelical world of talking about how Beauty must unfold into Goodness without immediately stepping on the landmine of "works righteousness." The idea that faith has to unfold into self-sacrificial agape somehow raises doubts about salvation so severe, that we are forced to stay stuck at step one, in "faith alone." Obviously, there is something wrong here, and something wrong with Luther's approach to combating *logismoi*, if when we follow it we are unable to handle this basic and needed unfolding of eros into a life of self-sacrificial works. After all, Christ himself did not preach "faith alone," but a rather more complex picture of salvation that also involved repentance and self-denial.[42]

Somehow, the scriptural command of Christ himself that the Christian should pick up his cross and die daily remains a stumbling block to the very people who most emphasize relationship with Christ and focus on his word. A truly Beauty-first faith would admit that salvation may not *depend on* works but that it is nevertheless *constituted by* and *looks like* a life of faithful actions, faithful words, thoughts, and prayers that render one's whole existence a "work of faith" – a liturgy. In that sense, failing to bear fruit in good works, failing to liturgize, is a sign that one's original faith has not found good ground, and has therefore not been effective for one's salvation.

A second problem with this "beauty-only" approach to salvation we saw earlier when we said that in the Jesus Prayer we long to "become sin" as Christ did. Not in the sense of committing sins, of course! No, not at all. Rather, because part of being saved is becoming willing to be regarded by the world as "lost," we may experience a deep longing to give our lives for the life of the world. We wish to be faithful to our leader, Christ, even unto death. The faith to which a Christian is commanded is not just a faith in Christ the resurrected and victorious Lord, but also a faith in Christ when He was despised and rejected. Therefore, the way to silence *logismoi* about our future salvation is not only to reassure ourselves that we

---

[42] This fact of Christ's own preaching, of course, was noted by the Lutheran theologian Dietrich Bonhoeffer in his *The Cost of Discipleship* (London: SCM Press, 1948). In Bonhoeffer's description of what he calls "costly grace," we can see that anointing must *always* be twofold, as in the Orthodox Christian view, and that faith should flower into works of both asceticism and agape. The gospel of what he called "cheap grace" was for Bonhoeffer the death of Christianity, not its perfect fulfillment.

are on the winning team, so to speak, but also to love God and his Church so much that we would rather "lose" than abandon our Savior whenever we find him on the cross.

Many commentators have worried that there remains something materialistic in American Christian faith; we want a Christ who will do all of the suffering for us, leaving us to enjoy only a sweet resurrection of wealth, health, and the earthly preeminence of our American nation. This materialist emphasis is not only found within the right-wing prosperity gospel but perhaps even more so in its more respectable left-wing cousin, the social justice gospel and its angry attempts to create a this-worldly utopia through social reform. Both of these visions are insufficiently familiar with the importance of "dying daily" as we follow Christ. A little *more* faith is needed by the Christian; enough faith to reject anxiety about the world and even about our own salvation.

Thirdly, we see that the Evangelical approach to salvation is presented as something static and individualistic. To be saved is thought to involve a stepping outside of time that grants us a personal insurance policy against all of our later sins and future betrayals of God. By contrast, in the early Church's vision of salvation, to be saved meant to be dynamically participating in two coinciding movements: eros for God and agape for one's neighbor.

In a sense, "faith in God alone" is sufficient *if* we understand that the God in whom we have this faith became man and gave his life for the life of the world. Therefore, if you really have faith in him, and not just in your own glorious and guaranteed future in heaven, you will also give your life for the life of the world. You will walk along the path of *both* of the two greatest commandments – and not just of the first one by having "faith." From the moment we set out on this more complete path of faith, we are saved.

For salvation is always a crucifixion of the self for the other, with the "other" being both God (faith crucifies the self because faith is an eros which involves an ecstatic self-forgetting and a trust in God) and man (whom we serve self-sacrificially through agape at the cost even of our own lives). Since the state of salvation is so clearly an "ever-moving rest" of love for God and neighbor, how could I then conceive of my salvation as a static commodity that I possess in isolation outside of a set of developing relationships with God and others? I mean, I don't want to press that perspective too far. You have to have some confidence in your heavenly future because it can seem like we do nothing but fail in those relationships – we see too clearly how we fall short of the gospel.

These three points, all closely related to one another, leave us with a question: what is more important to us, our own salvation or our Lord and God and our neighbor? If we have genuine faith, then we shall choose God and neighbor and launch out on an adventure of wild spiritual life and joy.

If we choose to remain focused on ourselves, then we shall find ourselves on unstable ground, wanting to be certain about our eternal fate, but still feeling doubt. Then, in the face of this doubt, we can either retreat more deeply into the self and choose the way of self-help, worldly success, or even the post-Christian cults; or, we can look for some proof of our salvation in the next world, yet still on the basis of the self, and remain ever hungry for new or strange "spiritual" experiences.

To the extent that Protestantism is a genuinely Beauty-first approach to the life in Christ (and to a large extent it is), it will have to face one more hurdle. Beauty-first puts God in the driver's seat of our religious life. What is required is actual experience of Christ in the Holy Spirit. You need theophanies, or the whole process can't even get started.

Well, this creates a tension and a pressure. If we are honest about it, we realize that we must wait upon the miracle of God's acting before we can get going in our spiritual life. But since we do want to grow spiritually, we might feel a pressure to find more theophanies able to elicit actual eros. This could come about in a good way, through the cultivation of gratitude and the meditation on Scripture and the lives of saints – and by giving a careful attention to our own quiet conscience. But we may also be tempted to manufacture such theophanies through mental gymnastics, through sentimentality, or through employing whizz-bang techniques in music, worship, and preaching.

RTE: Don't we Orthodox also give care to art, music, and architecture in order to help the faithful prepare to experience God? And, are you saying there are no genuine theophanies among Protestants?

DR. PATITSAS: There are countless real theophanies outside of Orthodoxy, enough to keep our world as close to God as it is. Saint Paul says that even the human conscience is a real message from God.

But a mature faith requires eventually joining oneself to the Church, it requires leaving behind the milk of one's childhood reliance on intellectual insights, emotions, or psychological manipulations, in order to receive the meat given in the theophanies of the Church in the *mysteries* of baptism, chrismation, confession, and Holy Communion. Mature faith requires growing from the "baptism of John" into the "baptism of the Holy Spirit." Christ is the Word of God – we need to eat his Body and drink his Blood, or we will "have no life in us." Holy Scripture is the verbal icon of this Word, and therefore Scripture does indeed have even a sacramental power. But we are meant to be guided by Holy Scripture all the way to the Communion chalice. This was a hard teaching when Christ himself said it (Jn 6:52-59), and it remains hard today. But we finally have to take that step.

And as to your other point, about the Orthodox use of the arts in worship, the Church has placed strict guidelines meant to ensure that the arts are consonant with, not mechanically productive of, mystical experience.

Yes, human religiosity does require a sort of guaranteed access to theophany. But this cannot come through emotions or tricks. This is why Roman Catholics, Orthodox, Lutherans, and even Luther himself maintained a stress on the sacraments, which are God's guaranteed action in the Church. These "predictable theophanies" which we find in the sacraments are meant by the Holy Spirit to be granted to those who are within the Church. We do need such predictable theophanies. Now, should they come about through the latest pop music? Or, through the mysteries handed down by the apostles themselves?

To summarize this whole section of our discussion, ever since the time of Martin Luther this emphasis on controlling "thoughts" has returned to the central place in the public religious consciousness in the West. To an extent, this is a return to the Beauty-first way. Indeed, if we can focus on positive theophany and devote ourselves to the crosses we were meant to carry, we could begin to experience our God-given freedom in a healthy way.

The Scientology Cult: Taking Square Aim at Logismoi

RTE: How would this need for theophany and reliance on faith play out in the pseudo-sophisticated secular experiments in thought control, such as Scientology?

DR. PATITSAS: After the Reformation, the healthy religious concern with "thoughts" gets bound up with other, cultural and economic, factors. The rebirth of vital urban centers in Western Europe, the rise of capitalism, and the growth of technology together spelled the death of the predictable feudal order. In its place arose the necessity for each person to take an increased responsibility for himself and the desire or even ambition to do so successfully, in worldly terms. Even today, many of us in the West eventually come to the point where we want to vanquish "thoughts" less out of love for Christ than out of love for ourselves, and less out of hope in the next world than out of an unhealthy passion for this one.

Positive thinking and the other movements you mentioned had their precursors in the writings and sermons of Calvin himself. Christianity was deployed as an aid to a bourgeois life; or rather, the goodness of Christianity could be seen in the success it helped its faithful adherents achieve. Methodism, aiming at the material and moral uplifting of England's urban poor, utilized the discipline of the gospel to help the lower classes succeed within the new market economy created by the Industrial Revolution. Mormonism arose in the nineteenth century in a burst of religious zeal, but its aim was always the construction of a this-worldly kingdom prepared to receive Christ as an earthly king. Even our twentieth-century fascination with meditation and Eastern religions was quickly subsumed into the drive for a successful, efficacious life in this world. We use yoga and meditation to cope with the stress of our overachieving lifestyles.

By the time we get to the invention of Scientology in 1954, we are many steps outside of a Christian consciousness. Even Mormonism, though its doctrine is technically speaking more akin to gnosticism than Christianity, still tries to respect Christ. Scientology, however, does not even claim to be Christian; some say that it is not even exactly a religion.[43]

But why, then, does Scientology find adherents? Precisely because it takes aim at the problem of *logismoi* much more squarely, much more comprehensively, and, above all, much more systematically than do most other religions. Scientology is explicit about striving for freedom from intrusive thoughts, and it has even invented biofeedback machines and novel meditations to help achieve this. In this, the Scientology cult is just one more interior application of the American experiment itself, which is to promote personal agency universally and democratically.

On this point, the overcoming of negative thoughts and of negative influences acting through our thoughts, Scientology vaguely resembles certain emphases found within the Orthodox Church, and thus it is on this point that most of its strength rests. Scientology also holds out the hope that our own increased agency will lead to others' being "saved." There seem to be no "unconditionally damned" in Scientology, a fact which is also encouraging.

---

43 Although Mormonism is much more closely modeled on Christianity than Scientology is, it is another faith with vast business holdings whose "spirituality" is centered in the cultivation of a quite specific and controlled mental outlook. Both of these religions see the self as being all but equal to God, although in the Mormon case the equality of our nature with God's nature is a doctrinal position, not something expressed in worship or daily life. There is at least a family resemblance among these two American faiths. Tolstoy famously called Mormonism "the American religion," by which he seems to have meant that Mormonism fit well with our national desire to strengthen personal agency and achieve success in this world.

We must be very wary of Scientology, however. People in this spiritual group may be learning some habits about how to face self-defeating thoughts, but they also seem to be brainwashing themselves. That is how they appear to outsiders, anyway. They don't seem at all like people who are overcoming "thoughts" through eros and self-forgetting, in the process becoming more free and alive.

Let's leave aside for the moment the fact that any spiritual practices conducted in a cult-like atmosphere may involve us in demonic energies – not because this is a small thing but because the pagan ancients also were often tricked by demons and yet still did attain good sometimes. Well, here in Scientology perhaps we do find some good; the practice of Scientology does help a follower like the actor Tom Cruise to inculcate certain disciplines and good works that might put us to shame, and so I am loathe to criticize him. I would very much like to have his good habits.

But Scientology rejects Christ, his divinity, and his saving death and resurrection. The healing of this world requires the uncreated grace that the Church receives through the Orthodox Christian priesthood and the sacraments; our unaided human efforts will never be enough, no matter how intense or enlightened these efforts might be.

Orthodoxy also combats *logismoi*, and Orthodoxy also addresses the problem of how bad thoughts can fatally compromise our moral agency. But Orthodoxy does so through Christ, and without generating cultish tendencies. In particular, Orthodoxy is productive of a personality that is deeply free because it is complete. An Orthodox saint looks and feels like a sort of fulfillment of human life, rather than some distortion of our humanity which we tolerate because certain compromises seem to be the price of success or even of peace in this fallen world.

In Orthodoxy, you gain agency, or freedom, by admitting and embracing your interconnectedness with Christ and others. This sounds counterintuitive, but it works. In Scientology, by contrast, you are supposed to gain this agency by separating yourself, by making yourself harder, more willful, and more hermetically sealed from others. You change the world, but you first learn to stand outside and above the world. A scientologist is better than those he helps, while a Christian is "worse." In Christ, you change the world from the vantage point of standing in "the lowest place" in the world, at its center, in the life-giving tomb of Christ.

So, Scientology seems to some degree effective because, to a greater extent than most Christian faiths and unlike American therapy, it understands that *logismoi* are a huge source of our problems and are not meant to be investigated. In fact, Scientology despises American therapy, which it regards as leading to passivity and to getting trapped in the rabbit holes that *logismoi* invariably bring. But Scientology is a false doctrine because it just tries to double down on the Enlightenment mistake according to which willpower, rationalism, science, and individualism become the great Archimedean lever to move the world. And, absent divine grace, its very attempts to overcome "thoughts" come to resemble self-hypnosis and not a true awakening.

No, Christ is the one who saves the world, and his lever is his death and his self-emptying and his resurrection; his standing point is the tomb.

Friendship in America

RTE: Let's go back again to your comment in the trauma interview that therapy has threatened to destroy friendship in America. That seems extreme. Can we start with your understanding of friendship?

DR. PATITSAS: Ok, seriously, therapists are the only ones left, in a commercialized culture, who have the time and the willingness to attend to your soul – although they won't really listen and will constantly try to jam your life into their preexisting categories. Still, their at least partial willingness to care is not merely because they are the only ones who have figured out a way to monetize listening in a culture where everything revolves around the bottom line. They really do care about your inner world; they are your *only* friends, it turns out! And they do a good job of helping you clarify some of your motivations without imposing any kind of teleological reference point, which in a sense is all that they promise. So, truth in advertising; good for them.

A school friend of mine, who is now a Metropolitan bishop in Albania, said that in his opinion there was almost no friendship left in America. He said that once when one of his friends in Albania needed him, he quit his job and moved to the friend's city for six months and lived through that crisis with his friend. Well, I don't know if you still see that here in America, but I know that in a rich country like ours, economic pressures often trump friendship. And I know that "it's all good," because, "Well, too bad for them: I've got my life to live, too."

Look, friendship is a higher good than self-realization or the gnostic fantasy of freedom from codependency. Friendship is the highest good available to human beings. But what makes friendship tricky is exactly the question of agency; i.e., the extent to which we should carry other people's loads, neglect our own responsibilities, and so forth. How do we balance committed loyalty to our friends with also letting them know when they are in the wrong?

Sadly, therapy has created a situation where, a) we can't tell our friends to just shut up, and yet where, b) we also don't back them to the hilt, all the way, no matter how wrong they are, when they are in trouble. We see all their problems as a lesson and an opportunity to lecture, rather than as the reason why we are there in the first place. In-your-face insight and distant "space" have trumped normal balance, loyalty, and warmth. That's not friendship; it's just cold betrayal. Friendship is not a chess game between Cold War superpowers; it's being under the pile while playing for the same rugby team.

And the general richness of personality in America before therapy was greater. It's not political correctness, mainly, that's to blame but an approach to soul health that involves this odd form of self-awareness that is even hard to describe. People are standing next to themselves; they aren't inside themselves anymore.

The Twelve Steps: Soul Health through Service

RTE: If we aren't fortunate enough to have a fully conscious Orthodox therapist who is engaged in noetic prayer, where should we go to find help outside the "empire of therapy"?

DR. PATITSAS: Well, we now tend to think of "help" as a service we consume, whether from a therapist or from a priest. The troubled person is a consumer looking for an outcome, a relief from distress. The current model of therapy is economic, seeing you as a lone individual seeking to satisfy some need. "Getting better" is a product that the sick person must be persuaded that he needs and that he must shop for.

Part of what this means is that all the onus falls on the person who is suffering. In the early days of Alcoholics Anonymous, they put the shoe on the other, correct, foot. Those who had discovered the AA society and were getting well felt a pressing obligation to search for those who were still in the state of despair and drunkenness out of which they'd come. So there was this reversal where you had an apostolic, missionary sense. Those recovering were supposed to be in search of those who needed help.

If the sick person is understood to be in need of help and unable to take the initiative, then they can't also be fully and independently to blame for not finding help; we can't have it both ways, no matter how Republican we want to be about it.

In the original Akron days of AA, when that little society was just starting out, they would make a second, even nicer reversal. When they went to the hospitals and mental institutions (which is where you found alcoholics in the 1930s because AA hadn't yet made its huge impact) to offer their help, they phrased the offer with some precision. They said, "I was told that you might have a problem with alcohol. Well, I *do* have such a problem. And I have found a method whereby I can stay sober, but it only works if I help another alcoholic. *So you would be saving my life, if you would just give me a half hour to tell you about this program.*"

Confession as Communion

Now, is this admission of the helper's *need* to help present within the Empire of Therapy? Is this the message of those who style themselves spiritual fathers? Why are they so anxious to have us come to confession, only then to bewail our intransigent refusal to improve once we do come? Is their attitude that they need to offer their service of spiritual fatherhood for *their* salvation? Or is it rather that you are lost and they are found? In that case they do need you, but they also need you to be sick for their own ego validation.

Confession for a priest is not "helping," but it is, rather, communion with his own flock. It is not only witnessing another person re-enter communion with Christ, but it is also for the priest a deepening communion with Christ through Christ's image, you the penitent. Not because the priest wants to know more details of your life, but because in his own self-emptying love for Christ, he is nourished by souls who are also pouring out their hearts for Christ. Thus, the event is for both him and us a holy and life-giving one.

I can tell you that it is very clear that the person to whom I confess finds the act of my confessing salvific for both of us – not because he needs me to be sick, but because the grace coming through him must be given away. His priestly identity is inseparable from his offering consolation and encouragement. His greatest joy is to give away what he has – whether you are sad or happy, struggling or conquering. And he is in no rush to use terms like spiritual father or spiritual child, nor is he in a hurry to give advice nor to choose other people's life paths. He is not interested in possessing you but in witnessing your rebirth into greater freedom and dignity. Long term, his goal is not "good" spiritual children at all, but, possibly, friends!

And why is this approach important? Because trauma, addiction, sin, unhealthy shame – they all have the same effect, which is to cast us out of communion with the people we are trying to relate to, to isolate us. We don't usually need a commission of clergy to excommunicate us when we fall because we ourselves already feel it.

But when I am treated as an individual consumer responsible for my own healing, whether by a therapist or by a clergyman, then that excommunication is underlined, intensified, and made more permanent in my very attempt to overcome it through my turn to such guides. And when the priest or therapist presents himself to me as "healthy," "saved," "bearing with me patiently," then in that case revealing my soul to them is an act of self-destruction on my part – one which I've risked many times because, what was the alternative? Who else was there to talk to?

But it never works. At the end of that kind of meeting the differential between us has only increased. They have become even richer, and I have become even poorer – even if I have gained some temporary emotional relief. They are even more safely "in the church" or "in normal society," while my membership is even more provisional, hanging tenuously from my supposed ability to not sin until the next confession or to not act irrationally until my next therapy session. No reconciliation has happened, only a deepening of my distance from the church, or from "normal" society in the case of therapy. And any cognitive gains in self-understanding attained in the meeting must be measured next to this deeper cognitive loss signified by the fact that the society or church no longer "knows me" as its own.

War Trauma: Our Brother's Keeper

Think of the sinner, the addict, and the trauma victim in this way, as an essential limb of our body that has been severed through some mishap or mistake. Now, who has the greater responsibility to reattach that limb? The severed foot, lying there and going grey as the blood runs out of it? Or the entire rest of the body, still possessing most of its functioning? The answer is obvious, and lecturing the foot is cruel, pointless, and shows that the rest of the body actually thinks that it can survive without that foot – so it is also an insane act.

Let me go back to war trauma for a moment. We as a society – you and I – sent more than two million of our strongest and bravest into harm's way after 9/11 because we did not want to see another Twin Towers here in America. People in those towers were left with the choice of burning to death or jumping to their deaths. It was not right that free people should be put to that choice.

I know that not every one of our foreign policy actions previous to 9/11 was pure, and that the policies pursued afterwards often spelled death for innocents in other places. My point is not the policy but the suffering of the loyal soldier who said, "I will risk my life so that the people I love will be safe, and I will try to make other countries safer from religious extremism or political tyranny, as well."

And if some hundreds of thousands of those who went off intending to prevent a replay of 9/11 now remain excommunicated as PTSD sufferers – now are, figuratively-speaking, lying there, cut off and severed from normal participation in the social body, from normal participation in the body of their own marriages and families, how is that mostly *their* fault? And why should we think of it as mainly their responsibility to "get well"? That's not how we treat those physically wounded in war, so why should we treat those spiritually wounded in that way? And until we stop thinking of it that way, we as an American people won't get well, either, while our returned soldiers lie there, bleeding out spiritually.

RTE: Since you've come back to the subject of trauma, how would a therapist trained in an analytical approach move into a Beauty-first way?

DR. PATITSAS: There *are* therapeutic approaches, empirically verified as being more effective, for the treatment of PTSD. All of them conform to one degree or another to the Beauty-Goodness-Truth model. Therapists can hope and agitate that the better methods will soon be the preferred and even standard methods employed at the Veterans Administration.

For example, from what I can understand of it, Cognitive Behavioral Therapy (CBT) is not really "cognitive" at all, in the sense of being analytical. Rather, it identifies those of our thought-patterns associated with the debilitating effects of trauma as being, in effect, no more rational than *logismoi*, encouraging the patient to hang a "do not disturb" sign on those thoughts and instead practice other, healthier, thought patterns. This sounds to me similar to the unknowing associated with noetic prayer. In other words, despite its name, CBT is the opposite of this too-Socratic, too-intellectual therapy I have been deriding all along. It is an ally of the Beauty-first approach, not its opponent.

The "Cognitive" in Cognitive Behavioral Therapy is actually about unknowing the thoughts that accompany trauma flashbacks and trauma-related reactions and behaviors. But I cannot "endorse" this method because that would be stepping beyond my practical experience.

All I can tell my brothers and sisters in the counseling community is that a truth-first approach will have limited utility for *all* their patients, and could even harm the trauma sufferer, whereas the right Beauty-first approach would bring better results, especially when dealing with trauma. It is up to the professionals working with people's souls to re-think their own Enlightenment biases and go much farther still towards the light. I think they are only scratching the surface.

Maybe small societies composed entirely of combat veterans and a few chosen friends – some of these might be friends from the therapeutic or religious communities, some might be other trauma sufferers, some might be non-combat veterans – will develop their own traditions about healing from combat trauma that will be centered in drama, in beauty, in the ordinary tricks and habits by which we recover, and in the experience that the way to recover is to show empathy for other combat veterans. The *Iliad* works exactly like that, giving the veteran the chance to show empathy for other soldiers who lived before him.

And I hope that a diagnosis of PTSD will someday result in receiving the Purple Heart; it is not something shameful, but rather a qualified honor.

Honoring Our Parents

RTE: Until now, we've mostly talked about the difficulty of healing war trauma. How about healing other kinds of trauma, such as truly difficult childhoods?

DR. PATITSAS: I think that it would be similar in many respects; in particular in the idea that trauma generates within us a toxic shame. Therefore, trauma's healing will have to be centered on the cultivation of healthy shame. For example, the answer to the trauma of a bad childhood that can be so morally disorienting cannot be for us to shamefully disrespect our parents. It can only be to find a better, different father – the Heavenly Father. And it can only be for us to find an additional, supplemental, mother – Panaghia and the Church. We cannot trade one kind of bad shame for another kind of bad shame and expect to get anywhere.

Insisting that we not humiliate our parents can be very hard if their abuse or neglect was unimaginably painful. But I also know that while the other way – of criticizing our parents even publicly – may seem to be necessary for a season as a means of survival, it might make actual healing harder later on. If possible, we must avoid disrespecting our parents. Publicly disrespecting our parents is usually a berserk act. Not only is it crazy, in other words, but doing it makes you crazier still.

It's quite risky to discover through the intellectual analysis of your childhood that you were parented imperfectly. Far better would be to so experience the perfection of your Heavenly Father's love for you, that you can see in your parents' comparative imperfection not just a cause for sorrow. Your parents were only an icon of this ultimate parenting, and knowing this helps us to see them accurately.

And just as we don't look at an icon that is not well painted and become enraged at its imperfection, so we shouldn't condemn our parents. So often, when we "forgive" a poorly painted icon, we come to love it more, as we see how through even such a humble state it manages to convey infinite grace.

Since your parents are an icon, you see not their faults but their limitedness; and you do not denigrate their love for its imperfection but elevate it to the eternal significance in which it imperfectly participated.

Reverse Osmosis

Of course, when we're down, when we're weak, then incidents and memories from the past (whether involving our families or not) can be enough to defeat us. They loom large in our memory and they control our present feelings and reactions. It really seems as if they were the most important information about us.

But the main answer in such cases is to ignore these thoughts and complexes while we build up our strength. Once we reach a point where we are strong enough, and where God's grace is strong enough within us, then the positive forces within will naturally repel the dark power of these past events.

To give an analogy, after 9/11 the newly-formed Department of Homeland Security advised Americans to defend their homes from possible biological or chemical attack by choosing a room in the house that could be sealed airtight. People bought tape and clear plastic, and then sealed themselves in for a few minutes to practice for such an awful eventuality.

Of course, what people discovered immediately is that the official governmental advice was terrible. They were literally suffocating themselves. This sealing-in couldn't work as a solution to a chemical or biological attack.

A better answer was quickly found. It was learned that in some countries the strategy for defense from poison gas attacks was to fit one window of the home with a small but powerful air filter. This device would suck in air from the dangerous outside, and in the process rid it of toxins.

Then, the filter drawing in outside air would create a positive air pressure within the entire home, such that no bad air could enter through any of the unsealed windows or doors. In effect, this rush of clean air into the house gave each home an invisible "shield" of clean air, protecting the inhabitants.

That, by analogy, is what Elder Porphyrios meant when he said that no one ever became holy by fighting evil, or what Jane Jacobs meant when she said that you couldn't "fight blight" in a ghetto as if it were some sort of physical enemy. No, our first priority in all such cases must be to feed the good, to strengthen what is positive in the house (purified air), in the soul (eros for Christ and healthy shame, generally), and in the city (the elements of complex urban order that are working well), and then to let the power generated by these dynamic forces ward off all harmful influences.

The Saint and Shame

RTE: Thank you. Will you summarize, then, how we are healed?

DR. PATITSAS: Shay concludes *Achilles in Vietnam* with a surprising comment. He says something like, "I like the American method of therapy. I sometimes see good results, and for this both I and the patients are grateful. But I can't escape the sense that other cultures knew better than we do how to heal the soul."

Well, what if Orthodox Christianity turns out to be one of those cultures that knows better? In that case, we should treat our own spiritual tradition with more curiosity and more respect. Setting forth the importance of Beauty-first, of healthy shame, and of the limited utility of "truth" is my small contribution to that recovery of our tradition.

I mentioned before the story of the Christian ministers who had been trained in seminary not to see the relevance of Christ's resurrection for their terminally ill patients. Imagine how far we have fallen!

For in actual fact, the individual can only occasionally be cured through further reference to himself and his own feelings. Healing is fostered when we are able to interpret our experience in the light of our relationship to God. Or, to put it another way, when our experience becomes consciously anchored in some archetype of ultimate value, then we begin to see the eternal significance of what we have suffered. Until we can glimpse how our life relates to God's own life, we have a crisis of meaning. As the psychologist Carl Jung once said, for a patient over forty years of age, there was never more than one *real* problem – "What is my relationship to God?"

So you can see how the New Age return to gnosticism follows the therapeutic culture as night follows day. Since no God is offered in our culture's process of soul-healing and soul-meaning, the person is forced to elevate *himself* (the obsessive subject of American psychotherapy) to the position of God.

One principle for real healing can be seen in the American South, in the slave experience. Before 1865, all the feelings-focused therapy in the world could not have changed the facts of the slave's life. But *their religion* could offer *a meaning* to a level of suffering that would otherwise have driven people to despair, suicide, and madness. That religion saved them by showing them an archetypal people who had also suffered and yet had been delivered. The Bible showed them that they were like the Hebrew people in Egypt, that one day a Moses would come to deliver them.

Seeing that the saints and the people of God are our spiritual ancestors is one example of how to interpret your life theologically. Another is more general: that we try to balance any increase in self-knowledge with an increase in knowledge about the saints and about our archetype, Christ. We won't really know ourselves until we know the Person according to whose image we were made. American therapy is like trying to correct a copy of the Mona Lisa without ever looking at the Mona Lisa. Does this make sense?

For our individual lives to have meaning, they need to find a context that matters. Our nuclear family of origin can never be more than one sliver of that context, in particular if it was as dysfunctional as we claim! We need to locate our lives in the larger context of our nation's story, our Church's story, and most of all in the economy of God. We need to turn to both the Bible and the lives of the saints.

Cultivating healthy shame lies near the center of Orthodox Christian soul therapy because the main goal of the spiritual mother or father is to restore the priesthood of the fallen victim of sin. That would mean to unleash in us again the power and the skill to love God and to love our neighbor at our own personal expense. Our destiny – the standard of health – is Christ, but it is not simply Christ. Rather, it is Christ, and him crucified. The person who has not learned how to make of his life an offering to God for the life of the world will be neither at peace nor spiritually complete.

In other words, when we can no longer make any offering of our lives to God for the life of the world, at that point precisely we are in danger of losing our humanity. This can be the berserker; it can be the heroin addict; it can be the cruel intellectual in his cold ivory tower; the moralizing uncompassionate preacher; it can be the selfish rich. All alike have left behind both priesthood and shame, and thus are seeing their own humanity slip away.

Is the recovery of shame and priesthood what therapy preaches? Or does it preach an ever-increasing recollection within the isolated self, an ever more elaborate web of mental rationalizations, the dispensability of others, and an odd faith in a God who can never invoke awe, shame, and wonder in our hearts? When it takes away our unhealthy shame, what does it replace it with? And how could any system based on rational self-interest (including capitalism and socialism) really convene a culture of friendship, raise a people whose priesthood for one another was refined and reliable?

In meeting the saint, two things stand out inseparably: love and healthy shame. Love for Christ, for the Church, for the fellow man, for every leaf and blade of creation. And shame, evident in the perfect respect for all and for themselves that the saint carries. In the presence of the holy person you feel loved, and you also feel the energy of shame arising within you in a renewed and proper form. You recover your humanity. You again become embarrassed about your sin, while also realizing that it isn't really your true self. And you gain again the wildness and freedom from vanity you had as a child.

The saint is a person in whom coincide limits and no limits. They are at once utterly aware of their dependence and createdness but have been given the license to swim in a limitless ocean of divine grace.

CHAPTER FIVE

ONLY PRIESTS CAN MARRY

The Reconciliation of Men and Women in Christ

Our concern in this chapter is the mystery of gender, an issue which has become increasingly vexed in our society. A new way of considering gender difference is proposed which borrows elements from both the "left-wing" insistence that the genders are interchangeable and the "right-wing" assertion that the genders are complementary. This new way is chiasm, wherein men and women, in embracing the cross of Christ within their biologically given genders, come to symbolize each other's vocation while experiencing the transfiguration of their own.

For Orthodox theology, troubles between men and women, and frustrations with gender, can be traced to the Fall in the Garden of Eden. In fact, Christ's mission of reconciliation was also intended to heal this war between the genders that began when Adam and Eve first betrayed each other. In the light of Christ's death and resurrection, Christian marriage and Christian monasticism are born, two ways whereby we can experience a foretaste of the eschatological gender peace of the heavenly wedding banquet.

Finally, this chapter examines another split: that between Roman Catholic and Protestant conceptions of the human person. We briefly remark on the anthropological work of Dietrich Bonhoeffer, who attempted to overcome this rift and negotiate a middle way between the Scylla of Pelagianism and the Charybdis of predestination. By reframing his argument in language borrowed from patristic Christology, we can show how human nature, human will, and human personhood are each affected by God's saving work in Christ.

I. THE SHAPE OF GENDER RECONCILIATION

RTE: While our readers know you principally through these interviews, in Orthodox Russia and Greece it is your scholarly article, "The Marriage of Priests: Towards an Orthodox Christian Theology of Gender,"[1] that is sometimes discussed. What readers find most surprising about this article is the sheer elegance of its account of Christian gender.

DR. PATITSAS: Even to me, the approach to gender presented in that article seems like a work of art, like a revelation of beauty. It's beautiful because it is complete, simple, and yet contains these really liberating and consoling surprises that arise through the daring embrace of self-sacrifice. You never get the feeling that the account of gender in that article is suppressing some parts of the truth in order to promote other parts. Its vision is majestic, in that way; it has scope and depth.

When I go back today and read "The Marriage of Priests" article, almost fifteen years after having first thought about it all, I sometimes find that passages within it take my breath away, even though it is written in a kind of strict style that is anything but elegant. I wrote it in that engineering, point-by-point format because I never had the feeling that I was figuring out its ideas, creating them or reasoning them out. Rather, in a single flash, while at a typical Saturday evening vigil in the beautiful Russian Orthodox church of St. John the Baptist in Washington, D.C., I saw the entire thing. The almost mathematical order in the article is an attempt to avoid being overwhelmed by what I "saw." I almost fell down when the insight came to me because this new picture was so beautiful and sublime.

---

1 "The Marriage of Priests: Towards an Orthodox Christian Theology of Gender," published in *St Vladimir's Theological Quarterly*, vol 51 (no. 1), 2007, 71-105. For my first work-up of this vision of gender, see Chapter Six of "The King Returns to His City: An Interpretation of the Great Week and Bright Week Cycle of the Orthodox Church," Ph.D. diss., The Catholic University of America, 2003. The Chapter is entitled, "Chiasm: Relations of Genders and of Syndromes," and parts of it were revised and became the published article.

Not to say that this account is "revealed." I am an obvious sinner, and those who know me would smile at the idea that I was normally a seer of anything but too much television. In Orthodoxy we have a nice saying when it comes to mystical experiences: "Neither accept nor reject." In other words, neither be in a hurry to accept that you were last night counted worthy to see a saint in a dream nor be in a hurry to deny God's ability to speak even through a donkey like yourself. In my case, the wider Church will judge over time if what I presented about gender is correct in its approach or if it requires revision, or if it was simply a subconscious, emotional, passionate (in the Byzantine sense of "passions" as distortions of our healthy drives) attempt by a young and starving academic to make sense of part of his dissertation work.

RTE: And that is a process that is happening now, as more Orthodox Christians are gaining access to the article in Russian and Modern Greek. Can you provide a glimpse of what you perceived in church that evening and how it unfolded as you wrote about it?

DR. PATITSAS: My intuition, by the way, is that the vision of gender in that article is right, and the beauty of it is precisely what makes me think it's right. As a Christian meditation about gender, "The Marriage of Priests" article never separates Beauty from Goodness from Truth. It has mildness.

Why would the truth about the world created by a loving God look unseemly or jarring? The world sees gender as a source of oppression, as something ugly; the world is traumatized by gender, because in responding to it wrongly, the world has indeed made it a source of oppression. But that was not God's intention.

The vision I saw was basically this: men and women alike are called to the same three offices; that of priest (to offer sacrifice), that of king (to lead and to fight), and that of prophet (to bring forth a word of insight). What differs between the genders is that the primary calling among these three offices for women is the prophetic office, while for men, it is the kingly office.

What unites men and women, though, is that they are called to fulfill their primary offices in a priestly way – that is, in a self-sacrificial way. They are charged to inscribe the cross of Christ within their primary gender offices, within their respective gender callings. Their first task is *not*, in a sense, to fulfill their gender calling, but – a challenging paradox – to "crucify" that particular calling.

When they do so, three things happen. First, their primary office (prophecy for women, kingship for men) seems to be all but wiped out as they become chiefly priests; in other words, their gender office dies, is humiliated, as it is offered sacrificially to God and to each other. Second, their gender office is re-born in a transfigured and much higher form.

But the third point is the biggest surprise in what I understood, and is the reason why what I saw seemed so beautiful that I was filled with wonder. The real way that Christian gender is inverted from the world's is that in Christ each gender not only dies and is reborn, *but in being reborn comes to a dynamic rest as the truest symbol not of its own life but of its partner's role and life.* Men come to symbolize best the feminine prophetic office, while women come to symbolize best the masculine kingly office. Thus both men and women experience all three offices, but according to a Pattern or a Way that is unique to each. This is how the genders are deeply reconciled in Orthodox life, in a loving act of mutual indwelling and self-offering.

The Chiasm at the Heart of the Gospel

In literature and in art, we call the inversion of two elements a "chiasm," from the Greek letter Chi (X) that can be physically traced when each element is joined to its repetition, since in their second occurrence the elements have switched places. In other words, in poetry you have a rhyme scheme like a-b-b-a, in which the place of the a and b are inverted when they are repeated. Such chiastic connections also occur in painting, intertwining elements across a canvas, or across the length of a novel or other work of literature.

An artistic or even literary device like chiasm functions here in this new way of talking about gender because Beauty is inseparable from Goodness and Truth: any Orthodox account of the world is always also an aesthetically coherent account. Here, the chiastic inversion and reconciliation of the genders that occurs traces a pattern that is really gorgeous.

RTE: It strikes me that while our reflection in a mirror shows us ourselves accurately, as does a photograph, neither a photograph nor a reflection is us; it's just a projection, an image of us at that moment. Whereas, in chiasm, the "image" of the original element we see is actually the original but now in an expanded form. Is that right?

DR. PATITSAS: Yes. In chiasm, it is not a mere shadow but the thing itself that appears in the new place. And, in addition, in chiasm the thing itself in this new place is actually different, transfigured – it is not a mere repetition of its earlier form.

Even in poetry, when the word or meaning shows up in a new place in the subsequent line of verse, the element *has* changed, even if it is precisely the same word that reoccurs. That identical form now carries a fuller or nuanced meaning by virtue of its reuse in a different or surprising context.

Above all, Orthodox Christians should understand that chiasm is the very essence of sacramental life, of all Christian life, of the gospel itself: God became man so that man might become God (St. Athanasius of Alexandria). This chiasm is the gospel in one sentence. I think that readers will see this basic theological chiasm at the heart of the gospel directly and easily because in this case the chiasm of location in the sentence is also the chiasm of being, of existence. There is a "divine commerce" – one name by which the Fathers called chiasm – involved in our taking on God's divinity, while He takes on our humanity.

Let me draw it out, physically, so that people can see what we mean:

God became man
so that
man might become god.

A person might think that the gender chiasm is simply a metaphor, a clever literary effect. Ok, they might say, it looks elegant, but it's not real. They might even say, if they do not feel what real Beauty is, that the chiasm's elegance is itself the proof that it is not a worthy description of gender in Christ. When the beauty of chastity is ridiculed in the name of sophistication and "liberation," the chaste beauty of the chiasm will be treated in the same way – as an oppressive lie rather than a liberating truth. Chiasm is the mutual crucifixion of maleness and femaleness, though, and not some idyllic fantasy.

These days, people have been fooled so many times by fake beauty that they almost come to expect that truth should be expressed in ugly or traumatic ways. Well, they do have a point – Christians are commanded to preach Christ, and him crucified, not some fairy tale. But let us not go to the other extreme by forgetting that the crucified Christ conquered death and is now seated at the right hand of his Father in heaven. Within beauty there is a balance between form and roughness, oftentimes. Is the chiasm "just ugly enough" to be true, might be the question. Clearly, it is, because it is centered wholly on the Cross!

The very essence of our relationship with God is a chiasm – by his will, not ours. After all, in the Garden we wanted to simply usurp God's role and leave our own human place behind; much as those who disturb marriage and gender today also want to denigrate their own role and take on that of the other gender. Christ shows us a different way, a way based in self-sacrificial love and not in the desire for power. We experience this exchange of places precisely because we each honor and retain our own place, in a wonderful paradox.

Speaking of transfiguration, St. Maximos the Confessor was very keen to remind us that our *deification* is always and forever God's renewed *hominification*; that is, no one can be deified except God again become incarnate, this time in the person being deified. We actually see two things on Mt. Tabor in Christ's Transfiguration: God has become man, and human nature has become divinized.

Christ is the nexus, the crucial center point, of a chiastic exchange between the created and the Uncreated, and, in general, chiastic exchange is the very definition of love; there is no love without chiasm because love always means the willingness to make way for the other so completely that we come to be a sacrament of them, to live *our own* unique life in such a way that we also become the epiphany of *their* life to those who see us.[2] When in Christ we die "for the life of the world," we ourselves become the very best examples of what this world was meant to have been in Christ.

Lars Thunberg, a well-respected expositor of St. Maximos' theology, says that all of the saint's many theological concerns came down to two themes: to show that the unity and diversity in Christ's two natures mutually conditioned each other; and that the deification of man always implies God's ongoing incarnation. But both of these concerns the saint resolves through chiasm. Notice, for example, that:

>Without unity, there can be no diversity
>(for on what common basis could
>we then establish difference itself?)

>while

>Without diversity, there can be no unity
>(for what would then be left to be unified?)

---

[2] In 1994, neurologists in Italy first discovered "mirror neurons," the parts of our brain that are activated by what we see others doing, such that we are able to feel what another person feels. This may be the physical neurological foundation of our ability to relate to other human beings. Crucially, people who lack this ability not only cannot relate to other human beings, but they also are unable, in some sense, to become human themselves. So again, we see that in the chiasm – in my becoming you, and you, me – we become real.

Chiasm, above all, is the defining structure of the Confessor's theology in the seventh century, although the saint does not explicitly use this term. And it applies, it turns out, here in gender as well. My own gender article is merely an application of St. Maximos' style of reasoning to one of the five tragic divisions that the saint himself said that Christ intended to overcome – the enmity between men and women.[3]

The Process of Healthy Grief Is Chiastic

When we love, we become the symbol of what we love. This is such an essential point about the life in Christ that we should not be surprised to find it in the case of gender. Let me step outside the realm of gender for a moment to show how love is always expressed chiastically.

When we are mourning a lost loved one, don't we always go through a process where we see the dead loved one as still "alive," as having been uniquely real and permanent? And at the same time don't we always, at least for a time, see ourselves as "dead," as a kind of walking dead, or as not being as "substantial" as they were? When I meditate on the departed generations in my home parish of Akron, Ohio, my life in comparison seems insubstantial, as if I have done nothing all my days but watch cartoons and eat cocoa-puffs. This chiasm within grief, wherein the dead one seems truly alive while the living one experiences being "dead," is the sign of love and is even a confession of the Resurrection; in their death, our loved ones have become more alive (we feel) than ever.

---

3 In fact, only in the light of "The Marriage of Priests" could I begin to understand St. Maximos' theological program. Although chiasm is also centrally present (though again unnamed as such) in his predecessor, St. Dionysios, St. Maximos the Confessor uses chiasm to resolve a wider variety of theological problems. Lars Thunberg has his own term for chiasm – he translates what the saint himself calls the καλη αντιστροφη as "the blessed inversion." Exactly!

The Vietnam Veterans Memorial

There are few memorials that capture the basic chiasm of loving grief to the extent that the Vietnam Veterans Memorial in Washington, D.C. does. The living visitor descends into the earth gradually, becoming "dead" as he does so, while those buried below the earth, their names inscribed upon polished granite, gradually rise above us as somehow eternally real, immutable, forever young, and alive. Our death is their resurrection; although, in fact, they are dead and we are alive.

The experience of this chiastic exchange has a unique capacity to unfreeze trauma, at least temporarily, making us able to release the bitterness of what Jonathan Shay called "thwarted grief." When we climb back out and emerge from the other side, we are different people. Our union with the deceased is secure. Even the shape of the Vietnam Veterans Memorial is one side of the Greek letter Chi; the memorial literally draws you through a chiasm.

When we first fall in love and we and our beloved are safely in each other's arms, this chiasm again applies. We long for this exchange of identity by which we become the epiphany of them and they of us, though without losing our own identity. We long to become an icon of them, in a sense.

Chiasm, in other words, is not just some literary device or trick. It is actually part of the essential structure of love itself. It should not surprise us to find a chiasm at work in healthy gender relations.

The Divine-Human Chiasm Is a Gift
Received through the Mysteries

In the basic chiasm of the Christian gospel that we mentioned above – God became man so that man might become god – something new about God is revealed: He loved us so much that He would become us, and die for us as one of us. And here something new about man is also revealed: that his destiny and majesty would not be fulfilled until he became "god," had become a sharer in God's uncreated life. So your earlier observation is spot on – when we see a chiasm, we are seeing far more than a mirrored repetition of each element; it is more like a fulfillment through a deep transfiguration.

Sacramental theology (in Orthodox Christianity our preferred term for the sacraments is the "mysteries") is nothing but the study of chiasm; it's a meditation on God's condescension, his permitting things "to be what they are not," but without corrupting them or ruining them in what they are. And He allows this, He orders it in fact, because in his love for us He wants to become what He is not – incarnate in us. Yet at the same time, He will not cease to be what He is, the transcendent God.

And we don't just *receive* sacraments; we are meant to *become* sacraments for others and for the life of the world. You don't become who you really are until you attain this sacramental status, this level of symbol. We are meant to be the icons of God, his epiphanies in this world. We are not fully real until we also become "myth."

Even so, in the gender chiasm a woman fulfills the manly role *in a more paradigmatic way* than he can, while destroying *nothing* of her femininity. Likewise, a man fulfills the womanly role *in a more paradigmatic way* than she can, while destroying *nothing* of his masculinity. We will give examples of this later, but this is the reason why the Orthodox Christian sacramental priesthood will always be reserved to men: it is the duty of *men* to become the icons of the feminine office of motherhood by giving Christ's Body and Blood for Christ's children, while *women* are called to enact the masculine role by standing guard and protecting the performance of the offering. Orthodox Christian priesthood is too feminine a role to also be *symbolized* by women, as I will explain in a moment. Similarly, the foundation of a Christian society's protection always must fall back on the fortress of motherhood. It is too masculine a role for men to make good icons of, in this rich sense of "icon" that Orthodoxy uniquely preserves. You can't symbolize what you already are.[4]

---

4 In the chiasm, male kings will, through grace and experience, learn to express a female prophetic wisdom. Female prophets, meanwhile, will learn to express authority even while practicing the nurturing and hospitality involved in "bringing forth a word."

Moreover, outside of grace, apart from God, these paradoxes are impossible to attain, and women and men alike may either destroy themselves as women and men without bearing fruit or remain locked, seeds that never flower because they are unsure of how to be planted, how to die, how to remain themselves while yet becoming something totally other.

Yes, it's clear that in discussing gender in terms of chiasm we are approaching the central mystery of love rather than generating an optical effect. I mean, in the gender chiasm the husband becomes the truest and best symbol of his wife and she, of him. It is more like what has been said about the sacraments, that "they are what they are not." And moreover, in chiasm, in contrast to a photograph, the original doesn't really become its truest self until it reoccurs in the place of its opposite. I mean, it's the Virgin Mary who

---

This does not mean that women will necessarily become more "public," however, as they become more kingly. The general kingly calling of men means that as individuals they tend to play out whatever talents they have in ways more visible to society. Meanwhile, the general prophetic calling of women means that they may prefer to work more or less behind the scenes, especially when they are confronted with the inability of some men to understand the word they are bringing forth.

In other words, we human beings are operating on several levels at once, conducting delicate balancing acts in our expressions of gender at each level. For example, a particular man may not be drawn to kingly roles but will still face such duties whenever the interests of his wife or children demand this. And a woman may be more gifted than the average man in leadership and command but may still find herself inclined to "give way" if she sees that the men around her cannot respect her in this role; alternatively, of course, she may discover ways to express her authority that do protect the kingly calling of the men around her. When a woman in authority sees the impulse in herself to give way entirely, she will have to decide when to "lean in," as a recent book puts it, by insisting on commanding, or when to accept, as all warriors must, that discretion is sometimes the better part of valor.

Even so, there were Orthodox empresses in Byzantium and Russia, and pious queens throughout the Christian world. They had to overrule the feminine tendency within themselves to follow men, for this was simply not how God had arranged their lives. But they could not overrule their feminine calling so completely that they were seen as pretending to be men. The different levels at which a human life operates must all be respected, in a difficult dance. Even a Christian queen is going to base her political rule on her chastity and modesty. When women try to rule or lead based purely upon a machismo or the latent threat of violence, this almost never succeeds, once men are involved.

Men, precisely because they are more "public," have already-developed codes of how to handle this tension from their side. The very idea of chivalry is that the nurturing heart of the knight should never be divorced from the hard outer shell of his warrior nature. Conversely, the most sensitive man must still give the impression that to fight him would simply be too much trouble – either physically, morally, or legally.

is the Unconquerable General, not any man; she more than anyone but Christ himself shows us what the masculine office can mean.

The Inflection Point within Chiasm

There was a music trio in the late 1990s that would sometimes dress chiastically. The singer to the left would have a white top and black skirt, for example, while the singer to the right would at the same time have a black top and white skirt. Your eye unconsciously traces the chiasm formed by linking white top to white skirt across the middle of the picture and black top to black skirt, also across the middle. Well this chiasm acted to focus the music fan's attention on the third singer, the one in the middle – whose mother, it turns out, was the person designing the costumes!

Chiasm always acts to focus our attention on what is at the inflection point. In the case of this chiasm of genders, what is squarely in the center is the priesthood of Christ, or rather the person of Christ, crucified and resurrected. He is the inflection point because it is his priesthood that draws men and women together – but then his priesthood does even more than that. It turns men and women inside-out so that they are more than united: they actually come to symbolize each other. This is no mere "gender complementarity" at work here!

Thus, you have a marriage of priests. By priests I mean the man and the woman who each offer their gender self-sacrificially to God at the site of Christ's cross because in this self-sacrifice they become firstly "priests." Christian gender defeats and yet embraces both the worldly concept that men and women are complementary and the worldly concept that men and women are interchangeable. Men and women are meant to be *different* precisely so that they can experience that highest *unity* which can only come *through symbolizing someone different than oneself.* This is a unity at a far higher plane than mere interchangeability (which we wrongly call "equality," for if men and women were not distinct, then neither could men and women be equal – since in that case the words "men" and "women" would themselves have no meaning). This unity is also at a far higher plane than complementarity, a concept which is also partly correct but which, again, when pressed too far becomes destructive.

But let us bracket this now, and we shall come to it all in greater depth. We should approach this in a more measured way.

What Struck Me

You asked about how the gender article was written. The background is that I had been thinking about our culture's problems with gender for many years, and had even written an entire, never-published manuscript about it. And what happened to me could happen to anyone, that when you have slowly gathered all the pieces of a puzzle and then suddenly put them together for the first time, you feel almost overcome. The mind does feel overwhelmed. Happening as it did in church, in a church founded by two holy elders, St. John Maximovitch and Fr. Nicholas Pekatoras (1899-1996), the insight carried with it something more, some sweetness of grace that I also felt; but, again, I am not claiming divine inspiration. After all, perhaps the grace was just to be done with the striving, to come up with a vision that someone else would correct or perfect later.

I thank God that over many years I had become more committed to the lesson of my high school science and math teachers that we should not trust proofs and theorems if they lack elegance. My teachers had insisted that an account of the world that lacks Beauty is probably no good and is probably not true. Why this should be the case, I of course have been saying in all these interviews, but I also know that it *is* very much part of modern science to insist that proofs should be elegant wherever possible. If you think about it, this is another way of saying that Beauty, Goodness, and Truth like to run together. It is certainly not always the case in math or science, but it often is.

The gender chiasm is so elegant and powerful, I feel that it has to also be true. It shows that Christ has changed things so much that we can almost talk about four genders; i.e., manhood and womanhood in their fallen, worldly form and then manhood and womanhood in their transfigured Christian form.

On Double Standards, and On Being Careful Not to Pit the Feminine and the Masculine Types of Shame Against Each Other

RTE: As we unfold this, can we also discuss what has transpired around gender, both in the Garden of Eden when men and women first betrayed one another and in our recent culture?

DR. PATITSAS: Yes. We can understand gender much more naturally if we return to the question of culture and to our discussion about the three kinds of healthy shame.[5]

If you remember, I had been mulling over the concept of "shame" in connection to the health of the soul for many years, when I saw Jonathan Shay describe Achilles' loss of his humanity in terms of having become shameless.[6] But when I set out to write this book, I finally noticed that there are really three different kinds of shame and that each one can exist within us in either a healthy form or in an unhealthy form. Because Orthodoxy means "right glory," it seems natural that the practice of Orthodox faith and life would strengthen the three healthy shames within us. And of course this is exactly what we find expressed in that penetrating word *philotimo*, which describes that majestic person who is modest, bold, and unselfconscious in just the right mix. The perfected person is characterized by three concentric phases of healthy, all-glorious, shame.

---

[5] In Chapter Three, "Chastity and Empathy: Eros, Agape, and the Mystery of the Twofold Anointing," and more extensively in Chapter Four, "Shame and Sacrifice: Rescuing the Soul from the Empire of Therapy."

[6] My first encounter with the idea that shame can be either healthy or impaired came from Gershen Kaufmann's *Shame: The Power of Caring* (Cambridge: Schenkman, 1985).

We said that the first shame was chaste yet ardent eros, which we also called "unknowing." The second shame was a courageous yet longsuffering agape, which we identified as the willingness to be the "one man lost," or to take the fall so that others might survive. And the third type of healthy shame was, surprisingly, "glory," or the co-incidence unto our last limit of the first two kinds of shame, despite the fact that, as we said, they tend to pull us in different directions.

I bring up shame in a discussion of gender because the first kind of shame has traditionally been seen as more feminine and the second as more masculine. Seeing how the first two shames are meant to relate within our own soul will then help us to see how men and women are meant to relate to each other. In other words, if we are careful not to pit the first two kinds of shame against each other in our own souls, and if we can even manage to relate their opposing force artfully in our own personal spiritual journey, this will tell us a lot about how men and women are to be reconciled through the worship of Christ.

The basic problematic is this: outside of the Church, some people feel that in order to be courageous at the level of agape – to be brave and "shameless" in the way directed by the second kind of healthy shame – one must actively renounce the first kind of healthy shame, of chaste devotion to the Holy Trinity. Some parents even encourage their children to disrespect the Church, lose their purity, or at least to neglect the holy services, feeling that otherwise the young person will be captive to this first kind of healthy shame and become weak and vulnerable in a difficult world. Such parents' intention is to toughen their children.[7]

But the two shames – shyness and boldness – needn't be opposed. In fact, they shouldn't be. In Mediterranean and South

---

[7] I think that the felt opposition between the two kinds of shame will make sense to most readers in an age when the paradoxes of Christian morality are less well understood but will especially be recognizable to those who know spiritual and cultural life in Greece today. The most personal spiritual decision for Greeks is the decision of how to relate to the two different types of shame, of how to define a manifestation of shame as being healthy or not, of determining whether or not the Church (really, a particular priest or bishop known to us) has gotten the proper handle on shame, and of how to balance the two kinds of

American cultures, we expect that a very "macho" man will still be enormously sensitive; this is often true in the Southern states of America, as well, where men are often more sentimental. But some other cultures seem to pit strength against sensitivity so automatically that they aren't even aware that they are doing so.

Our Orthodox Christian experience tells us that the first two kinds of shame are not sequential, but rather concentric. The first shame is meant to be a seed which flowers into the second, and even into a third kind of shame (which I called "glory"). So pitting them *against* each other is spiritually and emotionally dangerous.

We in the Church have found that when the first, pious kind of shame is neglected, then the bravery displayed through the second kind of shame may become captive to cruel and sacrilegious powers. We can see this in tales of soldiers who liberate a captive city only to savage its inhabitants, or in the romantic lives of men who lose their natural awe of beautiful women only then to become serial abusers of women. In each case, the appropriate boldness, in the absence of the appropriate piety, makes these men cruel.

In fact, in treating the first shame as if it were the enemy of the second, we may find that at those times when being bold requires also being chaste, some essential energy in our soul is not available and we fail at both. The soldiers who commit atrocities sooner or later suffer from psychological complexes which render them unfit for military service; the lotharios who style themselves "lady killers" often turn out to be unable to marry or to be good fathers to their children.

Alternately, if we get stuck at the first level of shame and do not permit the chaste shame of piety to be rounded out into the fear-

---

shame. These are the questions that, spoken in whatever way, govern personal identity in Greece today.

The persistence in modern Greece of a worship-based category like shame is due to the fact that Greeks are not in general persuaded by the reductionism of the Enlightenment or by the idea that "reason" is reducible to discursive reason. The Hellenism of the Enlightenment is a desiccated Hellenism, and actual Hellenes today sort of pick and choose from it whatever they like. In particular, they have not yet been divested of their awareness that getting shame right is the central human question. All of this is captured in this word, *philotimo*, by which Greeks signal their conviction that healthy and proper shame is among the highest human qualities.

less agape of doing good, then we are no longer "a city on a hill," "a lamp on a lampstand." We may feel full of light, but the world around us remains as dark as ever. We may think ourselves pious, but we are not fully alive and the world rightly rejects us.

RTE: Isn't this also the meaning of the parable of the Unwise Virgins, who lack the oil of agape even though they are dedicated to the Bridegroom?

DR. PATITSAS: Oh, very nice. I have never understood exactly what their fault was, although I have heard that the Church Fathers said their lack of oil was a lack of virtue. But I never knew what they meant by that or which virtues they had in mind.

However, we must be cautious in all directions. I am quite sure that a false shame before God at the first level, the level of chaste unknowing, will make a person "pious" in false ways. A false shame at this first level would be a shame that has been subverted into legalism, guilt, fear, and a paradoxical obsession with the self as "worthless"; clearly, this would not be healthy or pleasing to God. And it is also true that such a diseased chastity will lead to passive-aggressive cruelty towards others. It is even true that we might take our "success" at the first kind of shame as a proof that we need never grow up, that we can always rely on some authority to make our decisions for us. Some are driven into fundamentalist thought-patterns because their fear of the second kind of brave shame keeps them stuck in a distorted version of the first kind of shame.

But if the first shame of chaste eros is sincere and represents a truly chaste devotion to Christ and not to one's own neuroses, then there is no obstacle to its unfolding into the bold, "shameless shame" required of agape (the second level of shame). We are not to teach our children to negate the first kind of shame in order to strengthen in them the second. We don't need to make our children hard, just to make them strong; quite the opposite, I should say.

Still, the unfolding of the more feminine shame – even if we get it just right – into the more masculine shame is not guaranteed; it requires effort and real skill. As we said, the transition from eros to eros-plus-agape can be treacherous. And, of course, like St. Paul we must all be willing to leave behind childish things. Responsibility is sometimes lonely, risks must be taken, and free choices must be made.

More prosaically, it will not always be clear when we must waive a fasting requirement or skip a church service in order to meet some other holy responsibility. However, although we are not to waive the traditions indiscriminately nor ridicule the Church, certainly times often come when we have to make these decisions.

The Real Struggle

But those Christian parents who try to "toughen" their children through belittling the first kind of shame, and the contemporary pop culture which through many little vignettes ridiculing Christian chastity aims to showcase the supposed lack of sophistication within purity, are both confused and doubly so.

For the primary competition in the healthy psyche is *not* between these two kinds of shame; not at all. Rather, the contest is between chaste devotion to the Holy Trinity, on the one hand, and obsessive devotion to the passions of one's parents and society or to our own neuroses and psychoses, on the other. This is the first test, however unconsciously we may face it, and pitting the two shames against each other merely obscures from view the primary task involved in growing up. Parents or educators (and mass culture is the greatest educator of our children, and of all of us) who oppose the two healthy shames to each other are putting their efforts in the wrong direction and confusing the young in the process.

The actual drama that needs to play out is the one that we see in Christ's remaining behind in the Temple at age twelve. Here He both perfects the first kind of shame through devotion to God the Father by putting God above even his parents, *and* He also displays a boldness before the Temple elders and before his holy mother and his guardian Joseph (Lk 2:41-50).

And as our Lord shows us by his own example in this case, this unfolding of the journey is something that all of us must face to some degree *without* our earthly parents and *against* "establishment" opinion – whether that establishment appears to be quite hip as in the case of either the Hollywood or the Rock Music Industrial Complexes, or is perfectly holy, as in the case of Christ's own mother. A certain loneliness is unavoidable in this transition between the two types of shame. Our ability to face that loneliness is the sign that our devotion to God has become mature and is ready thus to unfold.

When I see young people following their parents' or the establishment's promptings to earn their boldness (the second kind of shame) by neglecting chastity and piety (the first kind of shame), I believe that such young people are retreating, not advancing. They are becoming *more* dependent on their parents and on the older generation who run the mass media, at the precise moment when this dependence must be cured, not through blind rebellion, nor by learning to ridicule what their elders already so easily mock, but through a revolutionary dependence on their Heavenly Father.

Still, let us not be completely unkind to the parenting that seeks to toughen children by depicting pious attachments as childish. The transition by which we discover the second kind of shame *within* the first is not easy. I, too, sometimes find myself a prisoner of religious legalism, lacking in manly boldness; then, when I try to be more decisive, I fall down on the other side and become either spiritually lax or insensitive to others. So the transition is not so straightforward, nor is it usually completed by the age of 12 (although it has been completed rather early in the case of many saints, and some cultures seem to do it better than others).

One last caveat: On top of all this, we must remember that, yes, there *are* in fact people who pretend to be religious so that they may take advantage of your son or daughter's naïve piety; and it can be hard to warn the children of this without making them feel like we are the jaded old trolls who have lost all idealism and that we are moreover trying to corrupt their oh-so-shining young souls.

And should we even mention those who continually "warn" the young person that almost every apparent good is really false and unworthy of pious reverence so that, devoid of all shame and defense, the young person can become the victim of this vampire's own passions? But let me not be too hard on certain of today's professors, either; they, too, are doing the best they can within the impossible constraints of a truth-first approach to knowing.

If parents feel that the son or daughter butterfly is not emerging from the cocoon of childish innocence by their late teens, they may of course get creative and desperate in trying to catalyze that themselves. But a better way, paradoxically, is for the parents to redouble their own eros for Christ, for the parents to perfect their own "first shame" – but now as older adults, without trying in any special way to influence or control their young adult children. In this way they will find that the transition is smoothed in their children as well as in themselves. Saint Porphyrios says this, at least, and I trust him.

On Not Being a Cliché

One other thing: These last twelve years I have been responsible for the St. Helen's Pilgrimage, the annual journey of our seminarians to Greece and Constantinople. In Greece we regularly run into this same drama: some people assume that because the students are future priests and pious, they must also be weak or be hiding behind piety and thus need to be shocked or scandalized in some way, however small, to make them grow up.

Although these "liberators" have a point, for none of us on the pilgrimage has perfected both kinds of shame, and we may all indulge in false pietism at times, something else more interesting is evident in these clashes: only a person who has *both* of the first two kinds of shame can have the third kind – can be truly noble. They alone are the true icons of the "King of Glory."

The rest of us, in trying to be sophisticated by abandoning the first shame, or in trying to be safe by avoiding the second, come across as ignoble. And we also come across as uneducated and intellectually unsophisticated, even though we may hold advanced academic degrees, when we belittle either boldness in the world or piety before the Holy Trinity.

Shame and Gender – A Second Try!

Forgive me for so many digressions; let's get back to the subject of what the two types of shame teach us about relations between the genders.

Since naturally the women are the priests of the home and teach the first kind of careful shame, when the father (or even the mother herself) later comes along and seeks to impart the "masculine" kind of shame by *denigrating* the "feminine" kind, it represents an invisible "divorce" between the two parents and harms the souls of the children. Such parents are teaching the child to denigrate the feminine in general – a fatal lesson in any era but made even worse in the coming age of emergence and organic order, when the feminine side of life is rising again to its high role even in secular accounts of the world's order.

In fact, the version of this double standard about shame which existed in the pagan world before Christ, and which St. Paul and the Christian Church abolished, was the idea that women ought to hold *only* the first kind of shame – be chaste, in other words – while the men, in order to become fearless contributors in the world, should hold *only* the second kind of shame.[8] Many Romans of St. Paul's day even believed that men should use force, seduction, and trickery to sexually abuse minors, slaves of both genders, and women generally. These humiliations of others then became the subject of shameless boasting among pagan males, the proof that they were strong men able to make their way in the world. In general, pagan men were expected to respect *only* the second kind of shame, i.e., to show courage in their personal relations, while at

---

8 Cf. Sarah Ruden, *Paul Among the People: The Apostle Reinterpreted and Reimagined in his Own Time* (New York: Pantheon Books, 2010).

the same time usually preferring to marry women who followed *only* the first kind of shame.

Such an evil and stupid approach to gender relations came to an end with St. Emperor Constantine's vision of the Goodness present within all Beauty – the cross of Christ. He saw that true worship and piety were never opposed to the service of others nor to bravery in the world: "In this Sign (the Cross, which is a sign of chaste holiness), Conquer! (Be bold in the world)," he was told. After that, men as well as women learned how to balance the first two kinds of shame, and thus they finally gained the third: they became "noble" in the deepest meaning of that term, and a Christian aristocracy steadily arose.

Some mock the long age of the Christian kings and queens, seeing Christian monarchy as mere political oppression. Those who ridicule should also remember how *liberating* it was for *everyone* in society to see, for the first time in history, both of the two kinds of shame respected and practiced at the highest levels of society, by those with power. The nobility's embrace of the Cross healed gender relations and made romance possible. We could use more of such *noblesse oblige* among our cultural elites today.

Within the honoring of both the feminine brand of shame and the masculine brand of shame by women and men alike were the seeds of the reconciliation of men and women. The reunion of men and women in Christ is born in our imitation of Christ's devotion to God our Father and of his love for his fellow man. It is the careful respecting of both kinds of shame, by both genders, that makes gender peace a reality.

The Spirit of Doxology

RTE: You speak of the first two shames as having a sort of gender. What gender would the third shame, the spirit of doxology, be?

DR. PATITSAS: Well, there in doxology we see the unity of masculine and feminine shame, and so we understand another way that in

Christ, "there is neither male nor female." This is not because we lose our genders but because our gender difference no longer makes us enemies once we have embraced the priesthood, i.e., the cross of Christ. Through the Cross both men and women live out all three offices of priest, prophet, and king, but they live them out in the sequence uniquely appropriate to each gender. And the inner lives of men and women, through this proper relating to our bodily genders, come to be more balanced and understandable to each other.[9]

Of course, whenever we speak of gender we are speaking of icons and of fractals because the actual mystery of gender is rooted in the relationship between Christ and his Church, an event which we both live directly and yet also see only "through a mirror, darkly…" (I Cor 13:12). So we cannot exhaust entirely these subjects. We see the mystery's appearing and its many fractal icons across the long history of the Church, and we reverently hand down also the ethical limits that have been revealed as to our participation in this mystery. For example, we may not feel sure why certain principles regarding ordination or sexuality were emplaced, but until we do understand, it is best that we treat these guidelines as if they stored a kind of data that will someday be decoded by others more worthy than we.

Anyway, this is why I wanted to discuss shame at such length. Each soul must negotiate the ascending sequence of chaste eros (the feminine shame), courageous agape (the masculine shame), and noble glory (the reconciliation of these powers). Then, in our roles as men and women, we play out this progression a second time. For example, chastity and the "chaste eros" shame among women is the first thing we may notice in a Christian society; it is the priestly

---

[9] Is there another way in which there is neither male nor female in Christ and we return to a true interchangeability? The answer seems to be yes and no. No, because in heaven the Virgin Mary remains a woman, for example. But yes, in that the Fathers of the Church describe a more thorough overcoming of gender difference in the next life than we can experience here. I am not sure what to make of the Fathers' words on this point. When I asked a young monk about the verse from St. Paul that "in Christ there is neither male nor female," he just laughed and said, "That's easy! Because in heaven we will be as innocent as children…" In other words, there will be gender difference in heaven but not with the strong sexual connotations it has here. Let me just add one other thing: the loss of gender difference also signifies the loss of sexual relations. One simply cannot build a case for same-sex sexual relations from within the authentic Tradition of the Christian Orthodox Church.

expression of the prophetic office. And this Christian success by women should naturally unfold into and support the "fearless agape" shame among Christian men, which is the priestly expression of the kingly office. Taken together, this begins to make a marriage, and then a society, glorious and real.

I say "begins," because the ancient wisdom among most peoples of the world knew gendered marriage at not only two but in fact at three fractal levels – in the soul; between men and women; and between "the King" and "the City," i.e., between Rulers and People in society. This third, social marriage was thought to take place under the influence of the Priests, who as a social class held this particular function of reconciliation. Today, artists and other cultural visionaries more or less fulfill this role of calling us to higher values.

Before about 1600 A.D., almost every society on earth accepted the basic three-wedding cosmology. Everyone just knew that accomplishing these weddings – in the soul, in the family, and in society – was necessary before the world could be at peace.

Christians were the first to see clearly why it was all so, however. For they could see, through the eyes of St. Paul and of St. John the Theologian, that the Archetype which all things resemble when they yearn towards Christ is the Heavenly Jerusalem, the priestly marriage between Christ and his Bride, the Church.

It is just so great how often in the hymns accompanying Pascha, and in particular in the hymn "The Angel Cried," we see the Virgin, the soul, and the City (the New Jerusalem) all brought together and made equivalent in their need to be joined to Christ. And because these three are brought together *in a hymn*, we are also taught *how* the marriages are to be accomplished and *how* the genders are meant to be reconciled. It is through Christian liturgy, through Christian priesthood – through Christ's liturgy – that each of the three offices, in each of the three weddings, is respected, realized, and put into a rich harmony.

Wedding liturgy, *not* gender war, is the final human destiny.

Kings and Prophets: The Hard Sayings

RTE: Will you say more about how the three offices of Prophet, King, and especially Priest, relate to gender difference?

DR. PATITSAS: Christ has traditionally been viewed as a priest, a king, and a prophet – perhaps not only for the obvious reason that He fulfilled these offices but because these are the only three offices that in the Old Testament required an anointing. Christ is the Anointed One, and so it is understood that He was in fact anointed in order to fulfill these three particular roles.

I think the difference between men and women is related to the sequence according to which they are meant to live out these three offices. Men have an initial calling to kingship, which makes sense in our ordinary experience. And women have an initial calling to the prophetic office, which also makes sense to us.

So, really, the most surprising insight to me was not this simple correspondence, but the fact that priesthood is more a modality according to which the other two offices might be fulfilled, than a third office of its own. In other words, a priestly king will be a self-sacrificing one, while a non-priestly king will be a tyrant and a thief. He will pillage his people. Meanwhile, a priestly prophet will know primarily persons, while a non-priestly prophet will be a fortuneteller, a witch, or a scientist who uses reductive methods to the harm of living organisms. Non-priestly prophets insist on knowing *things*, rather than take the risk of knowing *persons* or organic wholes, in other words.

Women differ from men, in that women have this unavoidable responsibility to prioritize at first the prophetic office: to be knowers, seers, givers of counsel, inventors, and discoverers. Women are the primordial originators of commercial life and of the crafts and of agriculture. This was true in prehistory and it is very definitely true in many parts of the world today. Women do most of the crafts, much of the agriculture, and they predominate in the small markets of Third World countries. In truly primitive economies, it may be hard even to identify *what at all* men are contributing economically.

In Christ, however, women learn to express this prophetic gift in a way that is also priestly. They now become mystical "*un*knowers" – that is, they unknow facts, things, and attributes, discovering how and when to look past them, to know instead persons. They thus become the special ministers to those in liminal states, such as children, the dying, the sick, and those giving birth. In all these cases, they are better able than men to unknow the facts of diminished or unrealized human dignity and thus to affirm and nourish the personhood of vulnerable people. And women in their role as priestly prophets can lead us away from cruel uses of knowledge and towards humane uses. Scientists imitate priestly women when they rise through reductive explanations of the world and embrace the science of emergence and complexity.[10]

In turn, men have this unavoidable responsibility to prioritize at first the kingly office: to be leaders, commanders, warriors, and protectors. We men feel the kingly calling naturally, but it then becomes wrapped up in our passions of lust, anger, and pride, or is smothered by opposing passions of snark, cynicism, and self-deprecation. In Christ, men are taught never to suppress this kingly gift but rather to live it strongly in a priestly way. They are to become the "one man lost"; that is, to exercise these masculine gifts at their own expense. They have to hold the door for the woman, even if she is strong and they are weak. They have to be the sort of leaders or warriors who are not controlled by revenge or ego, nor by despair and passivity.

Becoming the One Man Lost

What I have in mind when I say that a man must become the "one man lost," is a prayer clung to by St. Silouan when he faced his

---

[10] What would a scientist whose vocation is one of the more basic kinds of science make of this? Surely, there is a vital need for the other two kinds of science! My point is that we need both the "conquering" ways of science and the cooperative ways – a marriage of the two, not an obliteration of one approach or the other. I admit, however, that it is hard not to get caught up in our societal frustration with reductive methods since they are so often used to denigrate and deny holistic approaches. We must be careful to validate all three approaches to science in their right place, as mentioned in Chapter Four.

great trial, the fourteen-year period during which evil powers visibly accosted him every night. Indeed, these demonic spirits were so brazen, they often appeared to him even during the daytime. Saint Silouan checked these assaults and received the salvation of his soul only when, in his mind's eye, he could look upon the entire world and say, "All these will be saved; only I shall be lost." Considering both those who loved him and those who troubled him, both holy people and those tyrants who were just then committing some of the greatest moral crimes in history, the saint cast himself as lower than all others. In other words, St. Silouan looked upon the entire expanse of human history and by saying, "All these will be saved, only I shall be lost," kept his mind in hell and despaired not.[11]

It took me years to realize that, "All these will be saved; only I shall be lost," is St. Silouan's concise way of saying what Our Savior Jesus Christ said upon the cross. "All these will be saved" – *Father, forgive them, for they know not what they do* (Lk 23:34); and "Only I shall be lost" – *My God, My God, why hast thou forsaken me?* (Mk 15:34).

Even a brief meditation on Christian leadership will show us that St. Silouan's saying is also the perfect motto for anyone who wants to fill the kingly role in a priestly way. I recommend that all Christian men who have been asked to lead try repeating inwardly the words, "All these will be saved, only I shall be lost." It will calm you and help you to forget yourself and focus on what you can do right now to serve others.

But *I don't recommend at all* that women adopt this particular saying, since they are not meant to live firstly in this way, but in another, equally priestly way. Women will pray in other ways and will just naturally turn out to have fulfilled the calling of "one man lost," as is evident in the case of mothers who "die" for their children on a daily basis, even though unknowing is the primary priestly act of a mother and a woman. But a woman praying, "All these will be saved, only I shall be lost," may accidentally distance herself from

---

11 The full life story of the saint is available in Archimandrite Sophrony (Sakharov), *St. Silouan the Athonite* (Maldon, Essex: Patriarchal Stavropegic Monastery of Saint John the Baptist, 1991).

a healthy familiarity with her body and her gender, would be my fear. It is too lonely a prayer, while the self-sacrifice of women is instead usually meant to come in the context of very deep personal relationships. And most women also need the support of those deep relationships if they are to live self-sacrificially.

Becoming an Unknower

RTE: What then is the woman's prayer that will render her prophetic office "priestly" in such a mystical way? How can she inscribe the cross of Christ within her own gender calling?

DR. PATITSAS: A different hard saying seems to belong to women: "I don't know *anything* (that I might know Someone)." A caution, though: "unknowing" things does not signify ignorance but rather the prioritization of persons over their attributes. "Unknowing," doesn't mean that you are unaware or incurious but that you insist on not reducing people to the facts about them. This is the call of *unknowing*, although this prayer is more of a noetic stance, rather than something a woman recites.

"I don't know *anything* (that I might know Someone)" means that when you see the person you love tortured and dying on a cross, you still see that person as your Life. You look past the humiliating outward appearances. This is the prayer of the Panaghia at the cross, in that she confesses Christ as her Son, her God, and her Life, despite his seeming degradation and defeat.

It's not that the facts don't matter but that in priestly prophecy (the first calling of Christian womanhood) all facts become joined to and subordinated to persons, to the mystery of personhood. Love makes us subordinate the mere facts we know about other people to their personhood.

This calling of women explains why there are women who actually marry convicted murderers on death row; they are able to unknow all the terrible facts of what that person has done and instead see their personhood. Women have this gift, that through their feminine unknowing they bring men to the point where they can become priests, where men can become the "one man lost," rather than the berserk opposite. We see here how the first shame, when practiced by women, unfolds into the ability of men to practice the second shame. Again, there is a sequence to the shames.

RTE: Couldn't this unknowing become quite negative, as when a woman stays with her abuser because she can see "more" in him – more that perhaps is there but won't manifest in time to prevent him from harming her? It also sometimes happens that women go too far and give too much to "save" people, trying to provide things for that person that only Christ can provide. Obviously, this can't be right, either.

DR. PATITSAS: We are called to be as wise as serpents and gentle as doves (Mt 10:16). In the case of Eve, she was *not* as wise as the serpent, who was exploiting her feminine call to the prophetic office in order to abuse her. There are serpents all around, and trust is to be extended only to those men who are living out *their* version of the gender "prayers" – men who are willing to die for their brides, in other words. In discerning the true intentions of men, parental alliance can be very helpful, for our parents will not likely be swayed by emotional factors.

Incidentally, if Eve was outwitted by the serpent, Adam sinned against gentleness (the "one man lost") when he blamed God and Eve for his own freely made decision to sin.

What Happens When Husbands and Wives Enact Not Their Own, but Their Spouse's Hard Saying

But it is very important that we each focus first on the priesthood appropriate to our own gender.

Because in families that are running out of control, the men are the unknowers, and in the wrong way; they *haven't a clue* about the inner lives of their wives and children. A world of oppression of the wife, between the children, involving the children, all swirls around such men, and they are just oblivious. Well, our obliviousness as men can also be our strength at times, because if both spouses are equally sensitive, then situations can get out of hand. However, we men must be oblivious in the right way. Men are not as sensitive as women to certain kinds of connections, and this helps to dampen volatility within the family; that is natural. But a man has to develop a certain sly cleverness about the inner lives of his family, or there will be no peace. His cluelessness should, with time, become mostly pretense, a way to steer things correctly without embarrassing anyone or provoking reactions.

And at the same time, in sad families the women wrongly take on the role of "one man lost" – of being bitter, unthanked martyrs. They come to feel as if they alone are carrying the entire burden of the family or of the marriage. They may even loudly proclaim to all who will listen that they are fulfilling this masculine office of the "one man lost." But when they proclaim their kingship in such a way, their subsequent cries for help are rarely answered because such a proclamation already sounds like the confession that she is not willing to be helped. I mean, she is taking her glory in the wrong role, and after that what can be done by anyone to help her?

If a woman wants to overcome the temptation to take the man's priesthood, she will have to be ready to see in God's and her husband's apparent silence to her pleas for help something more than the uncaring disinterest of a powerful authority. Rather, she will come to see that God is "absent" in these situations because He is being crucified anew in the sufferings of those in them, and that her husband may be "absent" due to what he is experiencing in his own humiliations, his own priesthood. A woman's faithfulness to the Crucified One is what is at stake in these situations. She is facing her own Eve-like temptation to eat of the Tree of the Knowledge of Good and Evil. She is demanding a more effective god or a more decisively helpful and aware husband than what has been given, and then she herself is tempted to fulfill those roles.

Even when she is "fixing" the troubling situations that she faces, a woman's focus – all of our focus, but women are the exemplars in this – has to be on nurturing the development of the good that is present there, not on combatting the evil. Evil is meontic, and to fight it directly is to war against shapeless, ever-shifting shadows. You thus exhaust your spirit and embitter your soul. Her warrior-role is to be taken up from the standpoint of motherhood.

But I ask the reader's forgiveness in what I have said here. These matters are quite subtle and complex, and I am sure that I have not done justice to all the nuances in which the two sayings of "one man lost" and "I know persons, not things" must be applied.

Still, there is a basic point that cannot be denied except at great peril: not only do we have gender *roles*, but, more importantly, we have gender-appropriate *priesthoods*. It is the gender-priesthoods that make gender roles life-giving, rather than oppressive, to others and to ourselves. And when we neglect these priesthoods, we suffer as men and women, and our children suffer terribly.

In our fallen states, men and women must consciously fight against the temptation to enact the other gender's priesthood. It comes too easily to a man to be the unknower in his own family; he just wants some peace when he comes home from work, and he cannot untangle the general clamor of hurt feelings, sullen silences, or complaints that greet him as he walks through the door. But his masculine gift of insensitivity must be balanced by a hidden radar that tells him exactly what are the true needs of all those in his family and the right moments to fulfill them. Otherwise, he becomes irrelevant in his own home. In fact, worse than irrelevant, he becomes a heavy obstacle to the attempts of his family to find life despite his awful spiritual absence looming over and blocking everything.

And it comes too easily to the woman to take on the entire burden of everything in the home because she loves to care. But the more deeply she co-opts her husband's calling to be the "one man lost," and the more consistently she neglects her own calling to be an unknower, the more bitter she becomes and the less she respects her husband. In her bitterness, she often resolves to double down on this mistaken approach to her sacrificial calling in the family by working even harder. The result of this mistake is that the more she does, the more she is resented for her martyrdom by both her husband and her children, and a downward spiral ensues as she neither accepts help nor elicits cooperation.

As the dad and the mom alike abandon their gender priesthoods, the ship of the family founders, then begins to sink. Sensing this, the children either act up or try to anesthetize their own feelings.

Rest assured that down the beckoning path of assuming your partner's gender priesthood while neglecting your own priesthood lies family dissolution, divorce, or at least a hard childhood for your children even if in the midst of material abundance. Our proper gender ascetic callings in Christ will cure us of the too-easy pleasure we take in fulfilling our spouse's role while not doing our own. We have to be priests, but according to the sequence of priesthood that has been appointed by God himself, I believe.

We Christians Receive our Genders According to the Logic of the Twofold Anointing

RTE: What does it mean to say that the priestly calling temporarily eclipses both of the two gender callings?

DR. PATITSAS: An example would be what we said in another interview: that we honor our American soldiers not as warriors but as priests. That is to say, even in those cases when the soldiers have been sent to causes that originated in the sinful passions of the voters or of the leaders, we still believe that our fallen heroes obeyed and gave their lives with the intent that others might live. In civilized society, and especially in a Christian society, we emphasize the priestly dimension of the soldier's death. If this doesn't capture the whole truth at times, then we should change the policies, not ridicule the symbolism.

I bring this up because it shows us how so much of all that we praise in life is the *priestly* flavor of what people are doing, rather than their actual vocation or contribution. I don't praise a scientist because he is brilliant but because he is self-sacrificial in keeping long hours, or because he accepted ridicule on the way to a new breakthrough and thus saved countless lives, or was kicked out of his position but persevered. And there are examples of this in every career, that what we really admire is the priestly dimension of a person's journey. It is this priesthood that inspires us to give praise and glory to a person because it combines the first two kinds of healthy shame into something amazing. Professions and vocations in themselves are nothing; without the "flavor" of Christian priesthood, the salt of a vocation is all but worthless.

Earlier, I asserted that in Christ there are really four genders, depending on whether men and women are acting in priestly or in selfish ways. A man or woman exercising their office in a priestly way is so radically transfigured from what he or she was before. And the society around them will be deeply renewed when men and women receive their gender callings according to the logic of the twofold anointing.

The twofold anointing, if you remember, was this ancient idea that to be anointed is to become both a "sovereign" and a "sacrificial victim." Orthodox Christian anointing – the descent of the Holy Spirit who brings Christ to and within us, making us little christs – always takes on this paradoxical character. Thus, the Messiah *is* a King, and He sits at the Right Hand of the Father, and He will come again in glory to judge both "the quick and the dead." But He *is equally also* a lamb, a victim, an offering who will bear for all eternity the marks of his crucifixion.

And this duality is just as true of his prophetic office as it is of his kingly office. Christ alone "reveals" the Logos – rather, *is* the Logos. Yet He also claims not to know or, at least, not to be able to divulge, the two things a Prophet was supposed to know above all else – the time of the restoration of Israel and the time of his own Second Coming! (Mt 24:36, Acts 1:7) And his mother imitates him in this kind of prophecy, for although she brought forth the Logos more than any prophet of the Old Testament ever did, she did it through her ever virginity and her noetic purity. And all these things, "she pondered in her own heart," never pronouncing them to the world.

So, our gender callings cannot be received properly, except they be received according to this paradoxical logic of the twofold anointing. To be a man is to be not just the "head of the family" but the king who *dies and is resurrected* for his family. And to be a woman is not just to be the helpmate, the prophetic counselor, but an *unknower and yet therefore a mystic* in as noetic a sense as she can muster.

If what distinguishes the genders is the priority they must give among the callings to prophecy and kingship, then what unites them again is that they both must turn to Christ, must allow Christ to activate his priesthood within them inside of their respective callings. Whether as kings (the men) or as prophets (the women), *they must first of all be priests*. And therefore the calling of salvation in Christ is different for men and women, but it is also identical.

Like so much else in genuine Christian faith, we find here a mystery. We preach neither that the genders are interchangeable nor that they are complementary. Instead, we preach that gender is an icon. And this icon is actualized when we accept our gender calling – and then promptly inscribe the Cross so deeply within it, that this calling seems all but lost.

Liturgy and Order

RTE: And all of this while, within their souls, they are also following the Beauty, Goodness, Truth sequence? This rich picture of salvation seems complex, but perhaps that's only because we need an explanation for things that were once intuitive.

DR. PATITSAS: We live in an age when science is at last coming to grips with nonlinear order, with algorithms that generate order at an infinity of fractal scales. Should we imagine that order within Christ, within God, should be less rich than this? After all, God is even greater than his creation.

If we insist on drawing the simplistic conclusion that, because men and women both possess a tripartite soul, the spiritual tasks we have been ordered to fulfill in our bodies and in marriage should also be indistinguishable, then how are we still worshipping the actual God who has called us into every richness of life and into mysteries beyond our understanding as well? Why should we reduce God's creative power to the most basic kind of Enlightenment science, which can only handle linear order?

Future generations will dismiss so much of what we now think of as being "cutting edge" regarding gender, marriage, and spirituality, and they will conclude that it was quite the reverse, a holdover from that Great Reduction which had persuaded us to trade the appreciation of complex order for the most basic kinds of early science. They will see that our iconoclasm around gender and gender roles was the last gasp of an Industrial-Age gnosticism that denigrated the organic, the natural body, and the feminine.

Just because it takes really hard effort to embrace actual life in all its fullness does not mean that we should curse God and complain that He has called us to this struggle. Gender, too, is an example of the twofold anointing: Being born as a man or a woman involves both a blessing and a cross, inseparably. It gives us certain joys but then demands that we live these out self-sacrificially. Trying to avoid suffering by avoiding the cross of our gender leads to psychological troubles in either ourselves or in the people around us.

Well, just as algorithms seem to be running in different parts of nature and, in running, to generate the entire cosmos we see around us, so in Christ we believe that it is the liturgical and repentant response of all creation to Theophany that underlies the richness of the life in Christ. And when our doxological response to Christ's appearing plays out in our own lives and families and cities, we then become a fractal profusion of further theophanies to those around us. And this means, to be as precise as possible about it, that we too become icons of the wedding liturgy in the Heavenly Jerusalem, at these three levels – within our souls, in our bodies and marriages, and in our societies.

This will all happen naturally if we can but let go of fallen nature and instead embrace nature's *telos* – Christ. The only way to halt the appearing of the icon of the Heavenly Jerusalem (of gender and marriage at all three of these scales, in other words) would be to kill the algorithm; i.e., to stop liturgizing. But only those who liturgize will be saved. As St. Paul says, "only he who believes and confesses," or, "only he who believes and is baptized," is saved. The soteriology of the Christian faith has always been a liturgical soteriology.

Monastic Life and the Three Weddings

RTE: But what of the monastic life, which seemingly does not fulfill one – or even two – of these three marriages? I mean, monastics don't marry, and they usually don't participate in worldly society.

DR. PATITSAS: Monastics, it is sometimes said, are called to replace those angels who fell away from God in the archaic rebellion. Monastics live the angelic life, although still in this body. But if others of us would renounce the direct bodily manifestations of the Heavenly wedding liturgy by not pursuing marriage, we must follow the same path of sexual purity, not twist our bodies in directions not intended by God.

Additionally, through their prayers and counsel, monastics *do* contribute to the good ordering of civil society and to the well-being of other people's marriages. Moreover, while they begin to transcend gender in some senses, they never leave it entirely behind. They fulfill the gender chiasm without marrying; they are not sexless, genderless gnostics, but are saved as men or women. Male monastics will still give this special emphasis to being the one man lost, and female monastics will still give this emphasis to unknowing.

This is why the liturgical life even of monastics continues to honor the reality of gender difference. Men are still needed at female monasteries as priests to celebrate the Divine Liturgy, while the men of Mount Athos and of all monasteries focus so much of their attention on the Theotokos.

Is Sexual Differentiation a Result of the Fall?

RTE: But let me press you further. Some Church Fathers and even some contemporary spiritual fathers write that sexual reproduction in the way that we now experience it is not the ideal. Other fathers stated that gender was created in anticipation of the Fall. How do we reconcile this view with the holiness of marriage, and where does the goodness of the body come in?

DR. PATITSAS: In heaven there still will be a King and a City; there will be the internal reconciliation of all our soul powers; and, above all, everything we see will be part of the wedding banquet of the Lamb. So, these three weddings exist even in heaven, although heaven does not have sexual relations. Those energies are transposed to a higher, more fulfilling, plane.

Gender is an icon. Perhaps in heaven when we see Our Lord "face to face," some aspects of the artistic icons of him painted on earth will look false, but only because a more rich and challenging reality will supplant them. In the services of the Church, we don't lose our gender, but we instead find it transfigured.

Liturgy reveals so much about who we are. Look at the conundrum that two women "marrying," for example, face when they enact the actual ceremony. If they choose to dress identically at their wedding, with both women wearing wedding dresses, then it is obvious that what they have is not a union of opposites but an improperly sexualized close friendship. But if they decide that one partner will dress as a male, then again in their liturgical action they prove that the fractal icon that is struggling to be born is in fact stillborn in their union. Absent the ritual, the problem remains hidden, since a gay couple can just come across as two loving friends – and what any two friends do behind closed doors in their own home is not something we would normally ponder. But in liturgy, the fault is made manifest.

The same when two men pretend to marry. Often, what we see are two men who look and dress so identically in the ceremony that it is clear that the weak eros they are experiencing cannot overcome their basic human self-love. I mean, they have come to look *so* alike that it is as if they were getting married to their own identical twin. But to love is to leave the self behind. And to love all the way, we must even love our enemy.

II. LOVE FOR THE SEXUAL ENEMY

The thing is, marital and sexual love in the form we have them here on earth are meant to overcome a specific kind of enmity in the world – the enmity between the genders, between men and women. According to Christian Orthodox theology, the source of this strife lies in what happened in the Garden of Eden itself, and one of the main reasons we needed a Savior was to heal the rift between the genders that started there.

To exclude the other gender from one's marriage would be to leave this task of reconciliation with one's "enemy" undone. And in fact, in the light of increasing male-male marriage, more women are left without partners; they have, in effect, been abandoned.

RTE: You mention the test of ritual in same-sex "marriages," where the religious ceremony reveals an underlying gap in the reality of love. Do we see anything similar in marriages between men and women?

DR. PATITSAS: Well, while I don't know any movie stars personally, the tabloid photos tend to depict the Hollywood marriage ceremony not as the union of a male person and a female person, but as an alliance of two visually perfect human *natures* who have concluded that their human *wills* can be temporarily satisfied through an interlude of consensual mutual exploitation. So there are two human natures, and two human wills, but there aren't two human *persons* present in the marriage, somehow. The gossip writers seem to think this is what we all aspire to, which may be why they write it that way.

While in same-sex unions we see the attempt to make sacred a friendship that was not meant by God to be sexualized, in the tabloid account of celebrity marriage we see an alliance of male and female that will never become a friendship – until the divorce is finalized, at least, when both publicists will release a statement saying that the couple will "remain good friends." The bodies are perfect, the wills are ever-to-be-satisfied, but the person, the "face," is undeveloped, afraid to be unique or to become visible through a priestly, self-sacrificial lifetime commitment. And this has been the fate of marriage in some of the larger population. Marriage in such cases no longer manages to join sexual attraction (eros) to practicality (goodness or agape) to permanent friendship (philia).

This is not to say that you should not marry until you have the perfect friendship but rather to assert the reverse: trust that having the attraction to your spouse's beauty, and being inclined to practice the goodness of caring for them self-sacrificially, that God will soon lead you to friendship; eros, and then agape, and then philia, is the sequence.

I think some people are getting divorced the very moment they begin to sense that they are about to be joined in this deeper, permanent way, as forever-loyal friends to someone who is also their lover and their responsibility. Others are refusing to marry until they are sure that the friendship that will follow the eros and agape will be perfect; but this cannot be predicted or foreseen outside of actual marriage. A friend is not an armchair that we test for its comfort, but something we "win" by consistently enduring discomfort on our friend's behalf. We *make* friends; we don't shop for and then "consume" them.

Same-sex marriage justifies itself to our society by arguing for the backwards approach which we said is adopted outside the Church, whereby you find Truth first (friendship); then argue for the practical Goodness of *any* true friends being married ("I was denied access to my gay lover's intensive care unit bedside! Let us marry so we can express agape!"); to be followed finally by the eros, the Beauty of a ritual blessing for sexual union – which of course is not beautiful to the healthy eye.[12]

The heterosexual version of this denial of true eros and agape is "friends with benefits"; it, too, is the death of eros, and it, too, is not beautiful.

You can't put Beauty "last" and expect to wind up with anything but ugliness. And to adopt the opposite of the *human* progression – to exchange Beauty-Goodness-Truth, for Truth-Goodness-Beauty – is to make ourselves post-humans, super-humans, gods. This temptation afflicts all of us who give in utterly to hedonistic pleasure, by the way; we know everything and lose both our fear of God and our shame. This is akin to the berserk state. And because homosexuality so often involves or increases reservoirs of suppressed rage within the prisoners of these inclinations, the increasing prevalence of its practice will make our society more berserk with time. Meanwhile, among heterosexuals, the "friends with benefits" approach just saps all eros, makes our soul flat and empty. Such a soul, in turn, cannot see the wrongness in same-sex unions.

The Anti-Semitism Outside the Church

Well, first-century Greek-speaking and Latin-speaking Roman society across the Mediterranean also oscillated between berserk and nihilistic, and for the same reason, which is that they had abused sexual eros for so long. Therefore, it follows (although this may sound surprising) that all that we are seeing going awry in sexuality today, stems from some odd "anti-semitism" in the West. The West today can accept Greek science and Roman technology, but it won't allow Semitic personalism, beauty, the sacredness of the

---

12 Incidentally, I find it hard to believe that in a truly Christian Orthodox society today, there would be persecution of same-sex couples as we are told occur in incidents like these in the ICU. If this is clearly the person's closest friend, why should they be denied a visit at such an important time? No one has appointed us to investigate their private sexual lives at such a moment. Pronouncing the Church's experience of the destructiveness of homosexual intercourse is not a license for a witch hunt against people who, though caught up in this sin, may be surpassing us in other areas of virtue. But neither can we allow Christian charity to be exploited by those who are defying nature, convention, and God. The Church adopts a middle road which leaves all of us in a profound tension.

body, gender, and revelation. As we said in our first interview, Eastern Roman Orthodoxy balanced all three cultural visions and attempted to be complete.

I start again empirically. The Church agrees with almost all human societies in thinking that we all have both a feminine and a masculine side – our softer desiring powers and our harder fighting powers. It is also our experience that as individuals we may wind up on either side of the larger social wedding – that is, playing a more kingly masculine role or a more feminine prophetic role in our jobs and professions. However, the Church also has seen that when it comes to sexuality, we shall have to live out what our bodies have given to us. Here, we cannot be artificial and contrived, but must be California-organic, non-GMO, and locally grown. Our bodies and sexualities are simply too important to our identity; they are who we are.

And so despite the fact that our classical Roman side has always despised the rights and bodies of women, and our classical Greek side has, since perhaps Plato, been tempted to denigrate the body, we are just going to have to walk the path appointed for us by the apostles at their first council and not adopt these fallen sexual practices (Acts 15:28-29). We are going to have to give the body its full due.

RTE: Didn't you say earlier that the Roman-Greek-Semitic aspects existed together in medieval Eastern Christianity?

DR. PATITSAS: Right, of course. A friend of mine, a priest, is right now being forced from his small Greek Orthodox parish precisely because a tiny coterie of his parish council members have decided that Christianity is "too Jewish." The body, the sacraments, the sexual morality, the way of the heart, the creation of a new people – they see it all for what it is, a humbling corrective to the way of the mind that their fantasy-version of classical Hellenism represented. They want discussion, debate, ethical virtues for their own sake, abstract and remote gods – in a word, they want philosophy and Ethics, and Ethics of the Truth-first sort. They are the kind of people who ridiculed St. Paul at the Areopagus in Acts 15. And they will never see that what they think of as Hellenism is even a distortion of Hellenism itself – because the real thing remained liturgical and bound up with beauty right until the later Enlightenment.

While I'm sad about the situation in that parish, at least everyone concerned is getting a good look at the honest truth about the centrality of the Semitic inheritance for the Church.

Not very many, but some Greeks today still feel this, still have that sneaking suspicion that Christianity was a Jewish plot which robbed Greece of its pristine ancient glory. Hey, mission work is never-ending, and *one* reason why Greek Orthodox Christian leaders promote the value of Hellenism is precisely because, if we don't give this civilization the due it so richly deserves, some people will check out of the Church entirely. Not that our pro-Hellenism is a ruse – no, for in fact the Church has always promoted Hellenism, Roman identity, and the "salvation that came from the Jews" as the three indispensable elements of a Christian civilization.

RTE: What would that mean for, say, "Chinese Orthodoxy" in some future mission? Must all peoples adopt these three cultures?

DR. PATITSAS: All cultures have the way of the body, the way of the mind, and the way of the heart since, after all, every human being has a body, a mind, and a heart. The Romans, Greeks, and Jews each had all three ways. But what the Church did was to take what in her cultural world were the ultimate examples of each of these three ways and then combine them into one civilization.

Once you do that, then you place yourself in a unique position to understand, protect, appreciate, and nurture every culture on earth. Someday I'll tell you the story, but although the old Halki Theological School grads were more "Roman" than "Greek," most of them were also fluent in Turkish. What I sensed in them was that the uniting of the pinnacle of the ways of body, mind, and heart, made the Orthodox Romans ecumenically and discerningly open to every possible human culture. It was quite obvious that the fusion of the three pinnacle cultures had had this effect of openness to all.

But let us get back to this issue of why Christianity, as an inheritor of the Jewish tradition, must defend the goodness of gender.

Look, Christianity is not a debating society but a revealed religion. In creating gender, God purposely tied us to our bodies, joined us to the goodness of all of the physical creation, and He purposely set us a deep, eternal challenge: that challenge is to face our existential dependence on someone outside of ourselves, someone even opposed to us because their gender is so unlike ours, and to do this with grace and not as an excuse to be constantly at war. And God also opened the proper and holy way for that need to be fulfilled in a pleasurable and satisfying way, full of contentment, in marriage.

And anyway, why should we renounce so rich a salvation, just because we are good Enlightenment bourgeois who prefer linear, tractable, controllable order and a life without existential discomfort? Of course it can be easier for many of us to relate as friends to someone of our own gender, so same-sex relationships can seem natural. But what do we think will save us: Christ, or the program of modern liberal order? The Cross, or the false comfort promised by cursing the Holy Spirit's bringing of that Cross into our lives? Choose Christ, and we can have both God and the real benefits of modernity. Choose the modern program, and we shall have neither.

Even knowing all this, I myself still struggle to choose life. So let us pray, not condemn, and be at peace.

The Liberating Surprise: The Symbol of Love

However, if you choose to receive your gender calling in a priestly way, a further surprise awaits you. This surprise is the heart of the Orthodox Christian vision of gender, in my opinion.

Many times in life, as we said, we can see that opposites can be naturally joined or reconciled in a chiastic way. It is best to give another example so that we can illustrate the surprise within "chiasm."

Darkness and light are opposites. But there can come a light so bright, that it blinds you – this light is the ultimate darkness, in a way. Or there can come a darkness so deep that only within it can you trace the light from the very faintest stars; the darkness opens your eyes, in a way.

You see, a crossover occurs in chiasm. The light in these cases just mentioned becomes a symbol of darkness, and the darkness becomes a symbol of light. If we write it this way, and connect the same thing in its two opposing manifestations, we see the Greek letter "chi" formed.

> In deepest Darkness, we often "see the Light"
>
> while, by contrast,
>
> In brightest Light, we often become Blind

There are many examples of this throughout life. Which countries have the strongest militaries? Historically, militarized states have not necessarily been the greatest powers. It is very often the more economically creative societies that defeat slave-holding powers, whether these be the Old South or the communist nations.

But, on the other hand, which countries have had the strongest economies? Frequently, it is those with the most self-disciplined rulers and the firmest rule of law. The flowering of Muslim civilization proved this. In the very best of those times, a small minority of Muslims exercised light control, a kind of firm justice, and reasonable taxation over predominantly Christian and Jewish populations.

But as Muslim oppression of non-Muslims steadily increased, with the result that many more Christians and Jews converted in order to save their children from being sold into slavery to pay punitive taxes, Muslim societies gradually became inert and their golden ages passed. This history proves the point – self-disciplined and just governments often produce economic prosperity, while corrupt and oppressive governments generate economic stagnation.

So, again we see a chiasm: strong economies lead to strong governments in the form of strong militaries, while strong, just governments are often the most important element in forming strong economies.

These chiasms show up all over the place, and at their best they are really elegant in the way they reconcile opposites while keeping distinctiveness intact. I like them, too, because wherever they appear they inscribe a Greek "chi" – the first letter of Χριστὸς – across the world, showing how opposite things are bound together in this chiastic way.

As I mentioned above, one Saturday night during a time when I was thinking about gender and its relation to kingship, priesthood, and prophecy, I entered a church in Washington, D.C. There, I noticed in the beautiful icons that while Adam is always at Christ's right and Eve at Christ's left, at the cross and elsewhere this gets reversed. Then, it is the Theotokos (the Virgin Mary) at Christ's right hand, and either St. John the Theologian or St. John the Baptist at his left. If you could place one icon above the other, it would look like this:

At the Resurrection
Adam with Eve

Panaghia with St. John
at the Cross

So if you were to connect the two women to each other, and then the two men to each other, the lines formed make a chiasm artistically, with the cross of Christ at the center of the chiasm.

Well, who cares, right? It is just an accident of art and probably means nothing, you could say.

But to me, noticing this chiasm in the icons was electric. I realized at a flash that this artistic chiasm corresponds to the fact that our gender callings are also to be chiastically inverted and unified. Men would start out as kings but wind up symbolizing prophets; and women would start out as prophets, but come to rest as the symbol of kings. And this means that gender difference is preserved, while at the same time the unity of all persons would be achieved through their gender difference, if we would only come into Christ's priesthood. This is another way that we can see that "in Christ there is neither male nor female."

The artistic chiasm of gender in the icons suggests a gender chiasm that follows a four-step unfolding. First, our gender callings to exercise kingship (as men) or to prophesy (as women) make us different. Second, when we accept our gender callings and, imitating priests, inscribe Christ's cross within them, it seems like we have lost our genders entirely – we each move from our unique gendered vantage point into the middle, into Christ and his crucifixion. Men and women both become priests and seem to lose their gender callings because these callings are being "crucified" so completely.

Now comes a third step. In this step, these original gender callings are resurrected and returned to us in a transfigured way. We attain Christian manhood or Christian womanhood. The Christian man is still strong, but now also just and kind. The Christian woman is still sensitive, but now just and stronger.

Fourthly and finally, though, there is this additional surprise. At the end of this chiastic gender transfiguration in Christ, we come to rest as the symbol not of our own office or calling but as the symbol of our partner's office and calling. A man, not a woman, is the ultimate prophet (St. John the Baptist). And a woman, not a man, is the "invincible general," the "fearsome protector" (the Theotokos).

Love Always Makes Us the Symbol of What We Love

The thing that filled me with such awe and happiness in the church that night was this notion of symbol. I saw that in the Church's approach to gender, the cross and resurrection of Christ makes us become the ultimate and perfect symbol – the best example, really – not of our own distinctiveness but actually of our opposite's, of our complement's distinctiveness! Women, not men, are the ultimate symbols of the masculine office! And men, not women, are the ultimate symbols of the feminine office!

Thus, the Orthodox Christian approach to gender is not that men and women are interchangeable, nor simply that we are complementary, but something much deeper, richer, and more alive than either the "left-wing" (men and women are interchangeable) or the "right-wing" (men and women are complementary) option.

In Christ, we embrace our biologically-given genders, only at once to surrender them to Christ and see them crucified. We then regain them in a renewed and transfigured and living form, a form that we could never have achieved on our own. We fulfill a gender role not by conforming to an image or an external set of requirements but by following the path of crucifixion that is unique to our gender. We do fulfill a gender role but without making our gender either an idol or a mask.

And none of that is even the best part: in loving Christ we become the epiphany of our beloved, of our partner. We become their very symbol to the world. In a Christian marriage, we are the "theophany," if you will, of our spouse.

We can see that a man who exercises his kingly masculinity in a priestly way will quickly become the ultimate prophet, the ultimate symbol of prophetic ministry. Thus, St. John the Baptist is the ultimate prophet; men imitate him in that by becoming the "one man lost," they prophetically proclaim Christ. A warrior who lives his life in a priestly, self-sacrificial way symbolizes not a king but a martyr, a prophetic witness to love and to all that is good in his society. He "gives his life for his country" – he feeds his country with his own life, he nurses his country to life; the brave soldier is our mother.

And we can see that a woman who exercises her feminine prophetic ministry in a priestly way – in a personal and personally loyal way – will quickly become the great guardian of the home, of the society, and of the Church. And thus we call Panaghia, the Mother of God, the "Invincible General." And it really is the women who exercise the warrior role in this way, who are the great fighters for social justice.

Panaghia's feminine priesthood helps us to enact our priesthood. Our Orthodox tradition shows both Christ enacting his ultimate priesthood and Panaghia responding to that by enacting a priesthood appropriate to her gender. This is how we are all saved. We can't even imagine our consolation or salvation in this life without Panaghia's priesthood. When we look at her icon, we understand her self-offering, her unknowing – in other words, her ever-virginity. This is also a mental and noetic ever-virginity, in that she never engaged with even one sinful thought.

In sum, chiasm gives us a lovely, mysterious coinciding of sameness and difference. As Christians, we can accept both the idea that the genders are complementary *and* the idea that they are interchangeable, provided only that we remember that both conclusions are true. As I said, with the chiasm Christian gender gets interesting and exciting.

RTE: Why then could Old Testament women be judges, and in a traditional Christian culture act as empresses, ruling queens, or nowadays, prime ministers; but still not be priests or bishops? If they have fully partaken of Christ's priesthood to the extent that they symbolize the male kingship, why can they not be ordained? And is there a masculine counterpart to this: a seemingly feminine role that a man can take on in the world but not within the Church?

DR. PATITSAS: I don't think we are trying to put limits on men or women and their roles. The logic of the chiasm is just that, whatever we do, we not violate our core calling. Men do what they do as protectors, in a masculine way; women must do whatever they do as nurturers, in particular of children, which is the most interesting way of bringing forth a new "word," a new person in the image of the Word. It does seem, however, that somehow it is a greater challenge for a woman to take on some leadership or fighting roles without violating their core calling of prophecy and motherhood than it is for a man to take on nurturing roles without violating his core of protectiveness. This is probably because woman's primary calling is more challenging, more all-encompassing, and more complex.

The sacramental priesthood remains at its heart a transfiguration of the ancient offering of blood sacrifice for the remission of sin and guilt. As such, it will always remain closed to women, who are not called to shed blood, even in a mystical way.

The chiasm is not at all about swapping roles, but rather about putting Christ at the heart of your own role. And it just so happens, that, invisibly, without anyone much noticing it, you then come to symbolize the other role. I mean "symbolize" in the proper Orthodox sense, of really "being what you aren't," and also of being able to honestly convey to others something that you aren't. You aren't playacting someone else's role, but, by at first seeming to eschew all roles, since you embrace the crucified form of your own role so completely, you come to enact this beautiful chiasm.

Hence, if you try to usurp the other side's role upon a foundation of renouncing or fleeing from your own role, you aren't symbolizing anything. You would just be avoiding your cross. At that point, anything you do is just not serious. It's frivolous.

As for women empresses in Byzantium, this is a role which women can fulfill, so long as they heavily emphasize the chastity, or unknowing, of fulfilling their prophetic office in a priestly way. If they come across as unchaste in any sense, no one will take them seriously as leaders. I noticed this with Margaret Thatcher when she was Prime Minister of England. Her unimpeachable chastity removed all concern about her gender. Because in fact, *both* genders have their characteristic weaknesses, and the way to neutralize these is to inscribe the cross of Christ completely within the genders, in the way that is an antidote to those weaknesses.

It's not that women aren't priests, let us emphasize, but that women's priesthood is exercised from within the prophetic office rather than from within the kingly office. This means that they unknow things and know persons; i.e., they minister to persons who, though perhaps weaker than themselves, through the female ministry to them, become stronger than the women. Well, the "weaker persons" whom women were first called to minister to were *men* – who could not be alone, who are existentially threatened when they are separated from women. Even as a very prosaic statistical matter, this is true: single, widowed, and divorced men in America, for example, have almost double the rate of mortality, from all causes, as do married men of the same age. When women accept the role of ordination, then they are no longer helpmates to men, but dispense with men entirely.

The Athonite devotion to the Mother of God is the sign that, even for monastics, "It is not good for man to be alone" (Gen 2:18). Male celibacy and male ordained priesthood are unthinkable without reliance on the Virgin. When women abandon this role of helpmate and usurp men's roles, men are lost.

When women try to be ordained as priests celebrating the Eucharist, their underlying foundation of chaste unknowing is somehow lost. Priesthood for men or women involves our whole self. In this case, the Christian priest at the altar is meant to be an epiphany of Christ's dying for the people. Men are to become the "one man lost," while women are called to be chaste unknowers. In crossing the boundary into the self-sacrifice of a man, a woman forsakes her femininity rather than allowing it to unfold along the surprising trajectory of the chiasm. It is a *flight from* her original role as prophet and helpmate when what is called for is something more difficult than flight – the *crucifixion of* those roles in unknowing.

The Liturgy Reverses the Gender Roles of the Fallen World

The chiasm then shows you why you don't have women serving at the altar in Orthodoxy. In the regular world, it is women who bring forth the child from behind a veil or prepare the food for the assembled multitude. Therefore, within the Divine Liturgy, gender reconciliation is achieved when men take on these feminine vocations. "Take, eat, this is my Body," and "Drink of it, all of you, this is my Blood," are above all *maternal* statements. I mean, these words are what the mother is saying to her child in her womb and at her breast.

And so a man is tasked to symbolize these gestures, to enact them publicly in liturgy. The women, in turn, stand guard while this happens. And since the majority of churchgoers are women, the male priesthood in practice is an icon of men serving the women who are protecting them.

If you upset these roles in the Church, you would upset the way in which, starting from difference, we are united as we come to rest as the truest symbols of our partner's role and life. The Divine Liturgy is precisely the place where the gender roles are being inverted from their fallen, oppressive form. To tamper with this in the name of extremely simplistic understandings of equality would be both philistine and tragic for all concerned. You would have the frothy, light, superficial unity of collocated sameness while jettisoning the deep, enduring, exhilarating unity of the chiastic crossover.

And that's what love is, in one sentence: To make oneself the symbol of one's beloved; not the identical copy, not the mere partner, but the *symbol*, whereby a thing "*is what it isn't.*" A symbol remains itself, in fact becomes more itself, precisely through it's coming to be something that it isn't. This coinciding of opposites is the essential core of love.

Snarky Male "Prophets"

RTE: And in what instances do men have to be careful to not usurp the women's roles?

DR. PATITSAS: Have you noticed how awful it is, how unconscionable it is, when men publicly criticize their wives, even their ex-wives? I think that men can to some extent enact a priestly prophetic role towards kings and rulers, but never toward a woman whom they are sworn to protect. While it is embarrassing and improper when a woman criticizes her husband in public, when a man does this to his wife, it signifies the imminent death of the marriage. And all men who have not yet lost their minds know this, and they never can nor do trust other men who have made this false "prophecy" against their wives a habit.

Another and more common form of this improper taking on of prophecy by men is this attitude of snark and cynicism which pervades and often dominates educated male culture today. This false form of prophecy is the heterosexual corollary to the adoption of homosexuality by other men. Men have become cold critics, with the result that they have absolved themselves of the responsibility to die for women or to stand up for what they believe. They can stand detached, on the side, because after all they have skipped right to the other pole of the chiasm and become prophets without first becoming the "one man lost," or so they imagine.

Not Gender Roles, but Gender Priesthoods

So, the Church does not stand on rigid gender roles per se, but rather on the firm necessity of inscribing the Cross within the gender which we were given. You don't have a gender *role* but a gender *crucifixion* – and you better not miss your appointment with this sacrificial altar, or you will be in danger of missing the whole point of your life. But if you "make it to the altar," this will produce a chiastic crossover which at times requires a distinct separation, as in the ordination of men and not women, and at other times produces an apparent sameness, as when we see ruling women empresses in Byzantium – an unimaginable phenomenon in pre-Christian Rome.

To flee from the gender *or* from our cross – to either reject our gender or to fail to achieve the surprising symbolism – would leave love absent from our little corner of the world. And it would replace a living organic order with something dull and linear and rational and dead.

RTE: But wait, you and I have both remarked on the female Lutheran priests we met in Sweden. They had not left their essential womanliness behind, and seemed to be mothering their parishioners and visitors as a teacher would. Is this because the Lutheran understanding of the ordained priesthood and the sacraments differs from the Orthodox understanding? Perhaps because Lutheran priests are more like ministers, it makes sense in that context?

DR. PATITSAS: The possibility of a revived female diaconate in practice depends on broader cultural attitudes towards femininity. In America, even our feminists seem to despise women. The female Lutheran priests we've met abroad had developed and enriched their femininity and their chastity through their service to the Church.

But you are right: a different, less biblical notion of priesthood makes women clergy possible, but at some theological cost. Also, I never saw any of these women priests serve at the altar, either, so I don't know how that would strike me. Outside of liturgy, these women priests seemed to function in a role that was like a combination of an Orthodox nun and a deaconess. But this is something that is already present and much respected in our Orthodox Christian Church, in the persons of Great Schema nuns and, especially, of monastic abbesses.

The Garden of Eden:
How the War Between the Genders Began

A failure to enact the chiasm is nothing small or inconsequential. Saint Maximos the Confessor says that Christ came to heal five great divisions, and the first division to be healed was the one between men and women.[13] Without healing of the gender war, in other words, the whole cosmic order becomes unstable.

Our Orthodox Church believes that men and women have been locked in a tragic separation since our first parents sinned in the Garden of Eden. And we also believe that Christ's *very first* task in his ministry of priestly reconciliation was to heal this division

---

[13] Lars Thunberg translates the five divisions as follows: 1. Between the Uncreated and the Created; 2. Between the Visible and the Invisible Worlds; 3. Between Heaven and Earth; 4. Between Paradise and the Inhabited Earth; 5. Between Men and Women. From the moment of his Incarnation, Christ begins to turn these hard separations into distinctions designed to be united in relationship, starting with the opposition between men and women.

between men and women. He does this through his first miracle at the wedding in Cana and through his other "first miracle," his birth from a Virgin.

It's nice to notice that while one "first miracle" is taken as a blessing of virginity, and the other as a blessing of marriage, in fact, according to the Church Fathers, both miracles act to reconcile men and women in Christ.

This rift originally started in the Garden of Eden, when Eve did not enact her prophetic gift in a priestly way, but instead sought a knowledge outside of personal relationship. Secretly from God and from Adam, she entered into a research program that reduced knowledge to an object, a shiny apple.

But, some saints say, Adam made things far worse and took the gender war to an exponentially higher pitch when he failed to enact his kingly responsibility in a priestly way – that is, at the cost of his own life, if necessary.[14] Adam was faced with a judgment of death; "for in the day that you eat of it, you shall surely die," the Lord had already warned him (Gen 2:17). Therefore, once the fruit had been eaten and the Lord was questioning the primary witnesses to the transgression, Adam was in effect turning Eve and God over to the judgment of death by blaming them for his transgression! (Gen 3:12). In effect, he was claiming that his Creator and his partner, not he, deserved death for what had happened.

Notice how both of the healthy shames are being violated here. Eve was bold where she should have been ashamed, curious where she should have been faithful. But Adam was ashamed and afraid where he should have been bold. Adam was supposed to (forgive me for putting it this way) "stand up" to God by just taking all the blame for the sin he and Eve had committed, and in this way protecting Eve. Perhaps it was God's will that Adam "defy" him in just this way! Instead, Adam threatens to become a killer (to commit, in fact, both uxoricide and deicide) by blaming Eve and God rather than himself for a sin known to be punishable by death. He directly

---

14 The saint is St. Silouan the Athonite (1866-1938), who wrote that Adam's sin was different than, worse, and more consequential than Eve's. See Sakharov, *Saint Silouan the Athonite, op.cit.*

reverses his calling to be a protector. He should have taken all the responsibility for his helper's mistake as well as for his own.

And isn't this what the Fathers say about each of us in temptation? Before the sin we are so bold and confident, really shameless, and just jump to our destruction. But once we have sinned, suddenly we are too shy to go to confession to a priest and own up to our mistake. We enact the right shames but at the wrong times and in the wrong sequence.

Why Only Males at the Holy Altar?

The fact that the ordained, liturgical Christian priesthood is reserved for men is perhaps above all attributable to this one fact – at the Fall, at the first onset of sin, Adam offered God and Eve to die in his place. After Christ through his incarnation, cross, and resurrection reverses the enmity between the genders, He will finally grant Adam's wish (the wish of all men under the sway of the fighting passions) to offer others for sacrifice. However, Christ will command men to offer this sacrifice in a surprising way, in a form where the offering is now an act of love.

In the Christian priesthood, men will still offer God's life for the world, but they will offer God *with* God and *in obedience to* God; they will offer God in a bloodless sacrifice; they will offer a God who goes willingly to become a victim; they will offer a God who has already risen from the dead for the life of the world; they will offer a God whose desire *had always been* to be poured out for the life of the world, long before Adam, in his petty cowardice, attempted to impose this upon God; and, perhaps most of all, men will offer themselves and not their wives as they are offering God, and thus not make the offering of God out of fear or out of self-justification. In Christ the New Adam, men now offer God as sacrificial victim for their own sin and the sins of others but now out of their desire to offer themselves as well for the life of the world.

In other words, where St. Paul saw women *excluded from the priesthood* on account of their sinful actions that led to the Fall (I Tim

2:9-15), we should also understand it to be even more the case that men *are bound to the priesthood* on account of their own (in the eyes of St. Silouan, far worse) sinful actions at the Fall. Adam's greatest sin was his attempt to "kill" God, and so the sons of Adam are bound now to offer a sacrifice that will transform this sin into life.

I am not trying to reverse two thousand years of consensus in Scripture and the Fathers that Eve's role at the Fall was a major reason why women are excluded from the sacramental priesthood. Rather, I am trying to close a parenthesis, by showing that Adam's role at the Fall is an even more important reason why males are bound inescapably to the priesthood.

Even if you think the Genesis account is mythological – not that it is fictional but that it is a paradigmatic truth – the male priesthood still makes sense. Men are too prone to brutal violence, and women too prone to conversations with smooth-tongued serpents, for the denial of women from the priesthood and the requirement of men for the priesthood to not be necessary.

Origins of the Gender War, Continued

But let us return to our theme of the gender war and its origins. Each gender calling is meant to be an anointing in a twofold way, since we must receive the priestly cross within our gender calling. If we are to be happy as men or as women, we will have to embrace the cross meant for our given gender. The healthy shame appropriate to each gender is expressed through enacting the priestly calling of that gender.

To be a man means that we accept again and again to be the "one man lost"; i.e., that we consent to give our lives for the women, children, and others in our lives. And to be a woman means that we embrace the cross of unknowing, of preferring persons over things, of disregarding all the "proofs" of others' unlovability, instead loving them for who they are in Christ. To be a priestly woman means exactly *not to do* what Eve did, which was to believe a lie about God and to disregard the welfare of Adam. In fact, Eve made a mockery of the priesthood when she "took, ate, and then gave" to Adam.[15] As St. Paul tells us, this is a major reason why the ordination of women now naturally strikes us as so wrong (I Tim 2:9-15).

Somehow, whenever we enter the sacred space of the Church, the gender callings are reversed, or inverted, through the leaven of a healthy priestly consciousness. Normally, the women cook and serve, but in Church liturgy the men take on these duties. Outside of liturgy, the men are served, but in liturgy the women accept this role.

But as we said, when Adam does not act like a priestly king – when he does not volunteer to die in order to save Eve; and, moreover, when Eve does not act like a priestly prophet – when she does not refuse the offer of a knowledge divorced from relationship – then, in those acts the two have betrayed each other, even to the point of risking the other's death. And from that point on, the genders are at war, pitted against each other, implacably hostile.

Most everything that goes awry in sexual morality is a result of this "war between women and men" that Christ came to heal. What was intended to unite us – our helpless physical need for each other, our awesome sexual attraction toward each other – well, that very positive force has flipped since the Fall of Adam and Eve, and now it so easily serves to further alienate us from each other. In very many ways, sex has turned us against each other and caused us to exploit each other rather than to serve each other.

Thus as an ethicist I try not to discuss pornography and masturbation, fornication and abortion, adultery and divorce, in isolation from the larger Good News that Christ has come to reconcile men and women. Christ has plundered these temptations of their power over us.

By the way, notice how in each of these three pairs of sins, it is the case that the passion of desire leads inevitably to the passion of conflict – i.e., the failure to embrace Beauty chastely (through pornography, fornication, or adultery) invariably makes us not Good,

---

15 This priestly connotation of Eve's act was pointed out to me by Rev. Fr. Calinic Berger, the author of *Challenges of Orthodox Thought and Life* (The Romanian Orthodox Episcopate of America, 2011) in a personal conversation in 2003.

makes us failures at empathy (in masturbation, abortion, or divorce). All sexual sin to one degree or another is the same: the misuse of our God-given sexual powers so that they become an instrument of separation and harm between the genders and between persons, rather than an instrument of sweet union and long-sought healing.

Nor, of course, do we confront these gender-war temptations as lone individuals. Whole societies and ages will be vexed by particular sexual temptations. There are clearly larger forces and misdirections in our cultures that leave us all sexually vulnerable in the same ways in a given cultural or historical setting. Right now, the malady that has become much more prevalent is same-sex attraction, and so we have even more reason to feel compassion for whomever has been caught up in something that is not, obviously, mostly their own fault. There has been an entire cultural shift that means more people are tempted in this way and that fewer people know how to defend themselves spiritually when this particular temptation comes.

We must not only repent for our own particular acts of sexual sin – our sins against the God-given gift of gender and against the other gender – but we must also repent of our contribution to the larger forces that drive such things.

RTE: In Genesis God warns Adam and Eve that, as a result of the Fall, they will now find themselves in conflict. How does this relate to the gender chiasm?

DR. PATITSAS: When God drives Adam and Eve from the Garden of Eden after their sin (Gen. 3:23-24), He does pronounce a judgment so that they can see what they have wrought, and so that they can be prevented from worse sins against each other until Christ's coming. He punishes them out of love, however, and in order to staunch the wound of gender separation. These judgments in Genesis, in other words, pit us against each other but also deepen our dependence upon each other. They are a temporary measure for the preservation of the human race until the coming of Christ.

In Genesis 3:14-24, God condemns the woman to suffer in childbirth, to desire her husband, and yet to be ruled by him. God condemns the man to rule in isolation, to labor, and to die. Thus, though the man and the woman will now struggle to live side by side, neither will it be the case that living apart will be much of an option for them. And this is a burden God gives to men and women, but it is done by God with the hopeful intent of their eventual reconciliation. By suffering together and because of each other, the genders begin to regain their chastity. Each one is made more unavoidably dependent on the other, in other words, and thus some will begin to eschew whatever leads them away from each other.

Ephesians 5:
Christ Reverses the Judgments of Genesis

But in Ephesians 5, St. Paul describes what it looks like when this gender war and the punishments of Genesis are overcome by Christ's death and resurrection, and human life now becomes the icon of the liturgy of the Jerusalem above. The subjection of the woman pronounced in Genesis becomes in Ephesians a *mutual subjection* of man and woman in service to one another. Moreover, this new and mutual subjection is intended not as a curse but as an act of loving worship towards a perfectly meek and humble Savior. The man is the head of the wife as Christ is head of the Church; that is, he will die for her – not "kill" her to save himself. Also, the man, rather than reacting helplessly to any sins of his wife or accusing her before God or others, will himself wash and cleanse her of sin by his own self-sacrifice. He no longer presents her sins to God but instead presents her purity to himself and to God; that is, he regards her sins as being his fault, not hers; she is ever-blameless in his eyes. The husband must, literally if necessary, wash his wife's sins with his own blood.

In turn, according to Ephesians 5, through Christ the woman respects her husband and makes her decisions in communion with him. She sees him not as an obstacle to her divinization, going behind his back to cut deals with serpents, but she sees him as an icon or sacrament who will catalyze her communion with God. She becomes an unknower, not as a means of avoiding mystery but because she sees that unknowing is the unavoidable component of her twofold anointing as prophet. In unknowing, she becomes wise and the indispensable helpmate to her husband. She sees past the attributes to the inner and deeper reality of the person.

All of this is described in Ephesians 5, and we must see this passage as the direct antidote to what God had himself pronounced in exiling man and woman from Eden.

RTE: Might a man's reliance on his wife's prophetic counsel make her the de facto head of the household?

DR. PATITSAS: Let me answer that from the other direction. If her advice is genuinely rooted in chastity and unknowing, in love for Beauty, then she will not always be so intensely attached to her husband's reception of that counsel. That is, she will say a word, and a word to the wise will be sufficient. If the word is not received, it is not necessarily pressed – though its power will of course reverberate all the more without her insistence. A wise wife has mastered the art of, at least sometimes, unknowing the very advice she is giving; it is spoken and all but forgotten. Her husband's freedom is thus respected.

Of course, if he's falling asleep at the wheel, figuratively speaking, this is a different matter. She must become insistent in some cases; in those emergency instances what she is unknowing is her own self. She is risking herself because she sees the marriage will not survive unless her warnings are heeded.

This may seem like a sexist ideal, but in Orthodoxy we find this ideal also regarding counsel given by our holiest confessors. If an elder finds that his spiritual child resists his direct and Spirit-filled words, then the consensus is that the elder should not insist.

God may have other plans. Discernment is not a crystal ball, nor a political program. It is a Spirit-filled event involving more than one person.[16]

But to go back to one of men's faults for a second, because it is such an unmanly fault: a man who publicly accuses, condemns, lists the faults of, or exposes his wife is as wrong as a woman being ordained priest. They are mirror images of the same fault. There are some things that don't flip, since in the chiasm you don't abandon your original calling. So, a woman can give her life for her children, but let us hope she need not do so for her husband; and he should try not to hide behind her when the bullets are flying. And, a man accusing his wife has taken on a prophetic role toward her, which he cannot do. He must present her to himself, to the Lord, and to others as blameless, St. Paul says – even if it costs him his life.

Christ did not denounce *his* bride publicly. He never denounced *any* woman publicly that we know of. But He does denounce men publicly. And at his crucifixion He doesn't say, "Look what they have done to me," nor "Why, Father, did you give me such a bride?" Least of all does He say, "Father, I had to get down off the cross and hurt these people because You have given me an impossible task."

Instead, in his suffering He asks for his bride to be forgiven by God while at the same moment even denying that she has anything to be forgiven for; He simply says, "They know not what they do" (Lk 23:34).

---

[16] A person might want his spiritual father to be a kind of magician who can conjure up the truth. But if a guide's word is really true, it will also be inspired (the Logos and the Holy Spirit are never separated), and the spiritual child will probably feel peace when he hears the counsel. "Where two or three are gathered together in my name, there am I in the midst of them." If the spiritual child does not feel peace at the spiritual guide's words or if the words are clearly contrary to the gospel, then the healthy spiritual child will hesitate and resist. Of course, the question then arises, is our heart not feeling peace because the guidance is wrong or because *we* are not right internally? There is not always an easy way to know which is the case. This uncertainty can be a terrible burden, and so we may go to the other extreme and start to question everything that even a saint teaches us. But eldership works best when we see ourselves as entering into a *synodia*, a conciliar harmony, with our elders. And a true guide will accept our "pushing back" in a spirit of gentleness and love.

The Female Priesthood

But the reason women can't be ordained priests is expressible still more simply: women *can* be priests, but priestly prophets. Whereas presiding at a blood sacrifice (even if turning it into a self-sacrifice, as in Christian liturgy) is the action of a priestly king, which is something reserved to men. Women have another priestly expression of their calling, which is to know. They are, through the cross of unknowing, to turn this prophetic calling into its transfigured form – namely, motherhood in every possible form, which redeems human beings from the status of objects into full persons.

We must be careful of actions which are an offense against the calling for which each person was created with a particular gender.

RTE: I know you've read my interview with Alice Linsley, the Genesis scholar.[17] What do you make of her work?

DR. PATITSAS: The more I think about what she has written, the more my sense of the sacredness of creation grows. She says that all cultures understood the absolute necessity of keeping the blood of life separated from the blood of sacrifice. In order to protect women, men are called to bear the blood guilt that comes with the blood of death; they thus become like "shields" to women. Even pagan priestesses did not ever kill the sacrifice. And even today in most American households, the woman prepares the turkey at Thanksgiving, but at the table it is the man who carves it and serves it.

Alice Linsley tells us how absolute is this command not to mix the blood of life, which women alone possess (this meant originally the menstrual blood and, by extension, the feminine power of motherhood more generally), with the blood of death. Even in the ancient world the practice of mixing the bloods, when it rarely occurred, was understood to have an occult dimension, to be outside

---

17 Alice Linsley, "Stepping into the Stream: An Interview with Alice C. Linsley," *Road to Emmaus Journal*, Vol. XI, No. 1 Winter, 2010 (#40).

the parameters of what was permissible within civilization. Today, we would recognize such a practice as simply demonic. Pagan priestesses maintained rituals, guarded sacred hearths, and always their role was constructive – almost never did it involve killing.

And this is not just an Indo-European idea. Linsley tells us that worldwide all human religions resolved into two broad groups. In one, priesthood and a blood sacrifice were central, while the other type of religion was shamanistic. Well, it should tell us something about the elemental structure of human and cosmic reality that a) in none of the hundreds of cultures that practiced blood sacrifice was there a female priesthood involved in shedding blood, and b) even in shamanistic cultures that had no blood sacrifice custom, women were prohibited from the role of killing. In fact, in shamanistic cultures, women were often excluded from even being present while men were hunting nor could women be killed except at grave spiritual risk to the perpetrator.

Native American cultures, for example, concurred with this general shamanistic rule. The legendary American combat commander David Hackworth tells us that one of his Native American soldiers spared three female Viet Cong soldiers, even though they were heavily armed and were in the process of tracking an American platoon. This man came from a culture that understood the ancient prohibition against mixing the two bloods. "I was upset," the soldier said, "because they were women. In my society women are held in high esteem. Women are earth, mother of man." As a result, he purposely fired high and wide, something which he had not done before.[18]

RTE: Then should women not be in combat?

DR. PATITSAS: Female combat soldiers are essential in counterinsurgency settings where relationships with the local people are the whole point of the military presence. Moreover, women are doing

---

18 David Hackworth and Eilhys England, *Steel My Soldiers' Hearts: The Hopeless to Hardcore Transformation of 4th Battalion, 39th Infantry, United States Army, Vietnam* (New York: Rugged Land, 2002), 332-33.

great things in every branch of the service and in many cases raising the overall level of their units through their special talents as women.

But in general our focus should not be on women's abilities in combat but on the fact that it is somehow risky – an affront to the cosmic order that will right itself at the expense of those who violate it – to mix the blood of life with the blood of death.

Of course, in the current American case, the rates of physical injury and the rates of PTSD are much higher for women soldiers. Men have to step up and carry this cross, and we should return to national conscription if that is what it would take to limit our reliance upon women in combat settings. But one reason that we don't take this step is that military service has become a crucial link to certain educational and career benefits that are not otherwise available to women in our current system.

RTE: But should Christians be limited by these ancient cosmological considerations? In Christ, there is neither male nor female.

DR. PATITSAS: Well, St. Paul says that, but when Christ himself was asked about marriage and sexual morality, He goes straight back to the account of Genesis and God's having created human beings as male and female. In Christ's discussion of marriage, St. Paul's "neither male nor female" is expressed much more understandably as, "the two shall become one flesh." I think that this is a better depiction of gender peace and gender reconciliation than some vision that obliterates gender entirely.

So we have to use what our God and Savior says to clarify the meaning intended by his apostle. We mustn't be like those preachers (on television, they seem to be the majority of preachers) who talk endlessly from the Epistles and the Old Testament while mostly skipping over the Gospels themselves! And we can also see how for 2,000 years the Orthodox Church chose not to obliterate gender distinctions but rather sanctified and defended them.

The point of "there is neither male nor female" in Christ is that the two are reconciled in Christ without confusion and without separation. This occurs either through marriage or through chastity. In fact, perhaps we can apply all four of the Chalcedonian qualifiers to human gender union, as the couple becomes "unconfusedly, unchangeably, indivisibly, and inseparably" united.

RTE: Can we return again to your idea that each gender expresses its priesthood uniquely, so that women are firstly prophets and men are firstly kings? But in the Old Testament, both men and women were prophets and both men and women were rulers. Later Christian history also shows prophetic men and ruling women. How did that work?

DR. PATITSAS: The Old Testament realities are pointing to their archetypes in the New Testament. There, Christ is the sole priest, and all of prophecy – all bringing forth of a word – is revealed to have been a foreshadowing of the most important human prophet, the woman Panaghia.

Thereafter, in the Church, a new order is established. Men are to celebrate the bloodless sacrifice, thus honoring their protective natures while also dampening their fallen fixation on killing. At the same time, women become uniquely cherished for their ability to bring forth the icon of the Word, the human person – whether through motherhood or through some other calling, even as they are shielded from offering the sacrifice.

It is in this way that women in Byzantium could be empresses, more often as regents for their young sons: their calling in such a role is to infuse it with some extra dimension of motherhood and protective grace. Nevertheless, within the liturgy of the Church itself, where the Church is at its most ideal, men do not kill (it is a bloodless sacrifice) and women do not investigate the mystery. The full transfiguration of gender roles is most visible within worship itself, and from there radiates out in lesser ways to heal and transfigure gender relations within Christian society as a whole.

I think that it is significant that even though women were empresses and could call Ecumenical Councils, there were still not women priests in the liturgy. And paradoxically, it is also significant that, in the light of Christ's reconciliation of the genders, women could fulfill roles as leaders in society without betraying their femininity or their own core priesthood as nurturers of the Word. The first fact tells us that somehow the liturgical core of the faith, its liturgy, is held to be more archetypal, more structured according to a transfigured form of the ancient prohibition against the presence of women at blood sacrifice. The second fact tells us that this very reversal – where men are now peacemakers in the liturgy and bringers forth of Christ – will reverberate out into the wider society in such a way that we have much more freedom regarding gender roles than we did before Christ.

But this freedom comes with a caveat: the wider equality of the genders in Christian society is based on the more dedicated fidelity to the cross *within* Christian liturgy – and by liturgy I mean both the actual services and the spiritual life as a whole. Absent that embrace of the twin gender crosses there, what I expect we shall find is that in time the gender equality outside of liturgy will collapse and revert to something destructive. This is already happening, in fact. And in any case, in Christ we each have the roles of prophet, king, and priest, although according to a different sequence.

Again, each person is different in how we experience our gender. But the function of ritual is to safeguard and convey the kind of deep cosmological information that a culture forgets at its mortal peril.

Why We Resist Our Gender Callings

RTE: Since the 1970s, we've seen a growing social trend in Europe and North America towards denying our identities as men and women, to the point that people surgically alter their bodies in the hope of becoming the other gender. How has this come about?

DR. PATITSAS: There are a statistically very rare number of people who are born with ambiguous physical characteristics, such that hard choices are then required as to whether medical intervention is appropriate, and so forth. Such people face a different kind of situation.

Gender is a physical reality, but what the gender chiasm tells us is that it is also a personal and social *task* – a task at which we may fail. All cultural expressions of gender are, at bottom, simply more or less imperfect aids to enacting the gender chiasm in Christ. So we may fail to complete the chiasm for lots of reasons, perhaps involving our own choices, or our relationship to our parents and our family setting, or due to any confusion about gender in the culture that we grow up in, or even due to our fallen biologies and the challenges these present us.

In a fallen world, almost all cultural constructions of gender will be imperfect to some degree. Our own particular cultural tic since around 1970 – the idea that gender has no basis in physical reality – is yet another attempt to meet this universal challenge, and one that is even worse than the imperfect cultural guides that preceded it.

Going all the way back to Sophocles' *Antigone*, we can see that gender is often felt as a burden which must be overcome. Because the cultural guides to gender will always be imperfect, some percentage of us will live in tension and feel at times oppressed by what society or our families are telling us about gender. This is not only the story of *Antigone* but of many other works of literature. The Church records people who felt similarly oppressed by their culture's expectations around gender, but who found a way to receive sanctity in Christ without destroying gender as the icon it is meant to be. For us, we believe that the transcendence of gender begins paradoxically in the embrace of our gender callings.

Sex-change operations have become just one more cultural norm for dealing with the personal challenge of gender. But they are a terrible pattern, an immoral mutilation of the human body. They make the situation worse, and in about half the cases leave the victim of such surgical malpractice (after all, the surgeons aren't altering your DNA, so in what sense have they really changed your gender??) struggling with thoughts of suicide.[19]

---

19 The National Center for Transgender Equality and the National Gay and Lesbian Task Force, October 2010, confirmed that 41% of transgender respondents reported attempting suicide, compared to 1.6% of the general population.

Again, every society has guides to gender roles, ours being the new unisex approach, and none of them is completely perfect. Some come closer to being perfect. For example, I believe that there is an amazing coinciding of liberation and femininity among women within some Orthodox Christian cultures, for example, and of strength and tenderness among the men there. But none of these cultural approaches can take away the importance of uncreated grace in helping us to negotiate this challenge. When we turn any of these guides into idols we are in danger of being given over to sexual immorality, as St. Paul warns in Romans 1. The women's movement in America felt that gender roles here had become idols rather than guides.

Paradise vs. the Inhabited Earth

One particular tension around gender – the one where we seek to escape our own genders – concerns an even less well-known consequence of the Fall, a second division which Christ came to heal and unite. I mean, the one between Paradise and the Inhabited Earth. In this division, what is at stake is the way in which our circumstances in a fallen world are so different than what they were supposed to have been had we not been banished from the Garden of Eden.

This second division is another source of our difficulty with our own genders. It is harder to carry the real cross of our gender calling when the world around us is piling on top of us additional, non-godly crosses. The obligations we must fulfill as a man or as a woman, we must fulfill under less than ideal conditions.

For example, we perhaps did not receive the perfect parenting and mentoring we needed in order to take on these gender callings in a lovely way. Moreover, our heads are stuffed with a lot of nonsense from our wider culture about who we are as men and women. Spiritually, meanwhile, we find that we are undeveloped or out of balance in either our male or female side internally. Thus, where the cross of gender should rest upon our shoulders, we may have a "wound" that makes us flinch whenever we even think of shouldering that load.

If we sense personal difficulties, either in relating to the other gender or to our own gender, this is the opportunity to renew our relationship with Christ. This is also the time to understand that we have a Heavenly Father who is anxious to make up in our souls and psyches the missing pieces left over from our past.[20]

As for the various wounds in our gender formation, the worst thing that we can do is to panic about them or give up. Look, the very fact that human fertility begins to decline after age thirty tells you that biology and God did not intend for us to have sages or saints for parents: either a couple will be young and perhaps unready to parent maturely, or they will be less fertile.

Mothers and fathers, as we have said, are icons of God's care for us – they are neither the perfect virtual reality 3-D god-droids we demand them to be because we won't admit our need for the actual God, nor are they the forgeries we accuse them of being because we think that *we* are God and deserve better. They are usually just icons of a higher or lower artistic quality, sometimes even depending on where in the birth order we fall within the same family. So every single one of us is going to have to come to God for healing about our relationship with our parents, and this will include healing in our gender formation because mom and dad influence that so heavily.

Since we can neither deny our bodily identities as men or as women, nor neglect our complementary side (our feminine side if we are a man or our masculine side if we are a woman), we will have to turn to our Heavenly Father and ask him to heal and develop these powers within us, and to our mother, the Panaghia.

RTE: Then are male and female souls the same?

---

[20] A good if simplistic book designed to help us overcome these misappropriations of gender roles is John Gray's *Mars and Venus on a Date* (New York: HarperCollins, 2009). It contains practical examples of how a woman "unknows" when communicating with her husband or boyfriend and how a man can become "lost" for his beloved. Despite its title, I think it is a mistake to imagine ourselves as too sophisticated for such elementary aids. After all, marriage is collapsing and gender confounds us. We are indeed again beginners.

DR. PATITSAS: Yes and No. We all have the same three powers of soul – the desiring, the fighting, and the intellectual – and in this sense men and women are the same. But we must be careful never to forget how intimate is the union of soul and body in Orthodoxy. Because our biologies encode gender, our souls will feel different. The same Fathers who emphasized that our souls are the same also emphasized that pastoral care of the soul would be different for men than it would be for women.

Our gender identities cannot be enacted in the abstract, nor activated on the basis of isolated self-analysis, *since by definition they are relational powers*. We really only learn to be comfortable as men and women when we enter new and better relationships – with Christ, with our Heavenly Father, with the saints and Panaghia, with good mentors, with new friends that God in his providence sends us.

For most of us, the main thing in gender formation is probably to have good examples, good mentors. I remember in my younger days an aunt back in Greece who, during an argument, picked up a chair over her head and came at a man from her village who was illegally and deviously attempting to confiscate a bit of her land. Because she wasn't berserk or dramatic or sentimental about it, her very feminine strength settled a whole number of gender questions for me. Nothing of her femininity was lost. And she won her point without legal costs, too.

When faced with a person who has experienced a rupture in their childhood formation, Western therapy focuses on the patient. Through cognitive work, the gap is to be made up. In Orthodoxy, the situation is understood quite differently. It is expected that no one can, by themselves and solely through mental work, fill gaps which were meant to be resolved in the unspoken loving embrace of others. That would be just impossible, by definition.

Rather, if we are to be healed from a difficult childhood, then some *better* father and mother must be found.

Meanwhile, back in the United States of Therapy, public conversation about gender roles is dominated by the sort of hypochondriac busybodies who always stand ready to collapse at the first contact with the fresh air of an actual and unapologetic man or woman. I am talking about the way every sign of lively gender in our culture is now treated as evidence of gender oppression. As a program of renewal, I would suggest cross-cultural pilgrimage.

I myself was surprised to discover in my travels the extent to which the "ugly American" syndrome persists today, not because we act insensitively when we go abroad but rather because we are sometimes cold and correct about the hottest and sweetest things – eros and gender difference. People in more than one culture have told me how they started by seeing Americans as the freest and most fun people in the world, but in time were saddened by how controlled and self-oppressed we were, how calculating and unable to connect. Not in our terms, perhaps, where we may meet and marry other "Lawyers in Love," but by the standards of the non-Therapy World.

True enough, Americans can come across like robots, like some new form of human being. Same-sex marriage is the ultimate expression of this – so far. What is going on with us in America, though, is something more interesting than it at first appears. Americans are such democrats – so committed to the idea that the privileges of the elite should be shared with all, and without discomfort. Our "robot-like" quality is actually a secular version of Orthodox soul *apatheia*. Think of how remarkable it is to be so blasé about the fact that your spouse has previously slept with other people. Normal people don't accept that without some pain; only saints and robots can handle it totally calmly. But Americans, though neither, seem to do it routinely. Another example would be this post-gender world of homosexuality and transgenderism – it's a worldly, partial, and immoral version of the way that saints grow to overcome gender limitations.

As Americans, we seem to be seeking happiness through a kind of materialistic *apatheia*, attained through not having many children, not experiencing the pain of jealousy and loss, and so forth. This approach to satisfying happiness will not work, even on its own terms; as divorce and gay marriage have entered the vacuum left by the decline of the Christian family, the incidence of childlessness and spousal abuse have only grown. But it will have enough highlight moments to carry on for at least a while.

These bad turns in public morality are earning the support of some Christians – outwardly, the new gender order seems to be an advance in love and tolerance. But in the Church, passionless states coincide with fiery purity and limitless love, not with sexual uncleanness and indifference to our own falls.

As we love God with all that we have and are, and as we share that with a spouse, or in another way with God in the monastic life, we learn to carry our gender crosses. In this way, both the gender divide and the paradise vs. inhabited world divide are overcome in us by Christ. We no longer resent our embodiment in a particular gender, for the Cross teaches us that accepting such an "unjust" limitation is the essential starting point for a life that overcomes all limitations and all injustice. And we no longer participate in this harsh war between the genders. We become agents of reconciliation.

III. PERSONHOOD

The Tragic Divorce within Christian Anthropology: Catholic Nature vs. Protestant Will

RTE: Orthodox participants in inter-Christian dialogue have said that while the first century of ecumenical work aimed at finding an acceptable common understanding of the Church, the second hundred years will focus on who the person is, or anthropology. Do you think that gender will be part of these discussions?

DR. PATITSAS: This is already the case, and will become even more so. But in such theological work, our guide to what it means to be human must be Christ; He is the perfect man, the New Adam. If we cannot understand what we see in him in any aspect, including the role and meaning of gender, then we look also to the saints for clarification. Because without a clear understanding of human nature, we cannot correct our conclusions about ethics.

Now, for our purposes in this interview, anthropology is important because many people are not sure where to "place" gender itself. Is it part of our given nature or do we get to choose it? Is same-sex attraction part of the God-given nature for some people? Or, is the adventure of human freedom more complex than any of those choices? Thus, a rich discussion of the human person belongs in our discussion of gender.

RTE: The very definition of what it means to be human seems to be changing lately, doesn't it?

DR. PATITSAS: Ethics is said to be conducted based on conclusions reached in three "prior" areas: anthropology, teleology, and epistemology. In other words, our ethical conclusions flow directly from what we think the person is (anthropology); from what we think the goal of human life is (teleology); and from the method we use to make accurate moral determinations (epistemology). If we change our beliefs in any of these three areas, then we will have to change our conclusions about what it is moral to do.

An example would be whether we think that our salvation will depend partly on whether we have used our bodily sexuality in a Christian way, as Holy Scripture insists, or whether we think instead that God's real criterion of judgment includes only the human spirit. In that case, both our teleology will have changed (our thoughts about our ultimate destiny) and also our anthropology will have changed (we will think of our bodies as not essential to our identity). And following these changes, our beliefs about morality will obviously change, too.[21]

---

[21] In these interviews I have been attacking first of all the issue of how we know, or of how we approach ethical reasoning. I have been arguing that you can't start by establishing reason and logic, and *then* go on to investigate morality. You have to begin – even when doing academic theology – in responding aesthetically, chastely, and with purified eros towards Beauty, or theophany. Asceticism is therefore the first step of the intellectual life since it trains us to love what is genuinely Beautiful.

I also think that you don't come to know Goodness mainly through a truth-first approach. Paradoxically, you *contemplate* goodness *by giving alms to the poor* – i.e., by showing empathy.

So, how do ethicists see the human person? My very untutored impression is that within Roman Catholic ethics until at least the mid-1950s, theologians might have tended to base their definition of the human person on the common human nature. Human anthropology was handled as if it were reducible to some general description of humanity, and thus you rely upon Natural Law to tell everyone what to do. You look for what is universal in the human being, and you try to capture the laws that seem to guide or follow those universal components of the person. A moral person marches alongside all the other moral persons as part of God's undivided army, and ethics on this account is law-based rather than being tailored for each person therapeutically.

Protestant ethics reacted very negatively to this approach because in fact such a reduction does diminish, at least in part, human freedom. Everyone *is* different, and so a mass production approach to ethics can never capture all the situational and personal dimensions of the moral struggle. I am not saying that there are no fixed moral standards, but just that, in addition to the Natural Law, there is the adventure of moral development and even the necessity to enter into moral challenges that are unique to us, that we voluntarily take on.

Soul development itself teaches us that as we grow spiritually, our moral standard will become more demanding, so the Natural Law is a moving target in actual Christian practice. "Thou Shalt not Kill," is a fixed standard, but it is elevated for saints, some of

---

There is an even stronger rationale to my critique of the truth-first way: *whenever* we humans reason, we are not actually calculating like computers or logic machines. Rather, in *all* human thinking an idea somehow "comes to us" (which in itself is a kind of theophany, I would argue), and if the idea is pleasing to us at some level – somehow Beautiful, in other words – we then investigate its usefulness (i.e., its Goodness) to solve a particular problem or answer a particular question. And if it meets both criteria – if it is both pleasing and effective – then we conclude that it is probably True. *So, Beauty-first is the progression involved in the very act of thinking itself.*

This, however, does not exonerate the truth-first way but rather demonstrates that it involves a terrible confusion. If we are honest about what thinking is actually like, then it will be obvious that to think more clearly, we will need to purify the *primary* cognitive faculty, our aesthetic sense, by feasting and fasting in the context of celebrating God's revelation. "Thinking things through rationally" should parallel the act of thinking itself, not contradict it by cutting off the aesthetic and moral senses from the act of analysis.

whom come to repent of even harming a leaf and who even see a judgmental thought towards another person as a kind of killing. Meanwhile, the standard is lowered for soldiers in combat who sometimes *must* kill to fulfill their duty.

The whole point of the Protestant Reformation was for Europeans to break out of the limitations on freedom imposed by the Roman Catholic Church's theological system. But to achieve this liberation (which had a real political dimension, as well), Protestant theology will concoct its own version of the human person, reducing each of us to our individual human will. The person in this second view has *no* fixed nature except to choose and to be free.

Eventually, some branches of Protestant morality will become based in the idea that *any* consensual act is moral; any act that does not violate the human will, in other words, comes to be seen as permissible, since the will is the real kernel of humanity. And then the wider cultures influenced by this Reformation spirit continue and intensify this anthropological tendency independently of Protestantism itself. Thus, a woman who is certain that she is not a woman, despite her obvious nature, is held not to be a woman, and so forth.

For Protestants, Will trumps Nature – a predictable reaction to the fact that for the Roman Catholic Church, against which Protestants are reacting, Nature trumps Will.

A Vocation of Reconciliation

When Protestant ethics looks to Scripture, it is in danger of repeating this mistake but now regarding the nature of God himself. In emphasizing that the Holy Bible is God's Word, the connotation becomes that Scripture represents God's somewhat arbitrary, in fact implacable, will for the world. God's word is God's will, full stop. You would think a scriptural theology would lead to a Natural Law kind of reasoning, because the Bible shows you who God is and reveals insights about the world He made, but Protestant Bible study doesn't lead in that direction, and this emphasis on God's *power* is why. The theophany that Protestants are serving is not one of Truth (as in the Roman Catholic case) but of Goodness.

Protestantism wants to preserve our freedom from intellectual conclusions reached in the realm of Natural Law, and it feels that the way to do this is to reinforce the absoluteness of the Bible over against the power of settled Tradition and Reason. But to earn its freedom from the Church, Protestantism is prepared to subscribe to a biblically-revealed arbitrariness and absoluteness. It almost turns the Bible into the holy book of a certain other religion. Protestantism not only reduces the human person to his will but it also reduces God to His will and His power.

Thus, one side of Western Christianity tends to reduce human beings (and God, too) to their nature. The other side insists that, no, nature does not control; it is free will that is determinative of human identity, and God, by *his* arbitrary will, might declare us either saved or damned.

If we were reducible to our common human nature, then you could make much more sweeping and Natural Law-based moral judgments, but this would tend toward uniformity and oppression. The West originally liked thinking in terms of divine and human natures because once these were fixed, you could investigate them rationally. This was Lev Shestov's point about how Necessity and the erasure of freedom give a wider scope to reason; surprises, from God or from us, have been ruled out in these "nature-centric" systems.[22]

But if you decide instead to follow the Protestant reaction in anthropology and conclude that we are reducible to our free will, then such statements become impossible. Instead, you are left with a lot of competing assertions about what is moral. Maybe even God could change his mind and now bless what was formerly sinful. Each person finds his own truth within or outside of Scripture. Since all these individual moral differences can't readily be resolved, even by recourse to an inerrant Scripture, we declare a truce: morality

---

22 Lev Shestov, *Athens and Jerusalem* (New York, Simon and Schuster, 1968), 61-71.

is reduced to a contract that states, "If a behavior is consensual, then it is moral." Will trumps Nature. The Anglo-American Common Law tradition, with its presumption of limited government and limited interference by outside parties in our personal business, has now been hijacked by this trend, as well (I mean, its older basis in Natural Law reasoning is being jettisoned in favor of the maximization of liberty).

And so these are the two poles of Western Christian ethics today: Nature and Will. Or, if you like, Tradition (the ways that have worked for all humans and which are understandable expressions of the Natural Law) versus Scripture (God's infallible Will, interpreted by a wide array of free human wills). Orthodox Christians in the West are hard pressed to decide which to follow, for both elements of a human person are indispensable, and yet both are somehow insufficient to the full picture of what we actually experience of ourselves through our life in Christ.

In most things, I feel that Orthodox Christianity in the West has a vocation of reconciliation, a mission to reunite elements of life that were thought by Roman Catholics and Protestants to be implacably opposed. For example, does salvation come through works or through faith? Well, the tradition of the Church that received Holy Scripture is that salvation results in, and even follows from, a coincidence of pure faith and loving works that we call "liturgy" – and this liturgy is not even ours, but Christ's, to which we are joined like wild branches to a fruit-bearing tree. And this is just one of several examples where the Orthodox position reconciles the division between Catholics and Protestants.

As the Christians of the West recover their older theological traditions, they may see in the most ancient Church doctrines a reconciliation of Protestant and Roman Catholic views. What looks like contradiction is often paradox: conflicting views about God or salvation may sometimes turn out to be, by God's grace, held together in some larger frame. The ability to sustain paradox without descending into irrationality is a gift of God meant to be received in communion with the universal Church.[23]

Law and Freedom in the Realm of Politics

Let me take this one step farther to help clarify things. The Roman Catholic-Protestant split on the human person, or Nature vs. Will, should remind us of another split. In politics we often question whether a situation we are facing impacts all citizens in the same way so that we should enact a law, or whether the matter is really to be left to the free choice of individuals. For example, we do enforce conformity regarding speeding on the freeway, but we don't enforce conformity about religious choice, since in the first case a settled principle about the dangers of speeding covers the whole of human nature, while, in the second, we respect freedom of conscience. So much of political life is about deciding whether human nature in a given case is sufficiently the same that legislation is justified or whether, instead, the matter should be left to human free will.

But in fact, a person is more than law and more than freedom, and even, in some mysterious way, more than a constellation of both nature and will. We are *persons*. Precisely because politics only deals in the either/or of the nature vs. will question, it leaves us unsatisfied. Life can't be reduced to politics because neither legislating nor not-legislating can capture the full mystery of the human person. We long for something more, some more mysterious and personal dimension of existence that goes beyond both nature and will. And that more personal dimension is our personhood itself.

---

23 We Orthodox are fond of attacking the individualism spawned by the Enlightenment. But what if we think of this individualism as the beginning of a Western attempt to return to something like personalism, after centuries of an overly philosophical theology that pitted an abstract "human nature" against an equally abstract "divine nature"? Seen in this light, individualism might really be getting things going in the right direction. And in turn, individualism's direct offspring, existentialism, is still not quite the Orthodox approach to the person, but it was welcomed by an array of Orthodox Christian theologians in the twentieth century.

The Human Being

As an entry point to thinking about how personhood is distinct from nature and will, we might remember what is often argued about Roman Catholic vs. Orthodox Trinitarian theology. Allegedly, in the Latin Church, theology described God by starting with the common divine nature of the three Persons, while in the Orthodox Church God was described beginning with the Person – the word for person is *hypostasis* in Greek – of the Father. The "nature" approach was more amenable to logical argumentation because in thinking about God as "divine nature," you have something which will stay fixed while you analyze it. The person-first approach is more dependent upon specific Christian revelation and the ascetic response to Theophany; it is harder to make an academic theology when you start with the person.

Anyway, my point is that we all have a knowledge of and even some practical experience using the three basic terms of anthropology: nature, will, and person. We get these terms and concepts from both Trinitarian theology and Christology.

Now, all three of these elements are closely related in the mystery of being human, but the emphasis we choose to put on each term will more or less determine the tone of our moral theology. And for Orthodoxy, it is neither nature nor will that are quite the right starting point, but the person. This is tough to unpack, but let me try.

Nature

A human person, in a sense, is just a particular instance of human nature; in and of itself "personhood" is not even distinct from nature, and so the term "person" doesn't seem very special at all.

But because human nature itself cannot exist outside particular persons, we could look at the matter the other way around: what is human nature but a kind of inferred substratum which we never encounter *except* as it meets us through a particular face, through an actual brother or sister, no two of whom are identically alike? So taken in this way, it is human nature that seems insubstantial and abstract!

Moreover, since persons cannot exist on their own, no matter how human their nature, and since, in fact, persons always do require communion with other persons just to go on existing, human nature is dependent not just upon personhood but on personhood in communion with other persons.

Finally, although we all share a common human nature, we all share in that nature according to the unique way that makes us a person. "Humans" can climb Mt. Everest, but I never will. "Humans" can possess perfect pitch, but I don't. And there are female humans, but I am not one of them.

The above observations about the relationship between nature and person combine to say that, in practice, we have to start with specific persons and with our own cross of being a particular person, when we do moral theology. To give the theological analogy to this, there is a world of difference in a secular setting between using the term "God," which can mean almost anything, and the name "Jesus Christ," which is both much more divisive and much more liberating.

Will

Now let us look at the other term describing what it means to be human, the human "will." For one thing, this term has more than one meaning.

First off, the concept of "human will" is closely allied in the Church Fathers with the word "energy," a term which just means what a human nature actually does, in a general sort of way, including breathing, eating, or whatever. For example, the primary basis of St. Maximos the Confessor's argument that Christ possessed both a human will and a divine will of free choice is his observation that every nature, every existence, has its corresponding movement. When we use "will" in Orthodox theology, our first definition must include this basis of "will" in the characteristic energy or activity of a thing's being. This isn't "willing" as in deliberating and choosing;

it's more like our involuntary "will to survive," than a faculty of choice. Even plants and rocks have "wills" in that sense of involuntary patterns of action – we call a rock's will its energy, or activity; plants and rocks do the things that plants and rocks do. In the case of rocks, that includes weighty matters like being heavy.

In fact, since we can't know natures *except* as they act (for even *existing* is something a nature *does*, and thus existing is an energy or "will" of a particular nature), then the will or activity of a thing seems to be just a different word for nature! So at this point the term "will" isn't very impressive; it presents to us all that we can see about a nature: that it exists and that it is a particular kind of nature. But "will" is not otherwise readily distinct from nature.

Incidentally, the Church Fathers could not have conceived of a will without a nature, since they saw wills as the activation of the potential in a nature. A will without a nature would be like climbing a ladder with no floor beneath you; or, it would be like trying to sing without first having a throat, lungs, and vocal chords. In contrast, we of late have thought that through the exercise of our wills we could even choose to alter our nature – could change our gender, for example. Well, the ancient world knew plenty about the practice of surgically altering gender, as eunuchs were almost a third gender for them, though the Church always regarded castration as wrong and, if done voluntarily, as an act of self-mutilation.[24]

But there is also another meaning of "will," as the faculty of deliberation and choice. One of the things that humans can do is to desire and to choose. In a limited way, animals have a bit of that, also. With this, it looks like we are entering more radical ground, and might be able to pick ourselves up by our bootstraps, so to speak, and could even choose to alter our own natures.

---

24 Editor's note: The Christian Roman Emperor Justinian criminalized castration in the sixth century but continued to employ eunuchs in imperial posts. In other words, Roman Law did not penalize those who had been forcibly injured in this way but nevertheless tried to protect the young from this same fate.

Person

But there is more to this, since again will points to personhood. Because in fact, human will, just like human nature, can never exist except as expressed in and by particular concrete human beings. It is persons – each an unique instantiation of human nature – who exercise the human will and who do so in ways that are at times instinctual and automatic, at times deliberate, and at times the forthright and pure expression of deepest yearning. And therefore neither human will nor human nature can be considered as things apart from specific human persons.

So, in one sense both human nature *and* human will are fictions, or at least abstract categories dreamed up to make thinking about human identity easier. What we actually encounter are billions of human *persons*, and these persons each share *distinctly* in the common human nature while also willing a) according to the unique way that they share in the general attribute of human free will, b) in the exercise of a freedom that may even be sinful at times, and c) by the light of their personal identity.

While for the purpose of abstract analysis it would be nice to start our ethics with the common human nature, and while we might also want to disengage from thorny moral controversies by leaving things to each person's free will, in fact, a much deeper challenge has been given to us: to see the complex way in which a unique human person is both determined and free, both under the law and beyond it. And this third way we describe as personhood, a gift of grace. Thus, the Orthodox position is a wise one, although also a hard one to follow.

The Triumph of the Will

Today, however, the Reformation has left the Protestant churches and entered – really, become – Western Civilization itself. Our whole drive in Western culture is to enshrine our wills – through more refined political programs and policies, through technology, and through the religions that can serve these aims – in a place of ultimate significance. Yet for all this emphasis on our freedom and self-determination, we are not necessarily becoming more "personal," if by personal we mean something unique and deep. If anything, we have become less able to relate to other persons, which is the essential cornerstone of personal maturity. The will, in order to reign free, would like to reduce other persons to their base natures, paradoxically. Or, if allowing them freedom, to reduce them to the most minimal definition of that freedom, "consent."

We call the elevation of the individual and selfish will to this paramount status "democracy," but more and more it will come to resemble a berserk state, a self-deification through the collapse of concern for anything other than the self. Democracy presupposes citizenship, but we are constantly tempted to reduce our policy discussions to something more faceless – the supposed tragedy of any frustration of our wills. Citizenship requires honor, a deep sense of honor. Can honor survive the deadening of shame that therapy implies, or the worship of self that our public anthropology demands?

Today our *common* political and social program is the *self* – a paradox that either will open a window to the Church or will be seen as the suicide pact of the human race. I mean, the fact that it is necessarily a common project can lead us to see that we exist in and through each other, in communion, *or* we can choose merely to make a temporary alliance with others in order to expedite each soul's flight into gnostic aloneness and thus the abyss.

Losing Nature Means Losing Gender

Clearly, the "human nature" side of the divorce in anthropology – the Roman Catholic side – has been thoroughly routed by the Protestant "will" side. As a society we can see no fixed human nature, no fixed use of sexuality, and not even a stable definition of gender. For sophisticated Americans, "will" stands alone, with human "nature" operating only as a restraint that must be overcome. We don't even call it "nature" anymore; we just call it "bias," or "cultural prejudice," or even "hate"! But we use these terms to refer to anything fixed, anything received, anything that could make us find sin shameful and unworthy by reminding us that there are limits to our existence.

But to reject all such limits is by definition to be berserk. It is the shameless state of the tragic person who is rejecting all communion with God, with others, and with nature. And the main sufferers from the berserk state will be the berserkers themselves.

The Cost of Discipleship

RTE: A few moments ago you said that, until very recently, Protestant anthropology focused on human will and Roman Catholic anthropology on human nature. Is this also changing?

DR. PATITSAS: I think it really is. Someone as important as Dietrich Bonhoeffer dealt directly with this division. His *The Cost of Discipleship*[25] – as paradigmatic and respected a work of twentieth century theology as there is – describes *exactly* this impossible dilemma between will and nature in anthropology. He demonstrated that neither nature nor will, nor their combination, cover the whole of human personhood. Bonhoeffer doesn't use these exact terms, but this is the total meaning of what he is saying in that classic and well-known text. Had he been able to phrase his thoughts in these patristic terms, his work would have clearly linked up with the teachings of the Church Fathers and done even more to help heal the scars of the Great Schism, the Reformation, and the Counter-Reformation. Bonhoeffer is calling us back to a patristic anthropology.

Bonhoeffer re-classifies "faith" in personal rather than "will" terms, but he does not manage to do the same for salvation, paradoxically. Yes, he overcomes the truth-first notion of "faith" as merely a notional assent to the concept of "salvation through the free gift of grace." He does this by showing that genuine grace is always "costly grace" (what we have called the twofold anointing)

25 Dietrich Bonhoeffer, *The Cost of Discipleship* (London: SCM Press, 1948).

and by showing that assent to costly grace is neither from nature nor from will but from the *personal* response to the surprise of being called by Christ (what we have called eros in response to Theophany). For him, it is as persons that we are able to receive the cross imparted to every Christian. So far, so good.

But Bonhoeffer's discussion of salvation remains nevertheless mired in the classic Zeno's paradox of all Protestant and Roman Catholic soteriology: If salvation is not predestined, if we play *any* important role *at all* in our being saved, then have we not returned to a salvation by our own works? But if we don't play any role and salvation is thus a gift completely insulated from every possible dimension of human weakness, then what sort of humanity has God saved, in the end, but an apparently inert lump of clay? In that case, the entire drama of salvation becomes farcical, the image of God in man is lost, and problems of theodicy become alarming and irresolvable: if we are not meaningfully free anyway, then why indeed would God allow so much suffering in the world?

What sort of theological "calculus" can deliver Bonhoeffer and the West from this conundrum? Only the soteriology of Athanasios, Dionysios, and of the Church Fathers: The "gap" between God and man is overcome by the interpenetration of God's uncreated energies with human nature. This union occurred in Christ and was then made available to us through the Incarnation's resounding through the sacraments of the Church.

Once man *personally* consents to the visitation of the Incarnate Christ, then both his nature and his will begin to be transfigured, healed, and, most crucially, *man is now able to see his personal willing for God as both a free act and as an act that is wholly from God*. We live, in other words, the paradoxical Christology of the Council of Chalcedon in the most intimate possible way: our willing for Christ and his willing for us are united in a way that is unconfused, unchangeable, indivisible, inseparable. Only this Christology and this "sequence" of personal consent (faith, or eros) followed by natural transfiguration (Holy Baptism) and willing self-sacrifice (works of faith) can overcome the faith vs. works division of Western Christianity.

Martin Luther's Sleight of Hand

Bonhoeffer was a Lutheran minister and, without knowing it, he was reacting to a sleight of hand on the matter of Christian anthropology pulled off by Martin Luther himself. Luther appeared to be arguing that our human nature is so sinful, so unlike God's holy nature, that God has no interest in it. God wants only our persons, which He rescues not through an ontological, nature-to-nature sharing of uncreated grace through the sacraments but by an arbitrary fiat: Divine will simply pronounces us saved while leaving our natures just as sinful as before. What God really wants, Luther says, is not our worthless natures but our persons.

This induced a predictable Roman Catholic reaction, the Counter-Reformation's attempt to attach the human person even more decisively to human nature. The Western Church reacted to Luther's decoupling of person from nature by reinforcing the entire Natural Law edifice to the point of infallibility. The goal was to make this system so intellectually solid and so "Necessary," in intellectual terms, that it would be inescapable. From the Council of Trent to the First Vatican Council in 1871, Rome sought to close the last avenues of escape from the kingdom of Natural Law.

But Luther didn't care; he was happy to have the Roman Catholic Church distracted by the consuming attempt to subject the human person to human nature. The more they pressed on about that point, the more Luther and "real" Christians could escape out the back door of free will and grace. The Roman Catholics could have both person and nature; the Protestants wanted the will, which is still all Protestants, and especially post-Protestants (all of us, as Westerners), think we need.

Recent developments, though, have begun to break this logjam. First of all, by the early 1900s, the effects of the Counter-Reformation were being questioned in the Roman Catholic Church itself. Theologians and faithful alike understood that the heavy emphasis on philosophical system threatened to reduce the Church to a machine for salvation. Conservative Catholics may lament Vatican II, but it was convened in an attempt to step back from the precipice of the mass production, truth-first approach to human salvation.

And, in fact, something amazing has been happening. Over the last century or so, *all* the major traditions in the West pushed back against scholastic and abstract approaches to theology – against approaches that were too "nature-centric" and philosophical, too impervious to actual divine or human freedom. And, in fact, all major traditions have also moved to reposition the person, both divine and human, at the center of faith. In addition to Bonhoeffer in the Lutheran tradition, Pope John Paul II moved Roman Catholic ethics towards a personalist approach. And we should mention Martin Buber in Judaism, existentialism in philosophy, and Karl Barth for biblical scholarship. All of these movements sought to raise the person into equal importance with categories like nature and will.

And of course, Fr. John Romanides, as well as contemporary elders throughout Orthodoxy (the elders were always personalists), and some other Orthodox philosophers also helped warn Orthodox Christian theological faculties from heading toward impersonal, academic accounts of spiritual life – just as St. Symeon the New Theologian had also cautioned the Orthodox faithful with resounding effect in the eleventh century.[26] However, if contemporary Orthodox academic theology has seemed a latecomer to the personalist trend, this was largely because our theology was not caught in the war between nature and will in the first place.

So, there is a lot of convergence and room for hope.

In fact, just lately I have been reading the new edition and translation of *The Ambigua* of St. Maximos the Confessor.[27] In *Ambiguum* 65, the saint applies his famous triad (of being, well-being, and ever-being) in a way that all these contemporary anti-scholastics, and Bonhoeffer in particular, would have applauded. Maximos says that "being" concerns the common human nature; "well-being"

---

26 For St. Symeon's significance, see Archbishop Basil Krivocheine, *In the Light of Christ: St. Symeon the New Theologian* (Crestwood: SVS Press, 1986).

27 Nicholas Constas, editor and translator, *On Difficulties in the Church Fathers: The Ambigua*, in *Dumbarton Oaks Medieval Library* (Cambridge: Harvard University Press, 2014).

requires choice, and thus involves the will in addition to the nature; and "ever-being" brings us to eternal friendship with Christ, enfolding nature and will into a more permanent personal union with Christ. So you see that the three terms of nature, will, and person can be thought of as being related concentrically. We each, in fact, must make a journey from nature, to will, to person in an unfolding of our primordial response to God's having called us into being. All the anthropological categories are present within all the others.

RTE: Let me push back. For many people, the Roman Catholic Church before Vatican II did not feel oppressive, it felt liberating to stand on something so solid and sure. Whereas the move toward personalism was sometimes done so awkwardly that it seemed superficial and sentimental, as if it was being done to be "relevant."

DR. PATITSAS: There are real tensions between free will, Natural Law, and personalism. One seems arbitrary; the next seems forced; and the third can seem will-of-the-whisp. No merely human system can balance them. When you have all three in a healthy way, this is a miracle, a gift of divine grace. I wonder whether it can ever be fully attained, in a deep and enduring way, outside the sacramental communion of the Orthodox Christian Church.

However, I also think that although Western Christianity may seem like a shambles (particularly to Roman Catholic eyes!), this appearance is deceptive and hides the enduring grace and strength within each denomination. (And of course our appearance in their eyes is deceptive, as well.) We hope that whole Churches will struggle through and return to the Orthodox faith, in time. The only way through will be forward to an Orthodox Christian anthropology. The Orthodox way somehow works the miracle that grants Law, Freedom, and Personalism each their full due, despite the fact that they are in conflict.

Dying for Christ

There is a problem with human nature in addition to the ones we've mentioned above. It is something built-in: human nature is such that unless we deny ourselves and follow Christ, we cannot exist in a deep way. Human nature is not only incomplete without God, but, more challengingly, it also needs to die in order to exist at all; as a fixed or isolated thing, human nature has no future. This is because our Archetype, the model according to which we were made, is not only Christ, but Christ *crucified*. We need to live self-sacrificially – or not live at all. In the Old Testament, this was expressed as the need to live according to a particular code of holiness and by the notions of exile and pilgrimage, whereby one's life was dedicated to God and set deeply apart from the world.

And if this is true of human nature, the same goes doubly so for human will. One of the main reasons we *have* human freedom, is so that we can freely consent to our unavoidable and inevitable co-crucifixion with Christ! But that looks very much like the negation of the will itself, doesn't it?!

So there again, a merely human philosophy comes to a dead end: nature is incomplete until it dies, while our free will is tragically so bound up with protecting this mortally incomplete nature, that it is not of much help in achieving the thing that will save us: to die and be reborn with Christ. Therefore, neither of these elements of the person (the nature and the will) can be a proper place to begin a Christian ethics.

To be made in the image of God is a sign of highest dignity; so high, in fact, that outside of Christ no human being can even be said to fully exist, properly speaking.

To repeat, to be made in the image of God – of Christ – means that we are made in the image of the Crucified One. However, in the face of any real vision of Christ crucified, both nature and will break down. The nature wants to live, not die; the will quivers uselessly, unable to overcome this natural instinct. So, we are at an impasse. Insisting that our personhood is reducible to either nature or will – or in a last desperate attempt to avoid the inevitable adventure of the Cross, to some alliance of nature and will – we now find that neither will nor nature is of any real use.

In the face of our fear of death, it is only eros for the person of Christ that can help us know that we are *already* dead, insofar as we exist without Christ: it is personal eros alone that can show us the true source of both our nature and our will. Christ alone is Life – and He is often found in the grave. But if we can see that it is Beauty himself lying there in the grave, it may be the case that by the time we realize that the source of our Life is calling us to die with him, we shall have already "stepped outside of the boat" and be on our way to resurrection.

To succeed at this adventure of existence, what will be needed on our part is not only a nature and a will but first of all a face – a face that can see God face to face, or at least can feel upon itself the healing rays of Christ's resurrection. What is needed is some capacity for eros, for falling in love, some point where our childish nature and our foolish will can be caught up into a personal adventure, rather than merely being scolded, challenged to the breaking point, or humiliated.

Precisely because human natures and wills are only made concrete in persons, and persons know themselves to live in each other, there remains even in our fallen state the divine possibility of launching ourselves past the limitations of nature and will alike. What is needed is not an *individual* response to our existential situation but a *personal and therefore interpersonal* response to the loveliness of Christ's person, so that nature and will alike are crucified and we come alive as a person precisely because we see the limitedness of our wills and natures. We need, on some level, to laugh at ourselves.

Are You Saved?

RTE: Then how does the classic evangelical question of whether we "know Christ as our Lord and Saviour" work here? When asked it is irritating, yet it does seem to be about knowing a person.

DR. PATITSAS: Christ calls us into communion, into the Church. The question about "knowing Christ as Lord and Savior," in contrast, is meant to be, and is felt to be, intensely isolating. It is a question that strips you of the dimension of your faith that is familial, social, even cultural. It is meant to posit you as a lone, naked individual.

To a degree, this can be beneficial; we want our faith to mature and become personal. But even in the tone of voice there is the implication that this isolated beginning point will also be the ending point: your "inner assurance" in your isolated soul is all that there is or ever will be. There will be no Church, no Body, no Blood to follow.

We heard the story recently about how parents in Sri Lanka reassured their frightened children during the civil war there. Whereas in our culture we would think to answer something like, "Don't worry; everything will be alright," in this way attempting to assure the child of his or her individual survival, in Sri Lanka mothers would say, "If something happens and we die, we shall die together. You will not be alone."[28] I think this example illustrates a little of how different cultures can be in their ordinary thinking.

By definition the modern person will tend to ask and answer that question of salvation as if it were to occur outside of the Church; i.e., outside of the natural bodily need for a sacramental grace that will impact their physical nature and bodies. They may also ask it outside of the mystery of human communion. Even those who have accepted Christ have often rejected both his incarnation and his mission to establish his Church. Salvation for them becomes a question of intellectual cognition, and then of willpower, where it should really be a question about something as bodily as the blessing of marital union: to "know" the Lord is to marry him; that is, to become part of his bride, the Church, through the mysteries of Baptism and Holy Communion.

---

28 This anecdote is related in Chapter Two, "The Wave That Brought PTSD to Sri Lanka," in Ethan Watters, *Crazy Like Us: The Globalization of the American Psyche* (New York: Free Press, 2010), 65-127.

A lot of Christian spirituality has fallen into the service of consumerism and individualism. This is because, absent a doctrine of *uncreated* grace and thus the possibility of actual *perichoresis*, or mutual interpenetration between God and man, Christian spirituality remains Nestorian.[29] There is no real and dynamic interpenetration between divine and human life or between human lives. Sanctification of human life is not possible if we remain apart from Christ.

To accept a disembodied Jesus is to renounce the real Jesus. Why should a person accept Jesus but then renounce his Church, refuse to obey his command to eat his Body and drink his Blood (the only words in Scripture that an evangelical Christian will not take literally), and live in an isolated spiritual individualism that is the death of the soul? Should a person in such a state of separation from Christ actually be so confident of their salvation?

Besides, there is an implicit scholasticism in the Evangelical approach. The preacher doesn't begin with Beauty and Holy Scripture but with an intellectual attempt to create a dilemma, an anxiety, and a conundrum in the mind of his prospective convert. And then the preacher proposes Christ as the intellectual answer to this intellectual problem.

To submit one's soul to this kind of blank abstract intellectual system, this attack of intellectual brute force, is unworthy of your dignity in Christ. There is a better way.

Nevertheless, while it is only as persons that we possess a nature and a will and are thus able to reflect on the fact that this nature and will are finite and mortal, still the person cannot somehow float away from both *the necessity of choice* and the *dependence on nature*. Personalism doesn't mean that we don't have to make decisions or that we can disavow our natures. However, everything comes down to priorities

---

[29] "Nestorian" as a term of theological criticism relates to the way the fourth-century bishop Nestorius conceived of the unity of Christ's humanity and divinity. According to this hierarch, it was almost as if Christ were a union of two persons, one human and the other divine, joined in one body. There was no real unity of the two natures of Christ. We use the term "Nestorian" today to describe any lingering dualism in a theological argument, any sense that God and the world remain tragically separated, apart.

and to sequence. Try to fall in love with Christ in as childlike a way as possible – and only then allow yourself to make a very rudimentary and even hasty choice for him, and quickly be bodily baptized, chrismated, and communed into the Orthodox Church. This is the way to go.

And that's what an actual bona fide human person is, as opposed to a human nature or a human will or even some mechanical combination of the two. A person is someone who, in however small a way, has fallen in love with Christ and who, before he even realizes it, has begun dying with Christ and for Christ. Natures, Wills: these are big adult categories. But with Christ we must begin as infants in his arms, gazing up at his pure face.

Academically, this means that when we think about human beings, we prioritize neither nature nor will but person (*hypostasis* in Greek). And in practical application, it means that we are saved neither by forgiving ourselves (claiming that, after all, our nature is weak), nor by works, nor by faith – if by either works or faith we mean some action or decision on our part. Rather, our first goal will not be salvation at all!

Our goal is Christ: to embrace Christ, to try to be with him. The chaste eros, the healthy shame, the unknowing that arises in our hearts when we first begin to live in Christ: this is not a "decision for Christ"; no word exists for it except perhaps "motherhood." It is the conception of Christ within our hearts.

And so we personally take our wills and natures in hand and invite Christ to receive all that we have left of both freedom and nature, and then bury them with him in the life-giving waters of the baptismal tomb.

A "Second Baptism" for Orthodox Christians Entering Adulthood

RTE: Some Christians go so far as to say that infant baptism is an infringement of our free will. What is our response to that?

DR. PATITSAS: Yes, the persons who created us to begin with – *who, shockingly, brought us out of non-being into being without our consent* – did in fact take the next step and bring us to well-being, to the Church, again without asking us.

But you and I both agree that in a sense we do "will" our existence in the womb through the very biological processes that formed us from the moment of conception. I mean, once a person is conceived as a zygote, this tiny life-form kicks in and drives toward birth and development, or the person would never be born. So, there is a sense in which we do "will" to be born, at least at a bodily level. Well, something analogous happens in baptism. Having received that grace, our souls and bodies welcome it and cooperate with it. Parents have told me that after their child's baptism their baby settled down significantly, thus proving that the uncreated light conveyed in this mystery is being received within the soul. The very real changes and developments of our soul after this sacrament show another kind of free assent to this infant moment of salvation. This is undeniable. The infant *has* "made a decision for Christ" – but in the mode of decision-making appropriate to its station in life.

Another, more developed, form of choice follows later when the child has grown.

However, let's not try to show off our Orthodoxy by scandalizing our Protestant brothers on the matter of infant baptism. Historically, Orthodoxy *did* practice something that honored and answered the argument for adult-only baptism. And, let us bow to our Catholic brothers and even term it an "adult confirmation." I am talking about the fact that in Orthodox societies, young adults were typically either married or in a monastery by their mid-twenties, or even earlier.

The need to make this choice as soon as he or she had achieved a kind of "age of reason" gave the Christian a chance to make a mature, considered, and sacramental commitment to Christ that, like baptism, involved a new way of life and a new public identity. And like baptism, both marriage and monastic vows were accomplished through a sacramental transition achieved in a ritual infused with uncreated grace.

The experience of our Church is that the ideal situation would be infant baptism so that we would be raised with the protection of grace, and in particular with the nourishment of the Body and Blood of Christ, as full members of the Body of Christ (the Church). Then, in our late teens or early twenties, we would make an adult affirmation of what we received as infants, by re-committing our lives to Christ in a public way that involves a mature choice about life paths. Infant baptism should happen in the very first months of our life; if possible, even at our forty-day churching. There should be no artificially imposed spiritual starvation of our infant children; when a priest is available, they should be baptized and communed.

To us, it would be a mistake to not allow for *both* infant baptism *and* this mature decision for Christ. In fact, for us, the mistake would be to *limit* the adult ritual of accepting Christ to nothing more than what is customarily required of children. I mean, we might say that it's not adult baptism being practiced in that part of Christianity which excludes children but rather that they are taking the baptism that the Church offers children and reserving it for adults. But if we are adults, we need to go further and also make a sacramental determination that includes offering the gift of our gender and of our sexual powers, if we possibly can.

In Orthodox cultures, a person in their late teens or early twenties was expected to make a truly mature commitment to Christ by also being sacramentally committed to a path of service to the Body of Christ – a path that honored and respected their own *personal* body of Christ – in either marriage or monasticism. Saint Paul reminds us that "no one ever hates his own body" (Eph 5:29), but when we are caught up in sexual sin, we do in fact go through periods of hating our own bodies. In order to actually cherish our bodies properly, it really helps to make a mature commitment to Christ that inscribes the priestly vocation into our particular gender callings.

This is the liturgical path of salvation, and it applies to gender reconciliation when we fall in love and enact this "adult baptism" of marriage. One reason why infant baptism became so easily accepted in the early Christian Church was that society and the Church were now expecting a "second baptism" for almost all young adults.

Marriage and Monasticism

RTE: I can't let you go without your saying something about the idea based on the gospel story of Martha and Mary, that monasticism is the higher way. Some even make it sound like marriage is just a sop to our fallen natures.

DR. PATITSAS: I heard a much more pointed comparison between marriage and monasticism from my former spiritual father, the abbot of an Athonite monastery. He said that the monastic life is like trying to traverse a wide and long desert valley full of bandits, hungry predators, scorpions, quicksand, and other traps. I asked, "Well, then, what is the married life?" "The same thing," he answered, "only, at night."

I like this description because it is St. Paul's explicit point that in the world you have so many cares that you cannot give as much attention to the needs of the Church or to Christ. This is true. But St. Paul didn't denigrate sexuality because he could see that God's purposes were being worked out in many ways. We who are married need the monastics. And they need us – for financial support many times, for solace, to have someone to worry about and show hospitality to, and as the source of new monastics.

Is one higher? I think so, but I am not sure that we Americans can ever really hear the word "higher" with anything but imperfect understanding. We are Jeffersonians, Rousseauians, who oppose social gradations on principle, whereas the Orthodox Church invented the very word "hierarchy" itself, through the pen of St. Dionysios the Areopagite.

The story of America is to take what was once the province of kings and queens and make it available to every man and woman. This is true both in terms of politics and in terms of material comforts. And from the standpoint of health and material comfort, of opportunities in travel and education, the average American does live far better than the kings of two hundred years ago.

But America learned this equality from the Reformation and its approach to the spiritual life. It is a cornerstone of the Protestant movement since its birth that there should not be "first class" and "second class" Christians.[30] But in actual reality monastics do in fact form a kind of aristocracy in the Church in many senses: they devote a greater proportion of their time to the finer points of Church music, services, the arts, and so forth.[31] Or, if you prefer, they have also been called the "special forces" of the Church militant, since their spiritual training tends to be more intense and well-organized.

So, what does "higher" mean? The whole body cannot be the eye because then the eye itself would be weak and helpless. The Church is a body with many members, many parts and organs. In a true hierarchy, what is higher must serve what is lower, must cover its shame – not expose that shame and insult it and remind people of its weaknesses! Does the brain spend all its time insulting the legs? This would be contrary to the gospel. And in this way Christians are *both* directly equal *and yet also* hierarchically ordered. We all relate to Christ both *through* the chain of hierarchy and *directly*, one to one.

Anyway, Christ himself already resolved this competition between marriage and monasticism. He was asked, "What is the greatest commandment?" And He answered, "To love the Lord your God with all your heart, soul, mind, and strength" (Mt 22:37). This is clearly the monastic life, especially when we underline the bodily word "strength." And then Christ added, "And the second one is like it: Love your neighbor as yourself." To me, this is clearly marriage and even the sexual union within marriage. "For the two shall become one flesh," two neighbors forming one self.

---

30 And this is why, in speaking to my own American audience in these interviews, I have dared to articulate things that others have left unsaid. In our cultural setting, the complex teachings will have to be taught more widely before we can simply believe.

31 I have in mind here the special occupations of "Guardians," the warriors and aristocrats in all ages. See Chapter Seven for the discussion of the three parts of society: the commercial, the governing, and the artistic or spiritual.

The marital embrace itself is this profound way of combining the absolute self-forgetting love of eros with the cherishing love of agape. My body is no longer my own, for I have given all my strength over to another; this is eros. But I must cherish the body of my spouse with a tender, nourishing affection; this is agape. The marriage bed is beautiful empathy, it is almsgiving of a most sacred kind, when we are pure in our hearts.

So one path is first, and the other path is equal to it, although second. Of course, I know these two commandments have other meanings besides describing monasticism and marriage. In fact, the whole point of a previous interview was to say that *every* Christian is called both to eros and to agape, not that monks practice eros, whereas married people practice agape. But I think we are within our rights, at a time when people are troubled by this question, to use these two commandments also in this way.

But when my students ask how two things can be equal even though one is higher, I point to an American elder, the great Yogi Berra. He was asked to describe the key to hitting well in baseball. "Hitting," he said, "is 90% mental. And the other half is physical."

If at this point the person is still troubled, if even Yogi Berra can't help them to be comfortable with the paradox of equality within hierarchy, then I think it is because they are just trying to cause trouble for the Church. No one is forcing you to choose one or the other, so don't complain just because the one you chose is being labeled as "second."

Eros vs. Self-Love

RTE: How then have marriage and monasticism come to be pitted against each other?

DR. PATITSAS: As we know, one of the major tragedies of the twentieth century was the massacring or exiling of Orthodox Christians. In Russia, the Balkans, Greece, Asia Minor, in the Middle East and beyond, tens of millions of Orthodox Christians were either martyred or driven from their homelands.

So, how can it be that, weakened as we are, our main emphasis is not on repentance but on dissension? And yet the one-third of one percent of all Orthodox Christians who today happen to live in America sometimes speak as if the Church were a fixed thing, an institution to be taken for granted, rather than seeing that the Church is the ultimate gift: it is Christ, crucified – if also resurrected.

Both Christian marriage and Christian monasticism are absolute eschatological miracles of God's perfect uncreated grace. In fact, we now see more clearly, as the world around us swoons and becomes drunk with hatred and blasphemy, that Christian marriage *and* monasticism are both a kind of holy foolishness. They are both foolishness for Christ.

In the case of the person who falls in love, that foolishness also implies *poverty* because you don't wait to become a millionaire before you get married, you just jump in; and you don't wait to have kids, you just do it. So there's the poverty. It's *chastity* because you are chaste towards all the people you don't marry, plus marriage is not mainly about sex. Many married couples struggle to still have sex even though they do in fact love each other – just to find the time or the energy or the privacy from their kids. So there's the chastity and the *obedience* to each other, but more importantly the obedience to eros itself: to the calling to love and to forget oneself.

While in the Church some foolishly imagine marriage and monasticism as opponents, those outside the Church recognize them both for what they truly are: forms of ultimate freedom from slavery to the world. The world hates them both equally.

Monasticism operates in a way similar to marriage, in that when it becomes the thing that you must have more than anything in the world, you just do it. I think what spoils chastity in both monasticism and in marriage is this very worldly bourgeois kind of economic carefulness – that you should never give yourself completely to anything because that's not a wise risk. Or, "you should wait until middle age before you marry," or "you shouldn't rush into monasticism – you can serve the Lord more safely in the world." We do need to think practically, but there is a certain kind of selfish carefulness that would destroy both types of chaste and ardent eros.

And at that point, chastity becomes both impossible and pointless. Impossible for most, because excessive waiting deprives you of the social support found in marriage or in monasticism that is needed in order to remain chaste; and pointless, since chastity is a social virtue, a relational virtue, not a "private" one. I mean, chastity is not meant to make you as an individual virtuous or successful, but it is rather the purified form of eros, the power that commences your drive toward relatedness to others and to all of creation. Chastity is a quality of eros, not a "spiritual" form of self-love.

I think the Church is emphasizing the opposite of this individual self-preservation. When we encourage either marriage or monasticism, what we are really talking about is the complete liberation that comes through eros – freedom! So, the fallen world conspires to present even these two erotic choices as the opposite of freedom – as not erotic, as not a liberation. By "the fallen world," I mean even those who say, "Oh, marriage is just a concession to human weakness. If you really love God, you will become a monastic." They try to force the person into it. They try to conquer their minds into it. Or if you're more in the Mormon school of religious worldliness: "Oh, it's a sin not to be married." "You must be married by your nineteenth birthday..."

In both cases it outwardly looks the same as Orthodox monasticism or marriage, but it's actually the defeat of eros, since it has converted the liberating power of eros into fear and carefulness about success in this world or in the next. But really, we as the Church are for a definition of chastity that maximizes eros, that says, "I'm really going to go for this!" That's what we want.

When my students ask me what they should do with their life, I always say, "There's a shortage of truly happy people in this world; your first calling is to add to that supply. So, what do you really feel? Now let's see if we can find a practical way for you to go after that.

Our hope for you is that Christ becomes for you that thing, and that eros for him will empower you to forget yourself so completely that you can become happy by choosing the path that is perfect for you."

Advising the Young Person

RTE: What if a person feels equally called to both paths?

DR. PATITSAS: Each person is different, but in general the joy of life is not found in waiting around outside the party; you have to go in. "Marriage is about exchanging an infinity of possibilities for the possibility of infinity," I like to say. But you may, however, have to work to find the people who can give you the inspiration and courage and wisdom to go into the party. Eros has to mature into agape.

Of course, I speak as someone who has reached middle age without marrying or becoming a monastic, and so I can see that there are both upsides and downsides to such waiting. So, I am not condemning those who seem to have found a third way. With that caveat, here are my observations, and I encourage you to use them or discard them, as seems fitting to you.

If you are young, you are probably invited to several parties (the different persons you might pursue a relationship with) and perhaps to different kinds of parties (monasticism also entering the picture, let us say), so how do we choose the right one? I really don't know, but you and I both know that within the parties themselves is true life. Hanging around, or sampling from each – this can only go so far before you start to become annoying to others and even to yourself. So you will have to make a decision.

I can only say: you probably do know the right thing to do. Not necessarily, but probably. And, yes, the right thing to do might be "none of the above"; some people do live out that other life of celibacy in the world, and live it well. But in forcing yourself to choose, while asking for the prayers of others, the answer will be shown to you. We aren't meant to know "truth" in the abstract, as if we were bloodlessly observing our lives from a distance. Making a decision, is what will concentrate your intuition and help you to see the path.

But let me also warn the young person about two realms of bad advice that we run into as young American Orthodox Christians. When you turn to others to talk about who you are and what to do, you can easily find yourself bouncing back and forth between, on the one hand, the sort of spiritual father who is thinking entirely in terms of what sins you are committing and, on the other hand, the type of psychologist-counselor (whether a professional or an acquaintance) who is thinking entirely in terms of helping you further your self-knowledge.

The one keeps you trapped in the realm of Goodness and morality, and the other in the realm of Truth. If you can find the Beauty realm on your own, that is no problem; the moral correction and the self-knowledge will be folded into your own relationship with God and might actually help you decisively. But I think that, if you are in fact hesitating or you feel confused, neither of these two realms will be much help. Years can pass, and you won't see any progress.

What you actually need is an attention to your person that *immediately* places you before Beauty – the Father, the Son, and the Holy Spirit – and enlists you in doing the small spiritual chores which seem like a fitting offering of yourself to Beauty from within your present state of weakness. Not huge changes, based on detailed self-knowledge; not self-changes, based on a model of the Enlightenment individual self; and not even repentance, if by repentance we only mean trying harder morally. But falling in love with Beauty as the first order of business, and then looking at these other realms of moral struggle and self-knowledge solely from its vantage point.

RTE: Practically then, how do we place ourselves before Beauty?

DR. PATITSAS: Well, my point is what we have been saying already – that a certain kind of moral advice or self-reflection can actually try to usurp the primary place of Beauty in our soul, and thus, however pious or scientific such approaches look, they will harm your soul. Any emphasis on Truth or Goodness may be just a distraction if it is not wedded to this first step of falling in love and being inspired. An anxiety about choosing one path or the other, or trying to see which one is "better" or "higher," at some point just gets in the way. You have to fall in love.

The spiritual guidance you are receiving should therefore be *helping* you to fall in love with Christ, but even more than that, the spiritual father is to treat your soul like a tender plant and help it to unfold and grow, to share with it the light and warmth of the divine Son. In this way, you will naturally find your own very unique path, without force, without straining, without violence. I hope I am not giving the impression that we should all be in a state of anxiety and panic until we have either married or taken monastic vows.

My own spiritual father is not fixated on my moral faults nor has he offered much intellectual analysis of my character or hidden motivations. He is focused on Christ, and trusts that in time I will come to be similarly focused.

The big insight that following the Beauty-first approach has given me – after years of attempting the other two ways – is the realization that, in fact, I am not very much focused on Christ. Instead, I am usually focused either on a struggle for virtue that is mostly my own preening spiritual vanity, or on a struggle for self-knowledge that is mostly an escape from knowing God and knowing others, and that also happens to engender a despair in me that is total and then becomes the perfect excuse to be lazy.

The feeling now growing in me is different and is hard to describe in our cultural terms. I feel more ashamed than ever about how I'm living, but less oppressed than ever by my shame. It's like some odd combination of laughing at myself, which I take to be an indispensable part of eros; of seeing that my smallest actions are of infinite seriousness, which is crucial for both agape and eros; while also thinking that my heavenly Father is working it all out no matter what I do. I can't really think of these three opposite things at once, though, so I don't even try. I just go back to Christ and to those who bring me closer to Christ.

We don't choose monasticism or marriage, or any other path, in order to "grow up," but in order to preserve our childhood, our childlike purity. Because we have found that in returning as adults to the innocence of children, we are ready for these "holy foolish" callings, and we stop trying to be wise, or good, or anything at all – except simply alive and in love.

"The Kingdom of Heaven suffereth violence, and the violent take it by force." What does this mean? It means ignoring and not panicking about all the *violence* of passions and demons that inevitably assail you whenever you try to approach heaven and *forcing* yourself to just focus on the one thing needful, which is heaven, which is Christ. It means cultivating your eros and letting the world fall away around you.

RTE: What would you say to baptized Christians who secretly fear that their Christianity is a beautiful theory that they believe and act out in their church life, but that they haven't actually met Christ himself and don't know how to start that relationship.

DR. PATITSAS: Get around people who have met him, and just keep gazing in the direction they are all looking until your eyes adjust. There won't always be such people, which is good, because you must also look for Christ directly, even when He seems far away. There is a balance between the growing awareness of Christ within yourself and your ability to evaluate those who offer themselves as guides to Christ.

Your Heavenly Father is working directly in your soul in order that you may soon attain a fuller and even infinitely full life. As for the gaps and empty places in you that are preventing you from choosing, that are drowning you in fear and indecision, these are not nearly as substantial as you may think.

What is needed is a blend, first of the Orthodox liturgical way that puts you in the pure and blessed presence of God's Beauty; with the moral struggle that we hear stressed from people both within and outside the Church; with the slightest touch of the psychological way, that shows you how you perhaps are not letting God help you as much as He would like to. But always, Beauty comes first. When we use our willpower, we must do so in a mild way, in a secret way, so that the right hand does not know what the left is doing. I have seen this blend mainly in traditional Orthodox countries but also in many wise people who seem quite outside of traditional faith.

Starting with Beauty means starting with Christ – with his Person, not with abstractions about morality or self-analysis. Remember that the union we confess with Christ in the Jesus Prayer – that He has become the sinner that you are – is real. Your body is Christ's body; this is the body to which you owe a timely and brave decision for eros!

From Chaos to Cosmos

RTE: And how does this union with Christ bring us back around to gender?

DR. PATITSAS: Some of what we experience in ourselves is just chaos, or the result of chaos in other people, or of chaos in our circumstance. This certainly applies to gender and sex, for a lot of our sexual desires and gender impulses are ultimately not very meaningful, even though they might be quite strong.

But Christ came to bring a healthy and rich order to our lives, to replace chaos with cosmos. In his new City, we experience gender peace.

For fifty years now, we in America have been constantly ridiculing the gender icon; we've been calling every icon an idol and trying to smash it. But strength for men and softness for women are necessary icons.

Your gender role is is not only for you but also for others. This idea that "a man must be tough" is not meant only for your inner life but also for your social life. You do put on a little bit of a show, not in order to be phony or hypocritical, but because we all need a man to be this way. And besides, the show is fun because you realize it is partly a show; you hold loosely to it.

We are in a Trader age right now, an age where individualism and self-pleasing and efficiency are held to be the highest values. In a Guardian age you would be able to appreciate that prowess and even ostentation can be essential virtues at times. A Trader age will always denounce these virtues as hypocrisies, but sometimes they aren't. I will talk more about these approaches to life in another chapter, but it is basically the divide between merchants and warriors, where the one stresses efficiency and honesty, and the other prowess and display. And gender roles may "slow us down" as individuals, but they are invaluable ways to signal our love for others, for the larger world.

Ritual and Display

One place where "display" clearly makes sense is in rituals. In society, interpersonally, and within our souls, it is liturgy which is responsible for turning chaos into order. This includes both the "liturgy" of courtship and the liturgy of marriage. For others, it is the church ritual of monastic tonsure. While for still others, the ritual is the daily routine of turning to Christ in ways large and small. And through this liturgical conversion of chaos into meaning is born an ordered approach both to sexual desire and to the mystery of gender.

Because men and women are endowed with differing emphases in their experience of the two shames, which then are meant to be reconciled, and because both shames are ultimately concerned with worship, we can say that men and women can only be united, can only marry if they consent to become offerers of themselves and the world to God in worship. Only priests can marry because only within a proper and healthy shame can we be reconciled to each other.

All of the ancients thought that three kinds of marriage were essential for human flourishing, and they were right: The marriage within the soul, where the intellectual powers help the fighting powers and the desiring powers of the soul to reconcile; that between man and woman, helped by Christ and by the monastics; and that between the King and his City, through the prayers of the Church.

They are each fractals of each other and icons of the marriage between Christ and his Church, so that in fulfilling them we are united to God in a fourth and eternal marriage.

So let us not give up on marriage, nor on the ancient cosmologies and teachings about gender.

CHAPTER SIX

THE MYSTICAL ARCHITECT

The Conception of the Crucified Logos in Art, Science, and Nature

Eros for Christ makes us participants in his offering of himself to the world. Since Christ is the Logos, loving him so directly will inevitably make us and our actions more "informational" – that is, more concrete, specific, and meaningful. Thus, in loving Christ, we become more complete and also help to generate a refined order around us. At the center of our thoughts about art, bioethical dilemmas, and even science must be this sense that our vocation as creatures is to love the Logos and to offer a vigilant hospitality to his operation in our lives. We must be willing for Christ to be born in us.

The "mystical architect" Christopher Alexander sets forth a theory of architecture which is also based in hospitality to divine inspiration and which helps us to comprehend the ancient philosophical doctrine of the Forms in a fully Christian way. In particular, Alexander shows us an elegant way past the dilemma of whether God "had to" create or whether, instead, the creation of the world was an almost arbitrary act.

Alexander's discussion of Patterns which either do or don't have life provides a sophisticated yet flexible way to think about moral questions more generally. A discussion of biological conception and of marriage therefore follows. The emphasis here is on those avenues of relating to one's spouse in a manner that models the sacred hospitality of the saints towards God.

RTE: Thank you for this, our sixth interview. There are enticing loose ends from the previous conversations that I'd like to return to, such as an overview of the thought and work of the architect Christopher Alexander, whom you've mentioned with such warmth.

Readers have also asked that you say something about bioethics, and specifically about the attempt to aid conception medically.

Finally, we'd like to know more about a comment you made last time, that salvation is neither from faith nor from works but from our participation in the liturgy of our Lord and Savior Jesus Christ. These are very disparate questions, so where would you like to begin?

I. MOTHERHOOD

DR. PATITSAS: The three topics you've mentioned aren't so different in one respect, since they all involve conception, as well as the hospitality that will make conception possible. The Apostle Paul himself clearly says that all that he does as an apostle is, "until Christ be formed in you" (Gal 4:19). So, St. Paul sees each of us as being meant to imitate the Theotokos, in somehow "giving birth" to the Son of God, in ourselves and in others. This is a standard that is daunting and sobering and encouraging all at once, but St. Paul says that this is what is needed in order to be saved.

By the way, have you ever wondered if St. Paul knew Panaghia personally, and if so whether her manifest perfection in Christian life at all influenced his thinking? It would be interesting to reread his epistles with that one question in mind. He must at least have heard of her from others in the early Church. It's wild to think about things like that because we usually don't make such connections.

And as for the counterpart to conception, which is the hospitality we must offer if we would "give birth" to something or someone: well, showing welcome to visitors was one of the most important cultural obligations for pre-moderns. In an odd way, this applies to us today, as well: one reason we now find it so hard to practice hospitality to family and friends is that so much of our time and attention is already devoted to welcoming the inundating floods of information and entertainment coming at us through the internet. We are quite hospitable, although maybe not to people, or at least not to people in person.

The fact is, we all live our lives in the service of conception, but we may not be very discerning about to what and to whom we show the hospitality that will inevitably lead to conception.

The Theotokos, Our Lady Panaghia

In our last interview, we mentioned "motherhood" as the term for the way that wordlessly, beyond will and nature, Christ begins to be born ineffably within our hearts. This "wordlessly" has a very practical importance because when we struggle in ascetic and then moral effort, we may not notice any visible progress. But the Holy Spirit is still working within us, invisibly nurturing Christ's presence in our hearts, transforming our ability and inclination to give birth to Christ. Like a child being formed within a mother without her having to design the child consciously, so does our maturity in Christ unfold. A Christian, to mature, just has to "keep showing up" to receive the Body and Blood of Christ and to accept the humiliations of each day, as best we can. We don't have to get in there and actually "construct" a new identity within ourselves, atom by atom. And, in fact, if we try to, we will just spoil the formation of the "new man" (Eph 4:24), and drive everyone around us crazy.

While to a certain kind of eye, Orthodox devotion to the Theotokos seems pagan, or like an instance of "works righteousness," in fact, love for her cultivates the inner hospitality that will so help us receive Christ and his salvation wholly and completely as gift. The Birthgiver of God is both the proof and the refutation of Luther's "faith alone": the proof, because she believes and "does" nothing else; and the refutation, because there are degrees of faith, and a faith as perfect as hers worked itself out through an entire lifetime of vigilance regarding to what and to whom hospitality would be shown. Her level of vigilance, and thus her faith, was infinitely far beyond that of Luther himself or of any other known person.

Vigilance around hospitality (what we have earlier called, "Chastity," or "asceticism") is the work of faith, and it is at once both hard and easy. It is easier if we hear the Holy Spirit prompting us *not* to jump into some impossible situation involving people who are determined *not* to be helped, to live by faith and avoid all that confusion. Of course, at other times, the Holy Spirit may prompt us to get up and go to a far-off land to serve Christ. But in both cases, to show hospitality to the Spirit's prompting will involve an actual response on our part. Faith and works are only real – and are only combined – when we show hospitality to the will of God. This hospitality unleashes a liturgy within and among Christians through which the Holy Spirit accomplishes Christ's ongoing incarnation in the world.

We spoke of "chaste and ardent eros" as being the equivalent of what St. Paul meant by "faith." Eros is a good term for faith because it shows that faith is supposed to have an end in mind – loving union with Christ and deep acceptance of his salvific power. If this marriage of wills does not occur, then faith has been stillborn. But if it has *not yet* occurred, then Christ is still "being formed in you" (Gal 4:19), so let us not panic.

And anyway, in the Holy Spirit it is clear to what extent entering the tomb of "faith alone" – of baptism – involves a loving respect for the woman who understood that every single one of us is meant to become a kind of tomb for Christ. Is that not what happens when we invite Christ into our own particular "body of death" (Rom 7:24), so that Our Lord can resurrect us? Saint Paul speaks of being buried *with Christ* in baptism, but Christ is also buried *within us*, when, still trapped in sin, we must dare to receive him as Panaghia did. But dare to receive him we must, so that He might be born again within us and save us – by sparking *his* liturgy, his cross, his life within us.

Yes, if we would be *born again* as Christ commands us to be (Jn 3:3), then we must allow him to be resurrected, or born again, within us. Now, St. Paul uses the words, "formed within us" in Galatians 4:19, but he uses these words in connection with the "pains of childbirth," so "resurrection" is a valid paraphrase for being "born again." For us to be born again, Christ must condescend to be born again within our hearts.

RTE: Then, can we revisit a section from our last interview that has stayed with me? It's an image of birth *beyond* will and nature, and here is your quote:

> Academically, this means that when we think about human beings, we prioritize neither nature nor will but person (*hypostasis* in Greek). And in practical application, it means that we are saved neither by forgiving ourselves – claiming that, after all, our nature is weak; nor by works, nor by faith – if by either works or faith we mean some action or decision on our part. Rather, our first goal will not be salvation at all!
>
> Our goal is Christ: to embrace Christ, to try to be with him. The chaste eros, the healthy shame, or the unknowing that arises in our hearts when we first begin to live in Christ: this is not yet a "decision for Christ"; no word exists for it except perhaps "motherhood." It is the conception of Christ within our hearts.
>
> And so we each personally take our wills and natures in hand and invite Christ to receive all that we have left both of freedom and of nature, and then bury them with him in the life-giving waters of the baptismal tomb.

DR. PATITSAS: Thank you for mentioning that passage. It reminds me that in some places I've said that this unknowing or chaste eros is what St. Paul called *faith*, while here I have called it motherhood. These two terms seem to be closely linked. However, the word faith today has come to mean either an intellectual decision for Christ or a blind acceptance of some dark mystery. But real faith is a vision perceiving that which is "full of light" more than it is a form of blindness. Eros exists at the beginning of the "continuum of cognition" that Eric Perl spoke about;[1] thus, we can say that faith is already the beginning of knowing, is a down-payment on knowing.

1 Eric Perl, "Chapter Six: The Continuum of Cognition," in *Theophany: The Neoplatonic Philosophy of Dionysius the Areopagite* (Albany: State Univ. of New York Press, 2008).

Christ is born in our hearts "wordlessly." This is how, in Orthodox hymns, we describe Christ's conception in his mother's womb – the Word is conceived in some way that is *beyond* words. But this is true for all of us by analogy. It is not so much a decision of the will that we make for Christ as it is a falling in love with him. We then strengthen that love through the "easy way" of faith and asceticism, and this then flowers and appears as the various crosses of agape or empathy we bear in Christ's name.

I like in the passage from the earlier interview the explicit bond between salvation and motherhood, for this connection comes to us both from St. Paul and from Christ. For example, Christ's Parable of the Sower (Lk 8:5-15) is a story of motherhood, in effect. It is a parable of insemination, of a seed's dependence upon finding good ground (although we never hear it quite this way, and manage instead to moralize it and mangle it so that this gospel passage hangs over our Christian journey as a kind of rococo warning sign). The issue in that parable is *conception* and how we might help Christ to be born in us. This moment of the conception of Christ within us can't be merely an act of will nor merely the automatic result of some natural process, for while our wills and natures precede it, they also derive from it, are mystically constituted by it; it is eros for Christ that in arising makes us be.

So when Orthodox Christians speak of "starting theology with the person," very often they mean starting theology also with this particular person, with *Panaghia*. If you wish to become a theologian, then look to her and see how to conceive and bring forth a divine Word for the salvation of Israel. As we sing in her Akathist Hymn, she is the "good ground" that bore fruit a hundredfold; the Parable of the Sower should lead us to an appreciation of *her* more than of any other human person! And she imitates the Logos in acting in ways that are inexpressible. The vaunted "apophatic approach" of Orthodox theology is not an end in itself. Rather, such unknowing has a goal, it is dynamic. The "darkness" of apophaticism is meant to be the fecund darkness of the womb, a place of maximum development and change, a place out of which a trans-rational Logos can be born. Apophaticism is not the final word.

It is a sort of staple of Orthodox theology that the human person is *not reducible to* nature nor to will, but it was hard for me to see what this would mean in practice since personhood is also *inseparable from* human nature and free will. Personhood does not float in the ether. And yet personhood is also more than a mere combination of nature and will. A programmed robot can have hardware and software – a nature and a will – but it will not be a person. In fact, when we as humans act impersonally, there is something mechanical or animalistic about our actions. Some theologians have even said that this gives us a useful three-word definition of sin, "to act impersonally."

Yes, our personhood is inseparable from our human nature and our free will. But isn't it also the case that somehow, whenever we actually do relate personally to God and to others, we both are "born again" in a renewed human nature with a fresh and free will, and yet we also start to live in a way that transcends mere being, that goes beyond our mere humanity?

This is because when we love we become icons of Christ – icons of the God who exists but who also is *beyond* being. Personhood is thus *inseparable from* the particularity of human nature and unique will, yet it is also something *mysterious*.

Only the Face Shows

Many years ago, a nun at Fr. Sophrony's monastery in Essex told me that when she was robed as a monastic for the first time, Fr. Sophrony himself said, "You know, this is the most personal way to dress." She answered, "But Elder, every monastic has dressed in exactly this way for so many centuries. How could it be so personal?" And he responded very beautifully, "Because only the face shows."

It's in that face-to-face encounter with Christ, and with his mother, the saints, and our fellow man, that our personhood arises, and that every detail of our natures and wills has the chance to be gathered up into our personhood, made personal. And that is what is meant by asceticism – to gather up all our powers into our personal turn towards Christ. An ascetic is no longer a mere nature-will alliance but begins to attain the likeness of Christ.

Your nature and will may both prompt you to sleep with someone other than your spouse. But your personal regard for your spouse and your realistic, if also wonderfully romantic, sense that *you actually exist only by virtue of your relationship to your spouse* will be enough to save you from sinning. You realize that there would be no "you" if you were to do that, that you would no longer *be* a person if you were to betray this other person who is your spouse. That, and not willpower, is what keeps you on the straight and narrow path, and this kind of personal awareness is what will bring your nature and your desires into a uniquely personal expression. Your nature and your will are thus "gathered into" your unique personhood by these kinds of ascetic, faith-filled, erotic, and, in a word, personal considerations.

We have to develop spiritually to the point that certain sins will become "inconceivable." You should already be giving all of your hospitality to Christ, to your spouse, to others – until there is simply no more room in you to give hospitality to the sort of dark suggestions that are coming from the abyss.

By contrast, what we call "sin" begins when we turn our powers of thought, speech, will, or action not towards persons, and not towards objects still considered in the light of their relationship to persons, but blindly and impersonally towards objects in a way that makes them idols. In sin, our natural powers slip the boundaries of our personhood and run sort of pell-mell into the world; they get away from us. Later on, when we come to our senses, we may say, "What was I thinking? How could I have been so blind? How could I have acted that way?" We literally can't recognize our former selves, because we were acting impersonally – we were not behaving *as* our unique selves.

This is why shame is so important. It is our most personal feeling in a way, our most personal energy of relating to others and to God. It's as if all the other energies and drives we have are merely energies of our nature, whereas shame doesn't come into its own until all those energies and our entire nature are drawn into our own persons. Healthy shame is the crowning glory among all our energies and drives, the personal energy that renders all the other drives and energies uniquely our own and truly *human* because truly *our own*.

When confronted directly with the person we have wronged, at once shame arises to remind us that, even if all hell had raged against us, perhaps we might have been free in at least the very slightest way to have done otherwise. Shame makes us "super-human" – it helps us overcome our fallen natures and weak wills – even as it makes us comfortable being merely human, a limited human being who doesn't have to do it all. Healthy shame is thus the sign that we have become one with the *theanthropos*, the God-man, Christ our Lord. It is the sign that God "has made *his* face to shine upon us" (Num. 6:25).

RTE: Do you have another example of how a sinful act is an impersonal act?

DR. PATITSAS: Greed, for example. In living out this passion which is so natural to our fallen natures, we must ignore the sufferings of a thousand others who are starving now, of our spouses and children whom we neglect, betray, or put at risk while we obsessively hunt for excess. And we also must suppress our own shame about treating others badly, about acting in such a base way.

We are still acting when we act out of greed; or, we are still responsible, at any rate. But we aren't acting *ourselves*, we aren't really being who we are, we aren't living out our unique personhood. We've just become captive to some passion that looks the same no matter who is expressing it; there is nothing personal in it.

We don't exercise hospitality even to our own selves, in some odd way, when we fall into passions such as these. The visible social manifestation of this failure to be hospitable to ourselves will be the many people suffering around us as we pursue greed.

Attaining Freedom Through Hospitality to Others

The human being is constituted by hospitality to other persons, and by hospitality to theophany; that is, by communion. I mean, we aren't human until we open our hearts to other humans and to God. The two great commandments, to love God and to love others, could be expressed in another way: show perfect hospitality to God and to others. Or, in still another way, as: be yourself; be truly human, since being human is something that arises only in relationship with God and with other human beings.

I once knew a non-religious hermit who had cultivated an experience of total isolation. Recently, the hermit of the North Woods in Maine, when he was discovered after decades of never having spoken to or been seen by another person, said the same thing as my friend had, earlier: "I thought I would find my true self in absolute solitude, but instead I discovered that without others, I was almost a nothing." Isolation does work well for Christian hermits, because they are already at a place where this can lead to deepening communion with God, and later, through noetic prayer, with humanity and the entire cosmos. Alone, they received the entire world and all generations past, present, and yet to come, into their hearts. But a fallen isolation, an actual isolation that denies us all communion, dismantles us completely.

So, of course, the model for human personhood is not only Christ, in whose image we are made, but also *Panaghia*, in whom Christ took on flesh and then walked among us. Hospitality is primary in the human response to God because this welcoming is the essential support we offer to conception. For it is not just Christ but all those whom we love and whom we have granted space within us, that we must allow to be born within us.[2]

In fact, the people around us can't come to be in any other way.

---

[2] And this is why certain missionaries and evangelists in the modern world make us so uncomfortable – we sense immediately that in their hearts there is no genuine hospitality for us, their would-be converts. We are marks, targets, rather than brothers and sisters.

So let us circle back to the basic topic of conception and how it applies to all the themes you brought up: medical technology, of course, can run us into all sorts of moral difficulties surrounding conception. Oh, and we would also seem to be dealing with a type of conception when an artist brings some dimension of Beauty into being in order to remake the world. Also, the very act of thinking involves conception, as our language itself tells us.

And all of this must turn us towards this great issue of our lives – hospitality. Hospitality is more important than faith or works, one could say provocatively; or rather, hospitality conceals so mildly within itself the perfect synergy between true faith and true works that we call liturgy, that it overcomes the five-century-long war between faith and works. *Panaghia* stands to us as a kind of priest, a true mystic, and a worker of mysteries because her hospitality for Christ at his conception and throughout his life meant that her life was an angelic one, ministering day and night to the Holy One of Israel, and a priestly one, because she so ministered for the benefit of the people of Israel.

I tell my students that the serving tray is the foundation of human civilization, and I think that this is true. No home should be without a nice one, and we should never just hand a guest a glass of water when we could instead set even the simplest tray before them. A serving tray is a kind of portable altar table, presaging the cultic centers that will give birth to the first cities. Hospitality unifies faith and works, trust and offering, and it is a liturgical act. When it is offered with *philotimo*, we enter theosis.

Christ our God is a divine person who assumes human nature. But Panaghia is the human person who best typifies the art of our response to Christ, when she offers Christ that perfect hospitality which most of us are so far from showing. Because of this, she too can be described as Beauty, or at least as perfectly beautiful.

Great Art and High Art

And as for the other topic you mentioned – the work of the great designer Christopher Alexander – well, the very fact that you and I both comfortably refer to him as "the mystical architect" tells us that he is probably a good place to begin.

RTE: Yes. Do you remember where you acquired the habit of referring to him as the mystical architect?

DR. PATITSAS: That goes back to my one and only visit to Florence, Italy, to the Uffizi. These vast "Offices" belonged to the Medicis who, as you know, were the major early sponsors of the Italian Renaissance. The Offices are now the world's greatest museum of Renaissance art, arranged chronologically.

While walking through the galleries with a traveling companion, we turned to each other and said, "Did you notice how in the early galleries, where the art had not yet developed past the style of the Byzantine icon, we were constantly praying and even couldn't help but pray and repent? And do you notice how, since we've left that art behind, even though the themes are religious and represent a much more sophisticated offering to God, we aren't praying anymore and almost can't pray?" Even though it's great art, it also contains the beginnings of Hollywood: special effects, photorealism, Technicolor, mistresses playing madonnas, and the whole humanistic catastrophe of intense obsession with our own intellect and imagination.

As a complete aside, since I mentioned Hollywood: that wasn't the *whole* story of Golden Age Hollywood, which also may have involved an attempt to capture the Eastern European Jewish memory of court life of the Hapsburgs and of Holy Russia. The Jews who founded the great Hollywood studios had been on the periphery of this experience of royal life in the old countries, and they carried something of that with them.[3]

---

3 Neal Gabler, *An Empire of Their Own: How the Jews Invented Hollywood* (New York: Crown-Random House, 1988).

New Martyr Grand Duchess Elizabeth should be the patron saint of every Hollywood actress, right down to her difficulties with marriage and adoptive motherhood. What was expressed as "glamour" in Golden Age Hollywood was a memory of this European high court life – a royal life that itself was inspired by mystical accounts of the opulence and grace of life in heaven. In a sense, Orthodox Christian court life was an attempt to capture in art and ceremony the experience of the Uncreated Light.

But let's leave Burbank and return to Florence. There are exceptions within the Renaissance art displayed in the first half of the chambers of the Uffizi: the paintings done by an artist who is both an outsider and an insider to that movement, Leonardo da Vinci. In him, you see an additional kind of artistic technique alongside the astounding craft of the Renaissance. In a different way than most of the others, he can invoke the holy and turn a painting inside out, making it not a reaching up to God but God's coming down. I fell in love with Leonardo and, standing there, I began to think of him as "the mystical engineer."

Later on, when I saw that the writings of the architect Christopher Alexander made him a kind of St. Maximos the Confessor for architects and artists, I just transposed the term "mystical engineer" to him.

RTE: Before you go on, why would you say that Renaissance Art is great art if it doesn't make us pray or even suppresses prayer?

DR. PATITSAS: Since beauty is inseparable from goodness, every attempt at beauty – every work of art – has the right to be judged by and within the presuppositions of that art, according to its own canon of goodness. And if it receives and works out those canons faithfully and to a complex degree – if its goodness is intense and its complexity more or less profound – then it is great art.

I grew up on the old Speed Racer cartoons, the first introduction from Japan of *anime* to America, and those were just amazing, but at their own level and directed at a six year old. I recently happened to see the film *Polar Express* and, although also aimed at children, it *is* a story about theophany and the crosses that are inevitably hidden within theophany. So, even across the lower arts we have plenty to appreciate.

We can then consider the question of whether a particular art is not only great but also high, in the sense of being fitting for worship – and if high, then how high? Not every great art belongs in liturgy; this is self-evident. The Beauty of the highest art fulfills both of the two conditions of Beauty – of bearing Christ crucified within it and of evoking within us the mature and complete readiness also to be so crucified. The Divine Liturgy of St. John Chrysostom is itself the highest art, one of the highest products of human civilization.

In addition, high art always blends the two kinds of holy shame in a very seamless way. It lifts us up *and* chastens us with such a mild coincidence that we cannot separate the two differing movements. By healing shame, the primary and most personal energy, high art actually heals all of our energies, heals us of the passions that ordinarily make us potential crucifiers of Christ. Think of the way the very highest art – a masterfully painted icon of the Theotokos – is experienced in the Church as a gushing stream of healing. High art joins us to Christ in his self-emptying love for the world – as we said, within Beauty must be Goodness, must be Christ crucified. In high art, Christ's presence is more profound, even in those cases where it is more hidden.

And we experience such art as liberation, as complete liberation. This is because the higher the art, the more it will achieve its effect without "remainder," without leaving behind some negative residue inside you as it achieves its positive contribution. For example, Simone Weil said that most epic dramas move the listener to be nobler, but they do so through the device of making the audience hate some villain. Whereas, the *Iliad*, she said, does not achieve its positive aims by using negative means. It is more pure and high. It does not introduce a cheap dualism in order to accomplish its purposes. Simone Weil considered the *Iliad* to be the only true epic of Western Civilization because it was the only one in which there were no enemies, no villains, no moral shortcuts.

This consideration applies more generally. For example, country music probably excites *some* of your passions (such as sentimentality) in order to strengthen your embrace of *some other* dimensions of dispassion (such as a spirit of long-suffering). It leaves a "remainder"; its division throughout your being is not whole. To utilize such songs – or any art of this lower level – within worship itself would be to introduce emotional heresies into the faith. You would be treating as holy and sacred one of the artistic aesthetics that contains these misleading – though extremely difficult to avoid – trade-offs. Whereas, if in the services you have maintained a pure liturgy, a solid foundation in truly high art, then outside of worship you can filter out the bad in almost any lesser art and embrace that art all but totally. The key to cultural renewal in any society is for our artists to dive completely into the liturgy and the noetic prayer of the Church, and then do whatever they are moved to do in their artistic lives.

Very few artists can create without leaving something false behind; the struggle to be a high artist is the struggle to be a saint. It is the struggle to allow nothing false, nothing unreal to be conceived within your work or within your heart. Artists should be like Christians: great rebels – *against themselves!* And both theologians and preachers should aspire to this level of artistry in their teaching – to not cure one passion by exciting some other passion in their poor captive audiences.

Or, the difference between Holy Week and a passion play: a passion play tells the story more succinctly, with more emotional impact, but it also makes it a story, a drama. Orthodox Holy Week, on the other hand, is a work of art that passes through but also beyond all the usual devices and manipulations of scene, imagery, plot, etc. It leaves you with no sense of having been put through an emotional rollercoaster. It is not meant to be emotionally manipulative but, rather, emotionally transfiguring. As in the *Iliad*, in Holy Week we see the Hero struggling against forces larger than the merely human, and yet we are able to relate as well to the temptations and falls of the villains.

But in Holy Week, we also come to see the protagonist's suffering as the way that *He* identifies with *us*; it's his art that is being made in us.

Nevertheless, I don't know whether it is true to say, as I hastily did when I was in Florence, that some of the art of the Renaissance suppresses prayer. Perhaps it invokes a different kind of mindfulness of God than that experienced in noetic prayer. Or maybe, seen rightly, it can evoke even that. I have not been back to Florence since my years in Orthodox monasteries, nor am I an expert on the art of the Renaissance. Perhaps Renaissance art is the beginning of abstract art, in the sense that intellect and truth from that point forward come more and more to the fore in painting, until Beauty will be at last completely eclipsed by intellectual disclosure. And maybe even *that* movement can be holy in a foolish way, since this new art might manage to show us that truth is *always* inseparable from beauty and goodness, and thus that the Enlightenment's deep desire to separate truth from beauty could not, by definition, succeed. I don't know.

And besides: Fra Angelico! After we had noted our reaction to the art of the Uffizi, my friend took me to see Angelico's wall paintings in the painter's own monastery in Florence. You cannot really separate those paintings from icons.

One temptation most of us face, though, looks like this: this world, even in its fallen state, can be so beautiful that one does not want to lose it. It is natural to fear noetic prayer, to realize that in embracing such prayer one might "lose" the entire world. It is natural to wonder if, instead, one might have all that this present world promises and still be true to the next. But if at least some of us do not take the risk of renouncing that very question, our society can never mature nor even endure.

Some good things in this world, compared to nothing, are almost heaven; but compared to a full life in the Spirit, they only disappoint. Of course, some people are granted both and need both and that can be fine, too. We are not to be jealous if others seem to have both.

But if I am going to have both, as I hope to, I would like more da Vincis around to try to unite them, not just nervously juxtapose them.

The Timeless Way of Liturgy

RTE: Then would you say that Christopher Alexander truly unites Church and non-Church approaches? And, for the sake of readers who may not have heard of him, can you start with a short summary of his life and work?

DR. PATITSAS: Christopher Alexander was born in 1936 in Vienna, although he was raised in England. He was later a student of mathematics at Cambridge, earned his doctorate in architecture from Harvard, and in 1972 became the first person ever to receive the gold medal for a dissertation in architecture from the American Institute of Architects. He spent his academic career teaching architecture at Berkeley. One of his books, *A Pattern Language*, is a kind of bible for architects, with its 240-plus patterns guiding the design of everything from a door, to a doorway, to a house, a neighborhood, a city, and on to entire regions.[4]

Alexander's "pattern language" approach to creative order is even more popular among several schools of computer programmers than it is among architects. The pattern-language approach to programming is at the core of our anti-missile defenses, an architect of such systems once told me.[5]

---

[4] Christopher Alexander, *A Pattern Language* (Oxford: Oxford University Press, 1977). He also authored the classic text on architectural order, *The Timeless Way of Building* (Oxford: Oxford University Press, 1979).

[5] It was the computer scientists Kent Beck and Ward Cunningham who in 1987 proposed applying Christopher Alexander's pattern language approach to the architecture of buildings to the "architecture" of computer software. Their work, in turn, gained purchase when the so-called "Gang of Four" published *Design Patterns: Elements of Reusable Object-Oriented Software* in 1994. (See Wikipedia article, "Software Design Pattern," accessed December 2, 2017.) Today, the pattern language approach to computer programming is so ubiquitous that some reliance of missile defense systems on such patterns would be unavoidable.

Alexander has always been both behind the times and ahead of his time. Behind, because he sidestepped the entirety of the twentieth century's ideas about what was supposed to make great architecture. He spent his career ignoring the assumptions behind the Enlightenment while everyone else had accepted them; that is why most architectural theorists ignore him.

But he has also been ahead of his time, thinking in terms of nonlinear computer programming, paradigms for complex problem solving, and organic order – areas of inquiry and knowledge that surpass the reductive approach to science and nature implied in the truth-first approach to architecture.

Alexander attempted to unite natural science with theological intuition through one of the great points of contact between Orthodox Christianity and the Enlightenment West: dedication to empirical evidence.

When, in the 1330s, St. Gregory Palamas had faced the most persuasive and solid arguments against the possibility of seeing the Uncreated Light with one's created eyes, he responded, "Yes, your argumentation is extremely persuasive – but we actually *do* see this Light, and in fact hundreds of monastics see it. So the theory is just going to have to be re-done." That is the way to theologize, with our bodies placed at the center and theophany in the driver's seat!

Modern science is based on the willingness to reject any theory that cannot be verified empirically – and to the earliest modern scientists, religion seemed to be devoid of actual experience. To them, it was only an imaginary or theoretical construct. Of course, if we can have no contact with uncreated grace, then the critics are correct. Orthodoxy concurs with this Enlightenment assessment: theology has got to be grounded in the continued experience of miracle if it is to have any validity. If it has merely been devised in a university, then it *should* be rejected.

Well, Christopher Alexander found a way to test architectural style empirically, as well: the latest fads are all so fine in theory, he challenges, but why don't they ever work in practice? Why don't they produce *living* structure? And if you tell me – Alexander continues – that the quality that I am describing as "living" is just an opinion or a prejudice, then why, when I survey huge numbers of people about its presence or absence in a building or city, is their agreement so overwhelming about which buildings are living and which are dead? These are important practical questions that no amount of scholastic sophistry can silence. Right now our awful buildings and our destructive town planning endure because the sophists defending them are so persuasive and so well-connected to financial power. But this cannot last forever.

Alexander is a gifted philosopher, an observer of the actual constitution of the world, and this has given him a kind of Orthodox ethos. He is not literally an Orthodox Christian, for he was born a Roman Catholic and at one point in his life he cultivated Zen meditation. But "Zen Catholics" often seem to hold something like our Orthodox mystical cosmology. I hope that more and more people will read Alexander because he will help them to begin a Beauty-first approach to the world.

RTE: And how did you first hear of him?

DR. PATITSAS: When a very good friend in Virginia first told me about another one of Alexander's books, *The Timeless Way of Building*, I assumed that no book could be as good as what she was describing. But fifteen minutes of reading the book itself, and I reached for the phone to call a colleague in academia. I then made the extreme statement, "I was just given the book which our entire educational careers have been a conspiracy to keep from us!" This was not a wise introduction, of course, since my friend and I had both worked quite hard on our educations until that point, and no one likes to be told to start over! But I actually did start over after reading *The Timeless Way*, and this present book is the result, fifteen years later, of having done so.

The Quality Without a Name

RTE: Can you summarize *The Timeless Way*?

DR. PATITSAS: *The Timeless Way* starts with a kind of riddle: in the buildings and places that we most love and that feel to us the most alive, there is some quality that we cannot quite capture in words. Something "extra" is going on there which we recognize as very important, although we cannot name it.

Alexander then deepens the riddle: what if the undefinability of this quality is the result not of its vagueness but of its astounding specificity? This nameless quality is *too* precise for words, Alexander says. He refers to this characteristic of good places as "the Quality without a Name," and he goes on to argue that the search for this quality is the fundamental search not only in building and in the arts, but in every human life. We all are governed by an eros for something ineffable which, when we find it, will give order and meaning to our souls and lives.

Within the opening few pages of his book, in just a few short words, Christopher Alexander prompts you to recognize that you *do* know this quality that he is talking about, even if it is quite mysterious and can hardly be defined in any analytical way. And you must admit that this quality is so important that it, and not intellectual theories, has the right to judge art.

So, right there, our rationalist and reductive approach to life just evaporates; you wake up from it, as from a bad dream. There are truths – the most important truths – that you *know* but that reason cannot capture; and, moreover, these truths are universally understood by the human soul without the aid of prior argumentation and demonstration. All at once, through this realization, "truth-first" gives way to something more aesthetic. You are forced to admit that your capacities for knowing are not reducible to your capacities for thinking in a rationalist way, and that what you know in this way has an objective quality to the extent that almost all human beings know the same thing, when they allow themselves to know in this way.

The Mystical Architect

The Timeless Way is a mystical book. Everything Alexander writes in it, he expresses so simply and without violence or contentiousness. For example, he points out that just a few simple habits or patterns of action make up the bulk of what we do on most days of our lives. And then he gently asks if the quality of each day doesn't come down to whether these routines are full of life or are, instead, dead? For example, just the simple decision to have our breakfast on the veranda each fine morning, as opposed to inside, can give a much richer quality to our lives.

From this notion of patterns of action, he moves on to patterns in space – the characteristic relationships among elements that make every architectural style its unique self. For example, until less than a hundred years ago, windows in a building were almost always oriented vertically, corresponding to the shape a person makes when standing. Now we have a new pattern, the horizontal picture-window, which teaches us to see the outdoors as a product to be consumed through a television screen. This is not my idea, but is one of the main observations about bad Patterns that comes from the New Urbanist movement. They say there is something psychologically debilitating about walking below ranks of picture windows, and I know that I have felt this, as well.

Alexander says that if these patterns of relationship among the elements within our architecture are dead, then it follows that the buildings and towns made from them will also tend to be dead, no matter how gifted the architect who is employing the bad patterns. Well, open your eyes and look around: is the contemporary American built-environment alive or dead? And yet, isn't it obviously patterned, given that from coast to coast it has come to look almost exactly the same? So, something must be wrong with the underlying patterns themselves rather than with the architects or the planners using these tools.

Alexander lists more than two hundred examples of good patterns in urban design: "Four-Story Limit"; "Nine Per Cent Parking"; "Parallel Roads"; "Sacred Sites"; "Access to Water"; "Life-cycle"; "Activity Nodes"; "Promenade"; "Shopping Street";

"Night Life"; "Degrees of Publicness"; "Row Houses"; "Old People Everywhere"; "University as a Marketplace"; "Market of Many Shops"; "T Junctions"; "Network of Paths and Cars"; "Raised Walk"; "Children in the City"; "Carnival"; "Small Public Squares"; "Dancing in the Street"; "Holy Ground"; "Connected Play"; "Public Outdoor Room."

He lists still more within houses: "Intimacy Gradient"; "Staircase as a Stage"; "Common Areas at the Heart"; "The Flow Through Rooms"; "Tapestry of Light and Dark"; "Couple's Realm"; "Children's Realm"; "Sleeping to the East"; "Farmhouse Kitchen"; "Private Terrace on the Street"; "Light on Two Sides of Every Room"; "Bed Alcove"; "Windows Overlooking Life"; "Child Caves"; "Secret Place"; "Filtered Light; "Garden Growing Wild."

While you need to read his actual descriptions to see what they mean, you can understand just by reading the names of these patterns that there is some deep thought in each of them as to what it takes to build cities and homes in which human beings feel deeply at home, and therefore deeply at ease and completely alive. Just reading the list is somehow nourishing to the soul.

Each of these patterns works for different reasons. To go back to the example of the windows, it's fairly obvious that while it may be nice to look out from a picture window, to look up or across at a building with horizontal picture windows is just a soul-crushing, sickening experience. These buildings look like death, like naked ego imposed upon the world. Such windows should be banned in the interest of public mental health. And in places like Seaside, Florida that adhere to the New Urbanism, picture windows are, in fact, banned. The whole point of these awful horizontal windows is to objectify the person below. Picture windows reduce the world to scenery porn.

Or, such windows reduce the world to a vision seen through a sniper's scope. You don't want to walk around in a city where there are these cursed picture windows pointing down at you. It's like strolling along while someone points a gun at you. Normal people don't want to do it, even if the gun isn't loaded.

Those who object to such windows trace the problem to their shape. They say that when windows conform roughly to the shape of a human being, then the person looking out from them is letting himself be known as he knows others. There is a communion there. In sharp contrast, picture windows are Cartesian and objectifying. Through them, the knower is not known.[6]

For Alexander, a very central thing to realize is that the Quality without a Name will usually be mediated into our lives through good patterns, including both patterns of action and patterns of architectural design. And these patterns, in turn, will either possess or not possess this unnameable but essential quality which all humans desire. So it is to these patterns that we must look.

Existence Through Participation in God's Own Life

RTE: And what do you think this Quality without a Name really is? What is it that we participate in, in those moments when we are most alive?

DR. PATITSAS: Patterns are like rituals, whether in time or in space. What we are talking about in *The Timeless Way* is the difference between good rituals and bad rituals – between orthodoxy and its opposite.

The Quality Without a Name that arises in good Patterns, in good ritual, is a gift of the twofold anointing, of the Holy Spirit; that is why it can have a "bittersweet" quality, why the experience of it can make us sad. The Quality without a Name is God's uncreated glory, fed to us through the created world when we respond to that world liturgically. It is the two kinds of opposing shame at the moment when they coincide perfectly.

Now, the Quality Without a Name is not the Uncreated Light itself but a reflection of the fact that every existing thing is sus-

---

6 This is close to the heart of the Orthodox Christian idea of Creation as arising in response to God's Theophany, his self-revelation, in an act that is also a self-offering. What God creates, He creates by letting it know him. God does not know his world without letting it know him back. God is not a voyeur.

tained by some hard-to-describe participation in God's uncreated grace. *To be is to participate* in something divine. So, although the search for this quality can be termed, "the central search of every human life," to paraphrase Alexander, it is only when the Quality Without a Name is transcended in the grace that Christ discloses in the Mysteries (the "sacraments") that this quality takes on a character that is more permanently salvific. At that point, we can say more definitely in the words of St. Seraphim of Sarov that "the goal of the Christian life is the acquisition of the Holy Spirit."

That probably sounds obscure, so I should tell you what I have in mind. Saint Maximos spoke of a continuum of *being* – something in which all creation shares; *well-being* – which is a higher state of existence, given through the sacraments of the Church, and which involves a much more immediate and intimate experience of Christ; and *ever-being* – which is the condition granted at the Last Judgment to those who are worthy. Well, the Quality Without a Name, as wonderful as it is, seems to be only the presence of perfected being; the vision of Uncreated Light is much higher and comes with well-being. It is even a foretaste of ever-being.

Every human being can sense the presence of this uncreated grace in the form of simple being, if they allow themselves to. This is why aesthetic considerations are not mere matters of opinion or taste but can rise to actual certainty, as Alexander found. But I have heard that only those who are members of the Church through sacramental action can see Uncreated Light with their created eyes. I think this limitation may exist, even if saying so seems hurtful or exclusive.

I am pretty sure that Alexander's Quality Without a Name is the light of being, although "being" in the sense that being inevitably is a kind of image of God, and thus the Quality perhaps shimmers with something more than being. However, the Uncreated Light at the level of well-being is still another level – it is akin to the likeness to God, and we need to have the sacramental grace given by Christ through his Church in order to see it.

RTE: So, you are saying that the perfect garden wall attached to a farmhouse in the south of France, to give an example from *The Timeless Way*, reflects the presence of grace? In other words, that that space's participation in a true Pattern hints at something uncreated, although this isn't quite the same as seeing Uncreated Light? In appreciating this perfection, how do we not slip into a quasi-pantheism or at least an overly aesthetic approach to the world that distracts our attention from God?

DR. PATITSAS: All things that exist, bad and good, only do exist because God's uncreated energy, his grace, binds and fulfills and sustains them. This is an insight given to us by St. Dionysios the Areopagite. Nothing exists "on its own." We are not deists, for we do not believe that God created the world and then walked away from it. God is not absent from his world. He is present everywhere, sustaining all things through his uncreated grace.

But you're right; we are not pantheists, either, who believe that the world in itself *is* God. The Church calls her icons the triumph of Orthodoxy, because they show that in love, God became what He wasn't – a creature; while in God's love we can become what we can never be on our own – divine. In other words, the gospel message is that we are called to become divine by grace, never by nature. Creation is meant to be an icon, never an idol. If we were pantheists, we wouldn't emphasize the reality of chiasm, of exchange.

So, all being participates in uncreated grace. Well, in the Church a quantum increase in this experience and presence of grace is thought to be necessary if we would be saved. This renewed participation is then vouchsafed by God through the Church herself. To understand that God's grace operates *outside* the Church is not to deny that salvation exists *only within* the Church, nor that many who now seem outside the Church may be found at the Last Judgment to have been inside. We should feel some degree of healthy anxiety about our salvation – which pantheism does not allow.[7]

---

[7] How does all this discussion of a world imbued with divine grace differ from Neoplatonism, not to say pantheism? For one thing, the Christian revelation holds that a higher level of participation in God is meant to be received through the body of Christ. This

But a foretaste of the Light does come through Beauty in the created realm, and this is what Alexander is seeing – not the light of well-being but the light of simple being when it is truly anchored in participation in God. We need those who can mediate such experiences to us through their design. Such is the high calling of the artist.

Let us return to these paradoxes later, for they do have an order of their own.

The Forms as Archetypal Patterns

Again and again, Alexander stresses one idea: the good Patterns, whether of design or of action, are usually the key to this Quality Without a Name.

The Patterns of *The Timeless Way of Building* are much like the Platonic Forms. Or, in the terms of St. Maximos Confessor, they are the *logoi*, the archetypal ways that we participate in the Logos, in Christ. The patterns can carry a certain glory, can disclose this Quality Without a Name, because somehow they are a preliminary mode by which Christ makes *his* life available to creation – when you see a building, a room, or a city that possesses this ineffable character, you really do sense that this Quality is of life or death importance.

Remember that at the back of Orthodox Christian soul therapy and development is a particular and paradoxical narrative about the moment of Creation, which is not to be taken literally, but neither is it a metaphor; rather, it is an icon at the back of which lies a mystery that no language can capture completely. According to St. Dionysios and St. Maximos, the True God was so Good that He spilled over

involves not only the Eucharist now but the bodily incarnation, death, resurrection, and ascension of Christ in time. So, Christianity is not a "spiritualizing" religion but one which reaffirms the importance of creation.

Secondly, the assimilation of this grace in ways that really count, in ways that matter eternally (that save us) requires that we somehow embrace the death and resurrection of Christ with as much consciousness as we can muster.

We have to personally appropriate this grace which surrounds us, and to do that requires not only baptism and the Eucharist but most probably some kind of cross. All of creation must be inscribed with the Cross, if it is to be delivered from the self-contained and self-referential status which is its temptation.

"outside" himself. This appearing was so Beautiful that non-being also left itself behind and entered being. So, being is a kind of surprising marriage between the Uncreated and that which arises *ex nihilo*. Existence is therefore a sort of tentative zone that only takes on solidity when this marriage is secure. The world is a cosmos – a beautiful structured order – only when the self-sharing of the Logos is met by an appropriate receptivity; a hospitality, in other words.

Christopher Alexander stresses that an experience of actual Beauty is not merely a matter of your private opinion, prejudice, or emotion. I think this is because when you meet real Beauty, you are in a real way partaking of Christ, who is the Logos – the Logos who is the trans-rational ground of reason, and therefore the aesthetic sense is not something which is opposed to reason. Not that we can reduce what is beautiful to a propositional truth statement, for propositional truth statements themselves are at best icons of truth; they, too, retain an aesthetic dimension – despite themselves, almost.

Reason *is* part of Beauty. There are no "senseless acts of Beauty," Prof. Eric Perl used to tell us when we were his students, contradicting the bumper sticker that says, "Practice Random Acts of Kindness and Senseless Acts of Beauty" – unless by "senseless" we mean erotic, trans-rational, so *packed with* sense, that we can't describe such acts exhaustively in words.

Christopher Alexander conveys this certainty that the human awareness of Beauty is not something irrational or sub-rational, and that it is neither an opinion nor a prejudice. Alexander gives us a toolbox through which to make our way in the world as practical mystics. In *The Timeless Way*, you realize that the feeling for beauty is at once both our *simplest* intellectual act and – a point that we find also in Prof. Perl's writings – in some ways our *highest* intellectual act since it involves an insight that cannot be reduced to any number of prior rationalizations; there is a chiasm here, if you notice. And so the *feeling* for beauty is pure *intellection*, in a way.

The vision of the Quality Without a Name is pure intellection of being, while seeing the Uncreated Light is pure intellection of ever-being, of God's energies.

If there were one non-religious book that I would recommend be included in every Orthodox Christian school, it would be *The Timeless Way of Building* because it is the most measured and practical argument for the older way of thinking, the Beauty-first liturgical way that preceded our linear modern gnostic way. You start applying this book to the design of your home or to rethinking your daily habits, and what you are making is a proto-repentance. You acquire something closer to the mind that we find in the Church. To go farther than that, you have to enter the Church.

It is hard to make all the arguments for Orthodoxy from within Orthodoxy itself. You need impartial witnesses. You need allies from outside the Church who've seen the vision and fallen in love with it. My best witnesses for Orthodox Christianity are the people who've never much heard of it – Grossman and Shay on war; Christopher Alexander on beauty; C.S. Lewis on cosmology and gender.

I rely on all of them not only because they are impartial but because by finding the Orthodox Christian principle with a type of objectivity, they can help me overcome the blindness I suffer as a "crib," as someone born into the faith and needing help to see how it would look to another culture, to another mind. I often don't fully appreciate the primal and universal importance of the Orthodox Christian truths. Having ingested them since childhood, I am loathe to impose what I mistake as my own tribal allegiances.

RTE: Why "crib" instead of "cradle" Orthodox?

DR. PATITSAS: Well, calling someone a "cradle" seems to carry an implied disparagement, doesn't it? It says that having received one's faith as a child, one remains childish. "Crib," on the other hand, sounds like an infamous gang name; if I'm going to be labeled, I'd like a label with some street cred. "Cool Breeze," is another name I'd answer to, but not "cradle."

RTE: We'll remember that. Do you include *The Timeless Way* in your seminary classes?

DR. PATITSAS: Only in an advanced course, "The Ethics of Beauty." We read Alexander's *The Timeless Way* against the treatment of St. Dionysios the Areopagite in Eric Perl's *Theophany*, against the thought of St. Maximos the Confessor, against the life and words of St. Elder Porphyrios in *Wounded by Love*. With this combination you get the theology, the philosophy, the sanctity, and the practical application all at once. They explain each other, and each one safeguards us from the pitfalls we mere mortals tend to fall into when reading any of them in isolation.

For example, in that course we don't read Neoplatonism in a way that takes you away from Christ, and we don't read Maximos in a way that takes you out of your daily work, and we don't read Alexander as if he were the last word on mysticism.

But it's not an easy ride. Each of those thinkers will take us years of familiarity before we can make full creative use of them – and thus begin to *really* understand them. Even now, I'm sure that at least in some particulars I don't quite have them right, but since I believe that we are meant to understand matters like these only with time, I'm not in a rush to skip to the journey's end.

When intellectual work is done by such stars at such a high level, it won't be possible to assimilate it all at once, no matter how high our own I.Q. This has to be the case since the new understanding they give is really a "new mind" – the Greek word for repentance – and the mind must grow in mildness to really understand such truths.

Besides, understanding any of them on their own shouldn't really be our aim. We have to make them talk to each other about the practical spiritual and aesthetic questions that matter to us most. The point of reading such philosophies and theologies is to find them as aids to the abundant life that Christ wished for us. And that really took, in my case, more than twenty years of periodic exposure.

Christopher Alexander turns out to be doing a couple of things, though of course not explicitly, for which someone with a background in Orthodox Christian theology will be desperately grateful. First, he provides an empirical proof for the existence of the Platonic Forms. The Forms were a central feature at the very beginning of philosophy, in Plato's account of the world, and were used to explain how we are able to ever recognize anything in our world. They answer the problem of how we are able to reconcile sameness and difference – in other words, why we know that a horse is a horse, even though all the actual horses we ever see are slightly different.

What Alexander does is to show how we also recognize these same invariant Forms – Patterns, is his term – in architecture. In fact, he shows you how the struggle of the architect is to remain true to himself, while also descending into unknowing, into mystery, leaving behind every prejudice, opinion, bias, every image and rationalization, until he can simply give birth to a living Pattern – a living Form – in the place he is designing.

In the case of Alexander, the Platonic challenge of "how we know" is reversed: instead of asking whether it is possible to know, we are forced to admit that we just *do* know the difference between a "living" building and a "dead" one. Once you admit that, you are ready to see that this difference has to do with Patterns, and that these Patterns are invariant and yet never exactly the same.

Orthodoxy Is at Once the Most Image-less and the Most Image-rich of the Christian Faiths

Orthodoxy is at once the most image-rich and the most image-less of the Christian faiths. I will explain in a moment, but let me first say that if all you knew of the Church were this striking paradox, that could almost be enough to convince you that this is the true Church.

"Image-rich," because Orthodoxy, like Alexander, has an entire approach of how to capture the Patterns of the saints and of Christ in art. We believe that the world is theophany – or at least that the world finds its meaning and purpose when it has been captured into a mystical order (a sacramental order) and has therefore become the vehicle for divine self-disclosure. The very triumph of Orthodoxy, we say, are the icons, the art of the Church. If you think about this, it is quite remarkable: Which other Christian denomination holds up its art as being the triumph of Christianity itself?

But if Orthodoxy is the most image-rich of the Christian faiths, its churches and monasteries adorned so richly as to take one's breath away, it is also the most, and the most stringently, "image-less." No other Christian faith is both so concerned with the practice of noetic prayer and so suspicious of the intellectual approach to theology, so insistent on God's transcendence of all human ways of thought and depiction. There seems to be almost no room for the imagination in Orthodoxy; to us, the imagination is so often a drug, an escape, a virtual reality. It is so easy for human beings to turn religion into a videogame, but Orthodoxy will not abet this human impulse.

Why does Orthodoxy place such emphasis on the potential destructiveness of images when Orthodox faith is also on its way to render God visible in every corner of the creation? *Because of motherhood:* because the act of conception belongs to women and not to men, and therefore the creation of truly profound images ought to occur in a space before and beyond the typical human initiative – and beyond even the mind and its seeming power to create through imagination.

It is the heart of God's mother that we have been speaking of all along in this interview. I mean, because the image that we are trying to give birth to is not a realistic photograph but an icon, a living and miraculous participation in that which it presents, therefore we must give it actual flesh *on its own terms.* The presupposition of Orthodox icons is noetic prayer – that the iconographer is able to let go of all images, and allow a living form to be born through his or her eyes and hands.

The problem with preconceived images when you are trying to produce something beautiful in art or architecture is that these images may lead you to a dead repetition of earlier instances of the Form, rather than towards the creation of a living offering or to a participation in the archetype of Beauty itself in just the way demanded by your concrete condition. Adhering slavishly to a blueprint, or even having one ahead of time, may mean that you wind up with a cookie-cutter repetition. It usually means that what you are making will not be truly and completely sensitive to the exact situation in which it is being made.[8]

It's a problem you sometimes see in a live performer of music – the artists may not always be listening to what they are doing, they aren't really a part of their own audience, too. The rush is on just to execute the form, and so something personal is lost. Because what you are actually after as an artist of any kind is a participation in the Form that will be unique to you right now in this place and time – a marriage of universality and particularity. And to do that, you have to leave images and preconceptions behind, or at least hold onto them in a more personal way.

That is why when a true iconographer copies an archetype, he or she is so carefully devoted to the life of prayer. Something new is being born here.

Alexander applies this same spirit to all of architecture and all of art. He shows you the way these Patterns (architecture's version of the Forms) help turn chaos into order – how they impart Being, in other words.

---

8 How can Alexander simultaneously encourage reliance on good Patterns (one kind of image) while discouraging over-reliance on blueprints (another kind of image)? The answer is that for Alexander, Patterns express the living relationships among elements in a specific situation, while a static adherence to blueprints limits the ability of the builder to relate in fine freedom to forces in the building that only become evident on site during construction.

In his best example, cited above, he reminds us that there is no blueprint for a hand within your DNA; the perfection of your hand is inseparable from its uniqueness, which in your DNA is expressed more like a sequential relationship of actions.

Consequently, building according to strict blueprints rather than Patterns may render your final product more like a machine than like a living body.

Thus, in Alexander's ideal world, the architect and the builder would be the same person, and many elements of a building's design would only be finalized on site, as the building is erected.

Alexander's point is born out in the experience of Jeffrey Carson, the great translator of the Greek Nobel-Prize-winning poet Odysseus Elytis. Carson says that until very recently on the island of Paros, peasants building their own homes could spend an entire day discussing exactly where to place a window or a door. What were they talking about all day, specifically? Of course, they were bringing to mind every possible force in that situation, until all were acknowledged, honestly accounted for, and beautifully harmonized. No preconceived blueprint can compete with this level of on-site adjustment.

Jeffrey Carson, while lamenting the loss of the intense aesthetic focus of life on Paros, is far from despairing. For him, when such losses occur, the thing to do is simply to focus on high culture and on beauty wherever it can be found. He is confident that the conditions for a more widespread emphasis on art will someday return.

II. LOGOI, FORMS, AND PATTERNS

The Logoi as the Unique Way Christ Condescends to Share His Being with Each Bit of Creation

RTE: The Forms still seem a little abstract. Can you give it another go?

DR. PATITSAS: (*Laughs*) Ok, I'll try. For any bit of creation to take on a specific form, it has to be sustained by Christ, by his will, his love, and his power. But in his infinite mildness and goodness, our Divine Physician knows exactly what every part of chaos – broken and hurt chaos and non-being – needs in order to be whole, to be real. And so He shares himself, offers his own body in a sense, to each bit of non-being in just the way that each created thing is able to accept him with a maximum of joy and gladness.

The logoi – a term coined by St. Maximos to describe the distinct inner principles of each created thing – are themselves not "things" but rather are the particular *ways* that the Master kneels down and washes the feet of his creation. They are not so much "objects," these logoi, as they are tropes, or modes, or mannerisms through which Christ the Logos lends his life to the world.

Saint Maximos talks about how every created thing, literally everything that exists, exists because it participates in the Logos, in Christ. Christ is what gives to every being its being! In saying this, the saint continues the Neoplatonic tradition as developed by St. Dionysios the Areopagite.

But both saints also say that each thing participates *differently* in Christ, or participates in Christ according to the particular aspect of Christ in which it has been called to share. Each created thing falls in love with a particular aspect of Christ's self-offering. The particular aspect of Christ's self-offering which each thing loves, is that thing's particular logos, its "map" of what it must be.

Eros precedes, or constitutes, existence because every bit of creation finds the logos of its existence beautiful and so hearkens to it, and away from non-being. Of course, no created thing can contain *all* of Christ, and so it will only embrace one or a few aspects of him; each bit of creation will have its own particular doorway upon which Christ "knocks."

Saint Maximos, as we just said, uses the term logos, with a small "l," for each thing's specific and particular share of the self-offering of the Logos. By this, the saint indicates that the identity of each thing that exists is a dimension or facet of the "big L" Logos, Christ himself. Let us repeat, these logoi are not "things" themselves but the particular love with which Christ condescends to each created thing, so that each bit of creation will see in Christ's limitless self-offering to the world, a Beautiful "personalized" invitation rather than an overwhelming imposition.

It goes almost without saying that when something created participates in its logos – the unique aspect of Christ that imparts to it its very existence – it takes on a quite concrete specificity. At that point, it is just "this" and not "that." We have remarked elsewhere about the impressive *reality* of the saints, of saintly persons. When I stand before a saint, I feel myself almost a shadow! So we can see that these logoi which guide the concrete reality of things *are* the Forms, the Archetypes behind creation. They are the way in which the forces in a situation are absorbed and balanced so that creation can arise out of chaos.

This, in turn, tells us that the Forms are not pre-existing things but are more like sacraments or modes of God's self-disclosure in Christ. The fact that they are needed by creation in order to exist does not at all impose a Necessity on God's inner life. No, the Forms are the miraculous revelation of God's infinite freedom to give to each thing the being it desires.

Did God Have to Create?

As an aside, Orthodox Christian theologians these days are hampered by the fact that a false scandal has beset us regarding our greatest theologian, St. Dionysios the Areopagite. He is the font of much of what we have to say as Orthodox Christians about metaphysics, and yet he is dismissed by many contemporary thinkers as a non-Christian, a Neoplatonist.

The controversy surrounding this great saint comes down to this: if St. Dionysios is saying that *it was a necessity* for God to create, then in that case the saint would be saying that *God is not truly free*. If so, the argument goes, the saint would be a Neoplatonist and not truly a Christian theologian. The Neoplatonist system is felt by some to make God's act of creation so much a part of God's identity that God is "required" to make the world. God is dependent upon the world.

But *if God was free to create or not create*, then Dionysios is not a Neoplatonist, in which case why does he bother expressing his total system in terms that he borrows from the Neoplatonists?

Either way, the theology of St. Dionysios is thought to be suspect.

This entire controversy has an easy solution, in the end. In fact, no other non-Christian philosopher was more careful to preserve the freedom of God than Plotinus. Therefore, St. Dionysios also respects the freedom of God *because of* his dependence upon Plotinus, not despite it. That's why Lev Shestov, who more clearly than anyone else sounded the alarm that philosophy seemed to require a God who was not free (so that human reason could take the world as a given, something fixed, and then analyze it), himself thought that Plotinus was one of the very few philosophers who was innocent of this charge.

It's just that God's freedom is not expressed like human freedom, or like political freedom; God's decisions are not lawless arbitrary choices made in the void. God's freedom is rather the total activation of his inner truth and goodness, of his divinity and his love for the world.

Nevertheless, the more free God is, the more He appears concrete, fixed, and determined, in a wonderful paradox. Because his free decision to make the world results in a specificity of the world that is rooted in his providence. In the Incarnation, this paradox of freedom and determination reaches its climax in Christ. Do you want to see God's freedom in its ultimate expression? Look upon Christ in the grave, a corpse. That was a perfectly voluntary expression of his ultimate love.

So, in God, freedom and necessity coincide in a paradoxical way that we call simply, "Life," even when we look upon it in the grave. And once again, we see here a chiasm, where the proof of his freedom is found in his voluntary assent to necessity, and the proof of his good order is to be witnessed in his free overcoming of death in the Resurrection.

From Image to Likeness

RTE: If we human beings can only embrace our own particular facet of the Logos, in what sense are we made in God's image? Wouldn't that only be a partial image?

DR. PATITSAS: This is a good question, and it contains within itself two problems that need addressing. First, is Maximos implying that all of creation is just as much "made in the image of God" as human beings are? For him, no, not at all. Some additional participation has been given only to humans.

Second, if the uniqueness of every particular human being lies in its sharing only in some few aspects of Christ's full identity, can we really be said to be made in his image? Well, even Christ himself took on flesh and lived in a particular time and place, taking on a concrete identity. His hair was one color and not another, for example. He therefore shows how we become human, which is by starting with some particular set of limitations and then transcending these in the life of spiritual adventure.

Moreover, through your unique logos you connect to the Logos, and through him to the logoi of all creation, as well. As you approach Christ, you are becoming more uniquely you, more particular. In loving Christ, you embrace all people and all creation, while at the same time you also become more specific, so to speak. We call this growing from the image into the likeness, and again, here we see a paradox, where the more concretely unique you become, the more deeply you are connected to all of creation.

And think of Panaghia, in particular – she contained *the whole Christ* – she is, η πλατυτέρα των ουρανών (the one more spacious than the heavens) – which makes her the summation of all created things and an even more important "mother of all living beings" (Gen 3:20) than Eve was. And yet her personal uniqueness is not drowned in her union with God but enhanced and made eternal. She retains her identity as a mother and a woman, for example.

Patterns, Forms, and Logoi All Function Similarly

As we've said all along, for created things it's Beauty and *then* Goodness. And we said that Truth is not really a third moment, but if you have the first two, then you have Truth as well. And this is why: in Beauty we love Christ and him crucified, while in Goodness we consent to be crucified with him for the life of the world. And at that point, we *are* participating in our own unique logos so that we are true, also – we come to exist. We have been baptized in Christ and thus have put on Christ – we have attained our particular logos through union with the Logos.

All of creation does this, and this is the mystery of creation, its hidden side. Every existing thing is following this cruciform pattern, this path of loving God and loving neighbor, which is why when we sin against God or others it is so painful to us. *Because on the level of our existence as souls and bodies, as humans, part of us is still loving Christ (eros) in the logos of himself which He gives uniquely to us, and part of us is still choosing to die with him (agape) for the life of the world.* But when we sin, suddenly our free will and minds and the fallen dimensions of our nature begin simultaneously to head in the opposite direction.

Thus, when we sin, we ourselves are rending our very being by simultaneously loving Christ at one level of our life and rejecting him at another; and, we are in one way serving our neighbor and in another trying to kill or objectify him. You can see, then, why condemnation at the Last Judgment would hurt so much. On the one hand, so long as we exist, we are enacting a path of love for God and love for neighbor. But on the other hand, in hell we would also have set our free will permanently against God and our brother. We would therefore be tearing our own selves in two for all eternity.

This is how the invisible powers arrayed against Christ and against the Church exist, in this agonizing state. They can't repent, even, which is why some desert Fathers would weep for the demons.

But let us concentrate on the parts of the world which are *not* in self-conscious rebellion against Christ. In its own unique way, *every created thing fulfills these two moments* of both erotic self-renunciation *for* Christ and agapic co-crucifixion *with* Christ, and thus every created thing is automatically also "friends" with Christ, sharing in and even disclosing Christ according to its particular and unique logos. I mean, even a rock somehow is moved by eros for Christ, "consents" to suffer with Christ for the world, and thus discloses some hidden truth of Christ. The rock has this "friendship" with Christ because Christ does not hide from it the mystery of the rocklike aspects of himself which He himself received from his Father.[9]

And that is why effective soul therapy is not truth-first. God did not assemble the world from pre-existing parts but rather overflowed towards it, and in his Beauty drew non-being into falling in love with him. This is how the soul, too, was created, and this is the pattern by which the soul that has fallen or been damaged must now be re-created, to be set on a blessed and noble trajectory yet again. Truth follows, just flows, from our falling in love (eros) with the resurrected and crucified Lord and from our consenting to be crucified with him (agape).

One other thought I must share: some have this distorted idea that eros is a selfish love while agape is an other-regarding love. I

---

9 "Henceforth I call you not servants; for the servant knoweth not what his lord doeth: but I have called you friends; for all things that I have heard of my Father I have made known unto you" (Jn 15:15). What the rock knows in its friendship with the Logos is the very mystery of rockiness. Indeed, every created thing, in its being what it is, attains its own "friendship" with Christ. In reaching its particular logos, it becomes friends with the Logos. This is one reason why saints, who are also friends with Christ, are able to calm nature and befriend animals.

think we have addressed this in an earlier chapter, but let us now repeat that the Church does not share in this mistaken thinking. Eros is the total self-offering and self-renunciation of man or creation in the light of Theophany; agape unfolds this eros into a self-renunciation on behalf of others. Neither love is selfish; both are the renunciation of self-love; and both involve a twofold anointing that, in a fallen world, will have both a "pleasurable" and a "painful" side.[10]

The reason eros can seem to some more selfish is that a) it doesn't yet include the created other (although it is the very definition of rejecting self-love) because at first it is wholly for God, and b) it is not careful. I mean, we can love God with total reckless abandon, for He is infinite and He can take it. As we move on to agape, our renunciation must be refined and become more careful. A mere creature cannot bear the strength of all our eros, and so when we relate to others, eros must unfold into something not less loving, but rather more informed, so to speak. One reason why some reject St. Dionysios the Areopagite is that he promotes the eros which they so fear. Eros only seems selfish because it is more wild. But a people that fears wildness cannot truly be alive.

RTE: This sounds wonderful. And yet, Plato's Forms are controversial in Christian philosophy, are they not?

DR. PATITSAS: Yes, because the Forms can seem like some weird created thing, a demiurge floating between us and God that then acts to create us. But that is not what they are at all. They are just the logoi of St. Maximos – the way, unique to each of us, that we participate in the Logos. They aren't things but rather ways, paths, or patterns. They are just what the uncreated and eternal Christ looks like to us, from our very partial perspectives. "Behold, I stand at the door and knock," Christ says to us (Rev. 3:20a). And each bit of creation has a different "door" that Christ knocks on, unique to it. If we open this door, Christ grants us a share of his being: "If

---

10 As was argued in Chapter Three, lust amounts to a defeat of eros because a) it does not truly involve the forgetting of the self, but rather its elevation to one's sole concern, and b) lust does not unfold into the empathetic serving of another person.

any man hear my voice, and open the door, I will come in to him, and will sup with him, and he with me" (Rev 3:20b).

So, no, the Forms aren't "eternal," if by Forms we mean something created. But understood as logoi, the Forms *are* eternal because we then see that they are simply a share in Christ, a way of sharing in Christ. The Forms are the iconic way He appears to us in our created state. They are modes of God's self-disclosure to creation. They are ways, tropes, as we said above, made possible by his deepest eternal identity.

The main philosophical question about them has been whether these Forms existed independently at some higher level of being, eternally, or whether we ourselves make them up as devices by which to think about the world. Because if they *do exist* higher up, they would seem like a kind of eternal intermediary between us and God, a demiurge, and in that case the Forms would seem to limit God's *absolute* freedom to create without intermediaries and block us from contact with God.

But if they *don't exist* in that way, "higher up," then they seem more like an unnecessary holdover from a more primitive account of the world. Why bother with something that *doesn't exist*? We should then be sure to avoid talking about the Forms, and avoid completely the danger that they would lead us to a kind of polytheism.

Well, how can you resolve a question about the very being of all that exists? We can't see into such mysteries. But Alexander *does* help us to resolve it, once you realize that what he calls the "Patterns" in architecture really just operate in the same way the Forms do. He gives you empirical evidence that only through the Forms can good buildings come into being, and therefore it follows that the rest of the world also has its patterns, its ruling ways.

The Patterns/Forms don't exist privately above the world, but they are aspects of Christ the Logos, who is also the Archetypal Form. We could say that the Logos is to the logoi, what Christ crucified is to "Christ crucified in us." Or, in a third way to express the same matter, the Logos is to the logoi what the ultimate Form (Christ crucified) is to the many Forms (the ways in which Christ empties himself for us, which are also the ways we join ourselves to that self-emptying out of love for him and for the world). The Patterns/Forms are ways in which Christ shares himself with the world, ways He limits his self-disclosure so that we are not destroyed by meeting his ultimate and full Being to a measure completely beyond what we could take. They are condescensions of Christ towards the weakness of non-being, by which He gives each bit of creation only the share of him that it can bear. There are many Forms because Christ is God, limitless and rich beyond imagination.[11]

And, anyway, our emphasis about the Forms' existence should be the reverse of what we make it: *Whether the Forms exist or not is not the problem; the challenge is that the world itself cannot be said to exist unless it participates in these Forms.* The Forms don't "exist" in that sense because they are not something created to begin with. But they are patterns and ways according to which Christ empties himself and enters the realm of non-being, raising it up to existence. In the process, He too enters the realm of existence, of being.[12]

So, no, the Forms don't exist independently. But neither does creation exist until and unless it hosts one or more of these Forms –

---

11 As we shall see in Chapter Eight, the relationship between the Form and the many Forms is a hierarchy, but not the kind of hierarchy we usually imagine. Rather, we are dealing here with the kind of nested hierarchies that our science today knows either as fractals, or as nodes within networks. In a fractal hierarchy, the "parent" instance is repeated, but at different scales and in ways that are perfectly suited to the time and place of the "daughter" instances.

12 It has been noted by reader Georgia Williams that gender, too, seems to be a Form (or, two Forms). If that is the case, then male and female are two blessed ways according to which we are called to be human. This implies that a) a person who tried to erase every expression of gender in themselves, or who was set on erasing the gender they have been given, would be marring their own humanity. And this more or less fits with our experience, for even the saints, who have left behind the sexual expressions of gender, are still male or female in heaven; b) it can be quite hard to define in the abstract what makes a "man" or a "woman," because the Form of gender cannot be said to "exist" until it appears in actual men and women, who are all so varied; yet, c) gender, though nebulous in one sense, will be hard as a rock in another sense, since it is a manifestation (as all Forms are) of something that lies beyond existence itself, of something which is the basis for existence. Saint Paul in Ephesians 5:32 can therefore speak about marriage as reflective of a Great Mystery, the relationship between Christ and the Church. We can no more dispose of the Forms of gender than we could of the relationship between Christ and his Church. Finally, d) absent a relationship to Christ, the human race may find its hold on gender, and therefore on its own full humanity, becoming quite tenuous. This is happening today, as the collapse of Christian sexual morality has led to the loss, for many, of the positive appreciation of gender.

or, rather, until it walks the road of one or more of these patterns: "I am the Way, the Truth, and the Life," Christ said (Jn 14:6). Before that intersection of the Form with created matter – of Christ's humble self-offering with pure non-being – neither Creation *nor* the Forms exists. It is only in the intersection of Form with pure, formless matter that both the Forms *and* Creation enter into created existence. Being is a marriage between the beyond being and the *ex nihilo*.

There is only one point upon which I would disagree with Prof. Perl. He starts all his philosophical accounts from a single arch-principle, that of Parmenides (circa 500 B.C.). "To be, is to be intelligible," said this ancient philosopher; i.e., existing things are coherent. From this point, Prof. Perl is able to deduce and develop the entire Neoplatonist program.

However, it is possible to express the matter more dynamically: To be, is to be the intelligible icon of the Logos of the Father. Now, this Logos is itself *both* intelligible *and* beyond intelligibility (Christ is both "the Existing One" and "the One Beyond Being"). Therefore, while being is an intelligible icon (each thing is based in its logos), that intelligibility is only meaningful because it discloses something of the "beyond being," of the "beyond intelligibility."

Moreover, being's participation in the Logos, which gives to being both its existence and its intelligibility, is not fixed, but grows or fades with time as we approach or deny Christ. Therefore, our being itself lies somewhere on a dynamic continuum between non-being and perfect being, between un-intelligibility and intelligibility.

With these refinements, I think the danger that Neoplatonism should supplant the theology of the Church is avoided.

The Forms are Ways According to which the Logos Is "Crucified" for Creation – and through which Creation Is "Crucified" to "the World"

The Forms are "Christ crucified," because they are ways that, in pouring himself out for us, Christ for our salvation reveals only as much of himself as we each can bear. In this sense, He limits himself through the Forms. At the same time, the Forms are "Christ crucified" *in us*, because when we embrace them, we too become that which we uniquely are, laying aside all that *we could have been* or *might have been instead* – I mean, to be created at all is to be created as some specific thing, and therefore not as every other thing (if you see what I mean). We "die" to all that we might have been, when we become one actual thing.

The Forms are therefore a kind of Golgotha, the site of God and man's co-crucifixion, out of love, for the life of the world. I am describing the creation of rocks and insects as much as humans, but in the human case we can see the matter more directly. A person who tries to be what they aren't meant to be is in danger of not becoming anything at all, of not really existing as a concrete and beautiful thing.

I don't mean that we could have been made differently, because in that case "we" wouldn't have existed at all. Here I don't intend the conditional "could have been" in that full-blown sense. I am simply saying that *to be* one thing is by definition *not to be* every other thing; this is a death and resurrection that every created thing embraces.

We can see this in an analogy from the world of courtship: When married couples entrust their lives to each other, what they are doing is trading *an infinity of possibilities* for *the possibility of infinity*. Their being born to each other requires that they "die" to all other possible spouses. So the Form of marriage, just like the other Forms, is Christ crucified within us and we co-crucified with him in a way that will give us life.

Physicists working with Claude Shannon's Information Theory define creation in just this way, by noting that everything that is, only is by virtue of its not being something else.[13] The simplest bit of "information," the answer to a single yes/no question, coincides with our understanding of the Forms as a kind of crucifixion which is able to draw in chaos until the chaos becomes order. The confu-

---

13 Claude E. Shannon and Warren Weaver, *The Mathematical Theory of Communication* (Urbana, IL: The University of Illinois Press, 1949).

sions of chaos are harnessed by the Form into one specific type of creaturely existence. At that point, we know that a thing is, in part because we know for sure what it is not.

RTE: You have said that Christ enters being when He shares himself through the logoi, the Forms. But what does it mean when we say that we believe God is "beyond being"?

DR. PATITSAS: It is very interesting that, according to the Orthodox tradition, it is only when God "empties himself" for the life of the world, that He actually takes on being. Before that, God is not the "supreme being" but, in fact, beyond any conceivable categories of Being whatsoever. According to Western Christian theology, the essence of God is identical to his being. In the East, by contrast, theologians recognize a paradox; according to his essence, God is beyond any category like being or existence. It is only when God "spills over" in love "outside himself" that He becomes the Supreme Being – a role He plays out of love, so that He can create us.

Incidentally, this is why "theosis" has had to be ruled out as a possibility according to Western Christian theology. If God's being is his "highest and truest" self, then were God's being to suffuse us, we would know all that there is to know about God. We would in fact be God in the most ultimate sense possible.

Only if God's essence is even higher and totally other than his "supreme being" could his being flow into us as a gift of grace, deifying us by grace but not making us God by nature. God is not, in his essence, a being like us.

It is only when Christ does empty himself that He takes on being. And this act of self-emptying is his primordial "crucifixion," as well as his primordial "incarnation," in some way that we cannot fully understand or describe. It is a crucifixion because it is an act of kenosis, of self-emptying love.[14] It is an incarnation, in a sense, because He enters the realm of being for the first time, solely in

---

14 Rev 13:8 calls Christ "the Lamb slain from (or even, in some English translations, "before") the foundation of the world" – a mysterious saying to which we have referred before, in our discussion of the Garden of Eden.

order to save us from non-being – in other words, to create. And He enters the realm of being in ten million manifold ways, so that each bit of creation can find that rest in him which is all of him that that particular part of creation can handle. We call Christ's "logoi" these myriad "ways" of his self-offering, "for in him we live and move and have our being" (Acts 17:28).

It's just his tenderness and his mildness that makes him "divide" himself in these ways, like the director of an orphanage who knows each child so well that he becomes something slightly different to each child, since he loves each child in its uniqueness and knows exactly what each child needs and exactly how much of the director's love it can receive. These different ways according to which the director loves the children, each of them inspired by such infinite tenderness, are analogous to Christ's logoi in creation, each one suited to what every bit of creation is able to take and to what each creation deeply needs.

And this is why on Christ's halo in icons we write the words, "The Existing One," i.e., "I Am." He is the Father's agent in Creation in this intimate way of imparting himself as "the being *of* beings," as St. Dionysios the Areopagite so beautifully wrote.[15] He must be the being of beings since, after all, He only takes on being for the sake of all beings! And this is why a Christian glories in creation and glorifies God in the natural world. Everywhere he looks, the Christian sees Christ's self-emptying love sustaining the world.

Comparing the Logoi to the Forms and to the Patterns

Christopher Alexander, as we said, shows that the Patterns in *The Timeless Way* are the source of architectural order. This prompted me to ask whether these rational principles are like the logoi and whether we should therefore posit their participation in the Logos.

---

15 "It is the Life of the living, the being of beings, it is the Source and the Cause of all life and of all being, for out of its goodness it commands all things to be and it keeps them going." Taken from St. Dionysius the Areopagite, *The Divine Names* 589C-D, in Colm Luibheid and Paul Rorem, eds., *Pseudo-Dionysius: The Complete Works* (Mahwah, NJ: Paulist Press, 1987), 51.

In fact, I recently learned that centuries before Socrates, the Greek word "logos" had developed already to include in its meaning what he and Plato would much later signify by the term "Form" (*eidos*).[16] So the Forms of Plato are, by their very definition, roughly equivalent to St. Maximos' logoi.

More wonderfully still, the Pattern-logoi employed by Christopher Alexander are quite clearly "crucified," in the sense that they can exist, they enter existence, Alexander tells us, only by receiving into themselves and bearing *all* the physical and even emotional forces present in a particular building situation. The Patterns don't come into being until they have "gathered in" the entirety of the tension between these many conflicting forces. The Patterns come into being in a place, only when they have received into their "bodies" the entirety of the pressures present there. Only in this "consent" to "crucifixion" do the Patterns manage to become completely Passion-bearing and thus life-giving.

Well, the Patterns, I suppose, are always "willing," but the architect may either not bother, or might not have enough ability to pull it off, or is facing some external constraints on his work.

I should give an example here because this can sound abstract, when in reality it is so concrete. In a Pattern that I like very much, one called "South Facing Outdoors," Alexander notes that a garden or porch built on the north side of a house, no matter how lovely or well-designed, will almost always remain unused. One of the forces present in the situation – in the northern hemisphere, the movement of the sun's warmth and light is present more intensely on the south side of a house or garden – will always fight against the placement of a porch or veranda on the north side.

But in some cases, it seems to be impossible to place the porch on the south, and so the Form "South Facing Outdoors" is neglected and the porch is placed somewhere else. The building is not fully "crucified" by all the forces present – I mean, it neglects to bear the

---

16 Roy Rappaport, "Chapter Eleven: Truth and Order," in *Ritual and Religion in the Making of Humanity* (Cambridge: Cambridge University Press, 1999), 344-370.

weight of this one particular force (that people want to congregate on the south side, not the north) into its being – and so the order that is created is only partial. Such a house may not offer us solace.

Alexander himself thus shows how each of these Forms or Patterns is made present in the world only through its being crucified, suspended, by all the forces present there. And yet, these crucified Patterns are by this same act turning the chaos of the world into real, life-giving order. The well-built house "dies" to the world, the chaos of the world, and in this dying both comes alive and gives life.

Christopher Alexander does not say much of this explicitly. He is not writing as a theologian and probably does not know the cosmology of St. Maximos the Confessor. I believe, however, that in his arguments and demonstrations he proves the accuracy of that cosmology. Alexander shows that each Pattern is not only the presence of order, but also that to achieve order, the Pattern must carry within itself all the forces present in its situation. To me, this suggests that these Patterns (logoi, in my eyes) are "crucified," and that in this crucifixion they become life-giving. Living structure is Alexander's highest concern, and this structure arises only when the "nailing down" of the Pattern by every last force in its context is complete.

Alexander does not mean, however, that the building that is alive should necessarily be flawless, in our ordinary understanding of that term. The "imperfections" in living structure are not a rejection of the Patterns, but, rather, signs that the edifice is straining to the point of breaking to bear those Patterns. The Patterns are repeated not identically but fractally.

Modernist buildings, by contrast, try to avoid this healthy "shame" (the unavoidable imperfections within living structure) by attaining a flashy geometric perfection. They do not bear the tell-tale inexactness and roughness of fractal structure.

The Patterns discerned by Alexander become visible in a place only by a) being completely at the mercy of all the tensions in that place, yet b) also being able to hold that tension together, in their own "bodies," thus conquering them and turning them into life. The building elements that endure for any length of time only do so if they manage to participate in one or more of these Pattern-logoi. Only a building which "consents" to be crucified according to the Pattern of its logos exists, in other words. There is no Resurrection without the Crucifixion.

And thus, in attaining the Forms, buildings or natural things are nourished by and sustained by some dimension of the Logos' crucifixion *for* their sake yet also *in and through* their "bodies." The Forms are the modes by which creation embraces first eros for the Logos and, simultaneously, agape for every other element of creation.[17] Agape is at work in part because, as they allow the Pattern to be born in themselves, created things infused with Form are able to offer solace to the world. It is only through this double movement that they become true – in other words, that they exist.

RTE: Even though we know from St. Paul the concept of being crucified with Christ, it's not an easy idea for Christians who are trying to recover from the "depravity, sin, and guilt" mentality that has been a part of Western Christianity since the Reformation.

DR. PATITSAS: Before the Fall, before the first sin of Adam and Eve, this co-crucifixion was not painful in the way that it is now. Originally, it was the good pleasure of created things to pour out their "lives" for one another, to share their being with other beings.

But since the entry of sin into the world, human beings face exactly this reality that loving self-sacrificially can be painful, and

---

17 In this sentence I have described the threefold way both as if it were sequential (eros comes "first") and as if it were concentric (eros and agape occur "simultaneously"). My defense of this confusion comes in two parts: a) the subject matter demands both descriptions and b) our Savior employs the same rhetorical device when treating this phenomenon. That is, Christ describes the two greatest commandments both sequentially ("the first and greatest commandment") and concentrically ("and the second is like it").

Christ's incarnation is the substance of this paradoxical relationship between eros and agape: since He is both God and man, love for God and love for neighbor are both fulfilled in the single act of loving him; and, yet, Christ is a divine, not a human, person (i.e., He is a divine person who assumed human nature).

Incidentally, this close relation between eros and agape helps make animal therapies effective in the treatment of complex trauma. When presented with an innocent pet to care for, the empathy and care I am moved to show to that animal (something like agape) is instantly bound up with a pull out of myself (something like eros). Together, this constitutes the movement toward truth, toward wholeness.

this is one reason why we cry out continually for God's mercy! Yet and still, this is also one more reason why God so continually *does* show us his rich mercy. People don't ask to be born into such harrowing circumstances as they are, where they have to be practically superheroes just to preserve their own souls. God knows this, and He is therefore merciful.

When in our own lives we attain our likeness to the Logos and in this process are inevitably crucified, this crucifixion can be extremely hard to take. Moreover, it is not God's will that we make this self-sacrifice by force, unwillingly. His own crucifixion was voluntary, and forced crucifixion was not the path originally ordained by God. Rather, our forced sufferings are the tragic echo of two facts: a) that Adam and Eve took on their vision of the Cross while they were still too young and unready and b) in order to do so, "forced" their way to the Cross by entering the portion of the Garden that was forbidden to them.

But when we or creation become really true, the threefold way of Beauty-Goodness-Truth teaches us that even created things – rocks, rivers, animals – must also, in truly existing, therefore also necessarily have become friends with Christ. As his friends, all created things are therefore able to disclose some measure of Christ's secrets to us, if we will only listen. Having begun within, and remained within, eros and agape, created things also have attained philia. And this is what the beauty of creation means – the "friends" of Christ, knowing his secrets, share them with those "who have eyes to see," which is what accounts for the Beauty of the world.

To put this in human terms, when we love Christ through eros, we then find that we must allow him to be incarnate in us – but as the Crucified One. And this consent awakens in us agape, or readiness for co-crucifixion with Christ for the life of the world. Only then can we be called not just Christ's disciples but his friends. And only then can we be the true friends of those who seek healing from trauma or from any issue.

It is the friends of Christ who are beautiful. The beauty they radiate as they complete the threefold way and become further theophanies to the world, is some portion of the secrets that Christ, as their friend, has whispered to them.

So this raises a question for those who would, as artists, create something beautiful: Can the architect be chaste enough, if only for a moment, to conceive such a divine logos, such a Pattern in his work of building? Can the painter see past all that is, to the one thing needful, just long enough to give that one thing the chance to be born? Only in this way will the artist give life to some small corner of the world.

The one thing needful for that artist, of course, is not just Christ the Logos, but the Logos as we in particular have been called to follow him, in the manner we have been given "to see the light" (to paraphrase Abraham Lincoln). Our own peculiar manner of being is our logos. It is all the share in the Logos that we can handle.

Exercising Care for This World Through Liberation from the Cares of this World

We can see that the Pattern – the Platonic Form – once it is attained, is really a crucified logos: crucified, in that it bears suspended within its "body" *all* the physical and aesthetic forces in a given situation; but still logos, because in doing so it imparts an order that gives information and meaning to the situation. A well-realized architectural Pattern is like an appearing of the Holy Cross within the world, and we run to that cross for shelter because in the shade of the Cross we are protected from the withering heat of oppressive disorder, chaos, egotistical opinion, and vain obsession with appearance. In the case of architecture, the realization of the Patterns gives us life!

"Bear one another's burdens, and so fulfill the Law of Christ" (Gal 6:2). The Natural Law – the name we give to all Good Patterns, in whatever situation they are present – is the Crucified Logos, iconically alive in all things. In some cases, it may be better to say that the Natural Law is simply the Cross, or agape, rather than the actual person of Christ. But we can really see the "accomplishment of all things" (Acts 3:21) at every appearance of the Cross, and this "accomplishing" is no different than the creation of the world itself. Therefore it is to the "it is finished" of Christ upon the cross that the architect and artist must look, if they would create something truly complete. They must give birth to a crucified logos if their art is to endure.

The Cross liberates us from the cares of this world by absorbing within itself the entire tension and sorrow and anxious striving of the world, even unto the worst violence and ugliness possible, and then managing to turn that death into life. We, in turn, are to take care of the world by introducing the Cross within every situation of its life, for the Cross is that instrument which has overcome "the world," and can therefore save the world from itself.

When an architect (and we must include here both the client and the builder) captures a pattern in *exactly* the way that it is meant to be expressed in the particular and unique circumstances that he faces, then he has become, and he has allowed his materials to become, a God-bearer, for he is making room in this world for the crucified Logos. The successful builder has introduced into the world, in some small but infinitely significant way, the Cross – and in so doing, he has overcome the sorrow and chaos of the world. The wise team of designers has cared for the world, delivered it from decay and destruction, by liberating it from the cares of the world and therefore placing it in the consoling embrace of Christ crucified. They have helped to place within this fallen world its other-worldly *telos* in Christ God; not sacramentally, but to the extent that such a thing is possible for the world outside of the life-giving mysteries found within the Church.

The good architect may indeed give birth to a logos, but of course he is not *exactly like* the Theotokos. He *has* turned his corner of the world into a place where the act of creation, the incarnation of the logoi – being – is happening. But only in the Church do the next two levels of emergence/creation transpire; namely, well-being and ever-being. There, through the sacraments, a quantum increase in the depth of the Logos' presence is realized.

That is why "the Quality without a Name" is not the Uncreated Light but rather a bright shadow of that Light (if we could express it in this paradoxical way); it is real *being*. In plain fact, buildings that lack the Patterns aren't quite "real"; they don't exist completely. They won't last for long, for one thing – they fall apart *or* in time are rejected by their users and allowed to fall apart.

But still this wonderful and luminous quality is not *well-being*, and it is not yet *ever-being*. It is not the Uncreated Light – although it is an icon of that Light, since it may trigger within us an openness to that Light!

RTE: Why then does "The Quality without a Name" have this mystical taste – so vivid and real – when it isn't the Uncreated Light? Beautiful landscapes and towns, art, and nature can move you to the depths.

DR. PATITSAS: Because wherever the Patterns are realized, Being is realized – and there is something mystical in being itself, since all creation is a foretaste of the personal incarnation of the Logos. All creation takes its deepest being from Christ. Saint Dionysios the Areopagite described God as "beyond being" and therefore able to be "the being of beings." Creation itself shines with the light of theophany, not because it is God, but because it is suffused with the love of God for it and for us.

Symbols, Forms, and Sacraments

The Areopagite often speaks of "the symbols" when describing the structure of creation in the Church – and by "symbols," he means the Mysteries, the sacraments. And these symbols/sacraments can be understood as a kind of super-Form, because whereas ordinary Forms impart being when we participate in them, the "symbols," i.e., the Church sacraments, impart well-being and even ever-being.

This is why no ordinary soul-healer can equal the power of the priesthood and of sacramental grace. The healer may nurture your being, but your soul will feel incomplete until it receives well-being. And, at the end of our life, despite these ministrations by our priests, our soul will still long to be with the Lord and his mother more completely. No matter how much we experience this sacramental well-being, a time will come when we will desire to put off even this, or rather to see it "swallowed up," in order to accept the ever-being granted to us in the next life.

The dynamism that the Lord imparts to creation is imparted through the pull of his infinite Beauty, and this infinite pull gradually awakens an infinite push toward him on our part. This "push" has an unfolding aim: non-being longs for being; being, in turn, longs for the sacramental blessing of well-being; and well-being is progressively filled with the desire to put off this earthly life and be with the Lord in the state of ever-being. And then, even in heaven, our eros will still never be satisfied. We will progress endlessly "from glory to glory," as St. Gregory of Nyssa tells us. Or, as C.S. Lewis expressed this same idea, we will always desire to go "further up, and further in."[18]

Christopher Alexander also understood this progressive quality to human desire, for he says that once we have attained unto the Quality without a Name, then even the Patterns can be dispensed with. For then, *we* become the Pattern, or we become a new Pattern, in a way; our participation in the Quality is even more immediate. And this higher vision can reverberate back into art – for even the best architecture cannot be reduced to a "precious" attitude about preserving the correct building Patterns; innovation is possible and even necessary.

In the Church, we see this development when saints apparently "suspend" the laws of the Church, the ways or patterns laid down over the ages, because their approach to God is mediated by the super-Forms directly.[19]

---

18 C.S. Lewis, *The Chronicles of Narnia: The Last Battle* (London: The Bodley Head, 1956).

19 It seems to me that there is some hierarchy within the world of Forms. The Patterns are lower than the Forms, which are lower than, perhaps, scientific laws. Sacraments, meanwhile, are greater than all of them – but at a higher quantum level entirely. Perhaps the

The sacraments of the Church (what I am calling these Super-Forms, or even Super-Patterns) share in what the Theotokos accomplished because, although the Incarnation of Christ is a one-time event, everything in the Church points to this event and participates in this radical change in the fortunes of the entire Creation. In fact, by analogy, this unrepeatable Incarnation and Panaghia's role in it is also our surest guide for making art, as it teaches us exactly how we must approach the mystery of letting Christ be born within us.

Of course, the ultimate art is to live a life in Christ "for the life of the world."

The Triumph of Orthodoxy; or, the Logoi as Invitations to a Mystical Wedding with Christ

We say that the icons are the triumph of Orthodoxy, but why? Not only because they depict the fact that Christ God became incarnate man but also because they show that a merely human person, his mother, could receive God into incarnate existence.

They show, in other words, the possibility that human beings can worship God in spirit and in truth (Jn 4:24) and, in so doing, become vehicles for God's concrete and visible presence in this world.

I mean, icons show not only the triumph of God's love for and intervention in the world, but they show also the possibility that the world could bear God, could be a fitting place for God to dwell. Icons show us that a human person could bear the image of God, could through eros and agape be filled with the fullness of healthy shame (the glory) that enables them to attain the glorious likeness of Christ. They show that while remaining still human, we can further God's appearing in the world in our own persons. In icons,

---

canons of the Church belong in the same realm as the sacraments, not on an equal level, but in that their concern is the "way of salvation" for the Christian faithful.

Christ the Logos, meanwhile, whose self-sharing is the root of all these "ways" of being (and of well-being, and of ever-being), remains free with respect to all of them. He can help us make a bad Pattern in a building come alive; can redefine beauty when needed; and can suspend scientific laws, as in his own Incarnation.

we see that humans and creation can bear God's glory when they behave in an orthodox manner.

Icons are creation doing what creation does best – "capturing" the invisible God in a mystical reflection. They are the triumph of *orthodoxy* because they demonstrate that correctly glorifying God has the triumphal power to welcome God into the world, thus saving it.

The Patterns, the Forms, work in a similar way. They are God's interventions in the world, modes of the self-disclosure of Christ. But at the same time, these interventions are not rude impositions; they are more like invitations.[20] Like the gospel message itself, they summon, not crush. The logoi of creation are the self-emptying of the Logos in that they are his descending into the world, and also in that they are the manifold ways that He offers himself to the world.

The Patterns arise into being only when these invitations have been received by the realm of created matter. They are the evidence that creation (in the case of a house being built through the skill of an architect) has responded correctly by giving "right glory" to this condescension of God in the Forms. If the creation consents to receive the logoi in their vulnerable self-offering, then the world takes on form; both the world and the Forms/logoi come to be – exist – at the same moment, in a mutual embrace and a sacred wedding. The logoi are the wedding invitations of Matthew's Gospel (Mt 22:1-14).

---

20 I formed this idea that the logoi are "invitations" from a theme in Jane Jacobs' *The Nature of Economies* (New York: Modern Library, 2000). For the inner principles (of natural materials, processes, or even problems) the discerning of which is the basis of economic innovation, Jacobs uses the term "messages," even stating that these principles within creation are "invitations" for us to cooperate in the forming of a human-friendly cosmos – a humane, prosperous, well-rounded economy.

Of course, neither Jacobs nor Christopher Alexander uses the term logoi, and neither do they reference Plato's Forms. But I think that these authors are all the more valuable to us in that they are showing in an unforced, non-dogmatic way that these ancient concepts are still of vital practical significance. And, to an extent, their insights about these themes (for example, Jacobs' implication that the inner principles of nature are like messages or invitations) significantly adds to our theological understanding of what the Fathers must have meant. Of all the lovely aspects of this discussion, the idea that the logoi are *invitations to a wedding feast* is one of the loveliest. (Ed. note: Perhaps the "wedding garments" symbolize our willing participation in our appointed logos.)

But, if the world does not dare to offer hospitality to the Patterns – does not manage to glorify God – then both the world and the Forms remain outside of intelligible being. In the case of the world, because it remains chaotic and at war with itself; in the case of the Forms, because they somehow "hover" *beyond* created being, remaining aspects of God's *uncreated* energies that are still "hid with Christ in God" (Col 3:3). *Neither* the Forms *nor* the world exist until they *both* do, together, in a wedding embrace.

Again, in order for the creation to receive the Patterns, to show hospitality to Christ's condescension in his logoi, creation (and in the case of paintings and buildings, the human artist or architect) must consent to be crucified along with Christ. The world must respond to these invitations not only in admiring eros but in co-suffering agape. The building that would receive the Patterns must be built in such a way that all the forces in its environment are accounted for and borne within its structure and design. The building hosts the Forms by bearing within itself all the forces that the Form must "suffer" in order to appear there. This is the way a building is "co-crucified" with and within the Pattern/Form/logos, thus gaining its relative permanence.

In the case of the doorway to a home, the co-crucifixion is also the "death" that, for example, the specific doorway "dies" to the thousand other ways that it could be a doorway, but that would not fully capture the Pattern in this particular place. The precise shape and placement and materials used – all this precision, this fixing, all this "it must be exactly this and no other way," this *nailing down*, is of course a crucifixion – until the doorway becomes so Good, so fully carrying all the forces there, that it is True, and thus also radiantly Beautiful to an extent that cannot be pictured before the door has actually been built. This is not how we build doorways anymore.

RTE: Will the attempt to make the door of the building good then inevitably make it beautiful? Haven't you been saying all along that we go the other way, from Beauty to Goodness to Truth?

DR. PATITSAS: One of the mistakes of *our* using the truth-first approach is that this approach belongs properly to Christ. He is the Logos, the Truth, who consents to the Goodness of self-emptying, and thus shines out radiantly as Beauty. For him, the progression is Truth-Goodness-Beauty.

We ought to respond to this in the reverse: when we behold this Beauty, we are born, and then strive to become Good by accepting to live self-sacrificially, and finally, with time, we manage to become True. We *mirror* his progression, in other words, which is what marks us as "good and faithful servants." We ascend where He has descended.[21]

However, when you capture a form in art or architecture, both progressions are happening at once. You, going by your aesthetic feeling in response to the Beautiful Form, are adjusting and adjusting until what you make becomes good in the sense that it is faithfully and honestly bearing every force at work in your painting; if you manage this, you will have made a work of art that is true – i.e., that will last forever.

---

21 For Christ God, the order is truth-goodness-beauty; for us, his creation, the order is the mirror image, of beauty-goodness-truth. Reader Georgia Williams has asked whether the different gender callings of men and women spelled out in Chapter Five show a parallel to this symmetry. That is, man is called to kingship, inscribes priesthood within his kingship, and comes to rest as a symbol of the prophet. A woman, meanwhile, is called to prophecy, inscribes priesthood within that calling, and comes to rest as the symbol of the king.

Furthermore, she continued, a third pole on the parallel would be the way in which, in the world of Neoplatonic hierarchies, the same rules apply. The higher levels of a hierarchy unfold into the lower levels, while the lower levels ascend into the higher ones, in a relationship of desire and love. Woman is therefore the manifestation or the unfolding of man, and man is the enfolding or the embrace of woman.

I think these are excellent insights, to which I would add two points. First, St. Paul describes the following gender hierarchy: God the Father is the head of Christ, who is the head of the man, who is the head of the woman. We should extend this to say that the woman, in turn, is the head of the children, and the children, finally, are meant to crush the head of the serpent. That is, the children are meant to crush sin, death, illness, and the devil, while becoming forces for the victory of cosmos over chaos in the world. What is mothering, in the end, but helping children to conquer all these negative forces by nurturing and teaching them to become good, healthy, spiritually pure, and complete adults? Even in the act of nursing a sick child, the mother's aim is that the child will vanquish the illness and grow up to be an adult – that is, someone who is generating order in the face of the waves of disorder thrown at us by life.

As for the reference to the Neoplatonic hierarchies, this is a nice image because it shows why gender helps us to love, and how the mystery of marriage and gender enables a man and a woman to play out the primordial ecstasy of creation.

But while you, the artist, are making these adjustments guided by your aesthetic sense, at the very same time, from the other direction, the Form, the Truth – Christ – is condescending to shoulder more and more of the forces of chaos present in the particular artwork you are creating. That is, He is *doing* more and more Good and *being* more and more Good in that work of art or building. Until, when the artist has allowed the Form to be completely Good, the true building or painting at last radiantly appears, and in it Christ shines out as the Beautiful.

So even as the artist proceeds in one direction, he or she is mystically met by Christ, rushing to meet him from the other direction, rewarding the Prodigal's return.

But if the artist tries to be "creative" in some false, egotistical, *ex nihilo*, and truth-first way, or if at the other extreme the artist looks firstly to a pre-existing blueprint of Beauty which he intends to impose upon the world, then things won't turn out so well. Rather, he must be "stupidly" guided by his *feeling for* Beauty, or the building or painting won't come alive. Once again a chiasm is at work, for as God descends, we ascend, in a union that is also an exchange of places.

The reality of all this is so beautiful and so sublime: it is not by seeking to create a beautiful image but by falling wholly in love with Beauty that we ourselves become Beautiful. In this, what we do and make discloses both God's and our own Beauty to the world. By forgetting the world and ourselves, we help to save the world – and we ourselves (or our art) become immortal.

Patterns vs. Blueprints

RTE: How would that play out in the case of an iconographer whose work often increases in beauty and value as it comes closer to the original prototype? Surely that is looking to a pre-existing image of Beauty?

DR. PATITSAS: The purpose of a prototype in icon painting is to prevent the icon painter from imposing his or her own ego, in the form of his own mental picture, upon the wood. The process is designed, that is, so that the artist neither paints to his own blueprint nor seeks to create *ex nihilo*. The Prototype used in icon painting is itself a Pattern, a Form, which even if the final result seems to mimic, has guided a living birth and not a dead repetition.

When a Pattern is followed in icon painting, the question becomes, can the iconographer receive that Pattern of the archetype into the wood? When the iconographer first looks upon the original blank wood, he should see nothing less than his own "cross," a sacred, life-giving wood upon which his own ego and all his false images will be crucified, and upon which the world itself will be crucified to him – he will no longer be its slave. This is icon painting.

A Pattern, an archetype, is something living; it trembles, it sways with the passage of time. A blueprint, by contrast, is something fixed; it is suitable if you would guide the creation of a machine but not for the generation of a living organism. The artist is trying to give birth to a living being and so requires a living seed, not a dead one.

When Christopher Alexander designs a building, he first draws "clouds" of the rough shape and location of its elements, and is careful not to crystallize any part of the structure with a final shape even one moment before it is absolutely necessary to do so. When he designs a porch for example, the early drawings are cloudlike, and then as each additional Pattern is added to the project, the clouds "condense," thus revealing a more specific, but now living, form. But even at the end of the design process, a cloudlike element remains – final determinations will have to be made on site, by the builder himself during the process of construction. For Alexander, the architect and the builder should be one person, if possible.[22]

---

[22] Of course, there may be other ways of designing. We are highlighting Alexander in this chapter partly because he describes an arc of emergence that we find also in the natural world. In other words, in the history of creation, generalities steadily give birth to specificities, and these specificities in turn serve as the general framework for still further stages of refinement, development, or emergence.

In Orthodoxy, we even have our own equivalent to Christopher Alexander's *A Pattern Language* – entire volumes giving the Patterns for each type and style and part of an icon. The most famous one is by Dionysios of Fourna[23], and there is another by Photis Kontoglou.[24]

So, a prototype in the icon painting process plays the role of a theophany, a shining out of Beauty. And, in falling in love with this Beauty, the painter takes it as his "spiritual father," his guide to that path of asceticism and self-purification which every artist must pursue. The prototype is meant to be an aid to the denial of his passionate individualism, promoting instead his truly personal development. This is effective because by allowing himself to be led by the prototype, the painter repents of the passions within himself that would wreck his reception of the Form. He avoids the rock star individualism of the this-worldly artist.

His prototype is an imageless image – an icon – already, so the paradox is built-in, if you see what I mean; he is guided not by a "blueprint" but by the ultimate expression of artistic pattern language, Christ Incarnate.

RTE: Tradition tells us that St. Luke was the first iconographer. What was his prototype?

DR. PATITSAS: His prototype was that person who summed up and perfected the entire patterned response of Israel to God – the Mother of God. He had as his prototype the Person who had disclosed an invisible God as visible – yet without limiting God to his visibility.

The level of artistry required to paint icons takes repentance; that is, eros unfolding into agape. When an icon painter paints, there is as much emphasis on revealing the image of God within himself or herself as on painting it upon the wood before him. The two images of God (within himself and upon the wood) arise at the same moment, mutually reinforcing each other.

---

23 Dionysios of Fourna; trans. by Paul Hetherington, *The Painter's Manual of Dionysios of Fourna* (Oakwood Publications, 1990).

24 Photis Kontoglou, *Expression of Orthodox Iconography* (Ekfrasis Tis Orthodoxou Eikonografias) (Athens: Astir Publications, 1977).

Christopher Alexander is saying the same thing in a different way. For him, giving birth to a living form requires an act of repentance in the architect. This artistic repentance consists in forgetting himself utterly, stripping himself naked of all affectation and inauthenticity. For Alexander, too, the prototype being looked to by the ideal architect is not some ironclad law, but is the invisible Patterns seeking to be born in the building he is making. The artist must "look to the invisible," if his art is to come alive!

The icon painter prays to the saint that he is attempting to depict because the most we can offer to the Forms and Patterns is hospitality. Ultimately, it is up to the saint if he or she will consent to become present in the work we are doing. To prepare for this, the iconographer will undergo an inner process whereby the icon being painted will be something alive rather than a photocopy of the prototype. In looking to the sacred prototype, the iconographer is looking to the Form and also is being freed of his own notions and images. The invitation offered by the Form is met by an invitation of his own, a counter-offer, if you will, for the Form to take shape within his art. And then he must wait for the saint or for the Lord to "agree" to become visible in this art.

RTE: You say, "...if the saint will consent to be incarnate in the work we are doing." Does this mean the Forms are also somehow animate?

DR. PATITSAS: The Forms are sacramental, in one sense, for they are mystical ways in which Christ discloses himself to all creation. But because Christ is the Way, the Truth, and the Life (Jn 14:6), we can also say that the Forms are not only his self-offering to the world, the truth about the world, but that they are Christ himself – not in his full substance but because they convey a partial share in his life.

Scientific Laws Are Forms by a Different Name

Does this Neoplatonic account seem too mythical? But it was originally formulated as an attempt to give a rational account of the order found in the world. The ancients didn't have a crucial part of science, the scientific method. But they *were* trying to give coherent accounts of what they observed in the cosmos. And is their explanation really so different than our own creation story, the creation story of our physicists?

Physical scientists of our day also believe that the universe had a beginning, a moment when it came to be "from nothing." Our scientists also believe that from that first moment, the unfolding of order was guided according to natural laws that in a sense pre-exist the cosmos. Scientific laws are only made visible in nature, but they also control nature, and are not the same as the rest of nature in that way.

In some sense, the natural scientific laws that physicists and mathematicians study are the midwives of nature, and are themselves born into nature from some place outside of it. Our minds cannot capture every dimension of this puzzle, but I think it's obvious that when scientists today talk about universal scientific laws, they are in fact utilizing one of *our* culture's terms for "the Forms"!

And yet, the existence of scientific laws doesn't annihilate our freedom, even if they necessarily channel that freedom. Our entrepreneurs and inventors can only create a new technology or a new device by cooperating with and balancing among these scientific laws. Just as in the homes and cities described by Christopher Alexander, so also in a new technical product, the laws of nature are somehow "captured," made present, fully embodied. Knowing and discovering scientific laws can thus be a gateway to freedom – not submission to a sentence of slavery. Of course, we can also incarnate these laws of nature in ways that hurt or kill, but for Alexander this would only mean that we were behaving one-dimensionally. We need to see that the Patterns include and even transcend the lower-level Forms present in the scientific law in that they also apply artistry and art and moral feeling.

For we are not saying that a building that is well-engineered has somehow therefore captured all of the Forms. There are the Forms as scientific laws, by which perhaps something destructive yet sturdy could be created. And then there are the Forms within art and architecture, which are not only technically correct but which also shimmer with this aura of pure being. They are not mere matter but a cosmos; genesis has truly happened here.

I remember that when Wynton Marsalis taught a master class in jazz, he had these very advanced students memorize and play the greatest improvisational jazz compositions, really lengthy pieces, note for note, even though this would seem contrary to the practice of freedom that is synonymous with jazz. But this was not because he wanted to kill his students' freedom but rather because he wanted to refine that freedom, to let his students know how the freedom of earlier, truly great, "canonical," jazz musicians had felt in its frank and full expression. He could have instead insisted that his students simply "be creative," but for most, that would have meant throwing them back on their own self-generated, egotistical, and less than genius expressions of improvisation. So, submission to the canonical compositions was a subjection to necessity that taught these budding artists what *true* freedom is and feels like.

In this way, in this approach to teaching, what we can see is how pure freedom has at the same time a kind of absolute inevitability, a type of *Necessity* within it. The original musicians composed those pieces as expressions of unrestricted liberty. Yet once they had done so, a fellow jazz genius could see that these compositions had to have been *exactly* as they were, and not in the slightest way different than what they had freely been made to be, in order to express what they did and be as beautiful as they were.

This example of teaching by Wynton Marsalis is a good demonstration of the way in which law is needed to teach us freedom, and also of the way in which only freedom can give to law existence and life. Without freedom, the law cannot "come into being," cannot become visible. And yet without law, there is no substance to the product of freedom; its highest expression remains merely an arbitrary whim, a puff of smoke. Such one-dimensional freedom will achieve nothing, will produce no new state of being. Only acts of freedom which arise to ultimate significance – to a lawlike character – are truly inspiring. They *demand* our attention and our respect.

While in a truth-first approach law and freedom are continually at war, in the Beauty of Christ this grinding conflict is overcome. There is something more than law or freedom at stake, some other dimension. And this, I think we have already said, is why St. Dionysios truly was both a Neoplatonist who believed that God "had to" create, and a Christian theologian, who believed that God had created in pure freedom.

Obedience and Freedom as the Path to a Unique Personhood

Similarly, obedience in the spiritual life is not usually what we have made it to be – a martial and military affair of blindly following a command. Rather, we should normally translate the word "obedience" as fidelity, or faithfulness. Because when we are attempting to be faithful to another person, or in expressing undying love to another person, we can see how law and freedom are unified by some third force, some higher catalyzing power. A love that is stronger than death is a love that is the highest law, the force to which all else must submit – including obedience itself.

Therefore, what is needed in spiritual obedience is not for us to march like lemmings off cliffs, especially not in the service of those who have never dared to live themselves.

Because isn't it obvious, anyway, that in a genuinely loving relationship, at those moments when we must "break the rules" our beloved has set forth because an unprecedented situation clearly demands it, it obviously follows that in breaking the rule we still do not break the relationship. Rather, we simply move forward from dependence on the rules to an even more immediate dependence on the person who gave them. At such moments of "disobedience," the beloved person is suddenly the sole content of our thoughts and prayers and hearts and minds. We are conscious of the magnitude of what we are doing in disobeying, all of which only makes us closer to them. We have, in those moments where we must break a rule, become *more* faithful and obedient to the person, not less. We are positively obsessed with their inner heart – and are willing also to be rebuked, if we have perhaps understood the situation incorrectly. Saint Paul was very clear that freedom should not be abused as an excuse to sin (Gal 5:13).

RTE: And yet Christ was obedient unto death.

DR. PATITSAS: After He double and triple-checked what God's will was, all night in his prayers at Gethsemane! Christ was obedient to a Person, to his heavenly Father. And He was disobedient to the Law as it had been distorted and misunderstood by fallen human beings. We can't exactly match our inner experience to that of Christ. But when we have to "break a rule," as in the episcopal practice of *oikonomia*, this is because we are passing from a simple rule up to the Living Way himself. I think this is not hard to understand.

The canonical rule is like an icon, but sometimes we must *ourselves* become the icon, as the hierarch does when he lives out Christ's crucified love in exercising *oikonomia*. This is a kind of "stepping down" into the world, as Christ did. But at other times, a more ordinary way must apply, of helping the person himself to become "Christ crucified" by living out what the canons or ways imply. The canons are also Patterns, Forms, in other words, which transmit life. They have this sacramental dimension.

The tension between freedom and obedience that is always present within authentic life is also at work when an icon is painted from a prototype. One kind of dead law, a blueprint, is a product of my own or another's imagination, of someone's ego, perhaps. When attempting to perform a great piece of music, we may not always copy it note for note except when it is done as a practice or a homage, like Marsalis's students did. Even in classical music, an expert will remark as to whether a performer is playing mechanically or in a living way.

So, painting according to a prototype involves us in a dying with Christ because it is a joining of ourselves to a previous and greater iconographer's dying with Christ. In the case of the artist or iconographer, this co-crucifixion is experienced as the death of his passions; nothing of himself remains in the art, except what is completely personal between him and others and Christ. Nothing of his "general human nature" remains in the work, except that part of this nature that is now completely caught up in an utterly personal expression. This is a paradox – the work becomes *personal* only if the ego is removed. And so, despite the copy's fidelity to the prototype through this "death," some resurrection is granted – this new icon will be not only faithful to its prototype but also unique to the life and skill of its painter.

RTE: Is being itself always personal? Is every bit of creation personal, in some sense?

DR. PATITSAS: In Paradise before the Fall it was that way. Every bit of nature there was subservient to the personal communion of Christ with Adam and Eve. Only after the Fall and our expulsion from Paradise does our world become an impersonal one, where we often wrestle with nature, battle over resources, or even consider creation to be more important than God.

We are, since the Fall, afflicted with passions which are not submitted to our personal identity. These passions drive us in impersonal directions, expressing nothing more than our common fallen nature. But if we are able to re-capture the energies behind these passions by reinscribing the Cross within the very last farthing of our nature, then the powers they have distorted will become personal again. Then, "only the face shows," as we said earlier.

Information Is Always Physical: Making the Forms Exist

All of these insights are reinforced by something that Information Theory tells us about information itself: Information Theory[25] does not recognize anything as information *until* it is physical. This may originally have been because the main inventor of Information Theory, Claude Shannon, was concerned with modeling communication across telephone wires. He wasn't attempting to invent a metaphysics or a cosmology (although right from the beginning some people saw that his work had such significance) but to test ways to improve the quality and reliability of long-distance telephone calls.

Nevertheless, his insistence that "information" is always something embodied and concrete spares us from unhelpful abstraction. Even so, Christopher Alexander insists that we not think we have discovered a new Pattern about architecture *until* we have managed actually to create this Pattern in the world, physically, at least once.

Moreover, Alexander insists that the continuing physical existence of a Pattern in a specific instance in a building or town is imperiled unless *all* the forces of chaos are accounted for in that situation where the Pattern is being embodied. Unacknowledged forces – such as the fact that people simply don't feel comfortable with certain arrangements of their living spaces and cities – will tend to leak out and destroy those elements of the Pattern which *are* in good shape. For example, one reason really well-designed city neighborhoods become gentrified and even gaudy is that there are so many

---

[25] In the 1940s, Claude Shannon invented Information Theory, a branch of mathematics that describes communication as a special kind of entropy in which the relative unpredictability of a signal helps us predict whether it might carry meaning. Information therefore exists along a continuum between two extremes: pure randomness and incessant homogeneity. For example, if you meet someone new at a party, if they a) speak gibberish or b) drone on endlessly and predictably, you will realize that there is nothing to be learned and move on. Somewhere in between chaos and repetition, a new signal holds the possibility of actually having a message for us. It is worth noting that Information Theory leads to a philosophical conclusion: namely, that a thing only exists by virtue of its not being other things, and also by not being chaos. This is expressed with the little aphorism, "It from Bit," or Existence from Information. It is impossible not to think of the logoi when hearing this saying, and of the way they balance diversity and unity in a stable shape. Claude E. Shannon and Warren Weaver, *op. cit.*

poorly-designed neighborhoods, and so people are "leaking out" into the few worthwhile places, overwhelming them through their very appreciation.

So, a well-executed Pattern – or Form, or logos – must account for everything going on around it or soon fail. Apparently, this is very hard to do even in nature. Landscapes are constantly shifting, climates inevitably changing, and so forth. In fact, since scientists anticipate the eventual heat death of the physical universe (the end of all things through inexorable processes of universal decay), our world itself can be seen to contain "Information" only tenuously. The cosmos enjoys only a provisional existence; it cannot master all the chaos roiling within it.

At the Fall of Adam and Eve, a fatal warfare in the world was introduced which is permanently overcome only in Christ. As He is the Being of all Forms, whether artistic ones or scientific ones, only Christ can lend the Patterns and Scientific Laws any real stability, can order them all within himself properly and totally. He does this on the cross, and through his resurrection.

The existence of a Pattern in a town or building will not be even relatively stable unless the architect has really accounted for every single one of the forces in the context where he is trying to establish his Pattern, and has brought each of these forces within the body of the now-crucified Pattern. In other words, if the Pattern is captured poorly, it won't last; it will collapse, it will disappear from that place. But since Information Theory tells us that information has to be physical in order to exist, then this collapse, this erosion and washing away of what has been built, would mean that information was "departing" from this corner of the world. The loss of a good Pattern is like a reverse incarnation, a receding of the Logos present within that particular place. But this means, in turn, that the world gets "dumber" when we can't build according to good Patterns. Our world, when designed poorly, does not inspire or calm us, but leaves us struggling with feelings of meaninglessness.

The Absence of Good Patterns Makes Man a Stranger in the World

I can give you a simple example of the way certain "forces" in the built environment are or are not accounted for. In the very beautiful building where I work, the grand entrances were wisely placed at the center of the structure, off of central brickways and roadways, so that one could enter the building with dignity and then calmly proceed up the central staircases to whatever part of the building one desired.

But with time, the most beautiful entrance was closed because another force had to be accounted for – the need for the offices located near that entrance to have quiet and privacy once this mansion built for a family had become the workplace of dozens of people. Meanwhile, there was a need to alter the grand entrance on the opposite side of the building, because the larger number of visitors in an institutional setting means that we need to locate a receptionist where an additional set of central stairs would have gone.

So, these architectural make-do's are logical in their own terms and certainly do resolve certain forces, but they leave many other forces in the situation unaccounted for. Because now if we professors and staff come in at the second center entrance where the reception area is located, we must then proceed all the way to the far end of the building to find a staircase, climb the stairs, and then march all the way back to the other side of the building to our offices. One of the forces present in this situation is our need to make good use of our time, so instead we all use the less-welcoming far entrances – we enter past the dumpster on one side, or over a muddy grassy knoll from the parking lot on the other.

Now, we could recognize the Pattern trying to be born by examining the frustration felt by all who use the building, and then we could either build the central staircase to the upper floors that was never put in near the reception entrance, or we could put nice pavers along the goat path that some faculty have tried to wear into the grass over the decades. But – operating by a blueprint mentality –

we instead keep insisting on a pattern that is not real, and just keep reseeding those paths with grass.

Since not all of the forces in the "entrance" Pattern are resolved in the current configuration, none of these entrances is alive, and none of this is stable, and none of it makes sense – in other words, it is not "informational." That is, so long as major forces are unaccounted for, the Pattern-Form of "Building Entrance" is only tentatively present, and logos (Information) remains unwelcome in the experience of using these entrances. And so we who work there absorb these unresolved tensions into our own psyches and bodies.

I purposefully give this example from my own workplace, precisely because the *people* I work with are all so welcoming and humble, and therefore I am happy. But still the fact that every morning I enter work through a kind of furtive entrance, or over mud, or after a long out-of-the way back and forth walk, is typical of life everywhere in supposedly oh-so-convenient modernity, formed as it is by the truth-first approach to buildings and to art. You see these minor but telling assaults on human dignity in every corner of our built environment.[26] Our buildings are not beautiful, they lack utility, they don't promote human dignity, and we all secretly want to destroy them – they are not true, they are not "saved," and in some decades will not be thought worth saving.

Only the appearance of the Cross can make us feel welcome. In the case of buildings and cities, the Cross appears *only* when the Patterns are captured so that all the forces in a situation are accounted for and are allowed to work upon the shaping of the design. It's almost as if we have to allow every force its "shot" at crucifying the Form, for "that which is not assumed will not be healed."

---

26 There is a "best practice" way now being used on American university campuses that resolves the muddy goat path problem: don't put in *any* walkways between buildings, and just wait to see where people naturally walk by how they wear out the grass. (Search Google Images for, "desire paths," to get an idea of what this looks like.) Then, put your pavers there over the paths created by actual use, with the result that your paths will be more alive. This way, there will be no conflict between ontology (the actual forces present within your pedestrians and between your buildings) and ethics (what you are implying people must do, based on where you have put the sidewalks). And you won't have to ask people to keep off the grass, because they won't want to walk on it anyway.

Anyway, I am not trying to make myself out to be a martyr just because I have to walk a little; it is a small thing. But a Beauty-first culture is built on small things like this, as well as on the bigger things, like human rights. It keeps both. And in so doing, it promotes human dignity in ways that a truth-first approach, or a utilitarian approach, never quite will.

Existence is paradoxical in that *to be*, a creature must bear the twofold anointing. To exist, a thing must participate in a Form or a whole series of Forms, and through that participation must carry in some measure the crucifixion that its Form conveys to it – that the Form "knows" because the Form is a mode of conveying the energy of the Crucified One. Existing things won't exist, won't live, unless they can bear the dying taught to them by the Pattern, and bear this on an ongoing basis. The crucifixion of the Forms, as they bear all the forces in a situation, and the resurrection of the Forms, as this very bearing makes them glorious and real, are inseparable.

Bad art doesn't die thoroughly enough; that's why it never lives completely, and why bad art is almost always eventually discarded by posterity. Its novelty carries it for a little while, makes it seem like information, but when this wears off, the lack of good Patterns and deep information tells. Bad art from the past has historical significance, but it is not valued, it is not "canonical" (it does not itself become a Form or Pattern guiding future art).

Good art, by contrast, carries all the forces in a situation and carries them completely, without remainder, without shirking anything. Good art embraces and thus imitates the crucified Logos. Bad art may bear the crucified Logos, if only in part; but in its partiality, in its failure, it winds up also crucifying the Logos in yet other places, in the places to where its failures "leak," as Christopher Alexander says. One of the places to which the chaos of bad architecture and bad art leaks is into the souls of the people and cultures who behold it.

This isn't so abstract. Thousands of new pop songs are written every year, but 95% of them disappear without a trace. And how many of them will be around in a hundred years? It is simply not easy to say something profound; genius is rare. Authors of books know this equally well!

The Pattern is nothing, in a sense, but a unique way that being must allow itself to be crucified by *all* of the forces present in the situation that the Pattern is meant to heal – and yet, only being that conforms with these Patterns is stable, and only it exists. The Forms are eternal – not because they have always existed but because in bearing their crucifixion, they disclose the "beyond time" of Christ's self-sacrificial love.

The Natural Law is the same way. It, too, is a collection of Patterns that are fulfilled when all of the forces present in a situation are accounted for, held in tension, by our embrace of the crucified Logos. To fulfill the Natural Law around gender and sexuality, for example, always means a crucifixion, that you let the crucified Christ become incarnate within you. Bearing all the tensions in its situation, in each fulfillment of the Natural Law, we as people "bear one another's burdens, and so fulfill the law of Christ." But we could also call the Natural Law, "the Law of Christ," or even, "the Law, who is Christ," for his Law is his *Way* – the way of the Crucified One.

Emergence vs. Evolution

A hundred and fifty years ago, Darwin's theory of evolution captured the imagination of the imperial age of Europe with its account of a brutal yet blind battlefield of random collisions supposedly generating information-rich, living order. Darwinian evolution is best understood as a sort of early, crude name for what we now call "emergence," which signifies the way that in some corners of our world entropy is overcome and order increases.

Strictly speaking, Darwinian evolution was so incomplete a cosmology as to be meaningless, even if it was our best attempt at a rational materialistic account of order's increase out of chaos. Since when does randomness generate order without some intervening set of influences?

Today we recognize the same process by which order increases, but from the proper perspective, as emergence. "Evolution" is all about push and conflict. It was a martial myth appealing to a Europe and America that had conquered the world but were still unaware that they might soon be conquered back. But according to emergence, the greater forces at work in the increasing order on this planet have been pull and attraction and cooperation.

Chaos is chaos; it cannot produce order, except as occasionally in its randomness it may hit upon Christ's logoi, fall in love with them, find refuge in the shade of the cross they bear, and be "captured" by them. A blind battlefield can generate order only if, through the battle itself, information arises that permits some of the combatants to escape the battle. This is the true meaning of Darwinian "survival of the fittest" – some things, in flight from death, manage to run into their logoi and thus transcend, if only temporarily, the war that itself leads only to oblivion.

Knowing this, isn't it surprising how many of the Christians who are horrified by the theory of evolution are themselves relying upon a "survival of the fittest" approach when it comes to the gospel? They present the gospel, or the moral teaching that is inseparable from it, as if they were weapons that should slay all other accounts of the world, should humiliate all non-Christian accounts of right and wrong. It would be better if, in a Beauty-first way, they were to allow the gospel and its chaste life to attract those who are tired of living under the sentence of death imposed by the destructive, disordered desires that afflict all of us. They would then become practitioners of emergence rather than of evolution.

If we are trying to formulate the Christian position on marriage as an irrefutable argument that can conquer any person's mind, however implacably opposed to God or indifferent to faith the heart of that person is, then we have fallen into this evolutionist account of the cosmos. But the Natural Law is more like an *invitation* made to those who would live life abundantly; it is an invitation to their cooperation with the crucified Christ. The Christian teaching on sexuality and what to do when you find your desires going in diminishing directions is an invitation to co-crucifixion with Christ. It is an invitation to die for the life of the world, not a law of logical Necessity that can easily persuade all inquirers. It takes faith.

This is why the Resurrection is more important than the Cross, in a way. Until we begin to overcome our fear of death, have seen the light of Pascha, we cannot possibly begin to bear the many crucifixions necessary in making our lives a living art. We have to look to the Resurrection first, and then take up our cross.

To care tenderly for one's corner of this world, "to nourish it, as one does his own body," as St. Paul says in another context (Eph 5:29), one must consent to the incarnation of the crucified Christ both in the little place that we live *and* within oneself. One must permit our part of the world to become an image of Christ resurrected and yet still, though now joyfully, crucified, as we are all meant to be. One must conceive a logos that is true because its truth bears both beautifully and usefully all the truths of the situation in which it is placed.

Again, to care for the world in this way, one must *also* consent to be so crucified. One must leave aside all opinions and prejudices and dare to be *exactly* who one is, as Christopher Alexander insists the architect-builder must do. It is this exactness that makes up both our crucifixion and our existence. Only the Crucified One lives.

In the execution of a stable Pattern in building, art, or morality, no existential shortcuts have been taken, no easy reductions have been made for the sake of comfort, convenience, or just because it feels like fulfilling the Pattern would be the death of us since it seems so very demanding in this particular instance.

Facing the "crucifixion" of accounting for *all* the forces in some situations can indeed be simply too much for us; genius may be required. But art that endures does so by being comprehensive, by representing more than just some partial aspect of a story or situation.

RTE: Do you think that some might see your urging to be exactly who we are as a license to satisfy desire?

DR. PATITSAS: But for us as poor, weak human beings, desire will be a form of accurate knowing only when, as chaste and ardent eros, it induces us to renounce self-love and to launch out towards Christ in some way, shape, or form. It is only in the process of *that* journey that we are meant to then discover these difficult commandments and become moved to practice them. We can't be who we really are by falling into sin, but rather we become true by consenting to our eros for Christ. The freedom that eros grants is a freedom from death, from sin, from self-love – and from meaninglessness and chaos.

The so-called sexual freedom of recent decades is often a counterfeit version of this. Our weak eros is often nothing more than a greater immersion in self-love, and therefore it leads to the increasing rejection of the Christian commandments that teach us how to love others. This is readily apparent in our degraded sexual morality.

Freedom in Christ leads to diversity, to the uniqueness of the person. Sin leads in the opposite way.

Christianity vs. Neoplatonism

Let me now, in the light of all this, return to something I said before. Please bear with a little repetition. I had mentioned how one of our earliest and most important fonts of Orthodox Christian theology, the mystical theologian St. Dionysios the Areopagite, has come to be seen through the eyes of some scholars nowadays. When many experts look at the work of St. Dionysios, they are divided as to whether he is really a Neoplatonist philosopher masquerading as a Christian theologian or whether he is really a Christian theologian making use of Neoplatonist concepts.

The answer to the question hinges on one crucial issue: Does St. Dionysios depict a God who "had to" create the world? If so, the attribution of Necessity to God would make the Areopagite a Neoplatonist, it is said. Or, does St. Dionysios believe that God could have not created the world, or could have created some other world? If God's creation is described as arbitrary in this way, then in that case, God preserves his distance from creation and remains "free." This voluntarist account is alleged to be the Christian account of creation.

As we said earlier, however, a better approach is to reject all of this as a false dilemma and to see that St. Dionysios is *both* a genuinely Christian theologian who safeguards the freedom of God vis-à-vis his world *and* a philosopher in the tradition of Neoplatonism, for whom God's link to the creation is very deep, very organic. To be sure, St. Dionysios developed the Neoplatonic tradition using insights from Christian faith. But even within strict Neoplatonism, properly understood, it is not the case that God is subject to necessity.[27] Indeed, the alleged conflict between these two traditions is more apparent than real.

But in reading about creativity and creating in the works of Christopher Alexander, I finally saw the matter more viscerally. I could see why the same mystic might be taken by some as a proponent of God's freedom and by others as arguing that God was almost forced to create. It is very surprising, but these two opposite forces of freedom and necessity must be combined when we think about someone as "beyond" as God is. Freedom and necessity are intellectual categories, and neither one can fully capture the mystery of God. In *The Timeless Way of Building*, you are presented with a paradoxical coinciding of freedom and necessity within something that is higher than either of these terms: life itself.

As we've said elsewhere, Alexander observed that people and places possessing the Quality Without a Name express a paradoxical coinciding of the wildest freedom, the purest abandon, on the one hand, and an utter freedom from falseness, on the other. In other words, to be truly alive, to be truly free, is to be exactly and precisely *oneself* – with *no possibility of being in any way different than what one is.*

The "freedom" in which God creates the world is better thought of as a wild abandon, an immediacy that we see in children, in the saints – and in wild animals, too! And in such freedom, such wildness, there is no affectation, no falseness – a person at such a mo-

---

27 Cf. Perl, *Theophany*, 2-3.

ment is exactly who he "must" be. Only in this sense would a Christian Neoplatonist like St. Dionysios allege that God "had to" create. God is the Creator – we can give him that name – not only because He did create but because He *does* create, if you see what I mean.

Freedom and Obedience

This is not an esoteric matter. In what sense, for example, can we be free when we have to obey God's commandments or when we find ourselves in obedience to some authority in the Church? We mentioned this topic just a few pages ago, but it bears repeating. Have I not lost my freedom when I enter obedience? A common form of this question comes when people sense that they have found a real elder. They ask if we must be perfectly obedient to our spiritual fathers or if the relationships could be more of a conversation.

But as we grow in Christ, the opposition between freedom and obedience is itself transfigured and becomes something else – a vibrant and glorious fullness, a coinciding of these opposite terms. Yes, you come to see that sometimes when your father in Christ is asking you to do something, the only thing within you opposing him is a sort of foolish childishness. (Not always, of course! We must be wise.) But sometimes you also see that in obeying this difficult command and putting to death the "old man" in you (who in fact often acts like a spoiled, bratty child and not an "old man," at all), you will be fully free.

And the coinciding can run the other way. Not even our elder will know the secret name given to us by God (Rev 2:17). In fact, many times it will be the exercise of our freedom that reveals even to the elder himself the movement of God's will in our lives, the shape that our future obedience should take.

Therefore, empirically, we often see that it is only obedience that liberates and yet only the exercise of our freedom that can reveal a "commandment" – a "this must be so" – about God's will. You will recognize this as an occurrence of the twofold anointing, yet again. When we have arrived at this coinciding of freedom and obedience, then we have achieved the Form of "Christ (the Resurrected One) Crucified" within our souls and minds and bodies. We now exist "for the life of the world."

After all, the Only-Begotten Son of God is the original bearer of this paradoxical twofold anointing. "When" the Holy Spirit proceeded from the Father in order to rest upon the Son, the Son of God himself lived out this union of obedience and ecstatic freedom. In receiving his anointing from the Father, Christ "overflowed" himself and "gave himself" for the world; Scripture says that "through Christ" the Father made the universe (Heb 1:2). Therefore, we find within the creation of the world both the "Necessity" that is supposed to be the emphasis of the Neoplatonists (for Christ was given to the world by his Father, and the world was created through his obedience to the Father) and the "arbitrariness" within creation that is supposed to be the mark of Christian theology (for Christ's overflowing was an ecstasy, a free self-offering). It is neither freedom nor necessity that controls God's creation of the world; or, rather, both and more than both are at work, for the mystery of creation is something which can never be fully defined – although it definitely includes both freedom and necessity.

So what happens when a human artist fails to exercise his freedom as he "must"? When he fails, in other words, to achieve that coinciding of freedom and obedience that marks true creativity? Most probably, no deep Pattern or Form has occurred in his work – no substantial incarnation, in other words, of a logos. But this is not a trivial matter, for places where the Patterns don't exist remain in chaos. They may be dead places, or even killing places. They are not alive and, far worse, they typically rob us and others of life.

This points to a profound paradox, that until we renounce "the world" and all concern for the world, we cannot care for this world. The wrong kind of concern given to mere opinion or prejudice or even to an attempt to care for the world will itself destroy the act of capturing the Pattern. Only by living in exile from this world can we find our place within it and make it a place where others could live. In the case of freedom and obedience, only by this strange exile from the security both of blind following (necessity) and of arbitrary self-determination (freedom) do we, too, become persons in whom others can find rest.

A spiritual father is not to oppress or command but rather to be a midwife who works with us until Christ be born in us, supporting this miracle of new life which is our Christ-likeness (Gal 4:19). Here again, the spiritual child is like the artist, learning over time to balance the dictates of the artistic canon with the necessity of the new thing that God is calling him or her to do.

How great is Christopher Alexander! Here we have this ancient and vexing question about the operation of freedom vs. the operation of determination in God's creation of the world. Because we can't resolve this question, we remain scandalized by the very theologian, St. Dionysios, who is a crucial font of Orthodox Christian theology. And then there, in *The Timeless Way of Building*, you find this problem resolved just by looking at a mid-century anonymous photograph of gypsy women dancing. You see in Alexander's photos and buildings the perfect (as perfect as a person can bear it) coinciding of freedom and necessity, of freedom and obedience. And, in bypassing this misunderstanding about the conflict between freedom and necessity, you are saved. Moreover, you regain your access to the worldview and tradition of Orthodox Christian theology.

Whenever you meet a saint of the Church, you see this coinciding of freedom and necessity in an even more intense way than in pure art. To quote the American Orthodox architect Andrew Gould, "Any artist experiences a 'need' to create, so artists will have no difficulty understanding this quality of God."

And if such a person is your spiritual father, then you know that he is making this happen in you, as well.

III. HOSPITALITY

The Super-Form of Marriage

In human biological conception, in the act of conceiving a child, we also observe that the act of creation is at once an expression of freedom and a compassionate willingness to be bound to specific circumstance. In bringing a new child into existence, parents show an infinite care for the world by allowing another living icon of Christ, a unique human person, to come to be within them; the mother, of course, bears this especially. This conception occurs through an act that is an ecstasy and a liberation from the cares of this world, and yet which is also a crucifixion, a permanent fastening to one spot. I am talking both about the sexual act within marriage, by which we so powerfully gain and yet lose our freedom, and also about marriage itself.

Marriage is a God-given Pattern, a Super-Form or sacrament, that allows us to care for the world by first liberating us from certain of the cares of this world. In turn, it liberates us from these certain cares — loneliness, hopelessness, the struggle for survival — by accounting for all the forces in the situations of human sexuality and of family, social, and religious life, and then holding these forces in an equipoised fullness. To capture this Super-Form — to get married — is to participate not just in the rational logos but in a *crucified* rational logos. Few people "in their right mind" get married; they fall in love, first. And few people "in their right mind" conceive a child. It is almost always the beautiful rational madness of eros that drives us.

Of course, we could also think of the conception of a child as the opposite of a liberation: that now, with children, we must work so hard and always worry. And of course, this is true in part. In life, we have been saying, freedom and necessity often coincide; another example of the twofold anointing, it seems.

But the greater worry, by far, is shown by those who wish to conceive a child and cannot or by those who, against their will and wishes, live entirely alone.

The problem with our current culture is that we are trying to overcome the sorrows of this world – which include challenges presented by our sexual natures – by trying to avoid being fixed to any particular place. Given that gender itself is a relational force, ineluctably driving us toward and even pinning us to the opposite gender for companionship and sexual relations, if we still want to remain isolated "free agents," lone nomads in this world, then we will have to oppose gender itself. Or, occasionally, people try to make a romantic alliance with someone of their own gender in order to achieve this release from sorrow while avoiding certain sacrifices.

But for the vast majority of people, there are really two main Patterns, two Forms, two *Mysteries* whereby we are granted a transfigured and fully en-gendered experience of our sexes. In them both, gender is embraced. In both, we might be liberated from the negative aspects of gender while also bearing all the tensions that gender brings. These two Forms are monasticism and marriage.

In the case of marriage, it is through our very union as male and female that we receive our liberation from gender itself, to a large degree. It is in the marital transfiguration of gender that we experience the tremendous overcoming of all concerns imposed on us by a fallen world. The point of gender difference is that only it can help us to become "one flesh" with the other gender. This is *literally* true, since the one flesh includes not only the complementarity of male-female anatomy, but also the "one flesh" of the child potentially conceived in male-female sexual relations. And the "one flesh" has this other aspect, that only by respecting male-female difference and the necessity that marriage align one man and one woman, can we show genuine love to our opposite gender, whether we marry or not. No other path than the Christian one is completely loving of the other gender.

Each of Us Must Become Mystical Architects

RTE: Yes, that's very good. Now can we widen the field a bit? From what you are saying, we don't just fall passively into line with the Patterns, no matter how beautiful, good, and true they are. There is more freedom and struggle than that. So how *do* we reach them? Surely our will is involved in our response, and once we have responded, I would imagine that we would attract others who glimpse that particular wholeness in us.

DR. PATITSAS: Each of us must become mystical architects if we are to overcome the destructive attacks levelled at us by a *fallen* world, and show instead care for the *beautiful* world God created. The point of raising children in the faith, or of training any adult in Orthodox Christian faith, is not only so that they can learn Church history and dogma and learn to practice good works. They must first of all acquire the aesthetic sense, the "taste" of life in the Holy Spirit.

We must convey to our children the praxis of mystical unknowing and the practical application of "imageless prayer" by which alone their life can be delivered from control by vanities and "thoughts." And these vanities, which afflict us all, are legion – our own passions, feelings, resentments, our opinions, false leads promoted by educators, cultural blind spots, and so on. These cannot be overcome except by the art of dedication to Beauty. The young Christian must learn this skill so that they can give birth to the crucified and resurrected logos in the situations that they face, and so give life to others and to their world.

Christopher Alexander himself says that if our cities and towns are to come alive, we will need to rely on builder-architects who can apply the mystical process of capturing Patterns during the actual construction of buildings, as well as during the design phase. And he also says that more and more buildings will have to be designed by their own users, with many more of us schooled in this mystical Timeless Way. The example he brings in support of this idea is Japan where, until at least the 1920s, every child was taught how to lay out their own home according to the particular Pattern Languages which had developed from time out of mind in that country.[28]

In Orthodox Christianity, it is no different. Every Orthodox Christian should steadily acquire the taste of the Faith, a sense of its aesthetic quality. And our actions should more and more come to express this ethos. We are the mystical architects, or we must attempt to be, who will build a *cosmos* that provides others with shelter from *chaos*.

Iteration

Now, it is very useful and a big relief to learn that this birth of the Patterns almost never happens except it happen iteratively – or so Alexander tells us. I mean, we don't usually get the Pattern perfect the first time, but rather we make one attempt, see how it is going, and try again, and again, and again. Normally, we allow the Patterns to arise through successive rounds of creativity. And we allow the product of each round to become the starting point for the next round. We try, we pause to reflect on what we have wrought, and then we try again.

I think this is because we must constantly look to the theophany guiding us, rather than becoming so absorbed in our abstract thought about the image we are trying to make. In the same way, we look to Christ, rather than to constant evaluations of our own spiritual progress, as we allow his likeness to appear within us.

This cyclical – or rather, spiral (because as we repeat the steps, we *are* getting closer to our goal) – unfolding of the Patterns should remind us of something else within our Orthodoxy: the daily, weekly, and annual cycle of prayer culminating regularly in the Divine Liturgy itself. The birth of the Patterns and Forms requires liturgy because it usually emerges steadily, like a child developing day by

---

28 Christopher Alexander, *The Timeless Way of Building* (New York: Oxford University Press, 1979), 230: "And in later traditional societies there are bricklayers, carpenters, plumbers – but everyone still knows how to design. For example, in Japan even fifty years ago, every child learned how to lay out a house, just as children learn football or tennis today. People laid out their houses for themselves, and then asked the local carpenter to build it for them."

day within its mother's womb. Liturgy (that is, the general rhythm of Orthodox Christian prayer and worship) combines linear progress with repeated return in order to trace a spiral. Liturgy provides a matrix that is patterned and predictable while also remaining open to something that is always "new" – the ultimate Otherness and the unknown, which we encounter in God.

And, as we said above, the ultimate Patterns – the super-Patterns, the super-Forms – are the sacraments of the Church, "the symbols" that St. Dionysios the Areopagite spoke of. This is why it is wise to ask the Church's blessing on our creative work: we incorporate our artistic hospitality to Beauty into the Church's "super-hospitality" to Beauty.

RTE: How does this iterative character apply in the relationship with a spiritual father?

DR. PATITSAS: Alexander gives this wonderful description of design, as we mentioned before. He says that as a designer lays out a new home or building or what have you, he should at first draw rough shapes. The principle is that the artist should apply only as much specificity to each phase of design as is absolutely necessary. Then, as subsequent sub-Patterns are brought in, the architect can allow these rough shapes to gradually give way to a crystallized form of the overall and earlier patterns.

Alexander says that an architect can follow a design process that allows a building to unfold in much the same way that a new child unfolds within its mother's womb. Each part of the child's body only gradually acquires the full specificity that enables it to function and which also makes it uniquely a part of this particular person and no other. In ancient myth, it was held that the goddess Athena was born whole from the head of Zeus, but human creativity normally should not follow such a divine pattern.

A wise spiritual father usually – though not always – will operate in the same way. They will give you only the minimum of spiritual direction necessary to help you through the stage of your development where you currently are. They do not give you a truth-first final picture of yourself but rather a Beauty-first final picture of your goal – Christ the Resurrected One, triumphant over death.

In contrast, we all know the types of advisers who "call out" your spiritual destiny prematurely in order to show off their own discernment. The harm they cause your soul is great; they are forcing open the petals of a flower, perhaps preventing it from ever unfolding in a healthy way.

The Hospitality of Abraham

RTE: Will you give us an example of a living pattern?

DR. PATITSAS: Each time that I am in Moscow, I try to allocate at least one hour to standing or sitting in front of St. Andrei Rublev's icon, "The Hospitality of Abraham," which is safeguarded in the Tretyakov Gallery. This icon was originally painted for the Holy Trinity-St. Sergius Lavra in Sergiev Posad and for centuries was part of the icon screen in the church which houses the tomb of St. Sergius of Radonezh. In Orthodoxy, this Rublev icon is deservedly regarded as *the* icon of the Holy Trinity. Although a huge city, Moscow is off the tourist path for most people; so even though this is one of the greatest artworks in the world, you can more or less have the icon to yourself on slow days.

There are many profound descriptions of this icon's depiction of the Holy Trinity. All I would add to them is that no photograph of the icon that I had ever seen did more than suggest what it is like in person. One reaction you have when you actually see it is a feeling of relief, that some unacknowledged worry or care inside you is wiped away in its presence. This, to me, is still a surprising reaction.

I think this has to do with what Christopher Alexander says, that when a Pattern is captured well, then no hidden forces are left lurking within it, no subterranean tensions causing worry. Everything is resolved in such a work of art. The Form of the painting accepts all the forces in its situation.

Somehow, seeing the Rublev Trinity icon in a photograph does not convey this liberation, this Sabbath rest which is so longed-for by our tired souls. But you feel it in person. Since there is no falseness in that painting, no seductive or invasive use of the artist's craft, you feel free. And then what was false inside you *also* begins to come out, to float away.

One of the things I began to notice over many visits to this holy icon was a wonderful paradox. Rublev was a monastic, and his icon is held to be our best depiction of the mystery of the Holy Trinity. His is a painting that is perfectly suited to the highest human calling to noetic prayer. It was painted for the Holy Trinity-St. Sergius Lavra, as we just said, which because of its deep mystical life is really the heart of Holy Russia. As a pilgrimage site, the tomb of St. Sergius is second only to the Holy Sepulchre in its spiritual radiance and power; visiting it, you practically become a hesychast on the spot!

But Rublev's Trinity is also our best iconographic depiction of the mystery of human biological conception, for it is precisely in order to grant the gift of a child that the Holy Trinity has come to visit Abraham and Sarah. The Holy Trinity has come to announce to Abraham that his and his wife's prayers for a child were about to be answered.

The Five Hospitalities of Marriage

Our best icon of the Holy Trinity, in other words, is also our best icon of human conception, and the nexus of this surprising paradox is hospitality itself. Both monastic mysticism and marriage are constituted by hospitality.

So, in Rublev's "The Hospitality of Abraham," we may reflect upon the mystery of marriage and its relationship to hospitality, as well as upon the mystery of Trinitarian life and noetic mystical prayer. Within the setting of the icon, I count at least five ways in which a Christian marriage lives only by the exercise of hospitality.

First, in Rublev's painting we see hospitality being offered to the Holy Trinity, to its purity, presence, and creative power. This stabilizes a marriage and may also result in our becoming co-creators with God through childbearing.

Second, we see the paradigm of hospitality to the stranger, whether a saint, a guest, an angel, or God himself (Heb 13:2). This sort of hospitality may also be connected to the miracles of conception and creation because so frequently, by sharing the little we have with guests, we find that God blesses us with the paradox of abundance amidst poverty.

Third, the icon implies that special hospitality which is offered within a marriage to one's own spouse in their particularity and uniqueness. This kind of marital hospitality extends also to each other's emotional and bodily uniqueness, such that a deep peace comes into the home. This total hospitality to the uniqueness of one's spouse is the mystery of monogamy.

Fourth, the icon sets out the hope that we might offer hospitality to our spouse's gender, since it differs from ours. And this, too, leads to creativity and peace; in marriage, through this hospitality to the other gender, the gender war is overcome.

And fifthly, in childbearing, in the openness to receive children, we offer hospitality to the next generation of young people, those who will replace and succeed us.

In exercising these five modes of hospitality, we as married couples tenderly care for the world by renouncing our often *excessive* concern for the world. We are liberated from the cares of this world and are liberated for the proper use and enjoyment of this world. In each instance of hospitality, we realize our dignity as a human soul, the fact that we are each worth more than the entire world.

Hospitality combines eros and agape. It is a reaching out to otherness (an eros) that is simultaneously a taking in, a reception, a co-suffering empathy (an agape). Almsgiving, in the sense of offering each of these five hospitalities, is the substance of marriage.

RTE: In our third interview you mentioned the Natural Law approach to Ethics, and how it unfortunately can become a truth-first derivation of ethical law from meditation on the world as a given, as "Necessity." What do you think of the Natural Law argument that the purpose of sexual relations must always include openness to conception?

DR. PATITSAS: Well, "openness" is a rather expansive concept. The Orthodox Church certainly does not hold that sexual relations between a couple must cease if it is discovered that either the husband or the wife cannot create children.

But if we are trying to draw a sexual ethic from biological teleology, then certainly it must be remarked that a major physical purpose of human sex is the unity of the couple. In other words, evolutionary biologists believe that human sexual unions developed to have a stronger "imprinting" effect upon the partners due to the fact that our offspring are born so much more helpless, and remain so for much longer than those of other species. Sex with a partner makes us one with that partner for the protection of the children that may be produced. Sex is meant to produce a closely allied pair of parents so that they will both stick around to protect and nurture their young for as long as possible. Statistically, this unitive purpose of sex usually predominates over the procreative aspect, in the sense that every sexual union imprints the partners upon each other's five senses and makes them one, while only about one in twenty natural unions is going to result in conception. Therefore, the biological teleology of sex includes this unitive dimension, and even more so once we accept that sex's ultimate purpose is procreation.

In the Church, meanwhile, we see all of this spiritually. Even when children are not biologically possible, the sexual act is part of what makes the couple an icon of Christ and his Church. This holy union is our archetype, and moreover there are other, spiritual dimensions of fertility that arise naturally in the context of a loving Christian marriage.

But let us add another "hospitality" of marriage to our understanding.

And a Sixth Hospitality of Marriage...

The sixth and final hospitality, after which we may "rest," is the hospitality we offer to our son or daughter's spouse, for "the prayers of the parents are the foundations of a young family."[29] In seeing our children properly married, the work of the parents is complete – although this completion may, in fact, involve an "ever-moving rest," as St. Maximos described life in God! For you will certainly be needed to give more than your prayers to your children as they begin to face the challenges involved in marriage.

We can look at the Beauty-Goodness-Truth progression according to this parallel that we have been discussing today, the progression of Being, Well-Being, and Ever-Being. Through chastity and virginity – through our initial erotic harkening to Theophany – we receive our *being* (really, we avoid a dissipation that can easily destroy us). Then, as we enter adulthood, we choose the mode by which we will be good – whether marriage or monasticism – in order to exercise fearless agape. In taking this step, we receive our *well-being* in the Church sacramentally, when we embrace the blessing of one of these paths. Then, at the Last Judgment, if we have been chastely erotic and boldly agapic, we attain our *Ever-Being*, our acceptance into eternal life. We see how true we've been to our own logos, to the Logos – to Christ crucified both within us and around us.

Using this sequence as a measure, we can see that failure at chastity and virginity will threaten our very being, our life itself. This is all the more evident today when the sexually-transmitted diseases afflicting the promiscuous are more deadly. But the importance of chastity for survival is also evident in the fact that sex out of wedlock can lead to family responsibilities which we have no practical way to

---

29 From the Greek Orthodox Marriage Service, before the crowning of the bride and groom: "Remember also, Lord our God, the parents who have brought them up, for the prayers of the parents make firm the foundations of households."

carry, and thus our children may grow up in poverty. And the failure at chastity, in turn, can make it harder to succeed at marriage or monasticism afterwards, and thus to acquire well-being.

Proper Orthodox hospitality, both giving it and receiving it, has become something of a lost art in Orthodox Christian America. When a friend of mine went off to a long-term missionary assignment, his home parish made no provision for him nor even made mention of his upcoming departure, even though he had been an important helper for years in that parish! Or, sometimes my students will tell me that they are off to visit a monastery, and I wish them a nice trip, but I forget to offer a gift, together with a list of names to be given for prayer. We have forgotten some of the Patterns of hospitality.

Incidentally, there are important commonalities between Rublev's Trinity and the icon of the Theotokos with Christ. Both icons show the whole Trinity (because Christ is the express image of the Father, and the Holy Spirit is present in every icon of Christ, resting upon him in the symbol of his halo); both icons give evidence of a miraculous conception; and both teach us of the crucial centrality of hospitality for Christian faith: "Behold, I stand at the door and knock…"

Oh, and one more thing: offering hospitality in all of these ways, through all of these sub-Patterns, together makes us hospitable to the bigger Pattern of marriage itself. Exercising these five or six hospitalities is what makes a marriage, what makes a relationship between a man and a woman a welcoming host to the blessing of Marriage itself.

Promoting Conception Medically – A Living Pattern?

RTE: I like the fact that you've situated conception within this larger theme of hospitality, creation, art, and mystery. The parents of a child are artists, builders – mystics, too. So, to apply the Patterns to a pressing contemporary issue, what would a mystical architect say about *in vitro* fertilization? Is it an act of art and of giving birth or a technological imposition of human will upon the world? Does it take place imagelessly or is it an act of creativity that comes from the ego?

DR. PATITSAS: The issue is of course not the child nor the goodness of having children. The issue is the process of IVF itself as a pattern of conception and intimacy, and the sub-patterns within that larger pattern: stimulating multiple ovulations through injecting the wife with drugs; extracting eggs from her; the husband's being asked to simulate the sexual act in a lab setting, perhaps even alone; conception of the children in a glass dish; the doctor's implantation of the fertilized eggs in the wife's womb; the permanent freezing or fiery incineration of the unwanted zygotes when the couple rejects those of their children that, though conceived, they have no space for; and the involvement of outsiders at every stage of what is meant to be the intimate, hidden, and divine process of conception.

Well, are any of these elements themselves living patterns? Does even one of them resolve all the forces present in the situation it confronts? Taken as a whole, is IVF a process that is a liberation from the cares of this world? Or, is IVF an unstable pattern that leaks unresolved tensions into the surrounding world, causing harm and making us more bound up with the cares of this world?

In whichever way the Church comes finally to answer the question of the "life" present in the IVF pattern and its sub-patterns, these are at least the correct questions. Most of all, how can the desire for children really be the justification for this process when it almost guarantees the annihilation of the "excess" embryos this process creates?

Most of us have been sold a bill of goods in our youth: about education and about how long it should take; about how to prepare for employment; about marriage, about the propriety of sex outside of marriage, and about what it takes to find "the one"; about the importance of establishing a career before marriage or before starting a family; about the role the older generation should play in supporting us in our twenties; and about how difficult marriage actually is, and so forth.

It can happen the other way, too – there are those who play on our insecurities and try to deceive us into celibacy by painting impossibly horrible pictures of what married life will be like. Well, some marriages *are* presumably quite difficult, but if we don't have a real monastic calling, then these would-be pied pipers are introducing destructive delays into our lives and knocking us off our divinely-appointed course.

Well, this entire bill of goods comes due as we age and realize that it can be getting steadily harder to conceive. For one bad reason or another, whether because we have been caught up in the general gnosticism of our culture or out of a diseased piety, we realize that we have followed, not God, but our own or someone else's passions, and we cry bitter tears. Consequently, we turn to technology to make up for our mistakes. So perhaps it is fortunate that thanks to biomedical technologies, not all younger adults are paying the full cost of errors that originated not in them but in their larger society.

Nevertheless, I would guess that the pattern of artificial conception does not resolve all the forces in the situation of infertility, and that it does leak problems into the patterns to its left and its right. The Church has numerous reasons to counsel caution here – and, for heaven's sake, not even really to individuals but to an entire society that is organized around individual self-fulfillment to the exclusion of procreation.

How the Church Promotes Conception

RTE: Then, how does the Church respond to the problem of childlessness?

DR. PATITSAS: First, the Church has never seen infertility merely as a medical issue. In fact, infertility has been central to the divine plan of salvation. God saves Israel and later the New Israel through granting miraculous conception to infertile couples. So infertility is of great concern to God, and Orthodox Christian cultures abound with stories of divine intervention in conception.

Second, the Church believes that any Christian couple facing infertility potentially finds themselves within a different, distinct, yet still very sacred Pattern. The delay in becoming a parent is not to be taken as implacable disordered chaos but, instead, as just the difficult tip of a holy iceberg. The couple is to see that failure to conceive can itself become a holy Pattern – and then to learn what the other elements in that Pattern are so that they can help make it a *living* Pattern in their own lives.

For one thing, through the permanent or temporary experience of infertility, families are meant to be brought closer to God. There are ways that we go about this, that in Christ we react to infertility with prayer. These ways include repentance of all your past sins, the undertaking of pilgrimages, solemn vows, and, in general, a renewed relationship with Christ. The delay in pregnancy can also give the couple the chance to examine and nourish their physical health, which could be behind the delay. Above all, the delay can bring the couple closer and render their marriage more Christ-centered. If you know that this is the Pattern by which Christians face infertility, then your next steps become clearer.

Third, the Church is also cautious because the medical intervention to restore fertility might be made without repentance for the acts and in some cases the failures to act that may have led to the infertility to begin with. A good Pattern, says Christopher Alexander, will actually diagnose and heal the ills in a situation, including those ills caused by the failure to participate in the Forms elsewhere and by others. We may have to repent not only for our own sins but for the sins of others that have delayed our readiness for marriage and childbearing.

Sometimes this repentance may be the necessary prerequisite for the couple to become good parents. The *infertility* in these cases – the inability to bear children – was never anything but God's way of helping the couple *to bear children well*. Do we see that? If we rush to subvert every lesson being taught to us by God, then dark forces from our pasts will linger into the future rather than being repented of and resolved here and now. These unresolved forces will then hinder our ability to be good parents and impact our children.

RTE: But what about those who desperately long for children, try to follow the Church's patterns, and still never conceive?

DR. PATITSAS: I don't know. We can't know every mystery. Such suffering is very deep. The Lord knows that many people suffer in this and other ways to what can feel like a limitless degree.

But the Church is nevertheless cautious about our going to extreme lengths in order to conceive. People may be "sorrowful unto death" about lacking children on one day, and the next day calmly dispose of the "surplus zygotes" they have conceived. The Church respects and celebrates the desire for parenthood, but this desire must be an icon, not an idol. And some sorrows are so deep that they can only be consoled in the next life, it would seem.

And so, fourthly, the Church is cautious because this medical intervention to create life so often leads to the willful destruction of life. IVF is expensive, so the common practice – the bad pattern – is to create surplus human beings by fertilizing many eggs, and then leave them aside once the family has all the children that it wants. This is not right. When this destruction of life occurs, it raises the question of whether the medical intervention was being done without recourse to God, and without repentance in those cases where some prior sin led to the infertility. If in the process of IVF we destroy seven or eight of our children in order to have the two that our heart was set on, then how can this be from God? How can it be an act of restoration and repair of the bad patterns in our life? No – in addition to our prior sins, we now dispose of human life without even realizing it.

Fifth, because this medical intervention and others like it disrupt or intrude upon the sacred intimacy of the couple, the Church is again cautious. We would never promote that either a husband or a wife should practice a detachment towards the body of their spouse which has been consecrated to them, especially as regards their sexual powers. Rather, we welcome each spouse to exercise a jealous protection of their spouse's person and body. Thus, the involvement of others in the act of procreation through IVF is not preferred and perhaps may someday be regarded in the Church as proscribed, forbidden.

Sixth, to conceive a child – which is capturing the image of Christ, a kind of Form-participation itself – we must do so in a Form-filled way. That is, to achieve good Patterns, you have to use good sub-Patterns. This is why in the Church we even hear of parents who are careful in their sexual relations to conceive in a holy way. For example, spiritual fathers have reported that it is better for the soul of the child if the parents are not drunk on alcohol when they create the child. Or, they say that a child who was conceived on Good Friday would suffer some spiritual burden in his or her life. And there are other, more refined discussions about what constitutes a good Pattern of sexual union that I will leave for another time.

An issue like IVF will soon enough be taken up by the wider Church. As the hierarchs have begun to meet more regularly, issues like this will be more readily addressed. It would seem, though, from the synodal statements to date by hierarchs in many Orthodox lands, that the weight of Tradition is emerging against the IVF practice, and either we will rule against it softly, in the form of caution, or through outright prohibition.

And the big lesson to take away would be the importance of a wider cultural and social repentance that would make marriage possible and central again for people in their twenties. Today, it is not family that is central but individual economic readiness (which is not a totally bad thing) and individual ego fulfillment (which also has its place). But since these now come without much thought for family attached, we do face more obstacles in the attempt to have children.

Our cultural priority is on the isolated self, not on the family.

Hospitality to the Will of God

RTE: It's a common claim that a woman's body naturally passes some percentage of normally conceived and fertilized ova before they implant, without, of course, her ever knowing, and some IVF advocates use this to justify discarding these "extra" zygotes conceived in the lab. Assuming this account of passing fertilized ova is true, does this affect the ethical requirement that all the zygotes conceived in this way must be implanted?

DR. PATITSAS: In fact, it happens that most of those children which actually are implanted in the mother's womb through IVF processes do not "catch." Therefore, let *this* be the approach taken by those who would insist on using IVF, that over time they implant all of the artificially conceived children into the mother's womb, and let God decide what happens next. For by taking the tiny baby humans out of the freezer and reintroducing them back into the tender warmth of their mother's womb, you at least bring back a "force" in your pattern of conception that the normal IVF pattern partly excludes – the mystery of God's will, of divine providence. Without giving God that chance, you just won't ever know. And by allowing all the conceived children the chance to be born, you remove a bad force from the IVF Pattern, the willingness to abandon our offspring.

Unless, of course, the entire IVF pattern is against God's will. It seems to me that the statements of both the Synod of Greece and the Russian Church have taken this conclusion.[30] IVF really does take – has already taken – human conception outside of the marital embrace, and thus opened the door to every other form of "marriage." In that case, there is no good answer to the question of what to do with these embryos.

---

30 For the Russian Orthodox Church's statement, see "The Basis of the Social Concept," available at: https://mospat.ru/en/documents/87568-problemy-bioetiki/ (Use Google translate for a good English version) OR http://orthodoxeurope.org/page/3/14.aspx (English; scroll to Section XII)

For the Bioethics Committee of the Orthodox Church of Greece's statement, see: http://www.bioethics.org.gr/en/03_frame.html

The Greek Orthodox Archdiocese of America's position is at: https://www.goarch.org/-/the-stand-of-the-orthodox-church-on-controversial-issues (Scroll down to the section on Bioethics).

Although yet and still, once you've crossed the Rubicon and created life in the lab, you have to allow those children to be "held" by their mother. But even then, if too many zygotes do implant, the doctors will press you to abort some to save the others. This is another reason why the Church is unlikely ever to become enthusiastic about this practice.

In other areas of life, Western culture has moved away from reliance on artificial methods. For example, the elites in Western society have taken a good long look at how our food is grown and raised, and have concluded that some more natural approach is necessary to our survival and flourishing as a human species. Similar reactions could well occur in the area of sexuality and conception in the coming decades.

Divine providence – this is certainly a deep mystery, but we should remember that according to the theology of our Orthodox saints, God's will is not some empty intention, but is equivalent to his divine and uncreated energies. Our human will may come to nothing, but his divine will has actual *being*. In fact, it is *we* who only exist to the extent that we participate in God's will, through the embrace of his energies. Consequently, to frustrate the will of God in our lives is to reject God's very attempt to share his being with us! But this is equivalent to renouncing our participation in his uncreated life. In doing so, we endanger our own existence.

Moreover, there is an identity between God's "ideas" for you and his will for you, so that rejecting God's will in a deep way would mean that we no longer wish to be "thought of" by God: "I never knew you," are the terrible words of judgment heard in the gospel warning (Mt 7:23). I think it is better to be known by God, even if this means that we will be given a hard mission.

Eric Perl says that "thought-wills" would be a good term for the divine energies of God, the uncreated energies that St. Gregory Palamas and his fellow monks on Mt. Athos were experiencing.[31]

---

31 See Eric D. Perl, "St. Gregory Palamas and the Metaphysics of Creation," in *Dionysius* 14 (1990): 105-130.

These thought-wills are closely related to the Patterns, the Forms. And so, we create something lasting – we participate in divine energies – when we manage to cooperate with God's own will, his own thoughts.

Something Very Serious Is Happening in IVF

The mystery of God's will is what we face here in IVF. People undertake this process in order to create life. Their intention is not to harm; at the most, they may regard the discarding of certain of the fertilized eggs as merely mimicking natural processes of reproduction, where some zygotes never successfully implant in the womb.

But one of our students, himself a medical professional, had a very interesting and moving take on what is going on with conception in the lab. The student, Demetrios Wilson, pointed out that when we look upon a just-fertilized egg, a zygote in the glass petri dish of *in vitro* fertilization, it seems to be almost a nothing. The organism is too tiny to be seen by the naked eye, and so it seems to be of no significance, except for the significance that we might bestow upon it. He went on to say that in his hospital, many researchers think it of no moral consequence to destroy these human zygotes – unless, however, someone intends to use them for research, at which point they again become extremely valued.

But each of us, Demetrios pointed out, was at some point called into being out of nothing – *ex nihilo*, as we say theologically. Moreover, each of us passed through a stage when we were *just barely* on this side of nothingness. And indeed, we were each called out of nothing by the will of God, by *his* "conception" of us – his thinking of us and love for us. We were conceived as that zygote only because we were simultaneously conceived in God's thought and intention.

Demetrios went on to argue that to crush those zygotes, to destroy those lives, is also to trample upon the will of God at a moment when He, too, is utterly vulnerable to our decisions. Our freedom in this case comes through God's weakness, his dependence on our choice, and so to dispose of the zygotes or incinerate them as being of no further interest to us is to strike at God's uncreated providence and will. These are such serious matters.

I would add that nothing seems to have changed when we destroy the human zygotes – except that we may wrongly believe that we have in this way irrefutably proved that these cells were mere "biological material" and not real human beings. But if human beings are created in the image not only of Christ but of Christ crucified, if the Theophany that called the world into existence was Christ in his self-emptying love for the world, then killing these zygotes doesn't negate their human identity but rather only confirms it: we show them to be what we were meant to be, images of the Crucified One.

But at the same time, in killing these very small and undeveloped humans, we show *ourselves* to be *not* co-crucified with Christ – and thus we call into question our own identity as human. We have shown *not* that the zygotes possess a partial life, but have instead called the meaning of *our own* conception into question.

Still, let us not despair. Let us trust in God's mercy, for true Beauty is just this: the face of Christ whom we crucified, still loving us!

Sins, intentional or accidental, can never exclude the possibility of a new beginning, of "a new creation" (II Cor 5:17) through repentance, for it was repentance that has constituted us from the very beginning, from the moment we were conceived, as we said in Chapter Two. We discuss these grave matters never to condemn – St. Paul counsels us to "judge nothing before the time" (I Cor 4:5) – but to protect and to heal.

RTE: On the other hand, recourse to IVF might be avoided to begin with, in many cases. There are allowable medical interventions for infertility, such as procedures that Roman Catholic researchers have come up with over the past thirty years to fulfill the natural patterns rather than to circumvent them. For example, the "Creighton Model" seems to enjoy a higher success rate, at a far lower cost, than *in vitro* fertilization.

DR. PATITSAS: A few years ago, the National Health Service in Britain launched an advertising campaign to warn women that, if they waited until after age thirty to attempt to conceive their first child, they were more likely to face difficulties. The NHS was going to have to fund the IVF and other expensive medical interventions meant to cope with those difficulties, so for purely financial reasons it wanted to inform its clientele not to delay conception.

Well, the campaign had to be discontinued; absurdly, it was felt that mentioning bodily realities were an affront to women's rights to do exactly as they pleased with their bodies. Apparently, these days my "right to my body" rests on the right not to understand, show mercy to, or accept my body. So we do need reminders, and the folk wisdom of other ages can be a lifesaver.

However, let us not become overly materialistic, nor overly "biological," in our approach to marriage. So many times it seems as if God is willing the delay in marriage and conception so that the couple can mature and be better parents later. We aren't to become excessive about these matters.

Wendell Berry and Kindly Use

RTE: As a final topic, could you speak about the ways in which hospitality and conception, along with your observations on architecture and the material world, might relate to our care for the earth?

DR. PATITSAS: Yes, and I would like to draw in one last great contemporary thinker who can give us some insight into this seemingly esoteric idea of the Forms. I'm talking about Wendell Berry, an agrarian essayist, poet, and novelist.[32] Millions of American readers love him, and many people see him as being near the pinnacle of American Christian literary culture today.

He, like Christopher Alexander, speaks of something which resembles the Platonic Forms, but he uses neither that term nor the

---

32 Cf., Wendell Berry, *The Unsettling of America: Culture and Agriculture* (San Francisco: Sierra Club, 1977) and *The Art of the Commonplace: The Agrarian Essays of Wendell Berry* (Berkeley, CA: Counterpoint Press, 2003).

favored term of Alexander, the "Patterns." The term that Wendell Berry uses in his writings for the Forms is simply "the ways," or "the old ways" that people have anciently known, about how to care for community, for each other, and for the land. But Berry's "ways" are like Alexander's Patterns and Plato's Forms in that they are an ascetic and aesthetic principle that hold in tension *all* the forces in a situation, in order to give life.

Berry tells us that in the absence of a community these ways are hard to preserve and, even if remembered, are nearly impossible to cultivate as well as we'd like. For many of us, the old Patterns are lost and we cannot participate in them unless we link up with still-intact healthy communities. Berry also says that larger forces – of global finance and of the administrative state – have come in and scattered many of our small towns, small cities, and small farms. In the suburbs to which the refugees from our destroyed cities and farm communities have fled, new Patterns haltingly arise to fill the many gaps left by the loss of the old Patterns. Berry's account of modern America is at times depressing, but I'm also intrigued by the possibility of getting the old ways back.

In vitro fertilization, we can thus see, is a pattern that arose when community, and in particular the Pattern of young marriage, collapsed; as we said above, people are in these predicaments not entirely through their own choices. Back when families would all but determine the choice of a spouse for their children, many felt oppressed by this practice. Now, we have arrived at another extreme, that of absolute romantic individualism. In consequence, we may find ourselves oppressed in different ways, such as being unable to have the children our hearts desire.

RTE: Is it possible to return to a healthier way?

DR. PATITSAS: Dislocations and troubles have been the rule in human history, and so we must show resilience and never succumb to despair. Our ancestors dealt with much greater challenges than we face, and they are looking down upon us now, and wishing us to succeed with ours. The Patterns – the old ways – were discovered through much trial and error, as being the responses that made human life worth living. They can always be recovered again, if slowly.

One problem with reading Wendell Berry is that he's so incredibly elegiac that you feel a kind of delicious sadness in reading him. Alexander intends his work as a road map for the future, while Berry comes across like he's trying to convince you that the past was better. Well, it may have been, but so what? Today is pretty great, too, and the eternal Forms, the ways, can be learned again through repentance and attention. The traditions have been broken, or at least extremely marginalized, many times in history, and almost as many times they have been pieced back together and recovered.

In the case of the icons, which were nearly lost to the Church for a hundred and fifty years during iconoclasm in the East, the Patterns came back even stronger and more profoundly than before the cataclysm. Icons after iconoclasm were theologically richer, and better as art. Something similar may happen in another fifty years with Christian marriage and the beautiful gift of gender, which are the holy icons under direct attack in our day.

A Kind of Sweet Sadness Is Inherent in the Forms

It will help us not to despair if we know that while these eternal Forms are handed down from generation to generation, their eternity doesn't derive from their age, per se. The moment we capture them, we enter something older than the beginning of time – we enter Eternity Itself. So in trying to become "timeless" as counseled by *The Timeless Way of Building*, we mustn't be mesmerized by the past, looking back on what used to be until we nearly go blind with sadness.

I think Wendell Berry's lament involves a minor misperception. The ways aren't sad mainly because they are slipping away. In any age and even in the most ideal context, as Alexander points out, there *can be* something "sad" even in a perfectly realized Pattern or Form. The Patterns not only bear but also convey the twofold anointing that we spoke of in another interview. Or, to approximate

Alexander's words, their appearance in the world is poignant. To think of them always involves us in some repentance which, in a time-bound world, will include a twinge of sorrow.

In heaven there will be no sorrow, but there will be a calm strength free of superficiality – and sorrow is naught but the taste of this heavenly strength in a different mode, one that is at times appropriate in our fallen world.

The most perfectly realized Forms carry with them the strongness of death. I mean, they ennoble us, awaken in us both of the two kinds of shame we earlier spoke about. The Forms even innoculate us to their own possible later loss, for in this world all things are destined to pass, and a good painting or building gives us the courage to accept that.

Making Nature Personal

Still, Wendell Berry is in many ways an excellent theologian, and has a profound gift for showing us the practicality of Christian anthropology. According to Berry, the old ways – the living Patterns – teach us that the "kindly use" of the land cannot be imposed remotely or impersonally. It is only a face, a person who is present on the spot and truly aware of all the forces at work in a place, who can bring forth a Pattern that is responsive to every single force in that situation. For Berry, only a person who lives on the land and works the land will enter into a conversation and dialogue with that land. Ideally, for Berry, farmers would actually work their land behind draft animals when possible, and not from across the barrier of giant machinery. For him, only this kind of personal presence can "cultivate" the land – can render it liturgical, dialogical, and human.

Well, this is exactly the same with spiritual life. Hearken back all you want to some prior Golden Age in the Church, the fact is that that "perfect" time was bought with the prayers, sweat, anxiety, and blood of human saints who had no idea if God would answer their prayers for the world during their own lifetime, or only after their death. The truly idyllic order is in practice a gut-wrenchingly personal order, achieved through uncertainty, exertion, and even doubt. But God does grant answers to such prayers. We are sure of this.

Berry at times seems despairing. He emphasizes that a lot of the good that was present in American society was unnecessarily lost. But he also shows us that Good Patterns of use – the ways – will bring forth Good Patterns within land, community, and life. Land that is taken care of by an actual person will itself become beautiful, a consolation to the person who visits or views or lives on it. And this is the second appearance of the Forms in Berry's writing: not just the Beautiful Ways, but the fruit of those ways in the land, and in people and in community.

We don't all need to become farmers to experience this. Gardens and homes often have this exact feel, don't they? The city and village photographs in Alexander's *The Timeless Way* have it too. And when we see such places, we never forget them.

It is possible to understand, then, as Christopher Alexander does, that man stands on the earth as an artist, or a priest and a prophet, more than as a conqueror or a producer-consumer. And Wendell Berry, even more than Alexander, convinces us that land that is taken care of properly can become a garden, a paradise, and a work of art. In the aggregate, entire regions can become a liberation from the cares of this world, for as we work in them or just drive through them, our souls are nourished and fed by them. One thinks of examples of such landscape in every culture. And in the near future, I believe that our societies will learn these ways again on a wider scale.

The Holy Significance of Private Property

Interestingly, using Wendell Berry's writings, one can find a holy significance in private property, in the following sense: For the land to receive its logos, its care, its Pattern-Form, it must first be brought within the concern and love of a particular "priest" – I mean, a specific person who is acting out his or her God-given task of reconciliation. In the case of farmland, there needs to be an actual farmer. Private property can be distorted into a means to dominate or consume the land, true enough. But as a means to "enhypostasize" the land – to bring land wholly within the realm of personal relationship and relating – private property is an almost indispensable tool. Just as our natures and our wills must be personalized, so in time will we personalize the world, when we become saints.

RTE: And how would this apply to monastics who renounce private property? Also, can you say something about the term "enhypostasis"?

DR. PATITSAS: We use the term "enhypostasize" theologically to discuss how Christ, as a divine person, gathered his human nature into his own person, which is to say, made it fully his own. That is, Christ's human nature did not come with a second, competing human personhood; no, Christ was one divine person, and his particular human nature was instantiated within his divine personhood. This is what we mean, in the case of his incarnation, by "enhypostasize."

I would suggest that we could use the same term here, although analogously, to describe the gathering in of land and the world inside a human person, especially when that personhood is infused with divine grace. What follows is a holy use of private property, but also therefore a particularly *personal* use. *Some person in particular* has to give his heart and his body and his mind to that property, before it will come alive. Without that enhypostasizing of the land inside the concern and care of a concrete person, there is no one to discover the Pattern-Form that will account for all the forces present there and thus manage to make the land beautiful, useful, stable and true to its own inner nature. There has to be a person who learns and practices the ways – the timeless ways – of farming and care, and who then applies these to the land steadily and carefully. This means that private property is a necessary precondition for certain kinds of care of the earth.

Helping Wild Nature Become Still Wilder

This is not to say that wild nature is not already beautiful, but rather that even the most dramatic landscape benefits from – cries out for – the foundation of a small chapel and for the celebration of the divine liturgy within it. As I tell my students, the mountain isn't quite fully a mountain until the liturgy is celebrated there.

The cultivated farmstead represents a different kind of liturgy, for a well-tended farm signifies an intensification of our belonging in the world. We could imagine ourselves living stably in such a place, while wild nature is by contrast beautiful but not always welcoming. The well-looked-after homestead is a little taste of our recovery from the exile to which we were banished when Adam and Eve sinned. It is a promise of the "lasting city" which is to come.

Also, if we are going to actually build a chapel in a wild place, then it has to fit in aesthetically there. The environmental and conservation movements, although valuable in themselves, are also a rebuke to the builders and architects of the modern age, whose poorly-designed buildings have managed to convince tens of millions of people around the world that *any* human intervention in nature must inevitably be disastrous, a scarring of beauty. Because the majority of what we currently build is awful, people have no sense of how a building or even a city could be *part of* nature.

We need the land in order to survive; our need for food proves that this is true. But the land also needs us, it turns out. It needs us in order to become what it was meant to be – a complete sacrament of God's presence. And to be such a sacrament, we need builders and artists who know what they are doing. We need people who can show that humans belong to the world, and that the world belongs to us.

Of course, some monasteries have dispensed with the concept of property between the monastics themselves. Some families also do this – as a teenager, I had friends who had paying jobs, but who turned over their entire paychecks to their parents, and the resulting bond was very strong. In former times, some villages also managed to exercise farmland ownership in common – to a degree. But the property was *private enough*, at any rate, to allow a sense of ownership and the practice of personal, rather than expert or merely formal, care.

Besides, in a monastery we can think that in a sense all of the communal land of a monastery belongs to its abbess or abbot, and conceive of the nuns or monks as children in a family, as not something separate from their father or mother in Christ. The term "living in community" sounds unctuous and weird when we apply it to life in an Orthodox monastery because it implies a Hobbesian social contract among prickly individuals. A monastery is a *koinos bios*,[33] not a "community" in our current, desiccated sense: it is *one life*. Such a oneness demands hierarchy.

Private property, if we are exercising "kindly use"[34] of the land we own, is similar to the privacy of procreation. It is no one else's business how the logos takes on flesh in our own land, is what Wendell Berry implies. He doesn't mean that this use must be hidden, nor that we can harm the land if we please, nor that we are to be despots and tyrants on our private property. What happens on our land is no one else's business – *because it is our business*. For Berry, it is our *main* business.

Moreover, it's no else's business in an additional fundamental sense. Care for land is an occupation that no one but the owner can do because only the owner will be involved, with all his powers and all his personhood, in understanding and relating to that land. It is his personhood that must cooperate to make Christ more embodied there. For Berry, caring tenderly for the land requires living on it or near it so that you truly are aware of all the forces present there. There exists a limit, for Berry, of how much property a person can own before his relationship to it is no longer personal. In farming, towards the extreme upper limit, he says, would be a farm of about 500 acres.

The same principle of privacy goes for raising children. As much as others might contribute and pitch in, our children will always be "none of their business," since a child is designed to be

---

33 "Coenobia," is how this term is normally transliterated.
34 Berry's term.

cared for primarily by his or her parents (biological or adoptive), not by impersonal forces or institutions or drive-by busybodies. It is our business as parents – meaning, our sacred life-and-death responsibility – to act as persons and to nurture personhood in our unique children. There are good orphanages and other arrangements, but at the end of the day, even these will only be good if they recognize that it takes a person to nurture personhood in someone else.

And because Berry emphasizes the holy necessity not just of a farmer but also of a farm family and a farm community, his account of the land is hypostatic in that fuller sense. It isn't just that a person must care for the land but that the farmer *will himself not be a person unless he is in communion with other persons of his own kind* – in his farm community and in the past of his community – by having learned the ways they passed on. Berry thus shows that as far as the land is concerned, "one farmer is no farmer," just as the ancient Church through Tertullian believed that "*solus Christianus, nullus Christianus.*" It is the farm community that Berry cherishes, as much as the farmer.

What has replaced the farm community, Berry tells us, is "the machine" and "the mind of the machine," and "farming experts" who have been bought or beguiled or seduced or forced to serve that "machine mind."

In other words, what has replaced farming is the same truth-first approach to the world that has such a disastrous effect when it tries to fix the trauma victim through analytical psychotherapy. The desiccation of our farming landscape is the mirror image of the desiccation of our souls.

Wendell Berry is indeed a chief spokesman for the Beauty-first way of life.

RTE: But you yourself are not an agrarian – or are you? Your greatest influence is Jane Jacobs, who was the ultimate city theorist. She often accuses people of romanticizing life on the farm.

DR. PATITSAS: Strictly as a social theorist, Jane Jacobs is beyond both Berry and Alexander because she is handling a much wider array of social and civilizational forces and doing so with the greatest facility. Her "Form" of social life – the city – is truer because the number of forces and stresses within human life and the world that it can bear is much greater.

But this does not take away the good points that these others make. Berry is looking at one problem in particular – the loss of the farming community and its replacement by a truth-first approach to nature and to community that has damaged much of the agrarian lifestyle in America. For some of the displaced farmers who have been unable to find work in the non-farm economy, what has followed the destruction of the farm by big business, big government, and big science is a welfare-and-meth lifestyle. Poor whites are now the only demographic group in America whose life expectancy is falling.

And the biggest consumers of government welfare are the agribusinesses, whose vaunted efficiency at farming apparently requires about $150 billion a year in direct federal subsidies to keep afloat. This enormous dependence of corporations on government welfare is all the proof needed that our current Pattern of farming has *zero* staying power. Kick out the props, and it's unclear whether anything of the current agrarian structure will remain. And in the meantime, America's farming and rural communities have been mostly lost.

By the way, one thing we can say about our national addiction to welfare in general is that it is further evidence that we have lost the ancient ways. The ancient ways of production didn't need subsidies. They were self-sustaining. When we do offer charitable support to people, we should support them in such a way that we strengthen the Forms against the forces that try to prevent these hallowed Patterns from coming to be. The point is not to create artificial Forms that have no depth and no staying power, such as our current farming system, or the new family model of a single, never-married, mother living below the poverty line.

Anyway, the point of reading many authors is not to set up a cage-fighting match among them. These three great minds – Alexander, Berry, and Jacobs – promote worldviews that interlock. In the case of Christopher Alexander, his work in philosophy provides the necessary context for what Jacobs does. In the case of Jane Jacobs, her social theory provides the indispensable context for what Berry so beautifully does.

There is really only one element missing in the Berry vision, without which his social ideas can never work. Jacobs alone shows what is missing in his wonderful approach to the land, though she is a true "city girl." We are not meant to return to the Garden, and according to Jacobs, farming turns out to be city work transplanted into the countryside.

But let's save our discussion of cities for later; it's a rich topic.

CHAPTER SEVEN

BEAUTY WILL SAVE THE WORLD

Social Justice, Judgment Day, and the Human Need to Forgive God

In their attempts to be intellectually consistent, truth-first approaches to social justice offer prescriptions for economic and political life that are based on a single and consistent set of first principles. However, the many unavoidable paradoxes and contradictions inherent within dynamic systems such as economies and societies frustrate truth-first approaches to knowing.

The Beauty-first approach to politics and social welfare, by contrast, begins with the meditation on two theophanies – the vision of the Last Judgment revealed by Christ in Matthew 25 and the vision of the Heavenly Jerusalem described by the beloved apostle in the Book of Revelation. These two visions are combined in the Orthodox ritual of Holy Week, which pushes us to enact within our social relationships these two visions' difficult yet glorious picture of life in the City of God. What emerges through this Pattern of repentance in the light of Beauty, leading to contemplation of the Good through practice, is a civic icon of Paradise. Christian civilizations will, like their Heavenly Archetype, steadily emerge into the likeness of a joyful wedding liturgy.

Nevertheless, even the most loving Christian social order cannot "dry every tear," for it will not be until the final encounter with Christ that all trauma and injustice will be rectified and transfigured into seeds of participation in God's eternal glory.

This is partly because, for some, to forgive God himself for the hell that they have endured in this life will only be possible when they have beheld directly the mystical vision which Job once saw, and which alone can answer every doubt of the trauma sufferer.

I. SYMPHONIA: FIDELITY TO THE PROPHET-KING

The Now and the Not Yet of the Kingdom

RTE: Let's begin today with the question of social justice. In some of our discussions you've painted a very high picture of Eastern Roman Orthodox civilization – centered in what we know as the Byzantine Empire – as being the perfect blend of the Greek mind, the Jewish heart, and the Roman body (that is, Roman law and social organization). Can you explain what such an advanced society might teach us today about social justice, when we are used to thinking in terms of party politics and scientific public policy?

DR. PATITSAS: Because it is a question people sometimes raise, let me just say something about the terminology you mentioned. Western scholars first reduced Roman Orthodox civilization to the term "Byzantine" only a hundred years after New Rome (Constantinople) had fallen to the Ottomans; the Eastern Romans themselves certainly knew the ancient name of their city but, being Romans, never adopted it as their core identity. It is as "Roman" that many Orthodox Christians throughout the Eastern Mediterranean today still know themselves and their culture.[1]

I do feel a personal reverence for the civilization centered in Constantinople, both because of my frequent pilgrimages to Istanbul (since 1928 the official term for the city; the Ottomans after 1453 referred to the city by many names, but still in many official contexts as *Kostantiniye*) and because of the unforgettable impression made

---

[1] Constantinople was founded in AD 325 by St. Constantine the Great, the first Roman emperor to embrace Christianity. His official name for the city, *Nova Roma Constantinopolitana*, helps to explain why its inhabitants continued (and, if they are Christians, still continue) to consider themselves Romans of Constantinople. After 1453, when the Ottoman Turks controlled the city, its formal name became *Kostantiniye*, or "Constantine's Place." Istanbul, the present name, is probably a corruption of the Greek "eis tin polin," or "to the City" – confirming that "all roads once led to (New) Rome." The term "Byzantine" for Eastern Roman civilization, meanwhile, is of Western coinage and does not correspond to the historical self-understanding of the people who lived in the sole capital of the Roman Empire between 476 and 1453 AD.

on me by the surviving alumni of the Halki Theological School – a school which was forcibly closed in 1971 by the Turkish government.

But the Orthodox Christian Romans themselves (the Byzantines) felt that they were striving towards a social ideal, not that they had ever completely possessed it. We don't need to close our eyes to their faults in order to look up to them.

One of the meanings contained within their distinctive political philosophy – "symphonia" is the term often used to describe it – is the idea of an earthly polity continually striving towards a kingdom not of this world. It is hard for us to understand everything that *symphonia* implied to the Byzantines because this philosophy grew out of a still older and nearly universal worldview which is now all but lost to us. We mentioned that cosmology briefly in a previous interview; namely, that a true civilization is always a "marriage" between rulers and people under the influence of love.[2]

The "ideal" Byzantine civilization lived within the vicissitudes of history, and so it included all kinds of real-world difficulties, such as nearly constant foreign attack, many centuries of pressure to alter the Orthodox Christian faith in order to win the support of the West or to reconcile with the South (I mean, Egypt), an advanced hospital system that nevertheless was helpless before the bubonic plague, corruptions and violent rivalries, and a small but steady stream of their most elite citizens renouncing "the world" in order to take on the monastic life. The Orthodox Christian Romans were real people, struggling the best they could.

RTE: So, I notice that you personally prefer "Eastern Roman" over "Byzantine".

DR. PATITSAS: Since in Constantinople and throughout the Middle East today Orthodox Christians still know themselves as "Romans," we have to use this term at times. In 2012, I was watching an Arabic language television broadcast about the Holy Fire, and I could hear

---

2 See Chapter Five above, "Only Priests Can Marry: The Reconciliation of Men and Women in Christ," (Section I, The Shape of Gender Reconciliation).

the term "Roman" being used quite frequently! And indeed, when I first met the alumni of Halki, as I said above, I understood that "Roman" was still an accurate description for the Orthodox culture in Istanbul.[3]

But the term "Byzantine" through long use by excellent scholars has also become honorable. In some ways the idea of Byzantium very much clarifies, since we aren't thinking of Julius Caesar when we hear it, and in other ways it obscures – obscures the glory that Orthodox Christian Rome had attained in the East, and obscures the glorious personality that the bearers of the name "Roman" still possess there. But language is sometimes imperfect like that; as long as we know both terms, we should be fine.

Anyway, although *symphonia* included an emphasis on the endless striving for the kingdom, we are not saying that the Byzantines emphasized only the "not yet" of the kingdom. They, of course, also emphasized – and this is part of what makes Orthodoxy so distinct – that we do live the kingdom *from now* (Mt 4:17). In the Church, we *really do* experience the fact that the Kingdom of Heaven has already become present, even though we also await our hope at the end of time. This paradox has been termed "the now and the not yet" of the Kingdom of Heaven. And if you lose the emphasis on the fact that *already* "the Kingdom of Heaven is at hand," then you've defeated the very gospel itself and rendered Christ's first public words null and void! Christians don't repent in order to get to heaven; rather, we repent (and in the preaching of Christ we see this clearly) because heaven has come upon us.

By the way, this clear emphasis on the "now" of the Kingdom is one reason why the Orthodox Church has not been divided by discussions about whether you "get to heaven" by faith or by works. When people outside the Orthodox Church ask you whether you're

---

[3] Since 2007 I have been attending reunions of Halki Theological School alumni and professors and, as strange as this may sound, I can never escape the impression that I am meeting Greek-speaking Romans rather than Greeks – even though, since the forced closing of Halki, most of these men have come to reside in Greece. Their culture is different than Greek culture (which I know fairly well), and in their mannerisms they remind me of what Roman-era art suggests of Roman senators or noblemen.

saved, they often mean, "If you died right now, would you go to heaven?" But for us, this question itself sounds like a denial of the gospel: the Kingdom of Heaven is *at hand* here and now, whether we like it or not! It's not about our trying to get there, but about the fact that the Kingdom has come to us in Christ, so now how do we react?

Besides, not only are we already *in* heaven, we are also *all* "going to heaven" at the Last Judgment, whether we are in the Church or not, have lived pure lives or not, in order to experience this meeting either as salvation or as condemnation. The question of salvation is not only a matter of getting God to notice us favorably, for He already loves all of us. The question of salvation is really the question of how not to get crushed by the awesome purity and power of the Kingdom, now and at the end of days, when it has the mind to visit us. How should we react to the free and expensive gift of Trinitarian life being given to us now, so as to be ready to receive that gift eternally? Well, there is no need to speculate: we see saints and ordinary Christians experiencing heaven in a very deep way right now; we can just go up and ask them "how it's done."

In a sense, the Orthodox Church is the mirror image of the Christianities of Western Europe on the issue of the Kingdom's presence, and this will impact how we see the issue of social justice. Because we have the doctrine of uncreated grace and the experience of the Uncreated Light, we much more emphasize the full presence of the Kingdom from now, *within the Church*, and can see how this presence will radiate out to change every aspect of social life. Nevertheless, regarding *society*, we are perhaps more careful not to imagine that we could ever make this world a utopia; we don't use a term like "Christendom," for example. "The poor you shall *always* have with you," Christ said (Mt 26:11). We await with fervent hope that more complete redressing of all that is wrong with the world which can only be accomplished by the Second Coming of Christ.

In fact, I would say that for Orthodoxy, an acceptance of the "not-yet" of the Kingdom is the condition for peace on earth. If we are trying to make this place too perfect, we turn it into a living hell.

While, on the other hand, the acceptance of the "now" of the Kingdom gives us the strength to receive the foretaste of Paradise very richly and thus revolutionize our societies. We need both emphases.

Some Christianities, in contrast to Orthodoxy, seem to preach to their own Christians a God who may or may not someday return to the world; but to the wider society, they seem to insist that we can attain the immediate presence of the Kingdom of Heaven through better public policy.

Balancing "Show" with "Go"

RTE: A criticism of American Orthodoxy that one hears both inside and outside the Church is that we are so oriented toward our liturgical services and our inner spiritual lives that we don't have a strong culture of ministering to the poor.

DR. PATITSAS: I might have agreed with that some years ago. Growing up in America where there are so few Orthodox Christians and having been taught that most foreign societies are, when compared to America, somewhat inert in terms of their economic development, we can create images in our mind of a conservative, reactive, somnolent Orthodoxy, either here or abroad, that serves only private piety.

But now having actually traveled annually to Greece and Russia and having lived in Greece for long stretches, I am aware of an attitude that looks quite the opposite. Let me give you one example.

Ten percent of the population of Greece perished in World War II. Most of these died from starvation caused by the war, which means that the survivors were also terribly weakened. Greece had been the first nation to defeat an Axis power in that war. In fact, Russia's generals later stated that their country would not have survived if Greek resistance had not delayed the Nazi invasion of the Soviet Union by at least six weeks. After this suffering – with ten percent of the population lost – Greece's reward for having saved the Allied cause was to be made the target of a surrogate invasion sponsored by the Yugoslavian dictator Tito, who armed Greek communist guerillas. This plunged Greece into another five years of civil war, which we know is the cruelest form of war. My saintly father lived through this and saw the killing with his own eyes.

So, how did the Greek people react to ten years of war and devastating social dislocation? Well, within a year of the end of the final battles in 1949, Greece was a) sending fresh soldiers to fight and die for the freedom of far-off South Korea and b) sending Christian missionaries to Africa. Can you imagine what a basket case Greece was after ten years of war, civil war, and foreign occupation? Imagine if 15 million Americans had died in World War II (ten percent of our then population) rather than the 500,000 who did. And yet, Greece immediately reached out to help others, fighting and winning the very first two battles in the Cold War – I mean, the Korean War and, prior to that, her own struggle with foreign-backed communist insurgents.

I mean, how many times and for how many centuries do the Greeks have to stand at the gates and save Western civilization from annihilation – whether from the Persians, the Arabs, the Turks, the Nazis, or the Communists – before we admit that we need them and owe them?

It is so galling, so "ugly American" of people to disparage *any* of the Orthodox old countries as glibly as we do, when we have no idea of the crushing suffering every Orthodox society endured in the twentieth century.

You know, just because someone is poorer than we are doesn't mean they might not be as good or better than we are. I remember the first time I heard a starving Ethiopian peasant interviewed in her native language during the famine there in the early 1980s, and thinking, "Oh my gosh, they are a royal race! I will *never* reach the cultural and psychological level of such a person!" But, of course, in our materialism we easily imagine that poorer societies are also civilizationally more backward than richer ones.

Everywhere you go in Greece today you come across little associations that help the poor, help orphans, feed the hungry, support foreign missions. Greece's government, itself poor, has its own substantial foreign aid program. If Greek philanthropy is still imperfect, it's more because they have gotten caught up in Western secularism and "progress" than because their Orthodoxy is somehow deficient.

For example, a few decades ago Greek orphanages were taken away from Orthodox nuns so that the state alone would control the children's formation. But in reality, it was Orthodox monastics in Asia Minor and Constantinople who had invented the orphanage in the first place and who had cultivated seventeen centuries of experience in how to raise children in dire circumstances!

Still, criticisms that contemporary Orthodox cultures are not socially conscious should remind us to double-check that we are indeed doing the right things. A friend of mine told me that when she was considering becoming Orthodox, a colleague of hers at the Library of Congress exclaimed, "The Orthodox? Why, they're all show and no go!" I wasn't offended at all; I thought it was really funny! It's sort of a natural criticism of the Beauty-first way, to think that it isn't having any real impact.

But then you read books like Timothy Schwartz's *Travesty in Haiti*[4] or William Easterly's *The Elusive Quest for Growth*,[5] and you can see how too much "go" with too little "show" – too little emphasis on the Beauty-first approach to human relationship – is even more disastrous.

The End Is the Beginning

But let us begin our discussion of social justice at the end – since "at the end" is where it all started, it turns out. I mean, we have been arguing in all these chapters that we were originally created through our "beholding" (even before we had eyes!) our goal, our purpose, and that this initial vision was an event which so filled us

---

4 *Travesty in Haiti: A True Account of Christian Missions, Orphanages, Fraud, Food Aid and Drug Trafficking* (Charleston, SC: BookSurge Publishing, 2008).

5 *The Elusive Quest for Growth: Economists' Adventures and Misadventures in the Tropics* (Cambridge, Mass.: MIT Press, 2001).

with desire that we wanted to exist and rushed toward the end appointed for us. So, it really was our *end* that made us *begin*.

This is a basic Neoplatonic idea that St. Maximos the Confessor likes very much. Since things are created for a purpose, their end is actually the trigger for their very existence. Or, what first got creation going was the primordial appearing of that perfect Beauty that creation was destined to embrace – the anointed Son of God, the triumph of self-sacrificial love.

This is a paradox – how could we have "seen" our destination before we even had eyes? But let me give an example from everyday life, in the form of a story told by one of our students, of the way an "end" can be a "beginning," of how a vision can be the thing that opens our eyes from blindness. I was lecturing on this notion that when newly created matter first "saw" (in some way we can't conceive) Christ in his self-emptying love for the world, this formless creation was aroused by the vision of Christ's beauty, fell in love with Christ, and started to move toward him, thus coming into a defined state of being.

Well, after class a student told me that something like this paradox had actually occurred in her own life. She said that her parents had been completely non-religious until she was about eight years old, when they began attending the Orthodox Church. "Looking back," she said, "I can almost *not imagine* what I was doing or thinking before I first heard about God and the love of Jesus Christ. My entire life before hearing about Christ had been just a passionate obsession with dance and constant fighting with other little girls. I can remember almost no other thoughts or feelings of my inner world before that time." In other words, the first encounter with Christ was the beginning of her identity, of her humanity – in a sense, of her personal existence.

Wonderfully, you see in this example that "theophany" is not some impossible event but happened quite ordinarily in the life of a little girl in Texas – and then changed everything for her.

And we have tried to give other everyday examples of this, of that moment when falling in love with some person, some purpose, some perfection or ideal, really did mark the beginning of our lives. For me, one such moment happened when I was kneeling in front of the church at the Orthodox monastery in Essex, England, planting a tree, and I looked up to see Elder Sophrony (Sakharov, 1896-1993) for the first time. He was walking down the pathway towards me, leaning on the arm of one of the nuns. I was 22 years old at that time (he would have been about 92), and when I looked up at his face, in my heart I immediately laughed with joy and relief and said, "Oh! So *that* is what a human being looks like!" I suddenly was certain that I had never seen what a human being actually was until that moment – although such an idea had never before crossed my mind! And from that moment my life took a different path, and certain subsequent temptations have been easily "ignored" in the light of the memory of his countenance.

It is so much the case that Christian spiritual life begins with the vision of our end that I have sometimes wondered whether *all* Neoplatonic and patristic use of this description of creation's beginning is meant only as a metaphor for the philosopher or theologian's own personal spiritual life. That is to say, perhaps the philosophers and the Fathers themselves experienced how a vision (of Christ, or of the Uncreated Light, or of something holy) marked the real "beginning" of their existence, in much the same way my student did, and then simply applied this experience to creation by analogy.

I have concluded, though, that for the saints it wasn't merely a metaphor but rather that their personal re-birth was experienced so strongly when they saw the Light, that they realized that this experience was an image, an icon, of the beginning of *all* things. Their experience of being "born-again" (Jn 3:3)[6] was so deep that it gave them a Job-like insight into the origins of the very universe. My own experience in that garden in Essex, though enough to change my life, was but a pale shadow compared to what the saints saw in the Uncreated Light.

---

6 "Jesus answered and said unto him, Verily, verily, I say unto thee, Except a man be born again, he cannot see the kingdom of God," is the full verse. Perhaps what this means is that our response to theophany must include a willingness to accept our former lives as being a kind of *nihil* from which we will now be created anew, or the vision won't be complete.

Thus, while I did not see the implication for the cosmos of my encounter with holiness... some of the Church Fathers may have actually *seen* the cosmic meaning itself!

RTE: What about those who haven't had this revelation, at least consciously? How can they progress?

DR. PATITSAS: We can pray for such a revelation. This is how Bill Wilson founded Alcoholics Anonymous. He simply prayed for a "spiritual awakening" – while being very careful never to entertain an imagined picture of what such an awakening might look like. This was his successful attempt at "imageless prayer." And God visited him, after some time, and the rest of his struggle for sobriety and to build the fellowship of AA was really just the working out of that "primordial theophany" he had received in his hospital room.

Or, to be even more positive: if you are thinking to yourself, "Aw, shucks, why can't I have a vision!," just know that even this thought was not your own. It came to you from God. The desire for theophany *is* your first theophany. Only don't frustrate yourself unduly. "Be still, and know that I am God" (Ps 46:10). A student of mine just told me that a better translation of "stillness" in this verse is leisure or sabbath rest. So we needn't become anxious about it.

RTE: That's reassuring. Can we return now to how we reach a truly beautiful social justice?

DR. PATITSAS: As we said above, we really ought to begin our discussion about social justice at the end: we were created for Christ, and it is toward him that we are all barrelling at the speed of light. And we know that Christ will one day come to judge us. Incidentally, Muslims believe, too, that the "Prophet" Jesus will preside at the Last Judgment. The Jewish tradition is that "the Messiah" will judge humanity at the end of the world. And all three faiths believe that this judgment will take place in the valley between Gethsemane and Jerusalem. So, one half of the world's population is in rough agreement about our end, at least.

Now, speaking of the Judgment... We should remind ourselves that we already know the two commandments upon which "all the Law and all the Prophets hang," upon which we shall be judged. These are 1) the complete devotion to God and 2) loving our neighbor as ourselves (Mt 22:35-40). And we know, as well, that when Christ comes in his glory to judge us, He will ask six things: I was hungry; did you feed me? I was thirsty; did you give me to drink? I was naked; did you clothe me? I was sick; did you visit me? I was a stranger; did you welcome me? I was in prison; did you console me?

All of this is straightforward and well known to all of us. Nevertheless, three aids to the understanding of our ultimate end long eluded me.

To Love Christ Is to Fulfill both of the Two Greatest Commandments

The first aid is the relationship between the two greatest commandments and the person of Jesus Christ. Because we are commanded to love God with all our heart, soul, mind, and strength, and are also commanded to love our neighbor, our fellow human beings, as ourselves, it is proper that we should therefore place a special focus on that one unique person who is *both* our God *and* our neighbor: I mean, of course, Jesus Christ. Only in loving Christ do we directly fulfill *both* of the two greatest commandments because only He is fully God *and* fully man.

This is what Christ means when He says that all the Law and the Prophets are contained in these two commands – He means that the Law and the Prophets all pointed to him, to Christ, and to his divine-human nature! Devotion to Christ is therefore the simplest touchstone for a perfect and balanced life, and the fulfillment of the Old Law, the prophecies, and of human destiny.

Secondly, we can then see how this relates to the criteria of the Last Judgment, as described by Christ himself in Matthew 25. The six questions, of how we treat the hungry, the thirsty, the naked, the prisoner, the stranger, the sick among our fellow man, are all taken as referring to Christ God. If you love your fellow man (the least of these my brethren), then you have loved Christ (who is fully human), and thus you have loved God (for Christ is God). Your reward for this will be eternal life with God. However, if we *don't* love our fellow man, then we have not loved Christ, and therefore we have neglected God. So, there again we see the convergence within Christ's own person of the commands to love God and love neighbor.

In other words, once we see that the two greatest commandments meet within Christ's own divine-human self, we then can also see that the the six questions at the Last Judgment do not at all reveal a *different* standard of judgment than that given in the two greatest commandments. Rather, the six questions just expand the meaning of those two commandments, once you realize that Christ is fully man and fully God *and* that He has identified himself in particular with "the least of these." Don't love the poor, and you've betrayed Christ, and thus failed at the two commandments that matter most.

A third important point about the Judgment was harder to discern, but it relates directly to the issue of trauma and whether it is even possible for it to be healed. I didn't see this third point until one of my theological students, Dr. James Guba, pointed it out in class. In the story of the Last Judgment, all of humanity asks, "*When* did we see you hungry, thirsty, naked, sick, a stranger, and a prisoner?" Christ answers, "In the least of these my brethren." But, Dr. Guba pointed out, there really is another time *when we do see* Christ *exactly* fitting these six descriptions: at his crucifixion. There on Golgotha, Christ is a prisoner, a stranger, physically suffering, naked, thirsty, and hungry – all the states included in the criteria of the Last Judgment in Matthew 25.

Thus, the prophecy of the Last Judgment that Christ gives us in Matthew 25 in fact tells us that his own crucifixion is the moment of judgment for the entire human race! The six questions do not merely point us towards the poor but toward the mystery of the

God-man crucified. And thus, through these six questions, we are being told that, *Christ in his voluntary crucifixion will be the standard for the judgment of the world!*

To put this another way, when Christ poses the six questions to be asked of us at the Last Judgment, He is actually, in a humble way, saying that our reaction to him, whenever we find him crucified, is what will reveal the state of our souls and determine our eternal destiny. And thus it is before the Holy Cross that we will be judged, that we are *already* all being judged.

How we react to Christ crucified – this is what judges us. And, in fact, when Christ teaches us the two greatest commandments, He actually says that all the Law and the Prophets "hang" on these two commandments! So He really was, in stressing those two short precepts, in a hidden way not only pronouncing his own full divinity and full humanity, but He was also teaching us that the entire Old Covenant had pointed to his incarnation and to his coming crucifixion.[7]

In the Gospel of Matthew, Christ says of the Last Judgment, "When the Son of Man comes *in his glory* to judge the world..." Well, what if in this one instance the term "glory" functions in St. Matthew's Gospel just as it usually does in the Gospel according to St. John? What if the "glory" in which Christ comes at the end of the world is the full and undeniable revelation of his crucified love for the world?

And should it then still surprise us to realize that the vision that will judge us at the end of time is the vision that created us at the beginning of time: the self-emptying love of the Son of God for the entire world? To embrace and express such love is the end for which we were created, and therefore our judgment can be nothing other than the revelation of whether we have fulfilled that purpose. Our willingness to embrace the appearing of the Lamb slain "from before the foundation of the world" (Rev 13:8) is what tells us whether we have fulfilled the goal that originally drew us into being.

---

7 Moreover, Christ shows us elsewhere *how much* to love the crucified person. In John 13:34, Christ gives a "new" commandment – that we love one another as He has loved us. We are made in the image of Christ and of him crucified.

An Ancient Tradition about the Six Psalms of Orthros

There is a custom in the Orthros/Matins service that we are not supposed to walk around, bow, or even make the sign of the cross during the reading of the entire *Hexapsalmos* – the Six Psalms. We aren't to make our cross even during the middle when we recite, "Glory to the Father, and to the Son, and to the Holy Spirit."

A monastic tradition says that this is because these are the six psalms that will be read at the Last Judgment. And in as little time as it takes for the angel to read these six psalms, the tradition continues, all the people from all of history will be sorted out, the sheep from the goats, and placed at either the right hand or the left hand of Christ. During that time of final sorting, no more movement under our own power will be possible, no protests or acts of repentance, nor even making the sign of the cross will be permitted. We will be immobilized, awaiting God's judgment and determination; our time for action of any kind will have passed.

After the Last Judgment, a new and deeper adventure will begin for those counted worthy. And even in the service of Orthros, on Sunday in particular, the *Hexapsalmos* is followed immediately with the first announcement of the Resurrection: "God is the Lord and has revealed himself to us!" In other words, we begin to enter the Kingdom.

But why should this tradition at Orthros be true? Why would those six psalms in particular be the ones read at the final Judgment of the world? The answer is because each one of them is a confession of the thoughts of the God-man upon the cross. These Psalms judge us because they reveal the end for which we were created: Jesus Christ, and him crucified.

The earliest and still the most important prayerbook of the Church is the psalter, of course. The psalms are attributed to the *Prophytanax* – the Prophet-King – for, like Christ, King David fulfilled a prophetic as well as a kingly office. And while we may read the psalms as expressing the inner world of King David, in actuality they are prophetic books, too: The mystery that they often reveal is the inner life of the Messiah at various points during his ministry on earth. David mystically saw the inward life of Christ and shared it with us. When we pray the psalms, some of them in particular, we don't just petition or ask God as outsiders to God's life. No, we enter into and take on "the mind of Christ" (I Cor 2:16; Phil 2:5). We are privileged to think Christ's thoughts when we pray the Psalter! That is why it is the essential prayer book of the Church.

You know, Harold Bloom, the eminent scholar at Yale, wrote once that in the entire Hebrew Bible, only of David is it said that "God loved him."[8] And think now, in the light of what we have just said, what gifts were given to David because he was loved by God: David was granted to live the inner world of Christ and even to share in the sufferings of Christ upon the cross. What a prophecy David gave us! It is not just announcing that the Messiah will come or what the Messiah will accomplish, but a prophecy that declares the actual inner life and thoughts of that Messiah. Of how many of the prophets can this be said?!

So, this tradition about these six psalms being read at the Last Judgment teaches us that what we will behold there at the end of time, or understand fully for the first time, is the vision that once created the world and that once created each of us. At the Judgment we reach our *telos*, the end that by being so beautiful, began us. We see "Christ, and him crucified." For the first time, we shall understand perfectly his love and self-offering upon the cross. In seeing again, but now more clearly, our Archetype, our first love, the pattern-way-form-logos[9] according to which we were meant to exist, we will know for certain whether anything within us remains that could conform to that way of love.

---

[8] In his *The American Religion: The Emergence of the Post-Christian Nation* (New York: Simon and Schuster, 1992).

[9] See Chapter Six above, "The Mystical Architect" for the argument that the Forms are the logoi of Creation.

Avoiding the Unforgivable Sin

Let us weave in one more strand about the aim and end of human existence. Elsewhere in the Gospel of St. Matthew, Christ says that there is only one unforgivable sin, which is to blaspheme the Holy Spirit. Of course, when I was eight years old and read that for the first time, my thoughts immediately went in some silly direction and I asked my older brother if I had thus permanently lost my salvation.

But the Gospel writer himself probably had something else in mind. Saint Matthew uses the word "blaspheme" only two other times in his Gospel, the last time being when the passersby who beheld Christ hanging from the cross wagged their heads and "blasphemed." Those mocking him even said that Christ should come down from the cross and save himself. In other words, at what is Christ's moment of glory, the moment where the Holy Spirit fully anoints him as messiah, the moment where Christ's infinite sacrificial love for them is revealed and they are being saved, their only response is to mock and to curse!

How many times has that happened in my own life, by the way, that the very thing God has sent in order to help me, the very act of his self-emptying Theophany for me, appeared to me in such a difficult guise that I actually swore!

In fact, I wonder if almost all the time when we curse over some difficulty that this is in fact what we are doing? Not to say that cussing is the unforgivable sin, but certainly if we curse *every* blessing that holds a grain of difficulty, such that our entire disposition and our entire way of life becomes opposed to the Crucified One, what appeal would a heaven guarded by the cross still hold for us? Through this continual cursing, we would by then have become total thieves, ungrateful, blasphemers in our deepest souls. We would find no place in the eternal thanksgiving Eucharist of the Crucified One.

And not just our own crosses but when we behold the crosses borne by the "least of these," when we behold Christ crucified around us, do we bless or do we in fact curse? Do we embrace the Down Syndrome child as not only a cross but also a blessing, or do we undertake medical tests that could potentially harm even a healthy child in the womb, just so that we might detect Christ being crucified in a special-needs child and abort him before he can breathe his first breath? When we behold any suffering person, do we see that their suffering is a special anointing that we might, through empathy, also be privileged to share in? Or, do we see their suffering only as a curse and seek to run from it as fast as possible?

At the moment of our own worst crucifixions, when we are driven to the deepest despair, can we still cling to the Anointed One or are we tempted to blaspheme the difficult twofold anointing that we are receiving in the Holy Spirit,[10] and even reach the terrible point where we wish that we could end our lives rather than go on being anointed in this way?

Then, to top it all off, what happens when just a few hours after having contemplated such self-destructive thoughts, I am approached by a shifty beggar, whose affect suggests criminal intent? Do I remember Christ at that moment, or has the beggar's sin thrown me back into a place where I would be willing even to harm another person in order to survive?

Such is the instability of our reaction to the adventure of life in Christ! We long for an anointing but curse it when it comes. We wish for a theophany but without the cross that it is based in. We find our lives so difficult that they seem unbearable but are still willing to hurt others to survive. We have not found the middle way of patiently and gratefully bearing the twofold anointing that the Holy Spirit brings, and so we lose the chance to live stably within the Spirit's visitation, to find grace and God's good favor increasing steadily, permeating our hearts, bodies, and minds.

---

10 See Chapter Three above, "Chastity and Empathy: Eros, Agape, and the Mystery of the Twofold Anointing."

Acquire the Spirit of Peace

We are not stable in our reception of the anointing that the Holy Spirit brings, in other words. We have not "acquired" the Holy Spirit, as St. Seraphim of Sarov said we ought to, but instead are like leaves blown in the wind of grace's arriving and "departing."

What we cannot admit is that this suffering, this humiliation that the poor or the disabled undergoes, or that we ourselves undergo in our dark trials, *may well be or can become an aspect of our anointing by the Holy Spirit*. If we turn away in shame, or curse, or mock when we see others suffering, then we have begun to blaspheme the Holy Spirit. If, on the other hand, we hasten to show empathy, to share in the other person's suffering – and, in fact, to have compassion also for our own selves when we are humiliated – then in that case we will share, too, in the consoling and ennobling side of this anointing.

To repeat St. Seraphim, "The goal of the Christian life is the *acquisition* of the Holy Spirit" – not its mere reception. The Holy Spirit is given freely to all, but can we hold on to the Spirit? Since Pentecost, the Uncreated Light of God is shed abroad in the world without limit, but our eyes are not prepared to see it.

Saint Seraphim was saying that we are called to be the stable and trusting children of our Heavenly Father, gratefully receiving from the Lord's hand whatever He sends us. The warning about blasphemy of the Holy Spirit is of a piece with the Two Greatest Commandments, that we love God and neighbor, and also with the warnings of the Last Judgment. What the Holy Spirit brings to us is Christ the God-man himself, in his difficult twofold anointing upon the cross.

It was this vision of Christ crucified – for his crucifixion is an inescapable aspect of his anointing by the Holy Spirit – and it was the love that we felt when we first saw him there on the cross, that together long ago created the world, that once created each of us. I mean, even at the moment of our conception in the wombs of our mothers, it was by somehow beholding Christ in his self-emptying love that we were drawn into existence.

But, having lost this first love, we are now unworthy of it. At our beginning, we were willing to be crucified with Christ – that is, we were willing to bear the hardships of the adventure of life! "We didn't ask to be born," we say; but at some level, we *did* ask. We always, at a biological level at least, consented to existence, as the zygote underwent cell division and kept moving and struggling and striving toward life – and our bodies *are* us, too. So, yes, we *did ask* and we *still do ask with every beat of our heart* to be born and to have the chance to meet the struggles of life.

And yet later on, after God had done so much more for us and we therefore had so much more to lose, we were willing even to crucify Christ so that we would not lose what we now regarded as our own, or even had come to idolize. Once we saw more fully the cost of being made in the image of the Crucified One, we wanted to run away, to escape the adventure of freedom and existence.

We have rejected the twofold anointing in our own lives, and in the lives of the poor. We have rejected the working of the Holy Spirit.

And thus again, we see that it is the vision of the Cross that will judge us, wherever we find that Cross.

Responding to Christ in Need

RTE: How then would you answer someone who says that the real heart of Christianity lies in fulfilling the Lord's injunctions to feed the hungry, clothe the naked, visit the sick and imprisoned, and that going to church and praying is just too easy?

DR. PATITSAS: Helping is not enough. We have to see in the poor, and at times also in ourselves when we are poor, a theophany: Christ crucified but victorious. This is Beauty-first. And we have to consent to be co-crucified with the poor and as the poor for the sake of Christ. This is the Almsgiving, or Empathy, or Goodness that unfolds from Beauty. And if we do this consistently, then we shall be True – we shall be saved, and we shall befriend the poor in a real way.

As we help the poor, who are being crucified *by* the world, we helpers also have to crucify ourselves *to* the world. We have to give to and accompany those around us in such a way that we, too, are trading the vanities of this fallen world for life in the Kingdom.

This may not happen as much when we adopt the social cause of the moment or divert all our helping efforts into making our chosen cause politically popular. Paul Farmer, co-founder of Partners in Health, started his medical philanthropy in a setting of complete environmental and social desolation; so did Mother Teresa. Their genius was to resolve to add just one ingredient to their impossible situations: love. In starting a home to comfort the terminally ill as they lay dying, Mother Teresa wasn't impacting any metrics of social well-being, per se, but she was liberating the poor and herself from "the world" and its killing dominion over our souls. People might still die, she realized, but they would die loving and being loved, and thus they would depart having conquered the world.

All of that is not the same as trying to be good by "helping" someone who, unlike us, is poor, by throwing a few coins their way. And we very much need to expand our concept of poverty to include emotional and spiritual poverty because so many in the rich countries are literally dying from conditions stemming from their loneliness, boredom, and inner emptiness, as St. Paisios the Hagiorite (1924-1994) said.[11]

As for its being *easy* to go to church – well, our bishops and priests *want us* to come to church so that *they* can minister to *us* in *our* hunger, thirst, nakedness, and imprisonment. Philanthropy cuts both ways. In church we are also "the least of these." And we have to obey those set in authority over us, so let's go to church! We need it! We are poor, too, and this is how we are being helped!

---

11 Sometimes *literally* dying: towards the end of her own life, Jane Jacobs was very sorrowful and troubled by accounts of the elderly who had perished in the 1994 Chicago heat wave. Some had so few social connections that, out of fear, they wouldn't even open their doors to the social workers who came to save them from the heat. See her account in *Dark Age Ahead* (New York: Random House, 2004), 81-87.

Besides, it's not at all easy to go to church, or else everyone would be doing it. It's very hard to go to church. Sometimes, it's more than hard – it can seem like the very door of the church is closed to us, perhaps because of some inner disposition we are nurturing or on account of the habits we keep. At least, I can see that making time for chapel here on campus is something that sometimes I just can't do, no matter how hard I try, whereas other times it comes very easily, and I seem to be carried there effortlessly.

Most of all, the services and sacraments and teachings in church are the primary way that the Church feeds the hungry, gives drink to the thirsty, heals the sick, clothes the naked, welcomes the stranger, and liberates the prisoner – all these commands of Matthew 25 that will determine our eternal fate. I would rather have baptism, a short life, and a priest's absolution on my deathbed, than a long prosperous life outside the grace of the sacraments. If we don't believe this, then why go to church at all? Why honor the young martyrs who never enjoyed the things of this world? If we don't believe that church services are an answer and in many cases the best answer to the six questions of the Last Judgment, then we need to take a deep breath and reconsider.

RTE: This is true, but don't the Church Fathers usually view this gospel quote literally, as a command to physically feed, clothe, and visit?

DR. PATITSAS: Yes, of course. But we now live in a society where hundreds of billions of dollars are spent in this way, with very mixed results. Often, we can see in social justice movements a spirit that is quite empty, or even contrary to the gospel.

Our response to Christ's call to minister to the poor has to be quite discerning, quite rich. It should be, in fact, "fractal," meaning that it should take place at many different scales, and that within each scale of helping we should find the same crucial elements of doxology, repentance, asceticism, love for Beauty, and empathy.[12]

---

12 "A fractal is a never-ending pattern. Fractals are infinitely complex patterns that are self-similar across different scales. Fractal patterns are extremely familiar, since nature is full

Let me explain further why our response to Christ must be fractal whenever we find him hungry, thirsty, naked, sick, imprisoned, or a stranger. I mean, that a) this response should take place at several levels, and that b) within each of these levels we should find all the other levels, all the other ways of serving Christ, in a complex, abundant, and beautiful way. For example, not only social work but also motherhood, the church services, missionary work, and other acts all fulfill this gospel command to love the poor. But it is also crucial that within each type of philanthropy, we should be able to discern the other important types of philanthropy. For example, within motherhood we can clearly see a kind of social work, a liturgy, and a missionary endeavor. This should always be the case: in all of the ways of serving the poor, we should find discernible all the other ways.

RTE: Would that also apply if we are in a monastery or in another life situation – perhaps we are invalids – where we didn't have much contact with those in need?

DR. PATITSAS: Yes, I have come to see that even the life of a hesychast who lives in utter solitude is bound up with helping the poor.

My first clue as to how a life of the Jesus Prayer ministers to the "least of these" came through a puzzle that lasted many years for me. Father Sophrony Sakharov (whom we mentioned earlier) talks about how important it is for a monastic to "keep the commandments." But he seems usually not to specify which commandments he has in mind; he seems to be speaking about the commandments in general. Finally, I saw that he had written somewhere that he meant in particular the two greatest commandments: the monastic must, as part of everything else he or she does, seek to love God perfectly *and* to love his neighbor as himself.

---

of fractals. For instance: trees, rivers, coastlines, mountains, clouds, seashells, hurricanes, etc." From "What are Fractals?," on the fractalfoundation.org website.

But then my question was, well, how does the monastic keep these two commandments, especially in that he does not live a life of social service in the world? It turns out that Fr. Sophrony in yet another place insists that the struggle for noetic prayer is itself the struggle both to love God perfectly and to love our neighbor as ourselves.

First, because most especially in noetic prayer is "*all* our heart, soul, mind, and strength" really given to Our Lord; this is something we can all say from experience. In fact, such moments of total spiritual devotion to the Lord strike us as "noetic," even if we aren't literally reciting the words of the prayer when we have them. But, secondly, only in noetic prayer does our identification with the world become so complete that we really do "love our neighbor as *our own self*." Even marriage and motherhood cannot quite equal noetic prayer for this unity on the spiritual plane, in Fr. Sophrony's opinion.

Thus, the Jesus Prayer really does prepare us for the Judgment. Through this prayer, we do fulfill all the injunctions of Matthew 25.

Noetic Hospitality

Forgive me for another diversion, but something must also be said about the practical service monastics offer to the world, in addition to their prayers. When I was a young man making pilgrimage to Mount Athos, people would discourage me from going, complaining, "Why are they up there thinking of themselves, when they should be down here helping us? We are the ones who need help."

But then you eventually realize that a large Athonite monastery can host more than 30,000 visitors per year.[13] Not all of these pilgrims stay overnight, and not all of them even take a meal at the monastery. But still, a community of 120 monastics receiving 30,000 visitors a year is equivalent to a family of five people receiv-

---

13 These are the numbers I received when I visited the monastery of Vatopedi on the Holy Mountain in 2012. During my annual pilgrimages to the Holy Mountain on behalf of my seminary, I sometimes am surrounded by so many more pilgrims than monastics that at times I can hardly find even one person wearing black robes.

ing 1,250 visitors a year.[14] The monks at least have to greet them, make them coffee and the other three traditional gifts of Athonite welcome (a loukoumi sweet, a shot of tsipouro, and a glass of water), and clean up after them. And all this because St. Paul, thinking of Abraham by the Oaks of Mamre, commands all Christians to be scrupulous in showing hospitality (Heb 13:2).

So, this is just the obvious social outreach of the monastery. But then comes the fact that people are going crazy down here in the commercialized and over-regulated world of contemporary society, and a monastic retreat might be the only thing that saves their sanity and their soul. Many of those pilgrims travel to the Holy Mountain to pour out their most difficult problems, things they can tell to no one else on earth except a trusted confessor.

But in noetic prayer, the monastic (it is usually monastics, although not always) goes well beyond the physical and spiritual hospitality the monastery offers. In noetic prayer, a Christian reaches out and heals the world by receiving the world into himself as he offers himself to Christ. A Christian praying in this way can stop wars, heal the sick, and do so much else. If our sole focus were the results of our philanthropic efforts, we would arm a few of our philanthropists with *komboskinis*[15] rather than degrees in social work, and redeploy them to a life of prayer.

RTE: You're going to catch some flack on this one. Many people believe that we accomplish more for society by sending our young people to be doctors and social workers than cloistered monastics.

DR. PATITSAS: The problems down here are so complex that many times the most rational course is prayer rather than any particular

---

14 To be fair, we might only count the adult members of the family; so, 500 visitors a year coming to a home, if there are two parents and three children in the family of five. Incidentally, one of the biggest practical advantages of any monastic community is its high ratio of adults to children. Few families in the world match these ratios, and so families cannot usually give as much attention to the difficult points of Christian civilization that even a medium-sized monastery does: calligraphy, iconography, woodcarving, customs of hospitality, copying and preservation of manuscripts, care for precious relics, keeping the full cycle of services, specialized forms of social work, and so forth.

15 A *komboskini* is an Orthodox prayer rope, used especially when praying the Jesus Prayer.

social action. Besides, what percentage of physical maladies in the developed world have as their real cause, "the patient failed to live an ascetic life"? And without the monastic example, could we do that? One could argue that failure to keep the fasts and make prostrations is now among the leading causes of death among adults in the developed world. Meanwhile, failure to confess, pray, and commune is a leading cause of our psychological ailments.

Also, what percentage of poverty and social pathology in America is caused by the simple fact that we haven't bothered to support marriage in the right way? But how can most of us keep faithful marriages, if at least a few of us don't renounce marriage entirely? In practice, marriage needs the prayers and examples of the monastics. I don't know why, but it does.

In many ways our world is better off than ever before, while in other ways it seems worse. Did you know that *right now more than 150 million women are missing from the world because of the widespread practice of sex-selective abortion over the last fifty years?* Apparently, for decades now, parents in many countries have been testing the gender of their baby in the womb and, if it is a girl, ending its development because they want a boy instead.[16] How can we read such facts and not be almost crushed by the cruelty of human sin? But prayer, especially the imageless prayer of the Orthodox Church, changes everything; the very rules of the game are altered by its practice.

But my point was not to disparage social work nor any other calling. My plea is that we see instead that we need *all* the different responses to the appearing of Christ in the suffering person. We can't belittle *any* of the healthy ways of life, including the life of noetic prayer. And a person who pits one against the other – like people who claim that it is easy to go to church, although they themselves never do go to church (or even *could* go to church, perhaps because they are so angry at "the Church") is only going to introduce a lot of confusion when they give advice. They seem to be

---

16 When I was living overseas in one such country, I remember a woman quoted in the newspapers who had aborted five of her daughters because they were not boys. Upon finally reaching her goal of having a son, she simply stated, "I feel that I have plucked a star from the sky."

saying something significant but, in fact, are only burdening others with their own inner dramas.

Motherhood, Mission, Marriage

We must also look at motherhood as a way in which some women fulfill the six questions of the Last Judgment. Since the 1970s, and still now, people blame mothers for all our environmental and social problems. Not because they have children out of wedlock – no, this is fine in the eyes of a world that is so threatened by chastity – but because they have children at all. Supposedly, overpopulation threatens our planet. So they say women should "help the poor" by foregoing motherhood.

But if you think about it, when were any of us ever *more* hungry, thirsty, naked, physically vulnerable, a stranger, a prisoner, than when we were in our mother's wombs? Who is more naked than a person at the moment of his or her conception, when they possess only the barest thread of physical form? Is there anyone who fulfills the tasks of Matthew 25 more perfectly than a mother? And yet, in all the sermons on Matthew 25, who ever mentions mothers? Saint Paul promoted celibacy, but of mothers he says simply that if they persevere in faith and holiness they will be saved (I Tim 2:15). The perfection of their care for Christ is indisputable for him.

Furthermore, now that population growth in every single developed country (except Israel, the United States, and perhaps Russia) has collapsed, there will be no one left to pay for the social welfare of the sick and the old and to pay for schools and infrastructure for the wider society. The great Elon Musk, the most inspiring and gifted entrepreneur/engineer of our day, says that world populations are collapsing so quickly that the future will be dominated by the elderly and robots.

So, the Church services, monastic hospitality, noetic prayer, motherhood – these are all wonderful ways to answer these six questions that Christ will ask us at the Last Judgment. Each of them is real, to the point, perfect.

And let us hasten to add mission work. Is the sharing of the gospel not also a deliverance for the person imprisoned in sin and unbelief, who lives life as a stranger to Trinitarian life, hungry and thirsty for the Body and Blood of Christ, spiritually sick and naked of the grace of baptism and chrismation? Why should we not include mission work as an answer to Matthew 25, as well? When I was on mission in Korea, I remember asking a Korean university student if she didn't find it a cultural imposition to have Christianity brought to her country. She answered, "Don't be absurd! Buddhism came to Korea from China, and the Chinese got it from India – and all those prior cultural impositions occurred just to bring us the Buddha – *who wasn't even God!*"

Of course, to answer the six questions of Matthew 25, we must count actual charitable work, too. And the Church has always excelled in this labor. It was the Church that invented the orphanage, the medical hospital, the home for the elderly, and other social institutions. The idea of the welfare *state*, on the other hand, was invented not by Bismarck in the nineteenth century but by Julian the Apostate in the fourth, who hoped that if he could commandeer the Church's invention – care for the poor – for the Roman Empire, then he might break the appeal of the Church and return Roman society to paganism. Even in modern Greece, there was a cruel drive to take orphanage work away from monastic sisters and give it to the State, as we said. This is a perennial and darker side of government welfare, that it is often motivated by a fear that some loyalty of the citizens will remain toward a higher authority than the state could ever claim.

But let us now add to our list of real ways to respond to the six questions of Matthew 25, some of the hospitalities of marriage that we mentioned in another discussion: the welcome we show in marriage to God, to our spouse, to the gender of our spouse, to our children, and to visitors. All of this, too, is caring for people at their most vulnerable.

Here is a telling statistic: it has been claimed that 75% of the millions of foreign students studying in the United States complete their studies here without ever having seen the inside of an American home.[17] We spend billions of dollars on foreign aid but miss our chance to welcome the stranger when he or she is under so much stress and so far from home. The saintly elder Fr. Nicholas Pekatoras in Washington, D.C. (1899-1997) used to say that students were exempt from *all* fasting requirements because their lives are so full of challenges and demands. I liked his saying this because I myself was a student during the days that I knew him. But he was a tremendous ascetic himself, and a worker of miracles even in his own lifetime. So let us not underestimate the saving importance of the hospitality we show within our homes to hard-pressed people like students and others.

And, finally, in our list of ways to answer the call of Matthew 25, we can note that the Byzantines honored the work of the trades and commerce, and of government officials, as also contributing to the good ordering of society and to society's ability to take care of all its people, and especially of its vulnerable. Someone has to invent and make the things we wish to share with people; and, of course, a country with undefended borders and no real laws is naked in a fatal way.

The Fractal Character of the Response to Christ Crucified

All in all, I count eight beautiful ways that we react with perfect love to the presence of Christ in the crucified poor. These ways are: the services of the Church; noetic prayer; monastic charity; motherhood; mission work; social or philanthropic work; all the hospitalities of marriage; and our vocations in the world. I am sure that there are others, although some of them fit within these first eight. For example, teaching our children is either a vocation, or it is an aspect of motherhood; theologians/bishops who "rightly divide the word of the truth" are the heart of both mission and the divine services; and so forth.

---

17 According to the Christian non-profit International Students, Inc. Cf.: http://www.isionline.org/GetInvolved.aspx Accessed December 4, 2017.

Here is what I want to stress: in a healthy society, in a healthy Church, we shall find *all eight* of these main responses to the poor honored and promoted and practiced. And moreover, if any one of these eight is missing, this may be a sign that each of the ones we *are* still doing is somehow suspect; the good that we do witness may not be organic, not fractal, if parts of it are absent.

As an example, a society that cannot praise God properly may talk a good game about helping the poor, but if we scratch the surface we will find that its care for the poor is somehow amiss. In the communist case, "helping the poor" somehow always manages to make everybody poor, for example. A church with no mission work probably isn't feeling much devotion to its divine services. A society that humiliates its poor will soon enough find motherhood disparaged and its birth rates dropping.

There is something else which is even more wonderful: when the response to Christ is whole and genuine, we will find *within* each of the eight responses to the poor *all* of the other seven responses! This "nesting" of the eight ways within each other is what gives our social concern a properly fractal, an organic and alive, character.

For example, within motherhood we so clearly see mission work, as it is from their mothers and grandmothers that so many great saints learned their faith; we see hospitality, as the mother welcomes the child at every stage, no matter how difficult, of its life; we see care for the poor, as the mother so naturally extends her care to strangers *and because her own children are so infinitely poor without her*; we see religious ritual, as she lights the *kandili* before the icons at home and leads the family to prayer; we see noetic prayer, as she learns the great art of unknowing in her constant reliance on God, even if she has never even heard of the Jesus Prayer; and so on.

Again and again, we see that within any of these eight ways of helping the poor, the other seven are present.

Noetic Prayer and Helping the Poor

This next example of all the other seven ways being present in any one of them I like even better – although you will have to supply your own stories from the lives of saints and elders that you have read. Within the life of mystical prayer, also, we can see hospitality, Christian mission, protection against foreign invasion and civil strife, provision for the material needs of others, and a rapture that draws the whole world into a divine service to God in Christ. This last is the reason why sometimes the very hills around an ascetic begin to give off a myrrh-like fragrance.

A noetic prayer that did not ripple out mystically into such broader social and environmental effects would reveal itself as something odd, as something un-Christian. Such an asceticism would be a kind of yoga for the production of spiritual *individuals*, not an *ecclesial* event with intense *social, cosmic*, and even *environmental* ramifications.

That is why, even in our day, we hear so many stories of elders at prayer, who in the moment of most intense mystical *noesis* passed physically to places of need and offered physical help. An example from the life of Elder Paisios will help me to illustrate. One day in the 1970s, a father arrived at Mt. Athos with his young child and began searching the monasteries for a particular monk. It seems that just the month before, the child had wandered into the street and into the path of an oncoming truck. However, at the last moment, a monk had appeared out of nowhere, pushing the child to the ground and saving its life; the monk then immediately vanished. The good father had the thought to scour the Holy Mountain until the child should recognize his protector – which he promptly did the moment he saw Elder Paisios. But many, many such events involving either St. Paisios or St. Porphyrios, whom we mentioned in an earlier interview, occurred during their lifetimes. These saints were somehow in two places at once.

Another acquaintance of ours was pulled from the rubble of a collapsed building in the United States by a monk who at that moment was celebrating his feast day on the Holy Mountain. The monk, in fact, has never visited America, and it was only after his miraculous rescue of her that this woman first heard of him, met him – and then became a nun, taking the feminine version of the elder's name as her monastic name.[18]

A different friend of mine, a Ministry of Justice official in the former Soviet bloc, had been visited in Moscow by his elder towards the very end of the Soviet years, at a moment when my friend was in great despair. The visit surprised my friend very much, for his elder was at that time confined under house arrest hundreds of miles away. My friend offered tea and cookies to the elder, which he accepted, and they visited for over an hour. But afterwards, my friend could not say for sure how the whole thing had happened. Had he perhaps imagined the entire encounter? Years later, as the USSR weakened, my friend was able to see his elder again in person in the regular way, and ask if the mystical visit had been real, and the elder confirmed in a miraculous way that it had been.[19]

An American friend was often visited in his youth by a distant relative, a contemporary spiritual father who as of this writing is still living. These visits would occur after the boy had received Communion, and in the context of large family gatherings at the home on Sunday afternoons. But this elder, too, the boy would grow up to learn, had never actually travelled to America! The visits were miracles in the life of a boy who would grow up to become a priest.

Many other evidences exist of this link between noetic prayer and social concern, but, of course, the same people who dismiss such tales as mythological *also* then go on to condemn the life of noetic prayer as somehow selfish or self-concerned. Well if you make

---

18 Many years later, I happened to meet the architect who had designed the building that had collapsed. Its failure occurred through no fault of his own, for it was a cost-saving shortcut by the builders that led to the disaster. Although he is not Orthodox, when I told him of the miracle, he was completely unsurprised. He said that he also felt something spiritual happening that night as he rushed to the tragic scene with many others in order to rescue whomever he could.

19 The Russian elder was Hieromonk Nikolai (Gurianov) of St. Nicholas Church on the island of Talabsk (Zalit) in Pskov-Chudskoye Lake, who reposed in 2002. He was among the three or four acknowledged holy elders still living when the Soviet Union collapsed in 1989.

an *a priori* decision to dismiss all the evidence demolishing your conclusion that noetic prayer has no social effect, how valid will that conclusion be?

The Nesting of the Eight Responses

This nesting of each of the responses to Christ's suffering within the other seven tells us that we are dealing with something healthy, organic, and almost automatic – a fractal flowering or unfolding of orthodox response to God's revelation in the crucifixion and resurrection of Christ. We must choose between monasticism and marriage, to be sure – and perhaps choose one of the career paths. These choices are significant, of course. But if we stay close to Christ, we will also find that the choices we left behind all somehow re-appear, return, but now in a form appropriate to the path we have chosen. The parent will renounce monasticism, and then keep many all-night vigils with a sick child. The warrior will renounce social work, and then find himself giving his life for his friend. The mother will renounce making a difference in the world, only to realize that she has made the ultimate difference. Or, she will continue her career and, though fearing that she is failing as a mother, will in fact inspire her children with a pure love for the world and the ability to nurture others.

Fractals, we must remember, are not consciously "made" but rather are *generated* by some hidden algorithm, some responsive unfolding. To love Christ is to guarantee that we somehow fulfill all of these things He requires. Eros provides the energy for all this glorious unfolding.

And thus, we can see that in Christ all of life becomes both a doxology and a theophany. We see God enthroned everywhere, in every creature, leaf and blade of grass, and yet understand that somehow in his humility He also asks for our kind welcome and care. And so we praise God by conveying the mercy we receive from him to all of the creation around us. Saint Silouan once even chastised Fr. Sophrony, in his younger years, for the way he was cutting down branches to keep a forest path clear; St. Silouan thought it had been done without pity.

Creation remains creation, but it now functions as an icon of *Christ* in his twofold anointing as both resurrected king and sacrificial victim. The world becomes for us a giant procession; each part of the world becomes part of a liturgy *for the life of the rest of the world* – a liturgy for God in Christ, in other words, for *He* is our Life, and the world moves for him!

So these two tests help us to gauge or measure the health of our local church – we must see all eight of these responses to Christ in need present and functioning well in our communities, *and* we ought to be able to find, within any of these eight responses, all of the other seven.[20]

For example, overseas mission work that was not aimed at the future moment when "Christ be born in you" – a mission that did not also function as a "motherhood" by encouraging local churches to slowly become self-sustaining – would be suspect. Such a mission might create religious clones or political allies, but it would not be in keeping with the genuine ethos of the Church. A mission that did not engender noetic prayer and monasticism in its new place would be suspect; it would also be a partial gospel and would not manifest the otherworldliness and immediacy of the Kingdom of Heaven in the way that monasticism does. Without local monasticism, the new local church would always be dependent on "outside supplies" of sanctity and inspiration. And what would we say of a mission that failed to include care for the hungry, sick, lonely, and imprisoned people living there? Or of a mission that did not engender the immediate giving of such care within the new local church?

---

20 Of course, monastic communities like those on Mount Athos do not have biological motherhood. However, motherhood is respected and promoted in at least two ways on the Holy Mountain. First, many pilgrims to Mount Athos come to ask divine help for the conception of children. And second, the Mother of God herself is so nurturing and loving to the visitors and monastics, and the monastics are so conscious of her motherly nature and living presence, that everyone feels the beauty and centrality of this vocation of motherhood.

The Best Way

It is natural and not to be a cause for distress when representatives of each of these eight ways sometimes imagine that their way, in particular, is all that matters, or is really the best way to serve Christ. Saint Paul recognizes a genuine hierarchy among the callings within the Church, and he even encourages a healthy competition – while still praising all the offices and insisting that the Church, like a physical body, needs a differentiation of vocations (I Cor 12). But in our defense and marketing of our own way to answer the call of Matthew 25, we must also remind ourselves that, "He who would be the greatest of all must also be the servant of all" (Mt 23:11). And how can we serve the church if we imagine that only we *are* the Church? Better to praise all of the ways that we aren't doing, and, when it comes to discussing our own way, simply use it to praise God.

And, in keeping with good fractal order, we must remember the constant possibility of surprise. A friend reversed her parish's long-standing policy that only children of "members in good standing" and who regularly attended Sunday School could join the parish Greek dance troupe. In a poor city where more than half of the children were born out of wedlock, this policy had been counterproductive. After the change in policy, the dance troupe tripled in size, including many children who had no relationship to the Church or to Greek culture, and several of these children grew up to join the Church. So this simple hospitality contained more effective mission work than one hundred radio ads.

Or, who would have thought that the death of a "table server" – the proto-martyr and deacon, St. Stephen – would play a pivotal role in the conversion of the greatest missionary, St. Paul?

When the Holy Spirit is moving, life becomes unpredictable like that. It becomes fractal, and more than fractal; that is, fractals are a part of nature, but in the Spirit we enter the realm of the supernatural. Each of the excellent ways of ministering to Christ in the least of these his brethren is present within all the other ways. If this is not the case, or if some of these ways are being neglected or disparaged, then this is a clue that something deeper in our life in Christ may still be dormant. Our eros for Christ could be somehow lacking, and we must look to him, rekindle our zeal, and follow the promptings that He gives us.

A healthy Christian community will in time generate all of these eight ways and others besides – or in time generate *none* of them. Each one, when it contains all the others within it, is "enough," is enough to save the world. And all of them, if they are healthy, are generated in this "pull" way – by our falling in love with Christ, and him crucified – rather than simply being conjured into existence by some social engineer or church planner. Saint John of Kronstadt spent seventeen years in his city celebrating the liturgy daily and ministering to all before he took even the first step to organize his charity work formally. Wouldn't some of our contemporary activists have rushed to condemn him during those early years for not undertaking bigger programs? But he knew what he was doing.

These eight ways are fractal – let us be careful not to separate them in our lives, and let us be careful that when we *do* separate them for the purposes of effective sermonizing or to encourage our fellow missionaries or social workers or monastics, we do not encourage others to separate them in *their* lives.

RTE: Although we can't separate them, which of these responses has particularly nourished you?

DR. PATITSAS: I benefit most from hospitality in the homes of my friends, and even more from the special hospitality given in monasteries where noetic prayer is practiced. So I am happy when my students who are inclined toward marriage or monasticism are able with their parents' blessing to answer those callings.

But my special heart is for those who show hospitality to the weakest and most vulnerable ideas about the life in Christ, and about the life of civilizations, when those ideas are true. Oh, and artists, especially architects and musicians. I suppose at the moment they mean the most to me.

Is Justice Social?

RTE: What of the term "social justice" itself? Some churches discuss it so frequently that, as you said, we might feel like our Orthodox Church is somehow lacking. On the other hand, an American Christian talk-show host recently encouraged his listeners to *leave* any church that so much as mentions the term "social justice," so bound up with socialist causes has the term become. How do we do real charity, and how, as Orthodox Christians, can we escape from the left/right categories?

DR. PATITSAS: The talk show host probably got the idea that "social justice" is a pernicious term from Friedrich Hayek (1899-1992), the Austrian economist who was the great champion of bottom-up approaches to economic organization.[21] For Hayek and his followers, only transactions between individuals can be classified as moral or immoral; society is not a "person," and therefore there exists no social morality, per se, good or bad. I mean, Hayek has a point – how exactly do we hold "society" in the aggregate accountable for the individual actions of its members?

But to accept this view without qualification we would have to ignore the biblical and Church witness of judgments being visited upon entire peoples for the actions of their leaders or of a significant portion of their members. Although I appreciate Hayek's intent, which was to emphasize individual responsibility, still as Christians we do have an obligation to consider and improve the broad moral tenor of our society. Venerating the Old Testament prophets as we do, we know that the society as a whole will be judged for the actions of her individual members. Moral luck means that we have to tend to the broad moral tenor of our society because it will impact each of us.

Of course, as we see in Abraham's attempt to negotiate with God over the fate of Sodom, this works positively, too. We believe

---

21 Friedrich Hayek: Author of such books as *The Road to Serfdom* (1944); *Individualism and Economic Order* (1944); and, most tellingly for our purposes here, *The Mirage of Social Justice* (vol. III in *Law, Legislation, and Liberty*, 1976).

that a few saints among us are often enough to preserve us from the just punishment that we may deserve, giving us time to repent.

But, in general, we in the Church must be careful when we tread on grounds of politics or policy. The Church is so much older than the modern form of the struggle between "right" and "left." The Church remembers some things the modern world has forgotten, like the universal political philosophy that *must* underlie *every* civilization. So the Church knows ways that are more "iconic," that make room for mystery and miracle even within political organization, and which also are more faithful to the actual permanent features of life in community.

As for those who attack the Orthodox Church for not doing more on social issues, we should remember a few things. First, active Orthodox Christians in America represent at most one percent of the total population here; we may be closer to one third of one percent. The idea that we should be bossing around everyone else as to social policy is a bit funny, and it wouldn't be taken very kindly by other denominations and groups who happen to have their own coherent social ethical traditions, and who have worked harder and for much longer on social issues in America.

Second, until twenty years ago, the majority of our members were first- or second-generation immigrants struggling to maintain their faith after having been politically or economically displaced from native lands that they would never have left willingly. For a long time, the Orthodox in America were *themselves* the poor. Of course, the larger churches in traditionally Orthodox countries such as Greece, Eastern Europe, and Russia are often the first avenue of social assistance in those countries, but here in America we lack the numbers and the resources.

Still, Orthodoxy is the carrier of very ancient and deep ideas, some of which were either forgotten in the Western Dark Ages or were erased later in the Enlightenment. In particular, the old universal approach to politics, which we should discuss next, provides the best answer that I have ever heard, from any tradition, to the question about social justice.

II. THE ANCIENT VIEW: GUARDIANS AND TRADERS IN WAR AND PEACE

In the old way of thinking, social justice had two distinct – and in fact conflicting – meanings, and yet people accepted that you needed both understandings of social justice or else you would fail to maintain a civilized order. Moreover, the balance between these two conflicting approaches was felt to be very difficult to achieve; it would always take a certain art, a bit of luck, plus a healthy dose of divine intervention to pull it off. A third "presence" in life and society was thought to be necessary, in other words, simply to reconcile the first two ways. You couldn't just so easily find someone to blame when society was troubled, as we manage to, because this third force was felt to be a pure gift. Even the wisest policy makers couldn't guarantee its operation.

I guess we would dismiss the pre-moderns as superstitious, but they were right on in admitting how *rare* healthy political order actually is. There is an element of mystery as to why such peace is attained by some societies and not by others.

The first of the two main approaches to "social justice" was simply the idea that people in society should get their just desserts: criminals should be caught and forced to confront what they'd done, and punished neither excessively nor with a craven timidity. People who work hard and play fair shouldn't wind up as the servants of people who never try, or who manage to cheat big. Talent and effort and virtue should be recognized and rewarded. People should respect their elders, and the laws of society should be fair, honorable, and not malevolent or wrongly burdensome. Society should be peaceable, not caught up in pointless foreign wars, and the government should be chaste in its appetites, sophisticated in its diplomacy, and humble in its total approach to ruling the polity. The government should serve the people honorably and in truth.

In this first approach to social justice, what is emphasized is the "justice" involved when you get the fair results of your individual actions, and the sort of world where everyone has the opportunity to live a life unmolested by cheats, criminals, and tyrants. While the conservative followers of Hayek might not prefer the term "social justice," they do very much want to live in a "just society," defined in the terms I've described above and they might be willing to label such a society as "just" or even ideal.

A second approach to social justice turns the question around. This approach asks not about fair opportunity, but about fair outcome in cases when human moral agency is compromised. Because if outcomes are always skewed in favor of one race or class of people, then can it really be that the opportunities are equitable? Or perhaps some people in a society are in a better position to achieve worldly success? In general, this approach to social justice is worried more about the final distribution of the benefits of society and about the fact that, owing either to simple moral luck or to social biases, some people are losing through fault that is not their own.

In other words, in the first approach to social justice, we assume that everyone possesses perfect moral agency, whereas in the second, we acknowledge that many do not.

In early Christian times, the special groups lacking complete self-determination would have been those who were too sick to work, disabled, widowed, orphaned, or were even enslaved, rather than racial or ethnic minorities (although, even in the Book of Acts, there is a dispute between Greeks and Jews about cultural discrimination).

Today, this approach would also look at the fact that members of some classes or ethnicities face systemic obstacles – whether placed there by government or by private parties – such that their individual effort is less likely to be rewarded and more likely to be frustrated. Are we really content with a "just desserts" approach to social justice if it leaves certain groups to suffer?

In this second approach to social justice, we try to address the underlying inequalities that are beyond people's control. How might we take on the burdens of others, since after all we are aware of our own dependence on the good moral luck that we have received? The question of the second kind of social justice results from the fact that, if we are not hubristic but instead grateful, we all have to admit that we are benefitting from gifts we didn't earn. The old solution to this was for the rulers of society to attempt to purchase the allegiance of everyone in society by granting them all some benefits.

And this is roughly how we use the term "social justice" most often today. We not only want to make sure that everyone has a chance, but we want to see good outcomes for everyone. Moreover, we want to see something like an equal outcome, even in cases where people don't deserve it, strictly speaking.

Right away, you can see that the two approaches to social justice are in conflict. In one, you get what you deserve. In the other, we recognize that this will not be enough; the strong will have to sacrifice and help the weak. Furthermore, we can see that this second definition of social justice is more welcome to the ears of people on the left, whereas the first is more welcome to the ears of people on the right. It's not completely a right vs. left thing, but largely it is.

Our personal preference for one or the other meaning of social justice can also have a geographical or cultural origin. The Anglo-American tradition was all for the "just desserts" approach to social order, partly because people in England and America recognized that only a powerful central state could enforce equal outcomes, which would spell danger for liberty itself. Meanwhile, the emphasis within continental Europe has been on the equal outcomes approach to social justice that we as Americans, since the presidency of Franklin Roosevelt in particular, have also come to think essential.

RTE: Isn't this second approach what we most often think of as being the real meaning of Christian social justice? After all, "Bear one another's burdens, and so fulfill the law of Christ," says St. Paul in Galatians.

DR. PATITSAS: Well, if we manage to fulfill the first vision of a just society, then we have also, through our own strenuous work, lifted a great burden from the shoulders of our fellow man. Who would choose to live in a lawless environment, harassed by militarized police, his meager wages garnished to fund people who refuse to work, his grandparents' pension stolen by high-flying financial cheats, only then to be drafted and sent off to die in a misbegotten foreign war? Yet to defeat all these evils takes tremendous sacrifice and virtue from our rulers. So, both of these social justice visions have been addressed insistently by the Holy Scripture and the Fathers of the Church.

The reason that today we have come to think of "social justice" entirely in terms of the second, charitable emphasis is precisely because so much in our society already is well-ordered. Not everything, as today we still see speculation and front-running on Wall Street, for example, but to a larger degree than in many other societies. And not for everyone, because many of the poor inhabit communities where crime is rampant and simple order is hard to come by.

Really, both of these two social justice visions are Christian in the eyes of the Orthodox Church throughout history. We need both.

Guardians and Traders, in Brief

RTE: Did the ancients deal with categories like the political right and left?

DR. PATITSAS: The version of right vs. left that the ancients faced was just the universal fact that every human society must rely upon the two distinct visions of social justice, and be able to employ the distinct and opposing sets of social ethical principles and values that correspond to these two visions of society. There exist two entirely different sets of moral worldviews, and what makes everything complicated is that you will need both if you want to have a civilization.

Let us say more about this later in the interview, but for now we have to at least hint at how demanding it can be to attain both of the needed kinds of social justice. I mean, the ancients were so convinced that the two sets of social ethical values were deeply opposed, and that you needed both, that they openly said that only a miracle could bring them into harmony. This helped them to avoid *hubris*; they thought that civilization was a miracle, a gift of the gods.

Jane Jacobs, however, wasn't a social historian and didn't start with the distant past. Instead, she set herself to reading through the newspapers of her own day, asking which social values are routinely excoriated, which ones praised, and in what particular social contexts. Over about twelve years, she sorted and sifted through the lists of social virtues that she'd made until she saw that society is composed of two rival, almost fatally opposed, tribes of virtue loyalists.

One tribe of value-loyalists she called the Guardians, and the other tribe, the Traders. The Guardians have the vital task of protecting and administering territory, while the Traders are the producers and merchants. The two different sets of virtues – what she calls the two "ethical syndromes" – form coherent communities that resemble tribes because within each syndrome the ethical virtues make sense to all the participants, but neither tribe can really respect the ethical mores of the other tribe. For example, Guardians adhere to tradition, while Traders pursue innovation – and often both of these tribes secretly or openly despise the other side for being either too flighty (the Guardian view of Traders) or too stodgy (the Trader view of Guardians).

But that is just one example. Each syndrome has at least ten or twenty of its own unique moral values, and each of these values is considered by the other side to be literally *im*moral. Among the values Jacobs listed as being appropriate for commercial life, for example, were "collaborate easily with strangers; shun force; respect contracts; compete; be frugal; use initiative and enterprise; and, invest for productive purposes." In order to produce a culture of merchants who can seize their opportunities and generate prosperity, these values have to be enshrined and raised to an all but absolute level within the Trader syndrome.

Guardians, meanwhile, will succeed at their tasks of defense and protection only if they reject these very values, even find them morally repugnant. Guardians have their own, differing, set of social ethical values. These principles are necessary for the work of governing and defending territory. These include commands like "shun trading; exert prowess; be ostentatious; be obedient and disciplined; adhere to tradition; be fatalistic," and others.

And again, it seems to be a part of each syndrome that its members secretly or openly regard the other set of virtues as being, in fact, not moral at all. Guardians tend to regard Trader values as wrong – as perhaps weak or squishy or self-serving, and Traders tend to regard Guardian values as wrong – as pigheaded, wasteful, dense, and violent.

We may have heard of the syndromes from our reading of medieval history – the notion that there were merchants and noblemen and that their interests frequently clashed. But what we might still have missed is the ethical core of each way of life. The two syndromes are actually two competing and irreconcilable visions of what constitutes social justice – not just two different sets of financial interests or occupations. When we read about warriors and merchants in France in the 1400s, we may see that, yes, their jobs were different but not notice that, more importantly, *their ethics were naturally different and diametrically opposed.*

Jane Jacobs thought that what is actually going on is this: a civilization, she said, has to solve two fundamental problems – the problem of provision, production, and prosperity, on the one hand, but also the problem of governing, policing, and defending itself, on the other.

In the course of solving these problems, the people who've volunteered or been drafted to do these two broad kinds of work develop radically differing sets of values. This happens naturally, bubbling up from the bottom. You just see that to do that task, you have to cultivate the suitable type of values. The sense of morality appropriate to each is existentially and empirically necessary. You can't have entrepreneurs who are inefficient or not frugal, and you can't have soldiers who are in it for the money or disobey authority.

Let me stress: these virtues are not abstract but existential: if you don't keep them, you will fail at your task, full stop.

The Guardian* Moral Syndrome

Work: Protecting, acquiring, exploiting, administering, or controlling territories.

Shun trading
Exert prowess
Be obedient and disciplined
Adhere to tradition
Respect hierarchy
Be loyal
Take vengeance
Deceive for the sake of the task
Make rich use of leisure
Be ostentatious
Dispense largesse
Be exclusive
Show fortitude
Be fatalistic
Treasure honor

We might add:
use time lavishly – go slow
labor episodically
tempted to self-aggrandizement
remain stoic
have faith!
Temptation: do your duty!

The Trader Moral Syndrome

Work: Trading, producing for trade, science.

Shun force
Come to voluntary agreements
Be honest
Collaborate easily with strangers and aliens
Compete
Respect contracts
Use initiative and enterprise
Be open to inventiveness and novelty
Be efficient
Promote comfort and convenience
Dissent for the sake of the task
Invest for productive purposes
Be industrious
Be thrifty
Be optimistic

use time sparingly – go fast
labor consistently
tempted to self-pleasing
express feelings
have hope!
Temptation: give me my rights!

*Main body of both columns from J. Jacobs, *Systems of Survival: A Dialogue on the Moral Foundations of Commerce and Politics* (NY: Random House, 1992), 215; subsections are my own.

A Third Way

But, as anyone can see, these two sets of values are implacably opposed. They even generate two radically opposed senses of what social justice is. This is a dilemma: you need both syndromes, but their values are at war. So, we reach a dead end very quickly – except, Jacobs tells us, people improvised a way through.

The solution to the deadlock comes from the arising of a third way of looking at society and the world. Jacobs liked to call it simply the "third force." This third way wasn't really about survival in this world at all, Jacobs thought, but was *sui generis*. She said we might possibly call this third way by such names as love, or art, or gift. But in any case, the third way wasn't about making a living but about something else entirely. Love, she said, is what can bring two necessary, and necessarily conflicting, social justice visions into a harmony.

Jacobs' total argument about Guardians and Traders and their needing recourse to a third force amounted to a rediscovery of the ancient political philosophy of mankind. The ancients didn't have a "third way" that could *eliminate* the differences between the Guardian Left and the Trader Right, but rather they invoked a miraculous power that could help people in society to respect both syndromes and bring them together with love.

So the ancients weren't as dumb as they looked. At any rate, they weren't as dumb as we are! For we seem to think that you could run a whole society with just one or the other set of the two main syndrome values. I mean, it's clear that North Korea is a purely Guardian society, resolving everything through obedience and force, while in America we've got millions of libertarians or anarchists who think you could dispense with the Guardians entirely, turning everything over to free enterprise. So, the ancients didn't have that monomaniacal myopia that sophisticated intellectuals in the modern world have developed.

Let us now return briefly to our two opposing but necessary senses of whether social justice should be defined as "just desserts" or as "equal outcomes." It's clear enough that you need both visions operating in your society, but how? Remember that great dictum from Mount Athos, "Be easy on others and hard on yourself." In an ideal society, we would blame only ourselves for our own setbacks, in the sense of cheerfully looking for every opportunity to take the responsibility to better our fates (even if we know, in fact, that other people *are* to blame for holding us down). But we would also be very compassionate towards others, in remembering the burdensome influences that are pushing them towards failure.

But society is not ideal because almost every person in it is subject to the passions, and then the passions of each individual combine across society in various ways and cause great harm. And thus, many times when we promote responsibility and emphasize "tough love" in the right-wing sort of way, we seem to lose compassion. And later on, when we try to exercise compassion as good social democrats, we wind up promoting licentiousness and self-indulgence, with the result that we destroy the character of the very people we wanted to help.

We want to have it both ways in America: to "fight injustice" with a deep and even sentimental sense that we are very nobly battling oppressive forces, but at the same time to believe that anyone can succeed if they try. In a fallen world, however, this coincidence of what are in fact opposites – showing compassion and promoting responsibility – is often hard to come by. I think that in fact it is *impossible* simultaneously to promote responsibility and compassion *unless* divine grace and love come to our aid.

Thus the one-sided emphasis on the second approach to social justice, the welfare-state approach, has caused a decline in responsibility and, paradoxically, damages the equality of outcome that it claims to seek. The record of the War on Poverty is very mixed; not wholly negative, but certainly the successes are mixed up with very great harms inflicted upon the poor. Of course, we can all point to times in our lives where a little bit of unmerited mercy has been the thing that finally helped us to develop and become more responsible; somehow, though, you can't build social policy on this insight.

You can't square the circle of promoting *both* responsibility *and* compassion, except through love and uncreated grace. And paradoxes like that are the emphasis of the *third* approach to social justice: a society that is well-ordered, that balances the first two kinds of social justice specifically *because* it looks first of all beyond society, to God and to the Heavenly Jerusalem.

In this third approach to social justice, you are very much impressed when people show mature responsibility and thus become successful, however you also remember that the successful person always did benefit from at least *some* good luck. But in this third approach you also don't make a fetish of compassion, since compassion without responsibility would be like giving your child too much candy. Isn't struggle and hardship, figuring things out on our own, even living on a low income, often so much better than having someone else tear open our "cocoon" before we are ready to fly?

This – the remembering of our ultimate dependence upon God; the reminding us that we are judged by an other-worldly standard; the learning to ask God's help in achieving and then balancing the first two kinds of justice – is the Church's contribution to social justice, even more significant than its emphasis on helping the poor. And this is why the Church will always be needed, no matter how much charity the political parties distribute to the poor. For even as they do so, they will have difficulty promoting the love that is the key ingredient of a healthy society; worldly concerns of power and fear will naturally overwhelm these good impulses.

Look, sometimes helping the poor is just a worldly thing disguised as a Christian thing. It can be the Traders just buying the silence of the poor or trying to make them better customers; it can be the Guardians, who claim to love the poor, but who distribute benefits only because it brings them votes or shores up social stability – never mind if the charity program actually makes the poor poorer, for that will only make these unfortunates even more dependent on the "benevolent" leaders in their party or government.

The Concert of Social Justices

RTE: Does this third type of social justice – remembering our dependence upon God, with its emphasis on love and grace – take precedence over the other two? And speaking of a "third force," did Jane Jacobs believe in God?

DR. PATITSAS: She did not believe in God, although she and her husband did raise their children in the Episcopal Church. But she did believe in love and that love was more important than mere biological survival.

Incidentally, today some Orthodox Christian theologians exonerate Western atheists by saying, "Let us not judge. What if we had to choose between atheism, on the one hand, and the vindictive God of Calvinism or the Necessary God of the scholastic theologians, on the other? We ourselves would be hard pressed to choose." My point is, we can't easily evaluate other people's atheism until we see whether the "god" they were rejecting was some man-made idol, and perhaps a hideous idol at that. God will decide, in the end, who of us believed in him and who didn't.

Anyway, as to whether the third force *takes precedence* over the other two, I don't know if that is the way to express it. I think that maybe sometimes it does need to come first, but it would be more accurate to say that it always acts to *leaven* the other two approaches to social life. Love is the salt that gives the two syndromes their flavor, as much as it is something outside the syndromes entirely. This is a necessary paradox, that love cannot be love if it merely renounces all worldly occupations, but yet it also can't save them if it doesn't, in a way, disdain them. I mean, love transfigures Guardians and Traders; it doesn't annihilate them.

Love helps us to think about enforcing law and order, for example, without leaving certain parts of town feeling like the police are an occupying foreign army. Or, love can help us to think about providing homes for the poor, yet without taking away their dignity by forcing them to prove that they have no job in order to remain in those homes. Love can help a business to think about putting customers first, while not pushing its own employees to the point of desperation and humiliation.

If we want to exercise this leavening influence through the third force, we will need radical Christian empathy – empathy that leaves the other person stronger and us weaker – not an empathy that assuages our guilt but leaves the people we were helping worse off than before. This real empathy is impossible to achieve unless we pray, or at least benefit from someone else's praying for us. It takes clear-mindedness and wisdom.

What is required in order to have a civilization is *a concert* of the two social justices under the influence of love. Love is what makes it possible for us to balance the two opposing main kinds of social justice into one social harmony. This is why the Byzantines called their social and political theory "symphonia" – they were after a concert, a musical and artistic balance and proportion of the merchant approach and the warrior approach to social order.

Keep in mind this fact: since at least 800 B.C., the ancient Greeks had believed that training in music was one of the capstones and necessary culminations of a child's formal education. For them, a person ignorant of music was not ready to be a citizen because he had not yet developed the sophisticated feel for complex order that real civilization requires. Beauty not only came first for such societies, it also came last. Only a beautiful person – beautiful in speech, thought, manner – could take his place in society, and only a person trained to appreciate beauty could see that civilization itself was a concert of different social justices. You had to be an artist before you could develop a feel for the art of combining the two approaches to social order into some larger composition.

The Third Force Alone Can Purify Our Motivations

We have to think very carefully about when to employ which of these two sets of virtues. Public policy in itself is complicated but becomes much more so when we can't see which syndrome we ought to be relying upon.

As a general point, we all might admit that it *is* possible to start out with good intentions, to try to help another person, but then to make things worse by our attempts to be charitable. This happens in foreign policy; we jump in to protect one side in a foreign country, forgetting that they, too, have weaknesses and that their persecutors, too, have virtues. It has happened in our massive economic development aid to the Third World; this aid does some temporary good, and also very much harm, while developing very little.[22]

It also was the case that Urban Renewal and the War on Poverty in America began with good intentions and led to very bad results. These efforts fed so many, but they destroyed our inner cities and the families of the poor, setting back by many decades the goal of racial reconciliation. Welfare to the poor even became a justification for legalizing abortion, as a way to limit the costs of welfare! We loved the poor so much that we would help them, we said, but then when that help became burdensome we hoped that they would kill their children. And this reasoning unfolded among progressives without any right-wing involvement!

So, if we really want to answer the call to help, we have to be as "wise as serpents" in order to avoid "destroying the villages we are trying to save," to use a line favored by critics of the Vietnam War.

This is not easy. Urban renewal in America, which was Federal policy from 1948 to 1973, destroyed more than 2,000 of our city neighborhoods, 1,700 of which were populated by African Americans, in order precisely to "save" these neighborhoods.[23] Residents of the ghetto termed Urban Renewal, "Negro Removal" – and this was a policy enacted by racial progressives!

The balance of helping another person in such a way that we don't also hurt them takes experience, intelligence, and even miraculous intervention. Abroad, several books from African economists

---

22 William Easterly, *op. cit.*

23 Mindy Thompson Fullilove, *Root Shock: How Tearing Up City Neighborhoods Hurts America, and What We Can Do About It* (New York: One World/Ballantine, 2004).

in places like Kenya have *begged that we would simply stop sending* foreign aid, so distorting is the effect of aid on their countries.[24]

Those 2,000 American neighborhoods were destroyed in part to make work for unionized labor and to generate profits for the banks who funded the construction. And the constellation of interests pushing foreign aid is similarly bipartisan, a true miracle of cooperation among capitalist bankers, workers, and Christian religious people coming together to destroy foreign economies.

RTE: But that sounds like a type of *symphonia* of Traders, Guardians, and religion.

DR. PATITSAS: Which is why it has had such staying power, persisting for decades in policy despite doing real harm. I think the answer is that we have to think and really repent, in order to see what the net effect of our philanthropy is.

What would Christ say of so much of our philanthropy in the late twentieth century? "I was hungry, and you fed me" – but you also insisted that I leave my spouse in order to qualify for this food assistance. "I was thirsty, and you gave me drink" – but when clean water meant the population of my country rose, you pressured our women to be sterilized. "I was naked, and you clothed me" – but since clothing was the one thing my economy could produce at all, your gifts of clothing threw us out of work and cut off the development of our entrepreneurial skills. "I was sick and you healed me" – but not when we had more complicated illnesses, since you said it was not cost-effective to treat advanced disease in my poor country. "I was in prison, and you agitated for my release" – but you broke an essential link between the government and the people within my own land through your heavy-handed interference in my country, with the result that dictatorship flourished. "I was a stranger, and you welcomed me" – but what I really wanted was for you to permit

---

[24] Dimbasa Moyo and Niall Ferguson, *Dead Aid: Why Aid is Not Working and How There is a Better Way for Africa* (New York: Farrar, Straus, & Giroux, 2009). Also, William Easterly, *The White Man's Burden: Why the West's Efforts to Aid the Rest Have Done So Much Ill and So Little Good* (New York: Penguin, 2006).

my country to sell to yours so that we would not have to become exiles in your land just to find a job.

More of this goes on than you would think. When our friends Andrew and Georgia Williams founded the Russian Orphan Opportunity Fund (ROOF), their first act was to visit twenty orphanages near Moscow and make a survey. "What sort of help do you need? If we were to help you in the way that addressed your hardest burden, what would that look like? What would you need us to do?" The reaction they got from orphanage directors was *utter shock*. Dozens of foreign and domestic organizations had already offered their help, *none* of those charities had asked what the orphanages needed, and *all* of them had attached specific strings and demands to their offers of help. Had the orphanages accepted such help, they would have spent all their time fulfilling the outside organizations' goals and then filling out the paperwork to prove that they had done so.[25]

Philanthropy can become harder when the gap between the rich and the poor becomes wider. Without noticing, we can, through our very charity, trample the dignity of those whom we claim to serve. We are elephants; they are ants.

Room for Righteous Anger?

RTE: We see a tremendous amount of anger by social justice advocates today. Is this a righteous anger? Should we Christians share more of it?

DR. PATITSAS: Righteous anger is necessary and appropriate, but somehow these days what we get is its opposite – self-righteous anger. Politicians lead the way on this, since they are expected to be actors who can energize their supporters by exhibiting a continual sense of outrage and by teaching people how good it feels to be self-righteously angry. And, of course, the entire machine of Hollywood propaganda has trained Americans in how to cultivate and luxuriate in such feelings of self-righteousness.

[25] I am on the board of ROOF. To become a regular donor to the Russian Orphan Opportunity Fund, go to their website: http://eng.roofnet.org

In general, I don't think that social justice anger today is righteous, and I don't think we should be trying to cultivate anger in any case. Not because anger is always wrong or because outrageous things aren't happening, but because we are wandering in a kind of darkness about the proper relationship between the gospel and social improvement, to the point that only a striving for passionless love will help us.

Moreover, we live in a culture that since the 1970s has had very strong berserk tendencies, so for the time being we should be very cautious about our anger. Getting outraged often contributes to the further poisoning of the political atmosphere and loses us the grace we need to strike these very difficult balances among the three types of social justice. We have come to enjoy certain berserk states of outrage and retribution but, as we said in Chapter One, gods and beasts must live "outside the city." Politics is for mere humans, while self-righteous anger is appropriate for petulant gods, and righteous anger, for divinely anointed prophets. Just try to do and say what is right with as much love and patience as you can muster.

And we should be careful from the other direction, to not fall into a cold passivity. We should be careful about a false kind of patience, created simply by not saying the difficult truths because we think we will anger others. With discernment and love, we must overcome this fear and speak frankly to one another.

Giving Both Syndromes Their Due

According to the rationalist view of the world that the West has been saddled with since the Enlightenment, you should be able to work out an entire social system intellectually from a single set of first propositions. This type of ideological consistency is exactly what pre-moderns thought you *shouldn't* strive for in your political philosophy – in reality, you needed two opposing sets of logical approaches to the world, and only love and divine intervention could square the circle and give you both.

Right and Left each have slightly less than half of the full picture of reality, but each is spending more time trying to be logically consistent, hoping to solve all problems based on their partial outlook, than they spend on actually helping. This is where their anger comes from: "Look," they both say, "my position is logically self-consistent, so only a fool or someone of ill will could see it some other way." They rely upon their fellow tribal loyalists to confirm their sanity, and then return to shouting at and ridiculing the members of the other tribe.

The old vision of society, the very ancient vision, was more sophisticated. For example, within itself, the "just desserts" approach is rational and logical. But if you push that logic too far, it becomes absurd. Should children have to pay for their own food, or should their parents charge them for each hug they give? Similarly, within itself, the "equal outcomes" approach is rational, but when pushed to its extreme, it also becomes destructive. Should it be the case that a person who makes sacrifices and tries hard achieves a not much better result than someone who doesn't even try? Only love can sustain and yet reconcile these two opposing approaches. Only love can make real civilization possible, in other words.

In debates on television, very smart people try to impose one or the other logical approach to social justice. They accuse each other of being irrational, or willfully obtuse, or malicious. Both sides act as if a single set of social ethical values would be enough to build the entire social order. But it never works; social order is too complex. And when we, as a culture, insist that the world is a simpler place than it really is, the proponents of the first meaning of social justice (who might be called "conservatives") and the proponents of the second meaning of social justice (progressives) are forced to spend most of their energy trying to convince themselves and others *that the other meaning of social justice doesn't even exist!*

Meanwhile, the proponents of the third meaning of social justice – the Christian approach, the love approach – have had their minds largely captured by one or the other of the first two meanings. Instead of being the leaven who could civilize and then reconcile the other two ways, we Christians have become just clones of one or the other worldly approach. But both of these first two approaches to justice are concerned with a kingdom of *this* world. Christians must approach each of them very gingerly.

We Christians have sometimes lost our otherworldly focus. But without this dimension, we will never reconcile the first two perspectives, and we will see our society descend into a kind of civil war. When "the salt has lost its flavor," the third voice, love, may be terribly absent.

Jane Jacobs, who rediscovered this older view that society was a wedding between the first two types of social justice, thought that the needed alliance could never be achieved except through love, or as a kind of gift – a gift from where, she did not say. As I've mentioned, Jacobs was a self-identified atheist; perhaps you could even say that, in a sense, she was an agnostic. So if an agnostic is able to see that politics won't succeed without love and gift and, really, miracles, what excuse would a Christian social theorist have for not seeing that? And yet, even they are convinced that the right policy will solve all problems. For a Christian not to centralize love and mystery in discussions of social order would be madness.

Philotimo Is a Blend of All Three Types of Social Justice

And yet the blend between the two approaches to social justice is not only difficult, but easy, as well. The balance between compassion and responsibility can be achieved within the Church through an effortless effort. One of my students came to seminary when he was already middle-aged, after considerable success in the world. This student was later ordained and served as an assistant to a priest who was much younger and who asked of him an almost monastic obedience. Well, this is what happened, and it is wonderful.

There was a beggar, the sort of professional storyteller about his woes and needs whom we have all met, who was constantly hanging around the church where the two priests served. He was always asking for help, creating tales about why he needed help and where the money they had already given him had gone, and so forth. The successful and responsible person – my student – naturally balked at submitting to this transparent manipulation and sought the younger priest's blessing to send the beggar elsewhere. But the younger, senior-in-rank priest kept insisting that the bad behavior of the beggar was a result of the fact that no one had ever loved him in a truly Christ-like, selfless way. Many had given charity, but no one had loved him. Again and again, the presiding priest corrected his older protégé, until he practically had him washing the feet of the poverty-stricken man.

And what happened was that this poor but manipulative man was indeed transfigured through the experience of unconditional love and divine grace that he received from the newly ordained priest. Seeing a successful person serve him with such genuine love, changed him. He joined the Church. He took a simple job and found a place to live. He himself began to help the poor.

What had happened is simply that the newly ordained priest learned and practiced *philotimo*,[26] and this spirit was contagious; the poor man learned it, too. As the priest recovered his healthy shame, so did the beggar.

As an aside, some have asked if a Christian society could avoid usury, or charging interest for loans, entirely. Well, if we were to wonder what an economy without interest on loans would look like, this would be it: the recipients of help would feel themselves indebted out of *philotimo* and would pay back the help with interest anyway – as well as paying it forward to others.

So, in Christ we are not content either with showing pity (like the Left) nor with giving exhortations to try harder (like the Right), but we have some higher standard, that of love and uncreated grace which can touch the heart. Because it was the newly ordained

---

26 *Philotimo* is this spirit that combines the two opposing kinds of shame that we discussed at length in Chapter Four. On the one hand, *philotimo* is a shyness about doing evil and therefore encourages self-responsibility; and on the other, it is a boldness in doing good and drives us toward an almost reckless generosity to others. In this second step, we even blame ourselves for others' mistakes. We said that these two shames combine to produce a state of glory.

priest who also gained his humanity in this exchange, as well as the beggar whom he helped. And this is the essential core of Christian philanthropy: that both the helper and the helped gain their dignity and humanity – their salvation – in the exchange.

So much comes down to the spirit in which we give. If we would genuinely minister to Christ crucified, it cannot be through an act of "charity" that crucifies the poor man still further by humiliating or rejecting him – but which quiets our conscience because on paper it looks like an act of social kindness!

I asked a friend in the missions if there was really such a difference between aid that the poor in his country received from foreign governments and aid given through the Church. In his particular mission country, at least, he said that people felt as if foreign government aid was distributed in such a way that it violated their souls and stole their dignity. They took it, but they endured this soul violence only for the sake of their hungry children.

How opposite from the Orthodox Christian way! I remember the story of the monk who was asked what it means to be a monk. His answer was to take off his *exorasson*, hurl it to the ground, and trample it into the dust under his feet. In other words, a monk must allow himself to be trampled under foot like the new priest I just mentioned. Similarly, to serve the poor, we must become poorer than they are. Give me ten men like this newly ordained priest rather than an army of social critics!

But don't misunderstand me: by no means am I arguing against government aid for the poor. The Byzantines, and Orthodox princes in other lands, *all* felt that a very primary responsibility of government was care for the poor. As far as I know, this conception of politics began with the Church. But that does not resolve these other questions of *in what spirit* this help is given, in whose name, and with what skill?

Every society needs both the "mercy" and the "justice" types of social justice. Moreover, every society also needs representatives of a kingdom not of this world *who aren't, in a sense, concerned with justice at all*. Because we aren't aware of this complexity, because we won't recognize this dilemma, the proponents of each type of social justice spend their time trying to prove that the other type doesn't even exist, as I said. And sometimes we Christians have become extremely bitter promoters of one or the other of the two this-worldly visions of social justice, rather than studying the super hard path of co-crucifixion with Christ.

The third approach to social life – the Christian vision in which we turn more deeply to Christ for his miraculous grace – *this* is the spirit that should leaven the other two. It isn't so much a third view of society but a priestly approach which leavens the other two approaches. The two worldly approaches are also necessary and have so much to offer, but without the leaven of the third force, they are lost.

Discernment

RTE: Practically then, how do we help without also hurting?

DR. PATITSAS: Christ demonstrated how to help the poor in his every encounter, and yet look how impossible it is to classify what his approach exactly *was*!

Many times Christ offered forgiveness of sins, when what seemed called for was healing. At times He offered praise, although mission work seemed to be on order, as in the case of the gentile Roman soldier who asked healing for his servant. On other occasions He simply raised the very dead – a category of philanthropy that no army of social workers could ever manage. At times, Christ seemed to be alone with the poor person, although in the midst of a crowd of people who also felt they needed him. At other times, He seems to delay in helping the poor in order to shame the rich. The widow who gave her last farthing to the poor, meanwhile, He seems not to help at all, but rather He urges the rest of us to be more like her, even inviting us to see that poverty such as hers can be a great blessing in the eyes of God when, from within it, we remember to bless God back. And in addition to all this, our Savior prophesies that we will always have the poor with us – and we can see why, for the poor are his icons, and Christ has promised that He "will never leave us nor forsake us" (Deut 31:6). Poverty is relative, too, which means that even were we to raise all to a higher level, it would persist; it is not principally bad social policy that is responsible for poverty's persistence.

We can, if we like, go back and reread all of the gospels while holding in our minds the words of Christ in Matthew 25 about "the least of these." We may be surprised by how unconventional and unpredictable and divine is Christ's approach to suffering, if we do. You cannot put him in a box (although in his love for us He allowed us to put him in a "box" . . . temporarily!)

Our Savior was all-knowing. Unlike us, He always knew in every situation exactly what to do, whereas we have to try, experiment, and guess. Even those saints who "just know" how to help, themselves went through earlier periods of trial-and-error, when they simply were finding their way. I asked a contemporary elder what had been the key to his own gift of discernment. He is a saint still with us, whom we have seen perform miracles, but he humbly answered that the crucial key to discernment was "experience" and gave several examples of his earlier mistakes. But Christ's will in the Gospels was always perfect and was always illumined.

Friendship with the Poor

For us, it can be quite difficult conceptually to balance the first two types of social justice – to help the poor while also raising them higher. And, when we do find those few things that would really make a difference, it can almost kill us to do them, although they are so simple!

For example, when you leave the house and enter your city, have you thought already to have a few very small coins ready to hand, so that you can then look with love and kindness on at least some of the beggars and even engage them in a moment of conversation? Perhaps you can even pause long enough to share with them that you, too, are struggling and ask for their prayers? I know that if I am "surprised" each time that I see a beggar and then have to go digging around for my wallet, imagining it might be stolen in the crowd as I fumble through my cash, I just don't bother.

But in Athens, where I am spending my sabbatical, I am approached by beggars every day, since the country is in the midst of an economic recession far worse than our own Great Depression. So, why am I acting so surprised when I see a beggar, and why am I so unready? In fact, I am just being obtuse, even though in my mind I rationalize my lack of readiness in the moment by imagining the beggar is probably unworthy of help, although this country is in the midst of very trying times from which almost no one is escaping.

For another example, does any Orthodox Christian society today observe the major feast days of the Church as holidays from work, or at least as half-days off of work, as all European societies did until the Reformation? The most direct path to relieving people of the stress and anxiety of our hectic pace of life would be for us to spend at least part of these major feast days away from work and in church. Or, when we come face to face with the poor in our own parish or family, do we know how to help without humiliating? We may not.

This is the path to social peace, to friendship with our "adversary" (Mt 5:25), the poor, who will haul us before the Final Court in just a few short years when we die. Our brief lifetime on earth is but a journey to the court, to our own trial, and we are urged to make peace with our accuser *before* we arrive (Mt 5:25). Our "accuser" will be the poor in any form, the icon of Christ crucified, because the act of a rich person pouring himself out to help the poor is the *telos*, the standard we were made to live up to. The primordial Theophany which drew the world into existence was the shining out of Christ's self-emptying love for the world.

Any person, rich or poor, whose life in the world exhibits the twofold anointing, which is their share in Christ's original anointing by the Holy Spirit, is our judge. The Spirit who proceeds from the

Father in order to rest upon the Son, making him both King and Lamb, is moving in such people in an analogical way.

The first kind of social justice ("good order" and "just desserts") has so much to recommend it. But if it is all we have, then it leads to this awful coldness. It is shocking and sad when the government cannot guarantee the safety of its citizens on public streets; this should never be the case. But what sort of odd spirit has led to the frightening militarization of our police? Why has one entire political party, the Republicans, more or less abdicated its responsibility to fight for the poor in the general election campaigns? If they have better ideas about philanthropy, let them stress them loudly and repeatedly. They always tell us that without competition things won't improve, but then they don't even bother to compete on what is the central issue for the future of our country, the incorporation of the growing underclass into the middle class.

The destruction of our cities and of the families of our urban poor has been entirely self-inflicted; no foreign air force bombed our cities, although by the end of Urban Renewal it looked like it in many places. It was not ordinary racism but a poisoned philanthropy that produced those results. It was a philanthropy that erased responsibility, on the one hand, and that was not conducted in a Christ-like spirit of humility, on the other. It was only one leg of the "tripod" of social justice.

Wise attention, creative and spiritually-free attention, has to be given to social policy and not just to self-protection, as some Republicans would have it, or to self-justification, as some Democrats seem to maintain. Well, this is a harsh attack on both sides, and unjust to the many good people making huge sacrifices to do good – so I apologize for my hyperbole.

RTE: Then is it a mistake for us to align ourselves with political parties?

DR. PATITSAS: Somehow, God has designed us so that some of us can't help but identify more with one particular side of the social alliance and some of us with the other. It seems to be part of God's plan for social life that there will exist partisans and strong spokesmen for both approaches. But then, we are supposed to go on to discover that many of the people we love see things in the opposite way, and turn to God for guidance on our reconciliation.

Does this mean we don't need to organize to support the syndromes? No. Today's political parties are analogous to the great social castes of earlier history. Some parties push worker's rights; some push the need for free enterprise and the role of the merchants; others push for the need for state-backed philanthropy; and others, for a kind of perfect standard of universal love and peace.

Because God himself has designed society to function in this "marriage-like" way, as an alliance of the two syndromes under the influence of love, we will always need the corresponding political differences. We can't dispense with Right or Left any more than we could dispense with the third force and uncreated grace.

But let Christ leaven your heart with his grace, and let him, through you, leaven the actual policies of your party. The old vision, the vision of society as a wedding, teaches us that all three poles must be respected and honored – the Right, the Left, and the Church.

In this regard, I take to heart the beautiful example set by Orthodox Christians in Lebanon today, a country where almost every single one of the religions has both its own political party and its own armed militia. (Now there's an example of religious people standing up for social justice, for you; no hiding in the pews for them!)

Every religion has its own party and army, that is, except for one religion: the Orthodox. And, amazingly, they can be found working and serving in the political parties of *all* the other religions, including even that of Hezbollah! So this tells us something important. It tells us that to be an Orthodox Christian is to be utterly free of this world, even as we care so desperately about this world and the people in it.

And we must also remember that the representatives of the third way, the spokesmen for the Kingdom and in particular the clergy, will *also* be fallible human beings. So the other two sides – the this-worldly parties of Right and Left – should *also* not just roll over for whatever religious people claim is the third way! They should challenge us. I am really serious when I say that we do need *all three* approaches.

The City as Wedding Liturgy

The argument against the Republican approach is that "a lone Christian is no Christian – *solus Christianus nullus Christianus."* Persons, to become persons, need communion and lots and lots of free grace and love from others. No man is an island, and we are all the recipients of our parents' "welfare," at least. We all do live by positive moral luck.

The argument against the Democratic approach is that "for freedom Christ has set you free" – you have got to insist that people can be, are, and are meant to be largely in control of their own fates. If you see all of society as nothing but differing classes of victims, then what is left of citizenship? Calling everyone a victim is like calling everyone a slave, and then placing the whole country under the trusteeship of some elite class of policy makers. How can this vision inspire anyone?

The two political impulses each do have an element of the truth, but they also conflict and so they easily become, as I said, locked in a deadly struggle. And it is bootless to try to reduce them to some other, third set of social ethical principles – as if we were some far-seeing visionary who could dispense with the way God made the world, when really all we are is rather mushy-minded. We need elements of each of these two approaches even though they are in conflict, and we need for them to be leavened by the third approach, the way of love; we need a wedding miracle, in other words.

Of the three types of social justice – the individual "just desserts" approach (justice); the social "structural inequality approach" (mercy); and the Church's way, wherein we wash another person's feet (love) – we in the Church should put most of our emphasis on the third way, on the way that cherishes the image of Christ in the person.

The first approach is heavily emphasized within our American Protestant culture and concerns the free will of the individual; it is the older American approach, and it is beautiful. The second approach we owe largely to Roman Catholic and Jewish influence, and it concerns the common human nature we each possess; it, too, has become an honored part of the American tradition, and it is, of course, also beautiful. These are both good, and we need them both. We must honor those who fight for each.

But we are Orthodox Christians; let us bring to the fight for the poor and social justice the uniqueness of our own Tradition, of our own experience in the mystical way of Christ. This third approach can be the "little leaven that leavens the whole loaf" (Gal 5:9). It is the way that we turn almost any social situation into something just, holy, and peaceful. It is more personal.

Even in concentration camps in the U.S.S.R., imprisoned priests were able to practice this holy way of social justice so that those around them experienced paradise. It isn't only policy that is needed for salvation of the poor.

Or, consider how well-intentioned policies, if just slightly misguided, can wreak havoc. While in America our government housing projects for the poor became the locus of deep social pathology, in some communist countries the government housing projects, through a tiny change in the rules, were quite humane and healthy. These outwardly cold, aesthetically inhuman, and seemingly inhospitable concrete block flats were often a true refuge of humane living (in Moscow, for example). Families live there for generations, as do their neighbors, which gives them their stability.

Meanwhile, because our American "tough love" approach was that any family whose income slightly increased must move out to make way for those who were still poorer, our housing projects became dangerous and hopeless. Federal policy itself meant the continued destruction of the stable communities trying to form there. Perfect policy is not enough, for man shall not live by policy alone, but without grace we cannot even make a halfway decent policy.

Besides, why not just give the poor their houses, provided they have over some period of time lived in them responsibly, held down a fulltime job, and paid the utilities? This would be more like homesteading, the system that settled America's frontier. If a farmer lived on the land and improved it for five years, it was his, free and clear. If only we had handled government housing with as much common sense!

As a general rule, our aim should be to replace welfare with approaches that mirror homesteading. We have to give the poor the dignity of an independent share, not inflict upon them the wound of permanent dependency. The G.I. Bill or charter schools, for example, instill human capital and leave people free to use this capital as they see fit.

The Marriage of Left and Right

Let us reiterate what we have said until now, but add a new dimension: until the Enlightenment, most civilizations viewed society as a *wedding* between two distinct social ethical syndromes or "castes"; we have also been calling them "tribes."

One tribe was concerned with governance, while also arguing for equality of outcome because they wanted to have a wide "buy-in" from people for the overall social order. The other tribe was concerned with production and trade, and took the individual view that above-average skill and initiative should be generously rewarded.

Moreover, because these castes were then, as now, necessarily in conflict about their highest values – equality vs. freedom, is how we would phrase it today – everyone knew that you would need some third force to help the two tribes reconcile and "marry." This third force was supplied by religion. Or, in the civilizational wedding between the king and his people, it was the priests who presided.[27]

---

27 I said, "until the Enlightenment," but even the French Revolution of 1789, despite its cruelty and despite its being the pivotal event within the birth of aggressive atheistic secularism, marched under the banner of the ancient "social wedding," with the slogan, "Liberté, Égalité, Fraternité." The ancient political philosophy was so present in people's

What we are saying is that this marriage of the two ethical syndromes is what you get from a Beauty-first vision of political life, both because it is a vision vouchsafed to us by tradition and because it is an approach to political life that frustrates every intellectual system. In a truth-first approach, the wedding approach to social life is rejected for two reasons. First, the older approach explicitly relies on a miracle – the third force. It tells you from the get-go that civilization is not merely a human achievement. Second, the "wedding" vision gives equal respect to two opposing ethical syndromes that simply cannot both be explained from a single set of intellectual first principles. Real social order is nonlinear.

Again, I myself learned about these castes through the city planner and economist Jane Jacobs. In 1992, she published *Systems of Survival: A Dialogue on the Moral Foundations of Commerce and Politics*, which argued that every civilization exists at the nexus of two differing, and in fact conflicting, sets of social ethical values.[28] She termed the government caste the "Guardians" and the commercial/merchant caste she dubbed the "Traders."

And then, as we said earlier, she argued that because you will always need both of the conflicting ethical models in order to have a real civilization, and because they will necessarily be in conflict, it logically follows that there will have to be a "third force" – which she also called art, gift, or love – in order for us to reconcile them.[29]

---

minds that it at least had to be accounted for: only love (even if Fraternité/"brotherhood" does not capture every aspect of what love is) can unite the opposing ideals of Trader Liberté and Guardian solidarity/Égalité.

This slogan, although a clear holdover from the medieval political philosophy we are discussing here, animates French national discourse and education still today, such that French schoolchildren as young as six are taught its vital importance to social welfare.

28 Jane Jacobs, *Systems of Survival, op. cit.*

29 As I will mention in just a moment, all human relationships apparently involve a balance of these three types of activity. For example, not only is society as a whole tripartite (Guardian, Trader, Third Force), but so is the soul (consisting of the fighting or spirited powers, the desiring powers, and the intellectual powers), and so also is the family (father, mother, and Christ to reconcile them). This reoccurrence of an identical, though irregular, shape at three scales leads us to believe that we are dealing here with a fractal.

In the medieval period, the Guardians were called the Warriors or the Aristocrats; the Traders were called the Merchants; and the third force was exercised by the Clergy. But in one form or another, under one name or another, *every* civilization exists through the cooperation of the same two syndromes, under the influence of the third force, which is love or inspiration, and which traditionally was symbolized by the priests or some other form of the religious classes.[30]

In fact, it seems that this three-part structure is the universal and permanent anatomy of human societies *at every scale*, from the family, to the company, to the school, to the nation. At every level of social coherence, you will need the rules people (Guardians), the innovation people (Traders), and the inspiration people (the artists, clergy, or third force).[31]

---

30 Reader Georgia Williams remarked that, "In the American political system we structurally replaced the third force with something which is publicly defined, at least, as something a lot poorer – 'checks and balances.' I was taught that we have checks and balances because you can't trust any one branch of government too much. Maybe this is why France and America developed so differently in the end. Did we Americans actually enshrine lack of trust where the third force used to be?" This could be true. However, in the American system it is the judges, with their "monastic" robes, who are granted the role of referring to timeless and eternal absolutes which ought to guide the entire society to higher ideals.

Georgia's point is partly correct, though, because the American Constitution is a product of the Enlightenment and therefore attempts to engineer the state as a sort of "machine" for reliable governance. It therefore a) attempts to "capture" the third force within the courts, while also b) planning to make the third force's reliance on other-worldly ideals obsolete by pitting self-interests against each other in the form of "checks and balances." In theory, we could have criminals in all three branches of government, but liberty would survive as their passions drove them to fight against each other.

31 A genius of the United States Constitution was to treat the government itself as a tripartite fractal of necessarily tripartite society. In other words, within the Guardian realm of the Federal Government itself, you clearly delineate the Guardian again (the Executive Branch, or the President as the Commander in Chief and enforcer of Federal law); the Trader (the Senate and to some extent the House); and the "third force" (the Judicial Branch).

The Judicial Branch comes to resemble a third force rather than a Guardian institution in the Anglo-American tradition because of our "common law" tradition of "judge-made law" which demands that its judicial custodians continually ponder the paradoxes, unknowables, and even mysteries of life within civil society. This places the common law judge on a kind of mystical frontier in his duty to society, as anyone who revels in the study of this law's organic emergence can attest. Contrast this with the European continent's approach to law, which attempts to produce a once and for all time resolution of social imponderables.

Since the three nodes of Guardian, Trader, and Third Force exist within any society, clearly reproducing them within the American government itself was thought to be the best way to clarify and stabilize governance – which it has.

The tripartite fractal then appears a third time, within the regulatory agencies of the Executive Branch itself. Each agency under the President has its own divisions devoted to enforcement (Guardian), rule-making (Trader), and even their own internal courts and judges (Third Force). This fractal and tripartite organization of American governance is one of our greatest strengths.

If the ancients were right in thinking that this tripartite social structure is inherent to every civilization, then we won't get far if we ignore it. Indeed, I would assert that it is elaborate folly to think about politics when you haven't "beheld" the unavoidable core structure of social life vouchsafed to us by the Beauty-first way. Our ignorance of this basic "being" of society is one reason why since the Enlightenment domestic political disagreements have frequently devolved into violent civil wars. The social body is constantly regarding one or more of its three vital organs as a foreign transplant or an infection, and trying to expel or eliminate it!

I am thinking about the 1930s Soviet murder of the "kulaks," the term for those who tried to remain independent farmers and traders in the midst of collectivization, or who simply had had the bad luck to achieve prosperity in those difficult times. The Guardian approach to economic life could not abide the existence of this other syndrome, this other caste of people. And of course fascism, which elevated Guardian values of war and sacrifice to ultimate significance, naturally came to see the Jewish Trading classes as weak and therefore an existential threat to the new fighting identity being established.[32]

---

[32] As to our unique political philosophy, until very recently Anglo-Americans were supposed to be the "hobbits" in both governmental and world affairs; i.e., the sort of people who perceive that in great crusades lie the possibilities of great evils and great confusions, and who prefer the peace that comes with contentment and "good enough." In the twentieth century, in particular, it was the European continent whose political enthusiasms led to two world wars, communist tyrannies, fascisms, and now, in a sad parody of all that, the mess of the German-dominated European Union and in particular the euro. The drive for abstract social perfection has produced misery – which we Anglo-Americans suspect will always be the case. "My kingdom is not of this world; if it were, my followers would fight" (Jn 18:36). Apparently, in fact, *all* we would do is fight!

In law, meanwhile, Anglo-American judges are supposed to resemble Orthodox bishops, who believe that mysteries should be defined to the absolute minimum level required for peace in the Church (or, analogously for common law judges, for peace in the actual case at hand). Anything much more should be left undefined. This minimalism within the common law tradition could be an echo of the spiritual influence of Byzantium upon England, and upon Great Britain and Ireland more generally.

As we can see in our own day, those Americans who most reject the Anglo-American view that a society that tries to be too perfect will wind up a tyranny, will look especially to the courts to "usher in the kingdom," precisely because our courts function in this Third Force way. Our political progressives are more continental than Anglo-American in their conception of how much paradise can reasonably be expected upon this earth (not that

Communists vs. Fascists

Incidentally, American conservatives today cannot understand the historically deep antipathy between communists and fascists, when both are socialists and both tend toward aggressive foreign policies. They both seek to organize their economies to some extent upon Guardian lines. Conservatives keep trying to show voters how communists and fascists are ultimately the same. But an awareness of the syndromes makes all the difference to our understanding.

Fascists are hypertrophied Guardians, whose values are courage in war, social homogeneity, and sacrifice, which is why they so feared the foreignness and wealth of "international Jewry." Communists, meanwhile, at least begin by pursuing an ideal of internationalism, post-racialism, and material abundance. They are a cruel idealization of the Trader ideal, the materialism of which they learned from capitalists during the Industrial Revolution.

Thus, the Jews of Europe, who had been denied most Guardian roles in European society and were instead confined to commercial work, sympathized with the communists but not with the fascists. And this is also why communists and fascists were mortal enemies – their enmity typifies this "great divorce" between Guardians and Traders which marks the present age.[33]

Ages of Caste Preeminence

Twenty-one years after Jacobs wrote *Systems* – a book that has stayed continuously in print, being read by a large population that

they are always wrong, by any means!). When their political activism inevitably hits the wall of general American ambivalence toward utopia, they turn to both the courts and to religion (either formally or by themselves attracting a devotion that displaces religious belief) to attain their aims.

33 Winston Churchill made Peter F. Drucker's *The End of Economic Man: A Study of the New Totalitarianism* (NY: John Day Co, 1939) required reading for British officers in World War II. But as is obvious from the title, it is a book that inoculates one principally against the fascists' hatred of Traders. Communism, on the other hand, is a sort of Trader heresy; far from calling for the "end of economic man," communism elevates him to the pinnacle of importance. The communist society is supposed to be one of peace and abundant consumption.

apparently does not include political philosophers themselves – Jacobs' work on social ethics was corroborated by David Priestland, a professor of history at Oxford, in his 2013 *Merchant, Soldier, Sage: A History of the World in Three Castes*.[34] But although Priestland states more historically the argument that society is inevitably tripartite, and with a much more sensitive nuance about all the possible ways that the three syndromes can interact (principally, he points out that the symbiosis among the three is usually somewhat unequal, with one or another of the castes predominating), he never mentions Jacobs.[35] So, the field of recovering the ancient and universal political philosophy for today's world is really wide open to anyone who wants to claim it.

With the Enlightenment, intellectuals tossed into the trash can so-called "mythologies" about social weddings between kings and cities, word pictures about society as a liturgy, a dialogue, and an encounter, and then junked all emphasis on the permanent dependence of society on an irrational force like love. But, again, sometimes the ancients were pretty smart. And it is ten million times more rational to see that society is complex, and that it will only work if we all try to love each other, than to imagine that you could program people and policy like a machine.[36]

---

34 David Priestland, *Merchant, Soldier, Sage: A History of the World in Three Castes* (New York: Penguin Press, 2013).

35 Moreover, Priestland gives heavy emphasis to a "fourth caste," the peasants or workers, who represent a kind of swing vote; the Traders, Guardians, and Priests compete for the peasants and workers' loyalties, in his view.

36 Within the last year, I have come across other major contemporary works recovering the three essential components of the social organism. John Kenneth Galbraith's *The Anatomy of Power* (Boston: Houghton Mifflin, 1983) identifies the three foundational sources of social power, as being organization [Guardians], property [Traders], and personality [the charisma of the third force]. Kenneth E. Boulding's *Three Faces of Power* (Newbury Park: SAGE Publications, 1990) says that social cohesion derives from the careful wielding of Destructive Power [Guardians], Economic Power [Traders], and Integrative Power [third force]. Finally, the title of David M. Lampton's *The Three Faces of Chinese Power: Might, Money, and Minds* (Berkeley: UC Press, 2008) suggests the influence of Boulding and offers an indication of how a rediscovery of the classic social triad would be of some practical use today. Incidentally, I exclude from consideration a host of titles in the vein of Hans Morgenthau's

Freak States

RTE: So, every society is meant to be a wedding? You did say in our gender interview that where grace was operating, three marriages would appear. We discussed the one within the soul and the one within the family, and now this is the third?

DR. PATITSAS: Yes. And look how bizarro are the societies that openly reject the social wedding.

You have North Korea, in which the Guardians are the whole "civilization." No trade or dissent or innovation of *any* kind is permitted. All men serve ten years in the army – and all women serve six years! Hunger is constant, and is endured fatalistically. The country's only exports are weapons and slave labor. North Korea lives through the intimidation of its neighbors who, to quiet North Korean threats, offer her leaders oil or loans or what have you. And there is no third force permitted in North Korea – not even a trace of religion, and no culture except that which the State approves and commands.

This isn't civilization, but a hyper-rational, Enlightenment-based (after all, it is a Marxist country) intellectually-consistent lunacy. You barely had such one-sidedness anywhere in the world before the Enlightenment tried to replace love with logic. A rationalist age turns out to be also the maddest age, as G.K. Chesterton warned.

It is hard to think of a single freak-state of comparable distortion on the Trader/Commercial side of the spectrum because a "state" by definition has at least some element of the Guardian sphere, such as laws and police. But since just before the Reformation, the thrust of Western civilization has been to emphasize more and more the Trader values of individuality, comfort, and dissent,

---

classic national security primer, *Politics Among Nations: The Struggle for Power and Peace*, 7th ed. (New York: McGraw Hill, 2005) because such books tend to list so many sources of power and do not really group them according to the three central elements in social life.

To reiterate: Since none of the four main books listed above (by Jacobs, Priestland, Galbraith, and Boulding) are much aware of the other three, the way is wide open for someone to formulate a genuinely Orthodox Christian approach to political theory suitable for today by studying and integrating them in the light of Orthodox Christian history and theology.

and increasingly to classify Guardian values of loyalty, long-suffering, and obedience as pathological. This is partly the Protestant rebellion against the authority of the Roman Catholic Church, but it goes much beyond that conflict.

So I think that the world of the television talk shows, rather than any actual country, is the Trader counterpart to the hell of North Korea. The talk shows trap us in a different kind of misery, in which no one respects their parents or is loyal to their spouse, and everyone is drowning in their individual emotions and in their pursuit of individual satisfaction, without the life raft of divine Law, ethical duty, or the saving possibility of punishment. Being *only* Traders, the denizens of these shows have lost the fear of God, and this leads to hell.[37]

Christina Andresen, a friend and former student, once pointed out that we are all taught in school about the two extremist versions of the syndromes. Our two best books about possible future dystopias are George Orwell's *1984* and Aldous Huxley's *Brave New World*. In the first, fear and war reign supreme, and Guardian values take the place of the third force. In the second book, pleasure and production have become the highest values for society. So, those are your two possible hells, the Guardian version or the Trader version, and even our current educational system manages to warn us against both.

In an overdone Guardian world like North Korea, the state is continually inventing enemies and casting people out of society, much like Orwell warned; the social liturgy in such a place is twisted and lives by human sacrifice, both figurative and literal. In the talk shows, you may take a soft path toward an analogous result: you presume that anyone with a moral claim on you is your enemy, and yet the only reason that you aren't excommunicated is that there is no society left from which you might be cast out. We are all *already* excommunicated: we are individuals.

---

[37] As Americans we may have trouble hearing this, but many people in other countries view *our* country as the bizarro Trader counterpart to North Korea's ludicrously outlandish Guardianism. We appear to be obsessed with consumption, we push sexual license as a matter of state policy, we generate a cornucopia of disruptive technologies, and our foreign policy often seems, to them, to be either opportunistic or unprincipled.

A More Perfect Liturgy as the Aim of Philanthropy

Let us follow this thread: we have said elsewhere that possessing riches in coldness of heart and ignoring the cries of others will excommunicate us from the Church – and, indeed, from society. And we have said that on the other hand, poverty and need and sickness can also lead to our marginalization, our exclusion from the main arena of social life. Society sends the message that it doesn't want us, that we are not part of it, if it ignores us in our moment of vulnerability and refuses to help us. Society thus cuts us off, casts us from communion with it.

RTE: Isn't some degree of poverty self-inflicted? And what happens when the poor are engaging in destructive habits or even living comfortably on the largesse of others?

DR. PATITSAS: Many of us live in some form or degree of poverty, whether economic (lack of money), spiritual (lack of grace, inadequate access to the sacraments, etc.), physical (poor health), social (exclusion from the full range of normal relationships), or emotional (lack of strong marriages, friendships, and families). Even if these poverties are often partly self-inflicted, in fact, the most industrious person will also rely on good luck to escape them all. None of us can completely escape the reliance on good moral luck; there is always some element of outside involvement in our success as well as in our failures.

This does not mean that we should give up responsibility. Rather, as we said in Chapter Two, the reality of moral luck means that we should take responsibility both for ourselves *and* for others, in a way that is helpful to us and to them. It is love that will tell us whether solidarity or self-reliance is the correct path.

These days, of course, it has gotten harder to see what is really going on with poverty. Capitalism has been so successful that even quite poor people can dress well and be well-fed. Meanwhile, families with two jobs and college degrees can be continually at the financial breaking point, especially if there is even one sick child in the home. We can't judge by appearances alone.

Many of us who should be saving money while also giving generously are unable to do so, simply because we can't imagine disrupting the exact pattern of consumption that we grew up with, even when we don't have the money for it. All around us swirl problems with financial management, with addictions to consumption, with lack of virtue, with social and regulatory policies that discourage us from creating wealth, all of which together make the whole situation quite clouded.

As a result of our failures to conduct ourselves in a Christian way, whether personally, financially, or in our relationships, we have come to believe that we can neither help others nor right ourselves. Instead, we remain locked within our own mini-dramas of struggle and failure, and experience neither the self-possession of the disciplined nor the deep connections to family and neighborhood that could protect us. We tend to be happy, to a degree, but we aren't always very wise, and even our spiritual wealth may be brittle, a few setbacks away from total collapse.

So the issue of philanthropy is really the twin issues of re-communing the suffering poor, including the emotionally and spiritually and socially poor, *and* of re-communing the selfish rich, including the emotionally and spiritually and socially rich, all in the interest of activating a true "work of the *entire* people," an honest *liturgy*. Even those who are spiritually rich – who live lives of virtue and grace – at times may forget to suffer with, rather than look down upon, those who are far from God (although in this realm, at least, the failure to share will result much more quickly in our own impoverishment).

All of us are rich or poor, in one way or another, at different times. The presence of want and pain – the appearing of the Cross – in the world reveals not one but two vulnerable groups: those rich who neglect Lazarus, and Lazarus himself, the poor man at the gate (Lk 16:19-31). The sorrow existing in this world reveals one group – the poor – to be potentially marginalized in this life, and another group – the rich – to be potentially marginalized in the next. This dislocation, this failure to liturgize together, portends profound social and ecclesial injury. And thus poverty of every kind can be a flash of lightning that illumines the level of communion, both with the Church and with society, enjoyed by each person.

To go back to our first point: by "rich" I mean not just the financially rich, and by "poor" I don't mean just those who suffer from the second kind of social injustice, the failure to share equally in the goods of this world. Also to be considered as "poor" should be those who are cut off from the basic social justice of public safety, who live in neighborhoods where crime is rampant and police brutality is not unheard of. And therefore, also to be considered as "rich" should be those who can take such basic security for granted and can't even imagine what the alternate situation would be like.

Please keep both of the two kinds of social justice in mind – that which focuses on equal outcomes and that which focuses on properly earned outcomes – as well as the need for this other perspective captured in the third force. We should think of the poor as those who are denied participation in either form of social justice, and we should remember as well those whose poverty is that they are failing to give or to receive love.

In helping – whether by combating poverty or by combating lawlessness – we regain our communion with Christ and with his body, the Church. Helping the poor is this prophetic act by which we *unknow* the outward difference between ourselves and the one suffering, willingly seeing only the treasure of our common humanity, our respective personhoods, and our being made in the image of Christ. And if we manage to achieve such a chaste eye by comprehending our own and the other's humanity, then our whole body and our whole social body will be full of light. God will make his light to shine upon us, upon our countenances, and both we and the sufferer will recover our humanity.

As an example, I attend a parish in Athens whose front steps, like many in Greece, are occupied by Roma (Gypsy) beggars. Their presence used to bother me because the Roma whom I see in other parts of Greece can act aggressively or with a seeming disregard for the people who help them. Moreover, it is unclear whether they are really poor or whether they have simply chosen begging as a route to a certain income. But here in my new parish in this particular part of Athens, I can see that there is a genuine family relationship among the parishioners and the beggars, a mutual regard, a kindness. There is even a generosity from the beggars towards us "rich" in the form of their kindness and offers of help, and I realize that so much of this is just because the people in this parish, unlike me, have never had hobgoblins in their head that every poor person is learning dependency or is ready to attack them. So the steps of this church sometimes feel like a gateway to Paradise.

Marriage through Divorce?

To be achieved at a social level, this same communion of rich and poor requires a wedding between the realms of commerce and the state, but always under the influence of authentic love. Civilization is not just a liturgy, a common work of all the people, but specifically a *wedding* liturgy. It is a festival of love in which the distinctiveness of the Guardian and Trader tribes is neither obliterated nor exaggerated, but transfigured.

Every civilization must reconcile the two basic kinds of social justice (Right and Left) under the influence of love – or else it will collapse. But while all Christian societies until very recently knew this and could strive for this marriage quite consciously, today we have tried a new approach to achieving the social wedding: divorce proceedings. We think the way to achieve reconciliation of the two conflicting approaches to social justice is not to honor each and celebrate each under the influence of love, but rather to have them constantly insult and belittle each other, form political parties dedicated to erasing each other, and to have each constantly threaten to create an entire society that would be able to dispense with their need for the other.

Our "adversarial" approach to politics is borrowed from the adversarial approach to civil and criminal justice invented in Anglo-American law, which at election time is transposed into party politics. We in England and America believe that you get the best outcome in the courts if you have each side argue its case strenuously and to the limit. This makes a lot of sense; its origin is in a very "Byzantine" awareness of the weakness of human nature, which the English took to imply the necessity for many checks and balances within society.[38] However, when this adversarial approach leaves the courts and enters society, it can threaten civil war if people aren't also aware that our political arguments are, on one level, a game – a ritual – meant to be played with joy.

The Church must therefore stand outside the political process of elections and parties, and demonstrate to all parties the way of love and reconciliation. She must correct both approaches to social justice where they need it, and remind them both of their dependence upon each other and of their unavoidable need for love, miracles, and grace. Because now that we conduct the social wedding liturgy as if it were a divorce proceeding, many people have grown disgusted with politics altogether; they are checking out of the liturgy, out of civil society. They don't see what is really going on, and they only find it painful.

---

38 See Eamon Duffy, *The Stripping of the Altars: Traditional Religion in England, 1400-1580* (New Haven: Yale University Press, 1992) for background to the idea that the British Isles were the place in Western Europe where the spiritual ethos was most "Byzantine." Politics there therefore trended away from utopian ideals and toward a practical *iconicity* of the kingdom.

If we understand that the Kingdom of Heaven is present now, but also that it is never entirely so, then we are blessed to a) be cautious about political programs that promise to "wipe away every tear" and b) celebrate instead the perfection found within imperfection.

This is the principle of icon painting, in a way: icons aren't meant to be photorealistic in their accuracy, but when we accept the fact that they don't "capture" God, they do indeed become vehicles of divine grace. Even so, the old Anglo-American political mindset was to see that this world could never be utopia and yet also to see that fact as a paradoxical opportunity to experience a kind of heaven on earth. They thought that by accepting the grace-bearing potential of ordinary encounters and even objects, you could open the door to an experience of deep spiritual contentment.

III. THE WEDDING OF CHRIST AND JERUSALEM
The Chiasm between Left and Right

To put it another way, every culture has recognized a need for balance between a more feminine emphasis on mutuality and cooperation (the Trader respect for free contract) and a more masculine emphasis on law, authority, and obedience (the Guardian mandate for social solidarity). Not just social life, but all life, was felt to exist at the coincidence of these two opposites. As we said, marriage brings life at three levels – the soul, the family, and society.

In a culture like China, where Taoism represents the softer, less authoritarian approach, almost all of the practitioners of that faith also subscribe to other religions and cultural systems that are harder, rules-based, and more inflexible. Chinese culture itself is heavily Confucian in its social relating, as are the parts of Asia that were influenced by China. Thus, a balance between the masculine and feminine ways of relating arises organically.

Moreover, most cultures also understood that there was a certain chiastic quality inherent in these two approaches to social justice. I mean, it is the feminine, Trader approach that, although beginning with the concept of cooperation, ends up requiring rather strict adherence to principle, such as in legal enforcement of freely concluded contracts. While it is the Guardian approach that, although beginning with force and strength, very quickly realizes the need for benevolence in the interest of "team" solidarity, either within the army or within the nation as a whole. And therefore – to continue the Chinese example – the ideal Guardian and government form of social justice would be *ren*, a spirit of benevolence and humaneness that cannot bear to see others suffer. Meanwhile, the ideal Trader, commercial form of justice is *yi*, a feeling for justice that is also a loathing for the disruption of principle.[39]

---

[39] See Ping-Cheung Lo and Sumner B. Twiss, *Chinese Just War Ethics: Origin, Development, and Dissent* (Oxford: Routledge, 2015), 8-9.

RTE: It is interesting that you speak about the way of social solidarity being more Guardian, since we think of Guardian-warriors as males, though American male voters tend to prefer solutions that emphasize competition and free consent.

DR. PATITSAS: Yes, it is very interesting how certain cross-overs occur in the social wedding.

It is chiastic – if we recall Chapter Five – because the forceful Guardians become the spokesmen for compassion, while the luxurious Traders are the spokesmen for order and outcomes commensurate with our actual effort and abilities. Or, as Jane Jacobs wrote in *The Death and Life of Great American Cities*, it is the small business owners who hate crime and social disorder the most – they hate crime even more than the police hate it. But the need for a social wedding, and the necessarily chiastic character of that wedding, is a universal within human life.

Every society on earth is therefore a better or worse symbiosis between the two types of social ethical value systems. In the Indo-European and Semitic traditions until after the Middle Ages, this was captured in the idea that every city was a kind of "wedding" between a masculine King and his bride, the feminine City.

The Civic Wedding of Holy Week ...

RTE: And where would we see this in Orthodox Christian theology, beyond the motif that the Church is the bride of Christ?

DR. PATITSAS: Our corroboration as Orthodox Christians for the ancient view of political life, the view being recovered by Jacobs and Priestland, is truly hidden in plain sight – *right in the center of everything we do as Orthodox Christians.* I am talking about Holy Week, Pascha, and Bright Week.

After I read *Systems of Survival* and *The Death and Life of Great American Cities*, I asked Robin Darling Young, my dissertation director, if I could make my work a study of Jane Jacobs and the idea that cities can usefully be understood as liturgies. But Robin just thought a moment and said, "The title of your dissertation will be, 'The King Returns to His City: An Interpretation of the Great Week and Bright Week Cycle of the Orthodox Church.' You will demonstrate how this theme of 'the city as liturgy' is present in this currently-performed patristic text." In other words, she was asking me to pursue my interests in Jacobs through a careful reading of the Church's most important annual social assembly. Then she added, "Oh, and you will go to Patmos for Holy Week, to see where the Revelation of the Heavenly Jerusalem as a City-Liturgy was received."

It was she who pointed out to me that Holy Week is the paradigmatic example of this ancient political vision because it is the encounter between *the* King and his holy city, Jerusalem.

The Week starts off in just the way that the ancient cultures expected an encounter between a king and his city should start off. Christ wins a tremendous battle against a deadly foe – in this case, death itself – by raising Lazarus after he was four days in the tomb and in fact had already started to decompose. This is so unprecedented that Christ is described in the hymns of that day as, "slashing open the belly of Hades." The next day, Christ enters his city to be greeted as a conquering hero by throngs of people. He ascends the Temple Mount, where by rights He should have been met by the religious leaders who would be prepared to crown him as king, "marrying" him to the city. So far, this is exactly the ancient pattern of political life.[40]

But here on the Temple Mount, the ancient pattern is disrupted, and things begin to go astray. There is no one to greet the people's defender and hero, no one to welcome the liberator to his rightful throne.

---

40 Holy Week, like the Evangelist John and unlike Matthew, Mark, and Luke, separates Christ's Palm Sunday entrance from his cleansing of the Temple. This is probably because both texts wish to emphasize that Christ's kingdom is not of this world. Thus, the Gospel reading of Palm Sunday Orthros, although taken from one of the Synoptic Gospels, simply skips over the verses describing Christ's ascent to and cleansing of the temple. One thus receives the odd impression that Christ entered the city to great adulation, only to turn inexplicably and leave it at once.

Instead, Christ finds that the temple has become a "den of thieves" (Mt 21:13). It is no longer a "house of prayer," and there is neither a priest nor a prophet ready to anoint him. So his coronation is frustrated, delayed. In the pagan versions of the coronation rite, the new king would sleep in the city upon his coronation, since it was his and the city's "wedding night." Christ instead descends from the temple, and – a crucial fact given the old coronation program – Christ will never spend a single night within Jerusalem itself.[41]

Events unfold which seem to doom Christ, but which, in fact, He himself understands and controls. Rather than being crowned king of the earthly Israel, He will serve as the Priest of a new liturgy, a new offering – his own voluntary crucifixion. And, most shockingly of all, through his priesthood He himself will preside at the wedding of the Jewish people not to himself, but to the Emperor Caesar! This union is pronounced by the mobs at his trial who say "We have no King but Caesar" (Jn 19:15). We also read that from the moment of Christ's crucifixion and trial, Pilate and Herod went from being enemies to being friends. This marriage of Jews and Gentiles then becomes the cultural context of the Church. By marrying the Jews to Caesar, Christ paves the way for the arrival of St. Emperor Constantine.

Christ dies and then "sleeps" outside the city, at Golgotha. His tomb will be his "bridal chamber," so that he does not marry the earthly Jerusalem. Rather, through his death He both founds and marries the Heavenly Jerusalem.

... is a Civic Wedding Like No Other

In our gender interview, we said that in most societies three distinct weddings, fractals of each other, were regarded as necessary for human flourishing: the wedding between man and woman; the wedding within the soul between desiring and fighting powers; and, the social wedding of the king and the people.

---

[41] Jacques Ellul, *The Meaning of the City* (William B. Eerdmans Publishing, Grand Rapids, 1993).

Holy Week expresses a miraculous version of that third marriage, the social marriage which was the deep political philosophy of the human race. Christ the King goes on to become the servant of all. The people of the New Jerusalem learn (they are taught in Holy Week itself) not merely to receive their king as their liberator, but to die with him. They answer his crucifixion with a crucifixion of their own, expressed in chaste faithfulness to him and the renunciation of material things and appearances. Everything we said in our talk on gender about the virtues of men and women transfers, by analogy, here to the Guardian king and the Trader city, and then becomes the model for civilized societies and our own Christian rulers and Christian merchants.

In Holy Week, greed is specifically classified as *the* sin which, more than any other, led the human race to crucify its Savior; this is a rebuke to the Trader, commercial class. And the disciples are told that if they would lead, i.e., become good Guardians, they must do so not in the way of the Gentiles (Lk 22:25-26) but by washing the feet of all, and even by becoming the "one man lost." Christ's difficult example limits and controls the Guardian, ruler class.

Remember next spring, when you are participating in Holy Week, that the hymns of Holy Week condemning both greed and selfish political ambition were chanted for centuries in *Hagia Sophia*, just a few feet away from both the Emperor and from the richest merchants of a wealthy superpower. And then, notice that it is not just "the Jews"[42] who are depicted as the culprits but "the nations," that is, the Greeks (in other words, idol-worshippers) who did not yet understand that the Logos was a person who had taken on flesh. And note that it is *Roman* soldiers, obeying lawful *Roman* orders, who actually kill God. Finally, remember that all of this is being chanted and enacted just a few yards from the highest elites of Greek-speaking commercial society, and next to the Roman Emperor himself.

---

42 Holy Week's use of the term "the Jews" follows the practice of the Gospel of John, which uses the term not to describe a race but to designate the city leaders of Jerusalem, rivals to the real King of Jerusalem.

Here, in particular, to use the term "Byzantine" to describe this society – a term no one worshipping in *Hagia Sophia* would have understood – would be to erase the revolutionary social impact of the Holy Week observance on that civilization. *All three of its constituent cultures – Jewish, Greek, and Roman – were condemned in the crucifixion of Christ. All three stood condemned to death for having killed God.* And all three were resurrected by the Holy Spirit in the Christian Church as something new, something civilized. We shouldn't misinterpret the hymns as being anti-Semitic – none of us, and no culture, will escape Judgment Day.

The observance of Holy Week thus becomes "the little leaven that leavens the whole loaf" (I Cor 5:6) in the social ethical life of the Orthodox Church. Through grace, poetry, and ritual, the observance transfigures the two castes, the two tribes – Guardians and Traders – and the three major civilizations of that time, and turns them all towards a new direction of service, self-sacrifice, and mystical life.

Through this two-week ritual (if we include both Passion Week and Bright Week), set in the context of the nine weeks of preparation before Palm Sunday and the eight weeks of celebration after Bright Week,[43] the transfiguration of Guardians and Traders in Holy Week becomes the political program of the Orthodox Christian Church. Nineteen of the fifty-two weeks of the year – 37% of the year – are directly organized around these events, which further emphasizes the political meaning encoded within them. Whether we are living under a democracy, an empire, or even a dictatorship, the Guardians must rule at their own expense and must, like Christ, be willing to sacrifice or even die for the people. And whether our economic system is based in farming, trade, or venture capitalism,

---

[43] I arrive at a total of eight weeks *after* Bright Week by counting through not only the Feast of All Saints, but also to the next Sunday's feast, that of All Local Saints. For example, in the country of Georgia, this latter feast is celebrated as "All Saints of Georgia"; in Russia, as "All Saints of Russia." In America, the commemoration includes saints such as St. Herman of Alaska, St. John Maximovitch, St. Raphael of Brooklyn, and others. This celebration of all local saints made a truly lasting impression when I happened to be on the Holy Mountain for its observance. The sheer number of saints "local" to Mount Athos is astounding.

Traders must renounce greed and practice unknowing; they must always put persons ahead of economic considerations.

Symphonia as a Double Movement of Reconciliation

RTE: How did this view of Guardians and Traders play out in Byzantium, and would it have interfaced with the Byzantine political concept of *symphonia* you mentioned earlier?

DR. PATITSAS: Let me turn that question around. I think we moderns don't and can't know what *symphonia* really meant *unless* we have the work of Jacobs in *Systems of Survival* and of Priestland in *Merchant, Soldier, Sage* foremost in our minds. The ancients and the medievals took everything in those books for granted; it was the way that everyone thought. We don't carry the correct assumptions about the universal elements within ancient political life, so we make up other ideas about what *symphonia* might have meant. We tend to think of *symphonia* as the description of an alliance between a Patriarch (who today is no longer as powerful) and an Emperor (who has had no successor for almost 600 years). To us, *symphonia* therefore represents a dead letter, a vanished system reconciling two social elements, both of which no longer exist.

Symphonia has even been described as "the Church whispering into the Emperor's ear," as if there were only two real centers of power in Byzantine society, the Roman Government and the Christian Orthodox Church. Byzantine historians have tended to look at *symphonia* mainly in terms of those two power centers, but just by the numbers, they represent only a tiny minority of the total population. This description would leave out all of what we would call simply "the people" – an oversight which the ancients would have considered not only ridiculous, but fatal.[44] And it ignores the common polit-

---

[44] A recent book argues for the "Romanness" of Byzantium and also for the dependence of Byzantine emperors upon the will of their people. See Anthony Kaldellis, *The Byzantine Republic: People and Power in New Rome* (Cambridge: Harvard University Press, 2015). Kaldellis makes a strong argument that political order is an alliance between rulers and people that cannot be too one-sided if it is to survive.

ical philosophy of the Semitic, classical, and medieval worlds, whereby the king or emperor was the "husband" of his people, his city.

What *symphonia* really represented was a double movement of reconciliation.

On the one hand, the Church stood as the third force marrying the Emperor to the people, to his City, to his Empire. Thus, the Church blessed the new emperors and later conducted the rites of coronation, for example. And the Church insists that the emperor care for all his people by establishing hospitals and orphanages and providing for the poor. At the same time, the Church exhorted the rich, and citizens in general, to support the imperial commonwealth, to conduct themselves worthily, and to also care for the destitute. So in the first place, *symphonia* means that the Church stands as the "sponsor" of the *marriage* of City and Emperor which forms the kingdom of *this* world.

But the Church goes well beyond this. In a second act of reconciliation, she insists on attempting to conform the entire social realm – the this-worldly marriage of Emperor and People, or of Guardians and Traders – to the *heavenly* wedding liturgy, the New Jerusalem, which is the ideal social realm. In this second movement, the city *here* is helped to conform to the City *above*; or, if not conform, at least somehow to become fragrant with the divine aroma of the perfect liturgy enacted in the New Jerusalem. That is, the Orthodox Church prompts this earthly marriage between emperor and commonwealth to look always towards the other world, where Christ marries the New Jerusalem, the Church.

It was this second meaning of *symphonia* that made and should still make the Church such a powerful catalyst for social reform: pagan Roman entertainment, philanthropy, war, commerce, slavery, sexual hedonism, the widespread habit by pre-Christian Romans of killing off most of their female infants, the execution of murderers, the treatment of criminals and orphans and refugees – in Christian Rome, all of this had to be either transfigured or abolished, as the Church continually insisted that the earthly city must measure itself against the standard of the heavenly city. And none of it was ever good enough for the Church; she insisted upon perfection, she always wanted more! The Orthodox Church could not be satisfied with social progress because she was not interested in utopia, but in the Judgment.

As for the Church's pressure on the emperor regarding doctrine and other religious matters (a violation, to us moderns, of the sacred separation of church and state!), this was no different than the very ancient notion believed, throughout the entire world, that the liturgy of a city must be pure and orthodox or the city would lose divine favor and collapse. Political order had *always been* the concern of *every* ancient religion, *however* they defined their orthodoxy. The ancients had always believed that only a pure religion and pure rites and correct beliefs could invoke God's blessing – or the gods' blessings – and prevent the dissolution of a city. That was how the *Iliad* opened, for example: The priest of Apollo had been insulted, and so plague struck the army of the Danaans. Sure, the Byzantine emperors at times resented the Church's insistence on Orthodoxy whenever it complicated their relationships with their subjects or with their potential allies, but as products of that older culture, they would also have welcomed it, expected it, and hoped for material success from obeying that priestly and prophetic counsel.

Holy Week as a City-Founding Rite

RTE: Is this wonderfully integrated view of *symphonia* in the Byzantine sources, or is it something you've come to through your ethical and political studies?

DR. PATITSAS: I admit to being, as far as I know, alone in this view of *symphonia* as being a double or cruciform movement of reconciliation – between rulers and people, and between earthly city and heavenly city – and I admit that it is simply my most intelligent guess as to what *symphonia* actually meant. Also, I haven't read all the sources out there in Byzantine studies (and in fact there aren't many Byzantine sources dealing with political theory to begin with); perhaps this idea has been discovered by others already.

But Holy Week, which was the central religious observance of Byzantium, certainly *is* structured in exactly this way. Here, on a text that I know fairly well from having done my dissertation about it, I can speak with a certain confidence.

I am not a Byzantinist, but if almost *no* political philosopher today speaks the old universal political language of society as a wedding liturgy; if I can count on one hand the scholarly books that, very dimly, have begun to see the three universal elements within power (at least within social power); and, if our whole culture has forgotten this vision, then it stands to reason that the subset of political philosophers who are Byzantinists wouldn't know what to look for, either. They would have to read Jacobs and Priestland and the others I mentioned first, and then return to their source texts with new eyes. At that point, the political philosophy of the Christian Roman Empire in the East could begin to be filled in. If they are also reading Holy Week hymns for social messages, I am guessing they would make quick work of the matter.

I think what Byzantinists will someday come to see is that Holy Week itself was in effect the constitution of the Eastern Roman Empire. Anthony Kaldellis tells us that the Byzantines didn't have a constitution and that we shouldn't expect to find one, given that the political order there was more traditional and ritualistic.[45] I think, rather, that the constitution of the Orthodox Christian Romans is hiding right there, in plain sight, in the two-week traditional ritual observance of Holy Week. I think this is so for many reasons.

First, all the cities of the ancient world had annual celebrations in which they commemorated the events of their founding. Such cities were celebrating, literally, how they had first been "constituted," and by doing so, they were also proclaiming the standards and the

---

45 Kaldellis, *The Byzantine Republic, op. cit.*

principles, the highest values and protocols, which had to be respected in order for each particular city to avoid descent into anarchy.[46]

Second, think of what a perfect constitution Holy Week would make. For an entire week, you are plunged into an analysis of the sins of the whole society: the people betray their true king; the financially savvy turn out to be traitors; the fickle mob proclaims Christ king and just days later shifts and chooses a murderer, Barabbas; the earthly kings are craven cowards; the priests betray God and condemn him to death; the soldiers murder God. Therefore, you have a ritual cycle in which every part of the social order is forced to look in a mirror at its own worst potential faults.

Third, Rome in particular is humiliated in the Holy Week observance. It is the Roman governor who is too afraid to do the right thing, and lawful Roman orders which execute the most innocent man who ever lived. We make so much of how "the Jews" are portrayed in Holy Week because we forget that this ritual was

---

[46] The historian of ancient city liturgies, Fustel de Coulanges, writes, "The day on which men began to commit them [the laws] to writing [previously, they had been sung!], they consigned them to the sacred books, to the rituals, among prayers and ceremonies. Varro cites an ancient law of the city of Tusculum, and adds that he read it in the sacred books of that city. Dionysius of Halicarnassus, who had consulted the original documents, says that before the time of the Decemvirs [in the fifth to third centuries BC] all the written laws at Rome were to be found in the books of the priests. Later the laws were removed from the rituals, and were written by themselves; but the custom of depositing them in a temple continued, and priests had the care of them." Cf. pp 390-91 of Numa Denis Fustel De Coulanges, *The Ancient City: A Study on the Religion, Laws, and Institutions of Greece and Rome* (Baltimore: Johns Hopkins University Press, 1980); originally published in Paris: Durand, 1854, as *La Cité Antique.*

In other words, in ancient culture, secular law originally had a religious context. Ritual was where you went to look for the laws – for the guiding principles of public conduct. In Holy Week's case, such public principles are in a sense deeply buried; that is why we don't think of Holy Week as a political text. But in another sense, the public principles of Holy Week lie right at the surface, for the entire Week is the story of the perfect king in his attempt to found the perfect city.

It is in this general historical context of law and liturgy's intimate connection that we should at least ask whether the Holy Week ritual could ever have functioned as, in effect, the constitution of New Rome. The commemoration of the founding of Rome, as well as of New Rome (both of which were celebrated annually in Constantinople), lasted one day apiece. Holy Week and Bright Week rituals and readings, by contrast, already by the early 400s occupied a full two weeks of the civil calendar. Since the laws of the ancients were indeed originally sung, perhaps the citizens of New Rome would have understood Holy Week as having an authority superseding that of secular law and as providing the final and incontrovertible model for the Christian exercise of public power.

performed by and for Romans, who also come out terribly in the events of Holy Week. Imagine that throughout the history of the Orthodox Christian Roman Empire, the official religion is teaching the people that the worst, most dastardly thing a crowd of people can say is "We have no king but Caesar!" Holy Week is teaching this at mass public ceremonies, right in the presence of Caesar himself; it's astoundingly seditious. All of this together puts the markers and the limits on what Christian Roman governance can do, and on what loyalty the Roman people do and don't owe to Caesar.

Fourth, in Holy Week you are presented with what an ideal king and an ideal city would look like. You see the true King washing his disciples' feet, and the Mother of God in faithfulness to her King no matter how many earthly setbacks and failures He suffers. This is your constitution because it tells you how each part of society is supposed to behave in order to have a truly blessed public order. In this light, the repentance of the apostles who abandoned Christ gives hope to society, and the Roman soldier at the cross who confesses Christ's divinity – a powerful act of repentance for his role in these events – places limits on what is acceptable even in the context of military obedience.

Finally, in what way would a pre-printing press society have benefitted more from a written constitution confined to a parchment in a library than from a two-week long interactive, deeply immersive ritual that conveyed the society's highest principles, both religious and political, and imprinted these values in the deepest possible way on every member of society? Of course it would be better to create a way to live out, teach, remember, and enact the highest values of the society for two straight weeks than to have it locked up in a single document that only the literate and wealthy would have access to!

Symphonia at Harvard

But although these musings are strictly my own, I do have one other highly significant point of contact with my conclusion about *symphonia*: the greatest Orthodox social activist of the twentieth century – Aleksandr Solzhenitsyn. In 1978, he was invited to give the commencement address at Harvard. His words were so divisive and confrontational that literally no two commentators could agree on what he had actually meant! They could only agree, largely, that he was wrong – and that there was something deeply wrong with the Orthodox Christian culture that had produced him![47]

But in that address in the late 1970s, Solzhenitsyn was in fact saying the following to the West and, in particular, to America: during the Middle Ages, Western Europe took the Guardian side too far. It placed too much emphasis on martial obedience and duty. Then, with the Reformation and the Enlightenment, Trader values began coming on stronger and stronger in the West.

Now, the West has science, it has commerce, it has comfort – all the good Trader things. But in its reaction against its Medieval past, the West has neglected the Guardian values of courage and of long-suffering loyalty. And so (Solzhenitsyn continues) the West is in danger from this grave threat that has arisen from the Soviet Union. I am not asking the West to deny the Trader side, he says, but to balance it with the Guardian side. Then, in his final words of the address, the great Nobel Prize winner went on to say that this

---

[47] Ronald Berman, ed., *Solzhenitsyn at Harvard: The Address, Twelve Early Responses, Six Later Responses* (Washington: Ethics and Public Policy Center, 1980). When I read this book at the age of eighteen in Fr. James Schall's Political Philosophy course at the Georgetown University School of Foreign Service, it was a mild shock to my self-conception. It was the first time in my life that I realized the extent to which the Orthodox Christianity that I cherished and had been nurtured in could appear as something negative and even sinister to the eyes of both secular and religious Americans. In a sense, my writing *The Ethics of Beauty* – my attempt to get to the bottom of what makes Orthodox Christian civilization distinct – is the direct outgrowth of Fr. Schall's assigning this reading during my first semester at Georgetown. Also, while I know that justifiable criticism is levelled at Orthodox who glibly contrast their ethos with that of "the West," I have seen that there can exist a genuine antipathy and condescension in the other direction. As an American Orthodox Christian, both movements trouble me, and this book is an attempt to prepare the ground for reconciliation.

balance between Guardian and Trader is not enough: we need to remember something greater than both – the spiritual life.

This was Solzhenitsyn's message at Harvard, and in the light of all that we have just said, we can easily recognize his remarks as a perfect example of the Byzantine political philosophy of *symphonia*, exactly as I have surmised it to have been. No doubt about it. That is how an Orthodox Christian social activist like Solzhenitsyn would naturally think, I now realize, just from living life in the Holy Spirit.

Solzhenitsyn was speaking fourteen years before Jane Jacobs' *Systems of Survival* and thirty-six years ahead of David Priestland; we should count him as the first of five modern political philosophers to recover this older vision.[48] He doesn't use any of the particular terms these other authors would, and he never mentions the term *symphonia*. But I *did* read Jacobs, and let me tell you that the correspondence between Pennsylvania Yankee complexity theorist Jacobs, and Russian Orthodox Christian Nobel-prize-winning novelist and mystical apologist for the Russian people Solzhenitsyn, could not be more complete. On this point, the correspondence is one-to-one. In his commencement address, Solzhenitsyn was simply too far behind and too far ahead of his time.

If you speak from this ancient political philosophy of the city as a wedding liturgy today, of course, no one will know what you are talking about. And that is precisely what happened to Solzhenitsyn. Even some of the most respected American critics dismissed his speech as the ravings of a bearded, anti-rational lunatic. They said that his speech proved that Orthodox Christianity would always be irreconcilable with truth, reason, and Western civilization.

But Solzhenitsyn was simply saying that the *social wedding* had broken down in the West by becoming too centered on the Trader values of dissent and comfort and individual freedom, and that therefore the Western *soul* would also have trouble maintaining the wedding of things like self-interest (the desiring, or feminine, energies) with courage (the fighting, or masculine, energies). Is this an

---

48 The other four, as referenced individually in various footnotes throughout this chapter, are John Kenneth Galbraith, Jane Jacobs, Kenneth Boulding, and David Priestland.

extreme position? Or is it simply the most plausible interpretation of our situation, if you accept the common view held by all mankind until about 400 years ago?

What he didn't mention in the Harvard Commencement Address, but which we now know, is that as the social wedding and the wedding within the soul were both weakening, the third wedding, the one between men and women, would also begin to totter. And this we see now in fornication, divorce, and same-sex unions. The three ancient marriages that constituted the cosmos in the eyes of the entire human race for most of its history are all under siege.

Sooner or later, the neglected pole in each of the three weddings – the soul, the family, and society – always exacts its revenge. Some of the Guardian Popes suddenly began acting like illicit Traders and *selling* indulgences for profit, and their entire Natural Law social system began to crumble. Today, the Trader world stresses free "consent," but many feel that capitalism and the free market are really a harsh oppression. And within the political realm, we see Trader technology becoming the instrument for the perfection of state control and coercion.

What Holy Week and *symphonia* both agree on is that in order to have true social peace, true overarching social justice in both of its meanings, the Guardians and the Traders – Governments and Commerce – will each have to embrace self-sacrificial love. The Cross is, as we sing in the apolytikion of September 14th, our weapon against the barbarians because it is the necessary and indispensable weapon against the barbarism in our own hearts first. *We*, primarily, are "the barbarians" whom we call upon the Cross to civilize in this hymn! We can't have a civilized order, safe and prosperous, until both our leaders and our ordinary citizens inscribe the cross within their callings and embrace Christian love, or something very close to it.[49]

---

[49] I add the caveat "or very close to it" for two reasons: first, a society may not be explicitly Christian but still practice self-sacrificial love; second, even a society trying very hard to be Christian will never do more than approach the ideal of Christian love. Therefore, both the nativist and the nihilist should exercise charity in their evaluation of human civilization.

There is one exception where it appears that we can have social peace, albeit perverted, even while promoting selfish Guardians and greedy Traders. At the end of the world, in the Book of Revelation, we see an alliance of utterly corrupt kings and utterly corrupt merchants, who have settled into an arrangement of mutual exploitation. This is an alliance, we might say, of *unrepentant* "tax collectors and prostitutes" (Mt 21:31b), rather than a healthy marriage.

But let us remember that Christ did not spurn the company of tax-collectors and prostitutes, even as he saved them from living these worst examples of Guardian and Trader values. So let us have hope always.

What Poverty Means and How to Solve It

RTE: Can you describe how this vision would work for the poor, who are neither successful Guardians nor Traders?

DR. PATITSAS: Christians are meant to be the light of the world (Mt 5:14). That is, they are meant to become that theophany, that vision of Beauty, which will help to save the world by calling it out of darkness. They are to be this light not only by acting philanthropically but by developing philanthropy in new directions as the need arises and as God prompts. Saint Basil invented the concepts of the hospital and the orphanage, for example, and a St. Basil of today would certainly be equally creative.[50]

But this description of Christian life needs to be expanded because when we talk about philanthropy, there can still arise within our minds this dangerous though hidden enmity toward the poor,

---

[50] Jacobs pointed out how much good used to be done by the old for-profit boarding houses in urban settings. In a boarding house, a widow would lease the individual rooms in her home as though they were apartments but would also provide at least one meal a day to the residents. Such establishments were forced out of existence by zoning laws in the interest of "cleaning up" neighborhoods from the presence of unattached males (almost always a potential danger for criminal, or at least rowdy, behavior, it's true). Jacobs said that the demise of such houses contributed directly to homelessness and panhandling. We see a glimpse of the boarding house as an important and useful type of household in nineteenth-century London, for example, in the fact that a fictional character like Sherlock Holmes was depicted as living in such an arrangement with John Watson.

in which the poor are very much the *objects* of our concern and our initiative. We have got to phrase the matter with more subtlety.

If social life is really meant to resemble a liturgy, as I believe that Jane Jacobs herself showed in both the case of urban life and of economic life, then the main problem of the poor person cannot be reduced to material want. Rather, the problem is that they have been excommunicated from some dimension of social life, that they are excluded from this liturgy. They don't have a place in it.

In terms of the economic liturgy, a proper and full place comes only when a person gains a share of actual working capital within a functioning economy.[51] Handouts and welfare become, after a temporary crisis has passed, a mark of excommunication rather than a means towards reconciliation and unity.

In general, the poor require two things to escape poverty. First, they need access to the civic liturgy, or to a full participation in its markets, its legal systems, and its cultural life. It has been said that to prosper, the poor must have access to markets. But it would be better and more accurate to say that they require "full participation in a developing *city*, rather than just in 'markets.'" Because if we just say "markets," we are repeating the distortion of a one-sided Traderism.

Second, the poor require "ready access to the sacrificial object" – i.e., they need access to working capital and the possibility of engaging in public service. In these two ways, a person is restored to a place of more complete belonging and full citizenship.

But in order to attain a genuine degree of creativity about poverty, and in order to help in such a way that we don't excommunicate the poor further by choosing ridiculously counter-productive ways to help them, we actually have to be Christians. I mean, we have to have some vision that lies beyond this world. In order to make this world better and solve the sort of problems that will arrive

---

51 This raises the issue of lending money at interest and whether that practice constitutes the biblically forbidden practice of usury, even if the rates of interest are not punitive. I am not sure about this in the abstract, but I do know the spiritual quality to which "interest" corresponds – *philotimo*. Philotimo drives the person who receives a gift to pay the gift back, with generous interest, even absent any external compulsion.

tomorrow, we can't be closed-minded in the worst way possible; we can't have our minds *enclosed within* this fallen world. To see the truth about this world, we have to think beyond this world.

What Is the Meaning of Life?

It's like the question, "What is the meaning of life?" Well, what was the meaning of the last book you just read? If the book had a meaning, it's because the contents pointed to something *bigger than and beyond* that book, and because this something bigger was also present in some form *within* the book.

"The meaning of life" should be answered with a similar simplicity: if this life has a meaning, then this life must share in something *beyond* this life that is also present *within* this life. For us, that something is a someone: Christ the Incarnate Son of God, crucified and resurrected. Christ is "the very being of beings"[52] – He is within this world, through his incarnation, and yet He is the God beyond all being; He is beyond this world. The very logic of the question, "What is the meaning of life?" shows that only the God-man can be its answer, for only He is truly both within life and beyond life.

But if the salt has lost its flavor – if we in the Church come to imagine that social justice can be reduced either to just desserts or to social solidarity, or even to some materialistic and selfish combination of the two[53] – then in that case, our societies will become living hells. Some would say, judging by the numbers of Americans on antidepressants, that our own society has already become something unbearable. Unless we stand outside of society as well as within it, unless we renounce the striving for a materialistic utopia through our embrace of an *eschaton* that is *both* already present *and*

---

[52] Taken from St. Dionysius the Areopagite, *The Divine Names* (589C-D) in Colm Luibheid and Paul Rorem, eds., *Pseudo-Dionysius: The Complete Works* (Mahwah, NJ: Paulist Press, 1987), 51.

[53] In the Book of Revelation we see a reconciliation of Guardian and Trader during the end times, but in the form of a wedding that excludes God and is at enmity with God, as I noted above.

always to be hoped for, we will never experience Paradise, in this life or in the next.

The Church does not only *minister to* the crucified Christ in the persons of the poor – i.e., to all of us, for indeed all of us are poor and are in need of the Church's divine compassion – the Church is also *married to* the crucified Christ, whose death at Golgotha is a permanent sign of the limitedness and provisional nature of every this-worldly attempt at social justice. The Church, therefore, manages to improve the world without ever being captured by the temptation to idolize or trust in this world. And neither do we idolize either of the two basic syndromes and their particular values,[54] for we Christians are first of all to be the sign of that third force.[55]

What this means in practice is that the poor are for us an icon, not an idol. Not only do we not objectify them, we also do not romanticize them or idealize them, and we do not forget that their Master, Christ, sees in them a royal dignity.

Above all, we *are* the poor, and we simply wash each other's feet and ask each other's prayers. We invite each other into communion with Christ, in the hopes that through the intercession of those whom we rescue from exile, we too may be similarly delivered.

---

[54] I found a surprising example of how "this-worldly" social justice is limited while going through the Youtube channel "MedalOfHonorBook." In my watching, it seemed that about a third of the Medal of Honor winners interviewed had experienced an encounter with an enemy soldier in which they showed compassion and let the enemy escape, rather than doing their sworn duty to kill. In each of these cases, the decisive engagement in which the Medal of Honor winner earned his award followed just days or weeks later. (The most famous special forces soldier of all time, Col. Robert L. Howard, actually spared the life of a particular enemy soldier within the battle that earned him his Medal of Honor.)

It was spiritually evident that their prior compassion had unlocked the grace of their later bravery against others of the enemy, and that it also lay behind the protection from danger they received during these climactic battles. Now, this was not a "formula," by any means; the other two-thirds reported no such incident.

Also, many of these Medal of Honor winners expressed the sense that in killing their enemies they had killed a brother, and some winners also had countenances like elders. In the latter case, this was gained through their grief over the deaths of their enemies, balanced by the understanding that they had been right to choose the lesser of two evils in some cases.

None had won their medal by berserking.

[55] And this, rather than any insincerity in his belief, is why St. Constantine delayed baptism until his deathbed. In doing so, he sought to express that, whatever good he might do as the "Chief Guardian" (Roman Emperor), his priestly offering to Christ would have still greater importance.

Social Justice in the Church

In our last interview's discussion of the Forms, which we also called the Patterns or the Ways, we talked about how a Form isn't really present in a place until you manage to account for *all* of the forces in that particular place. To capture a Form, you cannot deal in partial truths; you have to be completely honest about what's going on and what needs to happen. The logoi, the Forms, are fractals of the Incarnate Logos, the Crucified One, and so to be real they must take into their bodies *all* the forces present within their setting, rather than seek to escape their appointed crucifixion.

Just so, the realization of the Form of the Heavenly Jerusalem in the Church and in society starts to become more real when we include *all* of the peoples of the world, as much as we can. "Social justice," if it is to capture the form "Justice" – if it is itself to avoid being *unjust*, as "social justice" movements themselves now many times seems to be – must include every one of the three differing and even opposing understandings of what social justice should be: just desserts, equal outcomes, and other-worldly love. It must include them all, and it must find a Pattern whereby all three are present, in the right way and at the right time and in the right union.

As we said, this Pattern, this incarnation of the Heavenly Jerusalem within society here on earth, the Byzantines called *symphonia*. *Symphonia* was the Christian transfiguration of the ancient political philosophy. It is still central to the Church's social teaching and is re-taught to us every year in the very heart of the Church calendar at Pascha, since Holy Week is an encounter between a Guardian King and a Trader City (a city that was undone by, of course, greed and cowardice). What Holy Week shows is how kings should behave in Christ, and how cities should also behave in the light of Christ. The "Liberation Theology" of the Orthodox Church – the new vision of social peace – is right at the center of our gathering *as the Church*, performed in Holy Week.

Symphonia might be ridiculed by modern historians as blessing despotic theocracy, when in fact it is the very jewel that we need in order to avoid political collapse and civil war. We need it because it shows us what moderns miss – that we need two distinct visions of social justice and that though these are implacably opposed, Christ's love can reconcile and transfigure them. We need to look to heaven or else find life on earth becoming hell.

The Being, Well-Being, and Ever-Being of Society

We can apply to all societies the progression that St. Maximos named as the concentric stages of creation: being; then, well-being; and finally, ever-being. We are meant to behold three successive visions of the Crucified One, and each vision grants us a different level of being.

Our personal being and the world's being came through the Primordial Theophany, which was already Christ in his self-emptying love for the world. We fell in love with his appearing and moved out of non-being into doxology, liturgy, and existence.

Well-being comes when we accept the earthly ministry of Christ, his crucifixion outside the gates of Jerusalem, through embracing the sacramental life of the Church in all our powers, including in the proper and blessed disposition of our sexual powers.

And ever-being will be granted to the worthy at the Last Judgment, when we see "the Son of Man coming in his glory" (Mt 23:51). We will see, that is, Christ crucified and yet also triumphant. This third and final vision of Beauty will reveal the disposition of our hearts and determine whether the love we received in the first two visions has found good soil within us.

Our social ethic must be also governed by these same three encounters with the triumphant, self-sacrificial love of Christ. Like all creation, our societies must be liturgical and complex or they won't long exist – they won't have *being*. Our social ethic must be ecclesial and sacramental, and here we receive the gift of *well-being*. Finally, our approach to social life must be eschatological and civilized, which brings us to the gates of *ever-being*.

A Final Note: How God Responds When We Judge Him

RTE: Before you finish, tell us about the title you've chosen for this talk. Can we say that humans must forgive God?

DR. PATITSAS: Although our interviews have covered such a wide range of interests, I really have had this matter of trauma and of the moral injury inflicted upon soldiers at the back of my mind throughout all of them.

I think I said somewhere that the Gadarene Demoniac was a kind of berserker, but that Job is a better example of the man who is afflicted by trauma, although he does not berserk. Job lost everything, and in such a violent and unpredictable way.

Job's "friends," meanwhile, the ones who urged him to "curse God and die" (Job 2:9), could even be looked upon as the healthy parts of his own body and soul, which look upon the ruin his traumatized life has become and urge him to end his own life. They are the personification of those thoughts which insist that ending our life is the only logical response, in strictly this-worldly terms, to the total failure of our earthly hopes and prospects. At least, I think that to commit suicide can be to "curse God and die," don't you agree? And it can certainly seem like the only rational course of action when all seems irrevocably lost.

Job endures and endures his sorrow, and he does not curse God. But finally he does *accuse* God, he does call God to account for what He has permitted Job to undergo. And then a miracle happens: God appears, so that despite all Job's trauma, God (really, Christ, according to our Orthodox tradition) *tests the justice of even the trauma victim's accusations against God.* Christ shows Job the expanse of His own wisdom and divine care for the entire world, the degree of our dependence on him, and the futility of using our limited minds to understand divine providence itself. God somehow has the right to judge even the victim of trauma.

But this initial vision and these unassailable words of truth do not heal Job. Neither the truth nor the goodness of God is enough to make Job whole or to restore his relationship with God.

Trauma victims, I think, might know what I am talking about: even should they understand the "reasons" for what they suffered or even if they manage to find the strength to accept rationally God's perfect providence, prerogative, and power to restore, still they might not forgive God. After all, did they ask to be born? And were they created just to suffer, like some kind of plaything for fate and for God himself? Is life really so insignificant here below that the most absurd and painful path should be so easily "made up for" in the next life?

But this failure to forgive God for what we have suffered, however we may justify it, could be sufficient to keep us outside the gates of heaven. What I mean is not that God will condemn us for it, but something worse. Even if offered heaven, some people have promised that they will decline to accept it because they will reject and condemn God for the suffering He has allowed on earth. Recently, one of my very favorite British actors made this precise claim, that having seen so much hell permitted by God here on earth, he would not be interested in heaven. This famous man said that if he were to meet God, he would accuse God of being capricious and cruel, and he would reject God's offer of heaven.

I remember a saying among some Vietnam veterans when I was a kid in the late 1970s: "When I die, I know I'm going to heaven, because I've served my time in hell." But as I just said, for the trauma victim, the matter can play out in just the opposite way. Having endured hell here, they may tell God that He can just go on and keep his heaven, over there. This is in fact *exactly* the argument that Dostoyevsky's Ivan Karamazov makes to justify his atheism. Not all of heaven, he says, is worth one infant having been tortured or murdered here below. Many people claim to feel this way, but perhaps the trauma victim at the beginning of his recovery, most understandably.

Well, we should not encourage such thoughts, in ourselves or in others. To do so is to play with fire. Too easily, our genuine outrage over the suffering of the world morphs into a self-satisfied smugness toward God. Even Abraham, who begged God to spare Sodom and Gomorrah if fifty righteous men there could be found (Gen 18:16-33), stopped his increasing claims against God at ten righteous men. We should be careful not to imagine that we can judge God.

Christ's Tender Mercy

And yet, see the compassion of Christ himself when faced with the judgment levelled at him by the trauma victim. Christ does something more for Job, the paradigmatic victim of traumatic loss, than simply justify his divine righteousness and goodness. Christ does more than display his infinite knowledge of truth and existence. Christ does something beyond what we can imagine. He does not only play the "I am God and I know more" card, or even the "Well done, thou good and faithful servant" card.

Rather, Christ appears directly to Job in the only form which can save and heal Job, the only form that can heal the trauma victim: Christ reveals himself to be the ultimate victim of trauma, and a willing victim at that.

What Job saw, I believe, and what healed him, was a direct mystical vision of Christ crucified, in all its meaning and profound significance.

At the Last Judgment, many of us – very many of us? – may still bear this resentment that I have described above. That is, we carry some trace of this wish to accuse God for what we have seen or suffered here on this earth, for what this human race has inflicted upon itself, even though we know that it is also our own fault and that God does love us.

And so I believe that all of us, and trauma victims especially, will be not only judged but also healed at the Last Judgment. Not just forgiven and saved but healed, set free, so that we can enter into the joy of our Lord – so that we can forgive God as He is forgiving us. And that healing will come because at the end of time we will see exactly what Job saw: we will see Christ crucified to the final measure for us, by us, because of us, but, most of all, *inside of us when we were suffering.*

When all those present at the last Judgment claim never to have seen Christ in the "least of these," it may also be because until that moment almost none of us have ever been completely, without remainder, ourselves. And it is in you, and in your life, that Christ wishes also for you to find "the least of these his brethren." And it is to yourself, as well as to the poor, that Christ wishes you to offer the pure consolation of forgiveness and compassion. It is for yourself, for your own life, too, that you must lay down your life and your obsessions with justice and truth, if you would be saved.

Since Christ crucified is the Pattern according to which we were made, until that final vision we won't truly reach our end or become ourselves. We haven't until then reached our goal. Only there and in the light of that vision of Christ can we be judged.

"Beauty will save the world," said Dostoevsky, although he knew full well that sensuousness could entrap and devour us. At the Last Judgment, the *actual* Beauty that will save the world will be nothing less than the ultimate revelation of Christ and of him crucified. Such Beauty will save us because it will wipe away any trace of estrangement we have acquired towards God through the trauma in our lives; it will enable us to "forgive" God. It is that vision that will judge but also heal us, and open the door to heaven from within our deepest hearts.

At least, I think some trauma sufferers would agree that nothing less than such a vision would suffice, if they were to develop even a desire for heaven.

Eros towards Christ means loving Christ in the least of these; agape means doing so at our own expense. Some measure of this, and then we may begin to experience philia – true friendship with Christ. And friendship with Christ means that at the end of all things you will "become" Christ – not as his copy but as his icon, as his sacrament, as his mystery to the world around you.

How can we say that we are saved by "faith alone" when all that we have discussed today talks of good works for the poor? Because in serving others we are merely confessing with all our power that we, too, take our identity from the Crucified One; that we, too, wait with him in the tomb for the resurrection. Christian works are "unworks"; we renounce relying on our food, on our money, on our self-justification for our salvation, and just give all these things to Christ in the person of the poor.

Not only by faith alone, and not just by these few verses from Scripture alone, are we saved – but truly *alone*, through faith in Christ joining him in the grave, on behalf of the entire suffering human race. This is where we want to be. If you think about it, the Good Thief managed this upon the cross. Whole civilizations have managed it, too. So can ours.

RTE: Forgive one last question. Should an Orthodox Christian try to "make the world a better place" – in other words, try "to change the world?" Or, should we rather live "a quiet life in peace" (I Thess 4:11), as St. Paul said?

DR. PATITSAS: If the world is an image and a symbol of heaven, then our task is to help it grow from the image of heaven into the likeness of heaven. And just as the icon painter takes wood and gradually "uncovers" Christ or the saint who is to appear there, so we must take the world and "bring out" the appearing of Christ within it.

Now, as the iconographer does so, he is also repenting, so that the image of Christ becomes clearer not only in the wood but within his own person. Thus two icons are being "uncovered" at the same time: one on wood, and one in the artist himself.

A social activist should think of his or her task in the same way, as a movement of helping Christ to become more vivid and present both in the world and in their own hearts. In this way, we cut off the arrogance, the self-righteous anger, and the impatience that mar so much of our social activism. I think this is the way of the saints.

CHAPTER EIGHT

THE CITY AS LITURGY

How Jane Jacobs Used the
Beautiful Science of Complexity
to Explain Cities and Unknowingly
Reconciled Science and Religion

In this chapter, we provide a powerful scientific corroboration for the Beauty-first way. The science of organic complexity presents us with a new cosmology, a picture of the world as a beautiful and fitting order. Our introduction to this new science will be through the life and work of one of its earliest proponents, the late city theorist Jane Jacobs. Jacobs discovered that this new kind of science was being developed and was an option for her own work, just as she was reacting to the disastrous impact of "truth-first" and "goodness-first" approaches to living city order.

Although this chapter does not deal with the subject of individual trauma, it does explain Jane Jacobs' efforts on behalf of the hundreds of American cities which had been cruelly wounded by the application of simplistic forms of scientific order to urban planning. Consequently, the chapter is meant to reinforce our confidence in the Beauty-first vision which alone can deliver our souls as well as our cities from disintegration, excommunication, and the loss of meaning.

Moreover, it could be said that, for Jacobs, the city is a kind of liturgy, a matrix for life-generating processes which are the opposite of events which produce trauma.

Finally, because the "liturgical" city which Jacobs describes is also an instance of organically complex order, in her work we find ourselves on the cusp of a new and therapeutic reconciliation between science and religion. Religion at its best generates complex, healthy integration within and between human beings; and science can now see in religion a testament to the liturgical nature of organically complex order.

623

I. JANE JACOBS, CITY THEORIST

Christ and the City

RTE: Dr. Patitsas, please say something about the main idea of your doctoral dissertation, which is that ordinary human cities can be understood as "liturgies"? What do you mean by liturgies in this case, and how does looking at cities as if they were liturgies help us to understand city life? Also, how did Jane Jacobs' book *The Death and Life of Great American Cities*, which is not a religious book, give you such inspiration that you felt that with it you could understand Orthodox Christian Holy Week much more deeply?

DR. PATITSAS: Once, as I was giving some books about economics by Jane Jacobs to my Holy Cross classmate, His Eminence Metropolitan John of Korçe in Albania, I exclaimed, "Forgive me, Your Eminence, they are more secular than spiritual." I said this because I was suddenly afraid that in his deep prayer life, he would not be interested in reading about worldly affairs.

But Metropolitan John responded at once, "No, Tim – many times such books are *more* spiritual than the ones that claim to be spiritual." I wanted him to have those books because Albania was at that time re-entering the world economy – a challenge which, if mishandled, can erode the cultural supports of a nation's spiritual life.

I will tell you why Jane Jacobs' books helped me to understand Holy Week: that entire week enfolds us into an encounter between Christ the King and his city, Jerusalem. This meeting then results in the founding of a new city – the New Jerusalem, the Church. Thus, Holy Week gives us all kinds of clues about how we can get along in ordinary human cities.

One of these clues we mentioned in a previous interview,[1] that the irreducible fact of human political life is its resemblance to a

---

[1] In detail, in Chapter Seven above, "Beauty Will Save the World: Social Justice, Judgment Day, and the Human Need to Forgive God," but also mentioned briefly in Chapter Five, "Only Priests Can Marry: The Reconciliation of Men and Women in Christ."

"wedding" of two complementary, but often opposed, social-ethical approaches to the world. Jane Jacobs called these modes Guardians and Traders, while in the Middle Ages they were described as "those who fight" and "those who work." These modes are represented in Holy Week by Christ the King and the people of Jerusalem, respectively. The rituals and readings of Orthodox Holy Week, Pascha, and Bright Week depict – as did most of the liturgies of the ancient world that commemorated and re-enacted the founding of a city – a marriage between a king and his city.

So, the more you know about the interaction between Guardians and Traders in general, the more Holy Week in particular will make sense to you. The reverse is even more true: the more you see the spiritual essence of Holy Week, the more you will see how rulers and merchants in any society might either go awry or succeed in their relating with each other and with God. The annual celebration of Holy Week gives you both the inspiration for and the Pattern of a just social order.

Another point about Holy Week that we mentioned in the same interview was that when the Christians of Constantinople prayed the services leading up to Pascha, they could see vividly how their own three constituent cultures – Roman, Greek, and Semitic – had been condemned through the role each played in the execution of the Messiah. For two of those cultures, this was more obvious – the Jewish High Priest had pronounced the sentence of death upon the Messiah, and the Romans had carried out that sentence with a cruel zeal.

But the Greeks, too, were confounded in their intellectual pride, when the rational logos which they worshipped turned out to be an actual person who took on flesh, lived as we do, and allowed himself to be murdered. Greek philosophy had for centuries been insisting that the mythic tales of personal, miracle-working, and incarnate gods were childish fabrications. Those intellectuals who met St. Paul at the Areopagus in Athens were scandalized by Paul's gospel because it was so concrete, bodily, and historical. It seemed a return to the fables of the childhood of the Greek race.

All three of Byzantium's core civilizations thus "died" in the mystery of Christ's death. But all three were then resurrected and transfigured in the Orthodox Christian Church. The Church thus showed its miraculous capacity to safeguard all of civilization when she purified these cultures of their destructive sides, and even brought them into harmony despite their mutual suspicion.

So how do I get from Holy Week to Jane Jacobs? Well, since Jane Jacobs' books are the best descriptions of city order ever produced, it follows that reading them alongside a city-centered and city-founding mystical rite like Holy Week will be an exercise in mutual illumination between Holy Week, on the one hand, and the drama of human civilization more generally, on the other. That, at any rate, is what I spent five hundred pages arguing in my dissertation – so I hope I was right![2]

And, of course, cities hold a special place for Christians, since only we and the Jews believe that heaven itself will be a city; all other world religions conceive of Paradise as something like a garden.[3] The Orthodox Church has always been deeply involved in city life, whether Jerusalem or the New Jerusalem, whether Rome or the New Rome – or through the diocesan sees being based in important urban settlements. The word "pagan" means country dweller, since those far from cities were the last to adopt the new Christian faith.[4]

It may sound too obvious to mention, but the word "civilization" comes from the fact that a more developed and complex human life is possible in cities. Therefore, Jane Jacobs' books about urban genesis and form are of significance for all human civilization

2 Timothy Patitsas, "The King Returns to His City: An Interpretation of the Great Week and Bright Week Cycle of the Orthodox Church" (PhD diss., The Catholic University of America, 2003).

3 From Jacques Ellul, *The Meaning of the City* (Grand Rapids: Wm. B. Eerdmans Publishing Co., 1970).

4 More recently, scholars have argued that the Latin word "paganus" also signified "civilian," as in, "one not enrolled in the army." In other words, the Church, beginning with Tertullian, classified non-Christians as "pagans" because they had not yet enlisted in the Christian fight for virtue and salvation. It seems likely, though, that to many Christian ears, since the Church grew first in urban centers, the other connotation of "pagan" also seemed fitting. I think this is a case where our newer understanding of a term does not completely invalidate our older one.

because she has intuited the universal structures within all urban life. No list of the "great books" of human culture can be complete without her three or four main works. I don't know anyone else recommending her as strongly as I do just yet, but with time I think more academics will see her central importance. Cities are the apex of human social organization; Jane Jacobs is the single best expositor of city genesis and form. She cannot be ignored.

What Is a City?

Jacobs demonstrated the two essential facts about life in cities that make cities completely different from all other forms of human association. One is that, in cities, you are surrounded by strangers; most of the people you see on a daily basis on the streets are not family, friends, nor even your acquaintances. They may not be of your tribe, ethnicity, race, or religion, nor even speak the same language as you do. But although the great mass of people in a city are completely anonymous to us, somehow together we make this really complex and fine-grained social order that is far more sophisticated than what is produced in less challenging human settlements where people can consciously coordinate their actions.

The second essential fact about cities is just as important. In cities, new work is continuously being invented and developed on the basis of older kinds of work. In rural areas, the work being done stays the same or changes only slowly; kinds of work, know-how, and crafts may even be lost as time passes. But cities are places where innovation and new work are a constant.

This second fact about cities is so important, Jacobs says, that any place where innovation remains constant cannot help but become a city. And any city where the processes of innovation die out, no matter how great a point of wealth or size it has reached, will steadily whither, until barely even the city's ruins remain.

These two features – being surrounded by strangers and constant innovation – together give us a concise and powerful understanding of why cities are inseparable from civilization: our abilities to cooperate and to innovate are centered there, are only fully realized there. Without cities, we wouldn't be human in the way we now know we can be.

In Holy Week, even the enemies of Christ come together in the city to accomplish a purpose greater than – and in fact the opposite of – what they intended. In their sin, they unwittingly accomplish God's ultimate purposes for the salvation of the human race. Christ wasn't just surrounded by strangers during his passion but by foreign occupiers, religious sell-outs, traitorous friends, and murderers. But in him, all this apparent chaos comes together and founds a new city, the Church.

The "innovation" accomplished in Holy Week, the "new work" invented by Christ, is to love our enemies, even as they murder us. This "new work" calls for the steady nurturing of our life in the Holy Spirit, until Christ be born in us.

The cross-fertilization between politics, Holy Week, and Jane Jacobs' discoveries reverberates in many ways from these two central facts of cooperation and innovation.

RTE: How was Jane Jacobs able to penetrate so deeply into the universal principles of urban order?

DR. PATITSAS: Well, she was a genius; this always helps! Second, she was living in what was perhaps the greatest city in the history of the world to that time, New York City before its astounding productive powers began to fade. This helped her to love cities, to luxuriate in their fascinating creativity and deep variety.

And, thirdly, because Jacobs happened to have become aware of a new kind of science that was just being discovered: the science of complexity, which is really the science of living things, as opposed to the Enlightenment science which preferred to think in terms of dead machines because they are controllable and predictable.

RTE: Many of us are unfamiliar with complexity theory, particularly as to how it relates to city planning or to a Christian worldview. Will you build us some bridges to Mrs. Jacobs and her thinking?

DR. PATITSAS: Well, I also needed someone to take me by the hand and show me an easy way into the understanding of organically complex urban order, which is part of what I want to pass on to my readers in this interview. If I had not had *The Death and Life of Great American Cities* as my own first introduction to complexity theory, I would never have understood the idea of what is also called "systems thinking," nor would I have known how to think about what makes some city neighborhoods so vibrant or some economies so prosperous.

"Complex systems" are just those systems where the whole is literally greater than the sum of its parts. This describes anything that lives, including animals, plants, human beings, and the many different types of human societies. Really, what complexity does is to take you past looking at machines, which are assembled from separate parts, so that you can study living beings, where the parts are generated by the organism itself through some larger life process; it is really this invisible process that is the soul of a living thing.

To prepare for our discussion of complexity, though, I would like to relate two simple stories about people. One story is about how the sister of Jacobs' grandmother was given an Orthodox icon while teaching school in Alaska in the early 1900s, and the other story is what happened when, in 2000, I gave Jane Jacobs an icon in conscious imitation of that earlier gift.[5] I think these two stories will be a nice way for an Orthodox Christian or anyone else who respects the art of holy icons to start thinking about Jacobs and her discoveries in city life and complex order.

---

5 I gave Jane Jacobs the icon at a private reception in her honor held by the Canadian Embassy on November 10, 2000, the night before she was to receive the Vincent Scully Prize from The National Building Museum in Washington, D.C.. If you are curious, you can see the icon itself, perched on Jacobs' desk, at 1:30 of the video "Jane Jacobs On Writing," viewable at https://www.youtube.com/watch?v=nlhX3oQkmOE

A Schoolteacher in Old Alaska

In 1904, the great-aunt of Mrs. Jacobs, Hannah Breece, was sent by the U.S. Government to the District of Alaska as a schoolteacher, a mission she fulfilled until 1918.[6] In the summer of 1911, she was teaching the children of the southern Alaskan village of Nondalton. In gratitude, the people in that village presented Hannah Breece with their most precious possession, a beautiful icon.[7]

This gift was presented to her at the close of a "vigil" observed by these Alaskan villagers in their parish church on the Feast of the Dormition of the Mother of God.[8] There was no priest or reader in this community and no one there could read the liturgical books, so the service consisted of the whole village assembling in church and then standing in reverent silence for two straight hours. This reverence is a testimony to the strong faith of the Alaskan people and to the love of the missionaries who planted this faith.

However, the gift to Miss Breece involved a true twofold anointing, a small "cross" as well as a "resurrection." She didn't speak the local language, but she could see that after the church service a very heated argument was breaking out between the older men and the younger men of Nondalton, and that it was about her!

---

6 "The District of Alaska" was not formally organized as "The U.S. Territory of Alaska" until 1912, although it of course had belonged to the United States since 1867. Alaska acquired its statehood on January 3, 1959.

7 The church where this happened was located near the summer fishing camp of the village of Nondalton in the vicinity of Lake Iliamna. In 1918, Ms. Breece retired to Oregon. Knowing that her grand-niece Jane Jacobs planned to become a writer, a few years later Ms. Breece entrusted Jane with the diary she'd kept during those Alaskan years, asking that it someday be turned into a book. Jacobs waited many decades, until the early 1990s, to fulfill this charge, by which time she had not only the confidence as a writer, but also the time and funds for the additional research on location in Alaska that the proper telling of her great aunt's story required. The resulting book is entitled, *A Schoolteacher in Old Alaska: The Story of Hannah Breece* (NY: Random House, 1995). When I was in Alaska in 2006, I was told that this book was required reading for all new Alaskan public school teachers from the lower forty-eight states.

8 This would have been on August 15th according to the "Old" or Julian Calendar, which even today is followed by the 110 parishes of the Russian Orthodox Diocese of Alaska. While the liturgical books would have been in both Slavonic and in the native language, many of the adults of this village were at that time illiterate.

There she was, inside an Orthodox chapel in remote Alaska, miles away from any other European person, while the native people were engaged in a vehement disagreement about her in a language she did not understand. She later wrote about that moment in her journal, saying, "I felt very much alone, far from my own people."

And yet, that nadir of her Alaskan adventure was followed by her being given the villagers' most precious possession, an icon sent all the way from Russia. The argument, it turned out, had been between the older men, who were grateful to Miss Breece but who also thought that she might ridicule the icon as they had seen other non-Orthodox do, and the younger men, who argued that she could be trusted with this special gift. Eventually, a compromise was reached, and the older men agreed to give her the icon, on the condition that she promise to treat it with respect.

In other words, out of one of her darker moments in Alaska, Hannah Breece received this theophany. I would even say that the gift of this icon was a visitation from the Mother of God, a sign of the protection of *Panaghia*, especially since it came exactly at the midpoint of Miss Breece's fourteen-year-long mission of teaching Alaskan children and was given on the Feast of the Mother of God's Dormition.

Jane Jacobs Saves the Enlightenment from Itself

Well, Hannah Breece's grand-niece, the great urbanist Jane Jacobs, can teach all of *us* to read the world more beautifully, especially if we are Orthodox Christians, by describing the inner nature of cities through the new science of complexity. As I will try to argue at some point in this interview, what Jacobs shows us is nothing less than a cosmic liturgy going on all around us, in both nature and in society.

In Jane Jacobs' work, the Enlightenment's virtues – and it is the Enlightenment that invented modern science – are maintained and extended, even as many of that movement's flaws are healed and surpassed. The glory of the Enlightenment had been its passion to see logos everywhere; i.e., its belief that reason would be richly rewarded in its thirst to understand the world. Its major flaw was that it also insisted that certain very simple kinds of rational order were the *only* kinds of order in the world.

Moreover, inspired perhaps by Descartes, the Enlightenment posited a kind of gnosticism, according to which humans were thought to exist somehow *outside of* nature. Forgetting that we, too, are part of this world, the idea was that humans would be able, through rational analysis, to dissect and control the world without any unforeseen impacts on themselves.[9]

I would even say that the logos the Enlightenment expected to find in nature was not a crucified and resurrected logos but an inert logos, because it was a logos that often did not inspire mercy for our fellow man.[10] The Enlightenment invented an approach to science that has left us, over time, tragically cold to beauty.

Still, Jane Jacob's work does more to seal the Enlightenment than to negate it. This was because she had happened to learn that a *post*-Enlightenment science had been discovered already – the science of biology and complex order. She presents this additional approach to reason that returns humanity to its proper place within nature. That way, you can use the "colder" science of the Enlightenment when studying non-living systems but needn't make a mess by applying it to living ones.

Moreover, right there in the pages of *The Death and Life of Great American Cities*, she said that this new science requires – on scientific grounds – that scientists be motivated by love for what they study and that they be restrained by pity and compassion for anything they try to improve.

---

9 In Chapter Five above, I argued that in the Modern period we have believed that we could liberate humanity from all constraint by using our wills to conquer and re-create our natures. In the case of the Enlightenment, the human will is reduced to human reason, and through genetics, this reason will soon attempt to recreate human nature itself.

10 I am not capitalizing "logos" here because I am referring to the many logoi of creation. As we said in Chapter Six, these principles within creation share in the crucifixion and resurrection of the Logos and are not just fixed rational principles. In art and architecture, it is the artist who must take care that the logoi be employed in a living way. And, it would seem, the more science advances in organically complex directions, the more our scientists will need to see themselves as being also artists.

Only the lover can truly understand an organic system, Jacobs tells us. And thus, through the new science of organic complexity, love returns to the center of the scientific enterprise after having been exiled for centuries by the drive for cold objectivity.

The reductive aspects of the Enlightenment vision live on still, many times, in ways that alienate us from the world and from each other. But that vision is broken where we most need it to be whole – in formulating a strong response to another impulse, the branch of postmodernism that rejects reason and science entirely and preaches a soft nihilism. Jacobs is able to save science from the deconstructionists, and even to show how science might possibly be reconciled with religion, because she first chastens Enlightenment science where it had grabbed things by the wrong handle.

The Theotokos Holds Back the Forces that Threaten Civilization

But now let us go on to my second story, of the icon that I gave to Mrs. Jacobs, in a deliberate attempt to imitate the earlier gift made to her grandmother's sister in Alaska.

Mrs. Jacobs of course was not an Orthodox Christian, nor was she a Christian, nor even a believer in the divine. In a private conversation with me at her home, she once said that she was an atheist, perhaps with a slight openness to being an agnostic. Yet she wrote her last two books with the icon of Panaghia I gave her practically on top of her typewriter – the same typewriter on which she had written all of her other books.

One of these two books, entitled *Dark Age Ahead*,[11] was about how some civilizations decline and disappear and about all that is lost when a civilization dies. She feared that we might be witnessing the decline of our own North American European civilization.

---

11 Jane Jacobs, *Dark Age Ahead* (New York: Random House, 2004).

I called Mrs. Jacobs when she was still writing this book and still wrestling with its themes in a creative way. She told me how dismayed she was to see the gathering threats to civilization, but then she said something I will never forget. She said in a very serious tone, "That icon you gave me, it's on the side of the right. And I don't mean the political right. I mean that *whatever force is trying to destroy civilization, that icon is against it.*" The moment she said this, she caught herself; I think she realized that she had stated the matter in terms that were too religious for her taste. After only a second's pause, she continued, *"I mean, whoever painted that icon understood the forces trying to bring down civilization, and how to block them."*

This is just the single wisest thing that I have ever heard said about icons. You know, I grew up Greek Orthodox, and so I gradually came to understand the Mother of God as the protectress of the Church, of Mount Athos, and of Constantinople, the Queen of Cities. I was taught to turn to the Mother of God in my own crises. But I had never seen that the Panaghia and her icons were this great force holding the powers of anti-civilization at bay on behalf of everyone, in every civilization. In contrast to me, Jane Jacobs, although being an avowed agnostic who maintained no religious practice or affiliation once her children had grown, understood at once the true meaning of an icon of Panaghia for the world. My own interpretation had been parochial – in actual fact, my understanding had been uncivilized and unloving, because it was too narrow.

So you see, spiritual insight can come from unexpected places; in fact, it often does. That's the whole point of theophany as being a gift rather than a result of our efforts.

But this story also explains why I am so glad to give an interview about Mrs. Jacobs' work on cities. Just imagine a person who could have such a natural and unlettered spiritual insight about icons and the Virgin Mary but who had also reinvented urban planning, reconceived economic science, and regrounded political philosophy – and who had done all this by incorporating the insights of the cutting-edge science of complexity a full forty or more years ahead of anyone else. Wouldn't you hope that someday *every* Orthodox social ethicist, professional or amateur, would be reading her?

Millions of readers love the work of Jane Jacobs. Her ideas are of universal significance. I'm convinced that our civilization won't have much of a future unless we either adopt her ideas or reinvent them for ourselves, which would be very hard to do. Many challenges confront us, and to face them we need a new economic science, a better understanding of urban order, a more sober yet also more joyful account of politics, and a richly inspiring reconciliation between science and religion. All of this Jacobs gives us to one extent or another.

A lot of people nowadays curse Descartes and the Enlightenment. They see in them only the cause of human alienation from nature, of rampant environmental degradation, of oppressive patriarchy, and of exploitation. In the period since World War II, people like the Bohemians, the hippies, and the New Agers have pushed back at the reductive tendencies within the modern approach to life. However, we must be very careful in our criticism of the Enlightenment revolution in human thinking.

Many anti-Cartesians seem unwilling to admit all the good that came out of the great movements for science launched in the Enlightenment. If some of these postmodernists and various New Age people had their way, we would lose science itself. Consequently, we must respond to them by showing how science is already able, on its own, to leave its overemphasis on reductionist and mechanistic models behind.

Jane Jacobs saves the Enlightenment because, although she was an early complexity theorist and a true holist, she also made the most convincing arguments for the goodness of reductionist techniques. She had the most coherent rationale for when such reductions should and shouldn't be applied. Reductionism isn't bad in and of itself.

However, there is one point on which we Orthodox Christians are in full agreement with the anti-modernists. In an age that is discovering the phenomenon of complex emergence, in an age when we see more and more clearly the maternal character of developmental processes in persons, in economies, and in nature, it is essential that we see how anything that disparages the feminine (including, at times, feminism itself) will bring us to absolute disaster.

As Orthodox Christians, our practice since ancient times is that we always come back to the Orthodox icon's picture of *the* mother holding her child, we always return to this vision of a chaste unknower who conceived the Logos and then was crucified with him, in her way, in order to remain faithful to that Logos. What was perhaps the greatest civilization that ever existed – Greek-speaking Rome in all of its Orthodox Christian glory – chose, after Christ, to look to this Mother and Child, to this one image, throughout its more than thousand-year long battle with the internal and external forces that try to destroy civilization. Jane Jacobs made me realize that *it was as if they had put everything the human race had ever learned about the importance and fragility of civilization, and about how to defend civilization, into those works of art*. We, too, must cooperate with and call upon the Mother of God if we are to preserve and extend civilization.

That icon, finally, is the key to our destiny in the centuries to come – if God grants such a long future to the human race.

The Biography of Jane Jacobs

RTE: After these marvelous stories about the icons, what else can you tell us about Mrs. Jacobs' life?

DR. PATITSAS: Much more, although I want to emphasize first of all that she was not a Christian or even a theist. I don't want to appear to put words in her mouth nor make her out to be some kind of "anonymous Christian." What she gave to the world in her writings, and some of the things that she said to me in person, suffice to establish her crucial importance to human civilization.

But I would be happy to say more about her because her life story unfolded to this point where she became a bridge figure between Cartesian modernity and the ancient appreciation of organic order.

She was born Jane Butzner in Scranton, Pennsylvania in May of 1916. Her father was a physician and an "early adopter" of the automobile, which he used to make house calls. It was he who insisted that his children pursue formal education but that they also learn a trade. Jane's trade was obtained during an eighteen-month stenography and secretarial program after high school which she then utilized while working for a newspaper in Scranton.

At age 19, she and her sister set out to find their fortunes in the most dynamic metropolis in the history of the world, New York City. Almost as soon as she got to New York City in the midst of the Great Depression, Jacobs began submitting freelance articles to magazines like *Vogue*, always about the intricate order and life in the city's diverse neighborhoods. An article might show the hidden side of the Diamond District or of the Flower District, for example.

She married Robert Jacobs, an architect, in 1944 and raised three children at 555 Hudson Street in Greenwich Village.

All told, from 1935 to 1968 Jane Jacobs lived, worked, wrote, and raised a family in New York City. That is to say, she lived from age 19 to age 52 in New York, and that city is really responsible for her adult identity.

She and her family then emigrated to Canada, where she continued to write for almost another forty years, until her passing in April of 2006, a month before her ninetieth birthday. In total, she wrote about eight books, almost all about cities and the organic structure behind and within urban order and city economies.

RTE: How did she move from freelance journalism to writing books?

DR. PATITSAS: Well, in the early 1950s, her work began to take on a growing seriousness. By then, Jacobs was an associate editor at *Architectural Forum* magazine. As the junior person on staff there, she was assigned to cover the new housing projects and urban highways which were the core of an ambitious program to renew America's cities. A Federal law, the Housing Act of 1949, had been passed, through which America would unintentionally wound, in some cases seemingly fatally, her own great urban centers, and this law was just then beginning to show its real, damaging effects.

Urban Renewal was a great tragedy for America; I can't help but think of it as a sin, of our own choosing, that God permitted us to commit because of what we had done to innocents in the cities of Germany and especially of Japan in World War II. Over the twenty-five years that the 1949 Housing Act was the law, more than 2,000 American city neighborhoods in over 300 cities were leveled to the ground in order to be rebuilt as simplistic parodies of their former complex order. This was done in the name of fighting poverty and wiping out slums.

Today, we don't have a clear idea of the ambitious scale and utopian hubris behind American Urban Renewal, but the belief was that, with enough money and public commitment, every slum in the country could be replaced by gleaming, immaculate "cities of the future." All that it would take would be the application of rational scientific principles, a ruthless willingness to evict millions of poor citizens from their homes, the cold-hearted decision to cast their communities to the winds, and the determination to dispossess tens of thousands of small business owners (principally in minority communities) with zero compensation. What could possibly go wrong with such a well-intentioned plan?!

Jacobs reported on what we now know as "the housing projects" (or, simply, "the projects") and on all the other bad patterns of urban renewal: expressways knifing through cities; gargantuan convention centers squatting sloppily and blindly in downtowns; cultural centers walled-off from their larger city contexts and "unable to support a single bookstore"; housing centers for the poor completely cut off from any urban context; and other blights on real city order. In the early 1950s, these kinds of projects were still shiny, new, and had not yet taken on that glower of menace or malicious neglect that they later did. Nevertheless, Jacobs saw at once that the gap between the glorious visions of the planners and the inhumane reality of what they were building could not be bridged.

To use that wonderful heuristic from architect Christopher Alexander, the city planners who ruled during the 1950s and 1960s started with a vain image, a blueprint, of what city life should be like, and then imposed that dead image upon the life that really did exist in those cities, destroying it in the process. The blueprint approach may be appropriate to the simpler kinds of scientific order but not to living cities. And these planners were not interested in the least in the actual forces in the neighborhoods they obliterated, nor in the actual forces of life that struggled on in the projects created by their brutal destruction of the old urban order. Consequently, their planning did not give birth to an eternal Form,[12] but rather attempted to create something that would be pretty by virtue of its conformity to abstract intellect.

To the Urban Renewal planners, the old Patterns of city order seemed chaotic, disordered. The order of the old neighborhoods was deep, but it was nonlinear and organic, and Enlightenment science couldn't cope with it. The Urban Renewal idea was that cities should look more like machines, or wind-up toys.

There was a conceptual confusion at work, too. Many of the people living in cities in the 1930s and 40s had been denied access to basic working capital and homeowner's loans. But in the planner's minds, the slums were downtrodden because of their adherence to the messy, living, ancient Patterns of city design – and not because the residents there had been denied all access to working capital, usually due to racial or ethnic discrimination. Wiping out the slums would therefore only be possible, the planners successfully argued, if a single master planner took total control over an entire neighborhood and stamped out all the bad uses of freedom.

---

12 Rome is known as "the Eternal City," and when you visit Rome you feel the absolute rightness of that title. But it is neither its antiquity nor its future alone that justify this designation, but also the fact that very few cities on earth have so completely and consistently captured living Patterns in all three types of human architecture – Guardian/Governmental/Civic; Trader/Private/Commercial; and, Third Force/Cultural/Religious – as well as in the linkages between and among buildings, for as long as Rome has. Vista after vista in Rome glows with the "self-maintaining fire" that Christopher Alexander said described The Quality Without a Name. This is a large part of what you are seeing when you "see" the eternal nature of Rome.

Christopher Alexander tells us that the Patterns in a city come to life when everyone in the city can contribute their dreams and talents to their creation and upkeep. The absence of meaningful participation by a broad cross-section of owners and residents due to racial or ethnic discrimination in the banking system is therefore the actual mechanism by which "slums" are created. People are barred from contributing to the formation of city order where they live, and so the neighborhood looks disordered. The obvious answer would have been to remove the barriers to home loans and self-employment in the slums, and then let the people take care of themselves.

When great masses of people cannot contribute to the development of their urban order except in a very constrained way, then their joint project – the city itself – of course will look broken. But the urban planners' answer in the 1950s was to make the original fault absolute: now, an even tinier elite, the planners, would control completely the city's shape and destiny, cutting off everyone from participating! Predictably, the result of this was that "the projects" created by the idealists were infinitely more brutal than the ghettos had been.

Any Orthodox Christian theologian reflecting on the actual facts about a city's dependence on broad public access to working capital would immediately recognize the actual issue at work in poor neighborhoods: what "creates" the evil of a slum is an absence of "liturgy." Without full access to jobs and capital among all its citizens, a city cannot be the true "work of the people" that occurs when average people are able to access capital and have the right to solve the problems and pursue the dreams that define their own lives and places. Racism, discrimination more generally, and much of what is called "central planning" are terrible sins against liturgy, as well as against persons, for they wrongly excommunicate millions of people created in the image of God from participation in the joint labor by which a city is continually re-created and maintained.

Lewis Mumford, the city theorist whose writings had captured the imagination of the planning elites up until Jacobs came along, had described the great American mega-city as a "necropolis." He coined this term not only because he could not fully appreciate the living order within the apparent chaos of urban life, but also because he postulated the ancient origins of all cities to be not liturgy, but rather the ancient human desire to live near the tombs of one's ancestors. Therefore, he tended to see the living, organic order of the cities as if it were indistinguishable from death and decay. Mumford's writings were broadly aligned to the Urban Renewal ideal, but they were based in a view of the city that found any association with death "unclean" and which aimed to build the deathless, antiseptic super-city of the future.

As it turned out, it was aesthetes like Mumford and the modernist planners themselves who not only built projects that had no life from an artistic perspective but whose "projects" became the epicenters of actual murder and violent assault, contributing mightily to the meteoric rise in felony crime in our cities. The failure of these housing projects radiated out and further injured ethnic and race relations in America, as well. In other words, it was the Cartesians, not the pattern-using citizens, who built cities of death.

Because Jacobs could see that poor citizens actually preferred their old neighborhoods; that the order in the old neighborhoods was more sophisticated, safe, and intellectually complex than that found in the vast empty "open spaces" of the rebuilt city; that the new city neighborhoods were destroying human community and generating social pathology; and, that the planners were too in love with their own, rather dull, creativity to notice the brutal harm their mighty intellects were inflicting, in about 1957 or so she began to speak out.[13]

Jane Jacobs quickly came to the conclusion that the Enlightenment-style science then used in urban planning in America and Great Britain had not only been a practical disaster but that this

---

13 Do the Cartesian "great minds" who destroyed rich, organic city order in favor of something more scholarly, precise, and dead have their analogues in many of those recent scholars who would reform the Christian liturgy, whether in the Protestant, Roman Catholic, or Orthodox Christian worlds? Like the city planners of modernism, the liturgical reformers have the weight of a certain kind of IQ and of a certain kind of science on their side; they are well-informed specialists, sanctioned by the academy.

But, in actuality, the order these liturgical reformers have generated, and would generate still more widely if permitted, is a less complex, less humane, and certainly less infor-

science was based on intellectually mistaken theoretical underpinnings. What was being accomplished by Urban Renewal, Jacobs said, was not the rebuilding of America's cities but their "sack" and their destruction.

The thinkers of the Enlightenment wanted a fixed and miracle-free universe so that science could operate without guidance from religion, which they saw as superstition. But living systems – complex and organic systems – live through cycles of death and life and, in some way that even science should recognize, *are always miraculous.*

In fact, the attempt to make the living world into a machine, an antiseptic and deathless mechanism, blew back and made the period since 1600 one of the deadliest in all of human history: mass trans-continental slavery; the decimation of indigenous peoples in the Western hemisphere; world wars; fascist concentration camps; communist gulags; the use of chemical and atomic weapons – the list goes on. While most of these horrors had existed to some degree and on some scale since the Fall of Adam and Eve, science and the scientific mind just scale them up exponentially. The imposition of dull, linear order upon a complex world is not a neutral project.

The Backlash Against European Culture Must Not Go Too Far

RTE: Your examples sound as if the evil of the modern age is mostly a European problem.

DR. PATITSAS: You mean, because I'm beginning to sound like some typical academic for whom Eurocentrism is the root of all the world's problems? But this goes back to my point in our very first

---

mation-rich order than that present in the seemingly imperfect and chaotic liturgies they denigrate.

Armed with the knowledge of every detail of liturgical development, these specialists lack only two things: the awareness that science itself has left behind the reductive style of rationalism which they have been taught is the whole of science, and a sophisticated feel for the beauty within the apparent chaos of organic systems. Everything about their training teaches them to miss the real order within what they study.

interview, that the integration of body, mind, and heart is not at all trivial. It is very hard to achieve. The Byzantines, I believe, can give us better guidance than either conflict theory or contemporary social justice movements.

Of course, Orthodox Christianity is not alone in critiquing the great hegemonic force of certain modernist Western European ideas. But I think that we Orthodox do have some unique insights into both the problems and the solutions. I hope that we are better positioned to admire and respect the West, even when we believe that it needs to refine some of its mistaken beliefs.

With or without racism, the larger challenges will still remain: how do we integrate mind, heart, and body? How do we blend linear, machine-style order (which is needed) with nonlinear, organic order (which is needed even more)?

What particular balance of mind and heart and body will be struck in America, and will it be a good balance, a sophisticated and life-giving balance? Or, will it descend into barbarism? These are the questions which every civilization must answer, whatever the relationships among its people.

For sure, my point is not that evil has some racial or cultural focus. When I'm at academic conferences and I hear the sessions attacking "whiteness" and cultural colonialism, I get the sense that it all really comes down to questions which I believe only Byzantium can help us resolve: Is it possible *both* to pursue the way of the heart preserved in non-Western cultures *and* to keep a complex and rigorous intellectual tradition as in the modern West? Will the victory of linear modernity mean the obliteration of all cultural difference, especially within the economically weaker segments of society whose wisdom and worldviews are thankfully not defined by the great reductive, linear intellectual movements of the past four hundred years? Racial discrimination is just one aspect of this challenge.

However, when opposing reductive modes of thought, contemporary opponents of the West swerve to the other extreme. In the name of preserving cultural distinctiveness, we hold up theologians or poets or musicians or architects who just aren't very good. Fleeing

Cartesian reductionism because it seems too "white," we then also abandon the basic tenets of rational discourse and aesthetics.

The task of integration requires that we combine the way of the heart with the way of the mind; the Orthodox Christians of Constantinople perfected this art. I say "art," but in fact it really is a gift of the Holy Spirit, wherever it happens. Outside of grace, there is only war. Look at what has sometimes happened to religious architecture in America, for example; tragic declines in quality are matched by the inability of people to even notice how bad it all is. This insensitivity is a sign of a civilization entering an eclipse.

Yet and still, I join some of these voices from the cultural margins who critique our culture to say this: a certain kind of scientific mind is so contemptuous of faith and religion, of the heart, the body, the feminine, and the other; it feels itself so superior to everything it describes as "primitive" or "irrational."

But hasn't it been science itself which has enabled killing and oppression at a pace and a scale never before possible? Why should these scientists look down their noses at the churches and temples because of "religious violence"? We weren't the ones who invented hydrogen bombs and biological weapons and all the rest of it. That's entirely on them. And so often the inventors of the technologies of mass destruction or oppression weren't particularly motivated by nationalism or hatred; they just enjoyed inventing, and it was in war work that the scientific funding was to be found.

Clearly, the way of the mind cannot be lost. But neither can it survive without the way of the heart. Jane Jacobs, by showing how to combine mechanistic, linear order with organic order, is indispensable to this balance. She is the sort of thinker whom the Roman Orthodox would have understood implicitly. We Orthodox living in the West (and by now almost the whole world is more or less "the West") will have to turn to her for help. This is my point.

The Death and Life of Great American Cities

About 1957, Jacobs gave a speech in New York City arguing that what city renewal was building was worse than what it had replaced. This speech became an article in *Forbes* magazine, and then the Rockefeller Foundation offered Jacobs a fellowship to turn her views into a book. That book, *The Death and Life of Great American Cities*, caused a firestorm. Brilliant and passionate, it was not only a cry for social justice on behalf of the millions of people being displaced or disrupted by urban renewal (who were typically poor and often black), but an attack on the validity of the actual science guiding the whole enterprise. She was determined to reinvent the science of urban order, and in this jewel of planning literature, she did precisely that. But she was also the prophet of a new kind of science, a living systems science that clearly contravened the presuppositions of the older Enlightenment approaches to reason.

The Death and Life of Great American Cities has been called the single best book ever written about urban planning, the one book more than any other that unlocks the way that neighborhood order in a city functions through both the built environment and through human relationship. It is a classic of American English prose, as well, just the most readable and enjoyable non-fiction book you can imagine.

So many people agreed with what Jacobs had written that she was thrust to the forefront of the Architectural Conservation Movement and is even considered one of its founders. She became the leader of the successful movement to save lower Manhattan's Greenwich Village from being leveled for a planned expressway. She therefore became the symbol of the effort to to frustrate Robert Moses, the person in the Greater New York City area who was masterminding all these destructive urban renewal schemes.

Robert Moses was a figure who at one time headed more than twenty different governmental and quasi-governmental bodies concerned with demolishing and rebuilding the New York City metropolitan area into the cold, lifeless Urban Renewal ideal, and his power was all but unchecked by either elected officials or citizens. Thanks to Jacobs, for the first time in more than twelve years, one of his destructive plans was halted; he never recovered his momentum in his great city-destroying efforts.

It will help our story if we mention Moses' sputtering reaction to his first defeat at the hands of Jacobs and her allies: "I've been beaten by a bunch . . . of mothers!" In the light of Jane Jacobs' later reaction to the icon I gave her, I would say that he had no idea how true that was.

Jacobs joined protests against the Vietnam War,[14] while also working on a second book, *The Economy of Cities* (1969). But after she'd been arrested several times while protesting, and with her two sons approaching draft age, her husband Robert Jacobs accepted a position as an architect in Toronto and announced to his family that he was moving them to Canada.

Sadly, Jane Jacobs' departure deprived New York City of the person who best understood that city's order, at a time when twenty further years of intensifying decline in the city's fortunes were set to begin. I have also been told that many of Jane Jacobs' former friends among the intellectual leaders in New York City, the brilliant lights who might have continued to push her still-unfolding ideas into the mainstream of American public awareness, somehow never forgave her for, in their view, abandoning this country. For whatever reason, her voice never became the central voice in American economic theory that it deserved to be.

But Jacobs' departure to Canada was significant in a positive way. No sooner had she arrived in Toronto than she learned that urban planners there (apparently infected by the latest fads in bad urban planning theory that had swept England and America) intended to destroy the entirety of that lovely city by imposing a vast spaghetti-maze of urban expressways. Jacobs took the reins of the

---

14 Vietnam veterans reading this book might wonder how I would react to her opposition to this war. In brief, I believe that the preservation of South Vietnamese independence was a cause worth fighting for. The country's borders were so long, however, that it was militarily impossible to defend them while Cambodian and Laotian territory were being traversed and even occupied by the North Vietnamese army.

foundering protest movement and saved Toronto – a city today regarded as so beautiful that many film directors who wish to depict American cities choose to shoot there, on its unruined streets and in its still-intact neighborhoods, rather than in any city in the United States itself.

Jacobs wrote more books after her emigration to Canada: *Cities and the Wealth of Nations* in 1984; *Systems of Survival* in 1992; *A School Teacher in Old Alaska: The Story of Hannah Breece* in 1995, which we mentioned earlier; *The Nature of Economies* in 2000; and, *Dark Age Ahead* in 2004. At her passing, a final book was in process, tentatively entitled *A New Hypothesis*, conceived in response to my dissertation's claim that her total insights about economies had amounted to a rediscovery of economic science itself.[15]

At a minimum you could describe Jane Jacobs' achievements in the following terms: she was a founder of the Architectural Conservation Movement; she saved two cities – lower West Side Manhattan and all of Toronto – from complete evisceration by expressways; she wrote the best book ever written about urban planning, *The Death and Life of Great American Cities*; and, she penned significant meditations about the way to improve economic science. To all of this you could add that, starting in 1961 in *Death and Life* and until her last unpublished book, she was an early employer of something called complexity theory (also known as the science of organic complexity or "systems thinking") in looking at both urban order and economic science. I think these of her achievements anyone could agree on.

But as significant as these are, they do not exhaust her contributions; there are other accomplishments, as well. *Death and Life* is also

---

15 In Chapter Eight of my dissertation, "The Future of Economic Science: Liturgical and Complex," in "The King Returns to His City: An Interpretation of the Great Week and Bright Week Cycle of the Orthodox Church," *op. cit.* in Footnote 2. It was reading this chapter that sparked Jane Jacobs to attempt *A New Hypothesis*, a final summary of her economic work, she told me by phone. Sadly, the completion of this book was prevented by her passing on April 25, 2006.

For a fragment of this unpublished work, see "Uncovering the Economy: A New Hypothesis; Excerpt from an Unpublished Work, 2004," in S. Zipp and N. Storring, *Vital Little Plans: The Short Works of Jane Jacobs* (New York: Random House, 2016), 406-31.

a brief against racial injustice, since 1,700 of the 2,100 American neighborhoods dynamited to rubble between 1949 and 1974 were African-American neighborhoods, and in all those places not only homes but also businesses, churches, stores, and cultural centers were obliterated with little or no compensation to their owners.[16] Racial relations in America today could recover from this blow far faster if we could consciously address the harm that Urban Renewal caused.

Also, Jane Jacobs didn't just offer critiques of economic science but, by the end of her life, had discovered an entirely new perspective on the discipline. I believe we will one day recognize Jane Jacobs alongside Adam Smith and perhaps Friedrich Hayek, as one of the two or three primary founders of economic science. Additionally, she effectively marks the end of the Enlightenment by both affirming the good that it had achieved while also showing that the new and more sophisticated science of organic complexity had relegated the old reductionist approaches to a subordinate, although still legitimate and useful, role.

Oh, and one other thing: Jane Jacobs laid the necessary groundwork for the reconciliation of science with religion.

Jacobs' Achievements

RTE: That she co-founded economic science and has reconciled science and religion are startling claims.

DR. PATITSAS: It took me a long time to recognize these additional accomplishments because a lot of it was not intentional on her part, nor even recognized by Jacobs herself. Some of what I see her as having accomplished is implicit rather than explicit in her work. Certain things – like her reconciliation of science with religion, or her defending, while also surpassing, the Enlightenment, or even that she succeeded in rediscovering economic science – were as-

---

16 See Mindy Thompson Fullilove, *Root Shock: How Tearing Up City Neighborhoods Hurts America, and What We Can Do About It* (New York: One World/Ballantine, 2004).

pects of her work that might have been apparent to any American Orthodox Christian theologian reading her work, though they seem not to have been noticed by her.

You will see what I mean as we go on, but the crucial questions and concerns that a person raised as an Orthodox Christian in America might bring to Jacobs' work were the key to my having discerned her additional contributions.

I sometimes like to think that anyone who had an M.Div. from the Holy Cross Greek Orthodox School of Theology in Brookline, Massachusetts and had read Jane Jacobs would have seen what I saw – and that perhaps no one who didn't have that background, would have! I don't mean this literally but rather as a way of describing just how "natural" these insights flowed together for me as an American Orthodox Christian once I had begun to discover them. And, to be honest, if there was some unique genius on my part involved, it was surely also "genius" in the classical sense of "divine inspiration," as well. It was a magical time in my life, when I noticed all these extra meanings within Jane Jacobs' work.

Jacobs was negotiating a boundary between two different ways of looking at the world, between different definitions of what it means to know something – between linear and nonlinear order, principally. But this boundary is familiar territory to any Orthodox Christian in the West.

So, even if someone else with my background might not have been able to discover what I'm about to tell you, still these findings are not hard to understand once they've been pointed out to you. I don't want readers to be intimidated before I've even had a chance to explain. It's really not that hard, or I wouldn't have noticed it, either!

Besides, by far the biggest obstacle to convincing others of Jacobs' three additional achievements – regarding complexity science, economics, and religion – is not at all their difficulty but rather just that the people who do love her books can't believe so much *further* richness might still be present in them. Her greatest achievements are hidden behind her other already dazzling achievements, if you see what I mean.

For example, the radical significance of her use of complexity theory escapes almost everyone, including the people who love *Death and Life* for the great urban planning book that it is. They don't really appreciate how astounding its final chapter is, where she announces that what her book has been doing is reinventing urban planning in terms of the newly discovered science of organic complexity, the close cousin of chaos theory. But just reflect on the fact that most social scientists have not even started to reconceive their fields in terms of complexity theory while Jane Jacobs did so explicitly and with perfect mastery – in 1961! The famous "butterfly effect" of chaos theory, for example, wasn't discovered by Edward Lorenz until 1963, two years *after* Jacobs took the new science by the reins and rode it to a complete reinvention of her entire field![17] It's almost disorienting that a person could be as far ahead of her time as she was. It's as if Jane Jacobs was a time-traveller from the future, sent back to guide us.

RTE: Did Mrs. Jacobs' economic ideas also figure in your dissertation, and did she ever have the chance to read it?

DR. PATITSAS: They are central to my dissertation. And in fact I presented them in a systematic form that she hadn't worked out herself. You see, the re-founding of economic science wasn't even Jacobs' goal. All her economic work was written in a spirit of, "I hope that someday we will have a true science of economics because so many of the core assumptions accepted by economists today are clearly wrong. I wonder who will manage to make that new science, where that new science will come from? In the meantime, I will add my insights about where we have been getting things wrong."

When she read my dissertation and its argument that she had already joined or supplanted Adam Smith as the founder of eco-

---

17 The "butterfly effect" describes the "sensitive dependence on initial conditions" of chaotic systems. For example, a tiny local difference in the weather in one place on Day One, will by Day Six lead to completely different end states in the weather on the other side of the world. Thus the cliché that a butterfly flapping its wings in one part of the world will make the difference in whether or not a storm forms on the other side of the world in one week's time.

nomic science, she was stunned. I will never forget my meeting with her in late June or early July of 2004, on the front porch of her home in the Spadina neighborhood of Toronto. She looked at me and said, "The first thing I have to ask you is, *How did you do what you did?*" She said this with so much gratitude and intensity and wonder that I was shocked. In my mind, I had merely summarized the economic discoveries of my heroine and made some new connections among them. Later on, in 2010, I saw a much deeper unity to her writing about economies – but let us handle that another time, for we can't do everything in one interview!

But my point is that until she read my dissertation, even Mrs. Jacobs herself hadn't realized how far she'd travelled as an economist. She thought she'd just made contributions to someone else's future reinvention of the science.

One of the last things she told me before she died was that in attempting to summarize her economic insights in response to my dissertation, she had discovered the real meaning of the business cycle.[18] But this, together with the definition of "economic development," which she also discovered, are the two greatest puzzles in all of contemporary economics. And she alone managed to figure out both.

As for the insight that the science of the Enlightenment had been surpassed in a very natural way by the discovery of organized

---

18 Jacobs' discovery of the meaning of development comes in two parts; first, in *The Economy of Cities* and, second, in *Cities and the Wealth of Nations*. In the earlier work, "economic development" is defined as the "bringing forth of new work upon the basis of older work, in the context of many others doing the same."

In *Cities and the Wealth*, this definition is extended to say that this process must happen in cities which are in "networks of volatile trade with other cities at similar levels of development." As she put it, "backward cities need each other," because trading with each other gives them practice in replacing imports with local production.

Meanwhile, her discovery of the meaning of the business cycle (which, as far as I know, neither she nor her heirs ever published) is that it is an epiphenomenon of the stages of city "refueling," a concept Jacobs' laid out in *The Economy of Cities*, in *Cities and the Wealth of Nations*, and finally in *The Nature of Economies*. At each stage, different pressures upon prices and employment arise.

Re-fueling is the process by which cities:
1. generate new exports as well as the support-work behind export work.
2. replace some of their existing imports with their own local production.
3. in consequence, shift up to the purchase of more sophisticated imports than they could formerly afford. (Footnote continues on next page)

complexity, and as for her laying the basis for the reconciliation of science and religion – those things were already right there in *The Death and Life of Great American Cities*, in 1961. However, they remained either unnoticed or underemphasized by everyone, including her, until I happened to see first the one, in about 2000, and then we both separately saw the other, soon after. She didn't consciously attempt to cap the epoch of the Enlightenment; it just happened that she did.

II. THE BEAUTIFUL SCIENCE OF COMPLEXITY

Warren Weaver, Ph.D. (1894-1978)

These two achievements of Jane Jacobs, the scientific one concerning the Enlightenment and the theological one helping to reconcile science with religion, flowed from a serendipitous event that occurred in 1958 while Jacobs was completing *The Death and Life of Great American Cities* with the support of the Rockefeller Foundation. An eminent scientist named Warren Weaver, the director of research in natural sciences at Rockefeller, was just stepping down after a tenure of almost thirty years. Weaver's departing address was a report summarizing the revolutionary discovery of organic complexity that he had helped to catalyze while at the foundation, and this report made a major impact on the thinking of Jacobs.

Warren Weaver, after taking over the direction of natural science research at the Rockefeller Foundation in 1932, had pushed

---

... 4. the city then enters a more inert phase, as it casts about for new export work and new local work supporting these exports, which may take some time to develop.

These more sophisticated imports are the "new fuel" of the city organism (thus, "re-fueling"), since they provide the possibility of new avenues of learning and import replacement. In Jacobs' theory, imports are among the greatest assets of a city.

The business cycle tracks the phases of this process of (1) export generation (a step which could occur either quietly or in a great "boom" of growth); (2) import replacing (the most expansive step, when both employment and prices are rising together), (3) import shifting, and (4) the interval until the process can begin again (often a rather downtime economically when prices fall and unemployment rises). The business cycle is thus not a sign of policy failure but a natural and necessary organic process.

the foundation to fund lines of inquiry that would quickly lead to the great twentieth-century advances in medical science and biology. It will help us understand the seriousness with which Weaver's contemporaries took him as a scientist if we know that he co-authored the first book ever published on Information Theory, together with Claude Shannon (1916-2001), who was the formulator of Information Theory and one of the most significant scientific minds, after Einstein, of the entire twentieth century.[19]

Through the medical and biological research he funded, Warren Weaver had been at the center of a scientific revolution that remains underemphasized, although this revolution affects our lives on a daily basis. I am talking about the scientific recognition of the special properties of organically complex systems.

Defined simply, in complex systems a whole is greater than the sum of its parts. In other words, in such systems the mechanistic and reductive approach of Enlightenment science doesn't work because the ongoing organic processes within such systems are as important to them as their fixed parts, their anatomy. You can't take apart an organic system, see what the parts are made of, and then put it back together in the way you could a machine. And even if you could, until you understood the dynamic processes in a complex system (its metabolism, one could say), you wouldn't have understood much of anything anyway.

One scientist of such systems put it clearly: "The behavior of a [complex] system cannot be known just by knowing the elements of which a [complex] system is made."[20] Nor, I would add, just by knowing the elements plus the laws of physics which "must" govern them; i.e., as *would be true* in the case of a machine of some kind. In a living system, something more is going on.

Another book describes this difference between a complex system and a mechanical one as being like the difference between *a cat*

---

[19] We will return to and define Information Theory below in "III. The City is a Liturgy."

[20] Donella Meadows, in *Thinking in Systems: A Primer* (White River Junction, Vermont: Chelsea Green Pub., 2008). Meadows describes complex systems as, "a set of things – people, cells, molecules, or whatever – interconnected in such a way that they produce

and *a toaster*.[21] It is clear that one of these two things *cannot* be taken apart and reassembled without serious harm to its functioning – no matter how white your lab coat nor how thick your glasses. In fact, to take apart the cat is not only to kill it but also to understand it more poorly than before. I think we can all see that it is not scientific to treat a living system with the same rational techniques that would be appropriate to inert machines. Rather, it is malicious and cruel, sometimes even an act of madness.

Warren Weaver, as I said, oriented research funding toward biology, medicine, Information Theory, and other related areas for almost three decades at the Rockefeller Foundation. Taken together, this research led to the quiet revolution I mentioned just a moment ago: the discovery of this new kind of natural order, a non-mechanistic and nonlinear order. Yes, this new type of "cosmos" could still be studied rationally, but only provided that you had mastered an entire set of alternative scientific techniques.

This discovery of an additional, third, kind of natural order alongside two other simpler kinds of order which previously had been discovered by the Enlightenment (which I will describe in just a minute) is what "seals" the Enlightenment. The existence of this new class of scientific problems marks a limit that the simpler kinds of science – Enlightenment science – cannot trespass, or else they become destructive, inhumane, and, in fact, unscientific.

However, we must also see this alternative kind of science as something positive for the simpler Enlightenment modes of thinking and not only as its limitation or rebuke. Precisely because the discovery of this new science curtails the reach of the Enlightenment into areas where it doesn't belong, it protects the Enlightenment methods from being rejected wholesale – which is, of course,

their own pattern of behavior over time ... the [complex] system's response to [outside] forces is characteristic of itself, and that response is seldom simple in the real world ... The [complex] system, to a large extent, causes its own behavior! An outside event may unleash that behavior, but the same outside event applied to a different [complex] system is likely to produce a different result ... " All quotes are from the first chapter, "Introduction: The Systems Lens."

21 See Douglas A. Hall, *The Cat and the Toaster: Living Systems Ministry in a Technological Age* (Eugene, Oregon: Wipf & Stock, 2010).

what has happened whenever the simpler approach has been used inappropriately and destructively. This third kind of science, the science of organic complexity (which is related to both chaos theory and the concept of "emergence"), marks the moment when the Enlightenment surpasses itself by discovering its own successor.[22]

RTE: Can you describe the first two kinds of science for us?

DR. PATITSAS: Each scientific approach is simply described in *The Death and Life* itself, and in a moment I will apply those summaries to our purposes.

However, let me just interject that the great surprise, the reason that I wanted to do this interview as a part of *The Ethics of Beauty*, is that it turns out that the organically complex approach to science is very much the Beauty-first approach to thinking scientifically. This, I think, will help resolve a question that many readers have had all along in this book; namely, what exactly is the role of reason when we approach the world through the lens of beauty and gratitude, rather than through the prism of cold analysis?

Furthermore, one of the most astounding things to me about all of this is the almost too-easy reconciliation of science and religion that flows from the artful use of the science of organic complexity. It turns out that, when you look at the world in the Beauty-first way, the first thing you will notice is that the world of complex order looks and feels completely "liturgical." A Beauty-first approach always means focusing on theophany and starting to doxologize, so this should not surprise us. But the degree to which the world through the eyes of complexity science looks like a cosmic liturgy is just astonishing, as we shall shortly see.

Let us move on, then, to our description of the three kinds of science. In the first kind of science, we look at *cause and effect*, or

---

[22] An observant reader might ask where quantum theory and quantum mechanics fits into this scheme of three types of science. Dr. Arnold E. Sikkema, a quantum physicist at Trinity Western University in Vancouver, Canada, recently told me that his field is actually a surprising mix of the last two kinds of science, probability/statistics and organized complexity.

causation. In the second kind of science, we look at *probability*, or *statistical patterns*. And in the third kind of science, we examine *organic processes*, or *living interrelationships*.

The First Kind of Science: Problems in Simplicity

In Chapter Four, I mentioned the 1958 address by Warren Weaver at the Rockefeller Foundation in which he summarized the history of science in a way that influenced Jane Jacobs so profoundly.[23] Although we paraphrased this address in that chapter, I want to do so again here with more thoroughness because Weaver's account is really the most necessary tool if we are to understand how contemporary science can be reconciled with the ancient wisdom traditions. Reading Weaver's address was the serendipitous event in Jane Jacobs' writing of *Death and Life* that I mentioned just now.

From roughly 1600 to 1900 A.D., science learned how to handle problems with only two variables; at that point, reductionism – reducing the behavior of one variable to its dependence upon a single other factor – *was* science. Scientists in this period perfected the asking and answering of questions such as, "How does increasing the pressure on a gas affect its volume?" Or, "If we drop two balls from an identical height, with the only difference between them being their mass, will the speed at which they fall differ?"

This level of complexity was all that science could handle for its first three hundred years, but it was enough to give us a great increase in our understanding of the world. Weaver points out that even this simplistic level of science made possible numerous useful technologies and the Industrial Revolution itself.

---

23 To remind the reader, Jane Jacobs presents the three main classes of scientific order in, "The Kind of Problem a City Is," the final chapter of *The Death and Life of Great American Cities* (New York: Random House, 1961), 428-48. She, in turn, borrows her account from Warren Weaver, "A Quarter Century in the Natural Sciences," in *The President's Review, including A Quarter Century in the Natural Sciences by Warren Weaver, from the Rockefeller Foundation Annual Report, 1958* (New York: The Rockefeller Foundation, 1958), 7-15.

What Happens If You Apply This Kind of Science to Living Systems?

Let me interpose at once, though, and say that this "problems in simplicity" approach can become destructive and is termed "reductionist" when it is applied to organically complex living systems. For example, it turns out that sending free food to starving areas of a foreign country (a simple two-variable approach: "hunger" *equals* "send food") often *increases* starvation in the place being helped. Locally-produced food cannot compete in price with the free food, and so farmers themselves begin to go hungry and leave the land, causing local food production to drop.[24] Or, trying to reduce the entire complexity of childhood development solely to discipline – or solely to mercy – misses the complex and interacting needs within a child's soul and will therefore inhibit the child's maturation. Many problems do not have simple two-variable solutions.

We can see that it is reductionist – although scientific in one sense, still it is not accurate – to say that a starving country's problem is lack of food and that therefore sending food will solve the problem. It was through a similarly low level of sophistication that Urban Planning science wounded our American cities. Plans based on two-variable thinking about things like the relationship between acreage of park land and total population of a city, or about the relationship between efficiency of traffic and road width, justified wiping out entire neighborhoods that, though poor, nevertheless possessed a richly complex and mature order.

The reason Urban Renewal spelled a Dark Age for American cities (and, in many ways, for American civilization) is that it involved the systematic substitution of simple, two-variable order in city neighborhoods that until then had been characterized by organically complex, multi-variable order. For Bostonians, this difference in scientific sophistication is the difference between the old

---

[24] See Timothy T. Schwartz, *Travesty in Haiti: A True Account of Christian Missions, Orphanages, Fraud, Food Aid and Drug Trafficking* (Charleston: BookSurge Publishing, 2008).

European order and feel of our beloved Italian North End, on the one hand, and our City Hall and its plaza, on the other.

There are numerous examples in all American cities of this "dumbing down" of neighborhoods. After you've read Jacobs, you walk through a typical American downtown and see where the lush urban order has been denuded, stripped, simplified way past the point of stupidity – all in the name of science! Urban Renewal represented not only a dumbing down of cities but also the triumph of dumb interpretations of their order and functioning over more information-rich and clever understandings; our cultural ideas of science had not yet advanced to the point where planners could understand organic and complex order. Even today, our urban planners have not caught up with the discoveries being made by complexity theorists.

However, Weaver's point, and Jacobs agreed with him, was also that we mustn't go to extremes. In many situations two-variable science *is exactly what is needed*. Many useful inventions and technologies resulted from a science no more sophisticated than the "problems in simplicity" approach; Weaver mentions the radio, the telephone, the diesel engine, and hydroelectric power plants as examples of technologies designed using the first kind of science.

Moreover, many times even in living systems we seek a binary, or simple, outcome: The patient will either live or he will die; the infection that is causing a stomach ulcer will either be defeated or it won't.

Reductionism, in Warren Weaver's wonderful account of the three kinds of science, is seen for what it is: only one of three ways to analyze the world, all of which are needed, but needed in different settings.

The Second Kind of Science: Problems in Disorganized Complexity

Weaver's account of science history continued: In the early 1900s a second kind of scientific problem, involving many more than two variables, was discovered. We are talking about statistical analysis, which mathematicians developed in order to handle huge numbers of variables and their interactions.

These sorts of puzzles Weaver termed "problems in disorganized complexity." In other words, scientific analysis learned to use millions of bits of information to work out averages and became able to predict the future of great chaotic systems by using probability. Thus, today a good health statistician can ask you ten questions about your health habits and then predict with a known degree of certainty your probable life expectancy.

But this does not mean that you *necessarily will* die the moment that your statistically-appointed hour has come! Nor, in and of itself, can the statistical probability tell you any biological reason why being obese will harm you. There is a kind of cloudiness to statistical analysis which must be refined through other means.

That is why, even though Weaver is careful to emphasize the usefulness of this second kind of science for understanding and predicting the behavior of all sorts of systems, he stresses that this kind of science has a narrow and particular place. He mentions that the design of a telephone exchange requires understanding the probable behaviors of a huge number of telephone users. So does planning by a life insurance company. Statistical studies are a valid form of science, even if their genuinely useful results suffer from certain constraints.

So far, both these kinds of science – problems in simplicity and problems in disorganized complexity – are discoveries of an Enlightenment-style approach to science. That is, both approaches reinforce the basic Cartesian assumptions of the Enlightenment: that the world is knowable by human reason; that objective knowledge ("objective" in the sense that the knower is not really involved in changing what he studies nor is he being changed by it) is actually possible; that the best kind of knower is one who is free from emotional influence of any kind; that knowing is not a moral (concerned with the Good) or an aesthetic (concerned with the Beautiful) enterprise but strictly a logical one (concerned only with the True); that the scientist can and should stand outside the world he is studying, knowing it from a critical distance; that the purpose of scientific knowledge is to augment human power and control over nature; and so forth.

All of these presuppositions are the core of the Enlightenment worldview. With the first two kinds of science, they all still apply; you can still hold onto your belief that "man is the measure of all things." With these kinds of science, you can still believe that the world is a mechanical toy, a dead thing. With simplicity and probability, you even seem to have drained the world of its mystery, its sacredness. You imagine yourself free of superstition, totally superior to the "savage" mind.

This notion of the world as a machine which we can take apart is the very approach to the world that lay holists (not yet getting to biologists and ecologists themselves) reject. Whether these holists be organic gardeners, alternative healers, or post-modernists, they do not think that the truth about the world can be known so clearly or so "cleanly." Holists of various stripes also think that knowing is always a moral enterprise, and perhaps even an aesthetic one.

All of these protesters against reductionism correctly discern limits to and problems with the Enlightenment kind of knowing. But what not enough of them seem to realize is that by 1961 one corner of science itself, biology, had already reached many of their conclusions and was finding a way past these limitations within the modern approach to science.

Before I mention that other way, I must say that even for some scientists, these first two kinds of scientific problem-solving are still assumed to be equivalent to science itself. It is all that they know of science, all that they believe their profession has to offer.

The Third Kind of Science: Problems in Organized Complexity

By 1930, science had made amazing progress using only the "problems in simplicity" and the "problems in disorganized complexity" approaches. The world and man's relationship to it were being transformed.

However, the fields of medicine and biology had meanwhile remained stagnant. Until that late date, says Weaver, medical science and the life sciences in general lagged far behind the "hard sciences" like physics, inorganic chemistry, and math. It has even been said that it was not until sometime in the 1920s when, for the first time in human history, going to a doctor was more likely to help you than to harm you![25]

This, Weaver says, was because it wasn't until after 1932 that scientists clearly understood that there was an additional, *third class* of scientific order, a *third kind* of scientific problem, which is operative in all living systems. This third type of problem is the "problem in organized complexity," or simply "complexity."

In this third kind of problem, science deals with a middle range of variables – not just two, and not tens of millions. These few variables are related through complex webs and pathways, feedback loops and connections, so that we can scientifically state that in these cases the whole is indeed greater than the sum of its parts. Whenever we are talking about the inner behavior of an organic cell, or about a cell's relation to the organs of which it is a part, or about how all the organ systems in a body interact to preserve our

---

25 Of course, this would depend on the doctor, the ailment, and the general level of medical knowledge within a culture. The Orthodox Christian Romans in Constantinople and Asia Minor, who in the 300s A.D. invented the hospital, certainly enjoyed some medical success or they would not have made hospitals a cornerstone of their urban life for the next 1100 years. See Timothy Miller, *The Birth of the Hospital in the Byzantine Empire* (Baltimore: Johns Hopkins University Press, 1997).

Others might read this statement about doctors no longer harming us, meanwhile, and protest that twenty-first century medicine remains insufficiently organic, and that it, too, (under the guise of "industrial medicine") sometimes causes harm. But at least we have turned a decisive corner, and we will go even farther in the years to come.

life, we are not employing reductive or statistical science but have instead entered the realm of problems in organized complexity.

With this third kind of science, we can discuss any system that is not a machine but which is, rather, literally or figuratively "alive." For example, we might look at the way a religion adapts to cultural developments around it and changes over time; the way an economy or a city maintains itself and adjusts to new shocks; the patterns and pathways whereby a person is able to produce meaning and attain robust psychological health not only despite, but in fact because of, the shocks and insults of life.

In other words, we use this third kind of science whenever we are no longer talking about machines or the random movements of imaginary particles but about actual living organisms. And this is why it is only during the 1930s that Western science starts to make real strides and gains in medical and biological knowledge because, before then, we were often using the wrong *kind* of science when we studied living order.

Incidentally, it is obvious that our contemporary pop-therapy culture remains largely rooted in the pre-1932 era, is it not? Our reductive psychoanalytic methods would be appropriate to toasters, but they have too often seemed to "kill the cat" of the human conscience, to refer to our analogy above. As I argued in Chapter Four, looking for the "causes" of our emotional poverty the same way your car mechanic tries to figure out why your car's check-engine light is coming on is not respectful to the true majesty of the human soul.

Teaching to Beauty

RTE: What does this mean for those of us who aren't scientists? Specifically, how does recognizing a system as being more like a living organism than a machine help us to understand it and deal with it? And how would this help us theologize about the world or find its meaning?

DR. PATITSAS: The third kind of science re-introduces the importance of relationship into our approach to the world. The world isn't just made up of dead objects but is composed of webs of relationships that even include us. The world actually reacts to our presence and even works on us. And with this type of science the world's operation becomes again mysterious; life and living order are not as simple as a toy. So, I find that this science helps us to think again about the world as an icon of some transcendent reality.

More prosaically, knowing the difference between the three kinds of scientific order helps us to decide whether we should don our Cartesian hats or our holistic hats when facing a particular situation. Because in life you will need to wear both hats but at different times, or for different aspects of the same problem.

For example, in keeping discipline in a school classroom, an elementary school teacher needs a full range of responses, from direct rewards and punishments of the children (problems in simplicity), to an awareness of which moments or days are on average harder for students and where the discipline must then be adjusted (this would be utilizing a statistical or problems in disorganized complexity approach), to the comprehension of the relationships among the students and the workings of their inner hearts (problems in organized complexity).

My schoolteacher sister used to spend part of every day with her eighth-grade students talking about their home lives before she even tried to teach a lesson. Life, death, family, meaning, the soul, their futures – it was all discussed in the light of what they were experiencing at home. When I asked her why she felt comfortable "throwing away" a chunk of each day's lesson time, she laughed and said, "Because otherwise *nothing* would be learned for the *entire* day." The challenges these particular students faced at home were too daunting to imagine that doubling down on discipline would have maintained their level of attention. The issue was the metabolic pathways (if you will) of the heart, mind, and soul by which students construct meaning out of the stressors and chaos of life.

But she also knew how to entice, too, when that was required, by promising interesting rewards for good behavior, and of course she knew just how to threaten in a way that made a student feel even more respected and loved. Nor did she choose to collapse the problem into a statistical one by saying, "Oh, they are from poor homes and have unsettled family lives; I should lower my standards."

Above all, what she did was to focus on the students' own power and responsibility to develop their immortal souls so that they could live a beautiful life. She always held out the possibility that a beautiful life lay ahead of them, if they could just learn how. That is why she began each day by catalyzing the processes through which her students could attend to life and find meaning amidst exposure to violence, instability, or, sadly, even murder. And she talked freely about God.

Tactics for Understanding Organic Complexity

When we know that a system is organically complex, we can change our approach to it in concrete ways. At the end of *Death and Life*, Jacobs listed the special research tactics needed when studying *any* living system, whether it is a city or a soul.[26] They are simple enough to understand, although employing them can be hard.

(1) First, in such systems you have to reason inductively rather than deductively. That is, you have to reason from general impressions down to patterns that slowly become evident within these impressions, and then you analyze further down to the specific processes that might be generating these discovered patterns.

In living systems, you cannot build your understanding out from first principles as if you were assembling a machine. This is because the behavior of the whole is not easily traceable, especially not at first, to a few simple factors.

So you have to kind of sit quietly with an organic system until it "lets you know" what it's really about. People who are good with

---

26 Jacobs, *Death and Life*, 440-443.

animals know that each animal has its own unique personality and that you have to cooperate with that in order to tame the animal. Living systems will let you know what's what, will seem to reveal themselves to you, if you listen in an inductive way. In these systems, your intuition is an essential part of your scientific apparatus.

(2) A second tactic in the case of living systems is that you have to pay attention to the processes even more than to the concrete parts involved. After all, the processes are what created the parts, what sustains them in existence, and still other processes are what the parts were created for.

Remember that when you studied the cell in high school biology, you had to learn the metabolic pathways that connect everything? Well, what are the metabolic pathways in the living situations you face at home, at work, or at church? What is the actual chain of interactions which determine your relationships with other people? When teaching, for example, the most brilliant lecture will not be received by most students unless there is an appropriate introduction to it. Learning is an organic process that requires appropriate catalysts, and cannot be reduced to the blunt download of data from one mind to another.

Through its metabolic pathways, a living organism responds to information in the world around it, and certain of its internal systems in response create information that still other internal systems will react to. Until recently, machines haven't been able to do that; even when they do so now, it is through feedback loops that are fairly simple. Processes, therefore, are of the essence in complex systems.

(3) Thirdly, Jacobs stated that in studying living things (as opposed to machines), you had to pay attention to "unaverage clues," by which she meant the tiny indicators that tell you more than all the statistics in the world about how some living system is functioning. You should look for such easy-to-miss signs that will disclose how an entire process is unfolding, in other words.[27]

---

[27] People who love a machine such as a car or a motorbike might also insist that paying attention to "unaverage clues" is an important tactic for understanding such devices. Interestingly, the sort of people who feel this way are often the sort of people who have come to think of their car or bike almost as if it were alive and not merely a machine.

In your body, one of many unaverage clues would be your Vitamin C levels. As a percentage of a human's total body weight, the difference between healthy and unhealthy amounts of Vitamin C is statistically insignificant, way less than a rounding error on the bathroom scale. But its presence or absence in those miniscule amounts is the difference between health and sickness. "Gross weight" does not equal "significance" in a living system. In a biological system, significance is not reducible to statistical preponderance.

An unaverage clue which Jacobs cited was the closing time of the stores of a retail chain in different neighborhoods within the same city. If one branch stays open a lot later, it's a safe bet that this particular part of town is lively and safe at night.

I once heard an Armenian entrepreneur who specialized in starting businesses in remote locations of America say that his "unaverage clue" was the presence or absence of a Greek-owned diner. If he came to a remote part of the country and found that no Greek restaurant existed, it was a sure sign to him that the area was economically hopeless; if it had any business life at all, an enterprising Greek would have already started a simple restaurant there. For this Armenian businessman, this was his unaverage clue, more reliable than any official statistical analysis of a local economy.

(4) But Jacobs then proposed something much more radical than these three tactics, which was that in studying organic systems, it was a *scientific* fact that *you would never understand such systems if you didn't first love them!* This, as much as anything else about the new science, tells us that it is a post-Enlightenment science.

Jacobs' logic was that living systems are so complex, so alive, that you almost have to "win their trust," or at least have to give patient, sympathetic attention to them, before you will ever come to see their surprising rational structure. This importance of love is very odd for a scientific method, and it is one more way that problems in organic complexity reverse the assumptions behind the first two kinds of science. Cold objectivity is no aid to the science of complex systems, Jacobs insisted.

The way I put it to my students is that organic systems cannot be understood or known unless we somehow let them "know us back." For example, you won't know a particular city until it has claimed you for itself, has changed you. This is not a principle of Enlightenment science by any means, but Jacobs says that in organic systems this is what you have to do. You have to love what you are studying, and you have to let it "know" you. You have to let this organic phenomenon you are studying impart to you a new intuition, a new faculty of awareness, appropriate specifically to it.

Soul Healing as a Complex Science

To go back to one of the main interests of this book – the finding of fresh approaches to the healing of trauma – my knowledge of organic complexity makes me suspicious of the talking and thinking approach offered by contemporary psychotherapy. When the therapist sits there like a wall and never reveals himself to the patient, he is apparently unaware of what Jane Jacobs is telling us: *scientifically speaking, no complexly ordered system can be known by an impartial observer.* Therapists are trying so hard to be scientific, but are they using the *right kind* of science? Or are they trying to exercise the cold objectivity appropriate to the first two types of science? If they are using the wrong kind of science, then it is unlikely their conclusions about us will be accurate.

When we express our souls in the deepest way, we need a loving response. We need to feel that we are not isolated individuals but persons in a loving relationship. Now, I grant that the therapist expresses his or her love precisely by listening so intently, but something more than this type of listening is usually needed. We usually do need to see that the outrage or delight we experienced is registering deeply within another person. In fact, we need to see that what we felt or still feel is also registering with God.

(However, could a healer ever convey such divine compassion to a sufferer, unless they themselves were very close to God?)

This issue of letting yourself be known by those whom you would know comes down to empathy and vulnerability, and how do we do that? Well, empathy and vulnerability – co-suffering love – are expressed in quite distinct ways by saintly people. They don't necessarily speak about their own feelings when responding to your confession, and they usually won't weep or dramatize their reactions. But in some hidden way, "noetically," they do make your problem their own. Their openness to you is total, and while you may know nothing about their personal life, you understand that not one thing of importance has been hidden from you, either.

Moreover, since they are at the same time open to God, they become a doorway, or a window, or an icon between you and God. They are not trying to change you or fix you; you are not a dead object upon which they are operating.

Finally, because spiritual guidance is being conducted in the context of the mysteries (sacraments) of the Church, there is less pressure for them to persuade you of some new intellectual understanding or alternative approach to life as the answer to your supposedly self-inflicted problems; both the helper and helped are waiting for God to work, invisibly.

I think that in secular therapy, even when it is done well, there is some unconscious pressure to make the patient better. The confessor, by contrast, sees that you and he are in the same fight, and that you and he are equally in need of divine grace to come out right. And the confessor is confident that this grace is already at work in both of you. The therapist, meanwhile, might sometimes be straining at the bit to fix you and inform you of your misperceptions about life.

So, the confessor doesn't fight against you nor try to change you – rather, he fights with you and for you against some other real force that is trying to drag all of us down. This is a force confessors know from hard experience better than their penitent does, so they don't have this notion that "Oh, I am relatively fine, while this person is quite dysfunctional." Rather, they see that you are under the same attack as they are. Thus, without saying anything, they have already revealed their deepest struggle to you, their greatest vulnerability, through the fact that they are treating you as a co-sufferer. Their non-panicked response to your crisis is not a professional technique, but the result of the fact that they believe themselves to be, in some ways, worse off than you are.

The elder's transparency comes down to his or her calm reliance upon the mysteries of the Church. It is neither by his skill nor by his virtue nor even by his insight that he is able to be a representative of God and an ally, but by his own childlike dependence upon the Church and upon Christ.

Loving and Being Loved – the Ancient Epistemology

One of my dreams is that someday every discipline in our universities would be accustomed to presenting their insights in accord with the Warren Weaver report's summary of the three kinds of science. Even the discipline of English Literature, just to name one example, is using reductive, statistical, and holistic methodologies.[28]

However, there is at least one discipline in the university that made the shift to an approach resembling organic complexity. At a certain point in the history of the science of cultural anthropology, the relationship between researcher and subject was changed radically. The result is that today, the doctoral student still goes out to some far-away culture for dissertation research, but now he or she doesn't just stand aside and take notes in an impartial and uninvolved way. Rather, the researcher learns the local language, joins himself to the life of the tribe, makes himself open to what is happening there in all details, is actually initiated into the tribe, and then through inductive reasoning describes the processes behind these behavioral patterns in terms appropriate to living systems.[29]

---

28 Cf. T. Patitsas, "Organic Complexity and the Healing of Our Epistemology," in J.T. Chirban, ed., *Holistic Healing in Byzantium* (Brookline: Holy Cross Orthodox Press, 2010), 297-310.

29 Perhaps the most famous practitioner of this approach was the late Clifford Geertz, author of *The Interpretation of Cultures* (New York: Basic Books, 1973). His significance for anthropology is precisely that he helps to shift the language of ethnography and religious studies away from reductive or even general "statistical" categories and towards more inductive ones. However, not even Geertz explicitly employs the language of organic com-

In other words, they allow what they are studying to know them, even as they know it. They resolve to love, or at least deeply respect, what they are studying.

Anthropologists don't explicitly identify this approach with the science of organized complexity – which is too bad, because if they did, and if many social sciences did use that term when that is the kind of science they have stumbled into doing, then we would be getting somewhere as a university culture. It would be clear to everyone that we are on the cusp of a scientific revolution for all disciplines, a universal passage into the liberating study of complex order everywhere it exists. We would have a "university" again, as opposed to the collection of rival "hermit kingdoms" we've got in the academy today, within which almost no academic specialty talks to any other academic specialty.

Two last points about tactics for understanding complex systems: (5) this can take a lot of time, and (6) you probably will need a mentor. Jacobs herself found mentors who unfolded New York City's hidden order for her, and she spent years living there, developing her awareness of what they'd shown her. The same will be true for us, whenever we study complex systems: we will need patience, and we should look for a guide.

By the way, I think some of Jacobs' mentors were clergymen in New York who worked on the streets directly with the poor.

RTE: It seems foreign to modern thought that, all of a sudden, love and empathy are essential to the scientific toolkit. That is the most revolutionary thing you've said about this new science.

DR. PATITSAS: The reliance on love in studying a complex system looks mystical, but in fact it may have a rather simple explanation.

---

plexity, such that the shift he makes seems "personal" to him or perhaps to his discipline, rather than part of a development in epistemology occurring simultaneously in many disciplines. Roy Rappaport's *Ritual and Religion in the Making of Humanity* (Cambridge: Cambridge University Press, 1999) comes much closer to defining anthropology as a science of complex human order. This is why Rappaport was able to assert general principles about human anthropology, rather than merely contributing to an improved method of observation, as did Geertz.

We have cognitive capacities far beyond our conscious, rational minds. It is said that only about thirty percent of our brains are specifically "human"; the rest of our brains we have in common with lower primates or even lower animals.

We would never have survived for so long as a human race if our puny rational intellects were all we had to go on. That is to say, in the whole of our brains, bodies, and souls, we possess a complex apparatus for intuiting and discerning the structure of the organic complex order around us (which happens to be the actual character of order in a living world) and so, by definition, the entirety of this apparatus needs to be tapped in order to understand complex systems. Loving involves a more expansive use of the mind.

Additionally, it may be that love is part of the new cognitive toolkit because when we love there occurs some hormonal change in our minds and brains that unleashes an openness to fine detail and a freedom from fear that makes knowledge of complex systems possible.

Or perhaps the matter is quite mystical, and living systems will only share themselves to those who love them, at least on some level. C.S. Lewis famously said that knowing what a star is made of doesn't tell us what it is. There is a spiritual dimension to nature, he argued. I would agree, at least in the basic sense that every created being came into existence through falling in love with Beautiful Theophany, as we've been arguing all along.

So, you see, right there in Chapter 22 of *The Death and Life of Great American Cities*, the chapter on "What Kind of a Problem a City Is," the Enlightenment does die, if only of natural causes, even as its achievements are preserved, though now in their proper place. The Enlightenment's ruling moment passes because the critical distance, dissection, objectification, and lovelessness of the Enlightenment mood are revealed as not being equivalent to science itself but as being permissible only for its first two, simpler, kinds of problem solving.

A third kind of science is brought forth, applied by Jacobs to show why the Enlightenment approach to urban planning had been such an utter disaster, despite being perfectly rational in terms of the first two kinds of science. Everything was done scientifically by Urban Renewal, but the result was the "witless murder" of American cities. The more we committed to the wrong kind of science, the dumber were our interpretations of city life; we couldn't see the forest for the trees. A new *kind of science* was needed.

Resistance to the Third Type of Science

Once you have all three kinds of science sitting in front of you, it's crystal clear that each has its particular place. Knowing this gives you the confidence to admit that some uses of the first two kinds of science are hopelessly, tragically unscientific. Moreover, all of a sudden you can think about the world in more sophisticated ways whenever you need to.

You might find, for instance, that although science and religion are distinct, still in the area of complex order they have much to discuss: the fact that religions themselves are organically complex, or the fact that the development within nature observed by science has no permanence (for "emergence" is ephemeral) unless we can also discuss categories like the Resurrection and eternity...

But Jacobs' *Death and Life* was initially criticized as being itself unscientific; the great urbanist who preceded her, Lewis Mumford, called her work a "home remedy" approach to urban order. And recently, a Nobel Prize winner in economics damned her writing about economies as "good, if amateur, work." He thought he was being generous, but if she is the only economist describing economies fully in terms of this new organically complex science, then it would be the Nobel Prize winner, not Jacobs, who is the "amateur."

Since modern science grew up in the three centuries from 1600 to 1932 by inventing only the first two, more inert, kinds of science, some social scientists and scientists still believe that these two approaches are *all* of science. And as a result, they may bristle when they confront dynamic, nonlinear order. It has become natural to some scientists to want things to be just one thing, to insist that objects be static and fixed and dissectable. But actual living order is complex and dynamic and organic, and in a living system a single variable may have many different meanings, depending on which of its relationships we are studying. And when you dissect a living system, you may not understand it better afterwards but rather worse, since you may well have killed it in the process of studying it.

It would seem today, getting on towards sixty years after the publication of the Warren Weaver report, that a large number of scientists and especially of social scientists never got the memo about the existence of this third type of scientific order. As a result, they still equate science with massive statistical analysis, to be followed by a few reductive explanations. That is, they think science is nothing more than problems in disorganized complexity, followed by problems in simplicity.

That describes, for example, the majority of our current economic science – a science which every few decades since 1900 has led Western civilization to the brink of cataclysmic collapse. We make economic policy through a statistical analysis that handles billions of points of data, which we then use to generate two-variable oversimplifications about the way either tax cuts or government spending will lead to economic growth. Is that really all we've got in the way of tools for economic policy? But since an economy, like other living systems, really is organically complex, such scholars are literally not dealing with the reality of life – and they are claiming science as their justification for their willful blindness, besides. It's just outrageous.

Well, some scientists may not even care to learn about organic complexity. Science sometimes seems to be five percent about understanding and 95% about power. The goal is not really knowledge but technology. Or, by generating reductive explanations to keep our sense of mystery and wonder at bay, scientists hope at a minimum to keep us from turning to religious belief, which they regard as a dangerous superstition. And the first two kinds of science do in fact preserve the illusion of distance and control, which is why they are loved by the Enlightenment types. When you study actual life, however, that distance between knower and known collapses and, moreover, control is really hard to achieve. Look at the fact that we can't cure HIV, for example, despite the billions of research dollars being spent on its study over many decades.

It is just so puzzling that we have not had explicit emphasis on organized complexity in our schooling or in the public understanding of science. The existence of problems in organized complexity was a published fact no later than 1958 because of the Weaver report.[30] Somehow, though, in the years since, we've heard far more about several close relatives of organic complexity which are appropriate to non-living systems. We've heard about chaos theory, which concerns turbulent systems; about emergence, which occurs even in very basic physical systems and is evident in something as simple as the way that water about to boil sets up convection patterns; and we've heard about self-organized criticality, which affects even sandpiles.

But what we don't hear about is the fact that it's the doctors, not the physicists, who are at the forefront of organic complexity science; we don't seem to appreciate the special character of biological science, and the need to apply its lessons more widely.[31]

Jacobs put a very big nail through the attempt to explain away organic order, burying the Cartesian conceit right there in *Death and Life*. As I said, she argued that it was almost impossible to know any organic system if you didn't also love that organic system. She drew this conclusion empirically: The great urban planning simplifiers, those who had committed the "witless murder" of our cities, also

---

30 Is the Warren Weaver report really a crucial turning point in the history of human knowing, an event of epochal significance? I can find only one ally besides Jacobs who might think so: Steven Johnson, author of *Emergence: The Connected Lives of Ants, Brains, Cities, and Software* (New York: Scribner, 2001). Sadly, he also seems to have discovered Weaver only through Jacobs' *Death and Life*.

31 It is odd that medical schools do not embrace Weaver's account of science history because doctors are actually our most able practitioners of the third, most interesting, kind of science. If Weaver's account is correct, then physicians replace physicists at the apex of the modern university. Yet American doctors sometimes bristle with a kind of arrogant inferiority, in which their patient becomes their enemy since he is the reason that the doctor is unable to exercise his science in a cold, linear, and reductive way, like a "real" scientist, a practitioner of the hard sciences, is supposed to. It's as if some American doctors aspire to be essentially car mechanics for the body.

all happened to hate cities, to deeply dislike them. The people who understood cities' deeper order, meanwhile, had first loved cities and reveled in their complexity.

From this observation, Jacobs constructed a hypothesis as to why, in the case of organic systems, cold Cartesian objectivity would make knowing impossible: To understand an organic system you had to befriend it. If you wanted to notice the "unaverage clues" that would tip you off to its deeper order, you would have to devote your time to it, make yourself vulnerable, and really try to love what you were studying.

Although not a religious person, Jacobs puts love back into the scientific project, to repeat myself from earlier, and no one has really ever parried that thrust, probably because it is just too damn wounding for the kind of mind that wants to be not scientific but two-thirds scientific. I mean, shouldn't science be the attempt to describe the natural world as faithfully as possible? Ecologists complain that Christianity sees man as the "king" and subduer of creation, but isn't it science that has really attempted to bend the world absolutely to its whims? What theologian ever produced poison bombs or radiation bombs? Did we in the Church ever cause the entire global climate to change the way the engineers of the Industrial Revolution have?

In a culture where we often still define being rational exclusively as exercising the first two kinds of science, all kinds of living things become "tough issues" for us. We want so badly to be scientific (we think) but our favorite *kind* of science is the two-variable type that reduces the behavior of one variable to its dependence on a second variable. Statistics is tolerated but only as a necessary accomplice to that. Science for us is about technology. For many, science is a mere accomplice to our desire to flip a switch and have things our way.[32]

---

[32] In his 1943 work *The Abolition of Man* (London: Oxford University Press), C.S Lewis noted that the same era that generated the birth of modern science (the sixteenth and seventeenth centuries) was also obsessed with alchemy. It was as if, he thought, the real motivation behind science was an almost occult desire for human control over the world, rather than knowledge itself. Both science and alchemy were trying to bring off a kind of "practical gnosticism" – aiming to achieve not an escape from the world through esoteric insight but control of the world through the unlocking of its secrets.

Only in the "problems in simplicity" approach do we completely attain what the Enlightenment types seem to really want, which is not insight or knowledge but control. Ah, to be young and scientific in the eighteenth century, when all seemed amenable to analytic dissection and technological manipulation, and *man* really did seem to be the measure of all things! Too bad for these types that probability, relativity, and especially biology had to come along and re-introduce nonlinear order, beauty, the interrelatedness of all things, and the centrality of love for any kind of real understanding of the world.

But some scientists and social scientists, Jacobs among them, far from being threatened by an approach to science that is different than what modern science was used to, can celebrate it. Ironically, in previous epochs of human history, organic complexity, and Beauty-first intuitive knowledge (the third kind of science) were all that they had, in a sense. They just followed their intuition and befriended the world as best they could. So, we have flipped our situation completely from theirs. The ancients had some degree of the third kind of science but not much of the first two; we have reversed this. What the ancients knew, we can't see; what we see, they never knew.

It is true that "systems thinking" introduces something new to us moderns. In this new approach, you have to love and befriend and give time to what you would understand. But the two simpler kinds of science still have their place.

Many times that is still the first place; but no longer *always* first, nor are we any longer forced to use *only these two kinds* of science. The Enlightenment ends in the pages of *The Death and Life of Great American Cities*, replaced not by postmodern despair, multi-cultural relativism, or the nihilistic multiplication of meaninglessness, but by something far more rich and mysterious – life itself, the living and developing cosmos.

Information and the Three Kinds of Scientific Problems

RTE: Dr. Patitsas, thank you for such a clear explanation of complexity theory. Now, can you explain the importance of Information Theory, which you've also mentioned, and how all of this fits into your earlier explanations of the Orthodox world-view and creation?

DR. PATITSAS: For our purposes, the main thing to know about Information Theory is that "information" is present in a different way in each of the three kinds of scientific problem-solving we've described above. Once you know this, you can see how even the ancients understood, in their own way of course, a bit of all three kinds of science and how to relate them to each other. The relationship among the three types of science is what our own civilization needs to clarify, and a bit of Information Theory will help. Such understanding will leave us poised on the threshold of wisdom.

Specialists in this theory ask us to think of information, in the technical sense of the term, as existing somewhere along a continuum between random chaos or white noise, at one extreme, and absolute homogeneity and cookie-cutter sameness, on the other. As a matter of Information Theory, neither one of these extremes qualifies as information, since in neither case can we discern a *meaningful difference* within our surroundings.

When being subjected to pure chaos or to absolute repetition, you aren't learning anything new and therefore you aren't experiencing information. You can't orient yourself, either, by what either of these two extremes show you; it's not a "world" you are discerning but some version, almost, of "non-being" when you meet either chaos or absolute sameness.

To make sense of our surroundings, we need to detect actual information. The differences within our impressions can't be absolute and infinite as is the case in situations of chaos, nor can they be utterly absent as in cases of mind-numbing repetition. What we need is "variation on a base of sameness."

That, by the way, is exactly what a trauma sufferer lacks – his recurring trauma flashbacks make his life a *monotony* of *chaos*, which would be the worst of all possible worlds, in terms of information. Orthodox Christian liturgy, by contrast, is the precise opposite: the ultimate example of variation upon a base of sameness. It is literally soaked in information.

I remember Jane Jacobs describing a lengthy walkway in a government housing project somewhere in lower Manhattan. Each section of the promenade was identical to every other section, so that the more a person walked, the more they had the feeling that they had no idea where they were! In fact, the effect was spiritual because this bad architecture of cookie-cutter sameness was taking you utterly out of the sense that you lived in a cosmos, a beautiful and good order. The ordered repetition was actually an instance of disorder; the "plan" of the architect had produced a built environment without any information.

Fifteen-year-olds may experience a similar feeling in high school. The more the days pass and the more they go through their identical daily routines, the less they can discern themselves as actually "moving" anywhere. Although they are learning information in their classes, they may feel that they are not experiencing information at a larger scale, at the scale of their actual lives. This drives them somewhat mad, and it confuses parents, who have forgotten that certain periods in our youth can feel endless in this way.

Information theorists are able to make another point. Any existing thing, by virtue of its being that particular thing and not something else, is an instance of "information" along this continuum between pure chaos and absolute repetition. Even when two atoms are identical, for example, they aren't in the same place at the exact same time; there remains some difference within the sameness.

Therefore, for Information Theory you can look at the creation of the world as a process where information and existence arise together, at the same exact moment. Only "informed" things exist, technically speaking. Information Theory even generated the saying, "It from Bit" or, nothing exists except it also be conceivable as information.³³ An existing thing can almost always be thought of as distinctly some "this," and not as some "not this."

So Information Theory carries insights that seem to correspond quite closely to St. Maximos' doctrine of the logoi. For Maximos, a thing exists only by its participation in the Logos, or by virtue of being "informed" by the Logos; it has to be "informed" by the source of all information, Christ. All created things are different, for St. Maximos, because all things participate in this Logos according to their own unique logos. But all created things are not *utterly* different, since they all have a common root in the same Logos, in Christ.

Oh, and if you remember from Chapter Six, we found that our mystical architect Christopher Alexander was making the same point about the balance between difference and sameness. He said that architects had to a) use the same and eternal architectural Patterns, but they also had to b) work like crazy to tailor each Pattern until it fit exactly and precisely in the unique circumstances where it was being used. Without this balanced use of Patterns, you have either architectural chaos or an undifferentiated sameness that is just killing. You don't have a "world," a beautiful and good structured order, but rather a chaos of disagreement or an ennui of repetition.

Therefore, we can see three thinkers – Jane Jacobs, St. Maximos, and Christopher Alexander – who all have similar instincts about what makes a world and about what makes something meaningful and informational.

The Origins of Information Theory

RTE: Then, where did modern Information Theory come from and how does it fit in with the three kinds of science?

DR. PATITSAS: Thank you for asking. An interjection, however, before I answer. I am interested in the three kinds of science and

---

33 See James Gleick, *The Information: A History, a Theory, a Flood* (New York: Vintage Books, 2011).

in the role of information in each for a number of reasons. This framework will tell us what is going wrong with our therapy of the human soul. It will give us an additional argument for a Beauty-first approach to life, and it will help us to understand why the things that we are sure we know when we are suffering from trauma can be at times so prescient and at other times wholly inaccurate.

Information Theory started out in two places, in fact: in America with Claude Shannon and in Russia with Andrey Kolmogorov.[34] It was initiated as a mathematical theory of communication, in Shannon's case, when he was a scientist at the old AT&T. In those days, "Ma Bell" was the only telephone company for the entire United States and had the resources to fund pure science research at an impressive scale.

Claude Shannon actually coined the term for the smallest possible unit of information, the "bit." He did this already in the research paper where he first laid out his mathematical theory of communication. The "bit" is defined as the smallest possible amount of information, and it is just the answer to a simple yes or no question.

Now, saying that a "bit" is the smallest possible unit of information doesn't tell you two other things – neither how much power over the world is contained in a particular bit of information, nor how much of a window that bit of information will open into the wider context in which it is found.

In dealing with the three kinds of science, I have found that we need to keep these three things in mind: *the quantity* of information present in a solution or situation, i.e., how many bits of information are present there; how *potent* that information is, in terms of how much power acting upon it will give you over the world; and, thirdly, the *quality* the information has, or the depth of the glimpse that it gives you into the workings of a larger context.

Quantity, potency, and quality are three quite distinct measures to keep in mind when we are learning new information. They also

---

[34] Andrey Kolmogorov (1903-1987): Russian mathematician who made significant contributions to algorithmic information theory.

will help us to distinguish the three kinds of science – simplicity, disorganized complexity, and organized complexity.

All of this will then help us to think about what kinds of soul therapy might help us to *become* information – to become more ordered, specific, and real, rather than chaotic or clichéd. As we go on, we will bring these topics back to our main concern: the Beauty-first approach not only to life, but to life and the soul together.

Information within Problems in Simplicity

Let me go straight back to our first type of science, the two-variable problem. In this type of problem, we are looking for very simple cause and effect relationships. Initially, this was all that science really wanted: to master relationships of causation and thus gain control over the world in a seemingly "magical" way.

In terms of their *quantity* of information, though, such problems are not impressive. By definition, knowing the dependency of one factor upon another only answers a single yes/no question; the first variable either does or does not depend on the second variable. Thus, at their simplest points, such problems contain only one "bit" of information and are therefore "information-poor."

The *potency* of the information gained in solving such problems, however, can be extremely high. Knowing the dependency of one thing upon another helps you accomplish a lot. For example, knowing whether or not this one switch will power down your whole house, even if you don't know why, is powerful information. We can think of many such examples where one bit of insight gives you a lever to move mountains.

Finally, such two-variable problems may or may not give you much insight into the larger working of their contexts, even when they are packed with enormous informational power. I would have to know a lot more about electricity and wiring before the bit of information about this one switch gives me much insight. Therefore, the information contained in problems in simplicity is not of very high *quality*.

In short, in problems in simplicity you deal with low-volume, high-potency, but often poor-quality information. Therefore, if your science specializes in only this kind of problem solving, your view of the world will be quite impoverished, even as it gains you huge power over the world. Such a combination of power and blindness obviously can be very dangerous.

Information within Problems of Disorganized Complexity

In our second type of science, the statistical or disorganized complexity approach, you have millions of bits of information. You are studying all kinds of movements and collisions, and the quantity of information about these interactions is astronomically high. For example, the IRS and the Federal Reserve have a seemingly infinite amount of data about the day-to-day and even moment-to-moment fluctuations in the U.S. economy. The *quantity* of information available to any study that relies on this data is hard to even imagine. You need powerful computers to handle it all.

However, the *potency* of all this information tends to be low for any particular application. In the case of random collisions in physics, a great mass of data is probably not of very high potency; that is, it doesn't necessarily tell you anything about how to influence these patterns. The information is not powerful until you can perform some analysis of it that enables you to convert the whole picture into the simpler reductive approach of our first kind of science. Without that key, understanding problems in disorganized complexity leaves you able to describe patterns of events but unable, except through blunt instruments, to influence them. That is one reason why, although we have all this data about our economy, policy makers can't really influence it except in very broad terms.

Also usually low in the initial phase of a statistical study is the *quality* of information gained. In the case of the random collisions among particles we mentioned above, a great mass of data doesn't necessarily tell you anything about the processes producing all those collisions. One reason why the medical advice we get about diet is so confused and changes so frequently is that it is based on these massive data crunches. Statistical correlations between the various things we might eat and how long we might live tend to tell us very little unless we can unlock the underlying metabolic pathways by which the body reacts to the food we eat. Again, you have to look elsewhere than statistical science for that, or else use this statistical kind of problem solving as a stepping stone to get to the other kinds of problem solving. In other words, the information presented by statistical patterns tends to be not only impotent, but it is not of very high quality.

In statistical situations you run into a high volume of information, but it is of low potency and of questionable quality. This is why, despite all our computing power, people cannot really predict the future movements of the stock market from studying all its past movements. They have access to unlimited data, but without some heuristic key (some way of decoding it all) the mass of information is neither potent nor of high quality.

Before I move on to the subject of information within the third kind of science, let us repeat a point raised in the beginning of our talk. Many scientists apparently believe that problems in simplicity and problems in disorganized complexity are the only two kinds of science. They start with statistics and get a high quantity of information. Then they apply reductionist analysis, looking to convert that high quantity into high potency.

But what they never acquire in using these two approaches, because neither of these sciences offers it, is any real quality in their information. Their view of the world is over-simplified.

Information within Problems of Organized Complexity

In the third kind of science, you come to organic pathways and organisms. Here, the *quantity* of information lies in a middle range between the first two. You have far more than two variables, but far less than millions. You may only have a few hundred variables, and you slowly try to answer questions about their interrelationship, adding a few bits of information at a time.

The *potency* of information in such problems is also in the mid-range because usually you cannot control an entire system from one variable for very long without damaging the system. Now, understanding an organic system properly does, of course, generate potency of a simplistic kind if you are looking to destroy that living system. In that case, you look for pressure points that will halt all its organic processes. But this kind of information only exists in one direction, in living systems; that is, there are no magic pressure points to restore a long-dead organism to life, and few to ensure its healthy growth.

The good news in living systems, though, is that any accurate information here will be of the highest *quality*. When you do figure something out in an organically complex system, you have begun to figure out the basic metabolism, the organic pathways generating and sustaining the living structure. You are answering questions at a sort of mystical edge, in a way, because you are learning just the way things really are.

In summary, in living systems the information to be discovered is at the middle-level in potency and quantity, but it will be of extremely high quality. Such information imparts to you a level of understanding close to what the ancients would have called "wisdom."

Applying the Three Kinds of Science

A good example of these three types of information is found in the raising of children. The moment you have "reduced" a child to one fact (perhaps an interest in music, or an ability to dance, or a failure to be assertive) the child will either notice this and change or will experience a kind of soul death. The very people they trusted to love them have instead labelled them and thus "frozen" them. Children resist all reductions of their souls, even positive ones. And, if they do accept such reductions, perhaps to please you or to please their own passions, they are creating problems that will have to be resolved later. The patterns of our interactions with our children do not number in the millions – probably there are ten or twenty that map an entire day, at any given age. Moreover, once you win the trust of a child, even the few insights gained into the workings of their souls do not put you in the position to control or fix or change them; these insights are not potent in that way.

However, if we are doing it right, our actions toward the child will be of a high quality, and our respect for quality information about our children is part of what will make them feel that they are surrounded by human beings, not machines or robots. Organic insight may also give you the chance to nurture the child and help it grow. Of course, at some point they may be ready to fly on their own, too.

Summary of Science and Information

So, these are our three choices:

In *two-variable problems* the information you get is of low quantity, high potency, but probably of a low quality. Tackling these kinds of problems gives you the science of causation, or cause and effect.

In *statistical problems* the information to be found is of high quantity, low potency, and even of low quality. Yes, through reductive analysis you may later flip it into something quite potent, but in itself the information is not potent and not of high quality. Tackling these kinds of problems gives you the science of probability, or statistical patterns.

In *organic systems* you have mid-quantity, mid-potency, but very high quality information. This is the science of life, or of systems that exhibit dynamic interrelationships.

Why does making this informational perspective clear in this way matter to us? Science is about knowing, and this rating of the information present within what you know shows you exactly how *powerfully*, how *broadly*, and how *well* you know something.

No culture until ours has ever had a conscious sense of the three kinds of science, but most *did* realize the distinction between wisdom, where you know a little but what you know is of a high quality, on the one hand, and a mere being informed, where you might know a little or a lot, but had not discerned the quality of what you knew. Have we forgotten this basic difference between the wise man and the well-informed fool?[35]

Even in Science There Is a Beauty-First Approach

RTE: I think I get your argument that "wisdom" is equivalent to a Beauty-first approach to deep matters of ethics and the soul. But is complexity really equivalent to a Beauty-first approach to the natural world?

DR. PATITSAS: Yes, and that is why I wanted to conclude our conversations on this note. Prioritizing for high quality, low quantity information *is* the Beauty-first approach to science because aesthetic quality really does have a cognitive significance in living systems. Health has a certain "look"; some doctors can almost guess your ailment by your appearance or, at any rate, by their noticing the right unaverage clues in your lab results. This is why we can speak rationally about the "art" of medicine. What people call "intuition" is really more like a sophisticated aesthetic sense about the rich

---

[35] How should we characterize the intellectual contribution of Nassim Nicholas Taleb, author of *The Black Swan: The Impact of the Highly Improbable*, 2nd ed. (New York: Random House Trade Paperbacks, 2010) and of several other books, since Taleb argues that a better application of statistics and probability will in fact allow us to avoid the pitfalls of high-quantity, low-quality information? But Taleb is the exception who demonstrates the rule; his entire project is a life or death struggle to demonstrate that statistical information will remain low-quality unless we can visualize the organically complex system with which probability must contend. Now, he also believes that we can then devise ways to work around the limitations of the second type of science, in order to account for the unique structures of living systems. But I would say that the Black Swan effect, in particular, can be better explained in terms of fractals than with mathematical equations. What Taleb is arguing here is that because organically complex systems are constituted by fractal hierarchies, a "one-dimensional," "fractal-blind" statistical theory will tend to overcount and magnify the high-probability, low-impact events. Taleb, in effect, turns statistics "on its side," showing that complex systems, their events all seemingly within one dimension from one perspective, in fact occur across multiple dimensions. Moreover, Taleb reminds us that the less probable events and features will tend to be of a much higher scale, and therefore can overwhelm all of the safeguards that conventional statistics has taught us will be sufficient to ensure our safety.

meaning of what is going on in a complex and dynamic situation. Intuition means having an eye for complex relationships in living systems.

In an organically complex system, the information you gather is of a high quality because it gives you an insight into the "big picture." It shows you in one glance the quality of the whole shape as it unfolds over time.

In contrast, knowing lots of facts or even systems of facts is a kind of *truth-first* approach to science. It makes you informed but not necessarily aware, not awake. Lastly, knowing a few decisive bits of information is more like a *goodness-first*, or "utility," approach to science. It gives you useful knowledge.

To me, this is the most surprising discovery of all of our interviews: that even in science a Beauty-first approach is often to be preferred over a truth-first approach, and that we already have such a Beauty-first method ready to be called upon in enlisting science in the healing of our world. Who would have thought!

Beauty-First and Financial Investing

RTE: Then please give us a real-world scenario in which we can see all three of these types of science and how the quantity, potency, and quality of the information within them tells us which science to use.

DR. PATITSAS: I was very surprised to discover that the three main approaches to stock market investing can be divided almost exactly into these three approaches to science, and that the strengths and weaknesses of these three basic types of investing are best demonstrated in terms of the quantity, potency, and quality of information present in each. In the process of figuring this out, I was happy to see how love and beauty give you all kinds of intellectual advantages, even in making your living.

I will start with the second kind of science.

Statistical Investing: Tracking Every Change in the Market

Most stock market investors are using a statistical/disorganized complexity approach focusing on huge amounts of information. They are making their decisions based on stock market prices and on the vast storehouse of stock market or economic data that could influence particular stock prices. They are forever phoning their clients with new information that they promise will determine where the price of a particular stock is headed.

Despite the huge fund of data which they monitor, even the best investors who use this approach, really smart people using advanced computing power, rarely are able to beat the return achieved by buying into a broad index fund that tracks the value of the market as a whole! Essentially, taking the advice of most investment managers is just a gamble, and not a very good one at that.

Why are they so impotent in their predictions? Because they are using the statistical or disorganized complexity approach to science, which has a *high quantity* of information and thus is complicated enough to occupy these great intellects (and to make them sound very well-informed to their clients), but the information they are using *is not* of a *high quality*, and moreover is not really predictive; it lacks *power*. But as I said, by relying on such a high volume of data, they can easily intimidate their investors, who feel that they could never on their own figure such things out.

Causation in Investing: Derivatives

Other investors start with statistics but sift through the data to structure derivatives, which are the equivalent of narrow two-variable relationships. For example, when inflation rises, then the price of gold will also rise by a particular amount. Or, when oil prices go up, so will the products of companies that make plastics, perhaps.

So, this approach has *less data* (once you've found the two-variable relationships hidden in the initial mountains of data) and also it has *much more potent data*. You just want to find a very straightforward one-to-one relationship that will tell you exactly what and when to buy and sell. This is the holy grail for derivatives investors: a little information with extreme potency.

But the problem with this simplicity or two-variable approach is that it doesn't tell you anything for sure about the underlying economy or about the businesses in the economy. Because it is reductive, *it is not high quality* information. It has made many people very rich, but their insight is powerless whenever the entire system shifts beneath their feet, which will periodically happen.

The American banking crash of 2008-09 was caused by exceptionally gifted analysts betting on these two-variable derivatives, but forgetting that the information provided by these derivatives was low quality information and contained only a very poor glimpse into the larger economic forces at work. When those larger forces turned unfavorable all at once, trillions of dollars in derivatives investments declined steeply in value. All along, the derivatives traders had been in reality flying blind because the *quality* of their information was so low. But that wasn't evident until the larger shift came.

This approach remains extremely attractive, however, because derivatives' origins in advanced statistical complexity meant that the very potent two-variable relationships within the mountains of data were hidden to all but the few mathematical geniuses who specialized in the study of the financial markets. They were modern-day alchemists who had discovered a secret code that enabled them to turn mountains of market data "lead" into literal gold. But the information was, as I said, of very low quality; no economic future could be built upon such shifting sands.

RTE: But they must have been making a profit or they wouldn't have continued working with derivatives, right?

DR. PATITSAS: With that approach you can make enormous amounts of money very quickly; no other approach is so *potent*. That is the point of this whole discussion, that "simplicity" approaches are fantastically effective. But their potency lasts only so long as the underlying and more basic forces in the economy remain stable.

The derivatives themselves actually give you very poor quality clues as to what those real forces are doing – until it's too late, and many of your prior gains have been wiped out.

Whenever we see over-reliance on "simplicity" science, it's a little bit like watching a bully picking on someone weaker. But the bully is not noticing that a reaction is building up which will eventually result in his being soundly thrashed! So long as the tipping point has not yet come, the bully seems to be the king of the world. But when the bill comes due, he has to run for help to anyone he can.

My point is not that these traders were bullies but that there was something parasitical about their approach to profit. So long as deeper forces were favorable, they could benefit from a very reductive and narrow-minded approach to the actual, real economy of people making their livings. When a bully picks on someone, it's a simple two-variable calculation: I press my advantage at some very narrow point; I get what I want. But the real life of the other person is so much deeper, and eventually, as I said, the bill *always* comes due. It came due with a vengeance on these traders and their banks in late 2008, such that our entire economy, caught up in their schemes, was nearly wrecked. Neither markets nor people will remain understandable as problems in simplicity for very long.

You know, I like understanding for its own sake, and I like telling insightful real-life stories. But these topics about Information and the three kinds of science really are life and death for our entire civilization. We have to know what we are knowing, when we know. The more complex our civilization becomes, the more deliberate we have to be about knowing.

Information theory, applied in this simple way to the three kinds of science, tells us quite clearly how to relate to what we know. That is, this discussion is important because it tells us how much trust to place in it. Without this awareness, we are liable to put our faith in people who lack wisdom.

I know these are new ideas, but it will prove so useful to put the matter directly in terms of the quantity, potency, and quality of information that are actually possible within each kind of science.

Organic Beauty in Investing: The Value Investor

The third way of doing stocks is the Warren Buffett approach, the organic complexity approach.[36] Here, your first step is to ignore information about derivative relationships and to ignore with even more determination the minute-to-minute movements in stock market prices. Your first step is to ignore most information.

It is actually the case that in Warren Buffett's approach to investing, *his highest priority is and his biggest effort goes toward "unknowing" most of the very market and stock data that everyone else finds central.* He is very open about this and about the effort it takes him to ignore what everyone else thinks "informational" and insightful. However, think how inexplicable this emphasis on ignoring large quantities of information is, except when viewed in terms of the three types of science, and through an awareness of the quality of information available in each type. Why should the first task of our most successful investor have been to ignore most of the data available?

Well, we can say it quite simply: because despite its high volume or, if you can ferret out these derivatives, its enormous potency, the *quality* of the information focused on in the other two approaches to investing is really low – just awful. So instead, Buffett selects a very few businesses, regards each one as a living organism, and studies a limited amount of moderately powerful but *extremely rich* data about that business.

And, just as Jacobs told us about organic systems, Buffett uses "unaverage clues." Buffett often says that he knows within the first five minutes of a new proposal whether the offer is worthwhile or not.

RTE: In what way is Buffett's "unknowing" analogous to the spiritual "unknowing" you spoke of in the interviews on shame and healing, and later on gender?

---

36 For Buffett's philosophy and worldview in his own words, see Warren Buffett, *Berkshire Hathaway: Letters to Shareholders, 1965-2014* (Mountain View, CA: Explorist Productions, 2015).

DR. PATITSAS: It is a fairly exact analogy. The priestly prophet unknows facts and instead knows persons. Scientists of organic complexity unknow great masses of statistical data so that instead they will have the chance to know biological wholes, living wholes – the "persons" of the non-human world. Buffett, in his turn, unknows stock prices and instead knows the companies and their leaders personally, conceiving of them both as life forms with specific moral characters.

In this approach to stocks (which Warren Buffett didn't invent; it's called the "value investor" approach), you have the best long-term results, if you are indeed able to unknow the information that everyone else is reacting to. The information you have chosen to follow is suitable for prediction in the longer term, even if it is not at all potent in the shorter term. When Buffett buys, he buys to hold the stock for years or even forever. But he can't predict the near-term value of the stock and would never try to, unlike the practitioners of the other two investment approaches.[37] He himself admits that his information is far less "potent" than that studied by other investors; it doesn't give him any power for short term gains or even to avoid short term losses.

In fact, because he really becomes a partner, in effect, in the firms he buys, it doesn't give him any "power" at all, except to live and die by whatever his new partners will experience. In the value investor approach, you actually "are known by" the company you

---

37 From time to time, Warren Buffett also stumbles across simple two-variable derivative-style relationships, but he usually won't let himself base investment decisions upon them. Based on low quality information, they are, in the end, just gambles, even if in normal times quite safe ones. And Buffett isn't gambling (or speculating); he's investing, in the sense that he is lending his money to companies whose future prospects he is willing to share, good or bad.

Now, in addition to such derivatives, he also notices unaverage clues, and these he does act upon because they are high quality information, whereas derivatives, though more powerful, are low quality information.

One of his favorite unaverage clues is the sales figure for men's underwear. These garments do not sell heavily when bad economic times are imminent or persistent. When their sales numbers suddenly return to normal, Buffett regards it as a sign that an economic recovery is taking place.

study because you become a co-owner of it. You *become* the company in the value-investing approach.[38]

But Buffett consistently doubles the market-rate of return – and has done so for sixty years.[39]

Anyway, all of this is to say that the third kind of science is the approach to science that deals with the highest quality information. Moreover, because this kind of science focuses on wholes and processes rather than on parts, it is also the Beauty-first approach to science. It is not concerned with amassing mountains of data for their own sake nor with finding magic keys for control, but it simply regards what it studies as beautiful and worthy of understanding for its own sake and on its own terms. When you study living systems, "reasons" almost don't come into play; life is a mystery, and the way it is, is the way it is. You are touching the edge of God's revelation in creation.

Furthermore, as we can see from Buffett's success, the third kind of science is the one that must regulate and order the other two. This third kind is the science that Jane Jacobs utilized to reinvent urban planning (a fact missed by all) as well as economics (a fact ignored by all). In this complexity approach, you know the

---

38 There is a religious reason why some people prefer value investing: they think that the other two forms of investing are "speculation" driven by greed and are therefore *ipso facto* sinful! Since Max Weber, it has been well-known that Calvinist morality sparked capitalism's rise, but here it was a number of "Calvinist" businessmen (Warren Buffett, his allies, and his earliest investors) whose emphasis on a Beauty-first approach to the management of money guided an unprecedented generation of wealth! For example, as Buffett himself describes his decision not to intervene in the management of the companies he owns, each CEO must be left to work on "his painting"; i.e., Buffett conceives of the firm as a work of art, a living work of art.

This raises the ironic fact that for "goodness-first" reasons, many Christians hit upon an organic, Beauty-first approach to investing. They espouse what is, in effect, an "investing as communion" approach to wealth.

39 A couple of people have asked me why, if I'm so smart, I don't invest like Buffett does? First, I happened to notice something very elementary about the quantity, potency, and quality of information across the three approaches to science and investing; such a simple discovery is not proof that I am smart. Second, I don't *love* business, and Jacobs is very clear that you will never understand an organic system that you don't love. These insights aren't magic.

I do love the Orthodox Christian faith – and yet I'm quite sure that I haven't yet understood even that perfectly correctly! But at least, because I love it, with the help of others I might someday understand it better. Buffett, having lived through the Great Depression, thought that the best thing he could do with his life was to give his investors a safe harbor for their hard-earned savings. He was right.

wholes as well as the rhythm that produces and sustains them, rather than bunches of disassembled parts.

RTE: We've said a lot about science and about information theory. Before we go on, can you say something about why all of this would be important to a theologian or to someone struggling to heal souls? Specifically, when some types of therapy require us to be purveyors of "information" about ourselves.

DR. PATITSAS: What we are after in soul therapy of any kind is that we should become "information" ourselves, rather than that we should get so bogged down in learning information "about" ourselves. The difference between these two is that the person who is information, has a coherence, a peace, and the freedom to focus clearly on what is outside of themselves – God and others. Whereas the person who focuses on self-knowledge in a pathological way is constantly mistaking their passions, their memories, or suggestions from outside forces for their real selves. We will have to renounce a host of information about ourselves, if we wish to become information – to become meaningful and real.

I mean this theologically, because as we conform more closely to Christ the Logos, we ourselves shall be more concrete, more specific, more unique, and more meaningful. We shall attain our logos, as icons of the Logos. And I mean this emotionally, since as we mature, our inner states should become more developed, more clear, and more stable. We aren't any longer to be tossed to and fro by the winds of our passions, our bad habits, or the memories of our troubled pasts. We are someone in particular; we are not shifty. And I mean it also in terms of healing trauma, because our trauma reactions are forever pushing us in directions that don't make sense for our current circumstances. They may be a telling clue about some past event, but they aren't appropriate to where we are now, and they don't allow us the peace to be who we are really meant to be. Persistent mobilization for trauma and danger keep us from existing comfortably in our skin, and they prevent us from being "accurate." We aren't really "informed" in a proper way, so long as trauma reigns in our hearts and minds.

And the key to all of this flight away from facts about ourselves and towards simply becoming a beautiful revelation of God's life on earth, the key to the way that we become "information" and attain our own unique logos, is our relationship with Christ and others, normally structured through liturgy. Trauma excommunicates; liturgy communicates, communes, and confirms our being.

III. THE CITY AS LITURGY

A Ballet in Many Movements

RTE: My original question was, in what way are cities like liturgies? Can we go back to that now? And, how does what we've just discussed about science and information relate to the "city-liturgy" concept?

DR. PATITSAS: Jane Jacobs' discovery was that cities and their economies are examples of organically complex order. You can't rely solely on the simpler kinds of science to plan urban or economic life without grave results. The information that a city planner or an economic policy advisor requires has to be of a much higher quality than what you get from reductive or statistical approaches.

Well, liturgies are also examples of complex organic order. And the center of economic life, the city, looks very much like a kind of liturgy. The close identity of these three phenomena – complex order, cities, and liturgies – gives you an entirely new and inspiring cosmology. It will help us to look at the cosmos as truly "beautiful" (the meaning of the Greek term, "cosmos," from which we also get the word "cosmetics," for example) if we see the identity of organic complexity with liturgy. This identity is most visible in cities.

RTE: What made you feel that you had discovered Jane Jacobs as a kind of "urban liturgist," and what does liturgy mean in this context?

DR. PATITSAS: Here, let's further clarify both "city" and "liturgy."

As we mentioned before, Jacobs defined "cities" in terms of two characteristics: cities are those human settlements where you are mostly surrounded by strangers, *and* where new work is being brought forth on the basis of older work, over and over again. These two criteria are what matters when we call a settlement a city, whether the place we are discussing has a few hundred people or many millions, is very rich or very poor, has existed for millennia or just now came into being. These are the indispensable elements that make a space a city.

By "liturgy," too, I intend something very specific. Liturgy is the public, mass-participation version of ritual, and rituals are actions or speech that, although freely undertaken, follow a form or pattern not entirely determined by us.[40] Rituals were either handed down to us by "the ancient ones" – i.e., by earlier generations; or, they are copied from heavenly archetypes. It was thought that sacred rituals ultimately derive from an inspiration given to a particular holy person; for example, Abraham received the command to institute circumcision, and Isaiah saw a vision of heavenly worship which inspired both Christians and Jews. As we see in the Eucharist, sacred public rituals seem valid because they have their source in God.

Similarly, in the city we may be free regarding where we go and what we do, but still the basic patterns of life in the city are largely set for us. These patterns include what language we can get away with speaking in our daily interactions, how we might earn our livings, the safe range of religious or political views we can express, what times of day we might shop, eat, or work, the roads or subways we take on our daily commute, and what sorts of foods we can buy and stores we can shop at.

Even when we try to be completely original in these things, we almost always find that our paths are smoothed by others who have

---

[40] Roy Rappaport defined "ritual" as "the performance of more or less invariant sequences of formal acts and utterances not entirely encoded by the performers," on p 24 of *Ritual and Religion*; see note 29. He also observed that religious liturgies require a plausible claim of antiquity or they will not be taken seriously.

gone before, who are being creative in the same way, or who are forging a path that we then follow, at least in part.

Thus, life in the city falls into broad, common patterns that we may influence but which also always influence us. We must partake at least somehow of the broad, repetitive yet always varied patterns of social life if we want to play any part at all in a society. Our life in cities is "liturgical" in this sense.

To see even better how cities are, in fact, liturgies, we can just notice that the city exists because of what we all do together there. The city is a common project generated by many people working, however tensely or tangentially, together. And this cooperation happens through the living patterns by which we interact.

Cities are a "work of the people" – the literal meaning of the term "liturgy" in Greek – in being created by the actions, plans, talents, desires, dreams, and efforts of many people all working together. Together, we fund the basic infrastructure of roads, schools, and government that we all require. But we are able to do this because we all follow, or at least enough of us follow, the same broad patterns of life.

Moreover, out of our daily interactions arise spaces and patterns that then shelter or encourage still more human flourishing. Jane Jacobs noted that even in something like shopping, our actions "pool up" and support each other. Stores tend to be more diverse in cities than elsewhere because when people congregate in large numbers they can support establishments that serve their less frequent shopping needs, which makes possible more variety. This variety then draws in customers from further away, supporting yet more variety. Here again, the city is a work of the people, as we work together unconsciously to make our city interesting and rich in opportunity.

However, what happens in a city is not just coordination but emergence. If we come to a city, we don't just bring our existing identity to the cooperation, but also the synergy at work in a city offers us new possibilities, and we quickly become something more (hopefully not less, though that can happen, too) than what we were before we entered the urban mix. We are then able, in turn, to offer this more developed self within the common matrix of coordination, discover new avenues of development, bring this new self to enrich the whole, and repeat the process again.[41] Cities are a whole greater than the sum of their parts – in other words, a living organism, not a mere machine. Since this is exactly our experience of life in the Church and of Christian ritual, it is additional confirmation that it is safe to think of cities as "liturgies."

But urban order turns out to be more analogous to liturgical order than in just the simple fact that both are "a work of the people." Part of the title of Jane Jacobs' very first book, *The Death and Life of Great American Cities*, was what triggered my identification of cities with liturgies. Cities resemble liturgies in their processions, their sacredness, and even in terms of their reliance upon various kinds of "deaths." After many years of reading her books, suddenly in a flash I understood that for Jacobs the city was in many different senses a kind of liturgy, and that therefore our liturgical theology would offer a whole set of practical applications to social life.

Jacobs coined the term, "the ballet of the city street," which is one of the most-loved of her observations about cities, to show how a crucial component of urban life is an interlocking system of human processions through space and time.[42] In order to show

---

41 One of the most important effects of this cooperation is the space it gives to those not explicitly involved in producing the order, to flourish through it – in particular, children. This raises the classic ethical issue of the "free-rider problem," where the efforts of some create an opportunity in which others who have not sacrificed as much may benefit. Jacobs would say, however, that in cities, we all both pull the load and enjoy certain free-rider benefits. I don't think she saw this as a major problem.

Orthodoxy, incidentally, handles the free-rider problem as follows: Those who sacrifice take honor in the generosity they have shown, and those who are pulled along in their wake, out of gratitude, long to someday also be so generous. This creates an unending chain in which *everyone begins* as a "free-rider," but *no one ends* that way. We are again talking, that is, about the virtue of *philotimo*. This approach to the problem works through the grace of the Holy Spirit.

We might also think about Trinitarian theology, since the original "free rider," is – excuse me for putting the matter in this way – the Son of God, Who is "true God *from* true God." The Son, in his turn, becomes the ultimate self-giver, "dying for us while we were yet sinners" (Rom 5:38). Thus, free-riding is not a "problem" but a tension intrinsic to divine life and to the adventure of reality.

42 This description of the ballet of the street begins on page 50 in the Vintage Books Edition (December 1992) of *The Death and Life of Great American Cities*, in the last few pages of Chapter Two, which is entitled, "The Uses of Sidewalks: Safety."

how city liveliness and safety depend on complex pathways of interaction and mutual support among people using the streets, she described in detail the precise rhythm which occurred on her particular block in lower Manhattan on a daily basis, hour by hour from about four a.m. until after midnight.

The rhythm of daily life on that street as people came and went, as stores opened and closed, as traffic ebbed and flowed, formed a basic pattern that was never identical on any two days. The "processions and returns" of city life, its basic "liturgy" in this other sense of liturgy as "ordered and patterned movements through space and time," are a major part of what turns the chaos of urban life into a stable, life-giving system. These predictable movements make a street safe, interesting, and commercially viable throughout such a broad stretch of the day that crime and other uncivilized behaviors are pushed out, she said.

"Continual variation upon a base of sameness" is one hallmark of liturgy, and this exactly describes life on Jacobs' street in Greenwich Village, as it does life on all lively urban streets. The daily balance between newness and form in our patterns of movement is a balance between freedom and necessity that adds up to "life." This balance is what enables so many unique people to come together and live in mutual peace, with all the differing life paths we choose reinforcing each other, supporting each other, sparking the best in each other – rather than collapsing into conflict.

It was through these patterns of movement that the many strangers on Jacobs' street in 1960 were working together as one body to support safety, commerce, and civilization. The first meaning of liturgy (the common work of the people in a city) is dependent upon this second, more explicitly ritualistic, meaning of liturgy (the interconnected patterns of procession and return, movement and behavior, through which we coordinate our efforts very naturally).

For example, if you do not have large numbers of people on a city's streets at almost all times of day, those streets begin to become unsafe (or *feel* unsafe, which Jacobs reminds us has much the same deadening effect on commerce and spirit as those streets actually *being* unsafe). Lack of safety, in turn, then freezes the cooperation and coordination among the citizens of the city.

The third sense in which cities are liturgies is the fact that cities are a matrix for the development of human personhood, just as most religious liturgies are supposed to be. We often say that "a lone Christian is no Christian" because without relationship to others, no human being can become fully human. In cities, the patterns of cooperation help us to "invest our lives in a number of significant relationships"[43] from the very close to the very distant, which enables our individual uniqueness to flourish.[44]

Jacobs noted this fact about cities, that they multiply both the number and the kind of relationships available to us, and that they also provide us with privacy and anonymity from unwanted relationships; something that we cannot find in more inert settlements like villages. Privacy is actually an important part of Christian personhood because privacy affords us the opportunity to transcend our merely natural connections to tribe or place. Privacy is part of our becoming more than just what our human nature gives us; it is essential for our development.

In that balance we all must strike between nature, will, and person in our practical spiritual development, cities are supposed to help us learn to coordinate our wills with others' desires, while allowing us to "enhypostasize" our natures and wills alike by making relationships with others *the* most important fact about us (far more important than accidents of genetics and birth, for example).[45]

---

[43] Jacobs, *Death and Life*, 136. "Statistical people are a fiction for many reasons, one of which is that they are treated as if infinitely interchangeable. Real people are unique, they invest years of their lives in significant relationships with other unique people, and are not interchangeable in the least. Severed from their relationships, they are destroyed as effective social beings – sometimes for a little while, sometimes forever."

[44] Tertullian is the recorded originator of the expression, *"Solus Christianus, nullus Christianus,"* which also counts as a succinct statement of why the human person is not reducible to nature, will, nor even to a combination of the two: our natures and wills are both useless absent personal relationship to others.

[45] This is one reason why same-sex attraction arises more often in cities, as do other religiously proscribed uses of sexuality, for in the city we come closer to transcending our belonging to nature and to the natural order. Christian experience, ancient and modern alike, however, teaches us to expect such temptations in cities, but also to remember that even in

The personal development and differentiation that can only occur through relations of interdependence are a major purpose and characteristic of cities as well as of liturgies. In cities more than in villages, we can see the paradox that our freedom and creativity are a necessary part of the fixed patterns that support a stable order.

Of course, you can also see – and there are enough biblical examples to prove it – how this cooperation in cities can go terribly awry, and how cities can become the place where we band together with others who share our fallen natures and passions in order to promote the most unnatural of human conduct (all the while calling this "personal," although in fact it is the death of our personhood) in defiant opposition to God and others. But I trust that, in the long run, the greater rationality of faith in Christ and the lightness of the burden given us by Christ (when compared to sin, since our Savior said, "my yoke is easy and my burden is light") will always remain a beacon for those seeking the highest possible civilization.

Time and Death in Cities

Yet and still, none of what we have said so far quite comes to the deepest meaning of this odd title, *The Death and Life of Great American Cities*. Within a few months of noticing the title's suggestion of something much more explicitly liturgical, I sent a letter to Mrs. Jacobs herself which commenced our friendship. And what I said was that, according to her writings, cities were sites where order was growing out of a cycle in which "death was embraced early and often," in the interests of promoting life. This is the fourth sense in which cities are liturgies.

Just walking down a street implies a kind of "death," since you must leave one place behind in order to be present in another. But the most important deaths in cities are really the trial and error, the

cities and despite the awesome power of technology, many natural limits remain for our protection. Life in cities often drives human reflection in gnostic, disembodied directions. Our goal, instead, should be to take up nature into a more personal life, not achieve our personhood at the cost of marring nature.

risks and sacrifices made in trying to start a business, reform a government, build a family, and so on. A city where all these death-defying offerings are being made, and being made by as many free people as possible, is actually a giant liturgy in which our time, treasure, and talents are the precious sacrificial object.[46]

Mrs. Jacobs loved my interpretation of her work, actually thanked me for "teaching her" what her own work had meant. So we have not only the logic of our arguments for this "liturgical" description of cities but the voice of an almost ultimate authority on urban order, as well.

Time is the crucial factor in cities, Jacobs had written. Time is sacrificed, because time is dedicated, in every significant enterprise and relationship. But the passage of time guarantees, eventually, death. Now in fact, *any* living organism lives only by managing the continuous death and birth within itself of its own cells, and any species faces the same dilemma at a higher fractal scale, as individual members come and go, but the species lives on. Only by accepting and managing death does anything ever live.

But this "living on" is possible only because the Patterns – which can be either the processes, the metabolic pathways, or the species characteristics of a living organism – continue across time though

---

46 Cities have been liturgies in a very dark way, as well. They have often been centered not on self-sacrifice but on *human* sacrifice. Many cities, for example, have been built through slave labor and the forced deaths of thousands of people. Moreover, Jacobs noted that even absent the dimension of political oppression, for most of human history cities have depended on rural in-migration for their existence, since, while the quality of life in cities is higher, so also is human mortality due to disease and natural disaster. This changed briefly with early twentieth-century advances in public sanitation so that cities were no longer "people-eaters." But the advent of wartime bombing and legalized abortion may have reversed this balance. I specifically remember a point where one in three conceptions in my hometown of Akron, Ohio was reported to be ended by abortion.

In point of fact, while cities may be ontologically liturgical, many times their corresponding religious liturgical programs have been quasi-demonic, or at least passionate. However, this is not sufficient reason to flee from cities, for wherever we go, we shall face challenges. Christ himself said that when weeds (bad liturgies) have been sown among the good crops (good liturgies), it is almost impossible to tear up the bad without destroying the good (Mt 13:24-30). We must stay where we have been called and do our best. However, different kinds of watchfulness are needed in the two settings. The monastic fathers contrasted the desert, where you face demonic temptations directly, with the city, where these are concealed behind idols.

the individual parts die. These processes, this metabolic order, these distinguishing elements are as important as the individual members of a species.

So it is that all living things live by mastering cycles of death and life. Every living thing lives only because it has a knack for this basic liturgical program of the passage through death to life, again and again. More than for any other reason, cities resemble liturgies because of their easy familiarity with death and resurrection at many fractal scales.

In contrast, the anti-cities that American Cartesian planners were building between the late 1940s and the early 1980s were all built on a directly-opposed approach to time and change and social cooperation. The planners tried to freeze time and change as a way to lock out death and decay. They wanted to annihilate the slums and replace them with an antiseptic perfection, built at one go, and fixed for all time. They aimed at an isolated, motionless, egocentric form of city order that was supposed to be born perfect in the mind of the planner, imposed on everyone else, and thereafter never change. But that "deathless" approach only guaranteed that these planned settlements would have no real life in them.[47]

Such planned cities not only feel dead, but their actual disorder (which is directly related to their being planned for superficial visual order) sparked an environment of crime and homicide; they became cities of actual death. In a real city, wonder, surprise, risk, sacrifice, disappointment, uncertainty, messiness, and the passing of time all mark the continuous transition between death and life, between what we know and what we will learn, between who we are and who we are able to become, between the plans we make and what actually happens. And by working death and the passage of time naturally into their life processes, cities become alive.

---

47 Roman cities, though usually built on strict grid patterns, had all of Jane Jacobs' four generators of city diversity (mixed primary uses; short blocks; buildings of varying ages; density), except perhaps for short blocks in certain monumental corridors.

Again, cities are places of wonder and surprise. They are scenes where we practice an openness to the unknown in our relationships, in our educations, in our cultural lives, and in our work. Cities are far more likely to be places where we meet new religions, as well. In all of this, we "die" to our old understandings of reality and awake to something new.

This opening of a window into the unknown is the fifth way in which cities are like liturgies, because religious liturgies are sites of concourse between human beings and higher or novel sources of intelligence. The very purpose of liturgies is to access or even create new information; cities fulfill the same role. This openness to the radical unknown in a city is not yet an openness to God, but it is the this-worldly equivalent of it.

Actually, in some cases it is *exactly the same* as an openness to God, since the surprises of relationship and new religions may be what help us to develop at our deepest level. And so there is something radically different in the fortunes of a city when Orthodox Christian liturgies are being celebrated there. A door has been opened that can then leaven the entire loaf of that city's urban liturgy, to mix metaphors with abandon!

Let me summarize and list the first five ways in which cities are usefully understood as liturgies: 1) They are a "work of the people." 2) They are generated and maintained through archetypally-patterned movements in space and time. 3) Cities are a matrix for the development of human personhood. 4) They are movements through death to life again, and again, and again. 5) They are sites where we are open to new information, to the absolute unknown, and often even to God.

Converting Chaos into Order: Externally and Internally

Sixthly and finally, I would like to point out that cities, like liturgies, perform an "analog-to-digital conversion" function. That is, they convert continuous, unstable, fleeting, or hard to define states, into stable, digital (yes/no), clearly defined, and dependable ones.[48] They take what is vague and make it specific. In generating this specificity, liturgies produce something that can be recognized as information by other members of the community.

My favorite example of liturgy performing this "analog to digital conversion" function is when the many shades of love between a couple are, through the very existence of the marriage ritual, converted into a simple state; that is, either the two lovers are "married" or they are "not married." The waves of love and affection will rise and fall through various degrees of intensity, but the ritually-produced digital state is harder to undo, and besides it is a status that is publicly understandable.

To better answer your question from a little while ago about therapy and the issues of complexity, information, and their relation to our inner life, let me point out that all these elements do become relevant. Liturgies and rituals perform the function of turning inner states into outer ones. They do it so well that we hardly notice it. But without these ritual conversions of analog fluctuation or of outright chaos into "digital" coherence and predictability, a common life of any kind would be impossible. Without rituals, we would have far less concrete information about who others are or what they intend.

For Christians, it is through the dramatics of baptism, confession, Holy Communion, and attendance at the various church services that the chaos of our inner lives is converted into well-ordered

---

[48] Rappaport's *Ritual and Religion*, cited in note 29, is the source for the analog-to-digital conversion function of ritual, and that this is a *sine qua non* for communication; see pp 86-89. Rappaport emphasizes that ritual serves this function not only for human beings but for other animals and even other phyla! Analog-to-digital conversion is similar to emergence itself, whereby things progress from inchoate states to coherent ones.

and even sanctified states of being. Orthodox Christian liturgy helps us to find a stable, reliable identity.

Contemporary psychotherapy, by contrast, tends to unravel this "digital" state of coherence to the extent that it puts too much of our attention on our inner chaos. A person's infinitely fluctuating and cloudy inner world becomes decisive for his self-conception. Then, if a day comes when we feel that we don't love our spouse any more, we may even conclude that the *ritual* is what's mistaken, and want to reverse it by getting a divorce. In our minds, ritual commitments have come to be seen as oppressive to the freedom that will supposedly be granted by a return to the formless abyss. But you can't be free unless you possess the basic form of existence itself – and rituals are what produce the foundation of basic existence.

Jacobs described city streets as the place where the drama between barbarism and civilization must be acted out again and again. This happens when our many clashing and amorphous desires are converted through stable city patterns into something that has permanence and clarity.

In other words, in cities people are converted from pure potentiality into the particularity of a stable culture, which then makes them able to communicate and cooperate with others. A stable order that feels and looks quite solid is produced in cities out of the chaos of many human passions, natural threats, and so forth. This solidity is partly illusory, but then so are most products of emergence in the social or even the natural world. But the solidity of a marriage or a religious conversion is certainly more sure when it is supported by ritual than not. Overall, in cities as in liturgies, it is the patterns that turn fluctuation and chaos into a stable identity.

The Illusion of Life's Fragility

A particular kind of nihilist loves to revel in exposing the fragility of ritually-derived systems of order. They will tell you that your church or your family or your nation amount to a thin veneer of order concealing great injustice or suffering. However, such smart alecks forget that the fragility of social phenomena is, in turn, an illusion of its own. After all, don't flowers and plants, though individually so weak, have the ability to crack boulders and bring down buildings? In fact, living rituals and religious customs, as well as biological life, have endured time beyond mind, while mountains have worn away, seas have vanished, and plains have arisen in their place. A loving family can absorb much chaos and yet still be the single greatest force for life, in our life.

The most accurate way to look at this question of the seeming fragility of ritual and ritually produced order is to say that civilization, marriage, and spiritual life remain solid only to the extent that they extend and deepen the liturgies that brought them into being in the first place – not that their seeming solidity is a fiction.[49] Quite the contrary; in reality, it is *only* liturgical states that are stable and solid. "Things" in themselves are *neither* fragile *nor* solid – except as the processes which created and still go on creating them are either resilient – able to digest shocks and insults – or not. And thus the divine Son's liturgy of the Cross and Resurrection is the only guarantor of solidity in this or any possible world.

In cities, the confused, chaotic "barbarians" that need to be changed into something solid and civilized are all of us, to one extent or another. This transformation happens with the support of others and as we support others, respect others, and learn from our interactions with others in the patterned repetition of city interactions.

The pressures of urban life can, if we approach them prayerfully, also help convert the wide range of our inner feelings into dependable states of service, responsibility, sophistication, open-mindedness, and cooperation. In cities, we may have all kinds of crazy ideas and opinions, but their expression generally must take into account public sensibilities and the love we cultivate for those who disagree with us. There are always opportunities to refine what we think.

---

[49] "Civilization, marriage, and spiritual life" – our three marriages from Chapter Seven. As we saw there, cities are not only liturgies, but in fact also wedding liturgies between the Guardian and Trader syndromes.

City vs. Country

RTE: This is a remarkable view of city life, but what about those who prefer country life, including many monastics, most hermits, and farmers?

DR. PATITSAS: Okay, that is an interesting question. Clearly, we get the word "civilization" from cities, so we can't deny that something special is happening there. But there are a couple of qualifications to our love for cities that we can add.

There is a definite value in being close to nature – although, as Jane Jacobs always pointed out, trying to turn a city into a suburban facsimile of nature is disastrous for cities and nature alike.

One thing that should make Christians ambivalent about cities is that we regard our main citizenship as being in the City Above, the Heavenly Jerusalem. The paradox for us is that it might take occasionally getting out of an earthly city and into the countryside to slough off some of the dangerous idolatry that inevitably coexists with liturgy in the cities of this fallen world. We should take the steps necessary to strive for a more direct heavenly "urbanism."

Second, today's country dwellers are often the refugees or orphaned tribes cast off from more developed cities of the past. In that case, their very rural isolation may keep them closer to certain ways and traditions they inherited from distant urban ancestors. That is, by living in the countryside away from contemporary cities, they can stay faithful to certain values or ways that their mother cities had long ago. If those lost mother cities were more civilized than the contemporary cities now available to these cultural orphans, then leaving behind their rural homes will be a mixed blessing. In that case, staying out of the available "lesser" cities may keep them more civilized, to some extent.

RTE: Did the ancients also see cities as liturgies?

DR. PATITSAS: After I noticed that in *The Death and Life of Great American Cities* the cities look just like giant liturgies, I was introduced to that greatest of texts about ancient religion, Fustel de Coulanges' *The Ancient City*.[50] On every page, you can see that cities of the classical world lived and breathed through ritual observance. In other words, in those cities the link between cities and liturgies was explicit.

How did a young man in ancient Athens become a citizen? By being initiated into the particular liturgy of Athens on the Acropolis at the age of eighteen. Why were women excluded from citizenship in the classical Greek world? Because the city liturgy of Athens revolved around blood sacrifice, and our forebears thought it extremely unwise to mix the "blood of life," which women possessed, with the "blood of death" handled by men in sacrifice and war.[51] In other words, originally citizenship was simply another term for the right to participate in the liturgy of a given city. Even the word for being "just" in Ancient Greek originally meant "qualified to worship." This shows us that ancient cities themselves emerged out of a kind of ritual field where everything that was public and civic was done religiously and ritually.

Every public detail of the ancient polis was steeped in ritual practice. Even within the home, family identity revolved around daily religious rituals. Not only are all cities liturgies in the sense of being patterned and repetitive cycles of death and life, but even before cities were born, human beings apparently lived together in settlements whose common life was structured through religious ritual. Liturgies are what gave birth to cities, while cities in their turn are liturgies in a different – in some ways shallower, in some ways deeper – sense.

---

50 Numa Denis Fustel De Coulanges, *The Ancient City: A Study on the Religion, Laws, and Institutions of Greece and Rome* (Baltimore: John Hopkins University Press, 1980); originally published in Paris: Durand, 1854, as *La Cité Antique*.

51 Alice Linsley, "Stepping into the Stream: An Interview with Alice C. Linsley," *Road to Emmaus Journal*, Vol. XI, No. 1: Winter, 2010 (#40).

IV. THE GENTLE RECONCILIATION OF SCIENCE AND RELIGION

So, we start with the historical fact that ancient cities organized their civic life liturgically. The city and its liturgy were one thing. And then we jump forward to the work of Jane Jacobs, and we see that cities with no explicitly religious character nevertheless still behave in ways that look liturgical. Is all of this a coincidence, or could something deeper be at work?

The science of organic complexity bridges this gap.

Cities are organically complex systems – and, in fact, they are among the most intricate of all human complex systems. Cities are also usefully described as "liturgies" in the very ordinary senses that we have depicted above. I mean, I am not getting religious here. I am just saying that when you look at how a city functions in view of its organically complex nature, you can't help but see that all its features look and act like liturgy in the five or six ways that we just finished discussing.

So far, this may not be impressive; perhaps it's just coincidence that the more organically complex cities are, the more they look like liturgies. But it does open a super intriguing possibility. What if other complex systems also look like liturgies, although perhaps less explicitly than cities do? In that case, even though we may not be religious, we might be forced to admit that science is demonstrating that *all* complex order is in some measure liturgical. We aren't that far off from saying that an accurate scientific description of the world is that it resembles a cosmic liturgy.

It is crucial to remember that cities are not *sui generis* in being complex systems; they aren't the only problems in organic complexity that exist throughout nature. Almost everything in the world obeys the laws of either complexity or of complexity's close cousins, emergence and chaos. Therefore, if cities organically and without anyone directing them behave like liturgies, will we find this also in other complex systems?

When I finally dared to ask myself the outlandish question of whether science was discovering, in scientific terms, that the whole world resembles a vast liturgy, I quickly came to see that all along the great chain of emergence, from atoms to biological organisms to religions, emergent entities only exist by adopting patterns that look "liturgical" in certain qualified but nevertheless very real ways.

And thus the science of complexity *does* reveal a cosmos that resembles a vast liturgical program.

RTE: So who discovered this reconciliation of science with religion, you or Jane Jacobs?

DR. PATITSAS: I think she saw it first, or at least glimpsed it. She then hinted at it to me in the vaguest of ways. I went back to *The Nature of Economies*, the book she had just written, without having any idea of what she was hinting at, and that is when I saw it for myself.

But it was several years before I dared to ask her about it directly, during one of my visits to her home in Toronto, and by then she was much more reserved about this deep correspondence between natural order and liturgical order. After all, to admit this correspondence is to enter into something like a "proof" of religion, and Mrs. Jacobs was a scientist, not a theologian.

The clear feeling I got in our one open discussion about this reconciliation between science and religion was as if she were saying, "This could very well be true. But if it is true, it is a fact so big that we had better take every precaution not to rush to such a conclusion. We should do everything we can to disprove it and not indulge in wishful thinking about it. It could easily be our imaginations running away with us."

This is exactly the method that Jane Jacobs liked to use in all her work: look at many different sources; allow yourself to slowly discover the underlying patterns; but then try as hard as you can to discredit those patterns until you are *forced* to accept them.

It was in my first letter to her that I said that she had described cities as if they were liturgies. In her letter back, she agreed that this was more like an identity than like a mere analogy or metaphor. Then, her hint to me, the sign to me that there was something even bigger that I had missed, was just her comment that in reading my connection of cities to liturgies she was "startled by how I had expressed so clearly what she had just been groping for" in her then-forthcoming book *The Nature of Economies*.[52]

Well, that book is about neither cities nor liturgies, so what could she have meant? I only had that one comment of hers to rely on, that I had grasped something she was groping for in that book. It took me two readings of *The Nature of Economies* before I saw it.

In the book, she was describing which behavioral habits would make us most natural, most at home in nature, and most able to arrange our economic life in a prosperous and productive way. And those habits all amounted to some primitive version of the religious, ethical, and liturgical impulses. It was such impulses that would make us at home in nature, she said, and prevent us from ruining the environment.

She arrived at this conclusion by asking which behaviors prevented animals from exploiting to extinction the resources available to them. Why don't cheetahs kill to the limit of their possible prey? Why don't cats hunt all the available mice in their every waking moment? Why don't elephants trample down their habitat as they feed and wander?

Jacobs looked at what such animals did instead with their ample "downtime." Animals, instead of "maximizing their productivity" and in so doing exploiting their ecosystems to depletion, instead socialized, groomed, played, rested, went swimming.

---

[52] The final paragraphs of this letter to me (dated February 12, 2000), read in part: "Next month, Modern Library is publishing my latest book, *The Nature of Economies*. Reading your letter, I was startled to realize how aptly your insights express just what I've been groping for. By this time you must be aware that my answer to your question about whether I think cities can usefully be understood as manifestations of liturgy is Yes. I think that's a splendid idea and as you say, 'really' so, not merely as an analogy. I might add that you are so much the best interpreter of my work that I'm aware of, that you are actually showing me what my own books mean in a way I hadn't grasped! Furthermore, in such an important and central way. I hope that when your thesis is finished you'll send me a copy. And again, thank you more than I can say for your enlightening, astonishing letter. Sincerely, Jane Jacobs." The full text can be found in T. Patitsas, "The City as Liturgy: An Orthodox Theologian Corresponds with Jane Jacobs About a Gentle Reconciliation of Science and Religion," in *Legacy of Achievement: Met-*

To Jacobs, all of this suggested that fitness for survival always had two faces: competitive success at feeding and breeding, but also cooperative success at living symbiotically within their environments. To her, this suggested that our standard accounts of evolution, written by men, were skewed in the direction of a "masculine" Guardian view of the world. Because such views overemphasized warfare and underemphasized "feminine" Trader cooperation, they were therefore incomplete.

So, Jacobs asked herself, what would represent what she called the feminine side of evolution – the drive to cooperation and self-limitation – in the case of our human species? As she put it in *The Nature of Economies*, "What could possibly have restrained our species?" – i.e., from destroying our own ecosystems. Her best guess included seven traits listed in the book: the capacity for aesthetic appreciation (beauty first, yet again!); fear of retribution for transgressions (the power of the good and of the true in one go!); the capacity to feel awe, expressed as veneration (fear of retribution and awe are, obviously, the second and first kinds of healthy shame which we mentioned in Chapter Four);[53] our linguistic capacities, or the ability to persuade ourselves and others to limit destructive behaviors (the necessity for logos); our abilities to correct our interaction with the world through tinkering and innovating (discovering the logoi in nature); and, our sense of morality (our reverence for the good).

All of this, Jacobs realized in reading my letter, added up to the dim outlines of religion, of religious life, and of liturgy itself.

So, this is one aspect of the reconciliation of science with religion: it is through the religious impulse that we integrate our primary powers and point them in directions that are friendly to nature. Meanwhile, pushing us in the other direction will be our intellects and our pride, gnostically driving us to regard ourselves as something set over nature, conquering, abusing, or abandoning it.

ropolitan Methodios of Boston, Festal Volume of the 25th Anniversary of his Consecration to the Episcopate, (1982-2007), ed. Rev. George D. Dragas (Columbia, MO: NewRome Press, 2010), 845-46.

53 Jacobs also says that, "One aspect of awe – the veneration of places because they're holy – has shifted in part to veneration of places because they have significant historic, aesthetic, or ecological value." *The Nature of Economies*, 128-129.

And this is why the criticism that environmentalism has become a religious faith is not decisive. Yes, environmentalism is a religion. The human religious impulse is our best bet for the marshaling of human energies to preserve and respect the planet. If environmentalism is incomplete on its own, this just tells us that we will have to rely upon real religion to achieve environmentalism's stated aim of saving the ecosystem.

Where Science and Religion Meet

In any case, the real reconciliation of science and religion, the meat of it, can be summed up like this: First of all, cities are liturgies. No, the identity is not total, but it is far more than a metaphor. Rather, organic order and self-organization in urban life look exactly like a liturgy. Cities cycle through death and life, trial and error, procession and return. They also summon concerted human attention and effort in the attempt to remain open to the absolute unknown for the preservation and furthering of human flourishing and human emergence.

Secondly, cities are not *sui generis* in terms of their type of order. I mean, cities are but one of a huge number of examples of complex order in nature. We find emergence in the creation of the universe from the earliest moments of existence, and all along through the chain of biological evolution.

This leads any rational person to the third point: If we can, broadly-speaking, describe cities (which, if they are healthy, are organically complex organisms) as liturgies, then is it possible to use a similar description for all the other many instances of organic order? Do other life forms also attain and maintain their organic order through patterned repetition, cycling repeatedly through death to life, do they pass through uncertainty and openness to knowing, etc?

Well, the answer there is mixed, but it is mixed in a very instructive way. All organic order in the universe looks liturgical to one degree or another. I mean, even electrons spin around the nucleus in a kind of procession and return, a motion of death and life, in a way. That's significant, but perhaps not very impressive.

But here is a fact that is impressive: The *more developed* nature becomes and the *further along* the evolutionary spectrum it lies, *the more it looks like liturgy.* The cycle of day to night, the seasons passing and returning, a plant's death and life cycle, and so forth, are already a proto-liturgy. Animals, too, exhibit ritual behavior. But political orders, cities, families, and societies are explicitly dependent upon ritual.

Not only does order increase through liturgical processes in the natural world, but the more order develops and the more sophisticated the cosmos becomes, the more liturgical the processes creating the world look.

Roy Rappaport, Anthropologist of Ritual and Religion

Again, it isn't just animals who exhibit ritual behavior. One of my favorite pieces of evidence for this liturgical or "ritualistic" view of all natural order is the following quote from the anthropologist Roy Rappaport. He first defines ritual, and then he talks about its ubiquity in living nature:

> I take the term "ritual" to denote the performance of more or less invariant sequences of formal acts and utterances not entirely encoded by the performers. This definition, being extremely terse, demands elaboration and discussion. Before discussing its specific features (performance, formality, invariance, inclusion of both acts and utterances, encoding by other than the performers), several general comments are in order.

> First, this definition encompasses much more than religious behavior. Psychiatrists, for instance, have used "ritual" rather similarly conceived, or the closely related if not synonymous term "ceremony," to refer both to the pathological

stereotyped behaviors of some neurotics (Freud 1907), and to certain conventional, repetitive but nevertheless adaptive interactions between people (Erikson 1966: 337). In sociology and anthropology "ritual" and "ceremony'" may designate a large range of social events, not all of which are religious, or may denote the formal aspects of such events..., and application...of the term has not been restricted to human phenomena. Ethologists have used it, virtually interchangeably with "display," to designate behavior they have observed not only among other mammals but also among reptiles, birds, fish and even members of other phyla....

[Rappaport continues ...] One may ask whether we observe, in the use of a common term by anthropologists, theologians, psychiatrists and ethologists, nothing more than a label stretched to cover phenomena of such diversity that little is gained from attending to whatever similarities may prevail among them, or whether the use of a single term for such widely differing phenomena as the courtship dance of fiddler crabs (Crane 1966) and the Roman Mass recognizes significant commonalities underlying their undoubted differences. Surely, some of the differences among instances of the general class "ritual" are both obvious and important. No one would be hard pressed to distinguish the genuflections of Catholic priests from the gyrations of impassioned crustacea, and it would be absurd to regard the former as no more than a mere complexification of the latter, or to minimize their differences in any other way. At the beginning, however, it may be more useful to attend to what is common to a class, or possible class, as vague or vacuous as these resemblances may seem, than to emphasize what may distinguish its members from each other, as striking as these differences may be. Prior attention to similarities does not preclude subsequent attention to differences, and it may help to place those differences in proper perspective.

By noting first the ways in which religious and other rituals resemble each other it may be possible to distinguish them from each other more clearly later, and distinguishing religious from other ritual will be helpful in fashioning conceptions of the sacred, the numinous and the holy.

Our definition, then, encompasses not only human rituals, but also those stylized displays reported by ethologists to occur among the birds, the beasts and even the insects.[54]

Clearly, as you proceed from the spinning of electrons around nuclei, up to star systems, seasons, plants, and animals, you find that emergent order looks more and more patterned, cyclical, and ritualistic. At last you come to human life and to the apex of human life, the city. And there, you see that organic, natural order looks *exactly* like liturgy.

Therefore, the answer to whether *all* organically emergent systems and organisms are "liturgical" is a qualified "yes," but the qualification pushes the identity rather than undermines it. Because the higher the level of development in nature, the more literally do organically complex systems look like liturgies. It's much like asking whether a man's seven children are biologically his own and having someone respond, "Well, we can see the physical resemblance very clearly in the older ones, whereas in the newborn infant it is hard to tell." Anyone can see that this qualified "yes" as to his resemblance to his children is stronger *because* it is qualified: the more the children develop, the more they look like him physically; they are *his* kids.

And this is what we can now say of Darwinian evolution, that the further along the evolutionary spectrum it travels, the more "liturgical" things appear. Therefore, it is not wrong to at least ask who the "father" of that creation might be. Well, let's not rush our answer, but at least the question has now become a valid one.

---

54 Rappaport, *op. cit.*, 24-25.

So, you see, it isn't just human cities that resemble liturgies. In fact, *every instance of organic life, of organic order, can broadly be termed liturgical.*

Meanwhile, there is a form of human development that is, in a sense, beyond even cities; at any rate, it can outlast any particular city. This form of human development, moreover, in the aggregate has had more impact on human emergence than any other human social organization, including even cities. That development, of course, would be religion.

When looking at the religions of the world, what we are seeing is the absolute pinnacle of human social organization. And what do we find within religions themselves? Well, that religions, even more than cities, derive their identity, their function, their existence, their persistence, their self-maintenance, and their self-organization, from and through ritual.

If we accept *homo sapiens* as the apex of evolution, then we can see that all of evolution has been pointing to, in the end, human priesthood within nature.

A Reconciliation, Not a Conquest

So far, it looks like the world exists by being "liturgical" and that, in fact, the more sophisticated and developed any piece of cosmic order is, the more blatantly that part of the world resembles liturgy. And it would also seem that "liturgy" – aka, "ritual" – is far bigger than religion. Liturgy is just the way that our cosmos happens to exist, whether we like it or not.

This is not yet a reconciliation between science and religion. One could argue that religions have evolved like all emergent organisms, and therefore they follow the universal cosmic laws of existence. So we don't yet have a reconciliation between science and religion, but things are starting to look mighty suspicious, at any rate. The key to achieving the reconciliation is what you look at next.

The fourth step is to turn the matter around. So far I've been claiming to discern liturgy, dimly or clearly, everywhere that complex emergence, or something like it, appears in nature. In other words, I've been asking what religion sees when it looks at the new science of organic complexity. And the answer is, "To religious eyes, science is obviously discovering a cosmic liturgy. The sciences of emergence and complex order are discovering the ubiquity of ritual order."

But now let's put the science of organic complexity in the driver's seat and ask what it sees when it looks at religion, and in particular at religious ritual. For Rappaport, the answer was simple enough: It is clear to objective scientific eyes that ritual in religion is *the* matrix through which human emergence has unfolded. Liturgy is the way in which chaos is converted to order, within religions and within human identity more generally.

And it is scientifically clear, too, that all of religion, not just religious ritual, functions in this way, as a matrix whereby chaotic forces are turned into information, nothingness into existence, death into life. Moreover, we must admit that human identity until very recently always emerged through the matrix of religious ritual and religion. Even Socrates was religious, and so were the early scientists of the Enlightenment.

This is the thesis of Rappaport's book, *Ritual and Religion in the Making of Humanity*. In the title, he means "making" literally, that what we call "humanity" is a *product* of ritual and religion. Rappaport is no pious fool; he rather strikes me as a hard-bitten agnostic anthropologist who knew what he was doing in his discipline. But humanity, for him, emerged through religion and ritual.

There is no fifth step: religion and science are now reconciled. a) religion believes that science has discovered a cosmic liturgy. b) science understands that religion, through its ritual character, is the organically complex system which produced human existence out of chaos.

This is as far as the reconciliation can be safely pushed. No, the one has not *conquered* the other – and, anyway, that would not be a *reconciliation* but the onset of a permanent *enmity* between science and religion. So, no, we haven't at all proven that the cosmos *is* a liturgy, any more than we can prove that religion *is nothing but* a further and very developed form of organic emergence.

But what we have achieved is a reconciliation. From the standpoint of religion, we can now say, and still be totally scientific, that the cosmos highly resembles a vast liturgy. In fact, it seems that we are part of some vast cosmic ritual order. From the standpoint of science, we can now say with no offense to religion that religion is yet another instance of biological, organic emergence, a complexly ordered system that in its arising has managed to defeat chaos, conquer death at least in some measure, and harness the passage of time in the production of increasing order, like other complexly ordered systems always have. Religions are alive. Many endure for centuries. And these living organisms have typically served to promote human emergence, even if imperfectly.

After the Reconciliation

At this point in the Reconciliation, we are welcome to find other things to disagree about.

For example, science ought to ask whether, having seen organic religion's close resemblance to other forms of chaos-defeating emergence, science itself couldn't attempt the conscious design of non-religious ritual social forms that accomplish the same tasks, such as the state, political parties, or major sports teams. Why not design our own complex ritual order, as we do in armies and in governments? This is exactly, of course, what many of those who oppose religion have argued for the last two hundred years or more.

So far, the attempt to create artificial social life has resulted in increasingly bloody wars and increasingly oppressive state control, even reaching the point of outright genocides. The attempt is not going well, it's plain to see, because scientifically it's almost impossible to design artificial life. Also, unlike nations, which have some basis in the organic order of blood or language, the modern technocratic state is a Frankenstein, a dead man walking. Divorce it from national sentiment, and it will fall to pieces.

Science can also, as it already does, interrogate religion for its actual effect on human emergence, and science can claim to be more organic and alive than certain kinds of religion which seem to limit, distort, or crush human dignity.

But the game can now be played in both directions. Religion will now have penetrating questions of its own to ask of science. Since religion appears to be an organic product of emergence, how can any rational person justify the scientific animosity against religion? Isn't it the place of science to respect and even venerate all natural order? Why does this one instance of natural organic emergence alone earn the blind hatred of science?

Is it possible that the scientific opposition to religion is just another example of the way in which Old Enlightenment Science prefers dead linear order to living nonlinear order? Why this preference for dead knowability over the uncertain chance for living participation in mystery? Such a preference would seem perverse by any human standard. Isn't scientists' fear of organically complex religion just a result of the fact that modern science's true aim is control and not knowledge – that science itself often isn't actually scientific, in other words?

Also, why has science, free of all superstition and claiming to be completely rational, been unable to design a non-lethal alternative to religion, in terms of an organically complex social organism? If scientists respond that they have so succeeded, in the form of the scientific community itself, then religion can respond, "Yes, there you have succeeded – but only to the extent that you consistently rely upon the falsifiable hypothesis and not on untestable theories or stale ideologies. You claim to reject Christianity, you say that it is a myth, *but your own community lives only by the death and resurrection of the word* enacted through the ritual of testing falsifiable hypotheses."

So I believe that we now have scientific evidence, if you care to see it, that the world is a cosmic liturgy. And you've also got scientific evidence, if you care to see it, that religious liturgies are one more instance of organic order in the cosmos.

Within this tension, science and religion appear to be reconciled. Not that one has conquered the other, as we have said, but that you have two perspectives on their relation, and both of them say the same thing about this relation, but in their own language. Science sees organic self-organization and complexity everywhere, including in religion and especially in cities and in religious liturgies. And religion notices that the whole cosmos seems to exist only by virtue of the operation of various liturgical patterns.

But this organic account of the cosmos is just what the Beauty-first account of creation would have taught us to expect. To this day, to this hour, Christ is still appearing to all that is. His beauty is still stirring non-being and being alike into eros for him. The creation still moves towards Christ and moves to share the life it receives from him with the creation around it. The whole world has fallen into eros with Christ and is imitating his ecstatic and self-emptying love by acting liturgically.

You see now what I mean by reconciliation of science with religion. They now exist in harmony with each other; they do not conquer each other. We are not to reduce one to the other.

RTE: This is incredible. I think I need a drink.

DR. PATITSAS: Wild times, ain't they? I am so glad to see the rise of a sophistication equal, in our terms, to what the Christian Romans had a millennium ago – and with air conditioning, electric cars, and antibiotics, to boot! I'm so glad to be alive in this age, with science learning what it is learning. We couldn't all be luckier.

Of course, things could still go horribly wrong for the world and the human race. One thing I think a lot about is the threat posed to Western civilization by bad economic science. Unless we drag our economic science out of the gutter of a wrongly applied reductionism, we will be too distracted by social chaos and decline to enjoy this perfect moment. Also, Artificial Intelligence looms menacingly. There will always be new mountains to climb.

RTE: Didn't you start by saying that Jane Jacobs wrote a book warning us not to fall into a dark age with an icon of Panaghia next to her typewriter?

DR. PATITSAS: Yes, and I had better find a nice icon right away as I now write my own book on Jane Jacobs' paradigm shift in economic theory. Thank you for that reminder of strong hope!

EPILOGUE

THE JOY OF ALL WHO SORROW

When the soul abides in the love of God – how good and gracious and festive all things are! But even with God's love, sorrows continue and the greater the love, the greater the sorrow. Never by a single thought did the Mother of God sin, nor did she ever lose grace, yet vast were her sorrows; when she stood at the foot of the cross her grief was as boundless as the ocean and her soul knew torment incomparably worse than Adam's when he was driven from paradise, in that the measure of her love was beyond compare greater than the love which Adam felt when he was in paradise. That she remained alive was only because the Lord's might sustained her, for it was his desire that she should behold his Resurrection, and live on after his Ascension to be the comfort and joy of the apostles and the new Christian peoples.[1]

St. Silouan the Athonite

Although this book began with a consideration of the issue of trauma, it by now has passed through an entire galaxy of subjects and themes. I believe that the reader who took up this book looking for answers on the issue of trauma will have found something of value in each chapter, and yet I want to circle around to the topic again because in my own mind so much seems clearer in the light of the many other discussions we have had until now.

Not all negative experiences are traumatizing. On a daily basis, we endure slights and injustices either small or great without any long-term impact on our ability to feel, to think, or to relate peace-

[1] St. Silouan the Athonite, in *Saint Silouan the Athonite*, ed. by Archimandrite Sophrony (Sakharov), trans. Rosemary Edmonds (Essex: Stavropegic Monastery of St. John the Baptist, 1991), 309.

fully with those around us. We even lose loved ones in the normal course of life without automatically feeling a fundamental worsening in our disposition towards the world. Usually, the dynamic organic processes by which soul equilibrium is maintained are enough to absorb these intrusions and protect our hearts.

A traumatic experience, by contrast, is a bad event or pattern of events that carries with it a force tending toward, or even seeming to reach the level of, a religious or mystical revelation. Such an experience is not just something awful that happens but something awful that seems to reveal, as if for the first time, that the truest and deepest character of the world is profoundly negative. Traumatic experiences are events which seem to pull back the veil on our everyday order, proving that life's beauty is only skin-deep, exposing the "fact" that beneath the world's beautiful surface lies a fundamentally cruel, meaningless, brutal, or amoral chaos.

Traumatic experiences, in other words, are anti-theophanies.

If they are to reveal their false "truth" about the world and about God quickly, such experiences must be particularly ugly or surprising. If they are to do so more slowly (for, as we now know, chronic neglect can be as traumatizing to a child as sudden horror), then it is not ugliness but an apparently meaningless monotony of pain or abandonment that will be trauma's most effective guise.

A tour of combat, an abusive childhood, and certain other life situations are distinct among traumatic experiences, however, in that they "hit us coming and going"; they combine the abrupt shock of hell with the slow, indifferent terror of being buried alive.

It has been observed that the same experience can be traumatizing for one person and yet can lead to greater integration and more stable character for another. This raises the hope that our attitude and response might insulate us from the painful effects of such experiences.

On the other hand, though, even the briefest consideration of the catalogue of horrors that have filled some percentage of childhoods over the long history of the human race brings us to the realization that there are almost certainly limits to the idea that it is "up to us" whether an experience will be traumatizing or not. Our best studies of war also confirm that some psychological damage from prolonged exposure to heavy combat is almost always a matter of "when," not "if." Sufficiently traumatic experiences are able to overwhelm human agency.

But even if it is true that there are limits to our ability to protect ourselves from trauma while it is happening, nevertheless we do have the strong desire to restore psychic integration to those who have been traumatized. Those who have been traumatized share the same desire, only more so. And we would also like to know how, if possible, to build our resilience so that we can endure at least some of the "slings and arrows of outrageous fortune" without the sustained damage to our character implied in trauma. In other words, we as a human race would like to acquire the art of how both to treat and to prevent the trauma wound.

Precisely here in the desire for prevention and treatment, however, a dilemma arises: not to hold out the possibility that a person can through their own thoughts and actions begin to assimilate or even become inoculated against trauma would be a condemnation to permanent exile, a prison sentence. Is there really nothing left of my freedom after a traumatic experience that I could use to dig my way out from my captivity to debilitating trauma reactions?

But yet it is the very character of trauma, as I said above, that it is not merely something bad that happens but an experience with a seemingly mystical force, the revelation of an apparently ultimate truth about the world and even about God. To hope for the impermanence of the trauma wound is therefore to contest the ultimate validity of the "truth" disclosed by the traumatic event itself. It is also, therefore, to question the judgment of the trauma victim about the force of what has happened to them, and so would seem like a further injury to an already wounded person.

If we ignore the claim to ultimate validity asserted by the traumatic event itself, by denying the apparent permanence of its effect, how will the victims of trauma ever feel truly heard – and thus, paradoxically, have the possibility of reintegration within their community?

What are we to make of this dilemma? How are we to give trauma its "due" as something experienced as revelatory *without* remaining forever the objects of its workings?

Three things need to be said. First, it is largely accidental which sorts of experiences are likely to be traumatizing to a particular person. At any rate, it seems not to be something that we can predict ahead of time.

Second, it is not entirely accidental. Some development based in our still-existing limited freedom might prepare us to see or endure certain things without a total loss of our psychic integrity, and even to recover that integrity if it has been taken from us.

Third, though, and above all, comes a specifically Christian – perhaps even specifically Orthodox Christian – point about trauma: it would take a superhuman chastity to handle literally any event without being traumatized. The capacity to handle anything, to endure any outrage, injustice, violation, or shock without suffering the destruction of our characters would require the gift of unmerited divine grace wedded to the purest possible eros for God. We would have to be the sort of person for whom "unknowing" things and knowing persons was a perfected art.

This brings us to the Virgin Mary, the Mother of God, whom Orthodox Christians also know as the Theotokos (the God-bearer).

The Mother of God faced what should have been the ultimately traumatizing experience when she witnessed the torture and cruel murder of the person who was not only her only Son but also her God. Yet she lived through this without sustaining a moral injury and without her heart becoming divided against itself. She was a human person, and yet in the face of a supreme trial that provided a glimpse into the drama of divine life itself, her character remained whole.

We have said elsewhere, inspired by Shestov's critique of truth-first intellectual systems, that to be exposed to traumatic experience is to be force-fed from the Tree of the Knowledge of Good and Evil. It is to lose grace and to find oneself "naked."

Now, the hymns of our Church state that the Mother of God also faced the Tree of the Knowledge of Good and Evil, which for her was the sight of the crucifixion of her Son upon the "tree" of the cross. However, we believe that, unique among human persons, she refused to eat of that bitter fruit. A sword pierced her heart and she nearly died of grief. But still she did not philosophize or speculate or doubt, she did not curse or "mourn like an unbeliever" (I Thess 4:13). Instead, she confessed the Crucified One as both "my Son and my God."

It therefore stands to reason that the Virgin Mary may have something to show us about how to endure, without the loss of our integrity, experiences which are meant to traumatize us. More than showing us, she has some powerful and consoling help to give us.

According to the Orthodox Christian tradition, the grief of the Mother of God was uniquely vast, both because her beloved, her Son, was unique and also because there was nothing partial in her love for her child. In the tradition of the Orthodox Church, not only did a sword pierce the heart of the Mother of God (Lk 2:35) but also her grief was so great that it took a special miracle from her Son so that she did not die of grief. And yet she lived on to behold the Resurrection despite the encounter with this ultimately traumatic vision.

You may remember Jane Jacobs' penetrating remark that, "Whatever is trying to destroy civilization, that icon is against it." Whether through sin or through trauma or through cold indifference, whether through our own fault or someone else's, many of us are beset by forces trying to "destroy civilization" – the sane and moral and beautiful order of a pure heart. We need the Theotokos and we need her icon so that we can belong again in society.

Timothy Patitsas
November 1, 2016
Brookline, Massachusetts

BIBLIOGRAPHY BY CHAPTER

Chapter One
The Opposite of War Is Not Peace:
Healing Trauma in the *Iliad* and in Orthodox Tradition

Calaway, Jared. "Polutropos: Much-Turned Speech in the Odyssey and Hebrews." *Antiquitopia* blog, March 18, 2009. Accessed February 16, 2018. http://antiquitopia.blogspot.com/2009/03/polutropos-much-turned-speech-in.html

Constas, Nicholas. "The Last Temptation of Satan: Divine Deception in Greek Patristic Interpretations of the Passion Narrative," in *The Harvard Theological Review*, Vol. 97, No. 2 (April 2004), 139-163.

Gault, Matthew. "The Problem of Drug-addicted Soldiers is as Old as War." *War is Boring* blog, May 8, 2015. Accessed on August 8, 2017. https://medium.com/war-is-boring/the-problem-of-drug-addicted-soldiers-is-as-old-as-war-5e3c5955f828

Grossman, Dave. *On Combat: The Psychology and Physiology of Deadly Conflict in War and Peace*. 2nd ed. Illinois: PPCT Research Publications, 2007.

———. *On Killing: The Psychological Cost of Learning to Kill in War and in Society*. Boston: Little, Brown, 1995.

Kaldellis, Anthony. "Edward N. Luttwak, *The Grand Strategy of the Byzantine Empire*," in *Bryn Mawr Classical Review*. 2010.01.49.

Kidder, Tracy. *Mountains Beyond Mountains: The Quest of Dr. Paul Farmer, a Man Who Would Heal the World*. New York: Random House, 2003.

Luttwak, Edward. *The Grand Strategy of the Byzantine Empire*. Cambridge, Mass.: Belknap Press of Harvard University Press, 2009.

Pope, Alexander, trans. *The Iliad of Homer.* New York: Macmillan, 1965.

Shay, Jonathan. *Achilles in Vietnam: Combat Trauma and the Undoing of Character*. New York: Maxwell MacMillan International, 1994.

_____. *Odysseus in America: Combat Trauma and the Trials of Homecoming.* NY: Scribner, 2002.

Weil, Simone. "The Iliad, Poem of Might," in *Intimations of Christianity Among the Ancient Greeks*. Boston: Beacon Press, 1958.

Yunus, Muhammad. *Banker to the Poor: Micro-Lending in the Battle Against World Poverty.* 1st ed. NY: Public Affairs, 1999.

Chapter Two
A Feeling for Beauty:
The Aesthetic Ground of Orthodox Ethics

Alexander, Christopher. *The Timeless Way of Building.* Oxford: Oxford University Press, 1979.

Dionysios, Areopagite, Saint. *The Works of Dionysius the Areopagite*. Translated by Parker, John. London: Aeterna Press, 2014.

Ferrell, Kirby. *Berserk Style in American Culture*. New York: Palgrave Macmillan, 2011. For an updated version of this work, see his *The Psychology of Abandon: Berserk Style in American Culture*. Amherst, Massachusetts: Levellers Press, 2015.

Finkel, David. "The Return: The Traumatized Veterans of Iran and Afghanistan," *The New Yorker*, September 9, 2013.

Maximos, Confessor, Saint. *On Difficulties in the Church Fathers: The Ambigua*, Vol. II, in Dumbarton Oaks Medieval Library. Nicholas Constas, editor and translator. Cambridge: Harvard University Press, 2014.

Meerson, Michael Aksionov. *The Trinity of Love in Modern Russian Theology: The Love Paradigm and the Retrieval of Western Medieval Love Mysticism in Modern Russian Trinitarian Thought (from Solovyov to Bulgakov)*. Quincy, Illinois: Franciscan Press, 1998.

Negel, Thomas. "Moral Luck," in *Proceedings of the Aristotelian Society Supplementary*, Vol. 50, pp. 137-155, 1976. Reprinted in *Mortal Questions*, Cambridge: Cambridge Univ. Press, 1991.

Nussbaum, Martha C. *The Fragility of Goodness: Luck and Ethics in Greek Tragedy and Philosophy*. New York: Cambridge University Press, 2001.

_____. *Cultivating Humanity: A Classical Defense of Reform in Liberal Education*. Cambridge, Mass: Harvard University Press, 1997.

Perl, Eric. *Theophany: The Neoplatonic Philosophy of Dionysius the Areopagite*. Albany, NY: State Univ. of New York Press, 2008.

Plested, Marcus. *The Macarian Legacy: The Place of Macarius-Symeon in the Eastern Christian Tradition*. Oxford: Oxford University Press, 2004.

Porphyrios, Saint. *Wounded by Love: The Life and Wisdom of Elder Porphyrios*. Limni, Evia, Greece: Denise Harvey [Publisher], 2005.

Shay, Jonathan. *Achilles in Vietnam: Combat Trauma and the Undoing of Character*. New York: Maxwell MacMillan International, 1994.

_____. *Odysseus in America: Combat Trauma and the Trials of Homecoming*. NY: Scribner, 2002.

Shestov, Lev. *Athens and Jerusalem*. New York: Simon and Schuster, 1968.

Sophocles. *The Oedipus Plays of Sophocles; Oedipus the King, Oedipus at Colonus, Antigone*. In a new translation by Paul Roche. New York: American Library, 1958.

Thunberg, Lars. *Microcosm and Mediator: The Theological Anthropology of Maximos the Confessor.* 2nd ed. Chicago: Open Court, 1995.

Tolkien, J.R.R. *The Fellowship of the Ring: being the first part of The Lord of the Rings.* George Allen and Unwin, London, 1954.

_____. *The Two Towers: being the second part of The Lord of the Rings.* George Allen and Unwin, London, 1954.

_____. *The Return of the King: being the third part of The Lord of the Rings.* George Allen and Unwin, London, 1955.

Van der Kolk, Bessel. *The Body Keeps the Score: Brain, Mind, and Body in the Healing of Trauma.* New York: Viking/Penguin, 2014.

Weil, Simone. "The Iliad, Poem of Might," in *Intimations of Christianity Among the Ancient Greeks.* Boston: Beacon Press, 1958.

Chapter Three
Chastity and Empathy:
Eros, Agape, and the Twofold Anointing

Alexander, Christopher. *The Timeless Way of Building.* Oxford: Oxford University Press, 1979.

Bergner, Mario. *Setting Love in Order: Hope and Healing for the Homosexual.* Ada, MI: Baker Books, 1995.

Bloom, Allan. *The Closing of the American Mind.* New York: Simon and Schuster, 1987.

Carbone, June and Cahn, Naomi. *Marriage Markets: How Inequality is Remaking the American Family.* New York: Oxford University Press, 2014.

Dalrymple, Theodore. *Life at the Bottom.* Lanham, MD: Ivan R. Dee, 2003.

Douthat, Ross. *Bad Religion: How We Became a Nation of Heretics.* New York: Free Press, 2012.

Eberstadt, Mary. *How the West Really Lost God.* Philadelphia: Templeton Press, 2013.

Feldhahn, Shaunti. *Good News About Marriage: Debunking Discouraging Myths about Marriage and Divorce.* Colorado Springs, CO: Multnomah Books, 2014.

Jacobs, Jane. *The Death and Life of Great American Cities.* New York: Random House, 1961.

⸻. *The Economy of Cities.* New York: Random House, 1969.

Kidder, Tracy. *Mountains Beyond Mountains: The Quest of Dr. Paul Farmer, a Man Who Would Heal the World.* New York: Random House, 2003.

Lewis, Clives Staples. *The Discarded Image: An Introduction to Medieval and Renaissance Literature.* Cambridge: Cambridge University Press, 1964.

⸻. *The Abolition of Man.* London: Oxford University Press, 1943.

_____. *Surprised by Joy: The Shape of My Early Life.* London: G. Bless, 1955.

Magnet, Myron. *The Dream and the Nightmare: The Sixties' Legacy to the Underclass.* New York: W. Morrow, 1993.

Papadakis, Aristeides. *Crisis in Byzantium: The Filioque Controversy in the Patriarchate of Gregory II of Cyprus (1283-1289).* Crestwood, NY: SVS Press, 1997.

Patitsas, Timothy G. "The King Returns to His City: An Interpretation of the Great Week and Bright Week Cycle of the Orthodox Church," Ph.D. diss., The Catholic University of America, 2003.

Perl, Eric. *Theophany: The Neoplatonic Philosophy of Dionysius the Areopagite.* Albany, NY: State Univ. of New York Press, 2008.

Porphyrios, Saint. *Wounded by Love: The Life and Wisdom of Elder Porphyrios.* Limni, Evia, Greece: Denise Harvey, 2005.

Renault, Mary. *The King Must Die.* New York: Pantheon, 1958.

Ruden, Sarah. *Paul Among the People: The Apostle Reinterpreted and Reimagined in His Own Time.* New York: Pantheon, 2010.

Schaff, Philip. "The Berengar Controversy," in *History of the Christian Church.* New York: Charles Scribner's Sons, 1910.

Schmemann, Alexander. "Appendix Two," in *For the Life of the World.* Crestwood, NY: SVS Press, 1970.

_____. *The Eucharist: Sacrament of the Kingdom.* Crestwood, NY: SVS Press, 1987.

Chapter Four
Shame and Sacrifice:
Rescuing the Soul from the Empire of Therapy

American Psychiatric Association. *Diagnostic and Statistical Manual of Mental Disorders: DSM-V-TR.* Washington, DC: American Psychiatric Association, 2013.

Bloom, Allan. *The Closing of the American Mind.* New York: Simon and Schuster, 1987.

Bloom, Harold. *The American Religion: The Emergence of the Post-Christian Nation.* New York: Simon and Schuster, 1992.

Bradshaw, John. *Healing the Shame that Binds You.* Deerfield Beach, FL: Health Communications, 1988.

Climacus, John, Saint. Trans. Fr. Lazarus Moore. *The Ladder of Divine Ascent.* Boston: Holy Transfiguration Monastery, 1978.

Desteno, David. "A Feeling of Control: How America Can Finally Learn to Deal With Its Impulses," in the online magazine *Pacific Standard*, Sep 15, 2014. Accessed on Mar 8, 2016.

Douthat, Ross. *Bad Religion: How We Became a Nation of Heretics.* New York: Free Press & Simon and Schuster, 2012.

Hall, Douglas A. *The Cat and the Toaster: Living System Ministry in a Technological Age.* Eugene, OR: Wipf and Stock, 2010.

Jacobs, Jane. "The Kind of Problem a City Is," in *The Death and Life of Great American Cities.* New York: Random House, 1961; 428-48.

_____. *The Economy of Cities.* New York: Random House, 1969.

Johnson, Steven. *Emergence: The Connected Lives of Ants, Brains, Cities, and Software.* New York: Scribner, 2001.

Kaufman, Gershen. *Shame: The Power of Caring.* Cambridge, MA: Schenkman Publishing Company, 1980.

Kreeft, Peter. *The Modern Scholar: Ethics: A History of Moral Thought.* Recorded Books: 2003.

Lewis, Clives Staples. *The Screwtape Letters.* London: G. Bles, 1942.

Middleton, Herman. *Precious Vessels of the Holy Spirit: The Lives and Counsels of Contemporary Elders of Greece.* Thessalonica: Protecting Veil Press, 2003.

Palmer, Gerrard, & Ware, Kallistos, translators. *The Philokalia: The Complete Text Compiled by St. Nikodimos of the Holy Mountain and St. Makarios of Corinth.* London: Faber & Faber, 1983-1986.

Pope, Alexander, trans. *The Iliad of Homer.* New York: Macmillan, 1965.

Rieff, Philip. *The Triumph of the Therapeutic: Uses of Faith After Freud.* Wilmington, DE: Intercollegiate Studies Institute, 2006.

Sakharov, Sophrony. *St. Silouan the Athonite.* Maldon, Essex: Patriarchal Stavropegic Monastery of Saint John the Baptist, 1991.

Shay, Jonathan. *Achilles in Vietnam: Combat Trauma and the Undoing of Character.* New York: Atheneum, 1994.

Van der Kolk, Bessel. *The Body Keeps the Score: Brain, Mind, and Body in the Healing of Trauma.* New York: Viking/Penguin, 2014.

Weaver, Warren. "A Quarter Century in the Natural Sciences," in *The President's Review, including A Quarter Century in the Natural Sciences by Warren Weaver, from the Rockefeller Foundation Annual Report, 1958.* New York: The Rockefeller Foundation, 1958; 7-15.

Chapter Five
Only Priests Can Marry:
The Reconciliation of Men and Women in Christ

Berger, Calinic. *Challenges of Orthodox Thought and Life.* Detroit: The Romanian Orthodox Episcopate of America, 2011.

Bonhoeffer, Dietrich. *The Cost of Discipleship.* London: SCM Press, 1948.

Chapman, Gary. *The Five Love Languages.* Chicago: Northfield Publishers, 1992.

Freud, Sigmund. *Moses and Monotheism.* London: The Hogarth Press, 1939.

Gray, John. *Mars and Venus on a Date.* New York: HarperCollins, 2009.

Hackworth, David, and England, Eilhys. *Steel My Soldiers' Hearts: The Hopeless to Hardcore Transformation of U.S. Army, 4th Battalion, 39th Infantry.* New York: Rugged Land, 2002.

Kaufmann, Gershen. *Shame: The Power of Caring.* Cambridge: Schenkman, 1985.

Krivocheine, Basil. *In the Light of Christ: St. Symeon the New Theologian (949-1022: Life, Spirituality, Doctrine).* Crestwood, NY: SVS Press, 1986.

Linsley, Alice. "Stepping into the Stream: An Interview with Alice C. Linsley," *Road to Emmaus Journal*, Vol. XI, No. 1, Winter, 2010 (#40).

Luther, Martin. *Martin Luther: Selections from His Writing.* Edited by John Dillenberger. Garden City, NY: Doubleday, 1961.

Maximos, Confessor, Saint. *On Difficulties in the Church Fathers: The Ambigua*, in Dumbarton Oaks Medieval Library. Nicholas Constas, editor and translator. Cambridge: Harvard University Press, 2014.

Patitsas, Timothy G. "Chiasm: Relations of Genders and of Syndromes," Chapter Six of "The King Returns to His City: An Interpretation of the Great Week and Bright Week Cycle of the Orthodox Church," Ph.D. diss., The Catholic University of America, 2003.

_____. "The Marriage of Priests: Towards an Orthodox Christian Theology of Gender," in *St. Vladimir's Theological Quarterly*, Vol. 51 (No. 1), 2007, 71-105.

Perl, Eric. *Theophany: The Neoplatonic Philosophy of Dionysius the Areopagite.* Albany, NY: State Univ. of New York Press, 2008.

Romanides, John. *An Outline of Orthodox Patristic Dogmatics.* Edited and translated by Fr. George Dragas. Rollinsford, NH: Orthodox Research Institute, 2004.

Ruden, Sarah. *Paul Among the People: The Apostle Reinterpreted and Reimagined in his Own Time.* New York: Pantheon Books, 2010.

Shestov, Lev. *Athens and Jerusalem.* New York: Simon and Schuster, 1968.

Sophocles. *The Oedipus Plays of Sophocles; Oedipus the King, Oedipus at Colonus, Antigone. In a new translation by Paul Roche.* New York: American Library, 1958.

Thunberg, Lars. *Microcosm and Mediator: The Theological Anthropology of Maximos the Confessor.* 2nd ed. Chicago: Open Court, 1995.

Watters, Ethan. "The Wave That Brought PTSD to Sri Lanka," Chapter Two in *Crazy Like Us: The Globalization of the American Psyche.* New York: Free Press, 2010; 65-127.

Chapter Six
The Mystical Architect:
The Conception of the Crucified Logos
in Art, Science, and Nature

Alexander, Christopher. *A Pattern Language.* Oxford University Press, 1977.

_____. *The Timeless Way of Building.* Oxford University Press, 1979.

Berry, Wendell. *The Unsettling of America: Culture and Agriculture.* San Francisco: Sierra Club, 1977.

_____. *The Art of the Commonplace: The Agrarian Essays of Wendell Berry.* Berkeley, CA: Counterpoint Press, 2003.

Dionysios, Areopagite, Saint. *The Works of Dionysius the Areopagite.* Translated by John Parker. London: Aeterna Press, 2014.

Dionysios, of Fourna. *The Painter's Manual of Dionysios of Fourna.* Translated by Paul Hetherington. Oakwood Publications, 1990.

Gabler, Neal. *An Empire of Their Own: How the Jews Invented Hollywood.* New York: Crown-Random House, 1988.

Gamma, E.; Helm, R.; Johnson, R.; Vlissides, J. *Design Patterns: Elements of Reusable Object-Oriented Software*. Reading, Mass.: Addison-Wesley Professional, 1994.

Jacobs, Jane. *The Nature of Economies*. New York: Modern Library, 2000.

Kontoglou, Photis. *Expression of Orthodox Iconography (Ekfrasis Tis Orthodoxou Eikonografias)*, two volumes. Athens: Astir Publications, 1977.

Lewis, Clives Staples. *The Chronicles of Narnia: The Last Battle*. London: The Bodley Head, 1956.

Luibheid, Colm & Rorem, Paul, eds. *The Divine Names, in Pseudo-Dionysius: The Complete Works*. Mahwah, NJ: Paulist Press, 1987.

Maximos, Confessor, Saint. *On Difficulties in the Church Fathers: The Ambigua*, in Dumbarton Oaks Medieval Library. Nicholas Constas, editor and translator. Cambridge: Harvard University Press, 2014.

Perl, Eric. "St. Gregory Palamas and the Metaphysics of Creation," in *Dionysius*, Vol. 14 (1990): 105-130.

_____. *Theophany: The Neoplatonic Philosophy of Dionysius the Areopagite*. New York: State Univ. of New York Press, 2008.

Porphyrios, Saint. *Wounded by Love: The Life and Wisdom of Elder Porphyrios*. Limni, Evia, Greece: Denise Harvey [Publisher], 2005.

Rappaport, Roy. *Ritual and Religion in the Making of Humanity*. Cambridge: Cambridge University Press, 1999.

Shannon, Claude & Weaver, Warren. *The Mathematical Theory of Communication*. Urbana: University of Illinois Press, 1949.

Thunberg, Lars. *Microcosm and Mediator: The Theological Anthropology of Maximos the Confessor.* 2nd ed. Chicago: Open Court, 1995.

Weil, Simone. "The Iliad, Poem of Might," in *Intimations of Christianity Among the Ancient Greeks.* Boston: Beacon Press, 1958.

Chapter Seven
Beauty Will Save the World:
Judgment Day, Social Justice, and
the Human Need to Forgive God

Berman, Ronald, ed., *Solzhenitsyn at Harvard: The Address, Twelve Early Responses, Six Later Responses.* Washington: Ethics and Public Policy Center, 1980.

Bloom, Harold. *The American Religion: The Emergence of the Post-Christian Nation.* New York: Simon and Schuster, 1992.

Boulding, Kenneth E. *Three Faces of Power.* Newbury Park: SAGE Publications, 1990.

Butler, Eamonn. *Hayek: His Contribution to the Political and Economic Thought of Our Time.* London: Temple Smith, 1983.

Coulanges, Numa Denis Fustel De. *The Ancient City: A Study on the Religion, Laws, and Institutions of Greece and Rome.* Baltimore: John Hopkins University Press, 1980. Originally published in Paris: Durand, 1854, as *La Cité Antique.*

Drucker, Peter F. *The End of Economic Man: A Study of the New Totalitarianism.* New York: John Day Co, 1939.

Duffy, Eamon. *The Stripping of the Altars: Traditional Religion in England, 1400-1580.* New Haven: Yale University Press, 1992.

Easterly, William. *The Elusive Quest for Growth: Economists' Adventures and Misadventures in the Tropics.* Cambridge, MA: MIT Press, 2001.

_____. *The White Man's Burden: Why the West's Efforts to Aid the Rest Have Done So Much Ill and So Little Good.* New York: Penguin, 2006.

Ellul, Jacques. *The Meaning of the City.* Grand Rapids: William B. Eerdmans Publishing, 1993.

Fullilove, Mindy Thompson. *Root Shock: How Tearing Up City Neighborhoods Hurts America, and What We Can Do About It.* New York: One World/Ballantine, 2004.

Galbraith, John Kenneth. *The Anatomy of Power.* Boston: Houghton Mifflin, 1983.

Hayek, Friedrich. *Individualism and Economic Order.* Chicago: University of Chicago Press, 1948.

_____. *The Mirage of Social Justice.* Chicago: University of Chicago Press, 1976.

_____. *The Road to Serfdom.* London: G. Routledge and Sons, 1944.

Jacobs, Jane. *Systems of Survival: A Dialogue on the Moral Foundations of Commerce and Politics.* New York: Random House, 1992.

_____. *Dark Age Ahead.* New York: Random House, 2004.

Kaldellis, Anthony. *The Byzantine Republic: People and Power in New Rome.* Cambridge: Harvard University Press, 2015.

Kidder, Tracy. *Mountains Beyond Mountains: The Quest of Paul Farmer, the Man Who Would Cure the World.* New York: Random House, 2003.

Lampton, David M. *The Three Faces of Chinese Power: Might, Money, and Minds.* Berkeley: UC Press, 2008.

Luibheid, Colm & Rorem, Paul, eds. *The Divine Names* in *Pseudo-Dionysius: The Complete Works.* Mahwah, NJ: Paulist Press, 1987.

Lo, Ping-Cheung, and Twiss, Sumner B. *Chinese Just War Ethics: Origin, Development, and Dissent.* Oxford: Routledge, 2015.

Morgenthau, Hans. *Politics Among Nations: The Struggle for Power and Peace.* 7th ed. New York: McGraw Hill, 2005.

Moyo, Dimbasa, and Ferguson, Niall. *Dead Aid: Why Aid is Not Working and How There is a Better Way for Africa.* New York: Farrar, Straus, & Giroux, 2009.

Priestland, David. *Merchant, Soldier, Sage: A History of the World in Three Castes.* New York: Penguin Press, 2013.

Schwartz, Timothy. *Travesty in Haiti: A True Account of Christian Missions, Orphanages, Fraud, Food Aid and Drug Trafficking.* Charleston, SC: BookSurge Publishing, 2008.

Wilson, Bill. *Alcoholics Anonymous: The Story of How Many Thousands of Men and Women Have Recovered from Alcoholism.* 2nd ed. New York: Alcoholics Anonymous Pub., 1955.

Chapter Eight
The City as Liturgy: How Jane Jacobs Used the Beautiful Science of Complexity to Explain Cities, and Unknowingly Reconciled Science and Religion

Alexander, Christopher. *The Timeless Way of Building.* Oxford University Press, 1979.

Breece, Hannah. *A Schoolteacher in Old Alaska: The Story of Hannah Breece*. Edited and with an introduction by Jane Jacobs. New York: Random House, 1995.

Buffet, Warren. *Berkshire Hathaway: Letters to Shareholders, 1965-2014*. Mountain View, CA: Explorist Productions, 2015.

Coulanges, Numa Denis Fustel De. *The Ancient City: A Study on the Religion, Laws, and Institutions of Greece and Rome*. Baltimore: John Hopkins University Press, 1980. Originally published in Paris: Durand, 1854, as *La Cité Antique*.

Ellul, Jacques. *The Meaning of the City*. Grand Rapids: Wm. B. Eerdmans Publishing Co., 1970.

Fullilove, Mindy Thompson. *Root Shock: How Tearing Up City Neighborhoods Hurts America, and What We Can Do About It*. New York: One World/Ballantine, 2004.

Geertz, Clifford. *The Interpretation of Cultures: Selected Essays*. New York: Basic Books, 1973.

Gleick, James. *Chaos: Making a New Science*. New York: Viking, 1987.

_____. *The Information: A History, a Theory, a Flood*. New York: Vintage Books, 2011.

Hall, Douglas A. *The Cat and the Toaster: Living Systems Ministry in a Technological Age*. Eugene, Oregon: Wipf & Stock, 2010.

Jacobs, Jane. *Dark Age Ahead*. New York: Random House, 2004.

_____. *The Death and Life of Great American Cities*. New York: Random House, 1961.

―――――. *The Economy of Cities.* New York: Random House, 1969.

―――――. *The Nature of Economies.* New York: Modern Library, 2000.

―――――. *Systems of Survival: A Dialogue on the Moral Foundations of Commerce and Politics.* New York: Random House, 1992.

―――――. "Uncovering the Economy: A New Hypothesis; Excerpt from an Unpublished Work, 2004," in S. Zipp and N. Storring, *Vital Little Plans: The Short Works of Jane Jacobs.* New York: Random House, 2016; 406-31.

Johnson, Steven. *Emergence: The Connected Lives of Ants, Brains, Cities, and Software.* New York: Scribner, 2001.

Lewis, Clives Staples. *The Abolition of Man.* London: Oxford University Press, 1943.

Linsley, Alice. "Stepping into the Stream: An Interview with Alice C. Linsley," *Road to Emmaus Journal*, Vol. XI, No. 1, Winter, 2010 (#40).

Meadows, Donella. *Thinking in Systems: A Primer.* White River Junction, VT: Chelsea Green Pub., 2008.

Miller, Timothy. *The Birth of the Hospital in the Byzantine Empire.* Baltimore: Johns Hopkins University Press, 1997.

Patitsas, Timothy G. "The City as Liturgy: An Orthodox Theologian Corresponds with Jane Jacobs About a Gentle Reconciliation of Science and Religion," in *Legacy of Achievement: Metropolitan Methodios of Boston, Festal Volume of the 25th Anniversary of his Consecration to the Episcopate, (1982-2007)*, ed. Rev. George D. Dragas. Columbia, MO: NewRome Press, 2010.

_____. "The King Returns to His City: An Interpretation of the Great Week and Bright Week Cycle of the Orthodox Church," Ph.D. diss., The Catholic University of America, 2003.

_____. "Organic Complexity and the Healing of Our Epistemology," in J.T. Chirban, ed., *Holistic Healing in Byzantium*. Brookline: Holy Cross Orthodox Press, 2010.

Rappaport, Roy. *Ritual and Religion in the Making of Humanity*. Cambridge: Cambridge University Press, 1999.

Schwartz, Timothy. *Travesty in Haiti: A True Account of Christian Missions, Orphanages, Fraud, Food Aid and Drug Trafficking*. Charleston, SC: BookSurge Publishing, 2008.

Shannon, Claude E. and Warren Weaver: *The Mathematical Theory of Communication*. Urbana, IL: The University of Illinois Press, 1949.

Taleb, Nassim Nicholas. *The Black Swan: The Impact of the Highly Improbable*. 2nd ed. New York: Random House Trade Paperbacks, 2010.

Weaver, Warren. "A Quarter Century in the Natural Sciences," in *The President's Review, including A Quarter Century in the Natural Sciences by Warren Weaver, from the Rockefeller Foundation Annual Report, 1958*. New York: The Rockefeller Foundation, 1958; 7-15.

About the Author

Born in Akron and raised in Kent, Ohio, Dr. Timothy Patitsas graduated from the Georgetown University School of Foreign Service (1988), received an M.Div. from the Holy Cross Greek Orthodox School of Theology (1994), and was awarded a Ph.D. in Systematic Theology from The Catholic University of America, Washington, DC (2003) with a dissertation entitled, "The King Returns to His City: An Interpretation of the Great Week and Bright Week Cycle of the Orthodox Church."

Dr. Patitsas taught at the St. Nicholas Orthodox Seminary in South Korea and at Marymount College in Arlington, Virginia. Following a lengthy residency in monasteries in Rhodes, Patmos, and Colorado, in 2005 he became Assistant Professor of Ethics at Holy Cross Greek Orthodox School of Theology, also teaching religion, business law, and literature at Hellenic College, Brookline, MA. He presently serves as the Dean of Hellenic College.

His publications include articles on Orthodox Holy Week and Bright Week, Ethics and Bioethics, an Orthodox Christian theology of gender, the economic theory of Jane Jacobs (one of his principal mentors), the pattern-language architecture of Christopher Alexander, and the implications of complexity theory. In 2019, he published *The Ethics of Beauty* with St. Nicholas Press.

Since 2006 he has directed the St. Helen's Pilgrimage, the study abroad program of Holy Cross in Constantinople, Greece, Israel/Palestine, and on Mount Athos. Professor Patitsas serves on the boards of The Russian Orphan Opportunity Fund, The Center for Byzantine Material Arts, and the Road to Emmaus Foundation. He is also the co-founder of Beauty First Films.